AA

SECRET BRITAIN

Published by the Automobile Association,
Fanum House, Basingstoke, Hampshire RG21 2EA

© The Automobile Association 1986

All rights reserved. No part of this publication may be reproduced, stored in a retrieval system, or transmitted in any form or by any means – electronic, mechanical, photocopying, recording, or otherwise unless the permission of the publisher has been given beforehand.
Published by the Automobile Association, Fanum House, Basing View, Basingstoke, Hampshire RG21 2EA.

Typesetting by Avonset, Midsomer Norton, Bath

Printed and bound in Italy by Pizzi, Milan

ISBN 0 86145 392 1
AA Ref 59527

SECRET
BRITAIN

COVER: *sanctuary handle at Adel – see Leeds, page 230.*
PAGE ONE: *Llanstephan Castle – see Tregoning Hill, page 152.*
TITLE PAGE: *Roman steps at Cwm Bychan, see page 130.*
THIS PAGE: *hay meadows at Muker, see page 243.*

Produced by the Publishing Division of the Automobile Association
Editor: Antonia Hebbert
Editorial Assistant: Rebecca Snelling
Art Editor: Dave Austin
Design Assistants: John Breeze, Neil Roebuck
Picture Researcher: Wyn Voysey

Special features: Dr Stefan Buczacki, Denis Harvey, Barbara Littlewood, Norman McCanch, Nigel Pennick, Tom Vernon

Side panel features: Jennifer Westwood

Descriptions of places: Paul Atterbury, Jan Beart-Albrecht, Alan Brack, Julia Brittain, David Brown, Roger Butters, Michael Cady, David Clark, Maurice Colbeck, Valerie Cottle, Ross Finlay, Julia Fisher, David Green, Roger Hamilton, Christopher Hanson-Smith, R.M. Healey, John Hudson, Robert Innes-Smith, Stan Jarvis, Andrew Jenkinson, Kenneth Lindley, Hilary Macaskill, Rob Neillands, Jack Rayfield, Colin Robins, David Robinson, Ron Sands, Roger Thomas, Francesca Turner, Peter Wenham, Valerie Wenham, Geoffrey Wright

Original Photography: Stephen Beer, Ted Bowness, Rick Czaja, Robert Eames, Dennis Hardley, Andrew Lawson, S & O Mathews, Richard Newton, Franki Raffles, Rod Richards, Martin Trelawny, Ronald Weir, Harry Williams, Tim Woodcock

Additional research: Publications Research Unit of the Automobile Association

Maps produced by the Cartographic Department of the Automobile Association

CONTENTS

INTRODUCING *SECRET BRITAIN* 6

INTRODUCING SECRET BRITAIN

There are some places whose beauty or importance has earned them a place in every regular book on Britain. Those places are not necessarily in Secret Britain.

Secret Britain *is about the unexpected, unexplored, mysterious, exotic and eccentric things and places of Britain. It opens up little-known corners, reveals hidden riches and tells strange tales. Many familiar places are included — but only if the book can offer less known corners to visit, a good story or an eccentricity to justify a mention. Why leave some important places out? Because it seemed right to devote space to those interesting and beautiful places which are hardly known outside their immediate neighbourhood. Because some of the best stories — stories about real-life people, bizarre legends, peculiar traditions — are attached to places which aren't well known. Because while organisations like the National Trust now have to limit the number of visitors to certain overcrowded, well-known sites, there are still immensely rewarding places waiting to be discovered.*

Secret Britain *tries to put Britain in a new light, bringing out interest and oddity where it might not have been suspected before. This is a book of discovery — a journey back into the history of Britain, that shows where the past lies hidden in the present. To read* Secret Britain *is to share the adventure, and share its secrets.*

HOW TO USE THIS BOOK

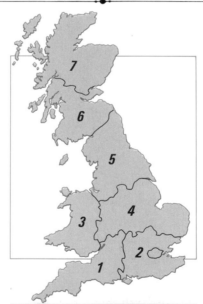

PLACE DESCRIPTIONS

Secret Britain is divided into seven regions. Places are given in alphabetical order in each region. The name of the place is followed by the name of the county in which it lies, with a map reference. Next comes a description, and in many cases a story linked with the place. People and other subjects mentioned may be described more fully in the side panel feature on that page. If not, there may be a side panel feature elsewhere in the book: check in the Subject Index which follows the complete Place Index at the end of the book.

MAP REGIONS

1 WESTERN ENGLAND
2 SOUTH-EAST ENGLAND
3 WALES
4 CENTRAL AND EASTERN ENGLAND
5 NORTHERN ENGLAND
6 SOUTHERN SCOTLAND
7 NORTHERN SCOTLAND

SIDE PANEL FEATURES

Side panel features appear throughout, on legends, personalities, architectural schools, traditions or other subjects relating to a place on each page. Place-names in **bold** refer to places described in *Secret Britain*: these can be found in the Place Index. If mention is made of a place which is not described in *Secret Britain*, the name of the county is supplied. The Subject Index lists all significant references to a subject, whether it is covered in a side panel feature or not, and is divided into types of subject: *Animals, Archaeology, Architects, Artists*, and so on.

JENNIFER WESTWOOD

Most of the side panel features in *Secret Britain* are written by Jennifer Westwood, who also writes and broadcasts under the name Jennifer Chandler. Born in 1940, a graduate of both Oxford and Cambridge, and by training a specialist in Anglo-Saxon and Old Norse language and literature, she has published several books for both children and adults, drawing on myth and legend. In 1986 she was selected as a guide on the Gothic images tour for American visitors, 'Magical Britain', and is a member of the British Hedgehog Preservation society.

FINDING A PLACE ON THE MAP

Each entry has a map reference, for use with the regional maps at the start of every region. *Secret Britain* places are shown on the maps in *red*. The map references are based on the *National Grid* system, and can be used with larger scale maps, if necessary (see *Using other maps* below).

The example on the right shows how to use the map references.

REGIONAL MAP

RIVER

TOWN

COUNTY BOUNDARY

'A' ROAD

MOTORWAY

VILLAGE

PLACE MENTIONED IN **SECRET BRITAIN**

MOTORWAY JUNCTION

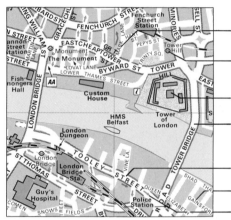

8 9 0 1 2 3

Beer

Devon   SY 2289

SY The letters show the area of the map in which Beer lies. This area is a square, whose edges are the lines numbered *0* along the edges of the map.

22 The first set of figures refers to the vertical lines, numbered along the bottom of the page. Lie a pencil vertically along *2*, then move it to the right, about *2/10* of the way to *3*.

89 The second set of figures refers to the horizontal lines, numbered down the side of the page. Lie a pencil horizontally along *8*, then move it up about *9/10* of the way to *9*.

The place you are looking for should be where the pencils cross.

LONDON STREET MAP

The street map of London on page 86 covers the places described in the Central London area. Districts which are mentioned but lie outside the Central London area are shown on an inset map on the same page. Street names which are given in the text are shown in *red* on the map. There is a London Street Index on page 314.

STREET MENTIONED IN **SECRET BRITAIN**

UNDERGROUND TUBE STATION

BUILDING OF INTEREST

AA RECOMMENDED THROUGHROUTE

MAJOR ROAD

OTHER ROAD

ONE WAY STREET

USING OTHER MAPS

The maps in *Secret Britain* show the main road network, but larger-scale maps may be needed to reach some of the more out-of-the-way places described. The map references can be used with any maps that follow the *National Grid* system, including the three-, four- and five-mile road atlases published by the Automobile Association, and the highly detailed 1:50,000 series of sheet maps published by the Ordnance Survey.

THE NATIONAL GRID system divides the country into 100-kilometre squares, each of which is known by two letters. These squares are sub-divided into 10 ten-kilometre squares, each of which is numbered.

VISITS BY APPOINTMENT ONLY

Some places in *Secret Britain* may only be visited by appointment. For reasons of privacy, we do not give full addresses, but in most cases inform- ation should be available from the Reference section of the local public library, from local tourist boards, or from the telephone directory.

If unable to find the correct address for making an appointment to visit, please write to The Editor, Secret Britain, Publishing Division, Automobile Association, Fanum House, Basingstoke RG21 2EA, enclosing a stamped addressed envelope.

GARDENS which are not regularly open to the public may be open under the National Gardens Schemes. Details of open days are given in the booklet 'Gardens in England and Wales Open to the Public', published annually by the National Gardens Scheme, 57 Lower Belgrave Street, London SW1W 0LR. For Scotland's Garden Scheme, write to 31 Castle Terrace, Edinburgh EH1 2EL.

Please respect the request for appointments to be made

FEATURE WRITERS

Six illustrated four-page features in *Secret Britain* look at aspects of the landscape from a different angle. The following writers, all of whom have extensive knowledge in their fields, were invited to contribute.

TOM VERNON negotiates a Roman road by bicycle. Page 30.

NIGEL PENNICK uncovers the network of civil and military structures under- neath London. Page 102.

NORMAN McCANCH looks at wildlife from the lighthouse keeper's point of view. Page 140.

DR STEFAN BUCZACKI reveals the secrets of six gardens. Page 182.

DENIS HARVEY introduces the Gypsy life. Page 232.

BARBARA LITTLEWOOD shows the inspiration behind the landscapes of literature. Page 286.

CORNWALL *circa* 1884.
Irish shellfish gatherers. They lived in the cave at Downderry, Seaton, during the week, collecting the shellfish which they carried in baskets on their backs and sold in Plymouth. At weekends they lived in Granby Street in the town. A familiar sight on the Torpoint ferry, the three were shunned for their strange appearance and 'foreign' tongue. Such itinerants were once a fairly common feature of Britain, but today the places they made their temporary homes are forgotten

WESTERN ENGLAND

*H*idden away in the western counties are such things as the Crocodile
Flamethrower, the Jack Spratt Clock, manticores and a pig called Gip. Less
obscure, but with much that remains unsung, are the moorlands, heathlands
and downlands, miles of wild coastline and delightful towns and villages.
Despite the dizzying changes of the 20th century, it is still possible to
discover places in the West where the old ways, ruled by the turn of the
seasons, are still today's ways. It's even possible to find the best of the old and
the best of the new fused in contentment. Find the Flamethrower, a machine
of World War II vintage, in retirement at Chittlehampton; the clock,
built of bits and pieces, is at Wootton Rivers; manticores are
imaginary beasts, and one is depicted at North Cerney. As for the pig, it was
the constant companion of the vicar of Morwenstow.

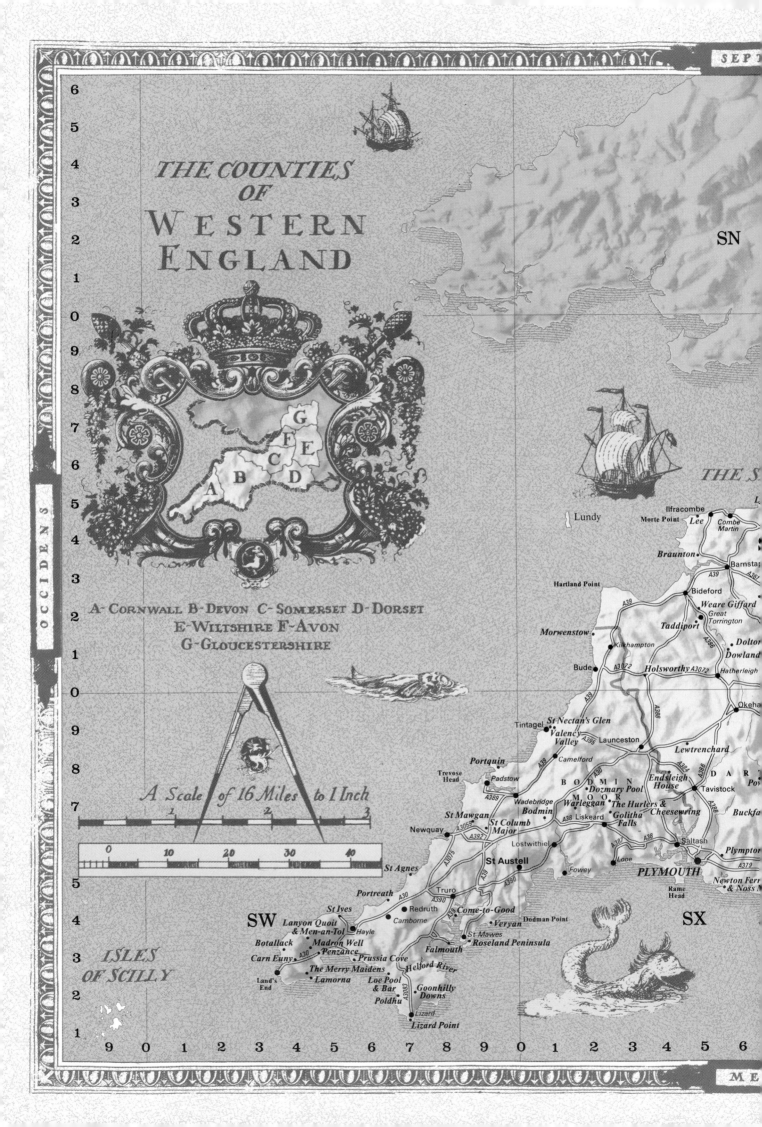

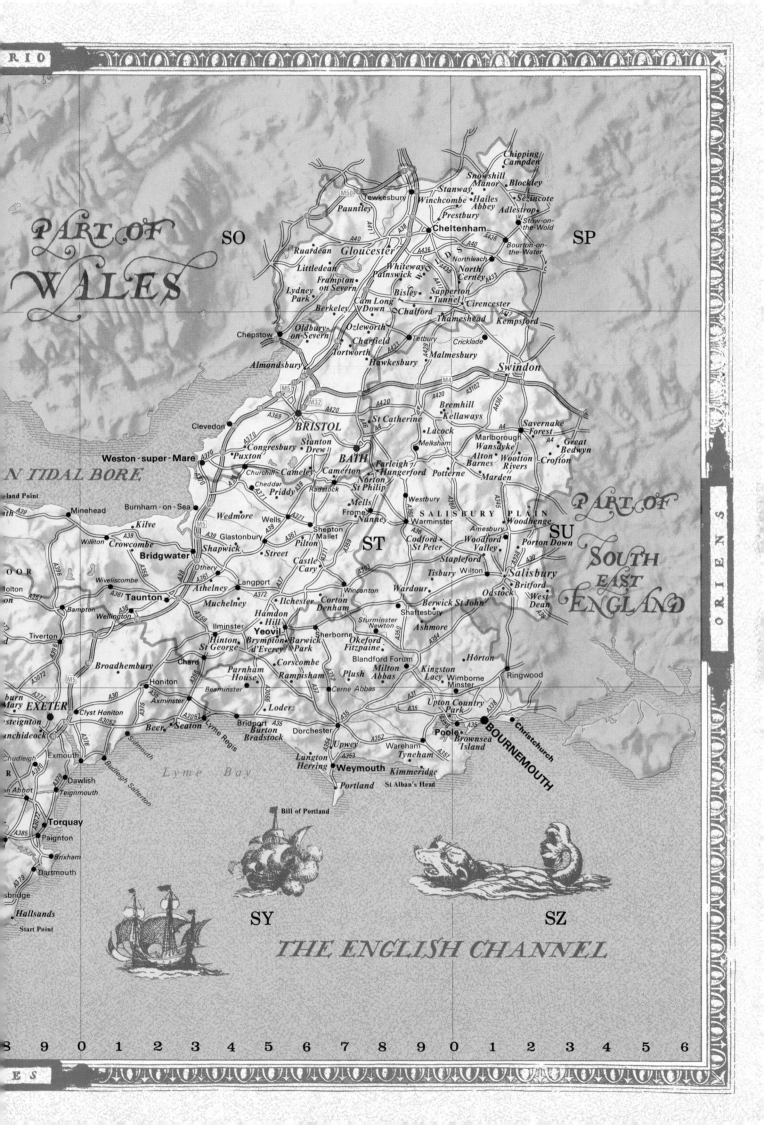

PART OF
WALES

SO

SP

Chipping Campden
Snowshill Manor • Blockley
Stanway • *Sezincote*
Tewkesbury • Winchcombe • Hailes Abbey • Adlestrop
Pauntley • Prestbury • *Stow-on-the-Wold*
Cheltenham • Bourton-on-the-Water
Ruardean • Gloucester • Northleach
Littledean • Whiteway • North Cerney
Frampton • Painswick • W.
Lydney Park • ott Severn • Bisley • Sapperton Tunnel • Cirencester
Berkeley • Cam Long Down • Chalford • Thameshead • Kempsford
Oldbury-on-Severn • Ozleworth • Tetbury • Cricklade
Chepstow • Charfield • Malmesbury
Tortworth • Hawkesbury • **Swindon**
Almondsbury

PART OF
SOUTH EAST ENGLAND

Bremhill • Kellaways
Clevedon • St Catherine • Lacock • Savernake Forest
BRISTOL • Melksham • Marlborough • Great Bedwyn
Congresbury • Stanton Drew • **BATH** • Wansdyke • Crofton
Weston-super-Mare • Puxton • Camerton • Farleigh Hungerford • Alton Barnes • Wootton Rivers
Churchill • Cameley • Norton St Philip • Potterne • Marden
Cheddar • Radstock
Priddy • Westbury
N TIDAL BORE • Mells • Warminster • Woodhenge
Minehead • Burnham-on-Sea • Wedmore • Wells • Frome • Nunney • SALISBURY PLAIN • Amesbury
Kilve • Shepton Mallet • Codford St Peter • Woodford Valley • Porton Down
Williton • Crowcombe • Glastonbury • Pilton • **ST** • Stapleford • Salisbury
Bridgwater • Shapwick • Street • Castle Cary • Tisbury • Wilton • Britford
Othery • Wincanton • Wardour • Odstock • West Dean
Wiveliscombe • Athelney • Langport • Ilchester • Corton Denham • Berwick St John
Taunton • Muchelney • Shaftesbury • Ashmore
Bampton • Ilminster • Hamdon Hill • Sturminster Newton
Wellington • **Yeovil** • Sherborne • Horton
Tiverton • Hinton St George • Brympton d'Evercy • Barwick Park • Okeford Fitzpaine • Kingston Lacy • Ringwood
Broadhembury • Chard • Corscombe • Blandford Forum • Wimborne Minster
Parnham House • Rampisham • Plush • Milton Abbas
EXETER • Honiton • Beaminster • Cerne Abbas • Upton Country Park
Clyst Honiton • Axminster • Loders • Christchurch
Mary • steignton • Beer • Seaton • Bridport • Dorchester • Poole • **BOURNEMOUTH**
nchideock • Burton Bradstock • Wareham • Brownsea Island
Chudleigh • Exmouth • Upwey • Tyneham
Dawlish • Langton Herring • **Weymouth** • Kimmeridge
Abbot • Teignmouth • Portland • St Alban's Head

Lyme Bay

Torquay
Paignton
Brixham
Dartmouth
sbridge
Hallsands
Start Point

Bill of Portland

SY

SZ

THE ENGLISH CHANNEL

ORIENS

8 9 0 1 2 3 4 5 6 7 8 9 0 1 2 3 4 5 6

ALMONDSBURY: *HOAX — Princess Caraboo of* **Almondsbury** *was a poor girl literally making a new life for herself. Other hoaxers have been more plainly mercenary — like the Tichborne claimant (see* **Upton Country Park**), *and the man who in 1925 'sold' Nelson's Column, Buckingham Palace and Big Ben in* **London** *to tourists. In the same year, the Eiffel Tower was bought for scrap (twice).*

In 1912, a skull found on Piltdown Common, Sussex established the 'missing link' between man and ape and brought acclaim to its finders — until, years later, it was identified as part orangutan. Tom Keating caused red faces in the art world with his highly prized 'Sexton Blakes' (fakes) of Samuel Palmer pictures.

Tradition said that only 99 yews would grow in **Painswick** *churchyard — until The Times of 8 June 1963 revealed that the scientist living next door to the vicarage had been quietly pouring acid on the roots of every hundredth tree planted. In 1957, Richard Dimbleby bamboozled thousands with an April 1 television programme showing Italians harvesting spaghetti. In the 1920s, four Abyssinian princes were given the red carpet treatment and a tour of HMS Dreadnought by the Royal Navy, turning down lunch for religious reasons. The 'princes' — Virginia Woolf, Duncan Grant and friends — were afraid their make-up would fall off.*

But the cleverest hoaxes are the ones that no one's yet found out . . .

ABOVE *Virginia Woolf and her chums fooled the Royal Navy when they dressed up as Abyssinian princes*

ATHELNEY *King Alfred is believed to have had a fort on Burrow Mump (right), now crowned by a ruined church*

Adlestrop

Gloucestershire SP 2427

Yes, I remember Adlestrop, wrote Edward Thomas, but lovers of this poem know it was the railway sign — '*only the name*' — that captured his imagination. The village itself, some distance from the now demolished station, is as remote as Thomas surmised it to be, a Cotswolds gem with golden cottages, a pretty church and a further literary tradition: Jane Austen stayed at the Rectory, now the private Adlestrop House, when her uncle was incumbent. The GWR sign that inspired Thomas when his train stopped there one summer afternoon is displayed in the bus shelter, with the poem on a plaque below.

Almondsbury

Avon ST 6083

In 1817 Mary Baker, a young Devonian, brought the village national notoriety when she appeared at the squire's door, fantastically dressed and speaking in mumbo-jumbo, and claimed she was Princess Caraboo, kidnapped by pirates in the Far East. She became the toast of society before she was exposed and given a one-way ticket to America by her embarrassed benefactors.

Just north of Bristol off the A38, Almondsbury is also noted for ghosts. A 'white lady' walks the ruinous Tudor Over Court; the popular Bowl pub is haunted by a French girl, Elizabeth Maronne, whose church memorial blames her death on her father's sins.

Alton Barnes

Wiltshire SU 1064

Cowboy decorators aren't new — in 1812, the painter commissioned to set out the perky White Horse on Milk Hill ran off with the £20 he had been paid in advance. But the sprightly animal, the largest in Wiltshire, is today visible from Old Sarum, 20 miles away. A better view can be had from the Barge Inn at Honey Street. Hidden away beside the Kennet and Avon Canal, this fascinating pub once incorporated a general stores and a bakery, serving villages over a wide area.

The tiny village church has stood under the great sweep of the downs for more than a thousand years. Its Saxon walls are crowned by a timber roof itself 500 years old.

Ashmore

Dorset ST 9117

Enter with care: such is the peaceful seclusion of Dorset's highest village, 700 feet up in the chalk of Cranborne Chase and encircled by trees, that ducks from its large round pond are likely to be dozing in the middle of the road. The long barrow north of the village gives a view southeast to the Solent and the Isle of Wight; in the other direction, Wiltshire rolls away green and empty. Radiating from the lonely pond are cottages of flint and stone, an old school, medieval Manor Farm and 18th-century rectory. The church has a 13th-century font and 20th-century animal carvings by John Skeaping.

Athelney

Somerset ST 3529

King Alfred let the cakes burn here, it's said, and certainly Burrow Mump nearby at Burrowbridge may have been his fort. It dominates the low-lying Somerset Levels, where 'withies', the shoots of pollarded willow trees, have been cultivated on a large scale ever since the Victorians developed a taste for wicker furnishings. They can be seen growing in spring, drying in summer and worked into every kind of basket at all times of year.

Topping the Mump is the ruined tower of a medieval church dedicated to St Michael, the traditional saint for hilltop sites. Below it is the new St Michael's, with a square bellcote; and a pumping station — very necessary in this low, wet landscape.

Four miles away at North Petherton, the Alfred Jewel (now in the Ashmolean Museum, Oxford) was found in 1693. Its inscription reads *AELFRED MEC HEHT GEWYRCAN* — 'Alfred had me made'.

Barwick Park

Somerset ST 5513

Jack the Treacle Eater comes down from the top of a spire at midnight to quench his thirst on treacle — or so it is said of the figure of Hermes on one of the fine follies at each point of the compass in Barwick Park. To the west a slender stone cone rises 75 feet from Gothic arches,

BARWICK PARK   *One story says that the Treacle Eater folly commemorates a murdered milkman, whose body was kept in the tower*

south is the graceful spire, slightly crooked, called Messiter's Cone, north is a 50-foot cylinder, the Fish Tower. Jack the Treacle Eater (east) is named from a runner who took messages to London and kept fit on treacle. By tradition the follies were a scheme of George Messiter's to employ workless glovemakers in the 1830s, but in her book *Follies and Grottoes*, Barbara Jones mentions seeing two in an 18th-century painting. Also here is a grotto.

Bath

Avon ST 7464

Behind the imposing classical façades and sweeping crescents, Bath is a labyrinth of side alleys and tradesmen's entrances which prove that while the great Georgian terraces are not quite as prepossessing from the rear, they are at least as interesting. Speculative builders who made their fortune here in the 18th century allowed their clients a considerable say in how their houses looked behind uniform front walls — and many of them had some peculiar ideas.

As if the sidestreets were not confusing enough, the 1980s have brought two purpose-designed mazes to the city. One, in Beazer Gardens, a prime site close to Pulteney Weir, is a mind-boggling circular footpath, while out at Batheaston, the vicar has laid an allegorical puzzle, based on a medieval French design, in paving stone at the parish church.

Bath ghosts are so thick on the ground that there are regular conducted tours of their favourite haunts. Perhaps best-documented is the Man in the Black Hat seen around the Assembly Rooms, while the jasmine-scented Grey Lady is a star of the Theatre Royal and the Garrick's Head.

The most eccentric local landmark must be Beckford's Tower, an early 19th-century folly in Lansdown with spectacular views over the city and across the Severn towards Wales. With 156 steps up to a belvedere, it is open on weekend afternoons from April to October.

A basement garden in Laura Place is the site of Mad Eli's off-beat collection of gnomes and royalty memorabilia. Amazed bypassers cannot resist throwing money down at this odd assembly, and Eli has donated thousands of pounds to charity over the years.

*A*THELNEY: ROYAL DISGUISE — The fenland isle of **Athelney** was Alfred's refuge when Vikings fell on his kingdom of Wessex in AD878.

He lived like an outlaw, stealing his food in raids on the Viking encampments and the farms of the English who had surrendered. Once he sought shelter in a herdsman's hut and sat by the fire cleaning his weapons. The housewife was baking loaves on the open hearth. Suddenly she spied them burning and, not knowing who he was, rounded on the king for not keeping an eye on them.

True or false, such tales of mistaken royal identity are part of a long, popular tradition. Charles II, who also went incognito on his flight from the Battle of **Worcester** (1651) is said to have been slapped for carelessness (to put suspicious Parliamentarians off the scent), and at Trent a woman assisted him believing she was aiding an elopement. Bonnie Prince Charlie is best remembered by some for being disguised as Flora Macdonald's maid on the flight to **Skye**, and where would fairy tales be without their princes in disguise as frogs and beasts?

Even in the 1980s, the Princess of Wales could hit the headlines by going shopping — incognito.

ALFRED   *in the Neatherd's Cottage — detail from an engraving, based on Wilkie's painting*

BOTALLACK: TIN-MINING — *Three thousand years of tin-mining are evoked by the engine houses of* **Botallack** *and* **St Agnes**. *Some say it began with the Phoenicians. But tinmining's most enduring memorial is probably the Cornish pasty. Those who have tried and enjoyed a genuine native specimen should remember that the pastry was originally the lunch box, and the lunch — it protected the vegetables (sometimes meat) inside from mine grime. Pastry initials identified each 'tinner's' (miner's) pasty, and two-course pasties had a fruit filling at one end.*

A hard life encouraged super-stition among tinners, and even today, whistling and swearing underground are frowned on. The reason — so as not to offend the 'knockers' — spirits who also worked the tin. The tapping of their hammers was a sure guide to rich lodes.

A miner called Barker once eavesdropped on them, intending to learn where they put their tools and steal them.

'I'll leave mine in a cleft', said one.

'I'll leave mine under the ferns', said another.

'And I'll leave mine in Barker's knee,' said the third.

Suddenly Barker felt a great clout and to his dying day walked with a limp. Hence the saying 'As stiff as Barker's knee'.

Apart from listening for these spirits, tin miners also made semi-magical use of a divining rod in order to find seams of ore.

BOTALLACK   *Tin mine engine houses recall the nearby disaster of 1919. People have lived on this rugged coast — called Penwith — for thousands of years, and it has some fine prehistoric sites*

Beer

Devon   SY 2289

Soft when quarried, hardening on exposure to the air, Beer stone was used for Exeter Cathedral and Guildhall and is thought to have been mined as long ago as Roman times. The spectacular underground caverns have recently been opened to the public in the summer.

This fishing village marks the most westerly extension of the white chalk of Britain's south coast cliffs; it may be approached by a pleasant walk over the headland from neighbouring Branscombe, where the rock changes abruptly to the familiar red Devon sandstone.

Berkeley

Gloucestershire   ST 6899

The fact that Edward Jenner pioneered vaccination in this sleepy spot in 1796 is remarkable enough, but almost as miraculous is the story behind the Edward Jenner museum, close to Berkeley Castle. In the early 1980s the house in which Jenner had lived came on the market, and a trust set out to buy it as a museum and immunology conference centre. At Christmas 1982, Ryoichi Sasakawa, a billionaire Japanese philanthropist, swept up in his limousine, examined the scene — and immediately promised £500,000. In the garden is Jenner's Temple of Vaccinia.

Berwick St John

Wiltshire   ST 9421

Those with a taste for expletives might try marching at midnight, cursing all the while, seven times round Winkelbury Camp, an Iron Age hill-fort north of the village. According to legend, the Devil, thus summoned, will appear on a black horse and grant one wish. A more benevolent local gesture was the tolling of the church bell for ten minutes every night at 8 o'clock, to guide benighted wayfarers on the lonely downs. Some 250 years ago the vicar left a legacy for this purpose and the peal was rung from September to March until World War II.

Bisley

Gloucestershire   SO 9005

Why did Elizabeth I have a fear of marriage, a baldness problem and a heart that beat like a man's? The answer is obvious to folks in Bisley, a beautiful but little-visited upland village near Stroud. As a girl she stayed at Over Court, a private house still standing, and when she fell ill and died her hosts were so fearful of Henry VIII's wrath that they produced a red-headed child to replace her. The match they found was perfect — except for the slight matter of gender.

Gothic wells are dressed in the village on Ascension Day, and in the churchyard there is another ornamental well-head, dating from the 13th century and known as the Poor Soul's Light. Legend has it that a priest once fell down the shaft, and as punishment the villagers were forced to bury their dead at Bibury, several miles away. A corner of the churchyard there is still known as the Bisley Piece.

Botallack

Cornwall SW 3632

Perched precariously on the steep cliff-side above the Atlantic are two recently-restored tin-mine engine houses. This was the scene of a disaster in 1919 when the 'man-engine' (a wooden beam used for carrying miners up and down the shaft) of nearby Levant Mine collapsed, killing 31 men.

The underground workings of both Botallack and Levant mines slope down under the sea and were at a later date incorporated into the Geevor Mine. On stormy nights, the sound of boulders rolling on the sea-bed above has been heard by the miners underground.

This is a spectacular stretch of coast. A bracing cliff-top walk leads you south to Cape Cornwall, the scene of many shipwrecks and the only cape by name in England and Wales.

Braunton

Devon SS 4836

A fine example of medieval strip farming survives in the Great Field, where the fields are still open and the strips clearly visible. It is some 365 acres in area and is protected from the sea by Braunton Burrows.

The parish church is dedicated to St Brannoc, who came from Wales as an evangelist in AD550, and according to legend built his church on the spot where he found a white sow with her farrow, a story depicted in the church roof.

Bremhill

Wiltshire ST 9873

In 1474, a market trader named Maud Heath died a pretty wealthy woman, but she never forgot the many times she had trudged with her basket of goods, cold and wet, to Chippenham.

Her will provided funds for the building and upkeep of a footpath raised above the flood level on brick and stone arches, a remarkable feat of civil engineering. Today, Maud Heath's Causeway runs four and a half miles.

ST BRANNOC   Roof boss

BRAUNTON: ST BRANNOC — *St Brannoc's Church at* **Braunton** *was begun on Chapel Hill, but every night the day's work was mysteriously demolished. One day St Brannoc saw a sow and her litter in the valley below the hill, and took this as a sign to build his church on that spot. Sow and piglets are commemorated in stone on one of its roof-bosses — his church stayed up.*

Similar stories are told of having to change the church site at Godshill, **Isle of Wight,** *and* **Shillington.**

The men who carved the Braunton pigs were probably borrowing a conventional design, used on the Continent. But when people wanted to 'explain' them and the name of Chapel Hill, they drew on an ancient native tradition. Pagan sites were often 'christianised' by the building of churches and stories of changes of site may be garbled memories of local objection to the practice. So the pig became the pagan party — for the wild boar was sacred to the Celts and probably the pagan Anglo-Saxons, as it was to their Scandinavian cousins.

BREMHILL   *Pedlar Maud Heath at Wick Hill, overlooking the flood plain she trod so often — her causeway, going almost to Chippenham, is also celebrated at Kellaways*

Blockley

Gloucestershire SP 1634

Unspoiled through being on the road to nowhere, Blockley is quite as handsome as many villages that have become tourist traps. Once a prosperous silk centre — its picturesque mills are now splendid homes — it was famous early last century as the village of Joanna Southcott, a prophetess who won national attention through her belief that she would bear Shiloh, the second Messiah. Her home, Rock Cottage, was the scene of many disturbing incidents until it was eventually destroyed by fire. Now rebuilt, it stands beyond gate-posts marked with a commemorative plaque.

Bodmin

Cornwall SX 0767

In and around this ancient market town are 11 wells said variously to have curative powers (the Eye Water Well and Scarlet's Well), to have been used for the baptism of Celtic chieftains into the Christian religion (St Guron's Well outside the parish church and a 5th-century well in the grounds of the priory Football Ground) or for more down-to-earth purposes — such as watering horses and washing tripe. Water still flows from St Guron's Well out of the mouths of two monsters (dated 16th century).

One of the earliest railways in Britain, linking Bodmin with Wadebridge, opened in 1830, and excursions were organised to allow the public to witness public executions at Bodmin Jail. The track is now open as a public walkway running from Boscarne Junction to Wadebridge and Padstow.

Bristol

Avon ST 5872

As in Bath, the 1980s have brought an elaborate new maze to Bristol — a circular one with water between the paths, in Victoria Park. Its pattern is based on a roof-boss in St Mary Redcliffe Church, to be seen in the north aisle, second bay west from the crossing.

Redcliffe Caves are a labyrinth of red sandstone passages, their origins obscure, below the city centre; organised parties are taken round by the City Engineer's Department if guides are available. Open less often, on selected weekends at Easter, May and in autumn, is Goldney Grotto in Clifton, a fantastic chamber lined with tens of thousands of sea-shells and 'Bristol diamonds', a rare quartz from the Avon Gorge. It was begun in 1737 and has been in a poor state of repair, through decay and vandalism, but a restoration programme is bringing it back to its full glory. The grotto is one of several Gothic follies con-structed in the grounds of Goldney House, now a university hall.

Still in Clifton, the Paragon, built in Regency times, must rank as that suburb's most eccentric terrace, with its concave façade contrasting with convex porches with curved double doors. Farther out of the city, Henbury has a variety of eye-catching oddities, from the Gothic fantasy of the hilltop Blaise Castle to the epitaph, incon-ceivable today, of slave Scipio Africanus in the churchyard: '*Born a PAGAN and a SLAVE Now Sweetly Sleep a Christian in my grave.*' Blaise Hamlet is a collection of ten ornate estate houses designed by John Nash in 1811, still greatly exciting to discover in the depths of a sprawling modern housing estate.

Bristol boasts three city farms, at Hartcliffe, the largest, with 60 acres, St Werburgh's and Windmill Hill. All are open daily and visitors are welcome to lend a hand. Crafts are also encouraged and the farms are geared to children.

In Southville lives human magpie Monty Maxfield, who has accumulated a huge collection of old comics, postcards, maps, newspapers and Victoriana.

BRISTOL *Under Goldney Grotto lies a fantasy world of cascading water, dramatic rock formations and a Neptune, made of marble*

Britford

Wiltshire SU 1628

Although almost a suburb of Salisbury, this hamlet is an unexpected and charming place, surrounded by the branches of the Avon. It has a moated mansion and a church many centuries older than Salisbury Cathedral. St Peter's has Saxon stone carving in the nave, dating from about AD800, with an arch turned with Roman tiles. As well as three pre-Conquest doorways, there is a mysterious ornate tomb, perhaps that of the Duke of Buckingham, who was beheaded in 1483 at Salisbury.

Broadhembury

Devon ST 1004

It is impossible to buy one of the picturesque cob and thatch cottages here because the whole idyllic village is owned by the Drewe family, and has been since 1603. They still live at the family home, the Grange, and have given their name to the village inn, the Drewe Arms. From 1768 to 1778 the Reverend Augustus Toplady, author of *Rock of Ages*, was incumbent of the 14th-century St Andrew's Church, built from local flint and Beer stone. Nearby are the relatively unknown Blackdown Hills, including Neolithic and Iron Age Hembury Fort, one of the finest earthworks in Devon.

BRISTOL *Each of the detached cottages in Blaise Hamlet is quite different in design and detail. They were all built from rubble, avoiding the smooth appearance of brick for a more rustic effect*

BRISTOL: MAZES
— *The maze at St Mary Redcliffe,* **Bristol,** *is one of the rare church mazes of Britain. Other carved mazes can be seen on the font of Lewannick church, Cornwall, and in the church porch at* **Alkborough.** *Ely Cathedral has a pavement maze.*

On the Continent, they are more plentiful, some also carved in stone, others laid out on the floor in tiles, the most notable being that of Chartres. Said to represent the toils of sin preventing a man reaching Heaven, they were sometimes known as 'Chemins de Jerusalem'. Penitents would go round larger ones on their knees, as a substitute for a pilgrimage to the Holy Land.

The maze is probably a pagan symbol adapted by Christians just as they adapted pagan temples and shrines (see **Braunton**). *Turf mazes (see* **Brandsby**) *seem to be pre-Christian, and some think that the rock-cut maze at* **St Nectan's Glen** *is Bronze Age.*

MAZES *at St Mary Redcliffe, Bristol (top), and Alkborough (above), where the maze known as Julian's Bower, cut into the turf, is repeated in the church porch. Such mazes seem to symbolise a tortuous route for body or spirit. Hedge mazes, just meant to puzzle, became popular later*

—◦◦◦◦◦—

Brownsea Island

Dorset SZ 0187

The raucous cry of peacocks wandering wild is a haunting reminder of the island's last private owner — wildlife loving Mrs Bonham Christie, who lived almost as a recluse and kept Brownsea as a sort of secret garden for animals, birds (including the peacocks' forebears) and flowers. An equally noteworthy owner was Colonel Waugh, who bought the island in the mid-19th century on the theory that the white clay which stuck to Mrs Waugh's umbrella here would be valuable for making fine porcelain. He invested lavishly in building the church, reclaiming the bay from the sea and founding the Brownsea Clay and Pottery Company, only to find in 1855 that the clay was solely good for drainpipes. Declared bankrupt, Colonel Waugh fled to Spain.

Today 100,000 visitors a year land at the Pottery Pier, but it is still possible to find seclusion on the island. Red squirrels thrive in woods free of the grey variety, the whistle and grunt of the male sika deer's rutting cry may be heard, and the island also has one of Britain's largest heronries. One foreign species which has settled here is the mink, first introduced into Britain in 1929. Among its victims on the island has been the tern and the colony has suffered badly over the years. Now owned by the National Trust, part of Brownsea is kept as a nature reserve but guided tours are available.

Brympton d'Evercy

Somerset ST 5215

England's longest single span staircase can be climbed in the delightful 16th- to 17th-century mansion every summer afternoon except Thursdays and Fridays. Close by are the sturdy Church of St Andrew, topped by a large square bellcote, and a Chantry or Dower House. A vineyard and cricket pitch add to the charm of the group in its lakeside setting.

Buckfastleigh

Devon SX 7486

Usually visited for its Abbey, it is perhaps less well known that Buckfastleigh boasts about a mile of spectacular limestone caves and passages. Probably never inhabited by man, they have yielded the richest collection of bones and teeth of interglacial mammals ever found in a British cave. Today the main inhabitants are bats; there are also spectacular stalactites like those at Cheddar and Kent's Cavern, Torquay. The caves can be visited, but check opening times at Plymouth Museum.

BURTON BRADSTOCK: COTTAGES — *Devon and Dorset villages like* **Burton Bradstock** *owe their beauty to the stone, slate and thatch in their cottages. Another popular material in these counties was cob — a mixture of shaly clay, straw and dung, built up and allowed to harden in layers. Once dry, it was shaved to form a rounded wall perhaps three feet thick. It needed a good 'hat and boots' — thatched roof and tarred ground level — but given these could stand for centuries.*

VERYAN'S *five thatched, whitewashed cottages were built so the devil had no corners to hide in and no north wall to enter by*

Rugged stone gives Yorkshire villages like **Luddenden, Heptonstall** *and* **Osmotherly** *their character, and honey-coloured stone is the glory of the Cotswolds, at* **Adlestrop, Blockley** *and numerous others. Good 'clunch' walling, with very hard chalk so accurately shaped that only the thinnest mortar is needed, can be seen in a few villages south of* **Cambridge** *and at* **Totternhoe** *church.*

Where oak was easier to get than stone, stud and plaster pre-vailed. A timber frame (the studs) was built up, leaving squares of oblong panels to be filled with lath and plaster. Typical of the black and white 'magpie' work of the north and west Midlands is **Pembridge***; in the south, such houses were often completely plastered, the plasterwork either left plain or decorated with pargeting, as at* **Clare.** *'Weather-boarding', with overlapping oak boards fixed horizontally to the walls, is characteristic of Essex.*

BURTON BRADSTOCK *The homes of stone and thatch are mostly over 300 years old*

Burton Bradstock

Dorset   SY 4889

Local fishermen are reputed to have landed a mermaid on Chesil beach in 1757; better authen-ticated is the smuggling that was rife along this coast. There are splendid views across the channel from the surrounding hills — many topped by prehistoric hill forts.

Despite a coastal caravan site, this is still an idyllic and unspoilt village. Lanes with names like Donkey and Darby are lined with thatched and ivy-covered cottages and the church (Perpen-dicular) has a central tower and 500-year-old roof. The clock is said to be from Christ's Hospital in London's Newgate Street.

Cameley

Avon   ST 6158

Betjeman described St James's as 'Rip-Van-Winkle's Church'. Unmodernised since a gallery was installed in 1819, it was regarded as a quaint anachronism until the 1960s, when an astonishing array of wall paintings was discovered, dating from Jacobean times back to the 11th century. Amongst them are a 14th-century jester, with his belled cap and multicoloured coat, and the foot of a huge St Christopher, stepping through water with a crab and fishes. Coats of arms include those of Edward I, his queen, Eleanor of Castile, and James I, while the chancel arch is dominated by two scrolls from the mid-17th century.

Camerton

Avon   ST 6857

The Ghost Train and *The Titfield Thunderbolt* took the line linking this mining village with the GWR: both films had scenes shot here. The line was axed by Beeching and the colliery went in 1950, but reminders are the *Jolly Collier* pub, with outside it a huge fibreglass miner, copied from a National Coal Board bronze for the 1951 Festival of Britain.

The early 19th-century diaries of local rector John Skinner are in the British Museum.

Cam Long Down

Gloucestershire   ST 7799

An outlier of the Cotswold escarpment in the Berkeley Vale, this lonely hill is steeped in mythology. Some say the Devil, carrying the Cotswolds away in barrow loads to dam the Severn, met a cobbler laden with shoes. 'How far to the river?' he asked. 'I've worn this lot out

CARN EUNY *fogou (left) and Culsh souterrain (above). Even today the Hopi Indians of Northern Arizona perform secret rites in underground chambers called 'kivas'*

CARN EUNY: FOGOUS

CARN EUNY: FOGOUS — *Found in ancient settlements such as* **Carn Euny**, *the 'fogou' is a passage-like stone-built structure, usually partly underground and covered with a bank of earth and stones. Fogous often include a corbelled chamber opening off the main passage, in which traces of occupation have been found. They span the late Iron Age to the Roman period.*

Some think they were hiding-places for both people and property, others pointing out that as refuges they were death-traps, and a more likely use would be as cold-storage chambers. Still others suggest that they stand at focal points for earth currents, and were used for mystic rituals in the dark — thought to assist psychic powers. A similar debate goes on over the 'dene-holes' of **Grays Thurrock***. Scotland has its underground chambers too — 'earth-houses' like those of Culsh, near Tarland. Tradition leaves no doubt as to their use: they were known as 'Pecht' houses, and the 'Pechts' or Picts were identified with the fairies. Ireland also has a tradition very like this.*

walking from it', was the reply, at which Satan gave up and tipped out his barrow. Others see this as Camlann, scene of Arthur's last battle, prompted by the legend that he crossed the Severn to fight it; and even sceptics have felt a strange affinity with the past here.

near-vanished England with its small shops and family businesses. The post office is an 18th-century house; the 1779 beehive-style lock-up still stands near the 1855 market hall. At the foot of the town, the war memorial rises out of the middle of a pond.

Carn Euny

Cornwall SW 4028

In the village centre, two miles west of Sancreed, are a deep circular chamber and an underground passage, 66 feet long, granite-lined, granite-roofed and known as a 'fogou'. Its use remains a mystery: was it a refuge, a cold store for meat or a place of pre-Christian ritual?

This is no ordinary village, but part of the Land's End Peninsula's rare prehistoric heritage — the remains of Carn Euny's interlocking courtyard houses and round houses date back to the Iron Age, about 500BC. Each house comprises a group of small rooms surrounding an open yard, and would have been thatched for use as living quarters and shelter for animals.

A similar settlement survives at Chysauster, north of Penzance. Most of it has been excavated and finds can be seen in the British Museum and museums at Penzance and Truro.

Castle Cary

Somerset ST 6332

Parson Woodforde, colourful chronicler of 18th-century life and eating habits, lived here and might still recognise the town centre — a bit of

Chalford

Gloucestershire SO 8902

Known as the heart of the Alpine Cotswolds, Chalford sprawls up the steep northern flank of the Golden Valley east of Stroud, a labyrinth of narrow lanes either difficult or impossible for motorists. Its pathways, dotted with shops and pubs, are best explored on foot, over the length of a full afternoon; for an easier walk it is relatively flat from Chalford Hill to the even more rural village of France Lynch.

Charfield

Avon ST 7292

Take the road south out of the village (near Wotton-under-Edge) for Charfield's hamlet of Churchend and the old medieval parish church. The Charfield Railway Monument in a remote corner of the churchyard remembers the victims of a local rail disaster in 1928. Twelve are named — but the tablet also notes two unidentified children, and the question of who they were remains unanswered. Some villagers talk about a woman in black who used to visit the memorial; others believe the two were not children but jockeys. The church is now redundant.

CHIPPING CAMPDEN: GAMES
— *Robert Dover, a Warwickshire attorney, got permission from James I to hold the Whitsuntide sports of* **Chipping Campden,** *at which he would appear in the King's old clothes 'but with much more dignity'.*

For nearly forty years 'Captain Dover' presided over the games — horseracing, hunting and coursing (a silver collar went to the best dog though not to the greyhound in Shakespeare's 'Merry Wives of Windsor', who was 'outrun on Cotsale') and traditional country sports such as wrestling, jumping and quarter-staff matches. Volleys were enthusiastically fired from a wooden edifice known as 'Dover Castle' and refreshments were served in tents for the gentry, or on cloths spread on the ground.

These jollifications were temporarily banned under Cromwell, and suppressed again in 1851 by Act of Parliament — as too unruly (though not to be confused with the type of unruly game found at Haxey, Humberside, **Atherstone, St Columb Major** *and elsewhere). Country sports held in other high places sometimes accompanied the 'scourings' of hill-figures such as the Uffington White Horse, Oxfordshire and the Chiltern Whiteleaf Cross, and some people see in them remnants of ancient ritual.*

HAXEY HOOD GAME   *A team of Boggans led by a Fool takes on all comers in the fight for 'hoods'. Shown here is the 'sway' — a kind of scrum which sweeps down all before it, in the effort to get the Sway Hood into one of three local pubs*

Chipping Campden

Gloucestershire   SP 1539

The old golden Cotswold town of Chipping Campden is never more enchanting than when a torchlight procession of thousands of people wends down to it from Dover's Hill after the Cotswold Olimpicks in late May or early June. The games, including shin-kicking, pikes and cudgels, were founded by Robert Dover in around 1612, and revived in 1951.

Even more colourful than Dover is the 'Campden Wonder', William Harrison, a respected old rent-collector who disappeared in 1660 and for whose murder two men and their mother were hanged. Two years later he walked back into his house with an amazing tale of robbery, kidnapping and Turkish pirates, an account none could believe or disprove. Campden House is one of the great lost mansions of the Cotswolds. Built by Sir Baptist Hicks, it was destroyed in the Civil War, though its distinctive gatehouses survive near the church.

Chittlehampton

Devon   SS 6325

Here can be found one of the most unlikely collections: the Cobbaton Combat Vehicle Museum, belonging to Mr Preston Isaac. He has collected World War II memorabilia over the last 25 years and the vehicles on display include a Churchill Mk VII Crocodile Flamethrower Infantry Tank 1944, a Centaur cruiser, a Leyland Lynx 1938 and a Standard Beaverette Mk III 1941. There are also domestic tableaux depicting everyday life in wartime Britain, set to background music by Vera Lynn, and hundreds of other exhibits. Open daily from April to October, otherwise by appointment.

Cirencester

Gloucestershire   SP 0201

Second-largest city in Roman Britain, Cirencester keeps most of its secrets buried but has some surprises above ground level too. A guide in the impressive parish church will point out the cat chasing the mouse in the lady chapel, an ancient craftsman's joke. And though the tower is no longer open regularly, the vicar will arrange ascents for parties. The view is spectacular, and reveals what lies behind the hedge round Cirencester House.

CHIPPING CAMPDEN   *A torchlight procession follows the Cotswold Olimpicks — once too unruly for the near-perfect Cotswold town*

Codford St Peter

Wiltshire   ST 9739

In the church is one of Britain's few surviving fragments of Saxon stone carving. Rightly described as one of Wiltshire's art treasures, its subject seems to be a dancing man, but its meaning remains an enigma. The figure may have been part of a cross; with branch in hand he may be celebrating a fruit harvest or worshipping a pagan deity. Only the force of the carving remains unquestioned.

Come-to-Good

Cornwall SW 8339

One of the oldest of the early Friends' Meeting Houses — where Quakers meet — stands surrounded by trees on the road from Carnon Downs to the King Harry Ferry. Dating back to 1710, it is built of cob with a thatched roof, and is whitewashed inside and out. Small latticed windows and simple wooden benches add to the charm of this most attractive building, which is still used for Quaker meetings. While seeming an apt name for a place of worship, Come-to-Good in fact derives from the old Cornish Cwm-ty-Quoit, which is translated as 'the house in the wooded coombe'.

George Fox, founder of the Society of Friends, regularly visited Cornwall and spent some time in Launceston Jail before the movement became legal in 1689.

Congresbury

Avon ST 4363

The yew trees in Congresbury churchyard recall the legend of a Dark Ages Saint Congar, who is said to have settled here, planted his stick in the ground, and 'on the following day . . . it put forth leaves'. One of the trees is said to be 'Congar's walking stick'. King Ine of Wessex was apparently moved to bestow land for a monastery, and the tenth-century King Edgar died after straying on the holy spot while hunting. To the north is Cadbury Camp, continuously occupied between the Iron and Dark Ages. Finds of Mediterranean pottery on this now lonely spot mark it as a place of sophistication during the latter period.

Corscombe

Dorset ST 5105

Squire Thomas Hollis, philanthropist, teetotaller and abstainer from sugar, milk and butter, lies buried as requested ten feet down in one of the local fields. A noted non-churchgoing liberal of the 18th century, he was also a benefactor of Harvard University in America.

Lying in lanes and rich in hamstone buildings, with mullion-windowed farmhouses all round, Corscombe offers beautiful views towards Wiltshire and Devon. The church has an impressive porch; the Fox inn is some 300 years old.

Corton Denham

Somerset ST 6322

Climb Halter Path Lane for the Beacon on Corton Hill, one of the county's best viewpoints. Below lies Sparkford Vale, punctuated by the superb prehistoric camp called Cadbury Castle — the likeliest contender for King Arthur's Camelot. Beyond it rises Glastonbury Tor — perhaps the Isle of Avalon where Arthur was taken after his last legendary battle in the west. Further north the view takes in the blue Mendips, the Beacon on the Fosse Way, Cranmore Tower and the Pensel Wood Ridge, topped by King Alfred's Tower. To reach Corton Denham and the Beacon, turn south off the A303 through South Cadbury.

CIRENCESTER *Looking from the top of the church, over the 40-foot yew hedge round Cirencester House and into the park — Pope helped create its 'amiable simplicity'*

C**HITTLEHAMPTON: COLLECTOMANIA** — *The Cobbaton Combat Museum at* **Chittlehampton** *is strictly 20th-century, but the collecting tradition goes back thousands of years. Sun-worshipping Amenhotep IV of Egypt had a special building for his collection of gifts in about 1300BC, and the Roman Emperor Hadrian was a noted collector as well as wall-builder. In the Middle Ages, the relic-collecting rage attracted further collections — of pilgrims' gifts — for* **Hailes Abbey** *and* **Canterbury.** *Eighteenth-century beliefs in knowledge for all led physician Sir Hans Sloane to leave his 69,352-item natural history collection for the public — the start of the British Museum — and also in* **London** *Sir John Soane set up his museum for architects. Dr Plume gave his 6000-volume library to* **Malden,** *and the Ashmolean Museum at* **Oxford** *began with a private collection.*

The Victorians opened numerous museums for public improvement, and the 19th century also saw great collectors like William Bankes of **Kingston Lacy,** *whom scandal forced to flee abroad. Today's museums cater for every taste — literally in the case of Guernsey's tomato museum at Castel. Those nostalgic for Wurlitzers will find all kinds of mechanical music at* **Napton on the Hill,** *and* **Snowshill Manor** *has exotica, but most extraordinary of all is Walter Potter's Museum of Curiosities at Arundel, near* **Burpham.**

ABOVE *Stuffed Kittens taking tea at Potter's museum. He is said to have been inspired by a nursery rhyme*

DOZMARY POOL: JAN TREGEAGLE — *Wicked Jan Tregeagle haunts* **Dozmary Pool** *and numerous other West Country places. He was a steward of the Earl of Radnor; he died in 1655 and was remembered as an exceptionally evil man, not least for killing a father and mother to seize the estates of their child.*

Most versions of his legend agree that he was called back from the grave by being named in court at **Bodmin.** *In a flash of lightning, Tregeagle appeared, saying it would not be so easy to dismiss as to summon him. The parsons of Bodmin decided to keep him busy with everlasting tasks. He was set to emptying Dozmary Pool (long believed to be bottomless) with a holed 'croggan' or limpet shell, and to weaving ropes of sand at Padstow. At Bareppa he had to clear the beach, carrying the sand away in sacks. When he dropped his sack one day the spilt sand formed* **Loe Bar** *(another sand-rope-weaving site). At Lands End, he labours still at the task of sweeping sand from Porthcurno Cove into Mill Bay, and the sighing of the wind is the sound of Tregeagle moaning as demons chase him over the moor.*

DOZMARY POOL   *According to tradition, the sword Excalibur has remained at the bottom of the lake since Arthur ordered Bedevere to throw it into the water as he lay dying. Legend also claims that this lonely expanse is bottomless, but in fact it completely dried up during a drought in 1869*

Crofton

Wiltshire SU 2662

The enormous steam engines in their neat Georgian engine house make an impressive sight at Crofton. The oldest working beam engines in the world (one was built by Boulton and Watt in 1812), they were designed to lift 11 tons of water every minute to replenish the Kennet and Avon Canal, here at its summit. They are 'steamed' periodically during the spring and summer by the Kennet and Avon Canal Trust, which also runs cruises along the canal.

Crowcombe

Somerset ST 1336

A mermaid, a Green Man, two naked men fighting a dragon — these and other arcane oddities can be seen carved on the bench ends of the 14th-century sandstone Church of the Holy Ghost. One of the benches is dated 1534, but the figures may well come from pre-Christian fertility symbolism. The font, possibly older than the church, is decorated with charming little carved figures. A split yew tree in the churchyard is thought to be as old as the nearby 14th-century cross. Outside the church is an appealing Quantocks village; the Church House is part Tudor and has splendid Jacobean mullioned windows.

Dolton and Dowland

Devon SS 5712 and SS 5610

These two tiny, obscure villages annually celebrate an International Festival during May and June. Events in previous years have included items from Italy, Africa, North and South America, France, Indonesia and the USSR, as well as more local topics such as a study of archaeology in Dolton and central Devon. Quite an achievement for a community numbering only 600 people! The villages themselves are worth visiting for a glimpse of unspoilt Devon life. Dolton is also notable as the home of photographer James Ravilious, whose work at the nearby Beaford Centre includes studies of contemporary rural life and the Beaford Archive, with over 4000 negatives dating from the early years of photography. There is exceptionally fine, well-preserved stone carving in Dolton's church and the font is made from parts of a Saxon cross. In the south aisle are three tablets by Lawrence Whistler.

Dozmary Pool

Cornwall SX 1974

It is said to be both bottomless and connected to the sea by an underground passage (its name means 'a drop of sea'). A white hand rose from its depths to take King Arthur's sword Excalibur. Jan Tregeagle, the unjust steward of local legend, was condemned to an eternity of emptying it using only a broken limpet shell.

True, similar tales are told of Loe Pool among many other places, and moorland cattle can be seen wading safely near Dozmary's centre. It dried out completely in 1869, when Neolithic arrowheads were discovered in the bed. And yet Dozmary Pool remains a most mysterious place, remote and haunting on the heights of lonely Bodmin Moor. It lies two miles south of Bolventor and Jamaica Inn — the original used by Daphne Du Maurier in her smuggling novel.

Drewsteignton

Devon SX 7391

Here are unspoilt thatched cottages in the square and a 15th-century church, but above all Drewsteignton should be visited for the Drewe Arms. It is known locally as 'Aunt Mabel's' after the landlady, Mrs Mudge, who has been in residence for over 60 years. The pub has no bar: beer and cider are dispensed in the back kitchen, along with a few spirits. Real folk music, singing the old songs to the accordion and fiddle, can be found here on most Saturday nights.

Close by is the National Trust's Castle Drogo, designed by Sir Edwin Lutyens in 1910 for Julius Drewe — a poor man's son who retired at 33 having founded the Home and Colonial Stores and claimed descent from a Norman nobleman.

Dunchideock

Devon SX 8889

Since time immemorial, rumour has said that there are treacle mines to be found at Dunchideock. No-one knows how this strange story evolved, but once every two years they can be visited. Mr Archibald Winckworth of Dunchideock House claims that the mines lie beneath his house, and on the biennial occasion of Dunchideock fete, held in the grounds of his house, is prepared to escort members of the public around for a small fee. It is possible that for the real enthusiast of industrial archaeology Mr Winckworth will open his mine by appointment, but this can be risky due to the highly explosive nature of the treacle.

A curious folly on the hills above the village commemorates General Stringer Lawrence.

Eggesford

Devon SS 6811

From the main Exeter to Barnstaple road (A377) can be seen the gaunt ruin of Eggesford House, the once-magnificent 19th-century home of the Earls of Portsmouth, famous for their love of hunting. The house itself is privately owned and unsafe, and cannot therefore be visited, but some of the history of the influential families of Devon can be traced from the marble monuments to the Chichesters, Wallops and Fellowes families in the estate chapel, Eggesford Church. A redundancy order on the church has made it the centre of a restoration battle, and as one of the few estate churches in Devon many feel that it deserves preservation. The Forestry Commission planted their first conifers on this estate in 1918.

Endsleigh House

Devon SX 4078

Some call it Endsleigh Cottage — no ordinary cottage but a *cottage orné* of the highly decorated and studiedly rustic 'Picturesque' style, and actually quite large. Built for the Duchess of Bedford in 1810 and now a luxurious country-house hotel, it was designed by Sir Jeffrey Wyattville to take full advantage of the fine views. The surrounding woodland and park was 'improved' (in fact transformed) by the landscape gardener, Humphry Repton. A staff of no fewer than 39 was needed to maintain Repton's much sought-after 'natural' gardens; today they still provide an idyllic setting for the hotel, which stands a mile south-west of Milton Abbot.

DOZMARY POOL: KING ARTHUR —

The story that **Dozmary Pool** is the last resting place of Arthur's sword Excalibur is one of numerous West Country associations with the legendary king, from a traditional birthplace at Tintagel to a last battle upstream from Slaughter bridge near Camelford, where 'King Arthur's Tomb', an inscribed stone slab, has been shown since at least Tudor times. The choughs once common at **St Nectan's Glen** were thought to embody his spirit, and the idea that Glastonbury was his Isle of Avalon led medieval abbey monks to search for his grave.

A suitable body was found — but was it Arthur? Or was it a plant by Henry II, who wanted the Welsh to know that Arthur would not be coming back to liberate them? Like the Welsh, Somerset people thought Arthur was not dead but sleeping, at South Cadbury, near Glastonbury, resting place of the Holy Grail.

Sleeping kings are claimed for **Richmond** Castle, Sewingshields on Hadrian's Wall and numerous other places — but research suggests that Arthur awake really was a sixth-century Celtic leader based in the west. The Tintagel link may be the Celtic monastery found there; and Cadbury Castle, South Cadbury, is a very likely contender for Camelot. Arthur or not, someone stopped the Saxon advance through Britain.

ABOVE *Arthur's death inspired the painter Archer and Tennyson: 'But now farewell. I am going a long way . . . To the Island valley of Avilion'*

EXETER: MISERICORDS — *The Knight of the Swan, fore-runner of Lohengrin, sails away in his swan-boat at* **Exeter**; *at* **Chester** *and Lincoln, Tristan meets Iseult under a tree in which is hiding King Mark, her jealous husband. At* **Norwich***, Reynard the Fox runs off with Chanticleer the Cock, 'Malkin with her distaff in her hand' giving chase, as in Chaucer's 'Canterbury Tales'. At Exeter again his mad career brings him to the scaffold.*

All these stories are carved on cathedral 'misericords' — the ledges hidden on the undersides of hinged seats, on which weary monks could prop their behinds when standing during mass. What a blessing this was shows in the name — 'misericord' is the Latin for 'pity'.

Carvers made the most of the opportunity they offered, and most interesting amongst their designs are the ones taken from medieval literature. This wasn't pure self-indulgence: the stories had morals. But sometimes we don't know what they were. Why does Sir Yvain trapped by the portcullis that cut off the hindquarters of his horse appear at New College, **Oxford***, at Chester and Boston?*

Ripon Cathedral has an exceptional series of misericords depicting among other curious tales, Jonah leaving the whale, a fox preaching, and pigs.

SAMSON *with the gates of Gaza — one of Ripon Cathedral's more conventional misericords by the local Carvers' Guild*

Exeter

Devon SX 9292

During the last war the Nazis boasted that 'Exeter was a jewel and we have destroyed it'. Medieval Exeter did largely disappear, but this cathedral city and county capital still has a wealth of treasures. Best known are the cathedral, founded in 1050, and the picturesque Guildhall in the High Street, but beneath the city runs a fascinating labyrinth of 14th-century underground passages, which once carried the city's water supply and can be visited. The Victorians built catacombs at St Bartholomew's, the first part of the city to be inhabited (by the Celts) and 15 people are interred here, while off the High Street is Parliament Street, the narrowest street in the world.

The area around the quay on the Exe (which brought Exeter its wealth as a wool-trading city) is full of history; and may seem surprisingly familiar: it was used in the television series *The Onedin Line*. The Maritime Museum is here, with a fine collection of unusual craft including the Cygnet, which used to ferry people aboard the Swan, a much larger luxury craft, which was once moored at Starcross.

A pleasant walk downstream passes Trew's Weir (dating from 1560), a paper mill and what is called the match factory — even though it actually made flax. Further out, past St James' Weir, St James' Leat leads to the ruins of another mill, whose owners fed their employees on salmon from the nearby Salmon Pool, which gives its name to the locality.

Falmouth

Cornwall SW 8032

A granite memorial opposite their home Arwenack House commemorates the Killigrew family (also connected with Lizard Point), who developed Falmouth from a village, at the suggestion, it is said, of Sir Walter Raleigh. Nearby, a pyramid celebrates 'the gallant officers and men of HM Post Office Packet Service' — from 1688 to 1852 this was the chief mail packet station for delivery all over the world. Local smuggling has its monument in the King's Pipe, a brick chimney on the slope leading down to

EXETER *The Cygnet ferried people to the larger, more luxurious Swan (seen in the painting behind), on which riotous parties were held. Both were built by a Captain Peacock*

Custom House Quay, which was used for burning illegally imported tobacco.

Steep alleyways lead off the main street down to the sea and two fine figureheads can be seen at the foot of Upton's Slip. On the south side of the Moor (the main square) a precipitous flight of 111 steps, known as Jacob's Ladder, leads up to a Wesleyan chapel. Falmouth working boats, some of the last under sail, still set off in search of oysters in the Helford River.

Farleigh Hungerford

Somerset ST 7957

Speaker of the House of Commons Sir Thomas Hungerford had to be pardoned for building the castle without permission in 1369, and a 16th-century Hungerford was executed for treason and unnatural vice after incarcerating his wife in one of the towers for several years. Claiming to own all the land as far as Salisbury, the Hungerfords were powerful and had a castle to match. Only the chapel, gateway and two towers survive, but even the ruins still make a very impressive sight.

Frampton-on-Severn

Gloucestershire SO 7407

The green of this pretty riverside village is often called Rosamund's Green, recalling the mysterious Jane Clifford, Henry II's 'Fair Rosamund'. Born locally, she was kept by him in a house surrounded by a maze at Woodstock, and bore him two children. Legend has it that Queen Eleanor found her way through the labyrinth to her bower by following a thread of the king's cloak, and once there, forced her to drink poison; all that is certain is that Rosamund was buried at Godstow nunnery. The green, some 22 acres in extent, is one of England's largest, and has three ponds and a cricket ground. A path across the water meadow nearby leads to the church and the nearby Sharpness Canal.

Gloucester

Gloucestershire SO 8318

The hidden gem of the city is Maverdine House, a towering four-storey mansion of great opulence occupied by Colonel Massey, the Parliamentarians' commander, during the Civil War siege of 1643. For this wonderful sight, go through the doorway beside Winfield's garden shop at 26 Westgate Street, which leads into a passageway just a few feet wide, and look upwards and towards the left.

The New Inn on Northgate Street is better known, but this superb medieval treasure, with its galleried courtyard, can still surprise visitors deceived by the building's later façade. Like the New Inn, the Fleece in Westgate Street was built for pilgrims to Gloucester Abbey, and one of its bars is housed in a stone-vaulted cellar dating from the 12th century. Also in Westgate Street the Dick Whittington (medieval behind a Queen Anne façade) was once owned by his nephew, and the Lamprey recalls the city's continuing tradition of presenting a pie of these eel-like creatures to the monarch on important occasions.

South-west of the cathedral and within easy walking distance of it, Gloucester Docks are a bonus to visitors who imagine this to be a land-locked city. Amongst other attractions is a museum of advertising and packaging, of great nostalgic appeal, and a converted barge, which serves as an entertainment centre and café. Ambitious plans exist for adapting the 19th-century dock warehouses.

Golitha Falls

Cornwall SX 2568

In a secluded valley of dense oak and beech woods, the River Fowey cascades over mossy boulders for half a mile. The falls are reached from the ancient packhorse bridge at Draynes, near St Cleer, and are seen at their best in the spring when wild daffodils are in bloom. Nearby, on the roadside, is King Doniert's Stone, an upright block carved with a Latin inscription and intricate interwoven shapes. It is dedicated to a Cornish king who drowned in AD875.

GLOUCESTER OLD SPOT *Females of the breed are noted for making good mothers*

GLOUCESTER: RARE BREEDS — *Lop-eared with black patches, the* **Gloucester** *Old Spot is an old-fashioned animal, also known as the Orchard Pig because it fattened on windfalls in the Lower Severn. It is one of Britain's rare breeds — displaced on farms as more commercially efficient breeds have evolved, but still valued for being an excellent mother and for other fine qualities.*

Selective breeding isn't new — most British pigs have 18th-century south-east Asian ancestors. So today stocky little black Berkshire pigs like Gip, companion of the vicar of **Morwenstow,** *are seldom seen outside the pages of Beatrix Potter's 'Tale of Pigling Bland' — the breed was too fat-prone to survive. But the attractive ginger-coated Tamworth pig still has the prick ears and pointed snout of medieval farm pigs, while among the sheep types the Cotswold and the Lincoln Longwool are probably direct descendants of flocks kept on Roman villa farms. It isn't only the breeds that are worth saving: traditionally, real Double Gloucester cheese could only be made from the milk of Old Gloucestershire cows (see also* **Middleton in Teesdale).**

Fortunately there has been a renewed interest in rare breeds. A remarkable selection can be seen at the Rare Breeds Survival Trust's centre, Cotswold Farm Park, Guiting Power, Gloucestershire. Several rare breeds are also kept at Rutland Farm Park, **Oakham,** *Leicestershire.*

FRAMPTON-ON-SEVERN *(left) rich in timber-framing, Georgian brick and dovecotes. The cat on this one is stone*

MASONS' *marks at Warkworth (top), probably a practical guide for stone cutting; and a mason of the mystic kind (above)*

GREAT BEDWYN: MASONS — *The stonemasons of* **Great Bedwyn** *work in a craft with a long tradition of secrecy. Travelling medieval masons devised a password to identify themselves among strangers, and masons' marks, such as the two found in the Wakefield Tower, Tower of* **London,** *developed from being a way for the pay-master to identify the work of pieceworkers or casual labourers, to become personal 'signatures'. Strange masons' doodles, like the manticore of* **North Cerney,** *added to their mystique.*

The very meanings of the word craft — from skill to cunning — reflect the mystery that crafts can hold for the uninitiated, and trained workers also had an interest in keeping their skills secret. Drawn by such mysteries, non-craftsmen came to masonic lodges in the 17th century in search of occult wisdom — the beginning of modern Freemasonry.

Among primitive peoples, black-smiths are still often linked with magic and secrecy. Their practices shed light on European traditions such as the legends surrounding Wayland's Smithy in Oxfordshire, and on prehistoric mysteries such as the smiths of **Stanhope,** *who lived apart from the community in a cave. Their craft seems to have involved rites using human blood.*

Ritual accompanied the practice of other early industries and crafts. In medieval England, charms and ceremonies attended the spinning and weaving of cloth.

Goonhilly Downs

Cornwall SW 7120

Surrounded by Bronze Age burial mounds, the 11 vast saucer aerials of Goonhilly Earth Station rise from a plateau of heathland on the Lizard Peninsula's serpentine rock, to pick up messages, phone calls and television signals which have been bounced back 22,000 miles through space via geostationary satellites.

From May to September there are guided tours of the Station. In early autumn the rare Cornish Heath is in flower on the downs.

Great Bedwyn

Wiltshire SU 2764

Peacocks scratch between fantastic tombstones, including an aeroplane with an 11-foot wing span, at Lloyds' Stone Museum in Church Street, a building decorated with tombstones painted their original bright colours. Tracing the history of carved and worked stone of all kinds, including stonemasons' secrets, the museum is run by the seventh generation of a 200-year-old family of stonemasons, still flourishing. Also here are the haunted Regency Bedwyn House and the tomb of one of Henry VIII's six fathers-in-law.

Hailes Abbey

Gloucestershire SP 0530

This was one of Europe's leading medieval pilgrimage destinations, for the Cistercians who owned it had a phial alleged to contain the Blood of Christ, authenticated by the Pope and presented to them by a rich benefactor. In an elaborate shrine, the relic drew pilgrims in their thousands, and is mentioned in Chaucer's *Pardoner's Tale.* When the monastery was dissolved, however, the fluid was dismissed as a fraud. Today the ruins of the 13th-century abbey are open daily, with an interesting museum.

Hallsands

Devon SX 8138

Gravel dredging for the Naval Dockyard at Devonport so eroded the village that in the violently stormy January of 1917, 29 houses collapsed in one night. Miraculously no-one was killed. The villagers were all rehoused except for one woman who lived on in the one inhabitable dwelling until her death in 1964. Now only gulls inhabit the ruins of walls and chimneys which remain perched above the sea, a monument to man's folly. It is just north of Start Point and close to the southernmost tip of Devon.

Hamdon Hill

Somerset ST 4717

Source of the golden, lichen-mottled Ham Hill stone which enhances cottages and stately homes for miles around, 400-foot Hamdon Hill dominates the surrounding plains — renowned as the source of Somerset fruit from strawberries to Cox's apples. The Romans quarried the stone and built a great fort here, close to the Fosse Way; below the hill is the ancient village of Stoke-sub-Hamdon. Interesting carvings in the church include two signs of the Zodiac, Leo and Sagittarius, symbols perhaps for summer and winter, or strength (lion) and evil (archer).

Hawkesbury

Avon ST 7687

In the porch of St Mary's, note the sign in which 'Jt is Defired That . . . the Women would not walk in with their Pattens on', below which someone has helpfully hung a pair of wooden overshoes. Up on the hill, Vulliamy's towering Chinese-style monument to General Lord Robert Somerset, built in 1846, is open at all reasonable times, although few people climb its 145 steps to enjoy one of the most breathtaking views from the spectacular South Cotswold escarpment.

Jane Austen referred to an inn at Petty France, nearby, in *Northanger Abbey*.

Helford River

Cornwall SW 7526

Hidden wood-fringed creeks, once the haunt of smugglers, border the peaceful waters of this sheltered river. One such winding inlet, Frenchman's Creek, was immortalised by Daphne du Maurier's romantic novel. A few boats from Falmouth still trawl the riverbed for the much-prized Helford oysters, and there is an oyster farm at Port Navas.

The waters of the Helford are also reputed to be the home of Morgawr, the Helford Monster, a smaller cousin of Nessie. There have been many sightings since 1926 and the beast has been described by one eye-witness as a 'hideous hump-backed creature with stumpy horns'.

HELFORD RIVER *Smugglers once landed contraband cargoes on its shores, but now the river is frequented by pleasure yachts and working boats from Falmouth, trawling for oysters*

HORTON *Did a wooden stair once climb 120-foot Sturt's Folly? A puzzle — like its builder*

Hinton St George

Somerset ST 4212

'Give us a candle, give us a light,
If you don't, you'll get a fright'
. . . is the song of local children on Punkie Night, the last Thursday in October, when they beg candles to light their intricately carved pumpkin and turnip lanterns. It is very unlucky to refuse them: the lanterns almost certainly represent spirits of the dead, thought to return at Hallowe'en.

Narrow lanes, a medieval cross and Ham Stone are among the attractions of the village, overlooked by a graceful Perpendicular church with scratch dials (early sundials) on the buttresses.

Holsworthy

Devon SS 3403

Unexceptional for six days of the week, quiet Holsworthy springs to life on Wednesdays with a fine old-fashioned market of the sort that's increasingly hard to find, selling local cheese and butter, Devonshire cream and good poultry as well as other standard market fare. In the church is a beautifully carved 17th-century organ, sold from Chelsea Old Church to Bideford in 1723 as 'worn out'. The impressive ex-railway viaducts reached from the Okehampton and Launceston roads can be walked with permission from British Rail.

Horton

Dorset SU 0307

A tower looms over the village and intrigues travellers on their way to Wimborne or Ringwood. Sturt's Folly, seven storeys of turreted and ivy-covered red brick, is said to have been built by Humphrey Sturt in 1700 for spotting deer from nearby Cranborne Chase — but may be much later. It can be seen close to: half way up is a fireplace — but no staircase.

HAILES ABBEY: RELICS — *In its heyday, the Blood of* **Hailes** *was a magnet for nearly as many pilgrims as the Virgin's milk at Walsingham. Items of Mary's clothing could be seen at* **Durham,** *bits of the Holy Rood at Bromholm Priory in Norfolk, and of the Crown of Thorns at St Albans. More exotic things even than these had reached the West in the wake of the Crusades — Christ's breath in a bottle, the tip of the Devil's tail, and, at Venice, Goliath's tooth.* **Reading** *was an important stopping point on the way to the shrine of Santiago de Compostela, because it owned among its relics one of the saint's hands — still to be seen at* **Marlow.**

Relics were believed to work wonders, especially on disease, and hopeful pilgrims brought rich offerings to the shrines that housed them. Consequently relics were not only acquired as gifts and bequests, but stolen, switched, manufactured and duplicated — Dorchester and Winchester both had St Birinus, and John the Baptist seems to have had several heads.

Great shrines such as Becket's at **Canterbury** *amassed staggering wealth from pilgrims — good reason for the Dissolution of the Monasteries, which administered them. To help justify the Dissolution, the Reformers mounted a campaign to discredit the relics and a principal scapegoat was the Blood of Hailes. Officially described as a yellowish gum enclosed in a beryl, making it look red, it was asserted in the propaganda version to be duck's blood in a conjuror's magical glass, furtively renewed by the monks as needed.*

ILCHESTER: ROMAN ROADS — *The Fosse Way past* **Ilchester** *was part of a ruthless new road network, built to serve the needs, not of local communities, but of central government. The roads shifted troops and stores by the shortest feasible route between legionary forts such as* **York** *and* **Chester** *and the Channel ports, or across country as between Lincoln and* **Exeter**. *If they deviated from the straight, it was only to facilitate descent of steep hills by loaded wagons, or to avoid natural obstacles.*

Construction varied: generally a foundation of large stones was topped with a layer of rammed gravel, but Holtye, East Sussex, has a stretch surfaced with iron slag from the nearby Weald furnaces. Unique in Britain is the paving of large stone setts on Blackstone Edge, near **Rochdale**. *The most impressive Roman road in Britain is the stretch preserved on Wheeldale Moor, North Yorkshire. Though its gravel has been washed away, its kerb-stones are in places intact, as are its drainage culverts.*

When the Romans had gone, this feat of engineering was attributed to the giant Wade, and known as Wade's Causeway (see also **Sarn Helen***). Even a lowly path leading to* **Silchester** *is known as Devil's Highway: like numerous other stretches of ex-Roman road it was thought by awestruck people who had forgotten Roman skills to be the work of supernatural hands.*

WADE'S CAUSEWAY, *a Roman road which originally ran 21 miles across Wheeldale Moor from Malton to Whitby, gave rise to the legend that it was built by a giant called Wade*

Houndtor

Devon SX 7581

The remains of a medieval village can be traced below the tor's irregularly-shaped rocks. A better climate made Dartmoor sites of well over 1000 feet above sea level habitable in the Bronze Age, and some communities hung on until the 14th century. Here the foundations of four typical Dartmoor longhouses can be seen, together with smaller buildings which were probably barns. It is also possible to see the boundaries of arable fields and pastures. As the climate deteriorated the villagers were forced to dry their crops artificially by means of fire holes or hearths in the barns until eventually they abandoned the settlement. It lies two miles south of Manaton village.

The Hurlers and the Cheesewring

Cornwall SX 2571

The Hurlers, three early Bronze Age stone circles, can be seen on desolate moorland near the village of Minions. Legend says that they were men turned to stone for playing the sport of hurling on the Sabbath. Close to the nearby quarry a stone cutter, Daniel Gumb, lived with his wife and children in a rough shelter of tumbled stones. He studied astronomy, philosophy and mathematics, and carved geometric figures signed 'D Gumb 1737' on the rocks. Local legend tells of a druid who owned a gold cup which held an inexhaustible supply of water for thirsty travellers. When a nearby ancient barrow was excavated in 1818, alongside a skeleton lay a gold vessel, the Rillaton Cup, now in the British Museum. Towering above the quarry is the Cheesewring, a strange formation of naturally weathered granite.

Ilchester

Somerset ST 5222

Foreteller of submarines, steamboats and aeroplanes, 13th-century friar Roger Bacon was born here and went on to become an outstanding thinker of the age. Imprisoned for his ideas, he would no doubt be pleased by the celebration of air transport close by at the Fleet Air Arm Museum at Yeovilton, which explores the history of naval aviation.

An important Roman centre on the Fosse Way Roman road, Ilchester is now a busy junction on the A303. England's oldest staff of office, a 13th-century mace, is housed in the Town Hall.

Kellaways

Wiltshire ST 9873

Maud Heath's Causeway (see Bremhill) runs here over 64 arches. The land and houses that she left to fund the causeway in the 15th century paid for the present-day bridge as well. In 1698 a ball and pillar were put up in memory of Maud.

skirting the property known as Batworthy, the North Teign River will be reached, wherein lies the Holed Stone. Passing through the huge round hole without falling in the river is said to cure anything from arthritis to barrenness. The river can be crossed by the 'Teign-e-ver' clapper bridge, leading to the Scorhill Circle.

Kilve

Somerset   ST 1443

Conger eels, or 'glats', up to 10 feet in length lurk among the great boulders lining the shore. They were once hunted as 'St Keyna's serpents' (after a legend of a saint who turned local snakes to stone) using trained 'fishdogs'.

Experiments in extracting shale oil from the rock ended in failure. To the west, East Quantoxhead, home of the Luttrell family for the last 600 years, stands prettily at the end of a narrow winding lane.

Kimmeridge

Dorset   SY 9179

Nodding donkey pumps rock back and forth in perpetual motion on the clifftop overlooking the bay — rich in oil, the shale rock around here has been known to burn for months on end. It also has remarkable numbers of fossils, and its thin laminated consistency gave the Romans a flourishing industry making jet-like jewellery. Discs from their turners' lathes — once known as 'coal money' — are on display in the County Museum at Dorchester.

Kingston Lacy

Dorset   ST 9701

A closed treasure house until very recently: the last owner, Henry Ralph Bankes, is said to have kept even Queen Mary at bay. He lived as a recluse, surrounded by pictures by Rubens, Van Dyck, Veronese, Tintoretto, Brueghel and Lely, and other riches. Most were acquired by the colourful William John Bankes who was descended from the house's 17th-century founder (whose own home at Corfe Castle was taken apart by a Parliamentarian rival) and said to be remarkably attractive. He had to flee home for good when charged with homosexuality in the 1840s. The house now belongs to the National Trust, which has spent three years preparing it for opening to the public.

Lacock

Wiltshire   ST 9168

The world's first photograph was taken here in 1835 and is on display inside the Fox Talbot Photographic Museum, housed in a 16th-century tithe barn. Outside, the subject, a latticed window, can be seen in the South Gallery of Lacock Abbey, home of photography pioneer, William Henry Fox Talbot.

Founded in 1232 and turned into a mansion in the Reformation by Sir William Sharington, the Abbey rapidly passed to the Talbots when Olive Sharington leapt from its tower, it is said, into her (Talbot) lover's arms, rather than renounce their love. Her billowing skirts saved her, the marriage was sanctioned and village and Abbey remained in the family until 1958.

The Dorset Coast Path as it rounds Broad Bench into **Kimmeridge** Bay leads to one of the most sombre stretches of this coast — yet most varied in interest — the rocky ledges of the Kimmeridge Clay, dark grey beds of banded clay and shales in which numerous fossils are embedded.

Ammonites (related to the octopus) are still abundant and in the Dorset County Museum at Dorchester are the remains of one of the great reptiles of the Jurassic period, Pliosaurus grandis. Further along the coast, 12-year-old Mary Anning came upon the remains of an ichthyosaurus on Black Venn near Lyme Regis in 1810, and ensured Dorset's place in the centre of the debate over evolution versus creation.

A popular explanation put forward for such relics was that they were animals drowned in the Flood. Others suggested that they were man-made, as country names for fossils like 'shepherd's crowns' suggest. The placing of an ammonite at the entrance of West Kennet Long Barrow has been taken to imply a belief in fossils' mystic powers, but might be for decoration, a use seen at Kimmeridge today.

ABOVE   A familiar sight on the Dorset coast millions of years ago? An artist's impression of the swan-necked plesiosaurus and the ichthyosaurus with its crocodile jaws

THE CHEESEWRING   *Many human abilities have been attributed to unusual stones, and it is said that the top part of the Cheesewring turns round three times on hearing a cock crow*

Kempsford

Gloucestershire   SU 1596

Local ghosts include a frightened mother, a penitent knight, a silent monk and a boy in lace and breeches. Lancastrian roses blooming in the roof-bosses of the church recall Kempsford's Plantagenet connections: Blanche, heiress of the first Duke of Lancaster, was the wife of John of Gaunt (who is credited with building the impressive church tower) and the mother of Henry IV. A horse-shoe on the church door is said to have been shed by the Duke of Lancaster's horse in tragic circumstances.

Kestor

Devon   SX 7087

From the ancient stannary town of Chagford (where the stannary court, for the regulation of tin mining, was held) winding lanes lead past the hamlet of Teigncombe to Kestor Rock and nearby ancient field systems, stone circles and rows, attributed to the Bronze Age Beaker Folk. The huge longstone inscribed with GP, C and DC marks the parish boundaries of Gidleigh parish, Chagford and Duchy of Cornwall land. If the double stone row is followed due north,

FAT MAN
ON THE
FOSSE WAY

Tom Vernon has been a minstrel, teacher and cave-tour-guide — but is best known for his cycling explorations, serialised on BBC radio as 'Fat Man on a Bicycle' and 'Fat Man on a Roman Road'. He lives in London with wife, sons and cat

A symbol of ancient power, running with uncommon directness through nowhere in particular . . . Tom Vernon explores the fascination of Roman Road Spotting as he follows the Fosse Way from south-west to central England

Roman roads are one of the great imaginative images of childhood: a grown-up stands you on it, points ahead and says it goes straight as far as the eye can see and then farther than that; and it is as if they said that there was a dinosaur on the other side of the hill, or a pyramid complete with Pharaohs. The road immediately becomes not an ordinary road, like the smelly, dangerous one you are forbidden to run into, but a symbol of ancient power and purpose, and every road with a straight in it becomes indisputably Roman.

When you are travelling the secret parts of the Fosse Way, this childish mysticism returns, so that you are constantly scanning ahead for the main road bending away while something else goes straight. Roman Road Spotting is the art of perceiving the ancient route, dashing boldly onwards, and apologising gracefully when you end up in someone's front garden. It is totally compulsive and only a little bit infantile, like most of the best amusements.

The Fosse Way is one of the medieval 'Four Royal Roads' of Britain — the Icknield Way, Ermine Street, Fosse Way, Watling Street — but it was built by the Romans, running straight as the flight of a fairly purposeful pigeon from the south-west to Lincoln. There is scarcely five miles deviation in all its 200-mile length, though in Dorset and Devon its course is uncertain. It is a road that is absolutely determined to go straight through nowhere in particular on the way to towns which were particularly important 2000 years ago.

Such a long road does not require surveying so much as navigating — and navigating by sun and stars, since the Romans had no compasses — with only the gleam of a beacon on a far hill at night to help the builders' self-confidence, although on shorter stretches they had a kind of primitive theodolite. Its fascination is that what was intended to be so purposeful and practical is now so random. It is nothing more than an accident of economic geography that makes one place a wilderness, one a city — and the accident has not endured. Where are the legions from Cirencester now, who had an urgent need to travel fast to Newark or Axminster? The Fosse Way feels like the road equivalent of a folly. Some bits of it have been developed, some have gone to grass; and the result is an unpredictable hotch-potch

THE FOSSE WAY   *After Cirencester, no longer a main road but 'a path through centuries of slow legs — pedlars, farmers' wives, drovers, labourers . . .'*

of secret places, which are secret because there is no possible connection between them apart from the long-dead logic of Aulus Plautius Sylvanus, the governor of Britain who planned it to maintain the wild western Celtic frontier.

There are advantages to this today. Travelling through my swarming England nowadays, I often feel like an alley-cat in a dustbin, picking out the bits that are only slightly tainted. Usually, it is the richer morsels that have gone off first. The Fosse Way does not suffer from being *nouveau riche, riche* or *nouveau* — which is how I like my country. A lot of it is pleasantly, unpretentiously traditional England, though it has few secrets and not a lot of charm beyond Leicester.

The road is thought to have begun on the Devon coast at the former quarries at Beer (*Beer,* Old English *Bearu,* a grove; not *beer,* Modern English, a blessing to humanity), but the first confident marking of ROMAN ROAD occurs after Axminster, a few miles up the winding river. Not far along the A358, at the top of Tytherleigh Hill, the first logical digression of the Fosse Way takes you by surprise — a nondescript slant off to Cricket St Thomas, where the big house is a tourist attraction and they breed shire horses.

From that point you have no choice but to become addicted to the doubtful science of Roman Road Spotting.

It is an easily missed spot, the turning north-east to Dinnington from the A30 at the top of Windwhistle Hill. A tiny lane thumps and bumps down the hillside in a tunnel of hazel, with ferns tumbling down the banks and creepers hanging from the branches. It is not always as straight as it begins, but it is certainly old, for the feet of generations of travellers and centuries of winter rains have cut it deep into the hill; and an unexpectedly beautiful house of golden stone from Ham Hill, not far distant at Montacute, seems to belong to a more imposing highway. The Way continues bracken-banked and very small to a field or two before Over Stratton, where it disappears into a footpath, and, though you can resume it on the other side of the village, it is not long to go before South Petherton, and it becomes the A303, too busy to be agreeable. The distance between the two main roads is less than ten miles, but the feeling of the lane is surprisingly remote.

At Ilchester, they have made a bypass and closed off the disused road with metal gates, but it is possible to walk through, and climb the bank before the roundabout where the A303 heads for London and the Way becomes the A37 to Shepton Mallet. Someone has made a two-plank bridge across a ditch in the

FAT MAN
ON THE
FOSSE WAY

central reservation to make sure the Way goes on. (There is a similarly thoughtful touch where Ermine Street crosses the motorway before Scunthorpe, for the traffic engineers have actually left a stretch of tarmac in the middle of the roundabout as a memento.)

It is a couple of miles before Shepton Mallet that the road starts scaling itself down again, and by the time it has come over the hill at Cannard's Grave and down to the old turnpike house where it crosses the Frome-Wells road, the A361, it is preparing to become very rough indeed. The turnpike has been built square across it; the lane goes diagonally down to a river and an old cider factory built in stone with mullioned windows, before it climbs the hill progressively shedding its surface until it is a torrent of rough boulders leading to a farm-track. There is no attempting this part of the Fosse in a car, but the whole of the section to Oakhill is less than four miles, and of great charm, with wood pigeons flapping out of the unkempt hedges as you pass and dog-rose, cornflowers and tumbledown dry-stone walls between hill meadows. A farmer has barbed wired

a small woody section so that you have to detour round lanes in the middle, but at last a grass track brings you to the plantation surrounding Beacon Hill, which was a hill fort before the Romans came, and an important Roman cross-roads. You can come at the fort from the hilltop road to Priddy, which is just as well, since the only way I could find past it was straight over the ramparts — fine if all you have to carry is a spear and shield, but tricky if you have any kind of obligation to a bicycle or a pushchair.

After the farm-track to Oakhill there is no going straight on — you have to take the main road to Radstock and Bath, which is by now the A367, and wait till it hits the Roman course again. Then, as it curves up and down the panoramic valley at Nettlebridge, the uncompromising line of the Fosse is clear again, part as lane, part as footpath, and there are two similar detours from the main road after Peasedown St John till you come on to

the Bath road along a tunnel of hedges floored by tree-roots. A derelict cottage along the track, with a rotten ladder still leaning against its apple tree, suggests that the days of the path being in greater use are not much more than half a century gone.

From Bath, the pleasure capital where Roman limbs loosened in hot water as a brief reminder of a homeland where it rained and froze and fogged far less, there is an adventurous stretch of Fosse Way to the second city of Roman Britain, Cirencester. It starts easily with a second-class road that climbs to the high ground from the A4 at Batheaston, runs the open ridge of Bannerdown to Mountain Bower (where it dips into a pastoral landscape of rough grazing and woody hollows) and eventually climbs out into the sunshine of the wolds a few miles before it goes under the M4 motorway.

It has long become a lane, and now dwindles periodically to track and foot-path, still following a course which is extraordinarily straight, even for a Roman road. Its feel is not at all one of marching legions, but of a path through

ordinary centuries of slow legs — pedlars, farmers' wives, drovers, labourers. It is a bit of the drive to some-body's house, loose stones put down by the water board, dry ruts, wet mud, a thicket, a brook bed with a single stepping stone, a dusty white road such as people must have ridden in the days of penny-farthings, a minute packhorse bridge over a quick, clear stream.

Wheels have to make frequent detours — one to Grittleton is specially worth making, for Grittleton House is built in several different architectural styles, and Fosse Lodge is a turreted fantasy of a cottage — and even legs need some determination to push through such obstacles as a farmyard on a derelict air-field with cows queuing for milking on the airstrip, thorn hedges, sloe bushes, nettles, and at last a live aerodrome, Kemble, just before Thames Head, where the river rises — or does it? There is a phone by the gate, so that you can ring the RAF to come and take you over, but it is not a courtesy to be relied on, for the telephone was out of order when I was there.

Through the Cotswolds the Fosse Way

is a moderately busy main road, the A429 to Stratford-upon-Avon until Halford, some miles after Moreton-in-Marsh. With the transition to the Midlands, the countryside ceases to be elegant, and becomes simple: butter-coloured stone and estates give way to red brick and farmsteads, the River Windrush to the Grand Union Canal.

Once again, the Fosse Way goes north-east with uncommon directness as a quiet road over everything, through nothing, never a town, hardly a village, until it reaches High Cross, the centre of Roman England, where it once again takes to the wilds, but far more decorously, as a foot-path, a yellow lane, a lighter-coloured strip of grass along the edge of a field.

So it continues until near Sapcote, not far from Leicester, after which city it has few secrets, for it is a main road through work-a-day countryside, and bequeathes its leisurely magic of lost purpose to

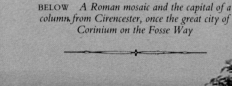

MAIN PICTURE *North of Halford, on its way to the Grand Union Canal. The Fosse Way is a lane here, bestowing its name on numerous farmsteads on its way*

BELOW *A Roman mosaic and the capital of a column from Cirencester, once the great city of Corinium on the Fosse Way*

other Roman roads elsewhere. Of course, the magic is in the imagination of the beholder: sitting in the sun by the church in Cirencester, which was the Roman Corinium, I met an old engineer who told me how, one day when they were digging up the road, he left his tea and climbed down the hole so that he might stand on the ruts that had been made by Roman chariot wheels.

The British rarely bury their past, and if it buries itself they dig it up again to make sure that it is still there. Every old town is a whole archaeology of legends, vanished societies, stories of individuals, troubles, labours, causes lost and won, fictions, accidents, happinesses: land-scapes hide an imaginative treasure trove.

Most of Britain is a secret place to most of us, for all of it is much more than its present-day appearance. It is an assembly of ghosts and fantasies, which mix with the present to make us what we are. All imaginings are equal, and only the imagining of the moment is more equal than others: but it is indeed a memorable journey to follow the pedantic spirit of a Roman surveyor along the Fosse Way.

SCHOOL IS OUT by Elizabeth Stanhope Forbes (1859-1912), a Newlyn School painting at the Penlee House Museum

Lamorna

Cornwall SW 4524

The tranquil hamlet of Lamorna nestles in a deep wooded valley which winds down to the sea. A gushing stream turns the waterwheel of Kemyel Mill and semi-tropical vegetation surrounds a small pond. The village inn is called the Wink: kiddleywinks were Cornish establishments where only beer was sold — no spirits. But a wink to the landlord often produced something stronger, and nobody asked where it came from! Behind the small harbour is a massive granite quarry where stone was cut to build London's Embankment and several lighthouses. Lamorna, the area and its people were much painted by the 19th-century school of painters who settled at Newlyn, some three miles north.

Langton Herring

Dorset SY 6182

Lying between Abbotsbury with its thriving Swannery (established by medieval Benedictine monks) and the seaside charms of Weymouth, Langton Herring offers one notable haven.

The Elm Tree is an old smuggling inn with beams festooned with copper and brass and an inglenook fireplace. Old-fashioned furnishings and a pretty side garden add to its charms; nearby is the quaint Church of St Peter.

Lanyon Quoit and Men-an-Tol

Cornwall SW 4333

Lanyon Quoit stands like a stone sentinel on high moorland beside the Penzance to Morvah road. A massive capstone supported by three upright granite slabs are all that remains of the Neolithic chamber tomb of about 2500BC. A man on horseback could once ride beneath it, but it was toppled during a storm in 1875 and the re-constructed quoit is now about a metre lower. One and a half miles to the north and reached by a stony track stands the Men-an-Tol, a holed stone between two uprights. Probably dating from the Bronze Age, it may have been connected with fertility rites. Ailing children were passed through the stone nine times against the sun to cure them of rickets.

Lee

Devon SS 4846

A beautiful little seaside hamlet near Ilfracombe, almost unspoilt, with a hotel in the former manor house. Thatched cottages stand in the idyllic setting of a wooded combe, running down to the sand and shingle beach of Lee Bay. Locals tell tales of smuggling and wrecking off this coast.

Lewtrenchard

Devon SX 4586

The Reverend Sabine Baring-Gould, author of *Onward Christian Soldiers* and Cornish saint enthusiast, was the incumbent here in the late 19th century. The tiny hamlet (which is just off the A30 between Okehampton and the county border) also boasts superb views to the 12th-century church on Brentor.

Littledean

Gloucestershire SO 6713

Open from April to October and often promoted as Littledean Hall, Dean Hall stands on a spectacular upland site overlooking the Severn. Ghosts range from a wandering monk and an ill-used black manservant to duelling brothers and slain cavaliers. The panelled Jacobean rooms are rich in atmosphere and hidden passages, and in 1984 the owner discovered one of Britain's largest Roman temples in the grounds.

Lizard Point and Lighthouse

Cornwall SW 6911

Ex-pirate (by renown) Sir John Killigrew built the present Lizard Lighthouse in 1751, replacing a 1620 original. Some say he wished to save ships from the Lizard's reefs only that they might founder on the rocks nearer his home town of Falmouth, where he owned the appropriate rights.

Lizard is the only village in mainland Britain lying south of the 50th parallel, and it was from the jagged rocks of Lizard Point, the most southerly point on the British mainland, that the Spanish Armada was first sighted in 1588. The chief rock is serpentine: marked like a serpent's skin and ideal for carving, it also supports a heathland which is a paradise for botanists. One of the rare plants, the Cornish Heath, is found nowhere outside Cornwall in Britain.

Loders

Dorset SY 4994

A deep narrow valley shelters this pretty place, just north-east of Bridport with Boars Barrow at one end and the landmark of Waddon Hill at the other. Under the hill nestles a picturesque church with a battlemented porch. The monks of a priory which once stood on the site of Loders Court are said to have made apple wine, thus bringing cider to Dorset.

Loe Pool and Loe Bar

Cornwall SW 6425

Like Dozmary Pool on Bodmin Moor, this lake separated from the sea by a high bar of shingle — Loe Bar — has supposed connections with King Arthur. His sword Excalibur is said to have been received by a hand rising from the water, and one of the punishments of legendary Jan Tregeagle was to weave a rope from the sand of Loe Bar. A walk leads round the wooded fringes of Loe Pool which is now owned by the National Trust.

Lydney Park

Gloucestershire SO 6203

A large Victorian house overlooking the Severn, Lydney Park opens its grounds only for a few days of the azalea and rhododendron season, in May and early June. Planted since World War II, the woodland garden is breathtaking at this time of year, more beautiful than Stourhead, according to people in the know. Also here are important finds from a temple site excavated by Sir Mortimer Wheeler in the 1920s; a herd of fallow deer; and memorabilia of New Zealand, of which the first Viscount Bledisloe, in whose family the house remains, was Governor General in the 1930s

LYDNEY: THE LOST GOD — *At the end of the fourth century AD an elegant temple-complex was built at* **Lydney** *to the god Nodens, who is otherwise unknown.*

Finds at Lydney show that he was a god of healing, to whom pilgrims offered votive figures of dogs, the mascots of healing sanctuaries elsewhere in the ancient world. He was probably connected with the sea: the temple had a mosaic (now lost) of fish and sea-monsters, and stood on hilly ground overlooking the Severn estuary.

In name Nodens corresponds with two figures of Celtic mythology, Irish Nuadha and Welsh Nudd, later Lludd. Lludd is the legendary king of Britain who fortified **London** *and was buried at Ludgate, and both Nuadha and he were involved in defending their kingdoms against invaders. At London and Lydney, he may have been a god of the headland guarding a great estuary and thus a national tutelary god.*

The patrons of Lydney were perhaps the wealthy Romanised Celts of great Cotswold villas such as Chedworth. Built in the closing years of the Roman Empire, when Britain was already under threat of barbarian invasion, and paganism was giving ground to Christianity, Lydney looks like an act of defiance against a new order.

LYDNEY PARK *Bold strokes of colour were the aim of the second Lord Bledisloe, who created the garden (a potato patch in World War II) with head gardener 'Mac' Stracey*

MELLS: PIES — The story gained currency in the 19th century that the 'Little Jack Horner' of the nursery rhyme was Thomas Horner, steward to the last Abbot of Glastonbury, Richard Whiting, who at the time of the Dissolution of the Monasteries sent him to London with a Christmas gift for the King — a pie in which the deeds of twelve manors were hidden. On the way, Thomas 'put in his thumb and pulled out a plum' — the deeds of **Mells**.

Horner took up residence at Mells soon after the Dissolution, and the idea that he had come by it dishonestly may have sprung from the fact that, when Abbot Whiting was tried for his life, Horner was one of the jurors who condemned him. As an old rhyme has it:

'Hopton, Horner, Smyth and Thynne,
When abbots went out, they came in.'

Even the pie is not impossible: **Painswick** had its 'puppy dog pies', and in his 'Accomplisht Cook' (1660), Robert May recalled the fantastic pies concocted for the amusement of the English court, out of which came flying birds and skipping frogs. His greatest triumph came when a pie was opened and out jumped, not 'four and twenty blackbirds', but a knight in armour — Jeffrey Hudson of **Oakham**, smallest of the royal dwarves.

LYNTON AND LYNMOUTH   *After the 1952 flood: it destroyed buildings and bridges, swept cars out to sea, and claimed 30 lives*

Lynton and Lynmouth

Devon   SS 7149 and SS 7249

The superb Exmoor coastal scenery reaches a climax around these two picturesque villages whose names are often linked. Lynmouth is the more widely known for the flood of 1952 when the river burst its banks and 31 drowned, and for the heroic launch of its lifeboat from Porlock Weir after a journey of 13 miles overland up Countisbury Hill, the highest sea cliffs in England. The cliff railway links Lynmouth with Lynton which stands 500 feet above. Just beyond Lynton to the west is the Valley of the Rocks where wild goats scramble among fantastically shaped formations: White Lady, Devil's Cheese-wring and Castle Rock. Continuing westwards the coastal road is extremely narrow and twisting; particularly beautiful are Woody Bay, with its steeply sloping oak woods, and Hunter's Inn, from where one can follow the River Heddon to the sea at Heddon's Mouth.

Madron Well and Baptistry

Cornwall   SW 4532

This mysterious holy well — little more than a small stone-lined hole in the ground — is reached by a path winding through dense woodland to the north-west of Madron village. St Madern is buried close by the well. Its waters reputedly cured children of 'shingles, wildfires, tetters and various skin diseases'. They were stripped, plunged into the well and passed round it nine times against the sun, then made to sleep on the marshy ground nearby, known as St Madern's Bed. Votive offerings of rags, spat upon to protect the site, are still to be found hanging from the surrounding trees. Close by is a roofless baptistry with its small stone altar.

Malmesbury

Wiltshire   ST 9387

In around 1020, a local monk named Oliver made an early attempt at man-powered flight from the tower of the Abbey, wearing a pair of home-made wings. Although crippled by the fall, Oliver lived for more than half a century and is said to have foretold the Norman invasion after seeing Halley's Comet.

The town is still dominated by the Abbey remains. This was the site of a Saxon monastery founded by St Aldhem in AD700, which possessed the first church organ in England. The surviving building shows some of the best Norman work in the south.

Marden

Wiltshire   SU 0857

The door of the church is claimed to be one of the oldest in England, and if contemporary with the church, is more than 800 years of age. The lock is some 300 years old. The church, with its twice-built tower, has atmosphere. It shows a fine Norman chancel arch and a decorated doorway.

The village is flanked to the north-east by an extensive Neolithic sacred site, dated to 1900BC. On the other side is 18th-century Marden Manor House, and in between them is a Domesday mill.

Mells

Somerset   ST 7249

A plum of a place . . . Wishing to placate Henry VIII, the Abbot of Glastonbury sent him a pie containing the deeds to the manor house. The emissary was Thomas Horner, who put in his thumb and pulled them out. So the story goes, and the property certainly stayed in Horner hands. The 104-foot church tower overlooks the village, one of Somerset's loveliest.

The Merry Maidens and The Pipers

Cornwall   SW 4324

The stone circle of the Merry Maidens, south-east of St Buryan, are said to be all that remains of 19 young ladies who dared to dance on the Sabbath. The Pipers who played for them were also turned to granite and can be seen in nearby fields. This perfect circle is thought to be Bronze Age in origin.

Milton Abbas

Dorset ST 8001

An 18th-century excursion into planning: deciding that the market town of Milton Abbas spoilt his view when he bought the property in 1771, Joseph Damon (later Lord Dorchester) demolished it and round the corner built the extremely picturesque village seen today. Protesters were washed away by temporarily knocking down the dam built across the stream to form the lake — although one villager was allowed to stay on in her cottage to add rustic charm to Capability Brown's landscape. Apart from the church and abbot's hall, the ruined abbey buildings (earlier given by Henry VIII to the lawyer who fixed his divorce from Catherine of Aragon) were demolished to make way for a Gothic mansion (now a school). East of the church, over a hundred turf steps lead to the tiny Norman Chapel of St Catherine.

Morwenstow

Cornwall SS 2015

The Reverend Robert Stephen Hawker, aged 31, arrived in this windswept parish high on the north Cornwall cliffs in 1834, and spent the next 41 years serving 'a mixed multitude of smugglers, wreckers and dissenters'. A much-loved eccentric, poet (*And shall Trelawny die* is his) and author, Hawker wore long seaboots and a fisherman's jersey and was much concerned with the loss of life on this rugged coast, carrying many bodies up the towering cliffs for Christian burial. He went on pastoral visits with a Berkshire pig called Gip, revived the Harvest Festival service, and once invited nine cats into the ancient church, excommunicating one for catching a mouse on Sunday. The vicarage below the church was designed by Hawker and its chimneys are based on his favourite church towers.

MORWENSTOW *The driftwood hut where the Reverend Robert Hawker liked to write poems*

Muchelney

Somerset ST 4224

The name means 'large island', and although the water has been drained, Muchelney Abbey (some 15 miles south-east of Bridgwater off the A372) still rises above the surrounding moors. Founded by Benedictines with a medieval monks' washroom and several 16th-century buildings, it also seems to have supplied the stone adorning the surrounding cottages. The church has a notable painted ceiling; in the village is a rare early priest's house.

Newton Ferrers and Noss Mayo

Devon SX 5447

It is necessary to travel winding lanes to find Newton and Noss; there is a lack of facilities for tourists when they do find them, but for some this in itself makes the journey worthwhile.

The two old fishing settlements sit on either side of the natural pool formed by the massive westerly sweep of the River Yealm, just before it flows into the sea near Plymouth. The natural anchorage provides a haven for the boating fraternity but the steep sides of the river valley have prevented too much change.

North Cerney

Gloucestershire SP 0208

A manticore, half man, half lion, is scratched in the outer south wall of this beautiful 12th-century Cotswolds church. On the west wall is a long-tailed leopard, and both graffiti are said to be the work of Tudor masons. Other faces peer down everywhere, from gargoyles, roof-bosses and corbels, and four peep out from the south doorway's Norman tympanum. For another view of the church, try the gardens of the Bathurst Arms, across the river meadows.

NORTH CERNEY: MYTHICAL BEASTS — *The manticore of* **North Cerney** — *traditionally a man-eater with three rows of teeth — is one of the surprising creatures found in churches which were drawn from medieval Bestiaries. These 'books of beasts' described real and imaginary beings, and gave them moral applications.*

One of the most popular is the mermaid (see **Aberystwyth**), *who with her comb and her glass in her hand on one of the misericords (carvings underneath the seats) of* **Norwich,** *represents the vanity of earthly delights.*

The dragon is a common symbol of evil, and he and the Devil are often one. Not only does St George fight the dragon over the door at **Linton,** *but so does St Michael, at Hoveringham, Nottinghamshire. This is another way of telling how Satan was cast out of heaven by the Archangel.*

In the church at Stowlangtoft, Suffolk, is the cockatrice (see **Saffron Walden***); human 'prodigies' include the blemya, with his face in his stomach, and the sciapod, or shadow-foot, who uses his one big foot as a sunshade, on a bench-end at Dennington, Suffolk.*

PAINSWICK: CHURCH CLIPPING — *The yew trees in the churchyard at* **Painswick** *are clipped each year on 19 September. The following Sunday the ceremony of Church Clipping is performed, during which children dance in a ring round the church. On Clipping Sunday 'puppy dog pies' used to be eaten — plum or meat pies each containing a small china dog. They were said to commemorate the occasion when the landlord of the inn, to meet the needs of the crowds at the Church Clipping, filled his pies with 'puppy dog'.*

The ceremony of Church Clipping has nothing to do with trimming trees — 'clipping' means 'embracing', as the children embrace the church in their dance. It may be the descendant of some pagan rite, later Christianised by the Church, during which the faithful encircled the object of worship, sometimes a tree, later a maypole, as at **Wellow**.

Church Clipping was really a spring festival — at Radley, Berkshire, it is held on Easter Sunday. Other churches — Painswick among them — observe it on or near the church saint's day. **Staplehurst** *also has a Church Clipping ceremony on Mothering Sunday.*

CLIPPING THE CHURCH *at Painswick. Afterwards, children used to run to the vicarage shouting 'Highgates'. A 19th-century vicar linked cry and ceremony with the Roman feast of Lupercalia*

Norton St Philip

Somerset ST 7755

Samuel Pepys and family stayed at the George in 1668 ('Dined Well, 10s'), and the Duke of Monmouth made his headquarters here before the Battle of Sedgemoor in 1685. It is little changed: built (by tradition) as a 15th-century house of hospitality for Hinton Priory and doubling as a cloth warehouse (the overhanging upper storey) it still boasts oriel windows, timber framing and an elaborate archway and gallery at the back. Local tradition tells of nine Norton men jailed here then burnt to death after Sedgemoor.

Nunney

Somerset ST 7346

One tradition maintains that Nunney Castle's sole pig was tortured daily in the Civil War siege of 1645 to make the attackers think there was plenty of livestock inside. Perhaps they went too far: it is also said that the besieged (one officer, eight men and some refugees) surrendered after only two days. The officer then offered his services to the Parliamentary forces, but was refused. It is as a romantic ruin that the castle is best known today, and for its water-filled moat, said to be the deepest in the country. Surrounded by cottages of grey Mendip stone, it was begun in the latest French style in 1373 by Sir John de la Mare, who had just returned from the wars in France.

Cross a footbridge over the moat, and another over a little stream, for the church. It has features from many centuries, but the best is the stone effigy of Sir John de la Mare.

Odstock

Wiltshire SU 1426

A curse hangs over Odstock's church. In 1801, a Gypsy of the prominent Scamp family was hanged in Salisbury and buried in the churchyard. The annual pilgrimage of travelling folk to his grave became a drunken nuisance and eventually the Rector locked the church door against them. The Gypsy 'queen' pronounced a mortal curse upon whomsoever should lock the church door ever again. The incumbent and his churchwardens and the parish constable all suffered violent or untimely deaths, as did subsequent challengers of the curse. No-one in recent times has cared to defy it and the door remains unlocked. The rambler rose reputedly planted by Scamp's daughter flourishes today.

Okeford Fitzpaine

Dorset ST 8010

'Ockford', as the locals call it, offers nothing extraordinary — except an unusually (and untrumpeted) harmonious appearance. Church, thatched and timbered cottages on a raised, railed footway, village stores and 18th-century rectory are attractively grouped on the curving main street. A footpath climbs up to Okeford Hill which has an earthwork and good views.

Across the River Stour are Hambledon Hill (with Neolithic and Iron Age earthworks), and Hod Hill, which has remains of a Roman fort on an Iron Age site. The Roman fort is interesting, because it seems to have been built at an early stage in the Roman occupation of Britain — perhaps to help enslave Cranborne Chase.

Painswick

Gloucestershire SO 8609

Only 99 yew trees will grow in Painswick's churchyard they say; plant another and the Devil will see it off. The ceremony of 'Church Clipping' takes place here.

Behind the churchyard is a fine pair of iron 'spectacle' stocks. The church, rebuilt in around 1378, has corbels said to represent Richard II and his queen, and there are signs of a skirmish and fire during the Civil War. The fighting of 1643-1644 is also recalled at Painswick Beacon, an exhilarating spot with fine views. Charles I, after watching his soldiers advance on Gloucester, found refuge in a hamlet below the hill and exclaimed: 'This is Paradise'.

Perhaps the finest view of Painswick is from remote Bulls Cross, to the south-east. This was the place of ghosts and gibbets recalled by Laurie Lee in *Cider with Rosie* with the words: 'As for Bulls Cross . . . I still wouldn't walk there at midnight.'

Parnham House

Dorset ST 4701

Senior US officers met here to plan strategy during World War II; today it is the home of the John Makepeace School for Craftsmen in Wood (where Viscount Linley studied). Monthly exhibitions allow visitors to admire contemporary craftsmanship and the 14 acres of lush gardens and woodlands where oak, ash, yew, sycamore and other timbers can be seen maturing. The house also has a huge four-poster bed, made from a single yew.

Pauntley

Gloucestershire SO 7529

Dick Whittington was born at the predecessor of the present (private) Pauntley Court — the church nearby has family monuments. No poor boy and no known cat-lover when he left Gloucestershire, he became even richer as a mercer in London, where he was mayor three times from 1397 to 1419 (Lord Mayors came later). The only other fact that tallies with legend was his marriage to Alice Fitzwaryn, daughter of a rich Dorset knight.

PAUNTLEY: DICK WHITTINGTON — *The tale of a poor boy whose fortune is made by a cat is found in many different countries — a famous version is 'Puss in Boots' — but why it came to be told of Sir Richard Whittington of* **Pauntley** *is a mystery, for his was certainly not a rags to riches story.*

In one of the earliest versions of 'Whittington and his Cat', Dick stops to rest as he is running away from **London** *at 'Bun Hill' (probably Bunhill Fields near Moorgate), but later he rests on a milestone at Holloway. The Whittington Stone on Highgate Hill, now surmounted by a cat, has since at least the 18th century been regarded as the stone, though it was never a milestone but a wayside cross.*

When in 1862 the carved figure of a boy holding some sort of animal was found in the foundations of a house in Westgate Street, **Gloucester,** *it was hailed as 'Dick and his Cat', and the idea got about that it had given rise to the story. This is doubtful — but whoever they are, the boy and 'cat' are now in the Gloucester Folk Museum, Westgate Street.*

OKEFORD FITZPAINE *Timeless charm where people have lived for thousands of years*

OLDBURY-ON-SEVERN *Two cows selected the site of St Arilda's. Looming below today's church is the massive bulk of the nuclear power station*

Oldbury-on-Severn

Avon ST 6092

Best known today for its nuclear power station, Oldbury is a tucked-away village with a rich tradition of salmon fishing and cider. A footpath skirts Iron Age earthworks, and the names of its pubs, the Anchor and the Ship, reflect busy river trading days. Its church on Cow Hill, a remote knoll with fine views over the Severn, is dedicated to Arilda, a pious virgin murdered at Kington, close by. The familiar story of its foundation is that a village site was proposed, but building work was invariably destroyed overnight. A wise hermit suggested the villagers should unleash two heifers and build where they grazed — and Cow Hill it was.

Ozleworth

Gloucestershire ST 7893

In the grounds of Ozleworth Park (two miles east of Wotton-under-Edge) is one of the Cotswolds' most remarkable churches. Set in a circular plot, it is dominated by a six-sided central tower, extremely rare and dating from the early 1100s. Although redundant, the church is often open and may be approached by public right of way through the imposing park gates and past the house. A fine walk may also be taken by following the right of way in a circle — shown clearly on the Ordnance Survey map.

BREAD STONES *record the changing price of a gallon of dough at Great Wishford. Dough for home baking was sold rather than bread*

PLYMOUTH: BREAD — *Jacka's Bakery at* **Plymouth** *has one of the few traditional ovens left 'in situ'. But traditional types of bread have been more resilient.*

Of crusty loaves — baked without tins, with a crust all round — one of the commonest today is the 'Coburg', a round loaf often slashed to produce four corners. The name is debated — but 'cob' is an old word for head and the four-cornered Coburg was sometimes known as a 'skull'. A nice variation with chequerboard cuts was the 'porcupine' or 'rumpy'.

Still popular is the 'bloomer', long with diagonal cuts. The name may come from 'bloom', used by bakers to describe the sheen on good flour. But bloomers are not what they were in days when they were made with high-quality flour, milk and butter.

The most distinctive of crusty breads is the cottage loaf, two round loaves baked one on the other. To most people this is the classic English loaf — although really it needs to be baked in the traditional way, on the floor of an old brick oven, fired by faggots, after the ashes have been scraped out. Bread is still made in the traditional way at the National Trust-owned, 17th-century bakery at Branscombe, Devon.

Penzance

Cornwall   SW 4730

Every schoolchild learns about the Armada; less well known is that the Spanish successfully sacked and burnt Penzance in 1595. The Georgian front of the Union Hotel hides an Elizabethan interior, and recently revealed scorch marks on the stonework of the door could be the result of that invasion. The victory at Trafalgar and the death of Lord Nelson were first announced from the minstrels' gallery in the hotel's elegant Assembly Room, and at the rear is one of the oldest theatres in Britain (not in use), where the first performance was held in 1787.

Enriched by tin, fishing and smuggling, Penzance is popular but worth exploring for its other notable Georgian, Victorian and Regency buildings. The quiet length of Chapel Street is probably the most distinctive and full of surprises: the Turk's Head is an ancient inn, the Admiral Benbow Inn has a model smuggler on its roof and across the street is the birthplace of Marie Brontë, mother of the Brontë sisters. Most eccentric building in the town must be the Egyptian House, an elaborate 1820s copy of a London hall and now a National Trust centre.

PENZANCE   *Smuggler on the roof of the Admiral Benbow — excisemen were perhaps more sorely tried west of the Tamar than anywhere else*

Pilton

Somerset   ST 5940

Pilton Manor's vineyard has become renowned — but the rambling, up-and-down village with its winding lanes is little known and worth exploring. The monumental stone tithe barn rises out of beeches and chestnuts on a hill, while the church with its Norman doorway stands on another. The manor was a summer house of the Abbots of Glastonbury.

Plush

Dorset   ST 7102

North of Puddletown, Piddlehinton and Piddletrenthide, turn right off the B3143 for Plush — site of an exotic orchid farm and of the Brace of Pheasants pub, locally renowned for food, wine and excellent atmosphere.

Plymouth

Devon   SX 4755

Eddystone Lighthouse can be seen, fourteen miles away, from the top of the Civic Centre, while red and white Smeaton's Tower, which did duty

for nearly 125 years at Eddystone, can be seen on the Hoe. This natural vantage point and promenade was used well before Sir Francis Drake's leisurely game of bowls, as a site for Iron Age religious meetings. Until the 17th century two giant figures were cut into its turf, either cause or effect of the legend that this was once the haunt of giants.

Jacka's Bakery in Southside Street is the oldest commercially working bakery in Britain and is said to have baked ship's biscuits for the Pilgrim Fathers, who left from Plymouth's Barbican. Near the bakery are colourful murals painted by eccentric local artist, Robert Lenkiewicz.

Plympton

Devon   SX 5356

Telegraph Cottage on Hardwick Hill was part of the Admiralty shutter telegraph system, devised in the late 18th century. Thirty stations linked London and Plymouth; on the roof of each was a frame containing movable shutters giving 64 possible combinations. Each station had a telescope for reading the messages. Telegraph Hill near Exeter was another such site.

Poldhu

Cornwall   SW 6519

In 1901 Guglielmo Marconi transmitted the first radio message across the Atlantic from Poldhu, north-west of Mullion. Massive aerials used to stretch between pylons on these high cliffs until the 1930s, but today the only sign of this leap in communications history is a small obelisk at the Poldhu Hotel, unveiled by Marconi's daughter.

The flat beach of nearby Church Cove is popular with treasure hunters: in 1785 a ship laden with silver dollars foundered here; and a 17th-century pirate is said to have buried a rich treasure in the vicinity.

Portland

Dorset   SY 6876

A bit of England which has been spread all over England and beyond. Portland stone, white, tough, but soft enough to carve, was chosen by Sir Christopher Wren for St Paul's Cathedral and has been in demand ever since. Convicts were brought in during the 19th century to keep up the supply; today a good deal of it goes into cement. Portland has become a giant quarry, but has a rare medieval strip field system, and Portland Bill, the southernmost tip, is a popular stopping point for migrant birds.

Porton Down

Wiltshire   SU 1836

Definitely *not* open to the public . . . in Service or Government occupation, uncultivated and closed off for more than half a century, Porton Down has become an outstanding example of unspoilt chalk downland. As well as rare plants and flowers (many now almost extinct over much of the countryside) there are the re-introduced giant bustards, birds once native to Salisbury Plain and a feature of the county's coat of arms, but wiped out by shooting in the early 19th century.

On a few occasions each spring and summer, Porton Down is revealed to organised parties.

PLYMPTON: SIGNALS
— From the chain of
beacons lit to announce the
Armada via the Admiralty
telegraph stations of **Plympton**
and *Chatley Heath* to the vast
'early warning' golfballs of
Fylingdales, *signals have been
whizzing across the countryside
for centuries.*

Fishing villages like **Portreath**
*can still show the high points
where 'huers' used to look out for
the tell-tale red of pilchard shoals
on the sea, and guide fishing boats
towards them.*

*Though more wideranging than
the huers, other early signal
systems, such as fires lit on beacon
hills, also depended on being seen.
(The beacons of* **Corton
Denham** *and* **Painswick** *still
give good views.) So did the more
sophisticated messages sent from
tower to tower between* **London**
and **Plymouth** *by the Admiralty
shutter telegraph. Invisible long-
distance message-sending came in*

*View of the TELEGRAPH
on the Admiralty.*

ADMIRALTY SHUTTER TELEGRAPH
*(above): ingenious but found to be
impractical*

*the later 19th century — Samuel
Morse started using underground
cables, Alexander Bell made the
first telephone call, and in 1896
came the wireless and Guglielmo
Marconi, who sent the first radio
message over the Atlantic from*
Poldhu *in 1901. Wireless had
really 'arrived' when it enabled the
police to catch Crippen.*

At **Jodrell Bank,
Goonhilly Down** *and*
*Fylingdales, communications have
entered a new era of transmission
by satellite across distances which
are hard to comprehend. The
Romans used fire, smoke and
semaphore signals. At
Goldborough, excavators found
what seemed to be two Roman
signalmen, one of them stabbed in
the back, with their great dog
killed beneath them.*

PLUSH   *A thatched village in an
idyllic setting, with a pub sign that
needs no words*

PORTREATH: GIANTS — Ralph's Cupboard, in the cliffs near **Portreath,** was long the terror of fishermen. Anyone who drifted or was driven into it by storm, was eaten by Ralph the Giant. After his death the roof of the 'cupboard' collapsed, leaving today's open fissure. Cornwall has long been noted for giants: according to a 12th-century author, it got its name from Corineus, when Brutus the Trojan founded Britain, because Corineus liked to wrestle with giants, and there were more here than anywhere else.

One reason for the many giants in Cornwall (though Devon has some too, at **Plymouth**) is its wealth of megalithic monuments. The huge stones of chamber-tombs such as those of Lanyon, Mulfra, **Madron** and Trethevy, were said

CORMORAN, the cattle-thief of St Michael's Mount, is the villain in one version of Jack the Giant Killer

to be their playthings — hence **Lanyon Quoit** and the Giant's Quoit at Pawton.

The giant Trebiggan (known since the 16th century) had arms so long that he could pluck sailors from passing ships, while the giant Bolster could stand with one foot on **St Agnes** Beacon, the other on Carn Brea.

St Michael's Mount was built by a giant, a giant hid his treasure in Trencrom Castle, Ludgvan, and of course Jack the Giant-Killer was a Cornishman . . .

PORTREATH The round white building above the tin-mines' harbour is the Pepperpot — a daymark and lookout for pilots and coastguards

Portquin

Cornwall SW 9480

The entire population of this tiny fishing village on the wild north coast of Cornwall is said to have disappeared one night in a mighty storm. Perhaps they drowned; some suggest that the men were press-ganged, others that the families left when the fishing worsened. Deserted for many years but now owned by the National Trust, the houses have been restored and are once again occupied. Nearby on the high headland of Doyden Point is a Regency Gothic tower, a folly used as a film location in the *Poldark* series.

Portreath

Cornwall SW 6545

West of the beach is the Wedding Cake, one of the high headlands around Cornwall's coast, from which 'huers' signalled the presence and position of pilchard shoals, enabling fishermen to encircle them with their nets. When fish were sighted the huer uttered the cry 'hevva' through a long trumpet, then used a pair of bats called 'bushes' to guide the ships with semaphore-like signals. Some fishermen still watch for fish from huers' headlands, and claim to catch more than radar-guided boats.

As well as a fishing port, this small resort was a centre for exporting tin and copper, and importing coal to fuel the mine engines. Behind the village are the remains of an inclined plane, a section of the Hayle railway which linked the harbour with the mines and carried trams down a 1 in 10 gradient.

Powdermills

Devon SX 6477

Gunpowder was manufactured here during the second half of the 19th century and was in great demand for the many mines and quarries on Dartmoor and further afield. At the turn of the century the industry ceased and the buildings fell into disrepair, but the granite ruins and two chimneys of the mills can be seen. Several small

businesses also thrive here: a blacksmith works in the former chapel and nearby is a pottery and craft workshop.

Prehistoric walled pounds (probably for cattle), hut sites and stone circles can be seen further north along the B3212 around Postbridge, which also boasts a three-arch clapper bridge (which is probably medieval).

Potterne

Wiltshire ST 9958

Take the turning near the George and Dragon for the Wiltshire Fire Service HQ, which has a unique museum of all types of bygone firefighting equipment and machines. Below, in the main street, is Porch House, a striking black and white timbered building which in its 500 years has been a priest's house, an inn, bakery, brewery and a barracks.

The fine church, contemporary with Salisbury cathedral, overlooks the village on the busy Devizes Road. It has a celebrated Saxon font, inscribed with a Latin verse from the Psalms.

Prestbury

Gloucestershire SO 9724

Site of a medieval bishop's palace, the village has at least half a dozen ghosts: a black abbot, Old Moses the groom, a horseman or two, a girl playing a spinet, a strangler and a man on a bike. Close to the racecourse and now a suburb of Cheltenham, Prestbury is also rich in thatch, timber and friendly pubs.

Priddy

Somerset ST 5250

A grey weatherbeaten church and cottages overlook a green where hurdles for the 600-year-old 21 August sheep fair are kept, not just stacked but thatched as well.

This lovely Mendips village is Somerset's highest. A mile north-east are the Bronze Age Priddy Nine Barrows and the Priddy Circles, sacred sites, while tumuli abound all around. Two miles south are the Ebbor rocks, rich in bats, badgers, hawks and Wych elms (resistant to Dutch Elm disease). Lemming, reindeer and bear remains have been found here in caves occupied by Stone Age man.

Prussia Cove

Cornwall   SW 5527

A hidden rocky inlet at the centre of Mount's Bay, Prussia Cove was renowned in the 18th century for the smuggling activities of the Carter Gang, led by John Carter, the self-styled 'King of Prussia'. On one occasion he fired on a revenue cutter with guns mounted on the headland.

Wheel-tracks are cut into the steep stone slipway leading down to the secret harbour, and several small fishermen's huts, their roofs held down against storms by stout chains, overlook the cove.

PUXTON   *The date 1557 is carved in the north porch of Holy Saviour, but the church is far older, with 14th-century windows*

Puxton

Avon   ST 4063

Just a mile off the busy A370 between Bristol and Weston-super-Mare, Puxton retains an air of remote calm. Farm buildings and apple trees surround the church with its spectacularly leaning tower; inside, untouched by Victorian restorers, are benches and box pews with a Jacobean pulpit, reading desk and altar rails.

Rampisham

Dorset   ST 5602

The voice of Britain has its jumping-off point here: above the village, 1000 feet up in beautiful scenery, rise the aerials which send the transmissions of the BBC overseas.

A mosaic pavement from a Roman building was found about a mile north of the village in 1799, but was soon destroyed — perhaps by people looking for treasure underneath.

Roseland Peninsula

Cornwall   SW 8435

This peaceful promontory of meadows, wooded valleys and winding lanes lies across Carrick Roads from Falmouth. The ancient Church of St Just-in-Roseland stands in a sloping churchyard of luxuriant sub-tropical plants on the edge of a tranquil creek. A bequest by John Randall in 1733 pays the rector ten shillings a year for preaching a funeral sermon on 27 December (the money will last until the year 2733). Across the winding Percuil River, St Anthony lies at the head of a wooded creek. A monastery (whose refectory is retained in the Victorian Gothic Place Manor) and the small church are said to have been founded after a visit by the young Jesus and his uncle, Joseph of Arimathea, who were sheltering from a storm at sea.

Ruardean

Gloucestershire   SO 6117

Close to the beautiful Wye Valley south of Ross, Ruardean church has recovered two fish that had got away for 700 years. On a small stone plaque, they were found in the 1950s in the lining of a baking oven in a local cottage. Identified as the product of the Herefordshire school of craftsmen, they were returned to be set in an inner wall, near the font. It is thought that they formed part of a frieze removed from an outer wall in around 1250 — so other sections may yet be discovered.

RUARDEAN: HEREFORDSHIRE SCHOOL — *The craftsmen who carved* **Ruardean's** *fish also worked on several other churches, mostly in Herefordshire and most remarkably at* **Kilpeck**.

The earliest was built at Shobdon by Oliver de Merlimond, who after work had begun went on a pilgrimage to the Spanish shrine of St James of Compostela. Going via France, he may have taken his master craftsman away with him — which would explain why the Herefordshire school uses native Anglo-Saxon and Viking styles alongside designs apparently copied from French and Spanish churches.

Shobdon church was pulled down in the 18th century, but its doorways were re-erected in Shobdon Park as a sort of folly. They are weatherworn, but enough remains to show that the Herefordshire 'school' was probably a travelling workshop under a principal master, who went on to Kilpeck, where the south door with its Viking dragons and nimble figures is his work.

His hand is also seen at Fownhope, while St Giles's Hospital, **Hereford**, *shows the influence of Shobdon.*

Other churches with work by the Herefordshire craftsmen include Brinsop, **Rowlstone** *and Stretton Sugwas.*

ABOVE   *Sheila-na-gig is the name given to female figures like this from Kilpeck. It shows an apotropaic gesture, meant to ward off evil*

RAMPISHAM   *Before the aerials came the Romans: a mosaic pavement was found nearby in 1799, but treasure hunters soon destroyed it*

SAINT AGNES: WEST COUNTRY SAINTS — *The Devil came to the Tamar and stood wondering whether to cross over into Cornwall. 'No, I won't risk it,' said he. 'Over there everyone's made into a saint, everything into squab pie.'*

St Agnes, St Columb, St Nectan's . . . *nowhere else in England are there so many villages named after saints, most of them rather obscure. This is because their churches, following Celtic practice, were named not after 'official' saints, but after their traditional founders. The same custom can be seen elsewhere in the West Country — hence* **Braunton** *(St Brannoc's town).*

Most of the 'saints' were missionaries who came from other parts of the Celtic world — Ireland, Wales and Brittany — sometimes by miraculous means: Piran of Perranzabuloe sailed here on a millstone, Ia of **St Ives** *on a leaf, Decuman of St Decumans on a bundle of twigs.*

Although only two of their missionary oratories survive, under the sands at Gwithian and Perranporth, there are many traditional 'remains': St Mawes' Chair in the wall of a St Mawes house; St Germoe's Chair, a stone seat in Germoe churchyard believed to be his shrine; St Levan's seat, on the south side of his church, which he split open with his fist and prophesied:

'When with panniers astride, A pack-horse one can ride Through St Levan's Stone, The world will be done.'

ST GERMOE'S CHAIR *seems medieval; the fifth-century saint may have preached on the spot*

St Agnes

Cornwall SW 7150

Relics of engine houses still surround St Agnes, a centre for high grade tin in the 18th and 19th centuries. The charming names of the mines, many named after the wives or family of the mine captains, survive: Wheal Kitty, Wheal Ellen, Wheal Music, Blue Hills, Wheal Friendly and Wheal Freedom. Beside the church, a row of miners' cottages known as the 'Stippy-Stappy' runs steeply down the valley-side.

The imaginary villages of St Ann's and Sawle in Winston Graham's *Poldark* books are largely based on St Agnes and Trevaunance Cove, a rocky beach at the foot of the winding valley. Thirty-one church towers and a span from St Ives to Brown Willy on Bodmin Moor can be seen from St Agnes Beacon to the west of the village, and a walk from St Agnes Head to Chapel Porth leads past the remains of Wheal Charlotte engine houses, poised half-way down the cliff.

St Catherine

Avon ST 7770

On a winding road north of Batheaston in a deep South Cotswolds valley, St Catherine is a hamlet of great charm, and can be the starting point of many a pleasant walk. There is an air of almost eerie peace in the countryside hereabouts, and of timelessness in the classic grouping of church, tithe barn and St Catherine's Court, once a priory grange but now a private house. The 15th-century church is chiefly the work of Prior Cantlow of Bath, who is depicted in one of several contemporary stained glass windows.

St Columb Major

Cornwall SW 9163

The ancient custom of Hurling the Silver Ball takes place in this old market town every Shrove Tuesday and the second following Saturday. The townsfolk split into two teams — the Townsmen and the Countrymen — and try to catch and carry the small silver-covered ball to one of two 'goals', two miles apart. The combat is often quite wild and all the shop windows are boarded up for protection. To touch the silver ball is said to bring good luck, and the game probably originated as a spring festival.

St Ives

Cornwall SW 5140

John Knill, 18th-century mayor, customs officer, privateer and — by repute — immensely success-ful smuggler, built the steeple to the south of the town, ostensibly as a mausoleum but possibly to help his contraband activities (it is still a useful daymark for shipping). Buried in Holborn, London, this colourful character left money and instructions for an eccentric but charming ceremony to be held at the monument every five years on 25 July (1991, 1996 etc). A procession of townsfolk is led by a fiddler, ten young girls and two widows. The girls dance round the steeple, then all sing the 'Old Hundredth' psalm. £10 is shared between the girls, £2 each is given to the widows and £1 to the fiddler.

As at St Columb Major, a Shrove Tuesday game of hurling a silver ball is played — but here only the children take part.

St Mawgan

Cornwall SW 8765

A bird released as a secret signal that Mass was about to be celebrated, during times of persecution of Catholics is said to have given its name to the Falcon Inn. The Catholic connection survives in a Carmelite convent here; next to it stands the church, dedicated to a sixth-century Welsh missionary, which contains a relic of the skull of St Cuthbert Mayne. In the churchyard can be seen a remarkable lantern cross of 1420, several fine Celtic crosses and a wooden memorial shaped like the stern of a boat, dedicated to nine men and a boy. They froze to death in their life-boat after their ship was wrecked on the nearby coast in 1846. The village is set delightfully in the leafy Vale of Lanherne, north-east of Newquay.

St Nectan's Glen and Rocky Valley

Cornwall SX 0789

On the road winding east from Tintagel, a deep valley leads up to a 40-foot waterfall which plunges down St Nectan's Glen into a 'kieve' (Cornish for a large basin). The saintly hermit is said to be buried nearby. The stream can be followed north of the road into Rocky Valley, a harsh place of slate and sea-spray. This was a former home of the chough, the red-billed crow once common in Cornwall and said to be the reincarnated spirit of King Arthur.

Salisbury

Wiltshire SU 1429

The quieter St Ann's Gate and the almost unknown de Vaux Place are two alternative entrances to the Cathedral Close. They not only avoid the awkward congestion of the High Street Gate, but also offer more interesting approaches to the many historic buildings within. The first is half-way down Exeter Street, the second at the foot of the same street, off the roundabout.

In the Cathedral are two special relics: the Library above the East Walk of the Cloisters contains one of the four surviving copies of Magna Carta, while in the north transept is a 600-year-old clock in working order, the oldest in Britain. By the west doors stands the 'Boy Bishop', said to have died by tickling. Elsewhere in the Close, the medieval King's House and Wardrobe, both on the West Walk, house the award-winning Salisbury and South Wiltshire Museum and the Museum of the Duke of Edinburgh's Royal Regiment.

In the city centre, almost any street can show buildings of four or five hundred years of age. Notable in the modestly-named New Street are the Old House and the New Inn next door. The first is nearly 700 and its young neighbour a mere 500 years old. The Odeon Cinema in New Canal encloses the town house of John Halle, a rich 15th-century merchant and Mayor of Salisbury; it can still be entered through the foyer, past the stills from space-age films. Queen Street, at the east end of the Market Place, shows buildings of every century from the 1300s in the space of a hundred yards. Among them are the so-called House of John à Port (about 1450) and next door the authentic house of William Russel, built not later than 1306 and, behind its younger front, very little changed.

SALISBURY: BOY BISHOP — *By the west doors of* **Salisbury** *Cathedral, on the north side of the nave, is a little statue traditionally said to be Salisbury's Boy Bishop. Choristers in the 17th century used to tell the tale that when the Boy Bishop was sad, the choirboys tickled him but so overdid it that they tickled him to death. Because he had died in office, the monument was made for him, showing him in his bishop's mitre and cope.*

During the Middle Ages, the choirboys of cathedrals would elect one of their number to be their bishop from 6 December, the feast of St Nicholas, the patron saint of children, to 28 December, Holy Innocents' Day. During that time the boy would perform the duties of a real bishop, except saying mass. If he died in office, he would be buried with the honours due to an adult prelate — as in the Salisbury tale.

On the last day of his term of office, the Boy Bishop would preach a sermon, before going in procession through the city to bless the people. A statute in 1518 required the scholars of St Paul's School, **London,** *every Childermas Day (Holy Innocents') to 'go to St Paul's Cathedral to hear the Childe-Bishop Sermon'.*

ST NECTAN'S GLEN   *(left) Legend says the hermit's bell can be heard signalling the approach of a storm*

A MAZE   *(below), one of two carved at St Nectan's Glen. They may be Bronze Age, or by a later local miller*

STANTON DREW: STONE CIRCLE STORIES

Stone circles like those of **Stanton Drew** and **The Hurlers** are said to be people turned to stone for breaking the Sabbath. The gist of Stanton Drew's story may already have been in circulation by the 17th century, when the stones were known as The Wedding.

In the early 18th century, three stones were known as the Parson, the Bride and the Bridegroom. The circles were the company dancing, and a group a little apart from the rest was the fiddlers or 'band of musick'.

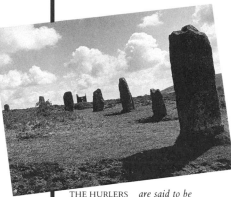

THE HURLERS *are said to be players, rooted to the spot*

Dancing on a Sunday was also punished by petrifaction at the **Merry Maidens**, St Buryan, the Nine Maidens (alias the Boscawen-Un Stone Circle), in Penwith, and several other megalithic monuments. There are petrified brides and grooms in Norway and Germany, and whole wedding parties in northern France.

The tradition probably stems from a popular medieval sermon against the custom of dancing in churchyards on high days and holidays. In England the custom outlived not only the Middle Ages but the Reformation, in defiance of both priests and Puritans. In Herefordshire and the Welsh Marches, 17th-century peasants danced to pipe and tabor in the churchyard 'on Holydayes and Holyday-eves', and survived to tell the tale.

STANTON DREW *A petrified wedding: the bride claimed she'd get a piper to play on the Sabbath, from Hell if need be. Satan obliged, but the party was turned into stone*

Sapperton Tunnel

Gloucestershire   SO 9403

Cutting through the wooded Cotswolds south of Cirencester Park, the 3817-yard Sapperton Tunnel was the longest in England on its completion in 1789. Bargees once 'legged' their craft through the tunnel by lying on their backs and pushing the roof with their feet; the Tunnel House and Daneway pubs refreshed them at each end. They are still open for those who come to admire the classical eastern portal at Coates and its Gothic counterpart at Daneway to the west, restored as part of a scheme to re-open the Thames-Severn Canal.

Savernake Forest

Wiltshire   SU 2266

Ghosts abound — a black dog at the Savernake Forest Hotel, an old man at the Savernake Arms and the Antlered Man who appears near Hut Gate to foretell the death of the sovereign.

Henry VIII courted his bride Jane Seymour at her family home, then deep in the Forest, now the site of a prep school in beautiful parkland. More than 2000 acres survive of the ancient forest, a medieval royal hunting domain. Massive oaks, beeches and some of the tallest Spanish chestnuts in Britain attract a rich bird life, including six types of warbler — and the odd bright blue Continental 'roller' bird.

Seaton

Devon   SY 2490

The Seaton and District Electric Tramway Company runs a six-mile round trip to Colyton and back on its rural tramway. The open-air

SAPPERTON TUNNEL   *Used from 1789 to 1911 — bargees pushed with feet against the roof for over two miles to get through it*

tramcars are maintained by a small team of enthusiasts who transported them in a total of 36 journeys from their place of manufacture, Eastbourne. Tramcars are popular off-season with ornithologists, who use them as a mobile hide to observe the abundant birdlife of the Axe Valley: the birds are used to the cars and accept them as part of the landscape.

Sezincote

Gloucestershire SP 1731

With its dominant onion-shaped dome, its once burnished copper now coated with verdigris, Sezincote is a most eccentric Cotswold mansion, a touch of the exotic in the gentle country south-west of Moreton-in-Marsh. Remodelled from an earlier house in 1805 by the architect brother of the owner, East India Company executive Sir Charles Cockerell, it predated Brighton Pavilion by several years and was visited by the future Prince Regent in 1807. The architect was helped by the Indian artist Thomas Daniell, and his oriental garden features still add charm. The grounds can be seen on Thursday and Friday afternoons and on Bank Holidays except in December, and the house on occasional summer opening days.

Shapwick

Somerset ST 4137

All round is a weird scene of chocolate brown, where Fisons are digging peat — but water violets, wild iris and marsh marigolds can be seen on Shapwick Heath's Nature Reserve. A permit from the Nature Conservancy Council in Taunton is needed. A public footpath north-west out of Shapwick village also crosses unspoilt heathland. If driving, take care: built on peat, the road is liable to subsidence.

Snowshill Manor

Gloucestershire SP 0933

South of Broadway and opened regularly by the National Trust, Snowshill Manor is an aston-ishing legacy to the enthusiasm of Charles Wade, collector and student of the occult. He moved

into this then dilapidated Tudor house in 1919, and eventually had so stuffed it with timepieces, toys, bicycles, carts, oriental furniture and other exotica that he found it would be easier to live in an outbuilding. Though the NT has tidied up after him, and played down his more bizarre interests, the atmosphere at Snowshill is still one of silent menace, punctuated only by the insistent ticking of clocks.

Stanton Drew

Avon ST 5963

There are three Bronze Age circles beside this pretty village, two in a field open from February to November, Sundays excepted. The largest is 120 yards across with 24 low stones; the monoliths of an adjacent circle tower above head-height; and there is also a spectacular group of three stones, known as the Cove, between the church and the misleadingly named Druid's Arms. There are no known druidical connections.

Stanway

Gloucestershire SP 0532

The view down on Stanway from the B4077 east of Toddington is one of the most enchanting in the Cotswolds for travellers with time to look, and the hamlet is well worth a visit too. It is full of impressive architectural oddities: an outstanding bronze of St George on the war memorial, an ornate gatehouse in strikingly golden Cotswold stone, a 14th-century tithe barn, a rustic cricket pavilion built on staddle-stones (mushroom-shaped), and a hilltop memorial pyramid. Stanway House, occasionally open in summer, was the home of Thomas Dover, the privateer whose rescue of Alexander Selkirk from a desert island inspired Defoe's *Robinson Crusoe*.

Stapleford

Wiltshire SU 0637

A charming village in the Wylye valley, above which is the site of the Norman castle once owned by Waleran, the Conqueror's chief huntsman. Its name indicates a ford with marker posts across the tiny River Till, and the spelling has remained un-changed in the 900 years since Domesday Book.

The church has impressive Norman pillars of green and white banded stone; in its porch a stone bench is marked out with the squares of Nine Men's Morris, the medieval board game.

Street

Somerset ST 4836

Cyrus and James Clark began selling fur slippers here in the 1820s, and so began the Clark shoe empire. Reminders of the Quaker Clark family's influence on Street include a handsome clock-tower gracing a factory in a garden setting, a Friends' Meeting House, the Bear pub — originally a temperance inn, selling non-alcoholic drinks only — and numerous shoe shops selling seconds. In the oldest part of Clark's shoe factory, the Shoe Museum has footwear, shoe machinery, fashion plates and related exhibits from the Romans onwards. Millfield School began in a Clark family house; while a master here, Robert Bolt wrote *Flowering Cherry*, to be followed by *A Man For All Seasons*.

ROBINSON CRUSOE *(above) rescued with Man Friday — the real Crusoe lived alone*
STANWAY *(top) The gatehouse of Stanway House, the home of his rescuer*

STANWAY: ROBINSON CRUSOE — *Rescued by Thomas Dover of* Stanway, *Alexander Selkirk (1676-1721), the original Robinson Crusoe, seems to have got his wish to go to sea only by making his hometown of Largo too hot to hold him. In September 1704, the ship he was on came to the uninhabited island of Juan Fernandez. Selkirk, having offended the captain by saying the ship was unseaworthy, asked to be put ashore. He regretted it, but wasn't taken back — and the ship was never seen again.*

After many days of distress, he set about building two huts against the coming winter. The island was full of goats, which he learned to run down on foot when his powder gave out. Using knives made from old iron hoops, he clothed himself in their skins.

He was rescued in 1709 and in 1711 reached England, where his adventures excited great interest. Based on accounts of these, in 1719, came Daniel Defoe's 'Robinson Crusoe' — and Selkirk was immortal.

TEDBURN ST MARY: CIDER — *Cider is still being made on a farm at* **Tedburn St Mary,** *but once every farm in the western counties had a few cider-apple trees growing in the orchard. In the 18th century it became the practice to pay part of a labourer's wages in cider. An average allowance was three to four pints a day, double during haymaking and harvest, but a two-gallon man was not unheard of. No wonder one old farmer told of halting work for fear someone got impaled on a hay-fork.*

Each farmworker commonly had a wooden cask called a costrel holding about half a gallon and marked with his initials. A lad would fill the costrels each morning and stand them by the cellar door ready for collection — by noon they were often back. Workers sharing a costrel would drink in turn from a horn cup, passing it round clockwise — widdershins (the other way) was unlucky. The last would empty a few dregs on the ground, a relic perhaps of libation.

The same superstition prompts the pouring of cider round a tree's roots during the custom of wassailing the orchard, still practised on Old Twelfth Night (17 January) in Somerset at Roadwater and Corhampton.

Costrels and other memorabilia of cider-making can be seen in the Museum of Cider at **Hereford.**

ABOVE *Cider making 1883 — a 'cheese' of apple pulp is pressed to extract the juice*

TYNEHAM *(right) The forbidden zone of Gad Cliff, in the area south of the village which is used for Army tank firing ranges, and often closed*

Swindon

Wiltshire SU 1484

The largest town in the county, this was the home of the Great Western workshops, which were sited, they say, by the toss of a half-eaten sandwich by Brunel from the downs above. Today a fascinating survival of this Victorian town planning is open to view. The Railway Village — 300 workmen's houses built in Bath stone excavated from Box Tunnel — shows a foreman's dwelling of about 1842, fully furnished in the original style.

Also in Faringdon Road is the Railway Museum, housed in the former 'Navvies' Barracks', which has a collection of preserved locomotives and Brunel memorabilia.

Taddiport

Devon SS 4818

Look down from Castle Hill, Great Torrington, for the best view of Taddiport's two very narrow strip fields, enclosed by hedges, running down to the River Torridge. These once belonged to the Leper Hospital at Taddiport, which fell into disuse at the end of the 17th century. The lepers' chapel, dedicated to St Mary Magdalen, remains today as a chapel-of-ease, and has a Leper Window of 1972 and a 16th-century Old Testament text, which refers to an unjust settlement over the lepers' strip fields. This inscription was renewed at the same time as the more recent window was commissioned, by the north Devon potter, Harry Juniper.

Tedburn St Mary

Devon SX 8194

Cider is still made at Lower Uppacott Farm. Sold on the premises, it can be tasted before buying, and the four varieties mixed to taste. Quite different from the more widely available carbonated ciders, this prize-winning brew should be approached with caution.

Thameshead and Seven Springs

Gloucestershire ST 9898 and SO 9717

With many of the streams that feed the infant Thames springing up in Gloucestershire, it is inevitable that several remote localities should be claimed as the source of that great river. The two strongest claimants, both with inscribed stone tablets to bolster their arguments, are Thameshead, a short walk through fields behind the pub of that name along the A433 Tetbury road three miles south-west of Cirencester; and Seven Springs, the undoubted source of the River Churn, some 11 miles to the north, beside the A436 at a busy road junction near Coberley.

Tisbury

Wiltshire ST 9429

More than a third of an acre of thatch is needed for the roof of the magnificent 15th-century stone tithe barn, nearly 200 feet long and reputedly the largest in England. It forms part of medieval Place Farm, once a property on the Abbess of Shaftesbury's estate and little changed, with its 600-year-old double gatehouse, and farmyard surrounded by stone buildings.

West of the village, Pyt House is a good example of a Georgian country mansion. It was the site of a battle between farm labourers and cavalry during the agricultural riots of 1830.

Tortworth Chestnut

Avon ST 6992

Noted by the Ordnance Survey yet visited by few, this gnarled giant lies minutes from Junction 14 of the M5. Fenced off in a readily accessible field, it looks more like an ancient copse than a single tree, its twisted limbs spreading along the ground. A plaque dated it as 600 years old in 1800; the diarist Evelyn described it as the 'Great Chestnut' of King Stephen's time, and there is a legend that King John visited it while hunting. A Spanish chestnut, it has special appeal in early spring, when it is surrounded by snowdrops.

Tyneham

Dorset SY 8880

A deserted village of controversy: the entire population was removed during World War II when the War Office requisitioned the area. Now part of the Lulworth firing ranges, it is strictly not open to the public — except on occasional open days, when visitors can wander the ghost-village of derelict cottages and gaze at an unused 40-year-old telephone kiosk. The medieval church has been restored. Like Porton Down, this is a haven for wildlife, including peregrine falcons and hobbies.

Upton Country Park

Dorset SY 9992

Roger Tichborne, subject of one of the most notorious hoaxes ever, spent his childhood holidays here. Years after his (presumed) death in 1854, the 'Tichborne Claimant' turned up demanding his inheritance — but was identified as a butcher from Wagga Wagga, New South Wales.

Today Upton offers a breathing space for Poole, with gardens laid out in the style of Humphry Repton, unusual corner icehouses and a nature trail passing by a pets' cemetery.

Upwey

Dorset SY 6684

Thomas Hardy used the mill as a setting for *The Trumpet Major* and is said to have drawn inspiration from the hills rising behind the village. Today visitors come up the B3159 from Weymouth for the ancient rustic wishing well. It was especially popular between the wars, when the colourful Surguran Shorey operated a horse-bus service to the site. Continue on the B3159 to Martinstown and turn left, or take the minor road via Portesham, for the Hardy monument — which doesn't commemorate the novelist but Nelson's flag-captain of 'Kiss me Hardy' fame. The area is rich in tumuli and other ancient remains, and numerous public rights of way, including the ancient Ridgeway path, are shown on the Ordnance Survey map.

Valency Valley

Cornwall SX 0990

This beautiful and little visited valley winds inland from the charming village and harbour of Boscastle. A footpath follows the riverside to St Juliot Church (drivers can take the B3263). The interior was restored and reglazed under the supervision of the novelist Thomas Hardy in 1872, when he was a young architect. Hardy fell in love with the rector's sister, Emma, and married her two years later.

Veryan

Cornwall SW 9139

Most remarkable feature of this village, beautifully set in a wooded hollow of luxuriant trees and shrubs, are the five early 19th-century Round Houses, thatched and topped by a cross. Tradition suggests that the shape was designed to baffle the Devil, who liked to enter by the north wall of a house, and to hide in its corners.

Wansdyke

Wiltshire SU 1264

Probably Dark Age, possibly built in the century after the Romans abandoned Britain in about AD420, perhaps to fend off the Saxons from the Britons, the Wansdyke (Woden's Dyke?) raises questions but remains an undoubtedly impressive bank fortification. The eastern portion, some 12 miles from Morgan's Hill south-east of Calne to Savernake, is walkable all the way and has been described as 'one of the most spectacular experiences in British field archaeology'. Fine views of the Wansdyke can be obtained from Tan Hill above All Cannings.

TISBURY: TITHE BARNS — Tithe-barns, used for storing the tithes (one-tenth of produce) payable by tenants of church lands, usually belonged to great monastic houses, as at **Tisbury**.

Normally stone-built, on the inside they have open timber roofs often supported on two rows of oak posts on stone bases, and so look rather like church naves. Sometimes there was a gabled porch on each side of the building to give access to wagons, and in one of the porches might be a tallat or small upper chamber for the use of the monk who checked the tithes.

*The barns are some of the largest buildings of the Middle Ages — the biggest on record being one at Cholsey in Berkshire, now demolished, which was 303 feet long. Among several belonging to the National Trust is a 13th-century barn at Great Coxwell, Oxfordshire, which belonged to the Cistercian foundation of Beaulieu Abbey in Hampshire. It is 152 feet long and the stone bases on which its roof-supports rest are seven feet high. Some other fine examples are at **Stanway**, **Pilton** and Bradford-on-Avon — a fine 14th-century barn which belonged to the Benedictine nunnery of Shaftesbury Abbey.*

GREAT COXWELL'S *tithe barn, said to be 'as noble as a cathedral' by William Morris*

WARDOUR: SECRET
PASSAGES — At
one desperate point in
his search for the legendary lost
passage of **Wardour** Castle,
explorer Eric Shipton is said to
have plunged down the gardener's
earth closet. He had good reason: a
passage was discovered in 1938,
and identified as a drain.

Drains seem to underlie most
secret passage traditions, including
tales of monkish routes to nearby
nunneries. But the most functional
chutes and drains actually were
widely adapted as hiding places, at
Harvington Hall for instance,
by Catholics sheltering Jesuits
from Elizabeth I.

Tradition links **Whitby's**
many underground ways with
smugglers, and tales of passages
exist at **Tamerton Foliot, St
Ives, Romney Marsh** and
countless other smugglers' haunts.
But remarkably few of them have
been substantiated, which may be
why the 18th century saw a craze
for gratifyingly romantic 'secret'
passage construction. Clifton,
Bristol has the Goldney Grotto;
at Welbeck Abbey the Duke of
Portland built himself a tunnel
system complete with railway, and
at **West Wycombe**, Sir Francis
Dashwood built a maze of tunnels
and caves for the Gothic exploits
of his Hellfire Club. A bizarre
warren of tunnels was built under
Liverpool by a 19th-century
eccentric, and **London** is rich in
20th-century underground
hideouts.

HELLFIRE CLUB *Banqueting
Hall in the West Wycombe caves.
Members and escorts came by
barge to 'meetings' lasting for days*

Wardour

Wiltshire ST 9326

In 1643 Lady Arundell, aged 61, and a garrison of
only 50 soldiers and servants held Wardour's
14th-century Old Castle for six days against 1300
of Cromwell's regular troops. She surrendered
only when offered honourable terms, which the
Roundheads immediately broke, sacking the
Castle and throwing its brave defender into
prison. But an old tradition tells of her escape via
a secret passage to Pyt House nearby. Later, her
son besieged the Parliamentary garrison in turn
and blew up his home rather than leave it in their
hands. The hexagonal courtyard, unique in
Britain, can still be traced in the ruins, which
stand at the end of a long, winding drive in the
grounds of the new (18th-century) Palladian
Wardour Castle (which unlike the Old Castle
cannot be visited). There is a grotto near the ruins.

Warleggan

Cornwall SX 1569

A steep narrow lane leads up to the lonely hamlet
of Warleggan, on the southern fringes of Bodmin
Moor, where the squat church with its clustered
beech trees and rookery recalls the sad story of
the eccentric Reverend Frederick Densham.

On taking up the post in 1931 he closed the
Sunday School, surrounded the rectory with
barbed wire and installed a pack of dogs to keep
strangers away. He painted the church interior in
garish colours and fitted the doors and windows
with numerous locks and bolts. A young musician
who applied for the post of church organist was
locked in his bedroom overnight and fled the
following morning. Parishioners stayed away; the
total annual collection one year came to just 17/6.
Eventually Densham preached to a congregation
of cards, each bearing the name of a former rector,
propped in the pews. One church register entry
reads: '*No fog. No wind. No rain. No congregation.*'

There are also many stories of the man's kind-
ness: he built a playground for children in his
garden — but they never came. He died alone in
the rectory in 1953.

Weare Giffard

Devon SS 4721

This tiny sprawling village just south of Bideford
is approached by winding lanes and over a
former toll bridge called Ha'penny Bridge. There
is a superb 15th-century manor house with
fortified gatehouse and hammer-beam roof in the
hall; adjacent is a charming church with 15th-
century glass. The disused railway line can be
followed, and there is much to be discovered; the
canal built by Lord Rolle in 1824 which joined
the River Torridge is also just a track now, but
once brought prosperity. A woollen mill and
earthenware factory thrived here, as well as the
lime kilns which can still be seen.

Wedmore

Somerset ST 4347

Capital of the low moors, picturesque, but off the
main tourist track, this stone village is rewarding
to visit with its good array of shops, pubs and
hotels, and high street known as The Borough.
The George is a rambling coaching inn with a bar
lower than its courtyard, but the most notable
building is the big church — Perpendicular but
with some earlier work that may be by Wells
Cathedral craftsmen.

Wedmore is renowned as the place where King
Alfred made peace with the Danes.

West Dean

Wiltshire SU 2526

Straddling the Wiltshire-Hampshire border (it
runs through the Red Lion pub), this tiny village
was a large Roman farming estate a thousand
years before Salisbury Cathedral was built. The
oldest building, dating from 1333, is the Borbach
Chantry, containing a remarkable collection of
sculptures of the diarist John Evelyn's family.
The flamboyance of the largest group is matched
only by the doggerel verse inscribed on the
brass-lined folding doors which enclose it.
Nearby at Church Farm is a notable brick tithe
barn of the late 15th century.

Whiteway

Gloucestershire SO 9110

Not the most picturesque spot: many houses look
home-made, and they are. Whiteway was
founded in 1898 when a group living according
to Tolstoyan anarchist principles settled from
Surrey. They refused all use of the post, police,
public transport or any other external service,
built their own homes, strove for self-sufficiency
and observed a personal code that raised conventional eyebrows. Much has changed since then in
this hidden community of winding tracks, high
hedges and eclectic building styles, but some of
the old ethos prevails, and it is still very much the
preserve of creative individualists who maintain
liberal views.

Winchcombe

Gloucestershire SP 0228

Once a capital of Saxon Mercia, the handsome old Cotswold town of Winchcombe is steeped in folklore, including a bloodthirsty tale about Kenelm, a martyred boy king. A street name recalls a once-thriving tobacco industry; and there is much speculation about the odd number of holes in the town stocks.

The church, one of the most splendid in the Cotswolds, has fine leering gargoyles. Up on lonely Belas Knap, a superb Neolithic long barrow an energetic walk away, would-be grave-robbers were deterred by a false entrance.

Also in Winchcombe, Sudeley Castle has the ornate Victorian tomb designed by Sir George Gilbert Scott for Katherine Parr, the sixth wife of Henry VIII and the only one to survive him. She remarried and settled here.

Woodford Valley

Wiltshire SU 1236

This little-used route from Salisbury to Amesbury is well worth trying. It starts with the fine old houses of Stratford sub Castle. William Pitt the Elder lived here as a child, and became one of the two MPs returned by the 'rotten borough' of Old Sarum — it had just ten voters.

To the east are the Norman (originally Iron Age) earthworks and redolent atmosphere of Old Sarum itself, deserted in the 13th century for New Sarum (Salisbury) but with the outline of Bishop Roger's cathedral marked out and traceable in the turf.

The three Woodfords include the celebrated Heale House gardens and fine views over the River Avon. Great Durnford has a notable Norman church and a beautiful cricket ground;

Lake has a well-restored Tudor mansion; and Wilsford a Norman church tower. The whole route, some seven peaceful miles, is a striking contrast to the busy and relatively characterless main road, the A345.

Woodhenge

Wiltshire SU 1543

One of the first archaeological sites to be discovered from the air, in 1925, Neolithic Woodhenge is an older counterpart to Stonehenge. It seems to have been a ritual temple, built of timber and aligned with sunrise on Midsummer Day. Concrete markers show the site of a wooden building in the centre of its acre and a quarter. A grim discovery was the skeleton of a child of about three, whose skull had been cleft, buried in the centre of the enclosure — it may have been a sacrifice of some 4000 years ago.

Wootton Rivers

Wiltshire SU 1962

On St Andrew's Church is the Jack Spratt Clock, made in 1911 by a local man from scrap metal. The villagers wanted a clock to celebrate George V's Coronation, but couldn't afford to buy one. With their donations of mechanical junk, old prams, bicycles, bedsteads — even a broken reaping machine — Spratt set to work. His clock face bears letters in place of numerals and the clock has a repertoire of 24 different chimes.

WARLEGGAN *'No fog. No wind. No rain.' wrote the vicar of the wonderfully remote church. In 1818, the spire was destroyed by lightning*

STONEHENGE *1776 — an object of speculation for centuries*

WOODHENGE: HENGES — *Something like a hundred henge monuments have been identified in Britain. The feature* **Woodhenge,** *Stonehenge and the rest have in common is a circular (or nearly circular) plan defined by a bank and ditch; the bank nearly always being on the outside. There are many variations on that principal theme. Even the name is somewhat confusing, since henge means 'to hang', and only Stonehenge has stones (the lintels) which hang. In this, as in so many other ways, Stonehenge is unique — a spectacular one-off.*

All the henges were built by Neolithic people between three and four thousand years ago. But why, and what for?

No matter how hard we try, we cannot re-create the world of pre-historic men. We can look at their bones, examine some of the objects they made, and visit some of the places where they lived, or were buried, or where they may have worshipped. But doing any of those things cannot tell us what they thought or what prompted their actions. So, to visit, or ponder upon, the henge monuments is bound to be a strange and possibly baffling experience.

Stonehenge itself was adapted and rebuilt several times during its active lifetime — we will probably never know just what it looked like at any one of those stages. Woodhenge is even more of a puzzle. Its post holes were discovered by aerial photography — nothing else remains. So what did it look like? A maze of wooden pillars? A roofed building? Arbor Low (see **Youlgreave***) is likewise a henge — but did its recumbent stones once stand upright or were they always flat?*

Many accept the theory that Stonehenge is, in part at least, a huge astronomical computer, capable of calculating the precise position of heavenly bodies at any given time. But what about Avebury, also a henge and only a few miles away? Its structure is quite different; was its purpose also quite different?

❧❈❧

KENT *circa* 1901.
Hop pickers. Nowadays nearly all the hops are harvested by machine, but until the 1950s work in the hop-gardens was done manually by poor Londoners, for whom it offered the chance of a country holiday. The pickers may be hard to find, but the hop-gardens are still very much part of the landscape of Kent

---
❧❈❧

SOUTH-EAST ENGLAND

A few examples will set the scene: in a Hastings pub are displayed two fossilised cats perhaps 400 years old; sea holly was once collected at Walton on the Naze for the purpose of making love potions; in Chaldon church are wall paintings every bit as nasty as scenes from a modern horror film; and the threatened bats in the Basingstoke Canal at Greywell are championed by enthusiasts who consider them to be little darlings and not little monsters. But to begin with, meet the giants . . .

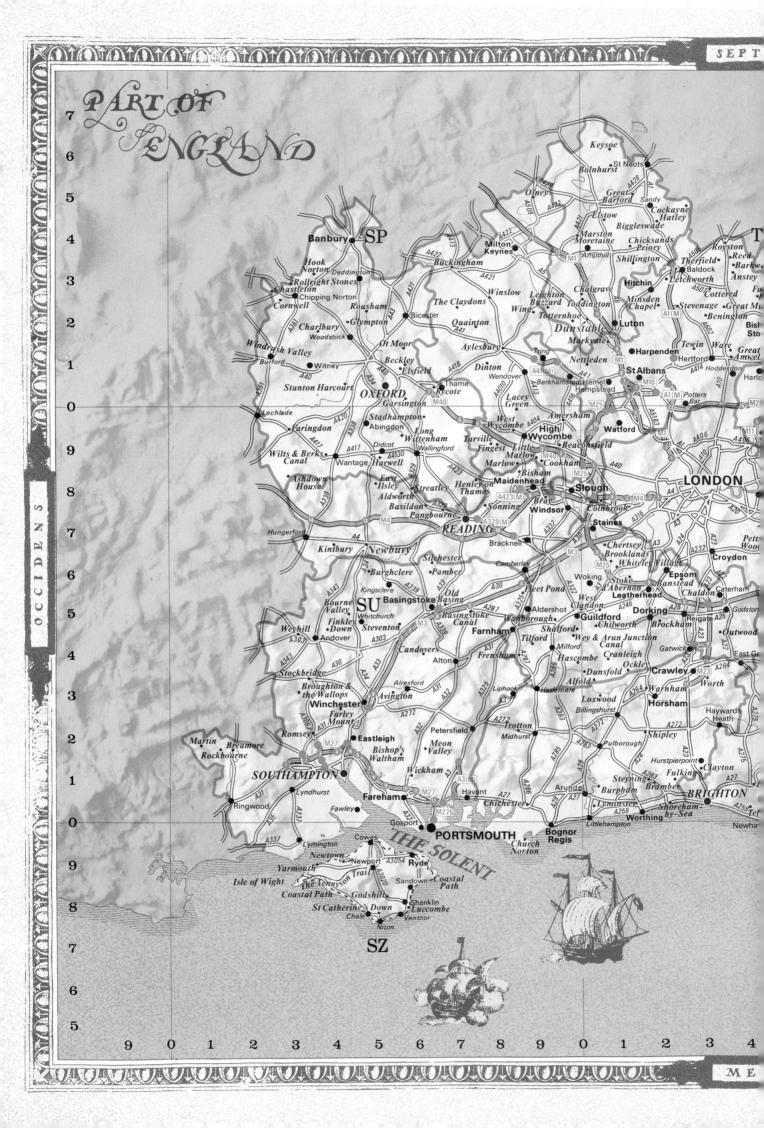

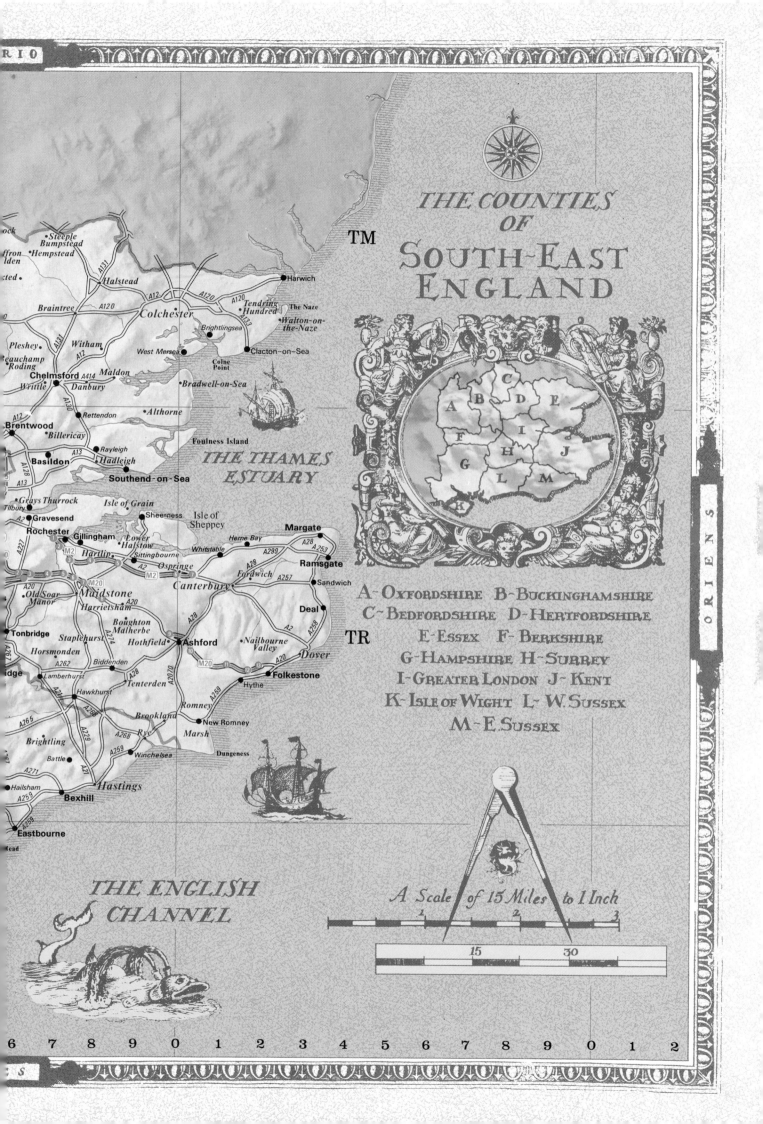

ALDWORTH: GIANTS

A LDWORTH: GIANTS — So remarkable are the **Aldworth** Giants that Queen Elizabeth I rode pillion behind the Earl of Leicester to look at them.

Tradition says that there were four giants — John Long, John Strong, John Ever-afraid and John Never-afraid. In fact, the 'giants' are stone effigies of the de la Beche family, buried here. 'John Strong' is Sir Philip de la Beche — his feet are on the dwarf who always accompanied him to Court, to show off his height. A Royalist officer called Richard Symonds sketched him in May 1644, with the caption 'The people call this statue John Strong'. He also tells us that there was an effigy on the outside wall of the church under an arch (now blocked). This, he writes, was John Ever-afraid, of whom the tale went that he had promised his soul to the Devil, whether he was buried inside or outside the church. But at his death he tricked the Devil, by being buried in the wall, neither within nor without.

Today Sir Philip has been defaced, but remains extremely impressive, leaning on his elbow with unusual nonchalance. A similarly relaxed pose is adopted by the much later Fettiplace family, awaiting the second coming in marble, at Swinbrook, in the **Windrush Valley**.

GIANT *effigy at Aldworth. The massive monuments to the de la Beche family are unusually impressive in size*

Aldworth

Berkshire SU 5579

The great yew tree which dominated the churchyard at Aldworth for nearly a thousand years has almost gone, blown down in a gale and reduced to a single branch, but the Aldworth Giants still lie within the church. Seen dimly in the gloom, these larger than life effigies of the de la Beche family date from the 14th century, when the head of the family, Sir Philip (who lies here with eight of his relatives) was Sheriff of the county and valet to Edward II. The church was visited by Elizabeth I. The effigies were knocked about by Cromwell's army, but they remain a remarkable sight beneath their fretted stone canopies along the aisles.

Little Aldworth is well worth exploring. The poet Laurence Binyon, who penned the World War I lines *At the going down of the sun and in the morning, we will remember them*', is buried in the churchyard; and the 372-foot well opposite the Bell Inn is one of the deepest in the country with a well-head consisting of great beams and heavy cogs and wheels.

Alfold

Surrey TQ 0334

Stocks and a whipping post can still be seen opposite a beautiful Tudor cottage by the church gate, in this remarkably pretty village. Along with Dunsfold and Chiddingfold, it was one of the early centres for the important Wealden industry of glassmaking, which may have provided glass for Westminster Abbey. The industry declined but was briefly revived at Alfold in 1567 by Jean Carré, who brought glassmakers in from Lorraine. Signs of the old glassworks still remain in Sidney Wood, to the west of the village. Carré is buried in the churchyard, and the probable site of his grave is marked by a very worn slab of Sussex marble (a material which is often rich in freshwater crustacea remains, and is known locally as winkle stone). The churchyard yew, almost certainly pre-Christian, is one of several claimed to be 'the oldest in Surrey'.

Althorne

Essex TQ 9199

Pre-dating the local caravans by half a millenium, St Andrew's has a fine flint and stone tower, built in the Perpendicular style. Inside the church is an octagonal font of about 1400, which still has its carvings of saints and angels intact. Purists have found them rough, but less severe minds will like their sheer vigour. A brass dated 1508 records that William Hyklott 'paide for the werkemanship of the wall'; an inscription over the west door remembers John Wilson and John Hill, who probably paid for the tower.

To the south, where Station Road meets Burnham Road, stands the villagers' own War Memorial: they themselves built the massive structure of beams supporting a big tiled roof that shelters the sad list of names. To the north, turn right off the B1010 as it leaves the village, for Green Lane and the golden-thatched, white-walled Huntsman and Hounds, which is partly 14th-century. A wicket gate leads through the garden to the saloon and a dark and timbered interior, with deal tables, high backed benches and the tiniest of bar counters, where the barrels are on view behind.

Amersham

Buckinghamshire SU 9697

The town lies in two parts, the old town down in the valley and the new one up on the hill above the River Misbourne. Halfway down the wide main street of the Old Town, which is well supplied with coaching inns, the red-brick 17th-century Market Hall once served a dual purpose as the town lock-up. It bears the arms of the local squire, Sir William Drake, who built the hall in 1612 and was a descendant of Sir Francis. According to John Leland, Amersham has always been '. . . a right prayty market towne on Frydy, in one strete well-buildyd with tymber'. It is still pretty and many of the houses and the King's Arms are timber-framed.

A footpath leads to the Martyrs' Memorial from the corner of the churchyard: in the 16th century, Lollards were burned at the stake on Amersham Hill for heresy. The daughter of one of them, William Tylesworth, was forced to light the fire.

Anstey

Hertfordshire TL 3833

In the grounds of a lodge-like cottage is what looks like the way into a narrow tunnel running eastwards. Not open to the public, Anstey Cave Gate is said to be the start of a lost passage to Anstey Castle, nearly a mile away. It can only be negotiated for a short distance, and drawings made after the cave's rediscovery in 1904 suggest that it was actually a Neolithic flint mine. Archaeologists working at Anstey Castle have failed to find an entrance at that end — but in 1862 a pair of massive iron doors was uncovered in the mud of the moat, and still lie there. Were these once the doors of the cave? Or does the Cave Gate lead not to Anstey Castle, but somewhere more mysterious, or much further?

The castle (only a mound remains), built by a Norman knight, was later given by Henry VIII to each of his first three wives in turn.

Ashdown House

Oxfordshire SU 2882

Set beautifully in the Downs above Lambourn, the house appears suddenly in a fold of the hills, looking just like a doll's house. It was built by William Craven in 1660 (tradition says that he intended it for the Queen of Bohemia), and is a delightfully formal composition at the meeting place of four avenues of trees. Chalk and brown-stone dressings, and the pretty cupola perched on top, add to the delight. A magnificent staircase climbs up to the roof through the heart of the house, there are family portraits of the Cravens in the hall, and a formal garden that is best seen from the roof. The house is opened regularly by the National Trust.

All around are the Downs, enhanced by a selection of earthworks, notably a hill fort known as Alfred's Castle.

Avington

Hampshire SU 5332

An unspoilt Georgian church, built of red brick and still complete with its original three-decker pulpit, box pews and gallery, is one of the gems of this charming hamlet. Another is the big hous

ASHDOWN HOUSE:
THE WINTER
QUEEN — *William
Craven's romantic* **Ashdown
House** *is one of the many he is
said to have built for Elizabeth,
Queen of Bohemia. Daughter of
James I, she married Frederick,
Elector Palatine, who in 1619
accepted the crown of Bohemia.
They were driven into exile after
just one winter, and Elizabeth
came to be known as the Winter
Queen.*

ELIZABETH OF BOHEMIA
*'By virtue first, then choice, a
Queen . . . Th'eclipse and glory of
her kind,' wrote Wotton*

*But she was also called the
'Queen of Hearts'. From her girl-
hood she exercised a charisma
celebrated by poets, including Ben
Jonson and Sir Henry Wotton.
Her most faithful admirer was
Lord Craven (later the first Earl).
In 1632, as a young soldier, he fell
under Elizabeth's spell, and for
the rest of his life he and his
fortune were at her service and
that of her children, especially
Prince Rupert. The 'little mad
mylord', as contemporaries called
him, was a knight-errant.
Captured with Rupert, who was
not yet 20, he offered twice his
own ransom of £20,000 to be
allowed to share his imprisonment.
With Rupert, he buried Elizabeth
in 1662 in Westminster Abbey.
He himself lived on until he was
90, amid portraits of her and her
circle (some are at Ashdown
House). Rumour later said that
they were secretly married — this
is untrue, but he never married
anyone else.*

— Avington Park — part of which has stood
here probably since the 16th century. Open to the
public on summer weekends, the house,
sweeping parkland and lake, which attracts many
wildfowl in the winter, can be seen from the road
that runs westward out of the village.

A web of quiet roads and public footpaths,
including a planned nature trail, links Avington
(near Winchester) with some of the Itchen
Valley's other delightful villages — Itchen Abbas,
Easton and Martyr Worthy.

AYLESBURY *The large, mullioned window in the King's
Head hall shows the Royal Arms of Henry VI and
Margaret of Anjou. Dating back to the 15th century, the
window, remarkably, still has some of the original, medieval
glass in place*

Aylesbury

Buckinghamshire SP 8113

Oliver Cromwell sat on one of the chairs at the
15th-century King's Head inn, which is also
notable for fine leaded windows and is now
owned by the National Trust. Outside in the
Market Square is a magnificent bronze statue of

John Hampden, the local squire who precipitated
the English Civil War by his refusal to pay Ship
Money to the King.

Modern civic buildings dominate this county
town of Buckinghamshire today, but at the
parish church, the vicar maintains an old tradition
by placing a fresh red flower on the tomb of the
Lee family, who lived nearby for generations.
The church itself has an unusual medieval door
and a Norman font, though the building dates
from the 14th century. The old County Hall at
the lower end of Market Square dates from 1740
and is attributed to the great John Vanbrugh, the
architect of Blenheim.

BASINGSTOKE CANAL: BATS — *Britain's biggest colony of bats, on the* **Basingstoke Canal** *at Greywell, has a loyal following — but for centuries these fascinating creatures have been regarded with fear and loathing. It was thought that bats were witches' familiars — an idea intensified by Bram Stoker's 'Dracula', and only just beginning to be dispelled by dedicated conservationists. About 40 groups throughout Britain are working to protect the bat, and to preserve its breeding and hibernation sites. The biggest of the known hibernation sites is the Greywell Tunnel, which may support up to 2000 bats of five species, two of those species being rare and none of them common. They enjoy a unique microclimate: a spring rising in the tunnel keeps the temperature constant. The collapse of the tunnel has ensured that the colony is undisturbed (although plans have been put forward to re-open it to canal traffic), and there is no access to the site.*

NATTERER'S BAT *Its natural habitat is woodland, but it is one of the many species that hibernates in the tunnel*

⊸∘❊∘⊶

⊸∘❊∘⊶

BARKWAY *The more splendid of the village's two milestones is carved with the arms of Trinity Hall and Robert Hare*

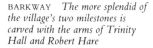

Banstead

Surrey   TQ 2559

Banstead Council still has a woolpack in its crest recalling the local wool industry, and various local place names such as Mint Farm confirm the importance of the peppermint crop. But easier money was gained, and lost, at horse racing. For a long time the racing on these Downs was considerably more important than that at Epsom. In November 1683 both King Charles II and the Duke of York are said to have attended the racing here; earlier that century one William Stanley had been killed 'running the race'. Whether he was a member of the Derby family who were to give their name to the two great horse races run at Epsom — the Oaks was named after the Derbys' home near Banstead — is unclear.

Barkway

Hertfordshire   TL 3835

The two tall milestones in this attractive village are part of what was probably the first example of regular milestone placing in Britain. In 1586, William Mowse, Master of Trinity Hall, Cambridge, left £1000 in his will to mend the highways in and around the university town and towards Barkway. His successor, Robert Hare, added £600 to the fund and between 1728 and 1732 a later master, William Warren, acted upon the will, setting up milestones along the whole length of the road between Cambridge and Barkway.

Basildon

Berkshire   SU 6178

The original Jethro Tull, agricultural machinery pioneer and inventor of the mechanical seed drill, is buried in the churchyard; another monument features two boys in swimming trunks, recalling the sad drowning of two brothers. Outside the churchyard is yet another memorial — the mausoleum built in memory of his parents by the late Mr Childe-Beale, and now the focal point of the Childe-Beale Trust wildlife park, with ponies and peacocks and deer. Rising above them all is beautiful Bath stone Basildon Park, built in 1776 and surely the finest Georgian house in Berkshire. Classical in style, it has some unusual features, notably an Anglo-Indian room and one containing an exhibition of shells. The house is owned by the National Trust and open to the public.

Before leaving Basildon, cast an eye at the railway bridge, one of the achievements of Isambard Kingdom Brunel.

Basingstoke Canal at Greywell

Hampshire   SU 7151

The red bricks which make up the villages hereabouts were the making of this canal, running from Basingstoke to the Thames. The railways heralded its end — but today it offers some fine canal cruising and walks, one of the best stretches left being that between Greywell and Odiham.

BENINGTON *In ancient times the Kings of Mercia inhabited the castle whose scant ruins were incorporated into the Lordship — a Georgian house converted into a neo-Norman folly*

Greywell itself is a delightful place, built mostly of red brick, and the walk begins in the middle of the village, where the canal emerges from the Greywell tunnel. Not far short of a mile long, the tunnel has collapsed in the middle and now provides a winter home for an estimated 2000 bats. Plans to restore the tunnel have frightened bat fans since it is probably one of the most important bat roosts in Europe.

From here the canal makes its tranquil way to King John's Castle, a flint structure that seems more like a castle in fantasy, since it is not much bigger than an average house. It was at one time a hunting lodge, and King John may well have visited it. The canal reaches Odiham at the Water Witch pub — and Odiham should be explored, especially for its Georgian town houses and excellent church.

Beaconsfield

Buckinghamshire   SU 9490

Enid Blyton lived here and might have been influenced by Bekonscot Model Village in Warwick Road, which has a wonderful display of miniature houses and people, spread over a large garden. Beaconsfield's other literary figures have included the Parliamentary poet, Edmund Waller,

who is buried in the churchyard — he lived at Hall Barn, as did the statesman, Edmund Burke, who lies in the church itself. G. K. Chesterton lived here while writing the Father Brown stories, and a noted American resident was the poet Robert Frost.

The town hosts a great 'Charter Fair' every spring, when stalls and side shows line the streets. It was once a staging post for coaches on the Oxford Road, hence the numerous and attractive coaching inns in the older part.

Beauchamp Roding

Essex   TL 5810

Local farm labourer Isaac Mead, who worked and saved enough to become a farmer himself in 1882, was so grateful to the land that made his fortune that he had a corner of a field specially consecrated as an eternal resting place for himself and his family. Their graves can still be seen in the brambly undergrowth, beside the present drive to Rochets house. The church of this village (one of the lovely Rodings group) stands alone in the fields, marked by a tall 15th-century tower and reached by a track off the B184. The raised pews at the west end have space-saving wooden steps, pulled out of slots by means of iron rings.

Beckley

Oxfordshire   SP 5611

The best way to approach Beckley is from the west, along a minor road that branches off the B4027. High on the side of a hill, this offers a wonderful view over Ot Moor, a great stretch of mysterious flatland, broken by a pattern of hedges and outbreaks of wood. Beckley is an old village, cut by the Roman road that runs up from Dorchester in the south, lined by thick hedges and blackberries. A feeling of age, silence and seclusion is still strong, despite weekend cottages and the spreading suburbs of Oxford. The stone houses encircle the hillside, all around the 14th- and 15th-century church, with its strong, rough stone tower, and the curious circular stair turret. There are plenty of enjoyable details, including a stone bookrest, a partly Jacobean pulpit, good ironwork, the remains of wall paintings and medieval stained glass depicting the Assumption of the Virgin. Beckley is best explored slowly, and on foot, with a pause at the pub (where the novelist Evelyn Waugh spent part of his honeymoon), followed perhaps by a visit to the little tree nursery.

Benington

Hertfordshire   TL 3023

For centuries the shattered remains of a keep destroyed by King John's men in 1213 lay disregarded on the castle mound of Benington Lordship. Then, in about 1832, a local landscape gardener named Pulham found a novel use for the ancient flint and mortar chunks — he incorporated them into a bizarre neo-Norman fantasy. Today on occasional spring and summer open days, the sham gatehouse, complete with portcullis, can be seen keeping company with a shrine for a Buddha. The toy-like 'medieval' decorations make it all the more endearing, and in certain places, red brickwork has been exposed where the 'stone' (made from Portland cement) has fallen off.

SEE THE FEBRUARY
STRAND

ANOTHER MYSTERY FOR SHERLOCK HOLMES.

ABOVE *'It was a prostrate man face downwards upon the ground . . .' A new mystery for Holmes, in the Strand magazine*

BISHAM ABBEY: LADY HOBY'S GHOST — *Built on an abbey site in 1557-61 by Sir Philip Hoby, **Bisham Abbey** is haunted by his wife Lady Elizabeth Hoby, whose splendid painted tomb can be seen in All Saints' Church. One of four sisters celebrated for their learning, and a friend of Elizabeth I, she is said to have murdered her son because he could not write without blotting his copy-books. One version says that she locked him in a cupboard where he starved to death, another is that she beat him so hard that he died. So great was her remorse that she has haunted the house ever since her death in 1609, perpetually trying to wash his blood off her hands.*

*Early in the 19th century, some blot-covered antique copy-books bearing William's name are said to have been found pushed between joists of the floor. But amongst all the children of twice-married Lady Hoby, there is no record of a William. Rather as at Aston Hall, **Birmingham**, the whole story may have been generated by a portrait. A picture of Lady Hoby, still to be seen at Bisham Abbey, shows her looking white-faced and dressed in black — certainly sinister enough to suggest a ghost — and descriptions of the ghost seem to have been influenced by this picture.*

BUSTLESHAM *or* BYSHAM MONASTERY *in* BERKSHIRE

THE ABBEY *began as a preceptory of the Knights Templar, became an Augustinian priory in 1337, and a Benedictine abbey in 1537*

Berwick

East Sussex   TQ 5105

At his enthronement in 1929, Bishop Bell of Chichester declared his intention of renewing the once close links between the Church and the Arts. The artist Duncan Grant, who was living nearby at Firle, produced a scheme for wall paintings at Berwick's church, and after much opposition, the work, by Grant, Vanessa Bell (no relation of the bishop) and her children Quentin and Angelica, was completed and dedicated in 1943. Like so many of the great medieval murals, it is firmly rooted in a local setting. The barn is a Sussex barn at Tilton; Mount Caburn at Lewes is clearly identifiable, and several scenes are based on the views from the church windows. A soldier (killed later in the war), an airman from the village, and a sailor from Firle are included in 'The Glory', as are the bishop and the rector of Berwick. Local shepherds carrying Pyecombe crooks are shown in 'The Nativity'.

Biggleswade

Bedfordshire   TL 1944

Rising up by the busy A1 road just south of Biggleswade is a fine, romantic-looking building that looks like part of a castle, but is in fact a pumping station. New Spring Works was built in 1904 for the Biggleswade Water Board and is still in use. The architect, George Deacon, was influenced by the Art Nouveau movement and succeeded in crafting from local sandstone a building with an almost ecclesiastical quality to it. Listed as a building of special architectural interest, it was recently restored, using moulded concrete and crushed sandstone, then faced with sandstone dust, as an alternative to using solid stone.

Billericay

Essex   TQ 6794

Evidence of local settlement has been traced back to the Bronze Age — but no one has yet supplied a conclusive explanation of Billericay's name. There is no doubt about the attraction of the High Street though, with its timber, weather-boarding and Georgian brick. The 1510 Chantry House was the home of Christopher Martin, treasurer to the Pilgrim Fathers.

The Peasants' Revolt of 1381 saw the massacre of hundreds of rebels just north-east of the town at Norsey Wood; today this area of ancient woodland is a country park, managed by coppicing (the traditional way of ensuring the timber supply) to encourage plant and bird life.

Bisham

Berkshire   SU 8485

A ghost and a curse haunt the little Thameside village of Bisham. The ghost is that of Lady Elizabeth Hoby, a lady-in-waiting to Elizabeth I, who is said to flit about Bisham Abbey, once in the possession of the Knights Templar.

The curse is that of the last abbot of Bisham, who vowed that no family should succeed to the abbey lands, and indeed, the Vansittarts, who lived there, never succeeded in a direct line, for all the eldest sons died. The Abbey, open only by appointment, now belongs to the Sports Council. Close by, the Hoby family, including Lady Elizabeth, lie buried under a fine alabaster

monument in All Saints' Church. Bisham is an attractive spot, set on the river beneath a long wooded escarpment.

Bishop's Waltham

Hampshire   SU 5517

Henri of Blois was the bishop beside whose palace this attractive little town grew up. A great flint-built structure dating back 850 years, the palace can still be admired as a massive ruin. The town is a harmonious jumble of building styles which give it great charm and variety. Reflecting the flintwork of the palace is that of St Peter's Church, crowned by an unusual 17th-century turret, while other buildings contrast half-timbering with sedate Georgian façades or surviving details of 1920s shopfronts with the rich red-and-grey contrasting brickwork that is characteristic of this part of Hampshire.

Bolnhurst

Bedfordshire   TL 0859

The church and a farm called Brayes on the edge of the village were among the few survivors of old Bolnhurst — most of which was burnt down in an attempt to stop the plague in 1665. The 15th-century farm is believed to have been a checkpoint manned by Henry VIII's soldiers at the time his first wife, Catherine of Aragon, was imprisoned in Kimbolton Castle, where she eventually died. Later it became the Plough Inn and today forms part of the larger pub Ye Olde Plough, which still retains part of the old moat around the property.

Boughton Malherbe

Kent   TQ 8749

On hot summer days, when the beautiful Wealden villages seem close to bursting with visitors, it is still possible to walk or drive up the stiffish climb to Boughton Malherbe, and there study a remarkably tranquil landscape.

The farm buildings originally formed part of the manor house, which belonged to the Wotton family for centuries, and stands next to the church. Snowdrops bloom in February on the grassy bank in front of the church, and sheep and lambs graze the sloping pastures below. Izaak Walton, in his biography of Sir Henry Wotton, the poet and diplomat, summed up Boughton's charm — 'the advantage of a large Prospect, and of equal pleasure to all Beholders.'

Bourne Valley

Hampshire   SU 4250

The haunting Iron Age hill fort of Fosbury Camp, just across the county boundary in Wiltshire, marks the head of this valley. A series of unspoilt villages stand on the Bourne Rivulet, a pure chalkland stream whose watercress beds, at St Mary Bourne, supply lorry-loads of fine watercress to much of Britain. One of the larger villages is Hurstbourne Tarrant — a frequent destination of William Cobbett on his *Rural Rides* in the early 19th century. In 1822, referring to it as 'a little village in a deep dale', he wrote: 'Uphusband, the legal name of which is Hurstbourne Tarrant, is, as the reader will recollect, a great favourite with me.'

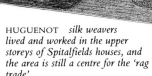

BRAINTREE AND BOCKING: HUGUENOTS —

*Huguenot names such as Courtauld continue to be attached to international enterprises. Samuel Courtauld's mill survives at **Braintree**, and Huguenot weavers' houses can still be seen in Spitalfields, **London**.*

Huguenots began in France in 1559 as an organised Protestant group taking their direction from Calvin and the Calvinistic Reformation in Geneva. At first they were able to live and worship freely, but as political and religious rivalries grew, the Catholic majority started persecuting them. Nearly a century of war, massacres and bloodshed followed. Sometimes the Huguenots were in the ascendant, but finally, in 1685, all their rights were taken away. In the ensuing chaos many more died, but thousands fled the country. It was to turn out a tremendous loss for France, since the Huguenots formed the most industrious and economically advanced elements in French society. France's loss was the gain of others; Huguenots poured into England, where their skills as builders, weavers and scientists soon made them valued members of the community.

BRADWELL-ON-SEA *Reconstructed in 1920, St Peter on the Wall — the little Saxon church with walls two feet thick — is sprayed by the sea at high tide*

Bradwell-on-Sea

Essex TM 0006

First there were the Romans, who built a huge fort here to keep the Saxons out. Two bastions and a fragment of wall survive. In around AD650, the Saxons used its bricks, stones and tiles under the direction of Bishop Cedd to build a tiny chapel. In the 14th century, the chapel was abandoned and forgotten for 600 years, except by farmers who used it as a barn.

In the village itself (two miles south-west down a Roman road), Erskine Childers, who fought for the Irish Republican Army and was shot by the Irish Free State in the 1920s, wrote the wartime thriller *The Riddle of the Sands* at Bradwell Lodge, an attractive and part-Tudor former rectory. To the north, Bradwell's vast nuclear power station looms over a nature reserve.

Braintree and Bocking

Essex TL 7523

These two small towns, on the crossing of two Roman roads, were knit together by a shared woollen industry in the 16th century. Flemish weavers settled here, followed by the Huguenot Samuel Courtauld who set up a silk mill in 1816. By 1886, Courtaulds employed no less than 3214 Essex people.

Mills still loom large, and the fine ex-Town Hall is one of many other Courtauld legacies, built in 1928 with oak-panelled walls, murals by Grieffenhagen showing stirring scenes in local history, and a grand central tower with a five-belled striking clock. The dome is crowned with a bronze figure of Truth, recalling the local motto '*Hold to the Truth*'. A smaller but very appealing reminder of Courtaulds is the 1930s bronze fountain, with boy, shell and fish, at the centre of Braintree.

Bocking has an impressive parish church and the sight of a postmill repays a walk down Church Street.

BRIGHTLING: FOLLIES — *Mad Jack Fuller of Brightling was one of the many who made his mark in a dramatically visible way — by building follies, including a pyramid, a hermitage and a cone. The latter is said to have been built after he had bet that he could see Dallington church spire from his window: when daylight came, he realised he couldn't, and put a substitute there instead.*

There are thousands of follies up and down the country. Some, like Lord Berner's Tower at Faringdon, served as eye-catchers; others, like Jack the Treacle Eater at Barwick Park, may have been intended to relieve local unemployment, while an obelisk at Farley Mount commemorates a horse.

The fashion of folly building began in the 18th century and still continues today, with such things as gnome gardens at Bath. However, it is the follies of the 18th and 19th centuries which have the greatest impact on landscape and eye. For all those towers, arches and sham ruins poised against the skyline, there are very many more mouldering away deep in copses and gloomy places. They were built to look mysterious and half ruined, and without the constant careful gardening needed to keep nature at bay they are slowly falling into oblivion. But such an end is probably entirely appropriate for a folly.

—∘◦❖◦∘—

BRIGHTLING *Jack Fuller built his tomb 24 years before he died. When he gave the church its organ the choir received smocks and yellow stockings*

Bramber

West Sussex   TQ 1810

Only a jagged 76-foot pillar of clotted flint remains of the great Norman castle protecting the River Adur. By the early 1800s the town had declined to such an extent that William Wilberforce could remark as he passed by that he really ought to visit, having represented Bramber in Parliament for 12 years. As well as magnificent views from the castle, Bramber has its House of Pipes, with a collection of smoking paraphernalia, including splendid sets of cigarette cards.

St Richard, Bishop of Chichester, is said to have blessed the nets of local fishermen, who promptly drew them up from the river full of fish; and the children of William de Brione, starved to death by King John, are said to still beg for bread near their old house in the town.

Bray

Berkshire   SU 9079

'Whatsoever King shall reign, I'll be the Vicar of Bray, Sir.'
So declared the tenacious vicar, who survived several reigns and various shifts in religious and political direction to become immortalised in English folk song. One can hardly blame him, for this is a pretty place, worth visiting as well as singing about. The church is both delightful and unusual, having the use of a chantry chapel and a 15th-century gatehouse which, until 1853, was a village inn known as the Six Bells. The vicar was probably Simon Aleyn, twice Catholic, twice Protestant, who held the living in the 16th century and lies buried in the churchyard.

Nearby Monkey Island in the Thames has a fishing lodge which once belonged to the Dukes of Marlborough. The ceilings are decorated with monkeys painted by Clermont. The lodge, reached by a footbridge over the river, is now run as an hotel.

Breamore

Hampshire   SU 1517

Walk up a lane bordered by Spanish chestnut trees, on to a hilltop farm track and make your way into the dense yew wood. Here, dark even in midsummer, is a turf-cut maze that feels like the very essence of ancient places. It seems small at first, but try walking its intricate contours and see how long it takes. Walking the maze somehow brings on a feeling of timeless magic — it is almost literally enchanting.

The village of charming thatched cottages close to the clear waters of the Avon has as its centrepiece Breamore House, basically Elizabethan but largely rebuilt after a fire in 1856. The house is open to the public and also here are a carriage museum and an excellent rural life museum. Close by the house is Breamore church, a Saxon gem complete with a Saxon inscription over one of its arches.

Brightling

East Sussex   TQ 6821

'Mad' Jack Fuller, 22-stone MP and local squire, is said by tradition to be buried sitting upright with a bottle of claret under the pyramid in the churchyard. Sadly, when opened in 1938, the pyramid was found to be empty, despite the broken glass which Jack (who died in 1834) had caused to be strewn outside, against the day when the Devil came to 'claim his own'.

Inside the church is a magnificent barrel organ presented by Fuller, who is chiefly remembered for his eccentricities and the follies he left around his pretty village — despite the fact that he was a philanthropist on a grand scale, and was perceptive enough to be an early patron of the young J. M. W. Turner. As well as the pyramid, he left behind a rotunda with a dome, an obelisk 65 feet high, a cone and an observatory, designed by Sir Robert Smirke.

Brighton

East Sussex TQ 3104

Phoebe Hassel, who for love of a soldier joined the army at 15 and served for many years without her sex being discovered, retired to Brighton and endured both poverty and some fame before dying there, aged 108, in 1821.

She is buried at the beautiful medieval church of St Nicholas, built outside the original village of Brighthelmstone, which became a town after the Prince of Wales decided in 1783 to sample its air and sea-bathing. The original Royal Pavilion, although built for the Prince, was 'owned' by his Clerk of the Kitchen, who paid all the bills. Menus of the feasts created for Prinny by his chef Carême can still be seen inside.

Before 1514, when the village was burned by the French, it was bounded by East, North and West Streets — South Street was washed away. Within these old boundaries today are the most ancient parts of Brighton, including the world-famous 17th-century Lanes.

Brighton has inspired some notable inventors. Magnus Volk's electric railway still runs along the front in summer; and Friese Greene, inventor of the cinematograph, lived here, as later did James Williamson, who produced short comic films. He used Hove locations such as Wilbury Road and George Street some years before the Mack Sennett era of similar films in America.

Brockham

Surrey TQ 1949

Badgers, or 'brocks', lived until quite recently on the banks of the River Mole where it curves around Brockham, and these shy animals are said to have given the village its name. (A less colourful explanation is that the name comes from the word 'brook'.) It has a fine broad green on which W. G. Grace once played cricket, and also enjoys the space of the Big Field — given by a mystery benefactor to the National Trust in 1966, on the understanding it would be used for recreation.

Nearby on the North Downs, Brockham Quarries still have the remains of late 19th-century kilns which were in use until the 1930s. Hearthstone and chalk were dug here. The disused quarries can be reached by footpath.

Brookland

Kent TQ 9825

Brookland church has a unique feature — a detached, weatherboarded belfry. Although it was almost certainly always separate from the church, several explanations have been offered, including the story that the appearance of a virgin wishing to be married so astonished the belfry that it leapt to the ground.

The magnificent framework supporting the bells is said to consist of timbers taken from nearby wrecks, and the origins of the splendid Norman lead font, with engravings of the signs of the Zodiac and the Occupations of the Months, are genuinely mysterious.

This was a great smuggling area, and the 'Battle of Brookland' in 1821, between the Aldington gang and Excise men, was one of the most violent of its type ever fought. On this occasion, as on others, it is probable that the local doctor, who lived in Pear Tree House in the village, was taken blindfold to tend wounded members of the gang.

Brooklands

Surrey TQ 0662

In the early part of this century, when motor racing became popular, Brooklands circuit was built. Around its steeply banked track were to thunder some of the largest and most powerful racing cars ever built. To it came almost all the legendary figures in the early history of motor racing. Yet at the outbreak of World War I, the track was abandoned, and by the end of the war nature had already reclaimed a large part of the circuit. Nowadays the outlines are blurred, and the British Aircraft Corporation's factory occupies much of the site. It is said that occasionally the roar of engines and the screaming of tyres can still be heard, while a figure in goggles and leather helmet, believed to be Percy Lambert, killed at the end of the railway straight in 1913, haunts the track.

BROUGHTON *When deemed fat enough to eat, the squabs (fledglings) were collected from their nests in the dovecote*

Broughton and the Wallops

Hampshire SU 3032

Lady Godiva owned the manor of Over Wallop — one of a string of villages linked by the little Wallop Brook, that richly repays exploration. Broughton offers a marvellous collection of cottages of many styles, quiet by-ways and an interesting church with an unusual 17th-century dovecote in the churchyard. Upstream, the villages of Nether, Middle and Over Wallop are perhaps most noted for their names. Nether Wallop gained fame not very long ago, as the venue for an off-beat arts festival, which became the subject of a television documentary. Its church is well worth a visit: the wall paintings above the chancel are now believed to be some of the earliest in Europe. The eye-catching pyramid in the churchyard houses the earthly remains of Francis Douce, an 18th-century local benefactor and doctor. The charm of Middle Wallop has been tempered by its 20th-century role as a big RAF base, but Over Wallop is still attractive.

BURGHCLERE: STANLEY SPENCER

— The artist of the Sandham Memorial Chapel at **Burghclere***, Stanley Spencer, trained at the Slade School of Art and was influenced by Post-Impressionism, but went on to develop an original and unmistakable style of painting. After a mystical experience at* **Cookham***, when he imagined himself to be walking in Paradise on Earth, he used the village for his paintings of Bible stories which his father had read to him at night. He portrayed the Bible characters as down-to-earth ordinary people, against a clearly English background.*

During World War I, he was in the Royal Army Medical Corps in Macedonia, and drew on this for the Burghclere paintings; during much of World War II he worked on a series of commissioned paintings of shipyards at Port Glasgow.

THE EAST WALL *of the Oratory of All Souls. Relatives of H. W. Sandham built the chapel as a memorial to him*

—⚬⚭⚬—

Buckingham

Buckinghamshire SP 6933

Printers Mews, off Market Hill, is the home of the Movie Museum, devoted to the preservation and display of home movies. As well as movie-making equipment and projectors going back as far as 1912, it also has a cinema, and is open daily from Wednesday to Sunday and on Bank Holidays.

Much of the town was destroyed by fire in 1725, so many of the present buildings are Georgian, but the Market Hall is medieval and retains a Chantry Chapel, rebuilt in 1475, with a Norman doorway. The Hall is topped by the great White Swan, the county symbol and badge of the Dukes of Buckingham.

Burghclere

Hampshire SU 4761

The outstanding feature here is the Sandham Memorial Chapel, whose interior is covered with an extraordinary series of murals painted just after World War I by the late Stanley Spencer. Spencer's wartime experiences, which included work as a hospital orderly, had made him acutely aware of the everyday, humdrum aspects of war and its impact on ordinary men: coping with laundry, rubbish, illness; moving baggage, dressing wounds. The reality and unreality of these unsung aspects of war form the theme of these strange and haunting pictures.

Two miles off is Old Burghclere, a peaceful hamlet with a simple medieval church built of flint, in contrast to Burghclere itself, which has more of the 20th century in its schools, shops and, formerly, a railway station.

The villages stand on the fringes of Hampshire's lovely Watership Down, the rabbit-rich landscape of Richard Adams' novel.

Burpham

West Sussex TQ 0409

Relatively few visit this beautiful place, so close to Arundel, but separated from it by the winding River Arun. Burpham can only be reached by a road from the A27, which leads around the village and goes no further. A stroll round Burpham is a journey in history. Here the Saxons built a defensive mound to repel the raiding Danes; today it gives a lovely view of Arundel Castle, which looks medieval but was completed in 1903. The church, with some beautiful and unusual ornaments, is mostly 12th- or 13th-century, although some parts are pre-Conquest. In the Middle Ages, there was a leper colony at Lea Farm in Wepham Down; and the George and Dragon has had smuggling connections through much of its 400-year history.

The Candovers

Hampshire SU 6041

These unspoilt villages are strung out along the valley which stretches southwards from the downland crest of Farleigh Hill, near Basingstoke. In winter, the villages are linked by a stream which, like many others on the chalk, dries up in the summer. Its valley has long been an important route. A busy turnpike road ran along it when William Cobbett came here on his *Rural Rides* in the 18th century, while a different kind of traffic used the parallel route called the Ox-Drove. This is now one of many public footpaths which criss-cross the area. The villages have their share of interesting buildings, from imposing residences like 18th-century Preston House at Preston Candover (not open to the public, but visible from the road), to Chilton Candover's curious 'underground church' — the surviving crypt of a Norman church which was demolished 100 years ago. Services are still held in it once a year. Further down the valley, near Northington, is The Grange (open to the public), a once magnificent neo-classical house of national architectural importance. The portico, with its huge, marvellously proportioned pillars, has been restored from the neglected ruin of a few years ago — though, sadly, not before much of the rest of the house had been demolished.

Canterbury

Kent TR 1457

Ever since the murder of Thomas Becket made Canterbury a place of pilgrimage, this city has been thronged with visitors. Little about it remains unexplained or less than thoroughly explored — but amongst its mysteries no one has conclusively explained the large conical mound in the Dane John Gardens. Is it a Roman burial barrow, a Norman motte, or has it some lost significance?

All visitors know that the cathedral is a must — but also worth seeing is the ancient church of St Martin's, outside the medieval city, which is probably the oldest surviving working church in England. Beautiful in its simplicity, it was considered an antiquity when Bede was writing in the eighth century.

The first railway locomotive engine to pull a train on a regular passenger service operated from Canterbury, on the line to Whitstable. But within eight years of the opening of the line, the *Invicta* was replaced by horses, and the railway

CHALDON *Woven into this frightening vision of punishments to come are grotesque images of the Seven Deadly Sins, such as Avarice — a figure with moneybags tied round him*

has long since gone.

On the edge of the city is Harbledown, the last village passed by pilgrims at the end of their journey, and mentioned by Chaucer. Henry II, on his way to seek forgiveness for Becket's death, made a gift of 20 marks a year to the village's leper house; and the village almshouses still receive payment from the Crown. Amongst the relics here is the alms box provided for pilgrims. A modern gift nearby is Golden Hill, two and a half acres given to the National Trust to be kept as a children's playground for all time.

Chaldon

Surrey   TQ 3155

Curiously detached from the surrounding suburban buildings in this small village is a little flint church, crouching close to the Pilgrim's Way. Its entire inside west wall is covered by the startling Chaldon 'Doom'. Painted in about 1200, it is one of the most important wall paintings in England, but having been covered over during the Reformation, was only re-revealed in 1870. On a dark red ochre background a ladder leads to Heaven, while below devils thrust souls into Hell — depicted by large cauldrons over blazing fires.

Chalgrave

Bedfordshire   TL 0027

Standing alone in a field, All Saints' Church was once at the hub of the lost village of Chalgrave. It was an important parish in the tenth century, with Watling Street forming its boundary to the west. One of the earliest existing Manorial Court Rolls (1278-1313) concerns the Manor of Chalgrave.

Part of the medieval ridge and furrow field pattern can be seen north-east of Tebworth, the site of Chalgrave's former East Field. It is known that the Black Death (1348-50) took its toll here, for records show that two Chalgrave priests died in swift succession.

Sir Arthur Conan Doyle took inspiration for the hero of his novels *The White Company* and *Sir Nigel* from Sir Nigel Loring, a local farmer and friend of the Black Prince.

Charlbury

Oxfordshire   SP 3519

Lying in the Evenlode Valley between two magnificent mansions, Cornbury Park and Ditchley, Charlbury is a compact little town with steep, narrow streets and a number of good 18th-century buildings, as well as old shops and pleasant inns. It is rather a smart place, popular with commuters, but its independent and self-contained air has so far survived the assaults of visitors. The best features are Lee Place, a beautifully balanced little 17th-century house just outside the town, and the railway station, a remarkably attractive white-painted and weather-boarded building with a generous roof. One of the best stations in Oxfordshire, it entices visitors to arrive by train.

Both Cornbury Park, buried in the mysterious Wychwood Forest, and Ditchley are largely private, although the latter is open occasionally during the summer; however, their splendours, the one 17th-, the other 18th-century, can be glimpsed from minor roads and drives with judicious use of the map.

The diarist John Evelyn planned some of Cornbury's garden. Ditchley was used by Churchill as a secret retreat during World War II.

CANTERBURY: PILGRIMAGES —

Pilgrims came to **Canterbury** *from all over Britain, travelling in bands for protection along the highways, where they could find lodging at inns or monasteries, and where the wealthier could hire horses. Like every popular shrine — whether that of Frideswide at* **Oxford**, *Thomas Cantilupe at* **Hereford** *or William at* **Norwich** *— the shrine of St Thomas of Canterbury could also expect a large number of more local visitors, from its circle of 'pilgrim villages', which would send a few members to represent the community.*

Motives for pilgrimage varied: some pilgrims hoped for cures, some for remission of sins, some for handouts from monasteries en route, many simply to escape the boredom of their villages. It was a holiday, and back home they would show their 'souvenirs': a phial of 'Canterbury water', or a leaden pilgrim badge stamped with the symbol of the shrine. Best known of these badges is the cockleshell worn by pilgrims to the shrine of Santiago de Compostela (see **Reading**). *Those who went to Canterbury might wear a 'T' for Thomas or a bell — hence the name of the flower, the Canterbury bell.*

For some, pilgrimages became an addiction. One man declared himself unable any longer to afford his wife's habitual pilgrimages, while a blind man 'cured' at Becket's tomb showed up shortly afterwards at the shrine of Cantilupe — and was 'cured' once again.

ABOVE   *St Thomas pilgrim badge — one of a collection at the Canterbury Heritage Museum, in the Poor Priests' Hospital*

HASTLETON:
TOPIARY — *Topiary,
the art of clipping shrubs
into artificial shapes like those to
be seen at* **Chastleton***, came into
vogue in England in the 17th
century. The fashion came from
Holland, where gardeners went in
for elaborate detail, such as the
laying out of highly intricate ornamental beds of clipped box.
Starting with simple geometric
shapes such as pyramids and cones,
the more ambitious topiarists proceeded to animals, people, birds
and chess-piece shapes.*

*Yew is now the preferred shrub
for topiary, but privet, box and
juniper were all once used. Most
favoured of all was rosemary,
which must have smelt even more
wonderful than yew when clipped.*

*Notable topiary can be seen at
Ascott House (***Wing***), which has
a topiary sundial; at Levens Hall,
Cumbria, where the trees, laid out
in 1692, are now of gigantic size;
and at Packwood House,
Warwickshire, which has a 17th-
century topiary representation of
the Sermon on the Mount.*

THE SERMON ON THE MOUNT
*The Lord, the four evangelists and
the 12 apostles are represented by
the yews at Packwood House.
They are traditionally clipped
during August*

Chastleton House

Oxfordshire   SP 2429

The spirit and appearance of this grand manor house are entirely of the 17th century. It is a dramatic place, with a bold façade whose sudden appearance through the arched gateway is a splendid piece of deliberate theatre. Theatre and illusion are also present in the topiary of the garden, where box hedges have been cut into dramatic shapes. Round the back are 17th-century stables, a brewhouse and a bakery, while in the field in front there is a curious dovecote. To the right of the house and hidden by trees is a pretty church from the 12th to the 17th centuries.

History has largely left Chastleton alone, although Robert Catesby, one of the Gunpowder Plot conspirators, once owned the estate. It is open on weekend afternoons in summer.

Chertsey

Surrey   TQ 0466

Chertsey is nowadays hardly recognisable as the place where the poet Cowley 'stretched at ease in Chertsey's silent bowers'. But Chertsey is no stranger to change. Its great Abbey, arguably the richest and most powerful in the country, was demolished at the Dissolution, and its stones used in the palaces of Oatlands and Hampton Court. Later, after the destruction of Oatlands, the same stones were incorporated into the locks of the River Wey Navigation. One of the Abbey bells is now in the much altered parish church; a romantic story attached to it concerns Blanche Heriot, whose sweetheart was condemned to die when the curfew sounded. His pardon was delayed, so Blanche clung to the clapper of the bell until the reprieve arrived.

Chichester

West Sussex   SU 8604

Chichester is a place of royal connections. Along West Street, where lime trees now grow between the cathedral and the Dolphin and Anchor, were the cottages where Mrs Shippam first produced her fish paste in 1750; the company is still based in Chichester, and its Royal Coat of Arms shows it is a supplier to HM The Queen. St Olave's Church, now a religious bookshop, is believed to

have been dedicated to a visiting 11th-century Norwegian king. Sloe Fair, nowadays held on 20 October, was first licensed by Henry II in 1107. It is said that Elizabeth I named Little London for its resemblance to a busy London street (although the name existed 100 years earlier). The Royal Arms is better known as the Punch House, because its owner was 'Manufacturer of Punch in Ordinary' to Queen Victoria.

Chicksands Priory

Bedfordshire   TL 1239

Around the romantic priory, which now stands inside an air force camp, the ghost of the nun Rosata is said to walk in search of her lost lover.

In the 17th century Dorothy Osborne wrote letters to Sir William Temple of her uneventful life at Chicksands, with nothing to look forward to except his letters. After a six-year engagement enforced by their disapproving parents, they married in 1654. The Chinese lacquer cabinet in which Sir William kept his letters from Dorothy is preserved in Elstow Moot Hall, near Bedford.

More prosaically, the diarist John Byng visited the Priory in 1791 and was reminded of a dairy. He said he would now think not of meditation, but of cream. The Priory is open on the third Sunday afternoon of the month, from April through to October.

Chilworth

Surrey   TQ 0247

Overlooking this long straggling village, St Martha's is a Norman church with a tradition that Christian martyrs were massacred here in the seventh century. It had to be rebuilt in 1850 after a gunpowder works explosion: Chilworth has an impressive history as a centre for making both gunpowder and paper.

Chilworth Manor was built in the 17th century, but the manor site has been traced to Saxon times and was recorded in the Domesday Book as a monastery.

CLAYDON HOUSE   *The Chinese Drawing Room with its large alcove carved with Rococo chinoiserie is one of the most extravagantly decorated rooms in the house — home of the Verneys for 400 years. It was regularly visited by Florence Nightingale*

CLAYTON *Jack — a brick tower mill of 1876, seen here without his mate Jill — a post mill of 1821*

Church Norton

West Sussex SZ 8695

Under ecclesiastical law, a church can be moved, but not its chancel. So when the church of St Peter's, Selsey, was re-sited in the 1860s, the chancel remained on a windswept rise over-looking Pagham Harbour, about a mile and a half from the rest of the church. St Wilfrid's Chapel can seem extremely remote when the tide laps close to the graveyard and rain lashes the 13th-century walls. The saint first brought Christianity to the South Saxons in AD680, and there is evidence to suggest that this is the site of his first church. Pieces of Anglo-Saxon stone found in the vicinity have carving identical to that on a cross erected by St Wilfrid in Northumbria. The stones now form part of Selsey war memorial.

The Claydons

Buckinghamshire SP 6926

'He who takes this banner from my hand must first hew my hand from my body,' declared Sir Edmund Verney, head of the Verneys of Claydon House and King's Standard Bearer at the Battle of Edgehill. His severed hand, still grasping the standard, was later found on the battlefield.

Claydon House stands in parkland just south of Middle Claydon and might have been much more splendid: the 18th-century second Earl wanted his old Jacobean house to rival Stowe, but ran out of money. He made it a place of Rococo delights first, though. Now run by the National Trust, the house also includes a museum to Florence Nightingale, who was a sister-in-law to the Verney family and often visited. The church at Middle Claydon is the Verney mausoleum, and is full of memorials.

Middle Claydon lies with Steeple Claydon, East Claydon and Botolph Claydon down rather remote lanes south of Buckingham. Thatched and timber-framed cottages make the area pleasant to explore.

Clayton

West Sussex TQ 3013

Hidden for centuries on the walls of the little Saxon church, Clayton's wallpaintings were only rediscovered in the 1890s, and found to be of a very high standard — higher perhaps than the modern work at nearby Berwick. The two sets of paintings provide a fascinating insight into the philosophies of different ages: at Berwick there is hope; here, eternal damnation is the reminder and threat.

On Clayton Hill, a little way above the quiet village of Clayton, stand the two windmills known as Jack and Jill; lower down the hill at the entrance to the long railway tunnel is a non-sensical Victorian fancy of battlemented towers complete with arrow slits.

Cockayne Hatley

Bedfordshire TL 2649

In the graveyard of this humble hamlet, a tomb-stone inscription reads:
'Nothing is here for tears
Nothing to wail or beat the breast
Nothing but what is well and fair.'

The grave is that of six-year-old Margaret Henley, the inspiration for Wendy in J. M. Barrie's *Peter Pan*. Her father, William Henley, who collaborated with Robert Louis Stevenson on plays, has words from his own poem *Margaretae Sorori* on his epitaph:
'So be passing,
My task accomplished and the long day done,
My wages taken and in my heart
Some late lark singing.
Let me be gathered to the quiet West,
The sundown splendid and serene,
Death'.

Cockayne Hatley Hall (not open) was the childhood home of Lady Diana Duff-Cooper, who wrote in her autobiography of '. . . a house in Bedfordshire that must always be remembered as a place where the clouds cast no shadows, where grass was greener, taller, strawberries bigger and more plentiful and above all where gardens and woods, the house and family, the servants and villagers, would never change.'

CHURCH NORTON: PAGANS AND FAIRIES — *Sussex was the last bastion of paganism in England, as St Wilfrid found out when he was shipwrecked near* **Church Norton**. *The high priest of the South Saxons cursed him and his fellow Christians, and attempted to render them helpless by magic.*

Twenty years later, the saint came back, to convert the South Saxons and build monasteries at Selsey (now submerged) and Church Norton. But the fact that paganism had lasted so long in the county may well account for its abundance of fairy legends: it is thought that tales of 'the little people' have their roots in memories of the old gods.

In 19th-century Sussex, many tales of fairies were connected with hills — and both the Celts and the Anglo-Saxons liked to worship in high places. Harrow Hill, two miles north-east of **Burpham**, *was a pagan sanctuary ('hearg' in Old English) and in the 1930s it was said to be the last home of fairies in England. Burlough Castle, near Arlington, was so haunted by 'Pharisees' (fairies) that no one liked to go there after dark. At Tarberry, or Torberry Hill, near Sedlescombe, they would dance at midnight on Mid-summer Eve, and at The Mount (Park Mound) at Pulborough, a fairy funeral was seen. Rudyard Kipling drew on local traditions for the tales of ancient magic in his book 'Puck of Pook's Hill'.*

FAIRIES *dancing in the moon-light, a 'fairy hill' that was prob-ably a tumulus, and the Green Man (in the tree). This woodcut is from a 17th-century chap book — a tome of ballads and stories usually sold by travelling 'chap men', or pedlars*

COLCHESTER: JUMBO THE ELEPHANT —

Jumbo, a six-and-a-half-ton African elephant, after whom the **Colchester** *water tower was named, was, with his mate Alice, a popular feature of London Zoo in the 19th century, until purchased in 1882 by Phineas Taylor Barnum, the American manager of 'The Greatest Show on Earth'.*

The removal of the elephant caused a great outcry, with thousands of English elephant-fanciers, including Queen Victoria, united in their distress at losing him. Telegrams were sent to Barnum by the editor of the 'Morning Post', enquiring on what terms he would return Jumbo. Barnum replied that with 50 million Americans awaiting his arrival, a hundred thousand pounds could not stop the purchase.

Protest songs were composed:
'Jumbo said to Alice, "I love you".
Alice said to Jumbo, "I don't
* believe you do,*
For if you really loved me, as you
* say you do,*
You wouldn't go to Yankee land
* and leave me at the zoo!" '*

But Barnum remained adamant, and the elephant was transported to America to become the star attraction of what would later be known as Barnum and Bailey's Circus.

When the elephant died, he was stuffed and exhibited in the Barnum Museum of Natural History in the USA.

JUMBO *leaving England. His export caused such an uproar that the 'Graphic' illustrated magazine featured eight drawings of his final journey to the docks on its front cover, on 1 April 1882*

Colchester

Essex   TL 9925

Jumbo was the name of London Zoo's first African elephant, sold to Phineas Barnum in the midst of a furore in 1882, and Jumbo was the name Colchester gave in his honour to its water tower, made of one and a quarter million bricks, 369 tons of stone and 142 tons of iron, to support a 230,000-gallon tank, opened on 27 September 1883. At 141 feet high, it makes an aptly Victorian answer to the massive Norman castle keep. The largest keep in Europe, half as big again as London's White Tower, it resisted England's worst earthquake, which had its epicentre here in 1884, and even the attempts of one owner to dynamite it for the building materials. The Normans had helped themselves to Roman bricks to build it, and underneath can be seen what is

COLCHESTER   *Used at one time as a warehouse, Tymperleys was formerly the home of William Gilberd, who experimented with electro-magnetism. His epitaph can be seen in Trinity church nearby*

left of the Temple of Claudius, the Roman Emperor deified here and immortalised in a different way in the novels of Robert Graves.

Renowned for a wealth of other Roman remains, including still-visible walls and the plan of the main streets, this capital of the Ancient Briton and chieftain Cunobelin (who may have been the original Old King Cole) still has its share of unexpected pleasures. An arch opposite the church in Trinity Street leads to Tymperleys, home of William Gilberd, who entertained Elizabeth I with experiments in electricity; in West Stockwell Street lived the Taylor sisters, writers of *Twinkle Twinkle, Little Star.*

COLNBROOK *Tame enough today, the Ostrich Inn is associated with a Sweeney Todd style legend. King John is thought to have stayed nearby*

Colnbrook

Buckinghamshire TQ 0277

The Cox's Orange Pippin came from Colnbrook — it was first cultivated here. A less wholesome culinary association can be found at the 15th-century timber-framed Ostrich Inn, where, it is said, unsuspecting travellers were on occasion boiled in ale.

Cookham

Berkshire SU 8985

Those who know Stanley Spencer's paintings will recognise Cookham: he was born in the village and based much of his work on local scenes. The Stanley Spencer Gallery and the house where he was born stand in the High Street.

The Bel and Dragon pub was open for business in the 15th century, and there is an old lettered sign on the wall nearby, warning 'All fighting to be over by 10 o'clock'.

Swan Upping, the annual ceremony when the Queen's swans are marked in early July, starts at Cookham, and the boatyard by the bridge belongs to the Queen's Swan Master.

Cornwell

Oxfordshire SP 2727

The great eccentric architect Clough Williams Ellis, the creator of Portmeirion in North Wales, rebuilt much of Cornwell in the 1930s and gave it a curious period charm that sets it apart from the conventional Cotswolds picturesque. One of the least known of the Cotswolds villages, it also has the advantage that the only road through it is private, so visitors can only see it on foot. Williams Ellis also worked on Cornwell Manor, whose mid-18th-century façade conceals an earlier house. It is splendidly situated on a little hill outside the village, overlooking formal gardens which are open occasionally in summer.

Cottered

Hertfordshire TL 3129

An Oriental paradise in the heart of the Home Counties was the aim of a wealthy china merchant, Herbert Goode, who transformed his three flat Hertfordshire fields into six exquisite acres of Japanese gardens. Pipes for wells and waterfalls were laid deep in the heavy clay, great mounds were heaped up to represent sacred mountains, while from Japan came rare trees and shrubs, a specially made Tea House of exotic woods, antique stone monuments and bronze lanterns, a wonderful bridge and many decorative blue stones — some weighing over a ton. Mr Kusumoto, a Japanese landscape artist, was engaged as a consultant from 1923. The gardens can be seen in summer on open days.

Cranleigh

Surrey TQ 0639

The people of Cranleigh *know* that Lewis Carroll's Cheshire Cat was inspired by the grinning head of a cat carved on the south transept arch of the church.

Also in the church is the memorial to Richard Mower, who discovered the value of lime in agriculture. Appropriately, the public school on the edge of town was founded for farmers' sons, and although it has long since expanded from its original 26 pupils, it still has a working farm where pupils can study. Long since expanded too is Britain's first cottage hospital, opened in Cranleigh in 1859.

An obelisk in the town records the distances to Windsor and to Brighton, confirming that the Prince Regent passed through on the trunk road.

CRANLEIGH *Lewis Carroll's Cheshire cat?*

Crowlink

East Sussex TV 5497

The pond beside the church in nearby Friston was the first in the country to be scheduled as an ancient monument. A lane leads from it to Crowlink, owned by the National Trust, and part of the Seven Sisters cliffs. Neolithic man lived on these cliff tops, where bowl and round barrows still survive, although the coast is disappearing at the rate of three feet a year. It has been estimated that the cliff-top Iron Age earthwork at Belle Tout was once on a hill some two miles from the sea.

The village of Crowlink, like so many in Sussex, has smuggling connections, and at Flagstaff Point, two smugglers and an excise man were killed in 1782. 'Genuine Crowlink' was a smuggled gin with a high reputation — and a price to match.

COLNBROOK: BOILED IN ALE — *The old Ostrich Inn at* Colnbrook *boasts a story as gruesome as that of Sweeney Todd. Tradition says that the inn was run in medieval times by a couple called Jarman, who murdered rich travellers by putting them in a special bed fixed to a trapdoor. When all were asleep, they worked the trapdoor, the bed tipped up and its occupants fell into a cauldron of boiling ale in the kitchen. Their 60th and last victim was a Reading clothier, Thomas Cole, whose horse was found wandering in the village after the Jarmans said he had left. When his body was discovered in the stream (thereafter named after him — hence Colnbrook) Jarman and his wife were both hanged.*

This local tradition, probably picked up in his travels as an itinerant weaver, was made famous in the 16th century by Thomas Deloney, in his 'Historie of Thomas of Reading'. 'Old Cole' became proverbial for wealth — he, not the founder of Colchester, *may be the original 'Old King Cole'.*

Most people's receptions at inns were not as ghastly as that, but inns could still be far from nice. The experiences of the poet John Taylor, travelling in the Quantocks in the 17th century, are quoted in 'Old Inns of England': he found 'the house most delicately decked with artificial and natural beauty . . . the walls and ceilings adorned and hanged with rare spiders' tapestry or cobweb lawn, the smoke so palpable and pernicious that I could scarcely see anything.' After trying in vain to get a decent supper, he retired to bed where 'I was furiously assaulted by an Ethopian army of fleas, and it may be freely admitted that I laid so manfully about me that I made more than 500 mortuus est.'

DANBURY: MEMORIALS IN WOOD

DANBURY: MEMORIALS IN WOOD — *The wooden funerary effigies in* **Danbury** *church are among the very few remaining in Britain. Early examples are rare because of the perishability of wood and other problems — two 13th-century figures at Reynes, Buckinghamshire, for instance, are hollowed out from the back to prevent cracking.*

But some fine examples survive: in **Gloucester** *Cathedral is the 13th-century effigy of William the Conqueror's son, Robert Curthose, carved in oak and decorated with paint. Edward, Lord Despencer, who died in 1375, kneels under a canopied niche in his chantry chapel at Tewkesbury. He was an original Knight of the Garter, 'much beloved of the ladies'. His colour and gilding restored, he gives a good idea of the original brightness of some of these effigies.*

Elsewhere are lesser mortals: at Much Marcle, Herefordshire, a cross-legged effigy of about 1350 (possibly of Sir Hugh Helyon) was carried into church at the head of every funeral, up until 1878. At **Pamber** *is a 600-year-old Knight; at Slindon, Essex, 16th-century Anthony Kempe or St Leger prays with his head supported on his tilting helm.*

DANBURY *Three rare, oak effigies of knights lie in the north and south aisles of St John the Baptist Church*

—◦◦❥✖◦◦—

Danbury

Essex TL 7705

Under a rare, 13th-century carved oak effigy, a crusader knight was found perfectly preserved in the pickle which filled his coffin when it was opened in 1779. One bystander tasted it and declared it to be 'partaking of the taste of catsup, and of the pickle of Spanish olives'. Fine carving is also a feature of the church bench-ends, and the oldest have inspired modern craftsmen to continue the same style of carving on all the pews. In 1402, 'the devil appeared in the likeness of a Friar Minor, who entering the church, raged insolently to the great terror of the parishioners . . . the top of the steeple was broken down and half the chancel scattered abroad'. In 1941 another devil, a 500-pound German bomb, reduced the east end to ruin.

Dinton

Buckinghamshire SP 7611

The most fanciful local building is the Castle, a folly built in the 18th century by Sir John Vanhatten, who used it to contain his vast collection of fossils, incorporating many examples into the building itself. The folly once housed the servants of the manor house, but is now open to the public.

More conventional attractions are the church, mainly Norman with characteristic zig-zag Romanesque decoration on the door arches, but with decoration over the doorway that is almost certainly Saxon. It shows two carved lions eating the fruit of the Tree of Life above a lintel carved with St Michael warding off a dragon. The village stocks, in urgent need of repair, stand under a canopy on the green, and are accompanied by a whipping post.

Dover

Kent TR 3141

Thousands of visitors throng the castle every year — but not many of them see the ghostly headless drummer boy, who was murdered during the Napoleonic wars, the period when the last of the great additions were made to the castle's defences.

Peverell's Tower in the castle bears the guilty burden of the death of an old woman and her dog — they were buried alive in the walls to appease the spirits who had repeatedly caused it to fall down. Surprisingly, she doesn't haunt the castle, but she did successfully curse the master mason, who died in a fall from the tower.

Much luckier was the highwayman from Frankfurt, who was captured after robbing a man from Waldershare and committed to the castle, only to escape the constables by sliding down the cliff on one of the ropes used by samphire gatherers.

Shakespeare's *King Lear* has the line '*Half way down hangs one who gathers samphire — dreadful trade!*' — which refers to the perilousness of collecting this edible rockplant, an asparagus-like delicacy. It has been culled from the Dover cliffs for centuries, and because of the Shakespearian associations, a local landmark is known as Shakespeare's Cliff.

A few miles north at Waldershare Park, Sir Robert Furnese's 18th-century Belvedere is one of the earliest examples of a building placed in a park for purely ornamental purposes.

Dunsfold

Surrey TQ 0036

Although Dunsfold is an attractive village, its main feature isn't in it! The church lies half a mile away on a mound, because (according to legend) all attempts to build it nearer the village failed when the materials insisted on travelling to the present site. The site may have had pre-Christian religious importance, and the well at the foot of the little hill is known to have attracted those seeking a cure from eye complaints.

Probably the village (not mentioned in the Domesday Book) was little more than a clearing in the Wealden forest when the church was built. This is a gem, virtually unchanged since it was constructed between 1270 and 1290, and including the original oak pews — rough, plain but immensely satisfying.

Dunstable

Bedfordshire TL 0121

A band of robbers led by one Dun is said to have given the town its name, and in coaching days, Puddle Hill was a favourite place for highwaymen. So steep was the climb that ten horses had to be used instead of the usual four. This route was abandoned in 1771 after a fatal accident.

Every Good Friday on Dunstable Downs (National Trust) children scramble for oranges rolled down the hill. This tradition is said to symbolise the rolling away of the stone on Jesus' tomb and may be related to 'pace egging' customs in the north of England. Dunstable's orange rolling is the only southern variation.

It was at Dunstable's Lady Chapel of St Peter and St Paul that Archbishop Cranmer declared Henry VIII's divorce from Catherine of Aragon. Much earlier visitors to the area are recalled to the west of the town, in a notable group of pre-historic burial mounds known as the Five Knolls

DUNSFOLD *In 1933, Caroe built this timber shrine over the Holy Well which springs up near the village church. The water, supposedly rich in chlorine, has traditionally been visited by those seeking a cure for eye disorders*

East Ilsley

Berkshire SU 4981

Horse-racing is the lifeblood of East Ilsley. The surrounding Downs are criss-crossed by 'gallops' where horses train; and in the village, horses, horsey people and racing stables are much in evidence, and have been ever since the first local racing stable was built by the Duke of Cumberland, victor of Culloden, in 1748.

Two hundred years ago, East Ilsley was also famous for its sheep market, the largest in the country outside London. Shepherds and drovers would bring their flocks to market here along the Ridgeway from Hertfordshire, Buckinghamshire and Wiltshire. This market flourished until World War I, and the annual Sheep Fair continued until 1934. The village is full of attractive 18th-century houses, running uphill towards the church, and there are good walks from the centre up to the breezy tops of the Downs.

Elsfield

Oxfordshire SP 5410

John Buchan, author of *The Thirty Nine Steps*, *Greenmantle* and other thrilling classics of the pre-war years, lived here for some time and is buried in the churchyard. The church itself, heavily restored by the Victorians, is not very thrilling, but Elsfield has retained some of the atmosphere of a small village, despite its proximity to the encroaching Oxford suburbs. Stone-built, it stands high on a hill, overlooking Oxford to the west.

EAST ILSLEY *Stan Ward's saddlery — specialists in horse racing equipment — has served the many local stables for over 30 years, on a 200-year-old saddlery site*

Elstow

Bedfordshire TL 0546

A granite block in a field marks the birthplace of John Bunyan near the hamlet of Harrowden, a mile west; on Elstow Green the Moot Hall (a medieval market hall) has a Bunyan collection. The Abbey where he was baptised has windows illustrating his *Pilgrim's Progress* and *The Holy War*, and the free standing church tower where he rang the bells is still there. Those wishing to seek out connections can find his 'House Beautiful' in the picturesque ruins of Houghton House, some five miles south. His 'City of Destruction' was most likely Bedford itself, where he was imprisoned and wrote part of *Pilgrim's Progress*.

A different kind of fame came to Elstow in the mid-1980s, when it was put on the shortlist of sites for the dumping of nuclear waste.

ELSTOW: PILGRIM'S PROGRESS — *Born in Elstow in 1628, John Bunyan was imprisoned in Bedford jail from 1660 to 1673 for preaching Nonconformism. There he began 'The Pilgrim's Progress': 'As I walked through the wilderness of this world, I lighted on a certain place, where was a den' (which has been interpreted as the jail).*

The story, of Christian's journey towards salvation, records Bunyan's spiritual experiences following religious conversion, but it also gains impact from realistic settings. His vision of the 'Delectable Mountains' in the book, with their 'gardens and orchards, the vineyards, and fountains of water', was inspired by Barton Hills in the Chilterns, described by Bunyan as 'a most pleasant Mountainous Country, beautiful with woods, vineyards, fruits of all sorts. Flowers also with Springs of Fountains, very delectable to behold'. The 'House Beautiful' has aspects of Houghton House, which is near Elstow.

BUNYAN'S DREAM *This engraving was used as the frontispiece to the first edition of 'Pilgrim's Progress'*

Bunyan's knowledge of Bedfordshire was extended by preaching around the countryside, staying at such villages as Willington, where he carved his name and the date, 1650, on the fireplace of the stables.

*He moved to Bedford in 1655 and is commemorated there by a statue, museum and library, but is buried in Bunhill Fields, **London**.*

FORDWICH: DUCKING STOOLS — *The ducking stool at* **Fordwich** *recalls the hoary myth that only women nag. Not to be confused with the older 'cucking-stool', for parading offenders of both sexes through the town and chiefly a punishment for dishonest brewers and bakers, the ducking stool was for dousing women in the village pond or river. It was sometimes used for witches and prostitutes, but its chief use was always for scolds.*

Ducking stools might be simple wooden chairs or elaborate iron affairs. Some were fastened to a permanent see-saw at the edge of the pond, or suspended from gallows-like structures over it; others (like the one in Leominster church) were on wheels, so the woman could be paraded.

Though the magistrate would prescribe an appropriate number of duckings, sometimes the woman died of shock before the ducking was completed. The earliest known use of a ducking stool in England was towards the beginning of the 17th century; the last recorded sufferers were Jenny Pipes (1809) and Sarah Leeke (1817), both of Leominster.

DUCKING WOMEN *A shocking way to cool tempers in the days when sharp tongues were not tolerated*

Emmetts Garden

Kent   TQ 4752

Local people maintain that Emmetts Garden got its name from the large colonies of wood ants — or emmetts — to be found up until the 1950s in the surrounding woods. Today this is a delightful National Trust shrub garden, usually by-passed by those anxious to sample the more publicised delights of the viewpoints at Toy's Hill and Ide Hill, but well worth visiting.

It all began in 1909 when many of the larger plants were bought by the owner of Emmetts from Messrs Veitch and Son, who were selling their Kingston Nursery, and brought up here by horse and cart from Brasted railway station (long since closed down). Some of the plants, it should be said, are now past their prime: a 100-foot tulip tree, which was the highest (if not the tallest) tree in Kent, fell down recently, and others are being replaced. But it remains a deeply peaceful place, with a formal garden, pond and fountain. It is open every afternoon (except Saturdays) from Easter to the end of October.

Faringdon

Oxfordshire   SU 2895

Not to be missed is the great tower standing just to the east of this handsome market town. Built by Lord Berners in 1935, this brick structure in a general Gothic style must count as one of the last follies in the true 18th-century manner. Its building created much argument, including objections from an admiral who, on being told that he would only be able to see it with a telescope, replied that he always looked out of the window with a telescope. Its completion on November 5 was celebrated with a grand firework party, featured in the *Tatler*.

The town has survived the assaults of the 20th century with plenty of 18th- and 19th-century buildings and a good atmosphere. There is an early market hall with an open ground floor, and, set up on a rise overlooking the town, a good church: long, low and powerful with a squat tower. Inside are fine brasses and monuments, the latter to the Unton family, while from the churchyard there is a dramatic view over the landscape away to the south. Well placed near the church is the entrance to Faringdon House, with a garden notable for its orangery, lake, trees and, above all, for its multi-coloured doves, tinted in bright hues. The house is private but the gardens are open a few days a year.

Farley Mount Country Park

Hampshire   SU 4229

The best of the panoramic views offered by this stretch of open downland, six miles west of Winchester, are from a pyramid topping an ancient burial mound. It was built in the 18th century in memory of a racehorse, which went by the name of Beware Chalk Pit. The name was earned when it safely carried its rider over the unexpected hazard of a gaping chalk pit. Shortly afterwards, the horse won a race. The full story is told on the memorial.

On clear days, the Isle of Wight, Salisbury Plain and the Berkshire Downs can be seen here. Both woodland and downland are rich in wild flowers — important enough to have earned part of Farley Mount the designation of Site of Special Scientific Interest. Look out especially for orchids, of which more than half a dozen species can be seen. But don't pick them!

Fingest

Buckinghamshire   SU 7791

Set in one of those long, deep, green valleys, or 'bottoms' as the local people call them, Fingest is one of the most attractive villages in the Chilterns. The very fine church of St Bartholomew's is Norman on Saxon foundations, with a tall yellow bell tower topped by an un-usual double roof. Just across the road is the Chequers Inn, where visitors have to pass through the kitchen to get to the dining room.

Finkley Down Farm

Hampshire   SU 3847

In an age when not even many country people get the chance of close contact with farm animals, places like Finkley Down are especially valuable. Here, horses, cattle, sheep, pigs and poultry — including some rare breeds — can be seen and children can feed them.

Along with the animals, there is an exhibition of farming equipment of yesteryear — a collection showing changes in farming techniques in the last hundred years.

trout were not freshwater fish, for when they were caught no food was to be found in their stomachs. The local museum has a ducking stool.

Frensham

Surrey   SU 8441

Four prehistoric bowl barrows are to be found on the high ground between Frensham Great Pond and Little Ponds. Both belonging to the National Trust, the ponds attract many species of rare wildfowl — as well as sailing enthusiasts — and there is a nature reserve near the Little Ponds. Stony Jump, the largest of three strange hills called the Devils Jumps, has a footpath to the summit. Popular folk tales claim that many such natural features were placed by the Devil.

Of most interest in St Mary's Church is the enormous copper cauldron, once believed to have belonged to a witch called Mother Ludlam, and earlier attributed to fairies.

Fulking

West Sussex   TQ 2411

A marvellously strong spring gushes out beside the village street at Fulking. Local shepherds used to dam it to make a sheepwash, and those vanished and lost sheep of the Downs are remembered in the name of the village inn, the Shepherd's Dog. Beside the spring is a Victorian well-house with an inscription on its tiles — some of the tiles have been wrongly inserted, producing an unintended rustic effect. Near the inn is Septima Cottage, named after Mrs Ann Septima Baldey who lived here for 80 years.

Fleet Pond

Hampshire   SU 8255

Reed beds and alder 'carr' — the kind of boggy land in which alders flourish — flank this broad shallow lake, and beyond lie woods of oak and birch. It all makes for a rich variety of wildlife. Perhaps the most exciting breeding species is a colony of reed warblers. In winter, great crested grebes and various wildfowl can be seen, while siskins and redpolls feed among the alders.

Fordwich

Kent   TR 1759

On the Kentish Stour just north-east of Canterbury is its one-time port of Fordwich. It was the highest navigable point of the river, and in medieval times was a 'limb' of the Cinque ports. Fordwich trout, still a local delicacy, attracted the interest of Izaak Walton, who wrote in his *Compleat Angler* of his theory that these

FULKING   *seen from Devil's Dyke. Legend claims this wedge-shaped cleft in the downs was dug by Satan as he tried to flood the area with the sea and thus drown all the churches*

FRENSHAM: FAIRY CAULDRON — *In* **Frensham** *church there hangs a cauldron that once belonged to the fairies. They used to lend out a variety of items: all you had to do was to knock on the great boulder on 'Borough Hill' (possibly one of the Devil's Jumps), stating requirements, and a voice would tell you when to come and collect it. But when someone borrowed the cauldron and returned it late, the fairies would not take it back, and borrowing came to an end.*

This 17th-century tradition resembles a story told of Wayland's Smithy, Oxfordshire.

WAYLAND'S SMITHY   *where a horse left at night with a coin will be shod next day, it is said*

Later Mother Ludlam, a witch who lived in a cave in the grounds of Moor Park, replaced the fairies in the tale. It almost certainly began as a way to explain why the church should have a cauldron in the first place. Probably medieval, it is likely to have been used for 'church-ales' — fund-raising feasts.

All sorts of things were once kept in churches. Guilds stored the utensils for their annual feasts there, and still to be seen in the church at Abbots Bromley, Staffordshire are the ancient reindeer horns used in the annual Horn Dance. In Low Ham church, Somerset, is a halberd, probably once used for pageants, and said to be the spear that slew the 'Dragon of Aller'. A sieve, said to have held the 'seven at one birth' fathered by Thomas Bonham, used to be in the church at Great Wishford, Wiltshire — and some of the seven's memorial brasses are still there.

Furneaux Pelham

Hertfordshire TL 4327

Still thriving here is the village brewery using equipment from the 1880s. Housed in a brick Victorian building set back from the road, it stands directly opposite the Brewery Tap, as plain and pleasantly English an inn as one could wish to find. The brewing firm of Rayment was founded in 1860 by a local farmer who up to that time had brewed only as a sideline. But his beer was good and the flourishing business remained in the family until 1931 — it now belongs to Greene King.

Garsington

Oxfordshire SP 5702

Spread over the hill south-east of Oxford, Garsington appears at first sight to be another dormitory suburb, with a hefty and over-restored church and a selection of rather self-consciously desirable cottages. But in Garsington Manor it has an architectural gem, a 16th- and 17th-century stone manor, a mass of mullioned windows, gables and decorative stonework.

From the road, it looks almost French, the handsome facade framed by a large stone gateway, and overlooking a courtyard enclosed by walls of yew as high as the house itself. Behind the house is a wonderful garden, much of it created by Lady Ottoline Morrell, who lived here from 1915 to 1926 and made Garsington a social and artistic legend, frequented by the painters, writers, designers and decorative hangers-on who formed the Bloomsbury Group. A series of formal beds, terraces and walks lead steeply down the side of the hill to an Italianate lake flanked by statuary with dovecote and stables, woodlands and a stream. The garden is open occasionally under the National Gardens Scheme.

Glympton and the Glyme

Oxfordshire SP 4221

One of the least known of Cotswold rivers, the Glyme runs an intimate and secluded course from Chipping Norton to the Evenlode near Bladon. There are moments, however, of unexpected splendour. It is the Glyme that flows through Woodstock and Blenheim Park, forming Capability Brown's huge lake, while to the north, other, smaller estates have in the past made the most of the river's potential. Kiddington has a lake, overlooked by Barry's 1850s mansion with its unusual stables, and a similar lake marks the course of the Glyme through Glympton.

This is a pretty village, though suffering a bit from traffic and suburban growth, with a pleasant inn. The best part is Glympton Park, an interesting example of a relatively modern model estate, well maintained and expanded during this century. The newer buildings reflect Cotswold traditions, while the mansion itself dates from about 1750 to 1846. Glympton Park is private, but much of the estate can be seen while visiting the church, which is in its centre; it is best to park in the village and walk to the church via one of the three entrance points.

FURNEAUX PELHAM   *In church decoration angels symbolised St Matthew; a lion St Mark; an ox St Luke and an eagle St John. Angels are used to support the 15th-century nave roof of St Mary's Church and also feature in one of the Victorian windows*

GRAYS THURROCK: DENEHOLES — *The long-held belief that the 'deneholes' of* **Grays Thurrock** *and other parts of the south-east were Saxon refuges from the Vikings sprang from confusion between the Anglo-Saxon word 'denn' (cave) and 'Dane', and was supplanted by a theory that they were grain-stores. Now they are generally accepted to be chalk-mines, whose product was used as fertiliser.*

Found in areas of Kent and Essex where there is an underlying layer of chalk, a typical denehole has a circular shaft about 2ft 6in across, sometimes with footholds still visible. On reaching the chalk it opens out, often in a double trefoil pattern. At Hangman's Wood, Grays Thurrock, the holes are joined to adjacent diggings. The shafts may be anything from 60 to 140ft deep.

The earliest surviving illustration of deneholes appears in the 1610 edition of Camden's 'Britannia', but from pottery fragments found in them and from their closeness to medieval field boundaries, they are thought to date from the 12th to the 15th century. Although of a much later date, they are of a similar design to **Grimes Graves,** *the Neolithic flint mines in Norfolk.*

ABOVE   *Grimes Graves: Neolithic antler tools have been found, and a chalk Earth Mother now in the British Museum*

GARSINGTON MANOR   *Part of the strangely beautiful garden which inspired artists and writers in the early 1920s*

Grays Thurrock

Essex   TQ 6177

Hangmans Wood at Little Thurrock (just off the A13) is the site of the mysterious 'deneholes' — pits dug 60 feet deep through sand and gravel, opening out into 20-foot long chambers and providing a bottomless source of speculation for archaeologists. Optimistic speculators of the South Sea Bubble era in the 18th century started a company to 'rework pits for gold', but it is more likely that they were chalk mines. There is a similar hole west of Grays Thurrock.

Great Amwell

Hertfordshire   TL 3612

This quiet village, celebrated in verse by the 18th-century Quaker poet John Scott, contains two contrasting curiosities. The more spectacular lies north of the church and is a perfect neo-classical tableau, begun by the architect Robert Mylne around 1800. Here on a pair of shaded islets in the New River (dug to take water to London) stand Mylne's urn memorial to Hugh Myddleton, the New River's 17th-century founder, together with two other inscribed monuments — one bearing lines by John Scott.

Amwell's lamp-post museum, situated off a back lane to Ware, is well worth a visit.

Great Barford

Bedfordshire   TL 1352

This was once an important port at the head of the Ouse Navigation, with extensive wharves and warehouses near the church. Now the offices form Church House, and part of the old wharf runs from Bridge Cottage to the weir. The winding mechanisms from the old lock have been dredged up recently and displayed by the new lock; on the opposite bank an old lion's head water fountain is preserved.

Great Barford's bridge, though much rebuilt from the medieval original, provides an attractive centrepiece to a group of period properties.

Great Munden

Hertfordshire   TL 3524

Puddingstone, a legend-rich glacial conglomerate of flint pebbles held together by silica cement, has been built into the walls of the church. It strongly resembles bread pudding and was once highly prized for its magical properties, including an ability to reproduce itself underground — it is also known as 'breeding stone' and 'mother stone'. It was said to ward off evil spirits, hence its use in church fabric and as 'markers' in churchyards (as at Nettleden). Lumps of pudding-stone are still occasionally turned up in fields in or around the Chilterns, and are religiously placed on the roadside by farmworkers.

Hadleigh

Essex   TQ 8087

Turn away from the traffic of the A13 as it thunders to Southend-on-Sea to discover the ruins of Hadleigh's Castle. From a hunting lodge used by Henry III, it was expanded by Edward III into the most important castle in the region. Constable's study of it is in the National Gallery; since his death in 1837 a landslip has furthered the depredations started by Lord Rich, who in 1551 bought the castle from Edward IV for just £700 and had much of it carted away to build houses and churches around the county. But walls and towers and the play of light on water that Constable recorded can still be seen.

GREAT MUNDEN: PUDDINGSTONE

— In Hertfordshire, pieces of puddingstone like those found at **Great Munden** were known as 'breeding stones', because the pebbles in them were believed to grow eventually into large boulders.

It was believed in most rural areas, and especially in East Anglia, that stones grew in the soil. In 1887, a clergyman reported having been told by a Suffolk farmer that it was a waste of time having stones picked off the land, as more would grow there. At Stone Farm, Blaxhall, Suffolk, the Blaxhall Stone has reputedly grown from the size of a small loaf to about five tons in the last century. The monolith which towers over the church at Rudston, Humberside, by contrast, grew there in one night. But the oddest 'growing stone' story is at Cricklade. A broken stone effigy in the church is said to have grown on the spot where a man fell from the top of the tower and was killed. Only later was the stone (which took his shape) moved inside the church.

RUDSTON MONOLITH
The tallest standing stone in Britain, it is over 25 feet high and is said to have grown overnight

ST BOTOLPH'S *A rare Anglo-Saxon oak door, once coated with skin. The iron strips are riveted to circular wooden bars*

*Flaying alive is mentioned as a punishment in the laws of Henry I, but these skins probably came from the bodies of executed criminals. Human skin was once in great demand, because of its supposedly magical qualities. Even in the 19th century, the skins of dead criminals were sold in strips as souvenirs, or in bigger pieces for more practical purposes: a book made from the skin of William Corder, the Red Barn murderer (see **Polstead**), is on display in the Moyses Hall Museum, Bury St Edmunds. The poor wretch at Hadstock — a man with fair or greying hair — undoubtedly had his skin nailed there as a warning.*

Hadstock

Essex TL 5544

A piece of human skin once covered the north door of the church. Tradition says that it was a 'Daneskin' — from a Viking flayed alive for sacrilege. Today the skin can be seen in the museum at Saffron Walden, some four miles south-west.

The door itself is a rare Saxon survivor from just before the Norman Conquest; the church also has pre-Norman 11th-century carvings, windows and arches. King Canute is said to have been associated with its founding.

Halstead

Essex TL 8130

Mechanical elephants, built life-size and weighing half a ton, were Halstead's most resplendent product. Made by W. Hunwicks earlier in the century, each one consisted of 9000 parts and could carry a load of eight adults and four children at up to 12mph.

Less fanciful but remembered with a love-hate nostalgia for their fumey warmth were Halstead's 'tortoise stoves', produced here by the Tortoise Foundry Company. But the most picturesque reminder of Halstead's industry is the white, weatherboarded, three-storey mill across the River Colne at the Causeway, built by George Courtauld in the late 18th century and still the most handsome building in town.

HALSTEAD *Courtauld's silk mill is an impressive sight with its double row of uninterrupted windows and the white weatherboarding so typical of Essex*

Harrietsham

Kent TQ 8652

Sir Charles Booth, who died in 1795, left bequests for the provision of Harrietsham's 'Bread Charity': a sum of £500, the interest on which was to be spent every week on bread, which would be distributed by the churchwardens to poor residents of the parish. The only condition was that the recipients had to attend Divine Service at the church. Though still handed out (by the local council), the Dole at Harrietsham has been rather overshadowed by that of Biddenden, ten miles south, where the Biddenden Dole is said to have been started by a pair of Siamese twins. Biscuits stamped with a picture of the sisters — the Biddenden Maids — are still distributed.

Booth's home, variously known as Harrietsham Place, Stede Court and Stede Hill, was later lived in by Robert H. Goodsall, a great researcher into the 'secrets' of Kent.

Hartlip

Kent TQ 8464

Set in the north side of the church tower is a small room with a tiny slit window. Once it was an anchorite's cell, the home of a hermit, man or woman, who was fed by parishioners in return for a life spent praying for forgiveness for their sins. It is now used as a vestry.

Orchard country surrounds the village, which has a reputation for being one of the best places for seeing spring blossom — traditionally cherry rather than apple.

Harwell

Oxfordshire SU 4989

The buildings of the Harwell Atomic Energy Research Establishment (AERE) can be seen for miles, dominating the rounded beauty of the Berkshire Downs. But the village is quite different, retaining a strong rural atmosphere. It is surrounded by apple orchards, glorious in the spring when all the blossom is out, and pleasant to wander through at any time, in search of the church which is lost among a little maze of streets. Dating from the 12th century, it contains brasses and memorials to the local Jennings family, who built the almshouses in the High Street around 1715. There is also a plaque for Samuel Smith, vicar for 50 years.

Examples of earlier brick and timber-framed thatched cottages with cruck beams are also quite common, but none is more splendid than the Dell, which dates from 1445.

Hascombe

Surrey SU 9939

A main street of tile-hung sandstone cottages and a church that is outwardly their perfect complement (though actually a Victorian re-build) are among the charms of Hascombe. Close to Godalming, it is nevertheless oddly off the beaten track, and surrounded by wooded hills. Splendid houses designed by notable turn-of-the-century architects, such as Sir Edwin Lutyens, can be seen in the area, as can gardens designed by Gertrude Jekyll, who lived nearby.

The half-timbered quadrangle of Winkworth Farm, to the north, was owned by Dr Fox — founder of the Roads Beautifying Association, formed in the county between the two world wars to embellish new roads with flowering shrubs.

Hastings

East Sussex TQ 8109

Two fossilised cats, said to be 400 years old, are owned by the Stag Inn, which also boasts a secret passage — essential in this town renowned for smugglers and pirates. The history of Hastings began well before 1066. A pot in the museum showing an ironsmith at work confirms a Roman connection; it was a Saxon port, and by 984 the town possessed its own mint.

In All Saints Church is a 15th-century 'Doom', all that remains of a large series of wall paintings. Christ is seated on a rainbow, while the damned are hanging from gallows. St Clement's has two cannonballs in its tower, one a 'gift' from a passing French warship, the other deliberately placed by the townspeople to balance the first.

Hastings' picturesque net shops, three-storeyed

Turpin, said to have been born at **Hempstead**, *lives in legend as a dashing people's hero, who defied an oppressive authority. Many of his supposed feats were actually the work of highwayman 'Swift John' Nevison who in 1676, really did rob a sailor at Godshill at 4am, then ride to* **York** *by 7.45pm to establish his alibi.*

Turpin himself was a cattle-thief and brutal plunderer of lonely Essex farmhouses. He did go to York, but only to continue the same sort of activity, and not in 15 hours on a horse called Black Bess. The romantic version of Turpin's life was created and popularised by W. H. Ainsworth in his book 'Rookwood'.

'DICK TURPIN *clearing the Old Hornsey tollbar gate — to the surprise of his pursuers,' says the original caption*

When he was hanged at York in 1739 for horse-stealing, at the age of 33, his body is said to have been rescued from a surgeon by the mob and buried in St George's churchyard, where his grave can still be seen.

So, they say, can the spot where Black Bess collapsed, on the present race-course. Opposite his reputed birthplace, the former Bell, Hempstead, is a circle of nine trees called Turpin's Ring; nearby, at Dawkins' farm is a great oak, in which, it is said, he took refuge. Another reputed hideout was the Old Swan Inn, Woughton-on-the-Green, Buckinghamshire, where he once stopped and reshod his horse with the shoes pointing backwards to foil his pursuers.

black-tarred wooden towers behind the beach, were built in the 17th century for drying fishermen's nets — but five of them are actually 1960s replacements, for the originals were burnt down.

Perhaps the greatest contribution made by the town to the 20th century is the one recalled by a plaque in Queen's Road. It was from here that John Logie Baird made the first television transmissions.

Hempstead

Essex TL 6338

Highwayman Dick Turpin was born here in 1705. His parents kept the Bell Inn, renamed the Rose and Crown and recently 'sub-titled' Turpin's Tavern. Logs still burn on the wide

HASTINGS *Fishermen have dried their nets in structures like these for over 300 years. Among the nethouses is the Fishermen's Church (1854), which is now occupied by a fishing museum*

hearth where gilt letters announce 'It is the landlord's great desire that no-one stands before the fire', and pictures all around celebrate the fame of the 'patron sinner'.

In the church, an impressively life-like bust on his tomb recalls the town's worthier son, William Harvey (1578-1657), chief physician to Charles I and discoverer of the circulation of the blood, as recorded in his *De Motu Cordis* of 1628.

The outline of the old village cockpit can still be traced, though the steep banks are now crowned with trees.

HENLEY-ON-
THAMES: BEER —
*Locally brewed beers,
such as Brakspear's at* **Henley-
on-Thames** *and* **Hook
Norton**, *have made a comeback
into British life, thanks to a large
extent to pressure from the
Campaign for Real Ale.*

*No two beers are quite alike,
because of different brewing
techniques and the malts, water
and hops which are used. The
taste of IPA (India Pale Ale), for
instance, relies on the rich mineral
well-water of Burton upon Trent.*

*Beer has held its status as
Britain's national drink,
weathering change such as the
introduction of hops into brewing
in the early 15th century —
viewed with deep suspicion — and
unfortunate incidents including the
bursting of a vat of porter at
Meux's Brewery, Oxford Street,
in 1814, which swept away houses
and drowned eight people.*

*It had a wholesome reputation,
from its earliest days as the sterile
alternative to milk or water
(although the Roman Emperor
Julian did comment that 'it smells
of goat'), up to its promotion in
the 18th century as a healthy substitute for the destructive gin. This
was the time when such great
breweries as Bass and
Worthington were founded.
Relative attitudes towards each
drink are reflected in the engravings of prosperous 'Beer
Street' and squalid, poverty-
stricken 'Gin Lane' by Hogarth.*

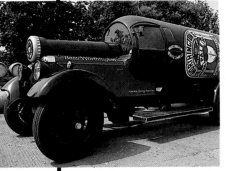

INDIA PALE ALE *Daimler truck
at the Bass Museum, Burton-
upon-Trent, which once had 40
breweries. Gypsum in the water
gives the beer its flavour*

Henley-on-Thames

Oxfordshire   SU 7682

There is more to Henley than the Regatta, even
though the impact of this annual carnival can be
felt throughout the year. Despite some over-
zealous prettifying, it remains a good town to
explore, preferably on foot (it is hopeless by car).
Unexpected treats include an elaborate Victorian
drinking fountain, the Kenton Theatre of 1805
(one of the earliest surviving in the country), the
splendid Victorian brewery building, and Friar
Park. This bizarre Hollywood Gothic folly was
created in 1896 by a rich and eccentric local
solicitor, who decorated his grounds with 'sham
Swiss mountains and passes decorated with china
chamois, and elaborate caves . . . festooned with
artificial grapes, spiders and other monsters'.

Excellent Victorian stained glass in the Roman
Catholic chapel, interesting Art Nouveau work
in the United Reformed Church and plenty of
boat yards for exploration by water are amongst
Henley's other attractions.

Hook Norton

Oxfordshire   SP 3533

Hook Norton is a curiosity, out of step with the
better known tourist villages of North
Oxfordshire and the Cotswolds. For much of its
life it was a small centre of industry, an incongruous island in a sea of traditional
agriculture.

Its prosperity was based on quarries, ironstone,
iron foundries and a brewery. Today, with one
exception, these have all disappeared, along with
the railway built to serve them, but they have left
as their legacy a handsome little town of brown
stone houses and terraces, full of old-fashioned
atmosphere. It spills down the side of a hill,
crowned at the top by the church, a powerful and
large building with plenty of Norman work surviving, a fine sense of space inside and an
imposing tower. Not to be missed is the Norman
font, boldly carved with lively figures, including
Adam and Eve, and some Zodiac signs. There is
also a 17th-century manor, and a couple of
chapels, but the most exciting thing is the
brewery. An independent concern whose products are highly regarded by real ale buffs, it is
housed in an extraordinary Victorian pile built
(seemingly at random) from bricks, cast iron,
slate, timber and other materials. The brewery
maintains Hook Norton's industrial tradition,
while outside the town is another, more silent
memorial. Striding across the valley are the stone
piers that used to carry the railway on a viaduct
80 feet in the air.

Horsmonden

Kent   TQ 7040

This is one of those villages, not uncommon,
which have drifted away from their church.
Called the Gunfounders' Church, it stands nearly
two miles away above the steep slopes of the
River Teise.

In the village stands the Gun Inn with a replica
of a gun made here in the 17th century; also here
is the large and attractive Furnace Pond. John
Brown, who made guns for Charles I and
Cromwell, is said to have employed 200 men at
his foundry; it seems likely that the villagers took
their homes to where the work was, and so left
their church stranded.

Hothfield

Kent   TQ 9644

The acid soil of Hothfield Common, one of the
County's best heathlands, supports the insect-
eating sundew, bog pimpernel, cotton grass and
yellow bog asphodel. Heathers (rare in Kent),
twayblade and heath spotted orchid can be seen,
as can oak, silver birch and aspen. More than 60
species of birds have also been recorded on the
site, while two species of sphagnum moss occur
in Kent only in Hothfield's acid peat hollows.

Lying just south of the A20, the site has been
designated a Site of Special Scientific Interest —
but not being legally a common, it has a long
history of encroachment, and now faces its
greatest threat — the advance of the market town
of Ashford, to the south-east.

Isle of Grain

Kent   TQ 8876

Tanker lorries thunder along the main roads, and
modern industry is all around — but those who
turn on to the byroads will find in the Isle of
Grain's brooding marshes a very different world.
The largest heronry in Britain is at the RSPB
reserve of Northward Hill, with paths leading on
to the lonely Halstow Marshes where rare birds
can be seen, particularly in winter.

ISLE OF GRAIN *Thames barges — those distinctive vessels
that can ride out sea storms as easily as they negotiate
inland waterways — lying idle on the bleak mudflats of the
Thames estuary*

Cooling churchyard is generally believed to be
where Pip met Magwitch in Dickens' *Great
Expectations*, although only five gravestones are
described by Dickens as opposed to the 13 here
to the Comport family. Nearby is Cooling
Castle, where lived Sir John Oldcastle, who led a
revolution against his friend King Henry V and
was cruelly parodied by Shakespeare (who denied
the charge) as Falstaff, fat and cowardly. At
Higham are the remains of Lillechurch Priory,
suppressed in 1521 after the nuns were convicted
of 'gross immorality'. The size of the 13th-
century church at Cliffe is a surprise, but long
before the present church was built, the village
had a great religious importance — the synod of
AD673 was held here.

The Isle of Wight

ISLE OF WIGHT *The Needles and the lighthouse which marks the western tip of the island. Another stack, the highest at 120 feet, collapsed in 1764*

ISLE OF WIGHT: THE MOVING CHURCH — *The church at* **Godshill** *was traditionally begun south-west of the hill where it now stands. But the foundations were found next morning at the top. Two guards were posted, who were disturbed at midnight by a rumbling sound: the stones were trundling up the hill. This was taken as a supernatural sign and the church was built on the spot the stones had chosen, thereafter called Godshill, because of the miracle.*

Another version says that it was the fairies who moved the stones. Stones are also said to have been moved up hill at **Shillington***, and at* **Braunton** *the new church was simply demolished until the builders chose the 'right' site.*

Pigs were involved at Braunton, as they were at Winwick, Cheshire, and Burnley, Greater Manchester. Mysterious forces were held responsible for a similar occurrence at Leyland, Lancashire. Many churches with this kind of tradition stand on artificial mounds or hill-tops: others are Breedon-on-the-Hill, Leicestershire, Church Stowe and Great Brington, Northamptonshire. There was also a medieval tradition that the less sinful of the Fallen Angels were allowed to haunt earth. They lived on hills and were known to men as 'elves'. Quite possibly, such stories reflect the conflict between Christians and pagans when Celtic hill-top shrines were Christianised, by the building of new churches.

BURROW MUMP *One of many artificial mounds topped by a later church. The 'Mump', on the Isle of Athelney, may have been King Alfred's fort*

Isle of Wight Coastal Path

Fortunately for walkers, there is an alternative to the island's roads, which can become extremely busy. The Isle of Wight County Council has planned several long-distance footpaths, which can be joined or left at many points. They provide an excellent, and comparatively peaceful, means of getting to know the island's landscapes, villages and wildlife.

The longest, at 60 miles, is the Coastal Path, which runs all the way round the island. It offers great variety, from dramatic cliffs and chines, mostly in the south, to the brooding saltmarshes on the Solent coast, or the promenades, piers and beaches of the east; and it crosses many acres of National Trust land. Leaflets detailing route directions and places of interest are published by the County Council.

Godshill

SZ 5281

The most visible part of Godshill, strung along the main road, is an extraordinary pixieland of knick-knack shops, wishing wells and model villages, which has a charm of its own but is not for the fainthearted in search of seclusion. Up the hill, decorum prevails. Here is a collection of pretty, thatched cottages and a church whose position is wreathed in legend. It has a late 15th-century wall painting of Christ crucified; a painting which may be by Rubens; and a series of Tudor monuments, some with alabaster effigies.

Luccombe

SZ 5879

Tucked in between Shanklin and Ventnor, busy resorts on the popular east coast, Luccombe owes its relative peace and quiet to the National Trust. They purchased the property in 1981 with funds from their 'Enterprise Neptune' scheme for protecting Britain's vulnerable coastline.

Seen from the main road above, or the downs behind, Luccombe offers the welcome prospect of a great, green bowl of unspoilt pasture and woodland, sweeping down to the sea at Luccombe Bay. A tiny lane leads down to the hamlet and to isolated Luccombe Farm, and the area is criss-crossed by public footpaths offering magnificent views.

Isle of Wight

Newtown

SZ 4290

The most ancient of the island boroughs, Francheville, as Newtown was once known, was the capital of the Isle of Wight. Its harbour sheltered great masted ships and supported thriving salt and oyster industries before it silted up. Now it is full of bright sailing boats in summer; in winter, wildfowl throng the mudflats.

In the village itself, the 17th-century town hall stands as a monument to Newtown's past importance. It witnessed many parliamentary elections (Newtown even produced a Prime Minister — George Canning — before it was declared a rotten borough in 1832). The town hall is now protected by the National Trust. The nearby church is Victorian, but stands on an ancient site; neighbouring Shalfleet has an impregnable-looking Norman tower.

St Catherine's Down

SZ 4978

Many would say that the best things on the Isle of Wight are the downs — the air, straight from the sea, is always a delight, the views are unfailingly fine, and, in the summer months, the downland turf is dotted with wild flowers that are little more than a childhood memory in most parts of the country. St Catherine's Down has all these qualities, and the added attraction of a charming 14th-century lighthouse, with, at the other end, a 72-foot monument built in 1815 to commemorate a visit by the Tsar.

Tennyson Trail

The Tennyson Trail crosses nearly half the Isle of Wight in its 15-mile journey between two of the island's most famous places — Carisbrooke Castle and Alum Bay (of the coloured sands).

From Carisbrooke the Trail heads for Brighstone Forest, the island's largest area of woodland, where red squirrels are among the wildlife that may be seen. Downland and magnificent views of the sea, island and mainland characterise the western section of the Trail, making a walk along it a breathtaking experience in clear, fine weather, especially when the chalkland flowers of midsummer are at their best.

After dipping down to the attractive cove of Freshwater Bay, the Trail climbs steeply to a great hilltop cross. This is the Tennyson Monument, erected in honour of the poet, who lived at Farringford House, which stands just below the downs here. Beyond, the route continues towards the Needles and their lighthouse, before descending to the sandstone of Alum Bay.

Yarmouth

SZ 3589

The castle was built by Henry VIII as a result of unwelcome attentions from the French, who twice attacked the town. Next to the castle stood the Governor's House, now the George Hotel. Across the square stands another historic inn, the Bugle, and beyond it the church — there were two churches here, both victims of French invaders, but this one survived thanks to a 17th-century rebuilding.

Yarmouth is a popular yachting centre: boats are admitted to the inner harbour by raising the delightful swing bridge. From here pleasant walks lead up both sides of the Yar estuary to Freshwater village and its historic church, where Tennyson's wife lies buried.

Keysoe

Bedfordshire   TL 0762

A rare surviving tract of ancient woodland can be found at Keysoe, north of Bedford: a half-moon moat marks the site of a large old farm, which included a stretch of old woodland carefully preserved as a deer park, for hunting. Names like Keysoe Park Farm and Keysoe Park Wood remain to this day, and within the wood are a deep ditch and an inner bank, designed to keep the deer inside the park. A footpath and a bridlepath can be followed round its edge.

Bumps and depressions in the fields at Hardwick End, near Keysoe Park Farm, show the sites of houses of a former settlement.

Kintbury

Berkshire   SU 3866

Tucked away near the River Kennet, the greatest attraction here is the quiet country atmosphere. The church has features from all periods, from a Norman south doorway to a Victorian roof above the nave, while the centuries between, when this church was the mausoleum of the Raymond family from nearby Barton Court, have endowed it with a wealth of tombs, busts and blazonry.

ISLE OF WIGHT: TENNYSON — *Farringford House, near the* **Tennyson Trail***, was Tennyson's home for 30 years.*

His early life was neither happy nor successful, and was clouded by the tragic death of his young friend Arthur Hallam, which inspired the poem 'In Memoriam'. But Tennyson's marriage in 1850 marked a turning-point, and shortly afterwards came the move to Farringford, where he wrote some of his best work, including 'The Idylls of the King' and 'Maud', his own favourite poem. Here he became successful, financially secure and contented.

The phenomenally strong, towering figure who had amused the youthful Hallam by casually picking up a Shetland pony and carrying it round the lawn, in later life never missed his daily walk on the Down that is named after him — he used to astonish neighbours with his imperviousness to violently stormy weather.

A few years ago, two boys walking from Farringford House to the Down saw a figure clad in Tennyson's characteristic cloak and black hat. But when they ran down the path to overtake him, he had disappeared.

ABOVE   *Tennyson created 'Maud with her exquisite face, And wild voice pealing up to the sunny sky,' at Farringford*

Lacey Green

Buckinghamshire SU 8299

The windmill at Lacey Green is of the 'smock mill' type, and is the oldest of its kind still standing. Originally built at Chesham, it was moved by the Duke of Buckingham to its present site in a field near The Whip pub.

The poet Rupert Brooke and his friends used to go drinking before World War I at the nearby Pink and Lilly pub (now a private house).

Leighton Buzzard

Bedfordshire SP 9225

Each Rogation Monday (in May), a procession of clergy, trustees of the Wilkes Charity, and choirboys walk along the High Street to Wilkes's Almshouses. On arrival, a hymn is sung, a prayer is read and the clerk reads an extract from the 17th-century will of Edward Wilkes, while a choirboy stands on his head. The reasons for this peculiar custom are obscure, but in recent years at least, a cushion has been provided for the up-turned boy.

Letchworth

Hertfordshire TL 2132

The most remarkable building in Letchworth is The Cloisters, a School of Psychology, with cloisters to sleep 20 students, and a central octagonal tower. It was designed by W. H. Cowlishaw for Annie Jane Lawrence (1863-1953), an heiress of strong principles, who settled in Letchworth, after a period of travel, in 1905. Despite her wealth, she boasted of living on ten shillings a week. Cowlishaw's building has the strong green veining of marble to represent Man's spiritual growth, and could also be cleaned by the 'hosing-down method'. Visits are strictly by appointment — it has been a Masonic Lodge since 1948. But some of the flavour of those early days, when Letchworth was the centre of burgeoning new ideas on social and spiritual progress befitting the first 'garden city', can be gained at the First Garden City Museum.

Lewes

East Sussex TQ 4110

Five thousand men are thought to have died at the Battle of Lewes, fought in 1264 on a now tranquil site overlooking the town. Fifteen hundred skeletons were disinterred near Lewes gaol, and at nearby Plumpton, wagonloads of bones were unearthed when the railway was built — and used to strengthen an embankment.

Memories of violence linger in the town: the museum in Anne of Cleves House has a marble table-top, said to have three times thrown off the weapons of the murderers of Thomas Becket when they rested at Malling. The harmless-sounding name of the Snowdrop Inn recalls that at this spot on Christmas Eve, 1830, eight people were killed when a great mass of snow and ice crashed down the hill, demolishing a row of labourers' cottages.

Violence against individuals is remembered every Guy Fawkes night in Lewes. The original purpose of the spectacular processions of the costumed Bonfire Societies (all of which used to be held on 24 November) was to remember the Protestant martyrs.

LEWES *The massive castle looks towards Mount Harry where, in 1264, Henry III's and Simon de Montfort's troops met at the Battle of Lewes: the king was defeated amidst much bloodshed*

LEIGHTON BUZZARD: CHURCH DOODLES — *In the 15th century, someone in All Saints' Church, **Leighton Buzzard**, drew a little sketch on a pillar of two people. Tradition says they are Simon and Nell who, unable to agree whether to have pudding or pie, first boiled and then baked their meal and so invented simnel cake.*

Graffiti, idle scrawls in words or pictures, have been with us at least since a Roman left the simple message 'Girl!' — but those found in churches tend to be more edifying.

The most poignant voice from the past comes from the tower of Ashwell church, Hertfordshire, where Latin inscriptions on the wall record the Black Death: 'The first plague was in June 1300'; '1349 pestilence'; '1350: wretched, wild and driven to violence the people remaining became witness at last of a tempest. On St Maur's day this year 1361 it thunders on the earth.'

***North Cerney's** church has a drawing of a manticore: it was perhaps a mason's trial run for one of the south transept carvings. Some drawings at All Saints', Leighton Buzzard, may have been designs for the stonework of the church windows. Certain coastal churches, for example at Blakeney, Norfolk; Newbourn, Suffolk; and most notably St Margaret-at-Cliffe, Kent, have pictures of ships, probably done by 14th- and 15th-century sailors.*

LYMINSTER: A DRAGON'S TALE —

The Knucker Hole at **Lyminster** *was once the bottomless lair of the Knucker, a terrible dragon who rose from its icy depths to ravage the countryside around, devouring cattle and people. The King of Sussex promised his daughter to the man who killed it, and a passing knight-errant fulfilled the task. Having married the princess, he settled in the area, and was later buried in the churchyard.*

Another version of the legend makes the dragon-slayer a local farmer by name of Jim Pulk. Either way, his tomb can still be seen: it is a medieval grave slab with a weatherworn cross on a herringbone pattern, which was explained as his sword, lying on the dragon's ribs.

The tombs of other dragon-slayers can be seen at Brent Pelham, Hertfordshire, Slingsby, North Yorkshire, and Sockburn, Durham. Misunderstanding of the tombs has undoubtedly given rise to their dragon legends. But at Lyminster it may be the name 'knucker' — found elsewhere in Sussex — rather than the tomb, that is the key to the story, for it comes from the Anglo-Saxon 'nicor', for water monster.

DRAGON slain on a carved bench-end at Crowcombe, Somerset. The vine growing out of the head (lower left) has been linked by some with a belief in dragons — or serpents — as the guardians of knowledge, perhaps teaching people about mysterious forces in the earth

Little Marlow

Buckinghamshire   SU 8788

Little Marlow, an attractive village, lying off the main road, has a 12th-century church dedicated to John the Baptist. Of especial interest is the swinging, centrally pivoted lych gate. Lych gates were erected to give shelter to the coffin and bearers until the priest arrived to conduct the funeral party on to consecrated ground. They were originally needed because coffins were not used ('lych' is the Saxon word for corpse).

In the cemetery extension near Bourne End, the novelist and thriller writer, Edgar Wallace, lies buried.

Long Wittenham

Oxfordshire   SU 5493

A Norman church, a fine thatched tithe barn and the 16th-century Plough Inn are amongst the attractions of this village, which is long indeed, straggling along a single street. But there are some other interesting features if you look about. The 'chipping cross' in the centre marks the place where bargains were struck on market days, and the Pendon Museum contains railway relics and displays on local life. Medieval mass dials (sun dials showing times of services) are cut into the stonework of the church, although the 'gnomen' — the centrepiece to cast the shadow — is missing. The font inside is Norman and made of lead; the south chapel contains a fine miniature effigy of Guilbert de Clare, Earl of Gloucester, a Crusader who died in 1295.

LOWER HALSTOW   A 12th-century lead font adorned with kings, angels and arches was discovered by chance beneath its layers of plaster

Lower Halstow

Kent   TQ 8567

Set at the head of a creek on the Medway, Lower Halstow is a place for lovers of saltings, open marsh, solitude, the sounds of birds calling and of wind in the reeds. Here the Romans produced pottery in quantity — it is still possible to find pieces, and occasionally whole pots, on the marshes around Halstow and Upchurch. There is also evidence of a third- or fourth-century brick-works, and the modern brickworks give a pleasing sense of continuity.

Roman bricks and tiles form a substantial part of the material of the bright little church, whose glory is a lead font. Not quite so spectacular as that at Brookland, it was only rediscovered when the vibration of the guns set around the village during World War I caused the hard plaster of the font to crack.

Loxwood

West Sussex   TQ 0431

In 1850 a meeting was held at Loxwood at which cocoa, imported from London, was drunk. The small religious sect which was founded at the meeting was formally known as the Society of Dependants, but its members have been called

Maldon

Essex TL 8507

At the top of this waterside town, a narrow staircase in a church tower leads to the Plume Library (open mid-week afternoons and Saturday mornings), which is still much as it was when the founder, Dr Plume, died in 1704. He built a home for the 6000 books he gave to the town on the site of a ruined church, and today the Public Library is below.

The High Street is lined with small, interesting shops as it runs down to the Blackwater Estuary — a scene of boats and barges, sails and spars — and the quay-side Queen's Head, which runs an annual mud-race across the river at low tide, in aid of local charities.

Markyate

Hertfordshire TL 0616

Lady Katherine Ferrers, who lived at the house called Markyate Cell (not open to the public) in the 18th century, was the original Wicked Lady of cinematic fame. She rode out at night, dressed as a man, and terrorised travellers, attacking and robbing them. It is said that a ghostly highway-woman still rides the Markyate to Dunstable road.

Marlow

Buckinghamshire SU 8586

Rich in Georgian buildings and renowned for its part in *Three Men in a Boat*, much-visited Marlow nevertheless has its share of the un-expected. The little Catholic church in St Peter's Street possesses one of the hands of St James of Compostela (once the prized relic of Reading Abbey), which can be viewed on application to the resident canon. The suspension bridge, built between 1831 and 1836 by Tierney Clarke, was a small-size prototype for a much bigger version which he went on to build over the Danube, con-necting Buda with Pest. Marlow's version gives delightful views of the Compleat Angler Inn and the foaming eddies of Marlow Weir. At the end of the High Street (lined with Georgian houses) is an obelisk, erected on the so-called 'Gout Track' to Bath, a milestone for sufferers of the Cecil family of Hatfield on their way to the spa. A fine brick gazebo dating from 1699 can be seen in West Street, and there is a beautiful square blue sundial in Dial Close by the river.

Marston Moretaine

Bedfordshire SP 9941

Two legends of the devil surround the 14th-century church of St Mary the Virgin. The first concerns its separate tower, originally a Saxon defence tower up which the locals would scramble, via an inside ladder, at times of attack. The legend gives the more colourful explanation that the church had an argument with Satan, who flung it away in anger. From the same tower, the Devil supposedly took three leaps. His first landing place was in a field 100 feet away, his second was marked by a pub called The Jumps (demolished in 1930), and the third took him over a road and into a field where three boys were playing leapfrog. He got them to jump with him and they disappeared down a hole in the ground, never to be seen again. An ancient stone, the Devil's Stone, stands on the spot.

MARKYATE: THE WICKED LADY — She was Lady Katherine Ferrers, and is said to have lived at **Markyate** Cell in the 18th century. The 'Wicked Lady' led a double life, riding out at night on a coal-black horse with white forelegs, to rob travellers on the Holyhead Road. Eventually shot, she crept back to Markyate, but was found dead at the foot of the secret stair leading to the room where she used to change into her men's clothes and put on her mask, before going out.

A colourful variation of the legend is that she took up robbery as an amusement after the failure of her early marriage to the teenage Lord Thomas Fanshawe.

When the old house was largely destroyed by fire in 1840, many of those helping to put the blaze out swore that they saw the Wicked Lady swinging herself on the branch of a large sycamore tree by the house. Certainly most people at the time believed that the fire was her doing.

MARKYATE CELL *The 12th-century priory of St Trinity-in-the-Wood stood here first: it was turned into a manor house and bought in the Dissolution of Monasteries by George Ferrers, and remained in the family. It was re-built in the 19th century in neo-Tudor style*

Cokelers by the locals ever since. They set up co-operative stores, first at Loxwood, then at several other villages. Assistants were required to wear sober clothes, and the sect still disapproves of dancing, singing and cut flowers in the house. Marriage, although not banned, was not per-mitted in the sect's chapel. At its height the Society and its shops flourished, but in recent years membership has declined and it no longer owns the store in Loxwood.

Lyminster

West Sussex TQ 0204

Beside the font in Lyminster church stand two ancient tombstones. One is said to be the repre-sentation of a sword — the sword of a dragon slayer, who killed the beast living in the Knucker (or Nucker) Hole. The hole can still be seen — it is one of a series of enclosed pools some 100 yards along the public footpath to Arundel.

Maidstone

Kent TQ 7555

An iguanadon appears on the coat of arms, and the town's history goes back to the Stone Age. On Penenden Heath, a quiet, enclosed public space, Susannah Lott was burned to death for the murder of her husband in 1769; also here, in 1748, Father O'Coigley was hanged for sedition (as a memorial in St Francis Church recalls). The last public hanging in Kent took place at the top of Maidstone's Week Street in 1868.

LONDON *circa* 1900.
An early milk bar. In the days before fast transport, it was dificult to get fresh milk into the capital, so cows were kept in the heart of London. Scenes like this are still just within living memory – but traces of them have virtually disappeared

LONDON

*F*or all its audacious modernity and seeming rejection of the
past, today's London of concrete, glass and steel is literally
rooted in history. Its foundations pierce layer on layer of older
Londons, going right back to Roman times. It could not
be what it is without those previous Londons.
In these pages are tales of buildings and people from all parts of
the long London story – Mithras, god of light of Roman
soldiers; Scratching Fanny, 18th-century poltergeist; Jack the
Ripper, mystery butcher extraordinary; Gilbert and George,
living 20th-century works of art; pie shops, hat shops,
tabernacles, pleasure gardens, tunnels, nature reserves, pumping
stations, cemeteries . . .

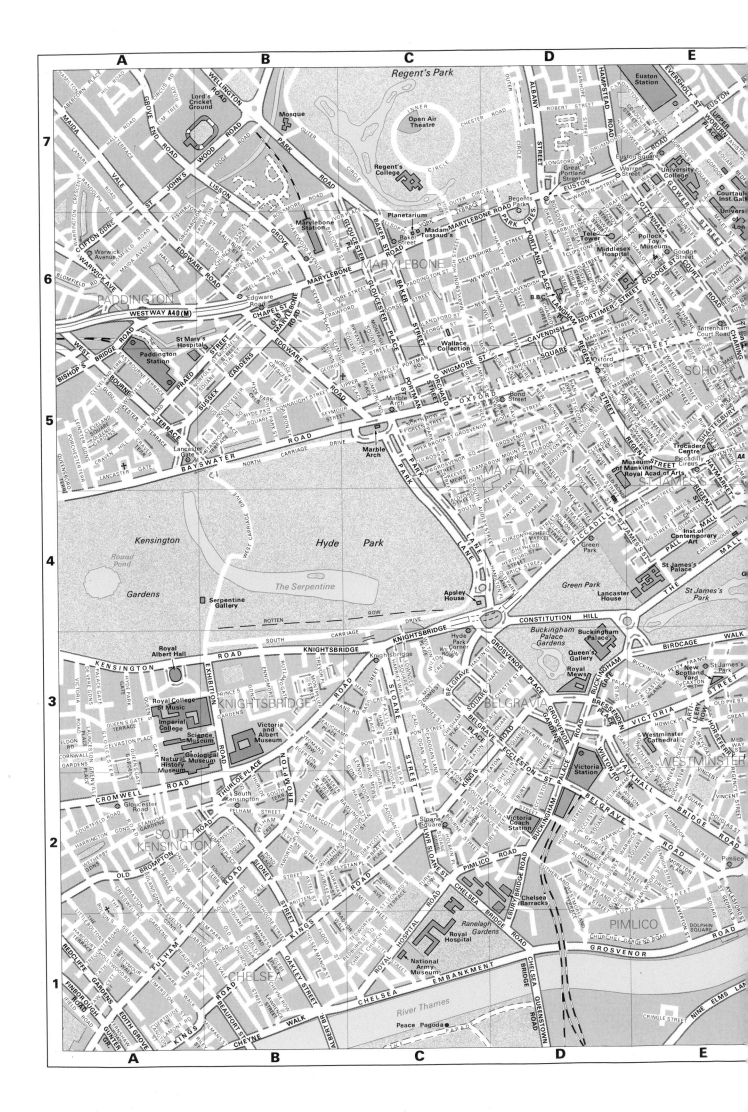

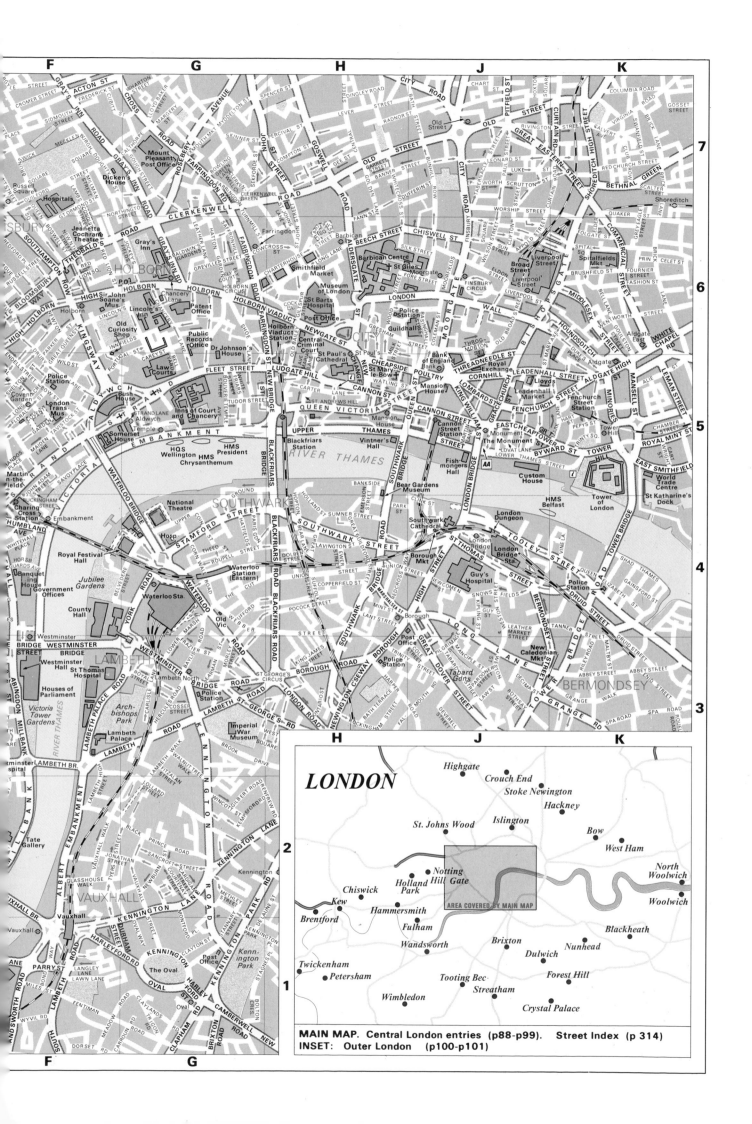

The City & Spitalfields

Every working day the City of London draws nearly half a million people into its square mile, and the 600ft National Westminster building dominates a skyline where once Wren's steeples reigned supreme

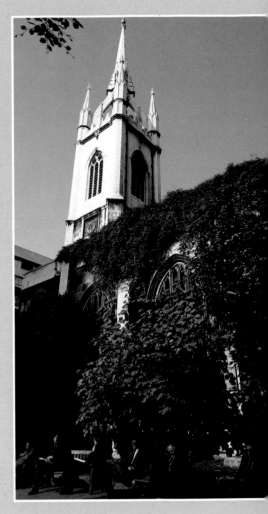

SWEETINGS *moved in from Islington in 1830*

JOHN STOW — *historian*

THE CITY: CHURCH CUSTOMS

Throats are blessed once a year at **St Etheldreda's,** *Ely Place. One of the numerous centuries-old customs celebrated in London's churches, the ceremony takes place on 3 February, feast day of St Blaise, patron saint of those with throat troubles. Two months later, on or near 5 April, the Lord Mayor and aldermen attend a memorial service at St Andrew Undershaft to the London historian John Stow. The quill in the hand of Stow's effigy is renewed annually at the same time. In fulfilment of a bequest made by John Norton in 1612, members of the Stationers' Company assemble every Ash Wednesday in the crypt of* **St Paul's Cathedral** *to hear the 'Cakes & Ale' sermon, the refreshments being served on their return to Stationers' Hall.*

In 1924 the Knollys Rent was revived and is presented by the churchwardens of All Hallows by the Tower.

ST DUNSTAN'S *The fig tree was planted in 1937 to commemorate George VI's coronation*

EVEN old *Billingsgate Fish Market*, stranded in Lower Thames Street since the market's move to the Isle of Dogs, is destined to become an international banking centre. But it is comforting to see that the *Billingsgate Christian Missionary and Dispensary* is still there with its 'surgery for minor casualties' round the corner from pleasant cobbled *Lovat Lane*. And lurking beneath the gleaming new glass and concrete monuments to Mammon, there are numerous other clues to an older, odder City. Perhaps Mithras, Zoroastrian god of light, still waits for blood baptisms and other occult rites favoured by Roman soldiers, at the second-century *Temple of Mithras*, whose remains nestle beside an office block in Queen Victoria Street. At the *Museum of London* on the first Tuesday morning and third Friday afternoon of the month, you can ask to see the entrance to the *Roman fort*, accessible from the car park.

A skull and crossbones over the gate shows the way to the peaceful churchyard of restored *St Olave's*, Hart Street, Pepys' church, one of the handful to survive the Great Fire and one of many casualties of the Blitz. Further along Hart Street is the splendidly cheery *Ship* pub, decorated with grapes in abundance and blue dolphins cavorting on its frontage.

Some say the east window of *St Katherine Cree* in Leadenhall Street represents the first Catherine wheel — a spiked one on which the fourth-century saint was tortured; certainly the church is a rare early 17th-century survivor. Close to Fenchurch Street Station in Mark Lane, and looking, as John Betjeman said, 'like a bit of stage scenery', is the 15th-century tower of *All Hallows, Staining* with a 12th-century crypt. (But avoid Monday and Thursday at lunchtimes unless you are stressed or strained, for then it becomes the Lincoln Clinic.) Services are in Welsh at *St Benet* in Queen Victoria Street, one of the least spoiled City churches; tiniest church in London is *St Ethelburga the Virgin* in Bishopsgate, which has a pond in its peaceful churchyard (open Tuesdays and Thursdays); while creepers festoon the windows, and trees grow through where the roof should be, at *St Dunstan's* in Great

Tower Street. Bombed in the war, now it has only a tower and skeletal walls, but the City of London Corporation has transformed it into a charming retreat.

A firm sense of purpose is required to see the *Spanish and Portuguese Synagogue* in Duke's Place — it is reached through the archway of Biba House on Bevis Marks, and is open regularly. Check on the telephone first (it is in the directory): the impressive gate across the archway is sometimes padlocked — but it is worth persevering, for this is England's oldest synagogue, founded in 1657 in Creechurch Lane, rebuilt here in 1701, and little changed.

Traditions endure, some older than others. At the *Tower of London*, the solemn passage of the Yeoman Warders round the ramparts in the *Ceremony of the Keys* can be witnessed nightly at ten (by appointment). Outside on *Tower Hill Terrace*, every Wednesday just the same as he has for years, Lord Soper, Methodist and exponent of peace, mounts his step ladder to talk.

Sixteen shire horses live in Garrett Street and pull the drays for *Whitbread's Brewery*, nearby in Chiswell Street, where the Speaker's Coach can be seen in the forecourt. The stables are open between eleven and three on weekdays, and also by appointment.

Amongst the many old-fashioned eating places, *Sweetings* at 39 Queen Victoria Street, London's longest established fish restaurant, has a pleasingly uncontrived air of great age. *Olde Wine Shades*, in Martin Lane, looks as it might have done in Dickens' day; it dates from 1663 and

18 FOLGATE STREET *where the owner has turned the clock back 200 years. This is the Punch Room*

ST OLAVE'S CHURCH *Dickens referred to these skulls as 'St Ghastly Grim' in 'The Uncommercial Traveller'*

ST KATHERINE CREE CHURCH *The East 'wheel' window*

SPITALFIELDS *takes its name from the priory of St Mary Spital, founded here in 1197. Charles II established the market*

claims to be the only City tavern to survive the Great Fire. Game and poultry can be bought fresh at *Leadenhall Market*, founded in the 14th century but rebuilt in 1881 with a splendid Victorian wrought iron and glass structure.

Fine Victorian Gothic iron and brick can be admired at *Liverpool Street Station*, off Bishopsgate; going north take a right turn off Bishopsgate down Brushfield Street to come face to face with Hawksmoor's *Christ Church*. Strange and strangely disturbing, it broods over *Spitalfields Market*, a lesser-known Covent Garden best seen very early on Tuesday or Thursday mornings, when fruit and vegetables and sprays of flowers combine the exotic scents of distant countries, under a sturdy Victorian roof with gable rooms. *Jack the Ripper* operated in the area — the pub bearing his name on Commercial Street has a list of names and places of death of his victims. But this area has also been the point of arrival for wave after wave of refugees, nowhere better symbolised than the *mosque* on the corner of *Fournier Street* and *Brick Lane*, which was once a synagogue but started as the New French Church and was later used by Methodists. Now a focal point for the Bengali community, Brick Lane has the air of a bazaar, with good eating places and a hectic *Sunday morning market* running down Cheshire Street. At the Aldgate end, the Art Nouveau *Whitechapel Art Gallery* stands next to *Whitechapel Public Library* — with 'Passmore Edwards Library' carved into the brickwork and a tile picture of rustic Whitechapel just inside the

door. *Blooms Restaurant* is a potent reminder of the once Jewish character of the area, with the best salt beef sandwiches in London and a frantic atmosphere engendered by the curious system of waiters buying food from the kitchen.

Amongst more recent arrivals have been eccentric and renowned artists and eaters-out Gilbert and George, living in a house without a kitchen. But it is the Huguenot character that seems particularly stamped on Spitalfields. It is still the heart of the rag trade, though sewing machines now hum in the big-windowed attics where Huguenots wove silk, stuffing the space between the floors with silk waste to deaden the sound of the looms. Some of the notable houses in *Fournier*, *Folgate* and *Elder Streets* are being restored to their 18th-century state, and a restored house in Fournier Street has sometimes been opened to Friends of the *Geffrye Museum*. Nearby in Kingsland Road, Shoreditch, the museum itself is a delight, arranged in what was once a set of almshouses, with rooms from different periods and a history trail for Spitalfields. But it is at *18 Folgate Street* that the greatest treat for those in search of another London lies. This is the only house in London to be lived in as it might have been in past centuries. The light comes from candles, with outside the door a flickering gas lantern. Three times a week, the owner lets others imbibe the atmosphere, scents and sounds of times past, with conducted tours round his home (telephone the house for more details).

THE CITY: MITHRAS THE BULLSLAYER — *The remains of the* **Temple of Mithras** *in the midst of the City of London's churches are a reminder that Christianity was only one of a number of Eastern cults introduced into Britain by the Romans. Christianity's greatest rival was Mithraism, originating in Persia and celebrating Mithras, god of heavenly light, who became the god above all of soldiers. Mithraism at one time was virtually the official religion of the Empire. Like other mystic religions, its rites were secret, performed in 'mithraeums' (such as one at* **Carrawbrough**) *often partly underground, to which only male initiates were admitted. Sometimes they wore costumes and masks according to their grade of initiation — there were seven grades, attained by ceremony and ordeal, including Raven, Soldier, and Lion. Central to his mysteries was Mithras's slaying of the primeval bull from which life on earth was created. He can be seen as Mithras the Bullslayer, a young man in a Phrygian cap killing a bull, on a third-century sculpture (above) now in the* **Museum of London**.

St Paul's to Fleet Street

Massive and magnificent still, St Paul's Cathedral, it is widely agreed, has the most beautiful dome in the world. It glorifies reason as much as God: geometry-trained Sir Christopher Wren solved centuries of dome-building difficulties by putting the weight on a sturdy cone and then putting the dome — a relatively fragile skin — on top

DOME or cone, the Cathedral's centuries of influence are clear in the network of alleys and passages clustered beneath it. The old *St Paul's Choir School* in Carter Lane, now a Youth Hostel, has rare Renaissance-style frescoes inscribed with Latin. Close by in Dean Court, almost opposite the fine Art Deco style *Tea Room and Dining Room* with its name engraved on the glass, is what used to be the *Deanery*. This gracious Wren house, dated 1670, is set back behind wrought iron gates, still lovely to look at though it is now an office. Just off Carter Lane, with an almost invisible entrance, is *Wardrobe Place*, a peaceful and surprising courtyard. Here was the King's Wardrobe, displaying ceremonial robes rather a long way from his home. Only the garden remains.

Amen Corner is a tranquil precinct leading off Ave Maria Lane, past a gatehouse with leaded windows. Home of the Canons of St Paul's, it has some houses of the 17th century, with occasional shell pediments, Latin inscriptions on the walls, a stone cat lurking over a doorway, and well-kept lawns where one can hear birdsong.

Gold labels show heralds' parking places outside the *College of Arms* on Queen Victoria Street. This is the national authority on coats of arms and pedigree. The Earl Marshal's Court is open weekdays; the Record Room for researchers by appointment only. Just round the corner in Blackfriars Lane is one of the City's many livery company buildings: the *Society of Apothecaries*, with a beautiful 17th-century court. *Blackfriars Priory*, a great Dominican monastery of the 13th century, dominated this area until destroyed by the Great Fire. Now the only traces left are a fragment of wall in *Ireland Yard* off St Andrew's Hill, and in *Church Entry*, off Carter Lane, the small churchyard of St Ann's, formerly the parish church in the precincts of the priory. The name lives on in *Blackfriars Station* where exotic former destinations are carved in stone — and in the *Black Friar* pub, which is bright with Art Nouveau mosaics, reliefs of friars and sententious sayings: Industry is All, Finery is Foolery and — an odd view so close to the City — Contentment surpasses Riches.

Up Farringdon Road and under Holborn Viaduct (one of the brightest bridges in London) is *Smithfield Market*, housed in wonderful wrought iron with green cupolas. Early morning visitors can mingle with the porters at nearby pubs like the *Fox and Anchor*, in Charterhouse Street. Smithfield's long vanished cloth markets are recalled by nearby *Cloth Fair* with its magnificent 18th-century bow-fronted houses at 41 and 42, overlooking the churchyard of *St Bartholomew the Great*. Secluded from Smithfield by a 13th-century gatehouse, the church is much bigger than expected. Hogarth was baptised in the medieval font; on the wall is a notice-board full of poignant pleas for prayers for the sick, the homeless and the faithless. On the other side of Smithfield, *Cock Lane* was troubled by an 18th-century poltergeist named 'Scratching Fanny'; on the corner with Giltspur Street is the gilt *Fat Boy*. *St Bartholomew's-the-Less* nestles inside the hospital

founded in the 12th century by Rahere, Henry II's jester. As hospitals go, *St Bartholomew's* — best known as Bart's — is magnificent. Through the gatehouse is a pleasant courtyard with a fountain, and the air of an Italian plaza. Take the door on the left for the staircase dominated by Hogarth paintings, leading up to the Great Hall, with original 18th-century panelling.

The Charterhouse, in the nearby backwater of Charterhouse Square, is London's only pre-Reformation monastery: there are guided tours from April to July on Wednesday afternoons (but not after a public holiday).

St John's Gate, spanning St John's Lane in Clerkenwell, just to the west, is a reminder of another priory — for the order of the Hospital of St John of Jerusalem, ancestors of St John's Ambulance — and has a small museum. The original *well* of Clerkenwell is at 16 Farringdon Lane: it can be seen through a window, but for access contact Finsbury Public Library at 245 St John's Street. Round the corner is *Clerkenwell Green*, and the *Marx Memorial Library* (Nos 37–38) where Lenin printed his newspaper, *Iskra*, to smuggle into Russia. Twisting *Clerkenwell Close* (where Clerkenwell Workshops continue the local artisan tradition) leads to *St James Church*, which still has box pews.

Running south from Clerkenwell Road, *Hatton Garden* leads to Ely Court, where *Ye Old Mitre* pub was founded by Bishop Goodrich in 1546 for his servants. *Ely Place* was a sanctuary — out of the jurisdiction of the police. It used to be the

FAT BOY *(above) Probably a pub sign, but said to mark where the Great Fire ended*

ST PAUL'S *(left) 'Different from all the Cathedrals of the Worlde' said one contemporary*

TWININGS *Founder Thomas Twining served tea as a novel change from London's thousands of coffee houses. Family portraits adorn the shop*

SOCIETY OF APOTHECARIES *Blackfriars Lane*

CLERKENWELL'S *original well*

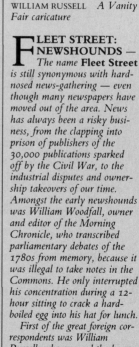

WILLIAM RUSSELL *A Vanity Fair caricature*

FOX AND ANCHOR *(above) Big breakfasts designed for Smithfield porters can be washed down with pints of beer, even at six in the morning*

WIG AND PEN CLUB *(left) Vanity Fair cartoons adorn the club, founded in 1908 and now open to members in law, journalism or business*

garden of Ely House, the 13th-century residence of the Bishops of Ely. All that remains is their lovely chapel, *St Etheldreda's*, the oldest Catholic church in London, built on Roman foundations.

Prepare for *Fleet Street* with a visit to the parish church of the Press, *St Bride's*. Its beautiful spire (by Wren) inspired a local baker to invent tiered wedding cakes. In the crypt is a Roman pavement. Not accessible, it can be seen reflected in a mirror.

Fleet Street has been the traditional heart of the newspaper industry and still has suitably colourful pubs and bars: *El Vinos*, where women, until recently, were forbidden to buy drinks, the *White Hart*, called by those in the know 'The Stab', and the hardly altered 17th-century *Olde Cheshire Cheese*, frequented by Dr Johnson, and still cooking a fine steak and kidney pudding. Said to be equally old, if a lot less picturesque, is the *Old Bell*, pleasantly tucked away by St Bride's. And there are newer ones like the *Poppinjay* and the *Cartoonist*, whose main distinction is the array of original cartoons.

The inviting looking alleys off Fleet Street

promise more than they fulfil, but *Wine Office Court* leads to the Olde Cheshire Cheese, *Bolt Court* to *Dr Johnson's House*, where he laboured on his dictionary in the attic, while across the road, *Middle Temple Lane* leads through a heavy wooden door to the *Temple*. Between this and the first office of the *Automobile Association* (opened in 1905 at Number 18) is *Prince Henry's Room*, by tradition the Council Chamber of James I's son, Henry, with panelled walls, a magnificent ceiling and a *Pepys* exhibition, in a gabled building of 1610, with overhanging upper storey. At 37 Fleet Street is *Messrs Hoare*, bankers to Gainsborough among many others, with its sign of a golden leather bottle repeated on the façade and street sign. Just across the road, two figures heavily but half-heartedly strike the hours, on the clock of *St Dunstan in the West*. Fleet Street's demon barber Sweeney Todd is said to have had a shop on one side of the church, while a partner dispensed pies on the other . . . In the church porch are figures of King Lud and his sons, taken from *Ludgate*, one of the main entrances to the City. Lawyers and journalists meet at the *Wig and Pen Club*, two ancient houses at 229/30 Strand, which unite the twin preoccupations of this area and can usually be visited in the mornings. *Lloyds Bank* customers can enjoy the wonderfully ornate interior of the 222 Strand branch — it used to be a restaurant — and at 216 Strand is *Twinings*, fragrant with tea, said to be London's narrowest shop and the longest established on one site. The 18th-century doorway is dominated by two colourful model Chinamen, a reminder that the company began by trading in China tea: Indian tea came in the 19th century.

FLEET STREET: NEWSHOUNDS —

The name **Fleet Street** is still synonymous with hard-nosed news-gathering — even though many newspapers have moved out of the area. News has always been a risky business, from the clapping into prison of publishers of the 30,000 publications sparked off by the Civil War, to the industrial disputes and owner-ship takeovers of our time. Amongst the early newshounds was William Woodfall, owner and editor of the Morning Chronicle, who transcribed parliamentary debates of the 1780s from memory, because it was illegal to take notes in the Commons. He only interrupted his concentration during a 12-hour sitting to crack a hard-boiled egg into his hat for lunch.

First of the great foreign cor-respondents was William Russell, who exposed the horrors of the Crimean War to readers of the Times. Tax changes in the 1850s were the making of cheap sensationalist papers like the News of the World; and news creation is generally agreed to have arrived when, presuming on a good story, the New York Herald sent Stanley to Africa to look for Dr Livingstone in the 1870s.

Bloomsbury to Temple

At the heart of Bloomsbury's publishers' offices, secondhand bookshops and elegant squares once frequented by the Bloomsbury Group is the great bulk of the British Museum. As well as being a treasure house of antiquities, it has the wonderful domed Reading Room (where Karl Marx worked on Das Kapital), which is really only open to researchers with readers tickets but can be seen on the hour between eleven and four

THE TEMPLE   *Haunted by Lord Brampton in wig and gown*

KING George I in Roman garb overlooks the area from the top of a copy of the tomb of Halicarnassus — the bizarre spire of *St George's, Bloomsbury*, in Bloomsbury Way, designed by Hawksmoor. Two duelling brothers have left their indelible footprints in *Tavistock Square*: it is said that the dips in the ground cannot be removed; and you can go to the *Sun* via the *Moon* — renowned free houses in Lamb's Conduit Street and New North Street.

The preserved body of *Jeremy Bentham*, bequeathed to his physicians, can be seen in term time at *University College*, which he founded — go in by the Gower Street entrance and ask for directions. Some say that he wanders by night, visiting the library and failing to return books to their proper places.

At 183 Euston Road is the *Wellcome Institute of Medicine*, with five historic pharmacies reconstructed in the entrance hall, including the frontage of John Bell's of Oxford Street, founded in 1798 with its elaborate pots and sets of drawers; a palatial 17th-century Italian example with majolica jars and handsome counter including inlaid figures; and a pharmacy from 18th-century Granada which has oil-paintings and hand-painted jars. But most captivating is the Arab example, a work of art with inlaid mother-of-pearl, glass mosaics, glowing jars and Islamic-arched cubby-holes.

Near Euston Station, at the end of Cobourg Street, is *Collectors' Corner*, offering an array of all sorts of railway artefacts from stop watches, lamps and station signs to waiting-room armchairs. Northwards on Hampstead Road and Drummond Street are the extraordinary *Laurence Corner* shops: the 'Boffins' shop sells anything faintly medical or scientific from instruments to specimen bottles; across the road are wigs, headdresses and ancient garments.

Covent Garden is theatreland and home of many a ghost: a skeleton with a knife in its ribs found in a blocked-up room at the *Theatre Royal*, Drury Lane, is said to be the origin of the 18th-century playgoer who still haunts the Upper Circle, from which he used to watch the actress he loved and lost. *Brodie & Middleton* sells stage paints and canvas at 68 Drury Lane; amongst other specialists *Philip Poole* at No 182 is hung above with a giant wooden fountain pen, and has a window — under the slogan *Vive La Plume* — dominated by a mosaic of pen nibs and a swan bristling with quill pens. Jars of artists' pigments, the finest paintbrushes and everything else the artist needs lie behind the attractive shop front of *L. Cornelissen & Son* at 22 Great Queen Street, a street overshadowed by the daunting and monumental *Freemasons' Hall*, which doubles up as a war memorial to masons who died in World War II. The eye-catching windows of *James Smith & Sons* on the corner of New Oxford Street and Shaftesbury Avenue boast sales of everything from sword-sticks to tropical parasols; ceremonial umbrellas for African chiefs are made here as well as repairs to ripped umbrellas.

In Holborn, the *Cittie of York* has been the site of a public house since 1430. Its back room is a galleried long hall with vats, a high, beamed ceiling and booths almost like confessionals. Usefully private, perhaps, for lawyers from the nearby green havens of the *Inns of Court* (and perhaps lawyers are not above using the French-style *pissoir* in Star Yard off Chancery Lane).

Grays Inn has a catalpa tree planted by Sir Francis Bacon; and at *Lincoln's Inn*, which survived the Blitz relatively unscathed, appointments can be made to see the old hall and the chapel. But best of all is the *Temple* — a complex of ancient buildings, courts and alleys; a small city of lawyers. Here Oliver Goldsmith worked, *Twelfth Night* was performed (supposedly with Shakespeare in the cast) and the 12th-century round church of the Knights Templar is still used for worship. The peaceful and blooming gardens overlooking the Thames are tended by the Worshipful Company of Gardeners, and the gas lamps are still lit nightly by a lamplighter.

Amongst the area's less frequented museums are the *Jewish Museum* in Adolph Tuck Hall, Tavistock Square, with Jewish ritual artefacts, and *Sir John Soane's Museum* at 12–14 Lincoln's Inn Fields. This is the home and collection of the great 18th-century architect, kept much the same as he intended. An astonishing array of antique fragments and sculptures is interspersed with work by Hogarth, Piranesi and Soane himself, some concealed behind folding panels (ask the curator). Just behind the headquarters of Channel 4 with its Video Box (where anyone can walk in and make a video, which might be used on television) is *Pollock's Toy Museum* at 1 Scala Street, tucked into two adjoining tiny houses with interconnecting rooms and winding staircases. Apart from the 'twopence coloured, penny plain' paper theatres made by Benjamin Pollock, who gave the museum its name, there are teddies and dolls of all ages and captivating miniature dolls houses.

Intrinsically interesting streets include colonnaded *Sicilian Avenue*, off Bloomsbury Way. Off Grays Inn Road close to Kings Cross is *Frederick Street*, with houses built in sets of three very different styles: it was used as the architect Thomas Cubitt's pattern book and he used to bring his clients here to choose what design they wanted. *Strand Lane* runs off Surrey Street from an entrance hidden among the exuberant red frontage of the former *Norfolk Hotel*, now part of *King's College*. A window overlooks the so-called *Roman bath* — built in Roman style, but probably 17th-century — into which David Copperfield plunged in the Dickens novel. Straddling the lane is the Regency *Watch House*, with a flowery, wrought iron balcony, from which a watch was kept for goods landing from the river. The river was closer then, and the 17th-century *York Gate*, at the foot of time-worn stone steps from Buckingham Street, marks the bank of the Thames before the Victoria Embankment was built in 1862.

MR. DAN LENO.

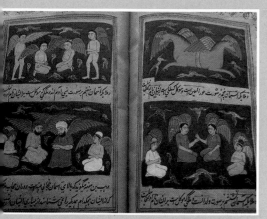

WELLCOME INSTITUTE   *Islamic medical textbook*

POLLOCK'S TOY MUSEUM   *Puppets, dolls, games . . .*

THE WATCH HOUSE   *(above) built in the 19th century with a view of the Thames traffic*

MIDDLE TEMPLE LANE   *(right) A corpse was found in the Hall when electricity was installed*

Westminster, St James's, Soho

Westminster Abbey is one of the most popular of national monuments. But even here there are surprises. Surprising objects like the oldest stuffed bird in England, a parrot that died in 1702 and is displayed in an exhibition of Abbey Treasures. Surprising places — tranquil and hidden places, many of them originating from the Abbey's days as a Benedictine monastery

ONCE a week on Thursdays, the *College Garden* and *Little Cloister* are open. The garden is said to be the oldest of its sort in England. In summer there are lunchtime concerts. Nearby are the few stone stumps that remain of the Chapel of St Catherine's.

Go through Victoria Tower Gardens and over Lambeth Bridge for the *Tradescant Museum of Garden History*. Here, in Lambeth's former parish church, John Tradescant and his son, gardeners to Charles I, are remembered. The imposing red brick Tudor gatehouse next to the Museum leads to Lambeth Palace (visitors by appointment only).

Back in Westminster, Henry VIII's *wine cellar* is under the Ministry of Defence building in Horse-guards Avenue, the only Tudor part left of *Whitehall Palace*. It can be seen on Saturday afternoons, by appointment. In Downing Street, the red Tudor brickwork just before Number 10 marks the site of Henry VIII's *real tennis courts*.

The *Cabinet War Rooms* are open to the public in a bunker under Government Buildings, Horse-guards Road, where Churchill and his Cabinet conducted operations during World War II air raids. The Transatlantic Telephone Room had a hotline to President Roosevelt, and also on view is the room where Churchill occasionally slept.

The block-like eyesore rising out of Horse-guards Avenue, where it joins the Mall, is the *Citadel*, used during the war for storage space. Across the road, on Carlton House Terrace, is London's one Nazi memorial: a small gravestone marking the *burial place of Giro (ein treuer bagleiter* — a faithful companion), the dog belonging to Hitler's ambassador.

CARLTON HOUSE TERRACE *A grand design by Nash*

CABINET WAR ROOMS *The Map Room*

The most surprising national embassy is round the corner off St James's Street where a stone-flagged, half-timbered passage leads to *Pickering Place*. Here a small plaque remembers the *Legation for the Ministers from the Republic of Texas* to the Court of St James 1842–45. Pickering Place itself is a charming corner with Georgian houses. Emma Hamilton lived here; and it is said to be the site of the last duel ever fought in Britain.

Local ghosts are doubtless urbane: this is London clubland, and oldest of the clubs is *White's* at 37 St James's Street, founded in a coffee shop in the 1690s. Even the chimps on the PG Tips advert had their bowlers made at No 6, *Lock's* the hatters, with its scratched and service-able counter, grandfather clock and walls lined with hat-boxes. The bowler, or rather the Coke, hat was invented here for Sir William Coke's gamekeepers. At Nos 7–9 is *Lobb's*, cobblers by special appointment — as a faded notice in the window says — to the Duke of Edinburgh and Prince of Wales. In 1872, that was, but it is still true today. Inside the door are glass cabinets full of ancient cobbling tools.

A footman of Queen Anne's progressed to establish his own business and became the founder of *Fortnum and Mason's*, just a stroll away in Piccadilly: he is commemorated on the clock which gathers a crowd of people on the hour to watch the performance of the figures. The *Fountain* restaurant below the store has wonderful milkshakes. The 18th-century auction rooms of *Sotheby's*, New Bond Street are worth seeing in their own right; for more intellectual pursuits, the *London Library* may be joined (for a hefty sub-scription). Tucked in the corner of St James's Square, it is a wholly pleasurable warren of ancient bookstacks, and the reading room has deep armchairs and writing desks just as every library should.

Off Jermyn Street, in Duke of York Street, is the magnificent cut glass of the *Red Lion* pub; to the north is Mayfair, with its slightly rakish image. The red light area of *Shepherd Market* is a trifle contrived, but it still has a village appearance with its narrow, curving streets.

To the east is *Soho*, well known to all visitors

LAMBETH: THE TRADESCANTS — *The Church of St Mary Lambeth (detail from window below) was rescued from demolition in 1979 and now houses the Tradescant Trust Museum of Garden History. This is a memorial to the John Tradescants, father and son, the great gardeners of the 17th century. They introduced numerous plants into England, including the red trumpet honeysuckle, the yucca and the tulip tree.*

A period knot garden lies round the tombs of the Tradescants and that of Captain Bligh of the Bounty.

HOUSE OF ST BARNABAS *with beautiful Rococo plasterwork and a fine staircase*

POCOHONTAS *The Indian princess died going home*

SOTHEBY'S *Founded in 1744 as book auctioneers, they now lead the world in fine art dealing*

LOBB'S *Keeps models of all customers' feet*

LOCK & CO *Nelson's hat was made here*

to London, but still capable of yielding surprises. Like Spitalfields, it was the home of the Huguenots and still has French influences, like the 'charcuterie' of *Randall & Aubin* in Brewer Street and the gateaux of *Patisserie Valerie* in Old Compton Street. The *French Protestant Church* in Soho Square was founded in 1550 and has a collection of rare bibles. In Leicester Place off Leicester Square is *Notre Dame de France*, with frescoes by Jean Cocteau. In Dean Street there is the *French Pub* (officially the York Minster), which was a meeting place for the Free French during World War II. Here the landlord dispenses drinks like Cassis, and on the wall is a letter from General de Gaulle.

Soho also has its *Chinatown*: the area around Gerrard Street is full of Chinese supermarkets, restaurants, accountants and acupuncturists. At the Chinese New Year the streets are festooned

with lanterns for the festivities and a magnificent lion cavorts and feeds on the paper money which is offered to it in plenty. Close to Soho Square at No 1 Greek Street is another unexpected treat. *The House of St Barnabas* (now a hostel for homeless women) is open on Wednesday afternoons and Thursday mornings for visitors to see the last remaining house to retain the magnificent decorations of 18th-century Soho Square. These include an 18th-century 'Act of Parliament' clock. In the garden is one of the oldest mulberry trees in England — a reminder of the days of silk weavers — and the tree under which Dr Manette in the *Tale of Two Cities* worked — giving his name to neighbouring *Manette Street*. The tiny chapel is open to the public for services at 19.30 on Monday and 12.30 on Wednesday, when the door into Manette Street is left open.

WESTMINSTER: A FOREIGN GRAVE —
London has been enriched for centuries by new settlers, and some have left unusual or poignant memorials.

No tears need to be shed for the Roman remembered by a graffito on a tile in the **Museum of London**: *'Every day for a fortnight Austalis has been going off on his own.' But what about King Theodore of Corsica, who died in 1757 and lies buried at St Anne's Church,* **Soho**? *The German dog Giro has a memorial at* **Carlton House Terrace**, *and an 11th-century Viking was buried at* **St Paul's** *Churchyard, watched over by a great beast. Outside London, there is the grave of the black slave Scipio, at Henbury,* **Bristol**. *And more poignant than any of these is the case of the Indian Princess Pocohontas, who saved the life of Captain John Smith in Virginia and came to England when she married another settler, John Rolfe. Struck down by illness, she tried to go back home, but was carried dying off the ship at Gravesend. She has a memorial window at St Sepulchre-without-Newgate, near John Smith's grave.*

Chelsea and Kensington

Chelsea was once a village far out in Middlesex, with its own porcelain factory, village church and Royal Hospital. The porcelain has long since gone — it was in Lawrence Street — but by wandering the cottage-lined streets, one can still imagine Chelsea as it was

ONLY accessible from the still flourishing *Royal Hospital*, where the red-jacketed Chelsea Pensioners reside, are *Ranelagh Gardens*, full of curving pathways, slightly shaggy mounds and hillocks, with hidden benches, pools and grottoes. There is also a distinguished summer house, once thatched, designed by Sir John Soane.

From the gates of Burton's Court, part of the Royal Hospital, the curious truncated mall with a double row of trees, running towards King's Road, is *Royal Avenue*, home of James Bond. Laid out by Sir Christopher Wren in 1682 for Charles II, who wanted a route from the Royal Hospital to Kensington Palace, it was never completed because he died only three years later.

The *Chelsea Physic Garden*, at 66 Royal Hospital Road, was England's second botanical garden; and the cotton industry of America grew from a cotton seed cultivated here. Open on Wednesday and Sunday afternoons in summer, this ancient walled garden with its dim green shade provides a tranquil haven. The delights to be seen range from a Chronological Garden to the Chinese

Willow Pattern Tree. There are splendid Sunday afternoon teas.

Round the corner, *Sir Thomas More* sits gazing out to the Thames in front of *Chelsea Old Church*, which still feels like a church in the heart of the country. Not a building can be seen from the windows and a torrent of bellsong peals out on a Sunday evening. It is still fashionable to marry here and then walk along the Embankment to medieval *Crosby Hall* for a reception in the fine dining room with its minstrel gallery. It used to be in Bishopsgate (where Thomas More lived in it briefly) but when threatened by road widening schemes at the beginning of the century it was moved bit by bit to its present location. *Cadogan Pier* is the finishing line for the annual *Apprentice Watermen's Race* in late July, and also in July is a commemoration of Sir Thomas More's last journey to the Tower. Otherwise, it is rather unfriendly in its notices, warning visitors off the colony of many houseboats on the Embankment.

Dracula author Bram Stoker lived in Chelsea, at 29 St Leonard's Terrace, one of the many notables that make Chelsea bright with blue plaques.

SIR THOMAS MORE
Statesman, Saint & Scholar, as the plinth records, gazes out from Cheyne Walk where he lived and rebuilt Chelsea Old Church. 'My neck is short,' he told his executioner

ALBERT BRIDGE *(left)* *designed by R. W. Ordish*
ROTTEN ROW *(right)* *fashionable since the 1700s*
ROYAL HOSPITAL *(below)* *inspired by Les Invalides*

THE PHYSIC GARDEN'S
gates with Apollo and a dragon

BATTERSEA PARK *Buddhist peace pagoda*

ALBERT MEMORIAL *Designed to top Albert Hall*

Turner lived at 119 Cheyne Walk in a tiny house with a basement front door; *Whistler* lived at 96. *Oscar Wilde* lived at 34 Tite Street. He would surely have appreciated the present-day view of Tite Street across the river to the *Buddhist peace pagoda* in Battersea Park, set up by Buddhist monks to help bring world peace. Just down the road is the magnificent *Tower House* with reliefs and striking windows. Other houses sport wrought iron, cupolas, turrets, and there are herons carved in the panels on the Lawrence Street side of *Carlyle Mansions*. By the riverside, elaborate wrought iron gates that once led into the *Cremorne Pleasure Gardens* are now the centrepiece of *Cremorne Gardens*, saved for posterity by a local brewery.

An underground river was dammed to make the centrepiece of what is the biggest pleasure garden of them all today — the *Serpentine*, in *Hyde Park*. Hyde Park was the site of London's first modern streetlighting on *Rotten Row* and it is here that Albert on the *Albert Memorial* has been quietly reading his Great Exhibition catalogue for over 100 years. Rotten Row is still a place for riding, and horses' hooves also ring out at *Gloucester Crescent Mews*, site of a riding school close to Belgrave Square. Those on foot in the area can join the Duke of Wellington and possibly George IV by drinking at the *Grenadier*, in Wilton Row. It boasts a sentry box outside, an occasionally fruiting vine over the doorway, and a notice saying that only customers who have arrived on foot or by taxi-cab will be served.

CHELSEA: PLEASURE GARDENS — Fireworks, balloon ascents and an appearance by the young Mozart were among the diversions of the **Ranelagh Pleasure Gardens**. *Canaletto painted them; Samuel Pepys sang on the river on his way home from the gardens at Vauxhall and Dr Johnson is said to have enjoyed the fun. Lightshows, music, fountains, grottoes, groves, pavilions and amazing spectacles made London's pleasure gardens places of delight. Leader of them all in the 19th century were the* **Cremorne Gardens**. *The biggest attraction was the spectaculars, including a naval battle with exploding ships and astonishing (and occasionally fatal) feats of daring by balloonists.*

There were the smaller gardens too: Mulberry Gardens, on the site of present-day Buckingham Palace, was a haunt of courting couples and **Islington** *had numerous Pleasure and Tea Gardens based around its many wells. Diversions included cricket, 'views of the Middlesex Alps' (Highgate Hill) and (in 1760) female wrestling starring Bruising Peg.*

The River and Docklands

Running through the middle of London, the River Thames has been both its lifeline and its big divide. No longer do great ships from all over the world sail up to the Pool of London to disgorge their cargoes, but all along its banks are the reminders of those days

---

THE RIVER: THAMES BARGES — One of the most distinctive sights on the Thames at **Limehouse** and **Wapping** until well into the 20th century was the rust-red sails of Thames barges. Sailormen, as Thames bargemen were called, used to say that their craft would 'go anywhere after a heavy dew' and 'turn to windward up a drainpipe'. These graceful vessels were put to uses as diverse as crossing minefields in both World Wars and taking hay up the Thames for London's cabhorses. They were built of wood in such famous shipyards as Everard's.

Features which made the Thames barges suitable for riding out sea storms as well as negotiating inland waterways, are the mobility of masts and gear, the 'sprit' crossing the mainsail diagonally, making it easy to gather in, and the enormous leeboard, acting as keel to give the flat-bottomed vessel a grip on the water when sailing to windward.

BELOW *Clyde, a 'stumpie' barge (short masted for low bridges) passes St Anne's, Limehouse, a mariner's landmark*

JUST east of Tower Bridge is *Wapping High Street*, once a thriving and busy dockland area. Now it has an air of ghosts, with only clues to its vivid past. Amid the toothless warehouses and new developments of *Wapping Pierhead*, a small and elegant oasis of Georgian houses stands with a *Custom House* around the grass of the filled-in dock, flanked by a laden fig tree. It is quite in keeping with this vague air of unreality that number 4½ is found between 6 and 7.

Nearby and next to *Wapping Old Stairs* is *The Town of Ramsgate* pub, where Judge Jeffries was caught, and convicts were held in chains in the cellar before being shipped to Australia. Outside on the terrace is a gallows, a reminder of neighbouring *Execution Dock*, where pirates were hanged in chains until three tides had washed over them. Across the road is a discarded church and a ruined school with the sign 'Infants' still discernible over the doorway. Further along *Wapping Wall* is Wapping Station, where the *Thames Tunnel* was the first to be driven under the river. It opened for public traffic in 1843, and was used as a foot tunnel until the advent of the Tube. Keep going eastwards, past the picturesque but tourist-packed *Prospect of Whitby* pub, to

Limehouse. Full of interest to all lovers of good Chinese food, it still retains a distinctive flavour of its once-numerous Chinese population.

The *Isle of Dogs* is like another world. There are bizarre images: windsurfing on the *Millwall Docks*, the jewel-brilliant sails highlighted against the background of recently arrived new developments. All sense of direction is swiftly lost as one comes across some tastefully restored complex like *Cannon Workshops*, now homes for small businesses. *Canary Wharf* has a growing collection of old ships and a *Museum of Dockland* is planned. Off Pier Street is the *Mudchute Farm*, with sheep and cows in a big, breezy, open stretch of land. And there is a history trail for the Isle of Dogs, available at the fine old *Dockmaster's House* in West India Dock Road.

At the very foot of the Isle of Dogs are the *Island Gardens*. The glass-domed building is the entrance to the *foot tunnel* under the Thames with a wood-panelled lift going down to the white-tiled passage. It comes out on the other side near the *Cutty Sark*, a perfect starting place for an exploration of *Greenwich Park* with the *Ranger's House*, where the Earl of Chesterfield wrote improving letters to his son in the 18th century, and *Vanbrugh's Castle* with its turrets and towers. Vanbrugh called it his 'Bastille', having been imprisoned for suspected spying in the real one.

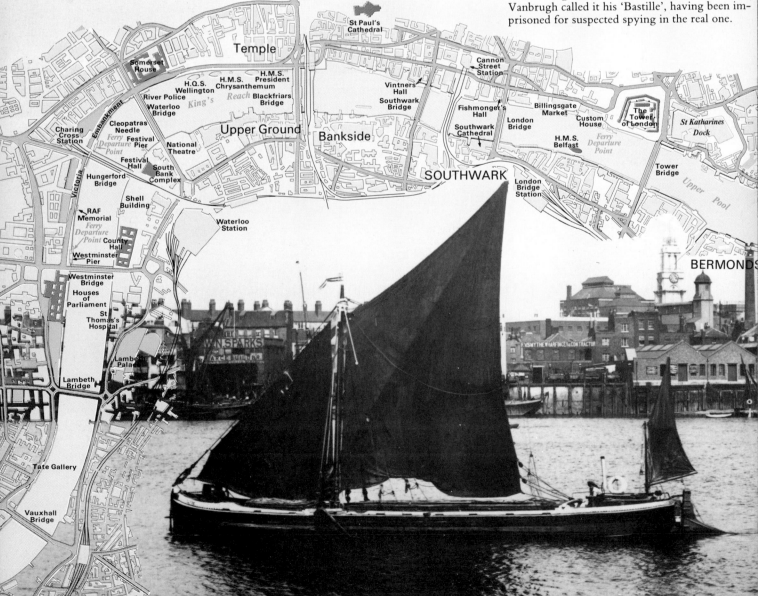

The south side of the river also has its sad decay, but there are hints of a grand past, like *St Mary's Church* in Rotherhithe. Nearby on the wall of a charity school are the two coloured figures of a boy and a girl. Rotherhithe has links with the Pilgrim Fathers who set sail for America in the *Mayflower*, hence the riverside pub of the same name round the corner. Just across the road is the *Rotherhithe Picture Research Library*, where scrapbooks of pictures on most subjects but especially costume and architecture, can be examined in a converted warehouse; while *sculptures* in massively thick rope overlook the river from a terrace by the pub. In *Bermondsey* are the riverside alleys and passageways needing just an old peasouper to conjure up images of Dickens. *Nancy's Steps*, just west of Southwark Bridge, is the scene of the grisly murder in *Oliver Twist*. Southwark has London's only galleried inn, the *George*, at 71 Borough High Street, which was a resting place for pilgrims; but rather more surprising in its setting is *Southwark Cathedral*, tucked away in all its Gothic glory between London Bridge and the fruit and vegetables of Borough Wholesale Market. Not far away is *Clink Street*, which once had a prison. Only the term 'in the clink' survives. Across the road is St Thomas's Street, and at 9a Cathedral Office is a most dreadful or delightful discovery, depending on taste: *St Thomas's Operating Theatre and Herb Garret*. Built in the garret of St Thomas's Church, because operating theatres had to be high up to catch the best light, it was linked with the surgical ward of the next door women's hospital — but was lost to the world when St Thomas's Hospital moved out of Southwark in 1865, and next door became a post office. Not until 1954 did Guy's Hospital surgeon Lord Brock rediscover the 19th-century operating theatre practically intact. It can now be

ST THOMAS'S *unique operating theatre*

VAUXHALL BRIDGE *One of eight statues representing the Arts and Sciences, holding what watermen call 'Little St Pauls on the water'*

seen on Monday, Wednesday and Friday afternoons along with the apothecary's garret.

One of the last bear baiting rings was along the river, and here at 1 Bear Gardens is the tiny *Bear Gardens Museum*. Despite a giant bear inside, it is mainly devoted to the story of the Shakespearean stage and has a small theatre upstairs. This part of town, called Bankside, was once both fashionable and risqué, out of reach of City jurisdiction and popular for gardens and theatres — including the Globe. Fine houses include *Cardinal's Wharf* (once a brothel) and the *Provost's Lodging*, now the home of the Provost of Southwark Cathedral.

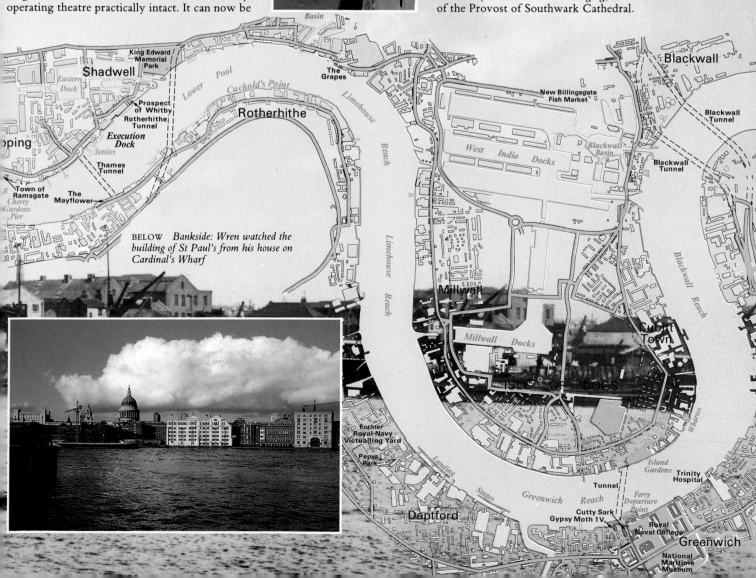

BELOW *Bankside: Wren watched the building of St Paul's from his house on Cardinal's Wharf*

WIMBLEDON (right)   The windmill, on the common where highwaymen and duellists used to lurk

CRYSTAL PALACE (below)
A dinner party was once held in
the largest monster

London — Out of Centre

*All around the heart of London is a galaxy of former villages and once-rural suburbs, all
long since overtaken, but not submerged, by the greedily expanding capital. Some of the
most interesting can be traced in two looping arcs running from east to west, south of the
Thames, and returning from west to east, on its north bank*

L ONDON: BY
WATER — On the
Thames, there are ex-
cursions to **Greenwich** or the
Thames Barrier in one
direction, and to Hampton
Court or **Kew** in the other:
contact the London Tourist
Board. Public transport across
the river survives at the — free
— Woolwich car ferry, and in
summer rowing boat ferries ply
for hire on the Kew-Petersham
stretch of the river.

The River Wandle can be
explored from **Wandsworth**
to Waddon Ponds, with the
remains of mills and manor
houses to be seen. It once
powered 90 watermills in its
11-mile course.

The Lea, scene of Isaak
Walton's 'Compleat Angler',
still has working barges around
Bromley-by-Bow. The New
River is a duck-populated
retreat in **Canonbury**.

The canals of London offer
towpath walking and narrow
boat rides. Contact the Inland
Waterways Association for
information on excursions.

The towpath of the Regents
Canal, part of the Grand
Union system, can be walked
from Limehouse to Paddington
and beyond, with a short break
at Islington, where it goes
through a tunnel.

S TARTING just south of Greenwich, the
green expanse of *Blackheath* (where a dis-
illusioned Henry VIII met Anne of Cleves
for the first time) is riddled underneath by
passageways and caves (ex-mines) — and ringed
by good Georgian houses. *Nunhead* has an
extremely eerie cemetery — a wildlife-rich forest
(now run as a nature reserve) with tombstones
leaning out of the undergrowth. A totem pole
stands outside the *Horniman Museum* in *Forest Hill*.
The eccentric towered building houses a delightfully idiosyncratic collection from musical instruments to an aquarium and an Indian sand
painting, given to London by Horniman, the tea
millionaire. Fake but lifesize prehistoric monsters
lurk in the *Crystal Palace Park*; *Dulwich Woods* and
Sydenham Hill Woods are genuinely ancient. *College
Road*, Dulwich, leads through London's only
working tollgate, in between the charming *Pond
Cottages* and the imposing pile of *Dulwich College*,
where Shackleton went to school, to the *Dulwich
Picture Gallery* and *Mausoleum*. It houses a collection of pictures started by Elizabethan actor
Thomas Alleyn, and the tombs of the Desenfans,
who expanded it to include pictures by
Rembrandt, Rubens and many other great artists
(it has been the target of burglars). Sir John Soane
designed the mausoleum with wonderful yellow
lighting. *Dulwich* itself was Alleyn's creation —
he developed the land and it clings to its exclusive ancestry with some success.

Brixton has a lively market, bright with yams
and other Caribbean exotica. It is also where Van
Gogh came to stay in 1872 and fell in love with
the daughter of the household. Conyers Road,
Streatham, has a pumping station built to look like
a mosque.

The *Surrey Light Railway*, drawn by horses, ran
through *Wandsworth* and Isaac Walton praised the
fishing in the *Wandle River*. *Wimbledon* has the
Lawn Tennis Museum, of course, at the *All England
Club* in Church Road. But it also has a *windmill*
on *Wimbledon Common* and the *Polka Children's
Theatre* which has an exhibition of toys and
puppets. *Southside House* on the edge of the
Common has been in the same family for three
centuries (descendants of the Scarlet Pimperne!)
and is open to visitors in winter. Emma Hamilton
sang from a special platform in the music room.

A very pretty and rural riverside walk can be
taken from *Kew* to *Hampton Court*. As well as the
Royal Botanic Gardens, Kew also has a fine
pumping station, in action at weekends. *Petersham*
has meadows, a farm and a pretty little church.
At *Twickenham*, larger than life-size stone nymphs
clamber in gay abandon over a fountain in *York
House Gardens*.

Returning eastwards, an ex-church at 368 High
Street, *Brentford*, is the home of the *Musical
Museum*, open on summer weekend afternoons,
with 200 self-playing instruments, from pianos to
musical boxes. Close to Lord Burlington's
Chiswick House lived the scourge of
Burlington's circle, William Hogarth: *Hogarth
House* in Hogarth Lane still has the mulberry tree
from which his wife made tarts for the foundling
hospital where he chose his models. In *Chiswick
Mall* is *Walpole House*, home of Barbara Villiers,
'fairest and lewdest of the royal concubines of
Charles II'. It runs into *Hammersmith Mall*, where
William Morris named *Kelmscott House* after his
Cotswolds home, and a previous resident, Sir
Francis Ronalds, laid miles of cables in the garden
to invent the electric telegraph. *Holland Park* in
the 19th century became the home of artists like
Lord Leighton — his *Leighton House* in Holland
Park Road can be visited and has a beautiful Arab
Hall. William Burges designed and lived in *Tower
House*, nearby in Melbury Road; later Holman
Hunt lived here. *Hippodrome Place* in *Notting Hill*
marks the site of a former race course.

High and fresh-aired Hampstead has very
attractive streets to explore, and the glorious
rolling acres of *Hampstead Heath*, which owes

100

HOLLAND PARK *was a private garden less than 40 years ago*

some of its nooks and dells to quarrying by an owner who wanted to develop the land. The *Admiral's House* in Admiral's Walk is an astonishing white mansion with more than a hint of ship about it and a bridge-like balcony from which the owner used to fire a cannon. Galsworthy finished the *Forsyte Saga* next door. *Fenton House* in Hampstead Grove is a late 17th-century merchant's house with a superb collection of musical instruments.

The new part of *Highgate Cemetery* is much visited for the tomb of Marx, but far more atmospheric is the old part — featured in Bram Stoker's *Dracula*, where monuments lean crazily in a near jungle. Legend says that Francis Bacon experimented with the preserving properties of cold by burying a dead chicken in snow on *Highgate Hill*. It remained fresh, Bacon caught a chill and died. Highgate's *Holly Lodge Estate* is a characterful Victorian Gothic enclave built by Baroness Burdett Coutts for workers; on North Hill are *Highpoints 1* and *2*, revolutionary 'point' blocks of flats designed by Lubetkin and Tecton, which influenced a generation of architects.

On the corner of Hanley Road and Crouch Hill in *Crouch End* is the former *Friern Manor Dairy*, with delicate frescoes portraying the stages of getting milk from cow to consumer. *Islington* has puppets at the *Little Angel Marionette Theatre* in Dagmar Passage. The *King's Head* pub in Upper Street (with theatre at the back) still charges pounds, shillings and pence for drinks (but accepts decimal coins). At *Canonbury Gardens* the New River appears — it was built by Lord Myddleton to bring fresh Hertfordshire water 14 miles into London. In Canonbury Place is *Canonbury Tower*, all that is left of the 16th-century residence of the priors of St Bartholomew's and now part of a theatre. *Stoke Newington* has a castle on Green Lanes — actually a pumping station modelled on Stirling Castle — and eerie avenues of monuments in *Abney Park Cemetery*. In Stoke Newington High Street, close to *Clissold Park* with its rabbits and deer, is the rare Elizabethan *Church of St Mary*. Kingsland Road in *Hackney* is the home of *F. Cooke and Sons'* eel and pie shop, founded in 1910. The third generation is now serving *the* London dish of eels or meat pie and mashed potato, covered with parsley sauce, in ornate surroundings.

A detour can be taken northwards over *Hackney Marshes*, with an amazing concentration of football pitches, and *Walthamstow*, with one of Europe's longest street markets. A. V. Roe made Britain's first powered flight in a triplane nearby. In the heart of Walthamstow's not over-beautiful streets is *Walthamstow Village* — a conservation area with a Tudor half-timbered manor house,

known as the *Ancient House*, and the *Vestry House Museum* in the old parish workhouse. It claims to have the first British internal combustion engine car — the *Bremer car*, of 1892. William Morris's childhood home in Blackhorse Road is now the *William Morris Gallery*. Cattle grids at the busy roundabout of the A503 and A104 indicate an early stretch of *Epping Forest*, East London's 6000-acre breathing space, where farmers let cattle wander free.

South-east from Hackney is *Bow*, where every Good Friday the *Widow's Son* pub in Devon Road adds another hot cross bun to its mouldering collection, said to have been started by a widow, who kept aside a bun, year after year, for her lost sailor son, expected home in time for Easter. *Abbey Mills Pumping Station* in Bisson Road, *West Ham*, is a glorious Victorian extravaganza which flourishes a wealth of wrought iron. Visits are by appointment. Locomotives and a reconstructed period waiting room bring colour to Docklands at the *North Woolwich Station Museum*. The *Woolwich Ferry* is a pleasant (and free) way to cross the river to *Woolwich*, depositing cars, cyclists and pedestrians near the glittering *Thames Flood Barrier*. The *Museum of Artillery* is in the *Rotunda*, John Nash's tent-like design. Oddly eerie *Maryon Park* was the setting for the 1960s' murder mystery film *Blow Up*. And so back to Greenwich . . .

HAMPSTEAD *(above)* The shipshape Admiral's House
BOW *(left)* Old hot cross buns at the Widow's Son

LONDON: BY LAND — *The best way to explore is on foot (or by bicycle). For guided theme walks, see London magazines like 'Time Out'. Walks can sometimes be designed to order.*

For the best view of architectural details, take a double-decker bus (top deck).

London Transport organises sight-seeing tours on old-fashioned open-topped buses, and the bright yellow Culture Bus stops at culture spots.

The Underground isn't always: it goes up and out as far as rural Amersham in the north-west, and eastwards through Epping Forest to Ongar (those markers by every track measure the distance to Ongar). The overground North London Line wanders from **Richmond** *to* **Woolwich***, through wildflower-rich wastes with backyard glimpses of life.*

A disused railway makes a fine walk from Finsbury Park to Alexandra Palace, through **Crouch End***. A grassy bank (actually over the Northern Outfall Sewer) makes another rural-feeling walk, from Stratford to near Becton.*

UNDERNEATH LONDON

A tram-ride through the Kingsway Subway at the age of five sparked off Nigel Pennick's lifelong interest in underground technology and lore. Here he reveals the intricate but unseen world below the streets of London

Beneath the streets of every great metropolis there lies another city, a honeycomb of structures and tunnels as vital as it is unseen. But nowhere has the complexity of the underworld that lies hidden under London — and goes almost wholly unnoticed by surface folk, except when making forays into the Underground.

There are church crypts and house cellars, which have existed as long as there have been churches and houses. There are artificial caves, like Jack Cade's Cavern in Blackheath, ex-chalk mines which have occasionally subsided (they swallowed a horse in 1798) and were such a notorious haunt of gamblers, prostitutes and pleasure-seekers that the authorities sealed them up in 1835. And there are secret passage stories, like the subterranean link from Sweeney Todd's salon to the pie-shop on the other side of St Dunstan in the West.

But the true subterranean network dates from the 18th century and later. London has — or had — numerous brooks and rivers flowing into the Thames, the biggest being the Fleet River, also known as the River of Wells, the Old Bourne or Holborn. Placenames recall it — Fleet Street, Holborn — and the springs and ditches that fed it — Sadler's Wells,

Lamb's Conduit, Chadwell and Clerkenwell. All have long since been put into pipes or arched over, but years ago they attracted health seekers. Sadler's Wells Theatre began as a spa and playhouse (with water shows on stage) and Bragnigge Wells, enclosed in a 'Grecian temple', sold water at 3d a glass or 8d a gallon, in the midst of trees and fountains. The Fleet itself was quite big, navigable until the Middle Ages as far as Holborn Bridge, but its condition became so foul that in 1732 it was covered over by Act of Parliament. Finally, in the 19th century, it was incorporated ignominiously into the newly built, much needed and still used main sewer system of London. But it has a claim to fame: it is said to support a herd of wild pigs living under Fleet Street. Like the alligators of the New York sewers, they probably belong to the rich underground mythology that can be found in modern cities.

Tyburn, the infamous place of execution now marked by the Marble Arch near Hyde Park, was named after another vanished London river, and the district of Bayswater recalls a stream which became the Ranelagh Sewer when it was put underground. Little evidence of this watery London remains on the

RAT-CATCHER *(above) at work in the sewers*

PNEUMATIC DESPATCH TUBE *(below)*
Opening Day at Holborn, 1865 — this early tube usually took mail, not people, but a lady is said to have been sucked down the line

POST OFFICE RAILWAY *(left)* *A pictorial map of 1926 shows its route between the sorting office and railway stations*

THAMES TUNNEL *An accident in January 1828 (top) and other difficulties beset Brunel, but when opened in 1843, the tunnel was visited as the 'Eighth Wonder of the World' (above)*

surface, but the cast iron conduit carrying the Westbourne can be seen above the platforms and tracks at Sloane Square Underground Station, and Effra Brook can be traced in the outline of the Kennington Oval cricket ground.

London also has its underground roads. Telephone engineers are said to cycle along the miles of the London Subway System (not an underground railway), the largest in the world, which was built to avoid constant digging by rival utility companies. As early as 1768 the Adam brothers had built underground service roads for their luxurious Adelphi development, and the idea was taken up all over London after 1860, with every street improvement including an underground passage big enough to walk in, reached by manholes and with gratings for ventilation. Major subways were built for the Holborn Viaduct, Victoria Embankment and Kingsway projects, and they remain valuable today.

In January 1863, the world's first underground railway opened. It still runs, as part of a much larger system, between King's Cross and Paddington via Baker Street (where the original platform area has been restored). A lady in a crinoline is said to have been sucked along the first 'tube' railway (1863), which carried mail from Euston Station to the District Post Office in Eversholt Street. It was a cast-iron, 30-inch diameter tube, through which a rail vehicle was sucked or blown by a large steam-driven fan — the 'pneumatic' system. By the 1870s the line ran between Euston and High Holborn, via Drummond Street, Hampstead Road, Tottenham Court Road and Broad Street St Giles. In 1874 it was extended to the General Post Office in St Martin Le Grand — but the whole system was abandoned as unreliable soon afterwards. The tunnels still remain: electricity companies used them illegally after they were closed, for power lines, and there was a big gas explosion in one at Holborn in 1928.

Lying abandoned, too, is the brick-lined pneumatic rail tunnel, twelve feet nine inches in diameter, some six yards beneath Great Scotland Yard near Whitehall. It was meant to go to Waterloo but the company ran out of money when they reached the Thames.

The first modern underwater tunnel, the Thames Tunnel from Wapping to

UNDERNEATH LONDON

Rotherhithe, was hailed as the 'Eighth Wonder of the World' when engineered by Sir Marc Brunel and his son Isambard, between 1825 and 1843. Intended for road vehicles and pedestrians, and now carrying the East London tube line, it was a financial disaster but was recognised as a brilliant engineering success — and was soon followed by several more.

The first true tube railway, using pre-fabricated cast-iron tunnel segments, also went under the Thames, from Tower Hill to Pickle Herring Wharf: like the Thames Tunnel, the 'Tower Subway' was more successful in engineering terms than financially. It became a pedestrian toll tunnel, and closed with the opening in 1895 of Tower Bridge, which was free. The London Hydraulic Power Company ran high pressure water mains through it until 1977, when the hydraulic mains network closed, and the entire system, including the Tower Subway, was sold to a cable telecommunications company.

But the success of the actual tunnelling of the Tower Subway led to the world's first electrical tube railway in 1890, the

CENTRAL LONDON RAILWAY *(above)*
Twopenny and threepenny tickets — the 'Twopenny Tube' from Bank to White City had flat rate fares

BAKER STREET *(below)*   *looks the same today*

City and South London from Stockwell to King William Street in the City. Boom years for tubes followed from 1898 to 1907, when the core of the present 'London Underground' was laid down. Leslie Green designed the original, Arts-and-Crafts style, ruby red-tiled stations of the present Northern, Piccadilly and Bakerloo lines. Notable surviving surface buildings of stations that closed in the 1920s and 1930s include Brompton Road, South Kentish Town, York Road and British Museum (and the tradition of striking design was continued under the aegis of Frank Pick). One station never opened: Bull and Bush, which was built between Hampstead and Golders Green on the Northern Line, but not connected to the surface for passengers.

Like the underground railways of Berlin, Paris and New York, the London Underground has acquired its own folklore with impressive speed. Covent Garden Station has a ghost who can be seen mounting the spiral emergency stairs but has always vanished at the top; the murdered actor William Terris catches his

train home from here. Tunnellers who inexplicably abandoned an extension to Lothbury from Moorgate in 1904 are said to have seen a phantom and fled (this was also the site of an all-too-real tragic accident in the 1970s) and a similar tale is told of the much more recent Victoria Line near Pimlico. Believers suggest that the spirits of the plague pits are responsible — the theory is not tenable if only because Tube lines go too deep, although a curve on the Piccadilly Line near Brompton Oratory is said to be due to such a cause.

Better documented is the role of the Underground in World War II. The City and South London had been extended to Moorgate in 1900, which meant that tunnels north of Borough Station were abandoned — but at the beginning of the war, the under-river section was sealed with concrete plugs and the section in Southwark was converted into a municipal air raid shelter for 14,000 people. The northern section was used privately and later became a repository for important documents. The Aldwych

Line was used to store the Elgin Marbles and other treasures in World War I; in World War II it became a shelter. The former station at Down Street, between Green Park and Hyde Park Corner on the Piccadilly Line, was converted into a bunker for the Railway Executive, in charge of wartime railway operations. Brick walls were built along the edge of each platform, with underground offices and eating and sleeping rooms on the platforms and in the tunnels. At the station entrance, a concrete shield four feet thick was built over the lift shaft to prevent bomb penetration, and ventilation fans and gasproof doors were installed. The brick walls for similar conversions can still be seen at British Museum (between Holborn and Tottenham Court Road on the Central Line), York Road (between King's Cross and Caledonian Road on the Piccadilly Line), City Road (on the City branch of the Northern Line) and Brompton Road (between Knightsbridge and South Kensington on the Piccadilly Line). Tube pioneer Harley Dalrymple-Hay was called out of retirement to build tunnels between the government offices in Whitehall in 1939.

In late 1940, a unique series of ten deep shelters was planned for government employees in case of mass bombing, or chemical or biological warfare. Sited in places where the tunnels could be used after the war for new express railways, eight were completed under the stations at Clapham South, Clapham Common, Clapham North, Stockwell, Goodge Street, Camden Town, Belsize Park and Chancery Lane. The most notable use was at Goodge Street, where the shelter was General Eisenhower's command post for D-Day. Later, and until a major fire in 1956, it was used as an army transit camp: bunks here have graffiti showing name and rank or simply 'Kilroy was here'. Eventually all the shelters were used by the public or as military barracks. They had twin tunnels, sixteen feet six inches across and twelve hundred feet long, and were divided into two floors. Side tunnels provided medical and cooking facilities, two shafts took stairs and lifts to the surface, and a stairway led to the tube station above. The concrete block-houses protecting the shaftheads can still be found near Belsize Park Sstation, on Tottenham Court Road north of Goodge Street Station and in nearby

Chenies Street, and at several places along Clapham Road. The entrances to the Chancery Lane shelter are in Furnival Street, off High Holborn. It became a telephone exchange after the war and operated until 1982. This one and the others are now either empty or used for storage of security archives as at Camden Town and Belsize Park.

A long barred-off ramp with rails close to Holborn Station, and a pair of doors on the Victoria Embankment under Waterloo Bridge, lead into Britain's only tram tunnel. The Kingsway Tramway Subway was open for traffic from 1905 to 1952. Unsuspecting motorists who drove in were forced by trams to go all the way through and several stunts among the trams were done by motorists for bets. The Subway forms a section of the underpass from Waterloo Bridge to Kingsway, and the rest is used for storage.

New ways are constantly being driven under London for 'cable runs' and other uses; old ways are constantly being put to new uses. Even those that have become obsolete can survive intact because they are forgotten and unseen by most of the world. Such places provide a fascinating source of study.

NIGEL PENNICK has been interested in underground structures since childhood. His books include 'Tunnels Under London', 'Early Tube Railways of London' and 'The Subterranean Kingdom'. He lives near Cambridge.

OSPRINGE: MAISON DIEU

OSPRINGE: MAISON DIEU — *The Maison Dieu at* **Ospringe** *would once have provided shelter for pilgrims on the way to* **Canterbury**.

It shows the link between the words 'hotel' and 'hospital': whereas the rich stayed in monasteries, and messengers, packhorsemen and the like could at least afford roadside inns, the poorer pilgrims were more likely to find lodging at 'hospitals' like the Maison Dieu, providing shelter, for the first two nights free of charge. Many would have been infirm, seeking cures at the saint's shrine they had come to visit.

Hostelries also grew up in the precincts of abbeys and cathedrals, and just outside the walls of towns, because the gates would be shut from nightfall until dawn. Some inns that came into being this way are the George, Glastonbury, the Falstaff, **Canterbury**, *the Star, Alfriston, the New Inn,* **Gloucester**, *the Angel, Grantham, the George,* **Norton St Philip**, *and the Bell, Tewkesbury.*

Ospringe's Maison Dieu is now maintained as a museum, with many Romano-British exhibits — the wealth of finds around here has led to speculation that this was the site of the lost Roman town of Durolevum. Other exhibits relate to the gunpowder industry of nearby Faversham — Defoe recalled an explosion at one powder mill in the early 1700s, a disaster which was repeated in 1917.

Martin

Hampshire   SU 0619

Take the lane westwards by the old village pump to arrive, after about half a mile, at Martin Down, a National Nature Reserve. It is a great sweep of ancient downland, complete with prehistoric earthworks and burial places; its flowers are superb, and so are the butterflies which feed on them. Some of the flowers are rare.

The village itself, on the far western border of Hampshire, and strung out along one long street, has many cottages which repay more than a cursory glance, since their architectural detail is often delightful.

Meon Valley

Hampshire   SU 6017

Of all Hampshire's lovely valleys, this is one of the most rewarding. The best bits are in the upper valley, along the A32. Start at West Meon: it has lots of half-timbered cottages, and an atmosphere that makes you feel you have stepped back in time at least 30 years. A detour along a leafy lane leads to the surprises of East Meon. Here, tucked into the folds of the downs, is an immaculate village with many substantial Georgian houses, all overlooked by a church with a massive tower. Continue south on the A32 through Warnford and Exton (both with buildings and churches of interest), to Corhampton, which has something very special indeed. Almost hidden by trees is a tiny, complete Saxon church. Many Saxon details can be seen, including the Saxons' characteristic 'long and short' stonework at the corners; inside is more evidence of Saxon work and a quaint assembly of furniture and fittings from many periods. Just across the stream is Meonstoke Church, with a timber top to its tower.

The last village in the upper valley is Droxford, with a church worth exploring for Norman details such as the zig-zag patterning of some of the stonework. The village is mostly Georgian, although there are earlier cottages.

Minsden Chapel

Hertfordshire   TL 1924

Though ruined from at least 1650, this 14th-century hilltop chapel had weddings celebrated within its walls up to the early 1800s, and there are numerous stories of illegal preachings here. Reports of hauntings include a ghostly Pan and a tolling bell, and in 1908 a spectral monk was actually captured on film. The historian Reginald Hine, who committed suicide in 1949 by jumping off a platform at Hitchin station, had his ashes scattered among the ruins. His cracked memorial plaque, and the numerous dead elms that form a backdrop for the broken outline of the chapel walls, contribute to the overpowering melancholy of this lonely, eerie place.

Nailbourne Valley

Kent   TR 1744

Flowing for some 15 miles through attractive and often quiet villages, the Nail Bourne is one of Kent's numerous 'intermittent' streams — streams which vanish and reappear. Starting at Lyminge (or very occasionally at Etchinghill), the Nail Bourne runs past Elham to Barham. Past Bridge it flows by Patrixbourne to Littlebourne, where it flows normally, as the Little Stour.

The Nail Bourne is the longest of the intermittent streams. Called 'nail bournes' or 'woe waters' (because their sudden reappearance can cause flood damage), they have attracted colourful explanations, often involving struggles between Christianity and pagan gods. Even geologists disagree about the phenomenon, but the most popular theory is that the chalk simply absorbs water until it is saturated, when the water is 'squeezed' out along the dry stream bed.

Nettleden

Hertfordshire   TL 0210

A tiny, hidden place of mainly 17th-century cottages, it nestles in a wooded crease of the Chilterns. Hellebore and bryony flourish in the shade of St Lawrence's Church, which is mainly brick of 1811 with puddingstone 'markers' and a moss-lined stone coffin close by.

Go past the lattice-paned Church House for narrow Spooky Lane (unsuitable for cars). It slices through the hill to Frithsdean by means of a sheer-sided cutting, which the Duke of Bridgewater's men faced with flint and brick early in the 19th century. Ascending or descending this lane is an eerie and dreamlike experience, even in broad daylight.

Newbury

Berkshire   SU 4767

The pride of the town museum (a 17th-century Cloth Hall) is the Throckmorton Coat. This was made for a bet: Sir John Throckmorton wagered that clothier George Coxeter could not turn the wool that was on the sheep's back in the morning into a coat for Sir John's back within the day. The task took place in 1811 and the time taken for shearing, spinning, weaving, cutting, fitting and tailoring was 13 hours and 11 minutes, after which Sir John wore the coat to dinner.

St Nicholas' Church was built by one of the town's great cloth merchants, Jack Winchcombe, called Jack o'Newbury, who became eminent enough to entertain Henry VIII and Catherine of Aragon at his house. The town was the scene of two fierce battles between King and Parliament during the Civil War, and the results of the conflict can be viewed at the splendid ruins of Donnington Castle, two miles to the north.

Ockley

Surrey   TQ 1440

Deep in the Wealden forest, Okewood Chapel (south-west of Ockley) was built around 1220 for those 'whiche dwell very ffar distant from ye parryshe churches'. It was clearly popular, for when in the mid-16th century the chapel was suppressed, two petitions were presented at Westminster by local yeomen, pleading for its restoration. Earlier, Edward de la Hale had endowed the chapel, after his son had been miraculously saved by an arrow from an unknown source, which killed a wild boar just as it was about to gore him.

Four bridlepaths still converge at the grassy mound, rimmed by a brook, on which the church stands. Today the forest is less dense, and oak has been joined by beech and ash, but there can be few more remote parts of Surrey.

Old Basing

Hampshire SU 6652

In its heyday, Basing House was the largest private residence in the country. Queen Elizabeth I was entertained there for three days by the Marquis of Winchester, a stay which cost so much that he had to demolish part of the house to pay for the visit. In the next century, Cromwell really did 'knock the house about a bit' during the Civil War, after it had withstood a siege of three years, and the locals completed the damage by taking bricks to rebuild cottages demolished during frequent bombardments. Ruins and cottages can still be admired.

Old Basing's huge church was used by the Roundhead cavalry as a stable, and had all its 'popish' images destroyed, except for the statue of the Virgin Mary over the west door (it was hidden by ivy). Somehow the 16th-century brick-built tithe barn survived the siege.

Old Soar Manor

Kent TQ 6154

Old Soar is a remote 13th-century manor house, partly incorporated into an attractive 18th-century red-brick farmhouse, with a solar or private living room, chapel and garderobe (lavatory). All these are on the first floor — probably to lessen the risks from the damp, vermin or enemies. Owned by the National Trust, Old Soar has a permanent exhibition on the history of the Manor and the surrounding countryside.

Olney

Buckinghamshire SP 8851

Amazing Grace was one of the so-called Olney Hymns written by the rector John Newton and William Cowper, the poet. Cowper came to live at Olney in 1757 and spent the last 20 years of his life here. His house is now a Cowper museum.

The village is a pleasant place by the placid River Ouse, with many fine 18th-century listed buildings lining the High Street, and a good

church. Today, it is the scene of a notable Shrove Tuesday Pancake Race, traditionally open only to local women aged over 16 and wearing head-scarves, but now run in competition with the ladies of Liberal, Kansas, USA.

Ospringe

Kent TR 0060

Kentish writers disagree about the age of the Maison Dieu at Ospringe but it clearly has a long history. It seems likely that Henry III founded a large monastic hospital, the Hospital of St Mary, or 'Dormus Dei', on this site between 1230 and 1239. Pilgrims on their way to Canterbury could lodge here, and there was provision for the care of lepers. A room was set aside for the monarch, and various royal personages are recorded as having stayed — including Richard II (twice) and John of France, who left rich presents in 1360. The timber-framed hall may have been built after the Dissolution of the Monasteries, and is now a museum with many Romano-British exhibits.

Ot Moor

Oxfordshire SP 5714

A slightly sinister sense of primitive isolation makes Ot Moor one of the strangest rural landscapes in the county. Six square miles of bleak and marshy farmland, accessible only from two tracks (one of them a Roman road), it is astonishingly rich in water lilies, wild flowers and butterflies, with yellowhammers, lapwings, reed buntings and corn buntings among its rich bird life.

Inevitably in so desolate a region, the military has made its presence felt. There is a shooting range on the moor and to the north-east are the huge storage depots of Arncott and Graven Hill, a vast and impenetrable secret world fed by miles of private railway line. Minor roads off the B4011 allow access for train spotters.

OLD BASING *Members of the Sealed Knot Society enact scenes from the siege which led to the destruction of Basing House*

OT MOOR: A PIECE OF THE PAST — *The wilderness of Ot Moor is a unique and exciting survivor in this highly cultivated area of east Oxfordshire, for it shows what much of England would have looked like perhaps two centuries ago.*

A bowl-shaped tract of land with many streams, it was originally wetland, and has been only partly reclaimed. Tall trees have grown up in the old hedge-rows, and the drainage ditches have become as wide as small rivers, producing a habitat that can support a rich variety of butterflies and other insects, birds and water-loving plants. Nightingales may be heard in the patches of woodland.

An attempt in the early 1980s to build a motorway across the moor was foiled by the determined resistance of Friends of the Earth, who sold small tracts of the land to members of their society all over the world, making a compulsory purchase order impossible.

YELLOW FLAG IRIS *Also known as the sword flag — one of the plants found on Ot Moor*

OUTWOOD: WIND-MILLS — *Windmills have featured in England's landscape since the 12th century: one of the oldest surviving examples is at* **Outwood**. *In certain areas of the country, they must have dominated the skyline: the post mill at* **Wrawby** *is a lonely survivor from Lincolnshire's 800 mills.*

Post mills such as this are supported on a huge post around which the wooden body, carrying the sails, is turned to face the wind. Smock mills represent the next stage in design and the one at **Lacey Green** *is the oldest in existence. Built at Chesham in about 1650, it was moved to its present site in 1814. The invention of a rotating cap to which the sails were fixed meant that they were much easier to manipulate. Instead of the rectangular shape of the post mill, a circular pattern was adopted, with a framework of strong posts tapering towards each other to make the characteristic conical shape of this type of mill. Its resemblance to a countryman in his smock gave rise to the name, with its variant of 'frock' mill. Despite their vulnerability to weather, smock mills continued to be popular.*

Tower mills, generally of the same design as smock mills, were larger and built of stone or brick. Handsome examples can be seen at Boston, Lincolnshire and Blackthorn, Oxfordshire. Unusual hybrid mills include the one on Wimbledon Common, **London**, *which is a post mill body on a smock tower.*

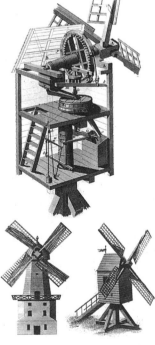

WINDMILLS *The cross section shows a post mill. Canvas sails were fixed to the wooden sail framework, and the rigging was changed with the wind's strength — as on a ship*

OUTWOOD *Villagers watched the Great Fire of London from the top of their post-mill. Staddle stones (foreground) were used to lift barns or hayricks away from mice and rats*

Outwood

Surrey TQ 3245

Outwood Common — National Trust land east of the village — used to feature two splendid windmills known as the Cat and the Kitten. The Cat has stood there since 1665 and is one of the oldest and best-preserved working post-mills in the country. For the past 200 years it has been worked by the Jupp family, using spring sails controlled by elliptical springs. This type of sail, invented in 1772, is composed of a series of shutters which can be adjusted according to the strength of the wind.

Unfortunately the Kitten, a late 19th-century smock mill which rivalled it, collapsed in 1960.

Oxford

Oxfordshire SP 5106

Architecturally, Oxford is extraordinarily rich. The medieval colleges are well known, as are the great buildings of the 17th and 18th centuries, such as Wren's Sheldonian Theatre and Gibbs' Radcliffe Camera. But some equally remarkable buildings are often missed. Iffley church, in a village now incorporated into Oxford's southern suburbs, is one of the best Norman buildings in the country, richly decorated. Among the colleges, William Butterfield's Keble College, with its vibrant polychrome brickwork and painted chapel, is a Victorian gem.

Even in the well-known colleges there are lesser-known features, for example fine stained glass from the medieval period, the Renaissance and the 19th century. A particular curiosity is the 18th-century glass designed by Sir Joshua Reynolds in New College chapel. Oxford is not known for its contemporary architecture, yet it boasts the Florey Building, an early design by James Stirling, the architect of the Tate Gallery extension, whose international fame now reaches far beyond this curious inverted pyramid hidden off the Headington road. St Mary's Church is familiar, but few bother to climb the tower to enjoy the view over the city centre.

Among museums, the Ashmolean and its varied treasures are justifiably popular, but Oxford can also tempt the visitor with a Museum of Modern Art, a Museum of Dolls' Houses and the University Museum, with its natural history collections and its splendid Victorian Gothic building, complete with wall paintings and John Ruskin associations.

Oxford's commercial, non-university side should not be forgotten. The factory where Frank Cooper's Oxford Marmalade was made is now used for other purposes, but there is a Frank Cooper marmalade shop and museum in the High. There is also the busy covered market which seems to have almost every cheese there is, and the occasional shark. On Wednesdays there is an open-air market.

But above all, Oxford is a city of waterways. Least known of all is Oxford's canal. Hidden among trees off Hythe Bridge Street is a quiet backwater, full of old narrowboats, with a graceful iron bridge and a lock leading into the Thames. A walk along the towpath reveals on one side the back gardens of dons and their families, who live in the genteel elegance of Oxford's northern suburbs, and on the other the wide expanse of Port Meadow, common land since Domesday Book, where horses roam.

OXFORD *A Bird of Paradise flower in the Botanic Gardens — an oasis of rare plants and trees laid out in 1621 (on top of a medieval cemetery) for the study of medicinal herbs*

Pamber

Hampshire   SU 6160

Some woodlands, forests and heaths have an other-worldly feel about them, and Pamber Forest is one of those. Mostly of oak woodland on acid soils, it still has the hallmarks of 'coppice and standard' management, practised in nearly all woods for hundreds of years. It both prolonged trees' lives and ensured a near-endless supply of wood, by a systematic cutting of new growth. Some of the massive oaks to be seen here are very old indeed.

Two miles south is Pamber Priory, embowered in trees and approached along a quiet lane. Still standing are the chancel of the priory church and the massive Norman crossing tower. Long, narrow lancet windows light the whitewashed interior, where a wooden knight nearly seven feet long lies with his feet resting on a lion. They have watched the sun slipping past the windows for something like 600 years.

Pangbourne

Berkshire   SU 6376

Those crossing the iron bridge which connects Pangbourne with Whitchurch must still pay a (very small) toll. This is one of England's few surviving privately owned toll bridges, and the right to toll has existed since 1792, when the ferry was replaced by the bridge.

Pangbourne takes its name from the little River Pang, which flows into the Thames at this point. Kenneth Grahame came to live here after writing the children's classic *The Wind in the Willows*. In the garden of his house, Church Cottage, is the old village lock-up, which he used as a tool shed. The village sign has an open book with willow trees as a memorial to Kenneth Grahame, and also shows a Viking longship with the figure of King Berhulf of Mercia, who owned the manor in the ninth century.

Petts Wood

Greater London   TQ 4467

The 1927 revision of the Ordnance Survey map (price 2/6) covering this area south of Bromley, where London sprawls into Kent, shows a great deal of woodland and open spaces, now remembered only in street names on the vast post-war St Paul's Cray estate. But one piece of the woodland, Petts Wood, was bought that year for the National Trust, by public subscription, to save it from such development. It still remains peaceful and remarkably unfrequented. Paths through the oaks and birches lead to a seat and a sundial, a memorial to William Willett, who devised British Summer Time.

Pleshey

Essex   TL 6614

'Alack, and what shall good old York here see,
But empty lodgings and unfurnished walls,
Unpeopled offices, untrodden stones . . .'
So Shakespeare has the Duke of Gloucester's widow bemoan the fall of 'Plashy' castle, and today it is emptier still (though open by appointment on summer weekends). Ancient Britons settled the site, hacking out a 40-acre enclosure; the Romans displaced them and added their own entrenchments; and the Saxons called it Tumblestoun, from the ancient mounds which were left.

The Normans in turn took over: today, the village, encircled by the massive Norman earthworks which formed their castle bailey, is most picturesque. A short walk to the castle mound, over the amazing 15th-century, single-span, brick bridge, brings a fine view of Essex farmland under a wide sky.

Quainton

Buckinghamshire   SP 7420

The chief attraction is the Quainton Railway Centre, which is open from Easter to October and contains a fine collection of vintage steam engines, some of which are 'in steam' on the last Sunday of every month.

Quainton lies on the North Bucks Way, and is a pretty place full of good pubs, while the parish church is exceptionally well endowed with large monuments and statues of the 17th and 18th centuries, including one to Richard Brett.

PANGBOURNE: THE WIND IN THE WILLOWS — *When Kenneth Grahame came to spend his last years at* **Pangbourne,** *he was returning to the sights and sounds of the river which had inspired one of the greatest of children's classics — 'The Wind in the Willows'.*

First published in 1908, and still the best known children's book after 'Alice in Wonderland', it has been especially acclaimed for its evocation of the English countryside around the Berkshire Thames, which runs like a thread through Grahame's own life.

Shortly after his mother's death in 1864, when he was five, he came to live with his grandmother at The Mount, Cookham Dean, close beside the Thames at the verge of what once had been Windsor Forest.

Though only there for three years, his time at The Mount seems to have been the happiest period of his childhood, to which he returned in imagination later as an escape from his uncongenial career at the Bank of England, and which provided material for his books 'The Golden Age' and 'Dream Days'.

When his own son Alistair, to whom 'The Wind in the Willows' was first told as an endless serial, was small, Grahame and his family lived at an old farmhouse known as Boham's in Blewbury, Oxfordshire — still not far from the Thames — and he died at Pangbourne.

ABOVE *The open road for Mole, Toad and Ratty — an illustration by Arthur Rackham for 'The Wind in the Willows': 'It was a golden afternoon; the smell of the dust they kicked up was rich and satisfying . . .'*

ROMNEY MARSH: SMUGGLERS —

Certain churches on **Romney Marsh** *are said to bear the smugglers' sign — a small ship painted on the wall to signify that the church was 'safe' for contraband.*

Smuggling became an efficiently organised, large-scale business in the 18th and 19th centuries, and look-outs were established along much of the coast (see also **Balcary Heughs**).

So widespread was resentment at high duties that whole communities were tacitly involved. As Kipling tells in his 'Smuggler's Song', there was 'brandy for the parson' (Parson Woodforde, the diarist of **Castle Cary**, *was not above receiving contraband) and 'baccy for the clerk'. In wartime, the French government encouraged the use of its ports by English 'free traders' (smugglers), in return for urgently needed gold and naval information: hence Kipling's line mentioning 'letters for a spy'.*

Certain customs officials (like, it is said, John Knill of **St Ives**) *were sympathetic to smugglers, or were even free traders themselves. At* **Theddlethorpe** *the customs officers may not have been so helpful, but at least they were easily seen over the flat Lincolnshire marshes.*

Notable among western England's innumerable smugglers' haunts is **Prussia Cove**; *in the south-east, a doctor from* **Brookland** *is said to have tended wounded smugglers.*

ST THOMAS BECKET CHURCH was built by an archbishop who fell into a ditch when crossing Romney Marsh, but was rescued after praying to St Thomas

Reading

Berkshire   SU 7173

The world's largest sculpted lion, weighing in at 16 tons, dominates the Forbury Gardens in the centre of town. Commemorating the Royal Berkshire Regiment's feat of arms at the Battle of Maiwand in the Afghan Wars, it was made in 1886 and is curious because the legs are wrong. If this lion ever moved, it would surely fall over.

Forbury Gardens were once part of Reading Abbey, founded by Henry I and destroyed by Henry VIII, who had the last abbot hanged at his own gate. The old gateway is almost all that remains of the ancient foundation. It was once a gathering place for English pilgrims bound for Santiago de Compostela in Spain, because it possessed one of Santiago's (St James's) hands, which was cut off at his execution and is still to be seen at Marlow.

England's earliest surviving part song, *Sumer is icumen in*, was composed here in about 1240 and is recalled by a tablet on the wall of the Chapter House. A less happy literary association is *The Ballad of Reading Gaol*, by Oscar Wilde, who did two years' hard labour in the town prison.

Reed

Hertfordshire   TL 3636

It is said that the Romans planned the 'gridiron' system of thoroughfares that distinguishes this spread-out hilltop village, but the only evidence is the site of a shrine among the woods towards Barkway. The medieval influence seems much stronger: there are three greens and six moated homestead sites, all concentrated in a tiny area and quite exceptional, even in this district of many moats.

The lonely church has a nave featuring Saxon 'long and short' stonework at the corners, and in the village's only pub, a weatherboarded gem, one can sit around a blazing fire in winter, gazing perhaps on to a High Street which can seldom see more than a dozen cars in a day.

Ringmer

East Sussex   TQ 4412

Commemorated on a local signpost is the name of what must have been Ringmer's most carefully watched resident, Timothy Tortoise. Timothy lived with Mrs Snooke, aunt of the 18th-century naturalist, Gilbert White, and was closely studied by White — indeed in 1780 Timothy travelled some 80 miles by post-chaise to join White at his own home in Selborne. The naturalist's appealing and astute observations of Timothy's life have been published, and Timothy's carapace is in the British Museum.

Rockbourne

Hampshire   SU 1118

Rockbourne is the archetypal pretty village, but it also has what few other villages boast — the remains of a sizeable Roman villa. The story goes — as such stories do — that it was first discovered by a farmer searching for a lost ferret. Subsequent digging revealed that the villa had nearly 50 rooms, and a treasure-house of Roman remains was uncovered, including a floor mosaic, coins and pottery. Many of the finds are displayed in a museum on the site.

Other testimonies to Rockbourne's past are its partly Norman church, a manor house with medieval chapel and barn, and several long barrows on the downs nearby.

Rollright Stones

Oxfordshire   SP 2930

Variously known as the King's Men, the Rollright Stones and by other, more local titles, this Bronze Age stone circle is the third most important monument of its kind in England, after Stonehenge and Avebury. Despite this, it is surprisingly little known. The circle, 100 feet across, stands in a field with magnificent views out over the Cotswolds and Oxfordshire, and

ROYSTON *The cave's strange, religious carvings may date from Anglo-Saxon times, but a popular theory is that they are the work of the Knights Templar*

across the road is a monolith, the King Stone. Standing on its own, encased in old iron railings in a grassy field, it looks like some caged beast in a zoo. A quarter of a mile away are the Whispering Knights, a set of upright stones that originally formed a chamber in a burial mound, long since disappeared. It is all very enjoyable, and the nearby village of Great Rollright is not bad either, with roses climbing over the stone walls and a handsome church which has some good carved details and a painted screen.

Romney Marsh

Kent TR 0429

The traveller passing down Appledore's lovely main street and over the Royal Military Canal still enters into an almost alien land. It has been said that the world is divided into Europe, Asia, Africa, America, Australasia — and Romney Marsh. Writers through the centuries, almost since the Romans first built the Rhee Wall and began the reclamation of the land from the sea, have tried to explain the fascination — and for some the dislike — of this large area of marshland. But the feel of the place can only be experienced by visiting and exploring it, and the church of St Thomas Becket, on the minor road linking Appledore with the A259, is an ideal spot from which to begin.

It is lonely, as is much of the area, and invariably deserted except for the sheep which are so much part of the marsh's history. The church sits among dykes in a field away from the road, and is reached along a raised earthwork. It looks, outside and in, much as it must have done over the centuries, although it has been restored this century. Legends surround it — legends of smuggling and legends explaining its existence, for it has no village.

Romsey

Hampshire SU 3521

This lively country town is a fascinating place to explore, though often eclipsed by its famous neighbour, Broadlands House, home of the late Lord Mountbatten. In its winding streets, medieval buildings such as King John's Hunting Lodge rub shoulders with 18th- and 19th-century civic buildings which reflect Romsey's days as a

thriving brewing and market centre. Watching over all is the great bulk of the Norman abbey — saved from demolition by the Romsey townsfolk, who bought it — for £100 — after Henry VIII's Dissolution of the Monasteries. The deed of sale can still be seen on display inside.

Rousham

Oxfordshire SP 4724

Overlooking the Cherwell is a garden virtually unaltered since its creation by William Kent in the 1740s. All the features of the Picturesque-style 'natural' garden are incorporated, with vistas, ponds and cascades, a castellated cowshed, statuary, a temple, an arcade and a planting plan that allowed for changes of colour throughout the seasons. A mock ruin on a hill a mile away serves as an eyecatcher.

Kent's work can also be seen in the house's parlour — an astonishing and extremely rare example of the English Baroque — and in the more restrained Rococo library.

The garden is open throughout the year, the house occasionally during the summer. The only disadvantage is that children under 15 are not admitted, even to the garden.

Royston Cave

Hertfordshire TL 3540

The extraordinary bell-shaped cavern that lies beneath a busy street in the centre of Royston is unique in Europe and yet remains one of Britain's least-known curiosities. Since its accidental discovery in 1742, by workmen digging a hole, there has been no shortage of theories regarding its age. Was it a Roman hermitage, an oratory, or a hiding place for the Knights Templar?

Astonishing chalk carvings form a frieze round the walls. The subjects are religious — crucifixion scenes, St Katherine and her Wheel, St Christopher, St Laurence, a variety of mysterious signs and symbols. The cave is open to the public on summer weekend afternoons, via a steep passage from the street. For further details contact Royston Museum, in Kneesworth Street.

THE WHISPERING KNIGHTS *Seen from the south-west in William Stukeley's drawing (1743), they originally formed a burial chamber. They are incorporated into the Rollright legend as the King's Men — hence also their other name*

Rycote

Oxfordshire SP 6604

Just north along the A329 off the M40 motorway is the little church of St Michael, an unexpected gem which was once the chapel of the great vanished Tudor mansion of Rycote Park. Outside are pinnacles and battlements, unaltered since it was built in the 15th century; inside is a treasury of 17th-century woodwork including pulpit, pews, altar rails, reredos, stalls and a gallery. Best are the two covered family pews on each side of the aisle. One has two storeys, the other has a wonderful canopied roof, like an exotic garden pavilion. They are enriched with carving and painting, including a ceiling painted with gold stars on a deep blue ground.

Rye

East Sussex TQ 9220

Most poignant of Rye's ghosts were the friar Cantator and the beautiful Amanda. They fell in love, were discovered, and buried alive. During excavations by builders of the South Eastern Railway, their bodies were uncovered, still wrapped in each other's arms. The lovers were reburied, and their ghosts, which had haunted Turkey Cock Lane for centuries, have not been seen since.

Henry James struck up an acquaintance with a spectral little old lady who appeared from time to time at his home, Lamb House; and the writer E. F. Benson was one of many to see the ghost of Allen Grebell there. Grebell was murdered by mistake in 1743, by a butcher named Breads. Part of Breads' skull and the chains in which his body was hung on a gibbet are still to be seen in the town hall. Breads had intended to kill Grebell's brother-in-law, James Lamb, mayor of Rye and the owner of Lamb House. Lamb was lucky on this occasion — but had a little less luck when George I stayed at his house and presented a newborn baby in the household with an inscribed silver bowl. Later examination revealed that it was only plate.

Rye has attracted artists as well as writers, and Van Dyck, not usually thought of as a landscape painter, did sketches of the town, one of which is in the Uffizi Gallery in Florence.

Rye has also been notable as a shelter for fugitives — despite or because of its long history of bloody battles with the French. A communion flagon brought by French Protestants in the 17th century is still in Rye church.

Saffron Walden

Essex TL 5338

Gog and Magog (or perhaps folk hero Tom Hickathrift and the Wisbech Giant) battle in plaster forever on the gable of the Old Sun Inn; at the museum, as well as the gloves worn by Mary Queen of Scots on the day she died, is a piece of the human skin which once coated the church door at Hadstock.

Though well on the beaten track, this lovely medieval town, built on wealth from the crocus's saffron dye, has its share of surprises. Henry Winstanley (born here in 1644) is said to have experimented with a wooden lantern on the fine church, before building the first Eddystone Lighthouse (which perished with him in a storm of 1703). Pre-dating all is Troy Town, one of Britain's rare and mysterious turf mazes.

Shalford Mill

Surrey SU 9947

The Tillingbourne is a river with a remarkable dual personality. Exceptionally pretty for much of its ten-mile length, it has been associated with virtually all the old, now vanished, Surrey industries, including gunpowder, paper and iron.

At Shalford the picturesque corn-grinding watermill survives, straddling the river. With much of its original gear intact, it dates from the early 18th century and was working until 1914. In the early 1930s it was acquired and presented to the National Trust by the mystery body known as Ferguson's Gang — even senior staff members of the Trust only knew the members of the 'gang' by false names, for all had sworn oaths of deepest secrecy.

Shillington

Bedfordshire TL 1234

Local legend tells that the church was meant to be built at the bottom of the hill, but that the stones used mysteriously to move up the hill overnight. After several attempts, the builders gave in and built it (successfully) at the top. Today it is a landmark for miles around, commanding fine views over the countryside.

Nearby is Knocking Knoll, the remains of a round barrow where, it is said, an old man can sometimes be heard knocking to be let out.

Shipley

West Sussex TQ 1422

Nowadays the history-steeped A272 neatly skirts the little toll house at its junction with the B2224, but for years travellers were forced to pay their dues as they passed by.

Fragments of Roman pots have been found at Shipley, and the hammer-pond of 16th-century Knipp Furnace can still be seen — it would originally have supplied the water to drive the waterwheel, which in turn powered the great hammers and bellows of the furnace.

The parish church has some untouched 12th-century features, but the outstanding feature of Shipley is the magnificent smock mill. It is very large, comprising five storeys over a brick base, and has been lovingly restored. From 1906 until his death in 1953, it belonged to the writer Hilaire Belloc, and there is a memorial plaque to him over the entrance.

Shoreham-by-Sea

West Sussex TQ 2105

Charles II escaped to France from Shoreham after his defeat at the Battle of Worcester in 1651; another notable local sailor was Captain Henry Roberts, who travelled with Captain Cook. He lived in one of the splendid 15th-century houses which surround the 'new' 12th-century St Mary de Haura — a superb church with a magnificent font of Saxon marble. At Old Shoreham is the 'old' Church of St Nicholas, the patron saint of mariners — it is a partly Saxon but largely Norman building.

The long maritime tradition is remembered in the museum at Marlipins, a 12th-century building of chequered flint and stone. It is thought to be one of the earliest secular buildings still in regular use in the country.

SHALFORD MILL *(left) Millers
used to say that when the
millstones were in action they
chanted 'For prof-it, For prof-it'
and as the mill slowed down the
stones' message changed to 'No
. . . prof-it, No . . . prof-it'
Both Shalford Mill and Newtown
Town Hall (above) were presented
to the National Trust by the
elusive Ferguson's Gang*

Silchester

Hampshire SU 6262

Once there were streets of houses and shops,
market places, civic buildings, public baths,
places of worship — all of the elements needed to
make for civilised city life.

It was the Romans who founded it (they called
it Calleva Atrebatum) — and when their empire
collapsed, it fell into ruins and was forgotten. It
is especially odd because almost every other
Roman town remains a town or city today —
Wroxeter and the elusive Durolevum (which may
have been near Ospringe) are the only other
known exceptions. All that can be seen here is the
great wall which surrounded it, Roman brickwork in the attractive little village church and
some finds in the small museum.

Sonning

Berkshire SU 7575

The eleven-arched, brick bridge over the river is
narrow enough to need traffic lights to control
vehicles, and is one of the oldest on the Upper
Thames. The ground slopes down steeply to the
bridge on the Berkshire side of the river, and the
main road is lined with old flower-bedecked

houses and fine inns. There is a picturesque mill
with a theatre restaurant on the Oxford side, and
attractive riverside walks can be taken.

Southampton

Hampshire SU 4211

To discover the delights of old Southampton, a
place rarely visited by busy shoppers, follow the
line of the old town walls and make a few
detours. The walls are preserved to their full
height in places and make up one of the finest
medieval defensive circuits remaining in England.
The stretch along Western Esplanade is particularly good, and incorporates parts of Norman
merchants' houses. From Western Esplanade
follow the little alley called Blue Anchor Lane up
to St Michael's Square and St Michael's Church,
which was founded in 1070 and is Southampton's
oldest building. Opposite is the Tudor House, a
half-timbered building that is now a museum,
with its own period garden.

Further round the walls, behind Town Quay in
Porters Lane, is Canute's Palace, a ruined 12th-
century merchant's house. Nearby in Winkle
Street is God's House Tower, one of the earliest
examples of artillery fortification in the world. It
is now a museum.

STEEPLE BUMPSTEAD: FOLKMOOTS

The Moot Hall at **Steeple Bumpstead** *takes its name from the 'folkmoots' of early Anglo-Saxon England. These were local assemblies where lawsuits were settled. Appeal was only to the King, up until the tenth century, when the country was reorganised into hundreds (or in some Danelaw counties 'wapentakes') and certain cases might be referred from the monthly folkmoot to the twice-yearly 'shire moot'.*

Folkmoots were held in the open, often at conspicuous landmarks — necessary in a land still heavily forested. These were frequently barrows — as at Mobberley, 'glade with a meeting mound', and Mutlow, 'mound where moots were held', both places in Cheshire.

Particular trees or stones were also chosen, as at Appletree, Derbyshire, Staine, Cambridgeshire, and **Maidstone**, *Kent. At Stone, Somerset, the Hundred Stone can still be seen, as can the Mottistone ('the stone of the speakers'), above Mottistone,* **Isle of Wight**.

Hill-top meeting places are recalled at Modbury, Dorset ('hill of assembly'), Spellow, Lancashire, and Spelhoe, Northamptonshire (meaning 'hill of speech').

Medieval and later moot halls also survive at **Elstow** *and Aldeburgh, Suffolk.*

MOOT HALLS *are relics of one of England's most ancient institutions. The Hall at Elstow (above) still has its original tie beam roof*

Stadhampton

Oxfordshire   SU 6098

The best thing here is Ascott Park, the site of a large 17th-century manor. Great gateposts, the formal plan of the gardens with its double lime avenues, and a Tudor-style granary and dovecote can be seen, although the house was destroyed by fire before it was completed.

A mile to the south is Newington, an attractive group formed by manor, church and a few cottages. The church, of the 12th and 14th centuries, has good monuments, a fine pulpit and some early glass. Beside it is the manor, a wonderfully formal classical stone house built in the 1660s and enlarged a century later, which is occasionally open.

Stanton Harcourt

Oxfordshire   SP 4105

An extraordinary group of Harcourt family monuments, ranging from the late 14th to late 19th centuries, can be found in the church: particularly good are the 17th-century ones, rich with Baroque detail. A curiosity is a memorial to a young couple killed by lightning in 1718.

Outside are thatched stone cottages and handsome town houses. Nearby, the manor house still has its great square medieval kitchen built of stone with an octagonal roof. A medieval tower of about 1470, originally a family room above a chapel, is known universally as Pope's Tower, as the poet stayed there in 1718 while translating Homer. The pretty gardens are regularly open.

Staplehurst

Kent   TQ 7843

Every Mothering Sunday, a charming little ceremony takes place at the beautiful old church at the top of Staplehurst Hill. The children in the congregation and their parents — and indeed all who wish to take part in the ceremony of 'clipping the church' — link hands and walk round the medieval building, to symbolise, it is said, the unity of Mother Church with her children. The church is situated at the heart of Staplehurst; old cottages and houses crowd the main street of the village, and the view south from the top of the hill is across Kentish orchards, hopfields and oast-houses.

Steeple Bumpstead

Essex   TL 6741

'...'Tis otherwise styled Bumsted ad Turrim, at the tower, from a Tower that stood near the road from Haverhill to Bathorne Bridge,' wrote 16th-century mapmaker Norden, disposing neatly of the problem of this pretty but steeple-free village's name. Edith Cavell worked as a governess here and worshipped at the church. At the crossroads stands the Moot Hall — 'moots' were originally Saxon meetings to settle disputes although this building was being used as a school by 1592. With its oversailing upper storey and formerly open-arched and timbered ground floor it is also likely to have been used as a Guildhall or market house at some stage in its existence. There is a stone lion, with a shield bearing the Tudors' royal arms, on the roof.

STADHAMPTON *St John the Baptist's Church, on the green: the tower, with its urn finials, dates back to 1737. Fifteenth-century brasses inside commemorate two John Wylmots and their wives*

Stevenage

Hertfordshire   TL 2324

Henry Trigg, an eccentric local grocer, requested in his will of 1724 that his body be placed in a coffin and that the coffin be laid on rafters at the west end of his barn. The executors complied with this strange wish and it wasn't long before both coffin and remains became a major tourist attraction for travellers changing horses in the town, once an important stop on a coaching route. Trigg's bones have long been buried, but his coffin can still be viewed in its original resting place. Apply to the Midland Bank in the High Street.

Steventon

Hampshire   SU 5447

This was the birthplace, in 1775, of one of Hampshire's most revered residents. More often associated with Chawton, near Alton, where she made her home in later life, Jane Austen lived and wrote in Steventon until she was 26. Her father was the rector of this tucked-away village, whose quiet is disturbed even today only by the trains on the Basingstoke to Winchester line, rushing past high above the village. A quiet lane leads to the little 13th-century church with its memorial to Jane Austen; the novelist is buried in Winchester Cathedral.

Steyning

West Sussex   TQ 1711

Steyning's rather grand parish church stands on the site where St Cuthman built his wooden church in the eighth century, on the advice of a stranger. When asked his name, the stranger replied, 'I am He, in whose name thou buildest this temple.'

A more recent (and less elevating) manifestation is associated with the cache of coins found at Chancton Farm in the 1860s. It is said that an old bearded man is sometimes to be seen wandering, as if searching, in the area known as Gurth's Barn, where the coins were unearthed. The coins, pennies of the reigns of King Harold and Edward the Confessor, are now in the British Museum.

Stockbridge

Hampshire   SU 3535

To the Romans it was a posting station on the road from Winchester to Salisbury; medieval travellers patronised its burgeoning market; and Welsh drovers brought their livestock through on their way to the markets of the Home Counties — the walls of a former pub, just south of the river bridge, are still covered with Welsh inscriptions. To pre-motorway 20th-century car drivers, Stockbridge was a stop on the annual holiday run to the West Country.

Now less of a staging-post (except for fishermen in search of the River Test's reputedly enormous trout) this is a pleasant place to walk and browse, with many attractive buildings, including a splendid petrol station that looks unchanged since the earliest days of the motor car. Built across marshland, parts of the town still float on peat.

The Test Way, a long-distance footpath, can be joined at Stockbridge. It follows the former Andover to Romsey railway, once endearingly known as the 'Sprat and Winkle' line. Nearby are good walks on Stockbridge Down — magnificent for its views — and Common Marsh, a riverside meadow rich in wild flowers. Both are protected by the National Trust.

Stoke d'Abernon

Surrey   TQ 1259

Over the centuries, the Mole, most charming and self-effacing of rivers, has been criticised by poets for its habit of avoiding close contact with humanity. Only one church is built beside the river bank, but that church, St Mary's, is the oldest in Surrey, and has several outstanding features. It stands on a wide curve of the river, sharing a site of great beauty and tranquillity with a 16th-century manor house. Behind the church the gardens of this house fringe the river, with a view beyond towards the M25. Roman bricks may be seen set in the church wall; part of a Saxon apse remains, and the much reproduced monumental brass to Sir John D'Abernon, dating from 1277 and the oldest in the country, still graces the chancel floor. His shield, still blue, was enamelled on copper and added later. Next to him is his son, also called Sir John, who is a little shorter. Fragments of 13th-century wall paintings and a bell cast by Joanna Sturdy of Croydon 500 years ago and still sound, are only some of the treasures which the motorway traveller will miss.

STOKE D'ABERNON: A WOMAN'S WORK — In the church at **Stoke d'Abernon** *hangs a bell cast in about 1450 by the bellfounder, Joanna Sturdy.*

Not all women in history were tied to the kitchen sink, certainly not the Abbess Hild, ruler in the seventh century of the double monastery of **Whitby***; nor Athelfleda of Mercia, daughter of Alfred the Great, who with her brother Edward planned and executed the reconquest of much of the Danelaw; nor Godiva, the 11th-century 'lord' in her own right of* **Coventry***.*

Phoebe Hassel of **Brighton** *served in the army for several years, and south-east England also produced numerous other, more eminent, independent-minded women: Dame Julian Berners, prioress of the nunnery of Sopwell, near St Albans, author in 1486 of 'A Treatyse pertayninge to Hawkynge'; Emily Faithfull of Headley, founder in the 19th century of a London printing-press employing only women; and Henrietta Vansittart of Ewell, perfecter of the Lowe-Vansittart screw propeller.*

EMILY FAITHFULL   *Born at a Hampshire rectory in 1835, she became Printer-in-Ordinary to Queen Victoria*

The contribution of women to literature is well known; less familiar is their contribution to crime. The legendary 'Wicked Lady' of **Markyate** *was a highwaywoman. Notable among pirates was Anne Bonny, who, with her companion Mary Read and her lover 'Calico Jack' Rackham, terrorised the high seas in the early 18th century.*

THERFIELD: MOATS
— To the west of **Therfield** there is a moat which belonged to a huge Norman Castle. But it isn't only castles that have moats: at **Reed** and other places in Hertfordshire, they can be seen gracing far more humble abodes. After burial mounds, moats are the most common archaeological feature in the British landscape — there are at least five and a half thousand of them, dug around manor houses, monasteries, farmsteads, chapels, hospitals and even windmills.

Many of them are dry or boggy today, but they would originally have been meant to hold water. They date mainly from between 1100 and 1500, and are usually square or rectangular, less commonly circular.

Sometimes the digging of a moat around a house coincides with a family's rise in fortunes — suggesting that a moat was probably a status symbol. Moats were also a sensible way of preventing theft, and may have kept out deer and other livestock liable to damage gardens. They were a defence against woodland fires as well, in days when many buildings were made of timber.

They are commonest in lowland areas which have a clay subsoil, and are pinpointed on Ordnance Survey maps. The deepest moat is said to be at **Nunney** (by tradition it is bottomless), and a fine example can also be seen at Little Moreton Hall, Cheshire.

LITTLE MORETON HALL   *A moated manor house and charming jumble of fashionable ideas, from three generations of 15th- and 16th-century owners*

STREATLEY   *Over 60 varieties of cheese made from the milk of cows, sheep and goats are on display in Wells Stores. Good cheese is dependent on many factors — not least of them being the weather*

Streatley

Berkshire   SU 5980

Streatley's beauty lies in its setting in a deep cleft of chalk — but its chief glory for those in the know is cheese. The finest traditionally-made cheeses from Britain and Europe may be bought at Wells Stores, under the guidance of proprietor Major Patrick Rance, well informed on the availability (or not) of rarities like Dorset's Blue Vinney cheese.

Streatley occupies an exceptionally pretty position in the Goring Gap, where the River Thames cuts through the chalk and separates the Chilterns and the Berkshire Downs. An attractive bridge over the river links it with the neighbouring village of Goring and overlooks the bustle of Goring Lock. Apart from several good pubs, there are some fine 17th- and 18th-century houses; and the village hall was converted in 1898 from a line of malthouses.

The ancient Ridgeway Path crosses the river at Streatley and climbs the juniper-dotted slopes of Streatley Hill, on to the top of the Downs.

Telscombe

East Sussex   TQ 4003

Flint cottages nestle in the coombe, much as they did when shepherds returned to them after tending the large flocks which once covered the Downs. The village can only be reached by a lane from the A275 at Southease, but also owes its unspoilt nature to the efforts of landowner Ambrose Gorham, who bequeathed the village to Brighton Council in 1933. Gorham ran a racing stable, and trained his horses on Telscombe Tye. The 1902 Grand National winner, Shannon Girl, was prepared here, and today the long tradition is carried on by the presence of racing stables at Findon.

The little manor house is owned by the National Trust but is not open; the lovely church is part-Norman.

Tendring Hundred

Essex   TM 1424

Thirteen local women suspected of being witches were sent for trial at Chelmsford in 1582. Amongst them was one Ursula Kemp, who heard her illegitimate eight-year-old son witness against her before she was hanged. Her bones were dug up from her St Osyth grave in 1956 and displayed in the witchcraft museum at

Polperro. In 1645, more local 'witches' were executed on the evidence of Matthew Hopkins, Manningtree lawyer and self-styled Witchfinder General. Such inhumanity may be contemplated today under the magnificent hammerbeam roof of Tendring's church.

The 'hundred' in the name comes from the Saxon county sub-division of which Tendring was the centre. It is still called the Tendring District, although the centre has moved to the Town Hall at Clacton.

Tenterden

Kent   TQ 8833

On a clear day, the coast of France can be seen from the steeple of Tenterden church, whose construction seems to have caused deep resentment. A bishop is said to have built it with the money or materials meant for keeping up the vital sea-wall at Sandwich — and so caused both the silting up of Sandwich Harbour, and the creation of the Goodwin Sands.

There may be something in the story, for the church is one of the largest in the county and must have been costly. Sandwich people may have had another cause to dislike it: seamen, who had hitherto used their port, could have used it as a landmark for Tenterden's nearby port of Smallhythe instead.

Tewin

Hertfordshire   TL 2714

It is said that before her death in 1713, Lady Anne Grimston of Gorhambury declared that if there was truth in the doctrine of the Resurrection, trees might spring from her grave. They did. Ash and sycamores have smashed through Lady Anne's splendid tomb in Tewin churchyard, lifting the stone into the air, and one tree trunk is busy consuming the surrounding iron railings.

Another Tewin grave is of quite a different type. The large inscribed stake lying at Oakenvalley Bottom, by the Bull's Green Road, marks the last resting place of Walter Clibborn, a piemaker turned footpad, who, having murdered several local farmers and merchants for their money, was himself shot dead by Ben Whittenbury of Queen Hoo Hall in 1782. This picturesque Elizabethan mansion on the road to Bramfield has changed little since Walter Scott visited it, probably after the death in 1802 of Joseph Strutt, whose unfinished romance, *Queen Hoo Hall*, Scott completed in 1808.

Thaxted

Essex   TL 6131

Soaring cathedral-like over the streets, light and graceful inside, Thaxted's glorious church was the incongruous scene of a pitched battle in 1921. Conrad Noel, colourful vicar and secretary of the Church Socialist League, hoisted the red flag of communism and the Sinn Fein flag high up in the church. Cambridge undergraduates tore them down and put up the Union Jack; Noel in turn ripped it down and, with his friends, slashed the tyres of students' cars and motorcycles.

Conrad Noel's wife is remembered for encouraging morris dancing in the town. Thaxted has numerous attractively pargeted and timber-framed houses, and a 15th-century Guildhall, built as a meeting place for the cutlers.

Therfield

Hertfordshire   TL 3337

Perfectly sited on a Chiltern ridge, with clear views northwards over the plain, Therfield is nevertheless a sheltered village of quiet, shaded lanes, where ancient plaster and thatch mingle gently with newer brick. From the green, a lane trickles past a picturesque cottage group to the church and former rectory, the latter a striking amalgam of 15th-century stone and Georgian brick. Therfield's incumbents have included the poet William Alabaster, whose verses were compared to Milton's, William Sherlock, a contentious divine, and Henry Etough, an 18th-century vegetarian and teetotaller. In the Rectory yard is a well, 270 feet deep. To the west is the moat of a huge Norman castle. Tuthill Manor, which combines fantasy with superb craftsmanship, stands to the north.

Tilford

Surrey   SU 8743

The King's, or Novel's, Oak at Tilford is surrounded by legends, and it is said to be 900 years old. Clearly it has been a magnificent specimen: Cobbett refers to it as 'by far the finest tree that I ever saw.'

The two branches of the Wey come together at Tilford, and are crossed by two fine medieval bridges. Tradition says that the monks of Waverley Abbey rebuilt the bridges after the disastrous floods of 1233, when the low-lying Abbey had to be temporarily abandoned. They now have cutwaters against the flow.

Toddington

Bedfordshire   TL 0028

On the ringing of the Pancake Bell at St George's Church, both children and adults head for Conger Hill, where they lie on the ground and listen for the bubbling of the witch's cauldron and the frying of her pancakes.

The custom takes place each Shrove Tuesday in this attractive village, just a mile away from the M1 at Junction 12. It once had an extensive market place and timbered market hall, as befitted an important centre for the straw plait industry — the plait was made by women and children for the booming straw hat trade of Luton and Dunstable, and sold here until the trade was killed by foreign competition.

Wentworth House is believed to be haunted by the ghost of Henrietta Wentworth, lover of the Duke of Monmouth. She is buried in the Wentworth Chapel in St George's.

Totternhoe

Bedfordshire   SP 9821

Old graffiti can often be seen in churches, although the subject is seldom industrial archaeology. But scratched on the chalk clunch walls of Totternhoe Church are drawings of windmills and the dates 1748 and 1753. It is thought that they represent the old post mill which stood between the church and the later Doolittle Mill, which incorporated some of its more ancient gear, built between 1815 and 1825.

Close by is the nature reserve of the Totternhoe Knolls, protected chalk grasslands, which are rich in plants and butterflies.

THE BOSCOBEL OAK *where Charles II took refuge. The original print for this engraving is dated 1695*

TILFORD: SACRED OAKS — *The legends surrounding venerable trees like the King's Oak at* **Tilford** *carry echoes of ancient beliefs.*

Once sacred to the European sky-god, under Ostrogothic law the oak had 'peace' and could not be felled, and particular oaks were held sacred.

From their connection with the sky-god arose a persistent belief that oaks were never struck by lightning — hence the 'acorns', originally charms — on the ends of blind cords. How unfounded this was appeared in 1879 when lightning destroyed the old oak in Wayland Wood, near Watton, Norfolk, under which the Babes in the Wood traditionally perished.

Certain oaks are linked with figures of legend, like Merlin (at **Carmarthen**), *Herne the Hunter (at Windsor), and Robin Hood (see* **Leeds**). *Others are said have connections with historical figures — Kett's Oak, near Wymondham, Norfolk, traditionally the rallying-point in Kett's Rebellion, Dick Turpin's oak, near* **Hempstead**, *and the oak (commemorated by a monument) at Hoxne, Suffolk, on the site of St Edmund's martyrdom.*

Best known is the Boscobel oak in which King Charles II is said to have hidden after the Battle of **Worcester**. *Oak Apple Day, once a widespread festival, ostensibly celebrates the king's lucky escape — but it may go back to an older celebration of the sacred oak. On or around 29 May, Oak Apple Day is marked by the Chelsea Pensioners in* **London**, *while it is celebrated as Garland King Day at Castleton, Derbyshire.*

TROTTON

TROTTON: SACRED YEWS — *The church-yards of* **Trotton**, **Aldworth**, **Crowhurst**, *and* **Painswick** *are only a few of the many in Britain with remarkable yew trees.*

Often a single tree near the lych gate (first built to shelter the corpse, or lych, awaiting the priest), the yew is traditionally planted in churchyards because, being evergreen and even longer-lived than the oak, it has from time immemorial symbolised ever-lasting life.

At English country funerals, mourners would carry a branch of yew to be laid in the grave with the dead person, or tuck sprigs of yew in the folds of the shroud. As an emblem of Christ's resurrection, yew is still included in church decorations at Easter.

But the yew is also the death-tree ('toxic' is related to the word 'taxus', meaning yew), sacred in Greece and Rome to Hecate, goddess of the Underworld and to witches. Slips of yew went into the witches' cauldron in 'Macbeth'. It also had magical powers: in Herefordshire, a girl would sleep with a sprig of churchyard yew under her pillow to discover in her dreams who she would marry.

In ancient Ireland, the Yew of Ross was one of the 'sacred trees'. Such age-old sanctity made it unlucky to cut down a churchyard yew, or to burn or damage its branches. The theory that church-yard yews were planted to provide wood for archers' bows is almost certainly unfounded: English wood was unsuitable, and wood for bows is known to have been imported throughout the Middle Ages. A statute of Edward I enforced the planting of churchyard yews, to protect churches from the weather, it was said, but conceivably because of half-remembered beliefs in their more mystical properties.

Trotton

West Sussex   SU 8322

A lovely 15th-century five-arched bridge crosses the River Rother at Trotton. Beside it is the church, where a 14th-century wall painting of the Last Judgement remains on the west wall, with faint traces of paintings elsewhere. A 1310 brass memorial to Margaret, Lady Camoys, is thought to be the oldest in the country dedicated to a woman. On the jambs of the west door are grooves alleged to have been caused by Trotton archers sharpening their arrows before their Sunday practice.

Turville

Buckinghamshire   SU 7691

The Church of St Mary the Virgin in Turville is mainly 14th-century, although the list of vicars in the porch shows that the first priest was granted the living here in 1228. An old but well restored windmill, complete with sails, now a private house, overlooks the fine medieval church, the Bull and Butcher pub and idyllic village.

Walton on the Naze

Essex   TM 2521

Somewhere off the 800-foot pier lies medieval Walton and much of the former Naze or head-land. The medieval church was lost to the sea in 1796: all were victims of sea erosion.

Neolithic flint-shaping implements have been found here, and fossil teeth and ears of sharks and whales have been discovered in the red crag cliffs. Walton was a source, in the 19th century, of sea holly for making love potions, but today offers donkeys, deckchairs and amusements on the pier. The great, grim windowless edifice on the highest point of the Naze is Trinity House Tower, built in 1720 to warn shipping of the treacherous off-shore West Rocks.

WARE   *Many of the walls in Scott's 18th-century grotto, dubbed 'Fairy Hall', are decorated with flints and exotic shells gathered from South Sea islands*

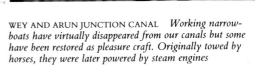

WEY AND ARUN JUNCTION CANAL   *Working narrow-boats have virtually disappeared from our canals but some have been restored as pleasure craft. Originally towed by horses, they were later powered by steam engines*

Wanborough

Surrey   SU 9348

Crouching just below the A31, on the north side of the Hog's Back, is a tiny village with the smallest church in the county. Built by the monks of Waverley Abbey, it was named for St Bartholomew, on whose feast day a fair was held. Beside the church, and dwarfing it, is a huge tithe barn, also built by the monks.

The manor was recorded in Domesday Book, and the present manor house is a mixture of 15th- and 17th-century construction. Between 1939 and 1945, special agents were trained there before parachuting into Europe.

Ware

Hertfordshire   TL 3514

Dr Johnson called it 'Fairy Hall' and vowed to write a life of its creator; and indeed the grotto built in his garden by Sir John Scott, a wealthy Quaker poet and literary critic, is Ware's own place of magic, though perhaps of a rather sinister sort. First inspired by Pope's grotto at Twickenham, it took at least ten years to build, starting in 1765, and cost over £10,000. The narrow passages and chambers (the Consultation Room, Committee Room and Robing Room are some of their grandiose names) are ingeniously ventilated and occasionally lit by sunlight.

After Scott's death in 1783 it was allowed to decay and is still being restored. It is open on the last Saturday afternoon of the month from April to September, or by appointment with the Leisure Services Officer at East Herts District Council, Bishops Stortford. Take a torch.

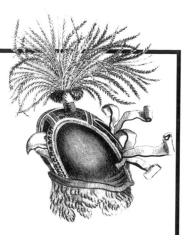

HOODS *keep the falcon calm when not in flight. The plumes and tassels enable falconers to put the hood on with one hand*

Warnham

West Sussex   TQ 1533

Percy Bysshe Shelley was born at Field Place on the edge of the village, and banished from home by his father who did not approve of poetry writing. Less renowned but far happier was local resident Michael Turner, a shoemaker who for 50 years acted as parish clerk and sexton. His viol, a tuning fork, some books and a photograph can be seen in a glass case in the church. It is said that he died with a fiddle in his hand, and his life is recorded in verse on his gravestone.

West Clandon

Surrey   TQ 0451

Clandon Park is well known, but perhaps less familiar is the brightly coloured New Zealand Maori house in its grounds.

In the south porch of West Clandon Church is a carved wooden panel — admittedly a copy — depicting a dog fighting with a dragon. This relates to a charmingly vague local legend about a dragon who lived in nearby Send Marsh. An army deserter, pausing in the village, was persuaded with the promise of a pardon to attempt to kill the dragon. His dog seized the beast's head, which was then cut off by the soldier, who was duly rewarded by the grateful villagers.

West Wycombe

Buckinghamshire   SU 8394

Glinting on the top of St Lawrence's Church is the golden ball which was added by Sir Francis Dashwood, founder of the Hellfire Club. It can hold up to eight people, and is said to have been used for card parties. Just below, a church-like façade conceals the entrance to the Hell Fire Caves, dug by Sir Francis' workmen to get chalk for a road they were building — but possibly used by Hellfire members for 'unspeakable orgies'. They now hold waxworks.

West Wycombe Park was built by the second Sir Francis Dashwood, founder of the Dilettante Society in the early 18th century.

Wey & Arun Junction Canal

Surrey   SU 9946

The canal's main problem was that it was constructed too late. By the time it opened in 1816, the Napoleonic Wars were over and a major problem for shipping in the Thames Estuary and the English Channel — French privateers — had been removed. Railways were soon to begin their destruction of the canal trade and the Wey and Arun was thoroughly 'dead' by 1868 when an Act of Parliament officially closed it.

In recent years attempts have been made to carry out restoration work on the canal. Its course can still be traced: the best way to discover it is by following the Wey-South Path from Guildford, which for almost two-thirds of its 36-mile distance follows the route of the canal.

Weyhill

Hampshire   SU 3146

Weyhill's busy fair was well known for more than five centuries and features in the work of writers as diverse as Langland, in his 14th-century poem *Piers Plowman* and William Cobbett, who found that 'tax eaters from Andover and the neighbourhood were the only persons that had smiles on their faces'. Today, Weyhill's rather different attraction is one of Hampshire's best wildlife enterprises — the Hawk Conservancy. Birds of prey of many species can be seen at close quarters, and the Conservancy carries out an extensive and successful breeding programme. There is also a heronry here.

WEYHILL: FALCONRY — *At the Hawk Conservancy at* **Weyhill**, *falcons and some of the skills involved in the ancient art of falconry can be seen at close quarters.*

Falconry came in with the Norman Conquest and remained popular until the advent of the sporting gun in the 17th century. It was one of the chief pastimes of the medieval aristocracy, which declared the best falcons and hawks protected birds. Class distinctions were strongly maintained: gyrfalcons were for kings, peregrines for earls, merlins for ladies, goshawks for yeomen and sparrowhawks for 'knaves', i.e. commoners.

The birds fall into two categories: hawks, including goshawks and sparrowhawks, which are short-winged and yellow-eyed, capturing their quarry at short range and thus ideal for wooded country; and falcons, such as merlins and peregrines, which soar above open country before dropping out of the sky (called 'stooping'), to kill their prey by sheer impact with their clenched talons.

The young, known as eyasses, were painstakingly trained to feed on the gloved fist and then taught to 'fly to the lure', an imitation quarry. Later the lure would be used to entice the bird back to the falconer, after it had killed its prey.

Falconry has seen a revival in recent years: would-be falconers can find out what is involved at Weyhill and at the Falconry Centre, Newent, Gloucestershire.

WING: TIME PIECES

*— Sundials, made in many elaborate and unusual forms such as the topiary example at **Wing**, were the most reliable means of telling the time until the 14th century. They were developed by the Egyptians during the 8th century.*

Churches often had a 'scratch' or 'mass' dial carved into the south wall, which is thought to have indicated to the priest the times for saying Mass.

The nocturnal, using the alignment of the stars, was the sundial's night-time equivalent.

Water-clocks were the chief ancient 'mechanical' recorders of time. Early examples would be powered by a waterwheel and as it advanced, step by step, water poured into a series of cups which emptied every quarter of an hour. Due to the inconvenience of water freezing, sand-clocks were invented, but these proved unsuitable for measuring long periods and were chiefly used on board ship.

*In medieval times, as time came to be regarded as linear rather than cyclic, a crude mechanical clock was developed and day and night were divided into 24 equal hours. But there was still a belief that knowledge of the celestial bodies was essential to most human activities, so complicated astronomical representations were involved. These large clocks, often with elaborate and theatrical methods of striking, such as can be seen in Wells Cathedral, Somerset, were used as calendars as much as time-keepers. They were generally one-handed, as at **Coningsby**, because the technical precision needed to measure minutes was not developed until Galileo developed the pendulum in the early 1600s.*

Man is believed to be the only animal with a conception of past and future.

ABOVE   TIME WITHOUT NUMBERS *told by a church 'scratch dial' at Hampton in Arden, and on the Jack Spratt clock, Wootton Rivers, by '*GLORY BE TO GOD*'*

Whiteley Village

Surrey   TQ 0962

In what estate agents almost certainly term a 'most sought after area', William Whiteley, who died in 1907, left a million pounds in his will to build a retirement village, originally intended for the staff of his large department store in London. Sited across the road from St George's Hill, Weybridge, home of many 'personalities', the village was designed and laid out in octagonal shape with a circular area of grass in the centre which has a monument to Whiteley standing on it. Four roads radiate from here and there are wide turfed diagonal paths as well. Several architects, selected by a competition, were engaged in the project, which aimed to provide a largely self-contained village with churches of several denominations, a hospital, shops and recreational facilities. It is best seen in summer: set in a well wooded and landscaped site of 215 acres, it is a blaze of colour with many flower beds, and hanging baskets on most of the houses.

Wickham

Hampshire   SU 5711

Despite one of the finest townscapes in Hampshire, Wickham remains quite remarkably modest and equally unspoilt. It consists of a very large square, lined for the most part with Georgian buildings or at least Georgian façades. Lovely silvery-grey bricks, sometimes mixed with red, and elegant doorcases give the little town its character. Winding down to stream and church is Bridge Street, and the best of the cottages here is undoubtedly Queen's Lodge, with its unusual doorcase and diagonally hatched bricks — a refinement that must have taken many hours of labour. By the stream is Chesapeake Mill, complete with early tin advertisements. It was built in 1820 and its internal timbers came from the American warship *Chesapeake*, captured in 1813. The use of ship's timbers is often claimed for old buildings, but is actually very rare.

Wilts & Berks Canal at West Challow

Oxfordshire   SU 3987

To explore this forgotten waterway is to come into contact with one of the more outlandish schemes of the canal age, a rural ghost of industrial ambition. Wandering for 51 mainly rural miles from the Kennet and Avon Canal near Melksham to the Thames at Abingdon, it was never a great success and was finally closed, after 104 years, in 1914.

But much of the route has survived and can be traced. A footpath follows the canal from West Challow to Grove. In West Challow itself, a village marked by a fine early 18th-century house, the canal is in a dip, its banks overgrown, full of reeds but, remarkably, still holding water. A branch canal leads into Wantage where some canal buildings can be found in Mill Street. To the south, and running parallel, is the Ridgeway, with all its prehistoric associations, another example of a long-abandoned transport network.

In Wiltshire, wharves, the occasional bridge and the site of locks can be explored, while in Oxfordshire, the route eastwards from Shrivenham towards Wantage can quite easily be tracked across the flat farmland.

Windrush Valley

Oxfordshire   SP 2811

Flowing as it does through Burford, Minster Lovell and Witney, the Windrush is inevitably popular. But some stretches remain little known.

Take the minor road due east towards Swinbrook from the centre of Burford to follow the river as it twists and turns along the valley, offering views of quiet Oxfordshire scenery at its best. Swinbrook is a collection of 17th- and 18th-century farmhouses, some pretty Victorian estate cottages and a former mill. This was the village of the Fettiplace family, whose grand mansion was demolished in 1805, leaving no trace. But the family lives on in the church, with its astonishing collection of splendidly sculpted monuments from the early 17th to the late 18th century.

A mile south-east is Asthall, where the Roman Akeman Street crossed the river. There are Roman and Saxon remains nearby. At the centre is a rather romantic and overgrown churchyard.

Wing

Buckinghamshire   SP 8822

With its rare Saxon crypt and Saxon nave, All Saints at Wing is one of England's best pre-Norman churches. From later centuries there are carvings, fine monuments and brasses, notably to the local Dormer family.

Ascott House, a mile to the east, has the extraordinary feature of a topiary sundial. The dial, with Roman numerals, is cut from box hedges, while the 'gnomen' casting the shadow in the centre is a rounded, well trimmed yew tree. Behind this, more box hedges are cut to form the words 'Light and Shade by Turn, but Love Always'. The house, 17th-century but rebuilt by the Rothschild family in the 19th, belongs to the National Trust.

Winslow

Buckinghamshire   SP 7627

A good starting point for an exploration of winding lanes and narrow streets is the Market Square. As well as Georgian houses, it has two fine old pubs, the Bell and the George — whose balcony came from Claydon House.

Wall paintings in the medieval Parish Church of St Lawrence illustrate the murder of St Thomas Becket in 1170; simple Keach Chapel was built for the Baptists in 1695. Winslow Hall was probably designed by Sir Christopher Wren between 1698 and 1702 and is now a museum.

Witham

Essex   TL 8215

Murder Must Advertise author Dorothy L. Sayers came to live at Sunnyside, Newland Street, in 1928, and died there on 17 December 1957, having enriched crime fiction with her aristocratic detective hero, Lord Peter Wimsey. Less familiar is her role as an advertisement copywriter for Guinness ('*How grand to be a Toucan — Just think what Toucan do*'). In earlier days, Witham thrilled to the gossip of Richard Sutton Cheek's local paper, *Tom Tit, for the Girls of the period and young men of the Day*. His allegations about the son of the Mayor of Maldon and the 'wife of a most respectable tradesman' brought him to court for libel.

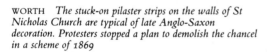

WORTH   *The stuck-on pilaster strips on the walls of St Nicholas Church are typical of late Anglo-Saxon decoration. Protesters stopped a plan to demolish the chancel in a scheme of 1869*

Worth

West Sussex   TQ 3036

Once in the heart of St Leonard's Forest, but now surrounded by motorways, roads and the ever-encroaching new town of Crawley, Worth has a reminder of a very different age. With the exception of the disastrous Victorian tower, the church is almost entirely Saxon, and is one of the more impressive in this country. No satisfactory evidence has been produced to explain why so large a church was built here, in the depths of the forest, and there is no record of it in Domesday Book.

Writtle

Essex   TL 6706

Out of a tucked-away corner of the minuscule St John's Green came Britain's first regular broadcasting service — experimental 15-minute programmes beamed out nightly by engineers at the Marconi works.

Opposite the green, the Cock and Bell is said to be haunted by a young woman who committed suicide on the railway, and up the street is the Wheatsheaf, one of the smallest pubs in the country.

In the church, a cross of charred timbers is a reminder of the fire which gutted the chancel in 1974. Ducks swim on the pond of the larger, and quite idyllic main village green, which is surrounded by lovely Tudor and Georgian houses — and all just two miles away from central Chelmsford.

GWENT *circa* 1900.
Fisherwomen with shrimp baskets. Dressed in clothes which served to protect them from all kinds of elements, the open air life the women led is reflected in their weatherbeaten faces

WALES

A *floodlit cavern containing 70 military vehicles, another cave where a brigand called Twm Shon Catti had his base, and yet another cave, this one with a blue door, behind which Merlin is supposed to sleep. And that is only a handful of treasures beneath the surface of Wales. Above ground there is much more, including Bird Rock, a cormorant breeding site four miles inland, Parys Mountain, once the largest copper mine in Europe, Carreg Cennen Castle, one of the most romantic ruins anywhere, and 5 Cwmdonkin Drive, a prosaic house in Swansea with poetic connections.*

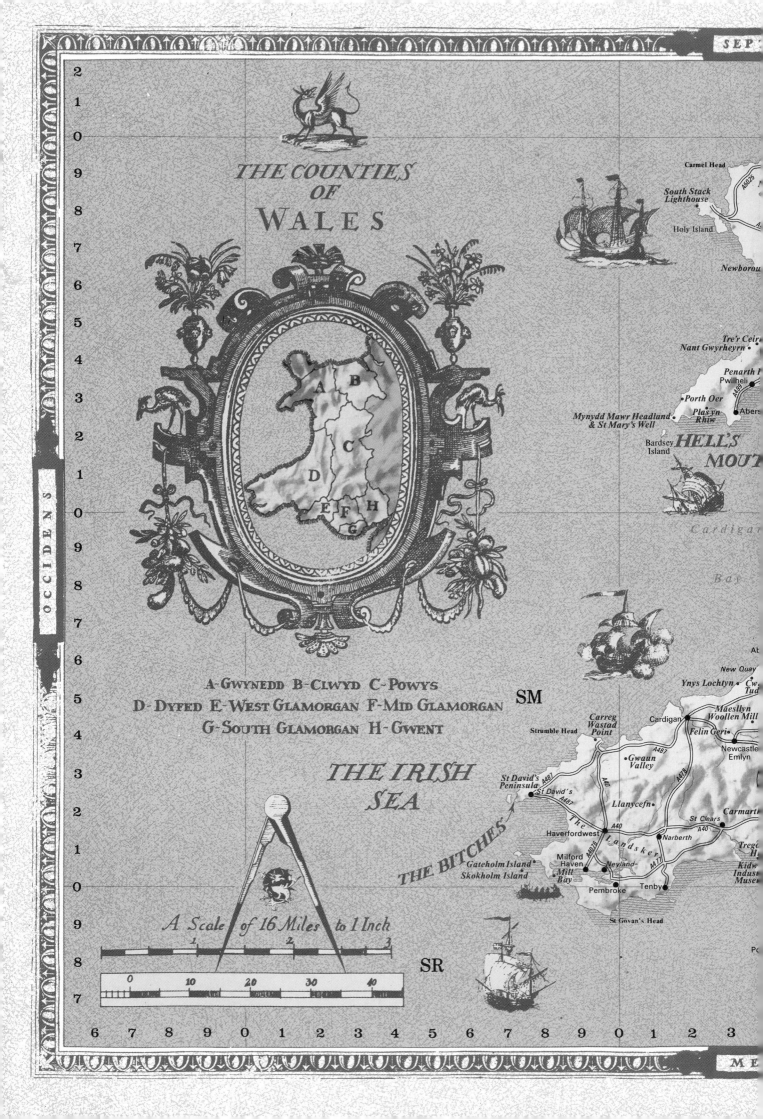

THE COUNTIES
OF
WALES

A-GWYNEDD B-CLWYD C-POWYS

D-DYFED E-WEST GLAMORGAN F-MID GLAMORGAN

G-SOUTH GLAMORGAN H-GWENT

SM

THE IRISH
SEA

A Scale of 16 Miles to 1 Inch

1   2   3

0   10   20   30   40

SR

Carmel Head

South Stack
Lighthouse

Holy Island

Newborou

Tre'r Ceir
Nant Gwyrheyrn

Penarth
Pwllheli

Porth Oer

Plas yn
Rhiw

Abers

Mynydd Mawr Headland
& St Mary's Well

Bardsey
Island

HELL'S
MOUT

Cardiga

Bay

Ab

New Quay

Ynys Lochtyn

Cw
Tud

Maesllyn
Woollen Mill

Cardigan

Felin Geri

Newcastle
Emlyn

Carreg
Wastad
Point

Strumble Head

Gwaun
Valley

St David's
Peninsula

St David's

Llanycefn

Carmart

St Clears

The

Landsker

Narberth

Trego
H

Haverfordwest

Kidw
Indus
Muse

THE BITCHES

Gateholm Island

Skokholm Island

Milford
Haven

Mill
Bay

Neyland

Tenby

Pembroke

St Govan's Head

Po

6   7   8   9   0   1   2   3   4   5   6   7   8   9   0   1   2   3

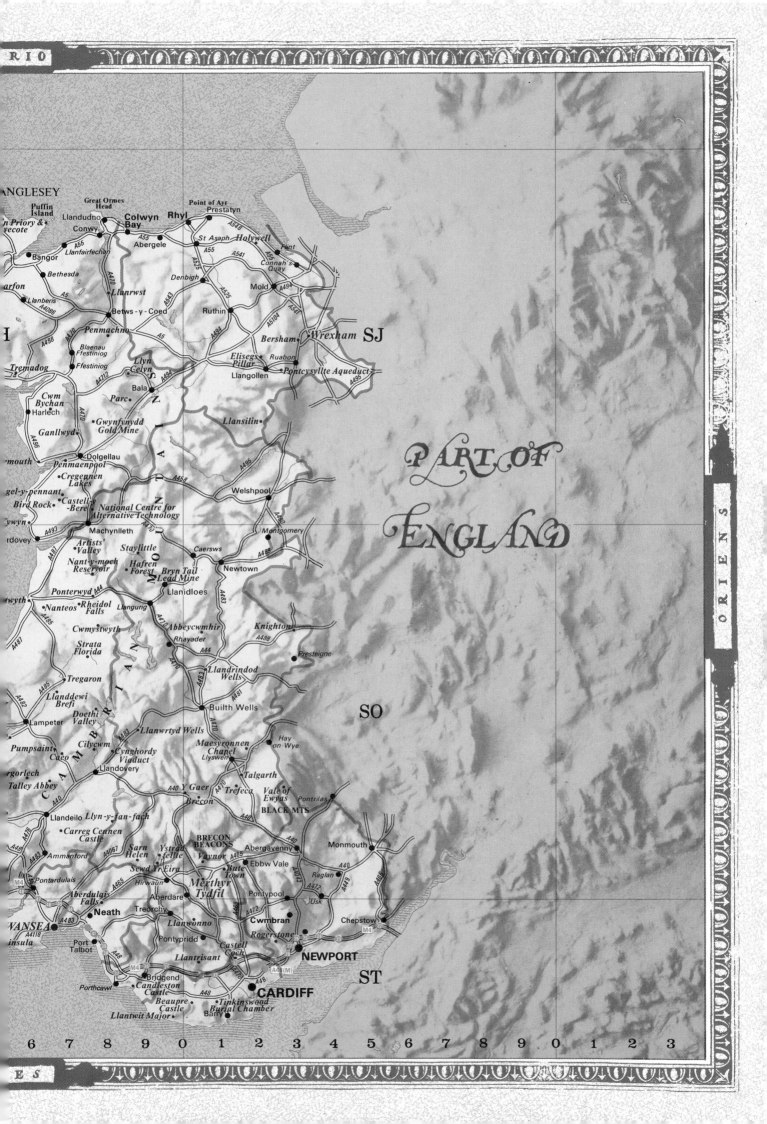

ABBEY CWMHIR: THE CULT OF THE HEAD — *A hawthorn among the ruins of* **Abbey Cwmhir** *was traditionally said to mark the grave of Llewelyn ap Gruffydd, the last native Welsh Prince of Wales.*

According to Adam of Usk (15th century), when Llewelyn was decapitated at Cilmeri in 1282, his head was washed in a spring which that day ran with blood.

The association of heads and wells goes back to pagan times, when the Celts were head-hunters. To them the head was the seat of the soul, and they carefully preserved the heads of notable enemies as both trophies and talismans.

Until quite recently, people in Celtic areas sometimes drank the water of holy wells from skulls — St Teilo's, for example, at Llandeilo Llwydarth, Dyfed. The washing of skulls in wells is also attested by custom.

Saints' legends have echoes of the cult of the head. St Winefride's Well, **Holywell**, *flows from the spot where the saint's head fell when she was decapitated by a rejected suitor. A similar story accounts for the well of St Columba, Ruthvoe, Cornwall.*

Abbey Cwmhir

Powys SO 0571

The silent, undiscovered settlement of Abbey Cwmhir is no more than a collection of houses, a church and an inn. Its name is taken from an ancient abbey, scant remnants of which still stand on a grassy river meadow beside the rushing Clywedog brook, a little way from the houses. Today, it is difficult to envisage that this Cistercian monastery, founded in 1143, had one of the largest churches in Wales and one of the biggest naves in Britain. Pillars taken from the abbey when it was dismantled during the Reformation found their way to Llanidloes Church, where they can still be seen.

Over the porch doorway of Abbey Cwmhir's Church of St Mary there is a relief of the Ascension which was copied from a tympanum of the old Abbey. Another carved tympanum, possibly from the Abbey, lies in the garden of a nearby farmhouse.

Llewelyn ap Gruffydd, the much-lamented last native prince of Wales, was killed by the English at Cilmeri, 13 miles to the south, in 1282. His body is said to have been brought here for burial.

Aberdulais Falls

West Glamorgan SS 7799

Turner was one of the many painters and writers drawn to these falls in the late 18th century. Since then, they have faded into obscurity and are only now experiencing something of a revival, thanks to the efforts of the National Trust.

The Dulais River tumbles here through a gloomy, atmospheric sandstone gorge — it is easy to see why the falls appealed to 18th- and 19th-century romantics — near its confluence with the River Neath.

Remains of old furnaces, weirs and water-courses can also be seen among the thick foliage: as early as 1584, this was a copper works, one of the first industrial sites in South Wales, and later, iron and tin were produced.

Abergorlech

Dyfed SN 5833

The River Gorlech flows down from the hills to join the Cothi at Abergorlech ('mouth of the Gorlech'), and clear flowing waters and cool, green forests dominate the surroundings of this lovely little village, in the back lanes of south-west Wales. The Cothi is a famed salmon and sewin (Welsh for 'sea-trout') river.

North of the village, an all-enveloping cloak of conifers covers the hillside and moorland. This is the Brechfa Forest, one of the Forestry Commission's largest plantations in Wales. Over the last ten years or so, the Commission has made genuine attempts to react to public criticism of its role, by unlocking the leisure and amenity potential of its woodlands. Good examples of this work can be seen at Abergorlech, where a scenic riverside picnic site serves as a starting point for a number of waymarked forest walks.

Aberystwyth

Dyfed SN 5881

Victorian amusement has returned to Aberystwyth in the form of a camera obscura. No self-respecting fashionable Victorian resort should be without such an attraction, which allows our film-, television- and video-besotted age the innocent pleasure of watching a moving landscape reflected on to a circular table screen.

Claimed to be the largest in the world, the camera obscura stands on the 430-foot summit of Constitution Hill, above the beach and promenade. Its huge, all-seeing, 14-inch lens captures no less than 26 Welsh mountain peaks and the entire Cardigan Bay coastline. The best way to reach it is by the Aberystwyth Electric Cliff

ABERYSTWYTH *seen through its camera obscura. The town developed as a port for inland lead mines in the early 18th century. Later it became a resort, and grand hotels were built for 'package tours'*

Railway, a 'conveyance for gentlefolk since 1896' — all of which is very much in keeping with a resort which has not moved away a great deal from its 'staid and respectable' image of the 19th century. Railway and camera obscura are open daily in the summer season.

Artists' Valley

Dyfed   SN 7094

Artists' Valley, or Cwm Einion (its Welsh name has no link with the English), is easily missed. A solitary signpost off the A487 at Furnace points in the direction of a secluded, dead-end valley, the haunt of painters 100 years ago. A narrow road climbs steeply at first before settling down to follow the course of the River Einion as it rushes through sheltered oakwoods. Tarmacadam turns to gravel within a few miles. From here, enthusiastic and well-prepared walkers can strike out upwards into the wild and partly forested moorlands of Plynlimon, a boggy dome filled with remote lakes and headwaters.

The strange-looking, barn-like old building at Furnace itself, right on the gateway to the valley, gave the village its name. Silver refining took place here in the 17th century. The present building — currently under restoration — is an 18th-century iron smelting plant. Its blast furnace was once reliant on bellows, which were powered by the Einion, courtesy of the strength of a huge waterwheel.

Barmouth

Gwynedd   SH 6215

For the payment of a small toll (at the Barmouth end) walkers have access to one of Wales's most unusual walks — a footpath which accompanies BR's diesels as they rattle across a bridge spanning the mouth of the lovely Mawddach Estuary. Mountain-backed Mawddach has been called the 'sublime estuary' which compares 'with the finest in Scotland' by no less than William Wordsworth, and BR's one-mile walkway affords unique, mid-channel vantage points of this delicious blend of sandbanks, luxuriant woodlands, green hills and bare mountains. From the north, approach from Barmouth. The southern starting point is the Morfa Mawddach Station, off the A493 north-east of Fairbourne.

Beaupre Castle

South Glamorgan   ST 0172

Be prepared for a walk of over half a mile: Beaupre (pronounced 'Bewper') stands quite alone, surrounded by lush meadowlands in the pastoral Vale of Glamorgan. This handsome historic site is more of a manor house than a castle. It belongs largely to the more settled Elizabethan period when preoccupations with attack and defence mellowed into a greater desire for creature comforts. It is no tough, rough-and-ready military fort. Mullioned windows add a definitely domestic touch to the walls of the courtyard, and Beaupre is also adorned by two richly carved and decorated porches. The first, on the outer gate, bears the date 1586 and the motto (in Welsh) of the Bassets (the family most closely associated with the castle): 'Better Death than Shame'.

The inner porch is even better — a splendid, three-tiered extravaganza.

Bersham

Clwyd   SJ 3049

Bersham, on the western approaches to Wrexham, was a pioneering ironmaking centre closely associated with the 18th-century innovator, John Wilkinson. Even before Wilkinson appeared on the scene, Bersham's early iron industry was producing a spin-off that is still with us, in the form of the decorative wrought ironwork gates made by the celebrated Davies brothers.

The Davies brothers of Bersham, Robert and John, were gifted craftsmen whose work was much in demand by the locality's nobility and churchmen. Their gates can be seen at St Peter's Church, Ruthin, and St Giles, Wrexham, and also at a number of country houses. The brothers' definitive accomplishment, it is generally agreed, stands at the entry to Chirk Castle. Chirk's gates, an incredibly complicated and delicate work of art in iron (dating from 1719-21), tend to steal the limelight from the castle itself. The site of the brothers' smithy, at Croes Foel Farm, which lies just south of Bersham, is marked by a commemorative plaque.

Bird Rock

Gwynedd   SH 6406

Craig-yr-Aderyn, otherwise known as Bird Rock, or Birds' Rock, looks for every inch of its 760-foot height a misfit. This craggy cliff soars — not above the sea, but over the flat, fertile hay meadows of the Dysynni Valley, four miles inland from the resort of Tywyn on Cardigan Bay. The sea has not always been at such a distance, but when the silting up of the Dysynni took the waves away, Bird Rock was stranded inland.

The shifting patterns of the Welsh coast have resulted in an ornithological as well as a geographical oddity. No one has informed the cormorants that their erstwhile sea-cliff is now landlocked, for they continue to breed and nest here. Ambitious birdwatchers should be aware that Bird Rock is also the home of a herd of wild goats. They are usually shy.

BIRD ROCK   *Now well inland, this cliff-like outcrop is still inhabited by cormorants who don't seem to have noticed that the Dysynni Valley is no longer an inlet of the sea. There is a path to the summit*

A**BERYSTWYTH: MERMAIDS** — *In July 1826, a farmer in Llanychaearn,* **Aberystwyth***, looked down from a cliff near his house one morning and saw what he took to be a young girl washing. But turning away, he was struck by the thought that the tide was in — so she must have been a mermaid.*

He fetched his whole household, including the servants, and they watched her for half an hour, sometimes swimming, sometimes sitting on a rock. She had white skin and short, dark hair. She often made a sneezing sound and frequently stooped as if to drink, revealing a black tail.

In the 12th century, Gervase of Tilbury remarked on the number of mermaids and mermen to be found off the coast of Britain. An early account describes the Wild Man of **Orford***, who was caught in 1197 by Suffolk fishermen in their nets and taken to Orford Castle, to be hung up and tortured to see if he could talk. Recorded sightings of mermaids often mention rough treatment: they were variously shot at (Irish coast, 1819), stabbed (Orkneys or Shetlands, 1701), and stoned (Hebrides, 1830).*

Like the manticore of **North Cerney***, mermaids were among the mythical creatures which were used in church carvings: there is a fine one on a bench-end in Zennor, who is said to have lured the town's best singer to her undersea home. Or perhaps to his death: 'marri-ed to mermai-ed at the bottom of the deep blue sea' (in the sailors' song 'Rule Britannia'), is one way of saying 'drowned'. But there was also an old belief that water spirits needed to marry humans in order to have souls.*

MERMAIDS   *were used by the Church to warn of the vanity of earthly delights*

CARMARTHEN: MERLIN'S TREE — *According to Geoffrey of Monmouth (12th century),* **Carmarthen** *was the birthplace of the magician Merlin. Carmarthen's Welsh name is Caerfyrddin, which Geoffrey probably took to be 'caer', a fortress, and Myrddin, Welsh for Merlin. In fact it derives from the Roman name Moridunum, 'sea-fortress'. Since Geoffrey, Merlin has remained firmly connected with Carmarthen. On Priory Street, there stood until recently an old stump, braced with iron and cement, known as Merlin's Tree or Oak. A 'prophecy' ran:*

'When Merlin's Oak shall tumble down.
Then shall fall Carmarthen town'.

So it was only after debate that in 1978 the Local Authority removed the stump as a traffic obstruction.

Merlin's end has always been mysterious. The best-known story is that he was imprisoned in a cave by the nymph Vivien or Nimue. This cave is supposed to be on the lower slopes of Bryn Myrddin, 'Merlin's Hill', up the Tywi valley from Carmarthen. Local tradition says if you listen at the right spot, you can hear him groaning underground.

However, in the 16th century, the poet Spenser placed the cave in the grounds of Dinefwr Castle, and the grave of Merlin is also shown at Drumelzier, Borders.

MERLIN *has been linked with Carmarthen since the 12th century, and is said to be imprisoned nearby*

Brecon

Powys   SO 0428

In January 1879, 141 men — 36 of whom were hospital patients — fought off an attack by 4000 Zulus at Rorke's Drift. Their story, and that of the entire Zulu War, is told in the Zulu War Room of the 24th Regiment Museum, alongside exhibits and artefacts that include campaign medals, Zulu shields and weapons. The museum is within Brecon's army base.

Bryn Tail Lead Mine

Powys   SN 9187

The green heartlands of Mid Wales seem, on the face of it, the most unlikely mining area in Britain. Yet in previous centuries — the 19th in particular — many prospectors moved in and many shafts were sunk in search of this area's rich deposits of lead, silver and gold. Today, sheep munch contentedly among grassy, long-abandoned mines, one of which overlooks the huge Clywedog Dam, in the uplands three miles north-west of Llanidloes.

This is the Bryn Tail Lead Mine, which reached its peak of production in 1851, when 384 tons of ore were extracted. It was a small mine even by Mid Wales standards, but a number of different processes took place on site, including ore crushing. Bryn Tail is open to visitors and makes special efforts to interpret to the public the work that took place here before its closure in 1884.

Bute Town

Mid Glamorgan   SO 1009

The old industrial communities of the South Wales valleys are characterised by the tightly packed terraced houses which are heaped, one rank above the next, along the steep hillsides. Bute Town, at the head of the Rhymney Valley, is something completely different.

This little self-contained village is laid out in an orderly and well-planned manner on a flat stretch of moorland. Bute Town was an early example of a model village, built by a far-sighted ironmaster for his workers in 1802-3. Attractive two- and three-storey dwellings in warm-coloured stone line the wide main street, and it was sympathetically restored during European Architectural Heritage Year, 1975.

Caeo

Dyfed   SN 6739

Peaceful Caeo seems the most unlikely place to have a murderous past. This forgotten village, on a little-used country lane between Llandovery and Lampeter, is dominated by its solid and sub-stantial Norman church, dedicated to St Cynwl. In the churchyard is the grave of Judge John Johnes, an eminent and respected pillar of society who was the victim of an infamous crime in the 19th century.

Johnes was killed by villager Henry Tremble in 1876, in a dispute about the running of a local public house. After murdering the judge, Tremble took his own life. Such was the strength of feeling against the murderer that his body was, in a macabre episode, removed for some time from the churchyard.

Considering its size, Caeo and its surrounds have produced their fair share of famous figures,

CANDLESTON CASTLE   *Fortified domestic buildings were added to the castle in the 15th century and an elaborate fireplace remains from that time. It was inhabited up until the 19th century*

including the 15th-century Welsh bard and poet Lewis Glyn Cothi, Roger Williams, the gifted 17th-century minister who founded Rhode Island, and the unconventional 'Doctor' John Harries, a self-proclaimed 19th-century 'Astrologer, Wizard and Surgeon'.

Caernarfon

Gwynedd   SH 4862

Visitors flock to Caernarfon for its world-famous castle, scene in 1969 of the Investiture of Prince Charles as Prince of Wales. They usually omit to visit a site of even greater antiquity, located on the hill above the busy town at the mouth of the River Seiont on the Menai Strait. This is the Segontium Roman fort, proof that the Romans recognised the strategic importance of this part of North Wales a good 1200 years before the medieval warlords.

The Romans' conquest strategy involved the construction of a network of forts connected by well-engineered roads. Segontium, poised between the mountains and the sea, and at the north-west corner of their military road system in Wales, dates from AD78. It served as an important garrison for auxiliary troops over the next three centuries, during which it was repeatedly abandoned and rebuilt according to military needs.

The stone foundations of its various phases of construction are open to view. Segontium is the only Roman fort in Wales where internal buildings remain exposed. Many of the finds from excavations here in the 1920s are on display at the excellent museum, just across the road from the fort.

CARREG WASTAD: THE LAST INVASION — *In 1797, three French men-of-war and a lugger, sent to seize Bristol, were driven north by the wind and landed at* **Carreg Wastad***. This was the 'Legion Noire' — 600 soldiers and 800 ex-convicts under the command of William Tate, a renegade Irish-American.*

Half-starved, they plundered Pencaer for its livestock, and took solace in the liquor they found stacked in virtually every cottage and farm (it had been salvaged from a recent shipwreck). Influenced by their spoils, it is said, they mistook a band of Welsh women in their red shawls for Grenadiers, arriving to reinforce Lord Cawdor's forces (Pembroke Yeomanry, militia and a naval detachment) — and surrendered.

There is a memorial to Jemima Nicholas, who captured Frenchmen single-handed with a pitchfork, in St Mary's churchyard; and the Fishguard battle honour is still worn by the Pembroke Yeomanry.

Lord Cawdor did make Tate think he was outnumbered, and Jemima Nicholas was real enough. But the story of the band of women seems to have arisen because people gathered on Fishguard's castle hill to watch, and, by accident or design, the tall-hatted, red-cloaked women may have looked like soldiers from a distance.

Candleston Castle

South Glamorgan   SS 8878

Now a neglected ruin, this castle was once the home of a Norman family, the de Cantelupes. 'Candleston' derives from 'Cantelupe's ton', 'ton' signifying a manor or farm. It stands where sand dune meets woodland on the eastern edge of the extensive Merthyr Mawr Warren, between Porthcawl and Bridgend. Originally a Norman fortification, the castle later evolved into a manor house. What we see today are the remains of a two-storey 15th-century tower, and time-worn, ivy-covered walls.

Carmarthen

Dyfed   SN 4120

Carmarthen — 'Merlin's City' — on the banks of the Tywi, is rich in Arthurian connections, and is especially renowned as the legendary haunt of Merlin the Magician. One can only hope that the supernatural powers of this ancient wizard have finally waned: in 1978, a frail old tree known as Merlin's Oak was unceremoniously uprooted from the town centre because it obstructed the traffic, despite the prophecy:

'When Merlin's Oak shall tumble down,
Then shall fall Carmarthen town.'

Its wizened remains were then taken a mile or so to Abergwili, on the outskirts of town, where they now reside within the splendid Carmarthen Museum. Nearby is so-called Merlin's Cave, marked by a blue door.

On the way to the museum, the road travels past an odd-looking break in the houses. Steep, grassy banks sweep down from a high terrace of dwellings into a great bowl, Carmarthen's Roman amphitheatre, one of only seven of its kind in Britain. It was built nearly 2000 years ago, when Carmarthen was known as Moridunum, a base established by the Romans.

Carreg Cennen Castle

Dyfed   SN 6619

Carreg Cennen is one of Wales's least known treasures. This spectacular, stirring castle has never attracted the attention it deserves, probably because of its position, well off the main road near the hamlet of Trapp — and also because of the stiff climb that separates the car park from the castle's lofty ramparts.

This is no second division historic site. Its walls and defences may be unkempt and ruinous by the standards, for example, of much-renovated Caernarfon Castle. But Carreg Cennen's gnarled medieval masonry is more than compensated for by its breathtaking position on top of a sheer-sided limestone cliff, overlooking the forbidding Black Mountain. The castle's extensive defences, dating from the 13th century, spread themselves out across the top of the hill — and down beneath ground level. One of the most intriguing features is a walled passageway, cut into the cliff, which leads to a cave beneath the castle where a number of prehistoric skeletons have been unearthed.

Carreg Wastad Point

Dyfed   SM 9340

The last invasion of Britain took place here on 22 February 1797. It was a farcical, tragi-comic affair masterminded by an American colonel in charge of around 1400 French troops. This ill-prepared army landed near the rocky, remote Carreg Wastad Point north of Fishguard, and, after a few desultory skirmishes with the locals, soon surrendered. They laid down their arms on Fishguard's Goodwick Sands. Invasion memorabilia — including captured weaponry and the table on which the surrender was signed — can be seen in the Royal Oak Inn, which stands in the centre of Fishguard.

JEMIMA NICHOLAS *captures one of the French invaders with her pitchfork. Her fellow women may have made the French think they were outnumered*

CASTELL COCH: WILLIAM BURGES

— *William Burges, architect of* **Castell Coch** *and* **Cardiff Castle**, *was one of the most extraordinary of the great Victorian architects.*

His best work is highly original,

and breathtakingly beautiful. He re-worked Gothic motifs in a brilliantly individual way, adding ideas from Oriental, Moorish, Eastern European and other architectural traditions to create dazzling effects. Interior surfaces tend to be covered in texture, pattern, colour — indeed, some of the more outlandish designs may have been engendered when Burges was under the visionary influence of opium.

Burges' work is at its most exuberant in the two castles he created, or rather re-created from ancient ruins, at Castell Coch and Cardiff. He was no dilettante, having studied medieval architecture for many years, so the ramparts, roofs, turrets and stairways are firmly based on architectural originals. Burges died in 1881, before the work at Castell Coch was complete, but the precise plans he left behind enabled the work to be finished. Anyone who has visited these two astonishing buildings will never be able to see the Victorian era in quite the same light again.

ABOVE *Moorish Room at Cardiff Castle, designed for the Marquess of Bute — like Burges, he dreamed of an ideal and romantic past*

Castell Coch

South Glamorgan ST 1382

This enchanting, fairytale castle should not really be viewed in isolation. It was built with the same flourish and exuberance as Cardiff Castle, five miles to the south.

Both castles are the 19th-century work of the eccentric architectural genius William Burges. And both were made possible by the astonishing wealth of his patron, Lord Bute, who controlled much of Cardiff's booming docklands and coal-exporting trade. Castell Coch was intended as a country retreat for Lord Bute. From the outside, its trio of conical towers evokes images of southern Germany rather than South Glamorgan. Within, the same elaborate decoration which characterises Cardiff is to be seen, especially in the drawing room, where flamboyant wall-paintings depict — among other things — scenes from *Aesop's Fables*. Historical purists, offended by Burges' flights of fancy, can at least take heart from the fact that Castell Coch, a mere 100 years old, stands on the site of a genuine 13th-century fortress.

Castell-y-Bere

Gwynedd SH 6608

In its prime, this rugged fortress would have commanded a route through the daunting, dramatic uplands of Cader Idris, but time, and the roadbuilders, have since by-passed Castell-y-Bere. Unlike the most famous castles of Wales, which were constructed by Norman and English invaders, this is an indigenous fortress, built by the native Welsh. It was founded in 1221 by Llewelyn ab Iorwerth, Llewelyn the Great, Lord of Snowdonia. From a distance, his ruined stronghold looks little more than a collection of stones. But first impressions are deceptive, for substantial sections of wall and elaborate defences can be seen close up.

Cilycwm

Dyfed SN 7540

This diminutive village, in the unexplored upper Tywi Valley, contains a fascinating little church. An ancient place of worship dedicated to St Michael, it may well date back to early Christian times in Wales. It has a 13th-century doorway and an unusual pair of roofs, one of the 15th century, the other of the 17th, but its greatest riches are the wall paintings which came to light during restoration work early this century. The most arresting is 'The Devil in the West Wall' in the back of the church, a frightening representation of death as a skeleton holding a spear.

Cregennen Lakes

Gwynedd SH 6614

These two lakes, sheltering beneath the northern escarpment of Cader Idris, are among the loveliest in Wales. They lie 1000 feet high on a largely treeless shelf of land above the swirling, sandy Mawddach Estuary. The direct approach, along the mountain road from Arthog on the shores of the estuary, is memorable indeed. This narrow road climbs sharply through woods and farmlands in a series of hairpin bends, before reaching the lakes, which are the property of the National Trust.

Cwm Bychan

Gwynedd SH 6431

A mountain road follows the course of the River Artro from the coast at Llanbedr, near Harlech, to the remote mountain lake of Llyn Cwm Bychan. This is just the start of a memorable journey, which can be completed only on foot. The lake lies on the doorstep of the desolate, boulder-strewn Rhinogs, a formless mass of heather, moor and rock, 2500 feet high, which is regarded as one of the last true wildernesses in Britain. Road becomes track beyond the lake. Soon, the mysterious 'Roman Steps' come into view, leading upwards into the Rhinogs. This well-engineered stone staircase, not Roman at all, is probably part of a medieval trackway used by pack-horse traders.

Cwm Tudu

Dyfed SN 3557

There are precious few places along the towering Cardigan Bay coast between New Quay and Cardigan where the sea-cliffs relinquish their grip. Cwm Tudu is one of the infrequent exceptions. A brief break in the cliffs gives way to a delightful little sand and shingle cove. A sheltered wooded valley opens up at the beach, which lies at the end of a confusing maze of country lanes, a few miles south-east of New Quay.

Cwmystwyth

Dyfed   SN 7873

The mountain road leading across from the Elan Valley lakelands to Devil's Bridge is a highly scenic one — apart from a single exception on the approach to the hamlet of Cwmystwyth. An alien moonscape of spoil heaps, scarred hillsides and the detritus of a long-abandoned mining encampment loom into view — a scene all the more surprising to visitors who stumble across it in mist or rain.

This was one of the largest lead mines in Mid Wales. The Romans mined it, but it was not until the 17th and 18th centuries that activity reached a peak, when silver was also produced. A complete community once lived and worked here. Derelict workers' dwellings stand below a large complex of rusting corrugated sheds, workshops and tramways. Close inspection of this site, which closed in 1916, is *not advisable*. It is in a precarious state and best viewed from the safety of the roadside.

Cynghordy Viaduct

Dyfed   SN 8040

Railway buffs, as well as seekers of the obscure and interesting, will be well rewarded by a visit to this viaduct, in the foothills of the Cambrian Mountains between Llandovery and Llanwrtyd Wells. This elegant structure is still in active service as part of British Rail's scenic Heart of Wales line, which cuts a path through some of the loveliest countryside in South and Mid Wales.

The line links Swansea to Craven Arms and Shrewsbury. Not the least of the many engineering problems encountered along its length occurred at Cynghordy, where the 18-span viaduct was constructed to carry trains 100 feet above ground over a broad vale. A little further on, the line plunges into a tunnel, 1000 yards long, burrowed into the hillside around the Sugar Loaf Mountain.

Doethie Valley

Dyfed   SN 7650

The source of the River Doethie, difficult to trace, is high in the boggy wilderness areas of Mid Wales, between Llandovery and Tregaron. The Doethie flows down a remote valley — where the only paths are sheep-walks — before joining another mountain river, the Pysgotwr, and then the larger River Tywi just north of the village of Rhandirmwyn.

Near the confluence we have Wales's answer to the secret glades of Sherwood Forest. High in the wooded hill above the watery junction is the cave in which Twm Shon Catti sought refuge from the Sheriff of Carmarthen in the 16th century. Twm, described *(continued on page 132)*

DOETHIE VALLEY: OUTLAW HEROES — *Twm Shon Catti, who lived in a cave near* **Doethie Valley**, *was one of those folk heroes forced to hide in inaccessible places — like Robert the Bruce in his cave, Hereward the Wake in the Fens, and Robin Hood in Sherwood Forest (but see* **Leeds**). *Clun Forest was the hideout of Edric Wilde, and* **St Cuthbert's Cave** *is said to be Cuddie the reiver's cave.*

Twm Shon Catti was really one Thomas Jones, who during the 16th century became celebrated as a Welsh Robin Hood. Humphrey Kynaston of **Nesscliffe** *was a similar figure.*

The last hiding-place of Owain Llawgoch, 'Owen of the Red Hand', is reputedly Ogof Pen-y-Llyn, a limestone cave in Craig Dorwyddion, near Carmel, Dyfed. With his band of men, Owain was walled up alive here by his enemies — a story some take to be true, because when the cave was opened in the 19th century, ten human skeletons were found. Others say he is not dead, but sleeping at Ogof Dinas, near **Carreg Cennen Castle**, *like King Arthur at* **Richmond**, *to be summoned to the aid of his country in time of danger. When he wakes, there will be peace all over the world.*

CWM BYCHAN   *Traditionally called the Roman Steps, because they are said to have been used by sentries going to and from Bwlch Tyddiad, these unhewn slabs more probably date from medieval times. Some believe a tunnel links the steps to Harlech Castle*

GOWER PENINSULA: WILDLIFE

*— Although the **Gower Peninsula** is quite small — barely 15 miles long — and is close to the Industrial heartlands of Wales, it contains a remarkable variety of unspoiled countryside. Habitats include open sheepwalks, forming the peninsula's spine, and cliffs, beaches, dunes, marshes and woodlands around the coast. Some of the coastal habitats are protected as nature reserves; one of the best is the National Nature Reserve at Oxwich. Here can be seen sandy beaches, sand dunes, salt- and fresh-water marsh and woodlands. Exciting communities of plants and animals are to be found in these habitats; for example within the dunes are permanently wet areas called 'slacks' which are home to nine species of orchid, the localised adder's tongue fern and much else besides; in the woodland are further fascinating plant communities under a tree cover dominated by ash. Buzzards nest here, and badgers may be seen.*

Limestone is an important factor in the make-up of the flora and fauna of the Gower, and there is a Limestone Nature Trail at the tip of the peninsula which takes in many of the most interesting points. The walk looks out over Worm's Head, where guillemots and razorbills are among the birds nesting on the limestone crags. There are other opportunities to see the life of rocky seashores on the peninsula's south coast, while the north is made up largely of mudflats, and is renowned for its cockle beds.

ABOVE *The guillemot spends months at sea, but in February jostles for a cliff-site for its egg — pear-shaped, so as not to roll*

(Doethie Valley continued . . .)

in conflicting reports as both a bona fide villain and a local hero, hid from the sheriff in a cave well concealed among the jumble of giant rocks on Dinas Hill. This distinctive, conical-shaped rise of land, clothed in oakwoods, is now an RSPB nature reserve. The rare red kite can sometimes be seen from the waymarked footpath which runs right around the hill, with a detour to Twm's cave.

North of Dinas Hill, a new road has been laid across desolate highland terrain that was previously accessible only on foot or horseback. This spectacular road, built to serve the huge Llyn Brianne reservoir, runs along the eastern shores of the lake. At the northern end of the reservoir, take the western fork across the mountain to Capel Soar. Farmers still travel on horseback to this small, whitewashed Welsh chapel, which stands completely alone in one of the emptiest parts of Wales.

Eliseg's Pillar

Clwyd SJ 2044

Eliseg, according to the long Latin inscription on this stone pillar, was the great-grandfather of Cyngen, Prince of Powys, who erected this eight foot high pillar cross in memory of his warlike forebear. The inscription, weathered and unreadable today, was, according to the 1696 transcription, a record of how Eliseg 'annexed the inheritance of Powys . . . from the powers of the English, which he made into a sword land by fire'. The pillar stands on a mound beside the main road two miles north-west of Llangollen. When the mound was opened it was found to contain a stone burial chamber with a human skull — Eliseg's? — and a silver coin. The skull was gilded — as befits a member of the Powys line — and was reburied.

Felin Geri Flour Mill

Dyfed SN 2942

This ancient, water-powered flour mill was rescued from oblivion in the early 1970s. It has since been restored to full working order, and is open to visitors from Easter to the end of September. Slow-turning wheels and cogs once more provide the mill stones with the power to turn grain into flour, in the way that it was produced in the 16th century. Fashion has caught up with Felin Geri: its high-fibre stoneground flour is now a best-seller among the health-conscious. The water is provided by the Ceri, a shady little tributary which joins the River Teifi a mile north-west of Newcastle Emlyn.

Ganllwyd

Gwynedd SH 7224

A gated road off the A470 in the village of Ganllwyd climbs up into a mossy mountainside of primeval beauty. Tall oakwoods and black boulders line the rocky banks of the River Gamlan as it tumbles down the valley. Within half a mile of the main road (it is better to walk than drive, for this side road is extremely narrow with no parking places), Rhaeadr Ddu, 'The Black Waterfall', comes into view. Rhaeadr Ddu, and its pocket of oak woodlands, are part of a National Trust estate, almost surrounded by the conifers of the huge Coed-y-Brenin Forest.

Gateholm Island

Dyfed SM 7707

Gateholm, in the far-flung south-west corner of Pembrokeshire, is totally insulated from crowds and commercialisation. Few visitors are inclined, first to drive all the way beyond Marloes, and then to leave their cars for the walk down to Marloes Sands, one of the loveliest, quietest beaches in Wales. Gateholm, an island accessible at low tide, stands off the western end of the beach. This ready-made stronghold bears evidence of an Iron Age settlement occupied until and during the Roman occupation of Wales.

Gower Peninsula

West Glamorgan SS 5090

Gower was, in 1956, the first part of Britain to be designated an 'Area of Outstanding Natural Beauty'. The most memorable stretch of southern coast lies in the far south-west between *Port Eynon* and *Rhossili*. Well away from all roads, it can only be explored by a spectacular six-mile path, which picks its way across the limestone cliffs.

Half-way along is Gower's most important — and inaccessible — prehistoric site. In 1823, the so-called 'Red Lady of Paviland' was discovered in a cave set in the cliff face. On closer examination, the 'lady' turned out to be the bones of Cro-Magnon man, nearly 19,000 years old. Visitors to the cave are rightly discouraged. In the words of the local guidebook, 'we do not recommend that you try to reach this cave which is very dangerous to inexperienced climbers'.

Rhossili is best known for its magnificent beach, a long, windy expanse of sands stretching northwards for almost three miles. Few visitors are aware that this was the home of Edgar Evans, better known, perhaps — as the memorial plaque in Rhossili's sturdy little church reveals — as Petty Officer Evans, who died in the tragic expedition to the Antarctic led by Captain Scott in 1912.

Although the peninsula's coastline captures the lion's share of attention, inland Gower is not without its interest. Evidence of prehistoric settlement is thick on the ground, most impressively at the *Parc le Breos* burial chamber, hidden in an isolated valley north-west of Parkmill. Visitors must leave their cars in this village and walk along a wooded vale to Green Cwm, a large meadowland completely surrounded by trees, where the well preserved outline of a tomb used by Neolithic people from 3000 to 1900BC can be seen. An even older prehistoric site lies further along the valley. This is roomy *Cathole Cave*, inhabited around 10,000 years ago, and within which the bones of such animals as the woolly rhinoceros and mammoth have been found.

Gower's empty northern coast begins in earnest along *Whitford Burrows*. This sandy spit, a National Nature Reserve of dunelands, salt-marsh and beach, points northwards into the mouth of the Loughor Estuary. In a wooded dingle at nearby *Cheriton* stands the most enchanting church on the peninsula. Dedicated to St Cadog, this ancient place of worship, which dates from medieval times, is graced by delightful interior carvings in light-toned wood.

Weobley Castle, further along the north coast, is also of medieval origin. This fortified manor house, ranged around a courtyard, dates from the late 13th century. Its position is stunning.

GOWER PENINSULA: BURIAL CAIRNS —

Built between 3000 and 2000BC, the Neolithic chambered cairns at Parc le Breos on the **Gower Peninsula, Tinkinswood**, St Lythans and Capel Garmon, are closely related to the chambered long cairns of south-west England, in particular those of the Cotswolds.

These chambered cairns are all wedge-shaped, with a distinctive funnel-shaped forecourt at the broad end. They were communal tombs, with the chambers approached by a short passage. Drystone walling was used to supplement the large upright slabs, and provide an even surface on which to rest the capstones.

The Parc le Breos cairn was first excavated in 1869, when no capstone survived. The badly dis-arranged bones of at least 20 people were found, the oldest about 25 years of age, all suffering from some disorder of the joints.

The cairn may have been deliberately built in the shape of a womb: one speculative opinion is that inmates were buried in the foetal position to symbolise their emergence as they passed from death into new life.

PARC LE BREOS *Chambered cairn for fresh or re-buried corpses, built by Neolithic peoples who had migrated from the west*

GOWER PENINSULA *No one can explain the walled-up opening called the Culver Hole, in the sea-cliff near Port Eynon. It may have been a dovecote or 'culver house'; inside there are stairs and floors*

KNIGHTON: OFFA'S DYKE — *Running past Knighton on its way from Sedbury Cliffs on the Severn to the sea at Prestatyn, Offa's Dyke covered 149 miles, going via the valley of the Wye and Herefordshire and across the Forest of Clun.*

Traceable for 81 miles, as an earthwork about six feet high and nearly sixty wide, with a ditch (usually on the western side), it was built as a boundary between the powerful Anglo-Saxon kingdom of Mercia and the Welsh princedoms. It was undoubtedly an agreed frontier — only in peacetime could such a work have been undertaken, and villages with English names left on the 'wrong' side of the fence indicate concessions to the Welsh.

*There are other linear earthworks in Britain — **Wansdyke**, Devil's Dyke, Cambridgeshire, and Grim's Ditch, Oxfordshire, for example — but this is the only one remembered (in both Welsh and English) by the name of its builder — Offa, King of Mercia from 757 to 796, and overlord of the southern English.*

He may have been inspired by tales of his ancestor Offa I, who built a great frontier along the Eider when he ruled the Angles in their homeland of Schleswig.

KNIGHTON *Inevitably, much of the great barrier (above) called Offa's Dyke has disappeared, but some of its best-preserved sections, seen left in this aerial view, run across the silent hills north-west of the town*

Gwaun Valley

Dyfed SN 0134

It is a case of turning the clocks back — quite literally — in this secluded, wooded little valley inland from Fishguard in north Pembrokeshire. The scattered, sparsely numbered inhabitants of the Gwaun Valley come together on 13 January to celebrate the New Year. This custom is explained by their adherence, during New Year at least, to the old pre-1752 calendar, which ran over a week and a half behind the times. Today's residents are still happy to stick to the old ways at the turn of the year, celebrating with traditional goose and plum pudding, whilst the children collect 'calennig', gifts of money and fruit.

Gwynfynydd Gold Mine

Gwynedd SH 7328

Deep in the heart of Coed-y-Brenin Forest, north of Dolgellau, lies a mine where 19th-century prospectors dug for gold. Gwynfynydd was one of the major mines during this Welsh gold rush, producing rich finds during the 1860s, 1880s and at the turn of the century. Mining continues today: indeed, plans to expand operations at Gwynfynydd have been a subject of controversy between environmentalists and industrialists.

Substantial remains of the old mine can still be seen among the trees, in a beautiful riverside setting. Gwynfynydd can be reached by a minor road which leads north-east into the forest from Ganllwyd on the A470. When the road ends, walk along the loose-surfaced track to the mine (a distance of about one mile). The effort is well worth it, not least for the two spectacular waterfalls which are close to Gwynfynydd.

Hafren Forest

Powys SN 8487

Two of Wales's most famous rivers — the Severn and the Wye — have their sources within a few miles of each other in the wilds of the Plynlimon Mountains. The Severn, in its infancy, flows through the Hafren Forest, a large conifer plantation on the eastern shoulders of Plynlimon (Afon Hafren is the Welsh name for the river). Enthusiastic walkers can follow a rough, wet path through the trees and beyond to peaty Blaenhafren, the source of the Severn, a strenuous round trip of at least seven miles.

Holywell

Clwyd SJ 1875

Although listed as one of the 'Seven Wonders of Wales' by 19th-century tourists, St Winefride's Well at Holywell is not today the best known of places. The well dates from the seventh century, when, according to legend, Winefride's head was cut off by a salacious local chieftain, Caradoc. She made a full recovery after her uncle, St Bueno, had replaced it, whilst the sinful Caradoc was swallowed up by the earth. The spring that appeared on the spot where her head fell to the ground became known, far and wide, for its healing powers. Called by some the 'Lourdes of Wales', it has been a place of pilgrimage for over 1000 years. The elaborate chapel built over it dates from the late 15th century.

Also at Holywell, the dramatic Grange Cavern Military Museum is a floodlit cave, hewn into the hillside, that contains over 70 military vehicles including jeeps and tanks.

Kidwelly

Dyfed SN 4106

A red-brick chimney, 164 feet tall, on the outskirts of Kidwelly, marks the site of a fascinating museum. The Kidwelly tinplate works, founded in 1737, grew into one of the largest in Britain during the booming 19th century. Today, it stands as the sole survivor of an industry that once flourished in this part of Wales. The entire manufacturing process — and the surprising scale of the operation — can be understood thanks to the preserved machinery, giant rollers, huge cropping shears and steam engines on the site. The coal industry is also represented here, in the form of pithead gear rescued from a local colliery. The museum is open during the summer.

Kidwelly's other most important historic site is much older. The town's remarkably well preserved castle still looks invulnerable, thanks to its massive, twin-towered Great Gatehouse and concentric rings of walls within walls.

Knighton

Powys SO 2872

Knighton's Welsh name, Tref y Clawdd ('The town on the dyke'), is a reminder that this is the only town that stands right on Offa's Dyke, the ancient earthwork constructed by King Offa of Mercia in the eighth century as the first official border between Wales and England. Knighton is now the home of the Offa's Dyke Centre, where information is available on the 170-mile long distance footpath that follows, where possible, the line of the dyke.

The Landsker

Dyfed

The Landsker, or 'landscar', is a ghostly line separating north from south Pembrokeshire. Although it does not appear on any official map, its historic influence has been profound. The line is generally thought to originate from the Norman invasion of West Wales in the 11th century. The native Welsh population retreated to the northern lands, blocked off from the south by a string of Norman castles. This division was reinforced by an influx of Anglo-Saxon and Flemish immigrants. English ways, customs and language subsequently gripped the south, turning it into the 'Little England beyond Wales'.

At one time, both sides kept themselves to themselves — inter-marriage, for example, was unthinkable. Although the Landsker's influence has obviously declined in this century, many Pembrokeshire people are still aware of its existence and the deep-rooted cultural differences that it implies. The line runs from Amroth, east of Tenby across to Newgale on the west coast, its route marked by a series of ruined castles. The divisions that it has created are summed up in the place names which straddle the border.

Llanddewi Brefi

Dyfed SN 6655

St David, Wales's patron saint, travelled widely as he spread the Christian message during the sixth century. In AD519, he came here for the Synod of Brefi, during which he took an important stand against the Pelagian heresy. At first his words were inaudible, but as he preached, the ground is said to have risen beneath his feet so that he could be both seen and heard. A church dedicated to St David still stands on high ground above the village square.

Llandrindod Wells

Powys SO 0561

Llandrindod, the purpose-built Victorian spa-resort, recreates its gracious golden era each September during Victorian Festival Week. Townsfolk dress in period costume, and appropriate Victorian entertainments — all properly genteel, we are assured — are staged amongst the ornate, gabled streets of this Mid Wales watering place. Llandrindod has even revived the practice of 'taking the waters': visitors can put the springs to the test once more, for the mineral waters are on tap in the renovated Rock Park pump rooms (closed during winter weekends).

Llanfihangel-y-pennant

Gwynedd SH 6708

Tyn-y-ddol, near this remote hamlet in the shadow of Cader Idris, was the home of Mary Jones, proudly remembered by the Welsh for her brave, unaccompanied, 25-mile walk across the mountains to Bala when only 16 years old. Her mission was to purchase a copy of the Welsh Bible from the influential religious figure, Reverend Thomas Charles, and it is said to have inspired the foundation, by Charles, of the British and Foreign Bible Society. A monument recalling Mary's determined deed stands amongst the ruins of the small cottage in which she lived.

LLANFIHANGEL-Y-PENNANT: MARY JONES — A ruined cottage in a remote village in **Llanfihangel-y-pennant** does not seem a likely place to be associated with a great worldwide organisation.

But it was from here that in 1800 Mary Jones, a girl of 16, set out to walk to Bala for a Bible. For years she had saved her pennies to buy her heart's desire, a Bible in Welsh, and she had heard that one could be obtained from the minister in Bala, Thomas Charles.

When she got there, unfortunately, she found that the last had been sold and no more were to be printed. But Charles felt so much compassion for her deep disappointment that he gave her his own. It was her burning desire for a Bible that prompted him eventually to found the British and Foreign Bible Society, making translations of the Bible available all over the world.

A memorial to Mary can be seen in her roofless cottage, and her Bible is preserved in **Cambridge** University Library.

THE BIBLE *that gave birth 200 years ago to a society translating the Scriptures for countries world-wide*

LANSILIN: WELSH PRINCES — *The remnant of warrior Owain Glyndwr's castle near **Llansilin** was one of many native Welsh fortresses attacked by English troops during Wales's last uprising against England. Glyndwr's daredevil defiance of Henry IV in 1401 rekindled the Welsh people's resentment of the English which had festered ever since Edward I's subjugation of the nation in the 13th century. Until that time Wales had been ruled for four centuries by the Welsh sovereign princes — tolerated by the Plantagenets only as long as they behaved peaceably. This uneasy truce ended in the 13th century when the rebellious Llewelyns held supremacy and Llewelyn I, 'the Great' (1194–1240), reputedly born at Dolwyddelan Castle and buried at **Llanrwst**, managed to regain a certain amount of autonomy. He was succeeded by his illegitimate son's son, Llewelyn II, 'the Last'. This accession was violently opposed by his brother, Owain Goch 'the Red', who subsequently suffered imprisonment for 23 years at Dolbadarn Castle. When Llewelyn II was killed by an English trooper in 1282 (see **Abbey Cwmhir**) all hope of Welsh independence died with him.*

*Castles built by the Welsh princes, such as **Castell-y-Bere**, can be identified by their defensive position high above landlocked valleys, by rather low curtain walls and gatehouses and by D-shaped or rectangular towers — a design influenced by the fact that these fighting men were spearmen, not archers.*

ABOVE *Llewelyn's tomb, Llanrwst. His remains, brought from Conwy to Maenan by monks, came here at the Dissolution*

Llangybi

Gwynedd SH 4240

Pilgrims have long come here for the cool waters of Ffynnon Cybi, St Cybi's Well, which flows through a peaceful little dingle beyond the churchyard. A ruined cottage stands next to the rough-stone walls that enclose the waters of this curative well, named after a Celtic saint who spread the Christian message throughout Wales in the sixth century.

Llanrwst

Gwynedd SH 7961

A magnificent treasure lies here — the sarcophagus (stone coffin) in which Llewelyn ab Iorwerth, Llewelyn the Great, was buried in 1240. Llewelyn, Prince of Aberffraw and Lord of Snowdon, is remembered as a wily, forceful and successful native leader who stood up to the English crown. The inscription on his beautifully carved coffin reads: 'This is the coffin of Leonlinus Magnus, Prince of Wales, who was buried at the Abbey of Conway, which upon dissolution was moved here.'

The sarcophagus is in the riverside Gwydir Chapel, just off the main square of this handsome old market town.

Llansilin

Clwyd SJ 2028

A mound seen from the road some two miles south is all that remains of Owain Glyndwr's once magnificent castle of Sycharth. Mercurial and romantic Owain was the last great Welsh rebel, rising against the English crown in the early 15th century. Initial success was followed by failure and the charismatic Owain, 'that great magician, damned Glendower' in Shakespeare's *Henry IV*, disappeared in 1412. All traces of his once splendid wooden castle have also vanished. The earthen mound in a private field is the only remnant from the 'most lovable of mansions' where Owain, according to Welsh bard Iolo Goch 'Upon four wooden columns proud, Mounteth this mansion to the cloud!' We now have to use imagination to fill in the details of the wooden defences, wide moat, private chapel, orchard, parkland, water-mill and dovecote that once existed here.

Llantrisant

Mid Glamorgan ST 0483

Vegetarianism, nudism, liberal attitudes to love-making and a fiery brand of politics were being preached by Dr William Price of Llantrisant a century before these causes became fashionable. Born in 1800, he lived in the old town, a jumble of narrow streets on the hill above sprawling, modern Llantrisant, and shocked his contemporaries. Everything came to a head in 1884 when Dr Price tried to cremate the body of his illegitimate son on Llantrisant Common. His son — named Iesu Crist (Jesus Christ) — had died in infancy. The cremation caused a furore, the affair escalating into a seminal court case during which Dr Price was declared innocent, a ruling that legalised cremation in Britain. He died at 93. A statue of this fascinating character, wearing his fox-skin head-dress, now stands in old Llantrisant's Bull Ring.

Llantwit Major

South Glamorgan SS 9768

If the journey to St David's Cathedral in the far south-west of Wales seems long, go instead to the little town of Llantwit Major in the pastoral Vale of Glamorgan, west of Cardiff. Historically, this is as important a religious shrine as St David's. It was here in AD500 that St Illtud founded his influential religious and educational community. It is close to the sea but in a protective hollow below the houses of the town, and although officially a church, it has cathedral-like dimensions. It is, in fact, two buildings in one — adjacent churches from the early 12th and late 13th centuries, built on the site of St Illtud's original monastery. A notable collection of Celtic crosses can be seen inside.

Just over three miles to the west, beyond the village of Marcross, is Nash Point. The layered cliffs of the South Glamorgan coastline are particularly dramatic here, with headlands crowned by two lighthouses and the remains of an Iron Age promontory fort.

Llanwonno

Mid Glamorgan ST 0395

Anyone who harbours the misconception that the South Wales valleys have only the kind of despoiled landscape portrayed in Richard

Llewelyn's *How Green was my Valley*, should visit Llanwonno. This pretty hamlet, high in the hills between the Rhondda Valley and Pontypridd, is completely surrounded by untouched mountainside and the trees of the St Gwynno Forest. It was from here that, according to legend, 18th-century runner Guto Nyth Bran sped across the mountain in the time that it took to boil a kettle.

Llanwrtyd Wells

Powys   SN 8746

Sedate to the point of sleepiness, the tranquillity of Llanwrtyd belies those heady, bygone days when 'taking the waters' was fashionable, and this spa town was bursting at the seams with holidaymakers from the industrial areas of South Wales. Tall, gabled houses are a reminder of those times — but the most evocative memorial to the town's heyday stands in the parkland beside the clear-flowing River Irfon, beyond the Dol-y-Coed Hotel. This is the old sulphur well, the appropriately named *Y Ffynnon Ddrewllyd* ('The Stinking Well'). The well buildings are currently under renovation as a tea room. Braver souls can forget the tea and sample instead the malodorous bluish sulphur waters that fill the circular well-head.

Old Llanwrtyd village further up the valley was where Welsh hymn-writer William Williams Pantycelyn was curate in the 1740s.

Llanybydder

Dyfed   SN 5244

On the last Thursday of each month, the obscure little Teifi-side town of Llanybydder, south-west of Lampeter, welcomes a cosmopolitan horde of visitors. Buyers from all over Britain and beyond make the long journey here for the horse sales — the town holds what some claim is the biggest horse-fair in Britain, during which hundreds of ponies and horses are auctioned off in the old market place.

Llanycefn

Dyfed   SN 0923

The chief attraction here is Penrhos Cottage, but a good map is needed to find it, hidden as it is on the narrow back lanes east of the B4313, between Llanycefn and Maenclochog (it is best approached from the latter).

Penrhos is thought to have been built as a 'moonlight house', a reference to a custom which allowed the overnight building of a dwelling on common land, as long as there was a fire burning in the hearth by morning. Today it can be admired as a fine example of the traditional Welsh thatched cottage, filled with original furniture. It has been renovated and is open at Easter and from mid-May to September (but not on Mondays or Sunday mornings).

L LANTWIT MAJOR: STONE CROSSES — In the church at **Llantwit Major** is a collection of stone crosses. Such crosses are the only monuments surviving from Wales's 'age of conversion', in the fifth and sixth centuries.

Although known as 'Celtic' crosses, their distinctive geometric patterns and other motifs derive from Saxon England, the designs becoming weaker as time went on. Many were erected to mark the graves of monks and important laymen in the cemeteries attached to the larger monasteries: King Hywel of Morgannwg set one up at Llantwit Major in the ninth century, to commemorate his father, Rhys. At **Strata Florida Abbey**, crosses were put up in memory of Welsh princes.

Crosses also marked church property and paths, or served purposes no longer identifiable. **Eliseg's Pillar** and the fine cross at Carew, Dyfed, bearing the name of Maredudd ap Edwin, king of Deheubarth 1033-35, are connected with the dynasties of Powys and Deheubarth, but why they were set up is uncertain.

STONE CROSSES   *and other memorials from the eighth to the tenth centuries can be seen in St Illtud's church, including a headless shaft bearing the saint's name*

LLANTWIT MAJOR   *Low tide shows the limestone platforms of Nash Point. A ship was wrecked off the notorious coast in 1886, but came so close in that the crew were able to walk ashore*

LYN-Y-FAN FACH: A LADY OF THE LAKE

— A fairy lady rose out of the little lake of Llyn-y-fan Fach to marry a widow's son from Blaen-Sawdde, Llanddeusant. On condition that he never struck her three causeless blows, she came to live with him on a farm about a mile from Myddfai, where she bore him three sons.

But one by one the three blows were struck, and at the third she returned to her lake. Her sons often wandered there, looking for her. One day, near Llidiad y Medygon (The Doctor's Gate), she met them, and taught them the use of certain herbs.

The eldest, Rhiwallon, and his sons became physicians to Rhys Gryg, lord of Llandovery and Dinefwr castles, who rewarded them with land around Myddfai.

These were the original Physicians of Myddfai, reputed to have lived in the 12th century. Their descendants continued late into the 19th century to practise medicine. The last to work in Myddfai itself was probably John Jones, who died in 1739 and is commemorated on a tombstone in the church porch.

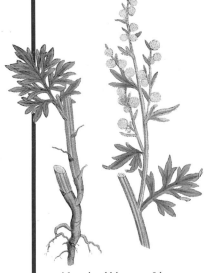

Near the old house at Llwyn Meredyd, home of one of the Physicians' descendants, is the site of the botanical gardens where some of their herbs were grown.

ABOVE *Common wormwood (Artemisia absinthium), widely used by medieval physicians. Infused in water, it was taken as a tonic and a worm-expellant. Its bitter taste gives flavour to absinthe. In the same family, mugwort (Artemisia vulgaris) was linked with magic and used to avert evil*

Llyn Celyn

Gwynedd SH 8640

When the water authorities created the lake of Llyn Celyn in the Arennig Mountains north-west of Bala, they consigned a tiny hamlet to a watery grave. A chapel and handful of houses were submerged when the reservoir flooded the valley in the 1960s. But all was not lost, for a modernistic chapel was built on the lakeside to replace the drowned original. The unusual nautical appearance of Capel Celyn Memorial is no accident, for it was 'designed to resemble a ship coming in from over the water'. Slate tablets within the chapel list those whose bodies are buried beneath the lake, in the original graveyard. Headstones removed from the drowned chapel grounds can be seen beside the memorial.

Llyn-y-fan Fach

Dyfed SN 8021

A beautiful fairy, who rose from the depths of the lake to marry a local farmer, it is said, taught her family magical remedies for all sorts of ailments, and so gave rise to the very real Physicians of Myddfai, who were famous throughout Wales for their cures in medieval times.

Llyn-y-fan Fach is an obvious candidate for such a legend. Its dark waters lie beneath a steep, curving escarpment that leads to the Carmarthen Van, the 2632-foot summit of the brooding, misty Black Mountain. The lake is accessible via the hamlet of Llanddeusant, south of Llandovery: it is reached by the stony path from the end of the tarmac road.

Maesllyn Woollen Mill

Dyfed SN 3644

Rescued from dereliction in the mid 1970s, Maesllyn Woollen Mill is one of the few survivors from the area's thriving 19th-century woollen industry. Dating from the 1880s, it is just one of the hundreds of mills, large and small, which grew up along the banks of the Teifi and its tributaries around Llandysul, and it has been renovated both as a working mill and as a museum of the woollen industry. The production process from raw wool to finished cloth is explained, together with the development in weaving techniques. The mill, open all year (though sometimes closed on Sundays), is four miles north-west of Llandysul.

Maesyronnen Chapel

Powys SO 1740

Tiny Maesyronnen helped plant the seeds from which a great religious movement grew, eventually spreading throughout Wales. Founded in around 1696, the church was one of the earliest places of worship for Nonconformists. Its out-of-the-way position among farmlands overlooking the Vale of Wye was deliberate: religious dissenters would meet here secretly.

A humble building that looks from the outside more like a stone cottage than a place of worship, it is filled with original furniture from the 18th and 19th centuries. It lies less than a mile from the A438 between Glasbury and Llowes — if the door is locked, instructions are given on where to get the key.

Mynydd Mawr

Gwynedd SH 1425

This is as far as you can go: Mynydd Mawr and the plunging cliffs of Braich-y-Pwll are known as the 'Land's End of North Wales'. A narrow road winds its way up to the windy 534-foot summit of this National Trust property, and from it are some of the most spectacular views in Wales.

The rugged, cliff-backed coastline of the Lleyn Peninsula leads off into the distant, great arc of Cardigan Bay. The dangerous waters of Bardsey Sound, a two-mile stretch which separates Bardsey Island (in private ownership) from mainland Wales, lie directly below the summit. Bardsey, Ynys Enlli in Welsh ('the Isle of Currents'), is also known as the 'Isle of 20,000 Saints' after a monastic community founded there in the seventh century. Three pilgrimages to Bardsey equalled one to Rome — perhaps unfairly, for the crossing of the treacherous Sound must have been a daunting prospect. Pilgrims would offer prayers and gifts for a safe passage at the headland church of St Mary's. Ruins of this ancient religious site can still be made out among the bracken. St Mary's Well, in the cliffs below, also survives. The spring, accessible by a rocky stairway, has legendary miraculous powers. Pilgrims clever enough to climb back up the cliffs and run around the church three times without swallowing or spilling a mouthful of its waters were granted any wish.

Merthyr Tydfil

Mid Glamorgan SO 0406

History books sing the praises of George Stephenson, who pioneered the world's first successful passenger railway between Stockton and Darlington in 1825, but a plain stone monument just north of the town centre of Merthyr Tydfil marks an equally significant world first. From here, in 1804, Cornish engineer Richard Trevithick ran the first steam-powered locomotive on a tramway route down the valley, to link with the canal at Abercynon. Its cargo was a ten-ton consignment of iron from the foundries at Merthyr. A model of Trevithick's locomotive can be seen at Merthyr's Cyfarthfa Castle, an imposing castellated mansion — now partly a museum — built by the powerful Crawshay ironmasters in 1824-25.

Mill Bay

Dyfed SM 8103

It was in this remote south-west Pembrokeshire bay, near the tip of the Dale Peninsula, that on 7 August 1485 Harri Tudur took his first steps to becoming Henry VII, founder of the mighty Tudor dynasty. A Welshman, born in Pembroke Castle, he landed on this rocky shore from France, with an army of 2000 men. In the next 16 days he marched 260 miles through Wales and the Midlands. Under the banner of *Y Ddraig Goch*, the Red Dragon of Wales, he gathered strength along the way before achieving victory over Richard III at the Battle of Bosworth, to become a renowned King of England.

MABINOGION —

The 'Mabinogion' is the title given to a selection of old Welsh tales by their translator, 1838-49, Lady Charlotte Guest. Taken from three manuscripts of the 14th to 16th centuries, the White Book of Rhydderch, the Red Book of Hergest and the 'Hames Taliesin', some of them are much more ancient.

Several have identifiable settings, among them 'Culhwch and Olwen' (see **St David's Peninsula**) and the story of Macsen Wledig (see **Sarn Helen**). Branwen, whose story appears in the Red Book of Hergest, is traditionally buried beneath the ruined cairn of Bedd Branwen ('Branwen's Grave'), near Llanbabo, Anglesey.

Also from the Red Book comes the story of Math, mainly concerning Lleu Llaw Gyffes — 'Lleu of the Skilful Hand' — rejected by his mother Arianrhod. Her castle, Caer Arianrhod, has long been identified with a reef within sight of the hillfort of Dinas Dinlle, Gwynedd, where her brother Gwydion brought Lleu up.

Later Gwydion and Math conjure a wife for Lleu out of flowers — Blodeuedd ('Flowers'). He takes her to live at 'Mur Castell' — the Roman fort and Norman motte of Tomen-y-Mur. But she proves unfaithful, and a tragic denouement takes in the Nantlle valley below Snowdon, the banks of the Cynfal, and Llyn y Morynion, 'the Maidens' Lake', above Ffestiniog.

ABOVE *Extract from the Red Book of Hergest — one of the sources of the Mabinogion*

A LIGHTHOUSE KEEPER'S VIEW

A rock no bigger than half a football pitch, surrounded by treacherous seas and reached by helicopter . . . For Norman McCanch, working as a lighthouse keeper was a chance to study the wildlife of the coast from a unique angle, and to do the pictures seen here

At 4am the eastern horizon begins to grow pale, throwing into sharp relief the twin summits of Ramsey Island and the conical peak of Carnllidi on the mainland beyond. From South Bishop Lighthouse, on the rugged coast of Pembrokeshire, you can tell the time of year by watching the dawn, for in summer the sun rises over the northern end of Ramsey, creeping around the shoulder of Carysgubor, while in winter the first rays of sunlight show above the cliffs of Ynys Bery at the southernmost end of the island.

It is early summer, Pete has completed his middle watch, through the dark hours from midnight to 4am, and gone to his bunk. For the next eight hours I am the morning watchman and have this tiny rock kingdom all to myself. Half the size of a football pitch, 120 feet high and mostly steep and barren, South Bishop is the most southerly and westerly of a string of dangerous rocks known as the Bishops and Clerks. The lighthouse was built in the late 1830s, originally with separate houses for two keepers and their families. Now there is one large four-bedroomed house, a squat tower about 50 feet high, a spotlessly clean engine room and a helicopter pad.

Early morning is a good time for bird-watching, with flocks of puffins and razorbills arriving to fish off the boat landing, and long lines of gannets, dazzling white with a six-foot wingspan, searching the waters for shoals of un-suspecting fish. Surprisingly, the rock sometimes rings with the songs of wood-land birds, for willow warblers and blackcaps, redstarts and flycatchers often stop overnight during migration.

Even the most forbidding tower light, poking like a defiant finger from a raging sea, has birds around it. Indeed, in an otherwise featureless ocean a lighthouse marks an unseen factor such as a rock or reef, which is bound to bring food to the surface and hence seabirds to exploit it.

However, the morning watchman has more to do than just watch birds. I sweep and clean around the living room, kitchen, radio room and bathroom, and then climb the spiral stairs to the lantern. About half an hour after sunrise, I put the light out. On an electric lamp it is simply a matter of throwing a switch, but in the old days oil-burning lights required a careful procedure, followed by a full

strip-down and clean every morning. I was fortunate enough to serve on an oil light during my training, and grew to like the simplicity of their giant Tilly lamp structure. Whatever the light source it is important to remember to hang the curtains in the lantern during the day, otherwise the sun's rays, focused by the lens, will melt the optical equipment inside.

Then it is down from the lantern, and into the engine room, where a new generator is started and the outgoing one is cleaned in readiness, every morning. Each of the three diesel generators runs for only 24 hours at a stretch, in rotation, so that there are always two on stand-by, in the event of emergency. After the fuel tanks have been filled it is probably about six in the morning — but before break-fast I must check the weather on the way in, and enter details of windspeed and direction, barometric pressure, temper-ature and general conditions in the log-book, to provide an independent record of conditions in the event of an accident to shipping.

Morning watch is special, for it is the only time when a real cooked breakfast can be justified on a lighthouse, so I look forward to a meal of bacon and eggs, toast, marmalade and lots of tea — to be followed straight away by washing

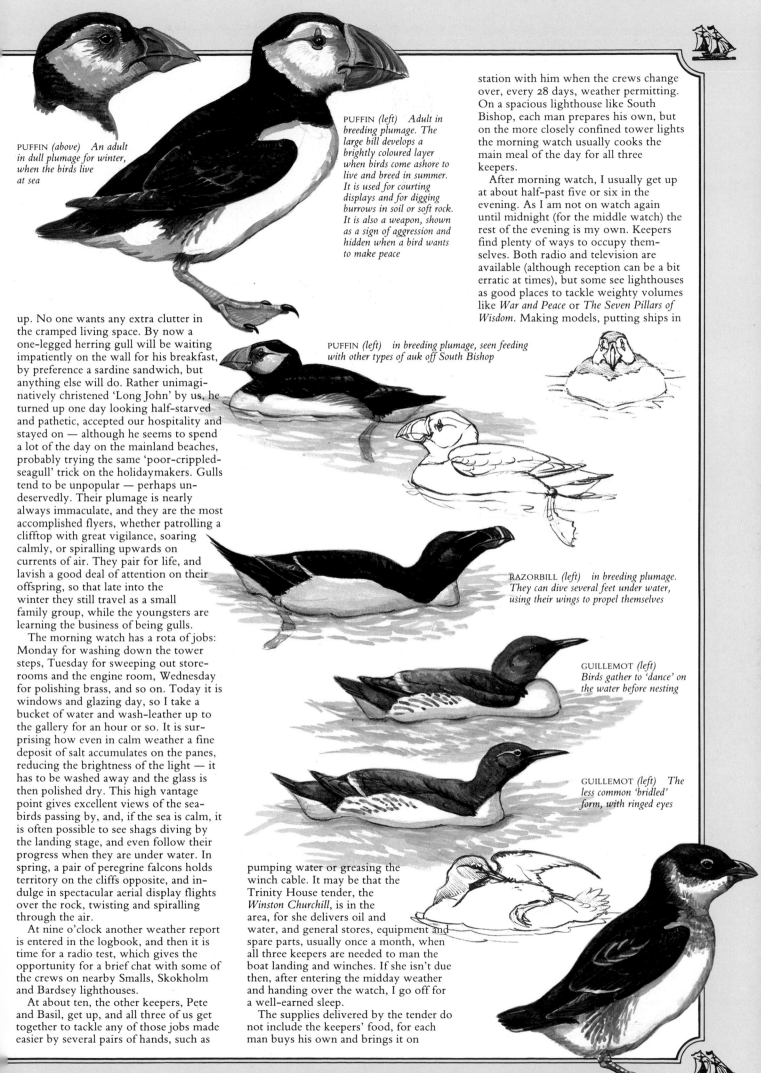

PUFFIN (above) An adult in dull plumage for winter, when the birds live at sea

PUFFIN (left) Adult in breeding plumage. The large bill develops a brightly coloured layer when birds come ashore to live and breed in summer. It is used for courting displays and for digging burrows in soil or soft rock. It is also a weapon, shown as a sign of aggression and hidden when a bird wants to make peace

PUFFIN (left) in breeding plumage, seen feeding with other types of auk off South Bishop

RAZORBILL (left) in breeding plumage. They can dive several feet under water, using their wings to propel themselves

GUILLEMOT (left) Birds gather to 'dance' on the water before nesting

GUILLEMOT (left) The less common 'bridled' form, with ringed eyes

LITTLE AUK (right) found killed by oil

up. No one wants any extra clutter in the cramped living space. By now a one-legged herring gull will be waiting impatiently on the wall for his breakfast, by preference a sardine sandwich, but anything else will do. Rather unimaginatively christened 'Long John' by us, he turned up one day looking half-starved and pathetic, accepted our hospitality and stayed on — although he seems to spend a lot of the day on the mainland beaches, probably trying the same 'poor-crippled-seagull' trick on the holidaymakers. Gulls tend to be unpopular — perhaps undeservedly. Their plumage is nearly always immaculate, and they are the most accomplished flyers, whether patrolling a clifftop with great vigilance, soaring calmly, or spiralling upwards on currents of air. They pair for life, and lavish a good deal of attention on their offspring, so that late into the winter they still travel as a small family group, while the youngsters are learning the business of being gulls.

The morning watch has a rota of jobs: Monday for washing down the tower steps, Tuesday for sweeping out storerooms and the engine room, Wednesday for polishing brass, and so on. Today it is windows and glazing day, so I take a bucket of water and wash-leather up to the gallery for an hour or so. It is surprising how even in calm weather a fine deposit of salt accumulates on the panes, reducing the brightness of the light — it has to be washed away and the glass is then polished dry. This high vantage point gives excellent views of the seabirds passing by, and, if the sea is calm, it is often possible to see shags diving by the landing stage, and even follow their progress when they are under water. In spring, a pair of peregrine falcons holds territory on the cliffs opposite, and indulge in spectacular aerial display flights over the rock, twisting and spiralling through the air.

At nine o'clock another weather report is entered in the logbook, and then it is time for a radio test, which gives the opportunity for a brief chat with some of the crews on nearby Smalls, Skokholm and Bardsey lighthouses.

At about ten, the other keepers, Pete and Basil, get up, and all three of us get together to tackle any of those jobs made easier by several pairs of hands, such as pumping water or greasing the winch cable. It may be that the Trinity House tender, the Winston Churchill, is in the area, for she delivers oil and water, and general stores, equipment and spare parts, usually once a month, when all three keepers are needed to man the boat landing and winches. If she isn't due then, after entering the midday weather and handing over the watch, I go off for a well-earned sleep.

The supplies delivered by the tender do not include the keepers' food, for each man buys his own and brings it on station with him when the crews change over, every 28 days, weather permitting. On a spacious lighthouse like South Bishop, each man prepares his own, but on the more closely confined tower lights the morning watch usually cooks the main meal of the day for all three keepers.

After morning watch, I usually get up at about half-past five or six in the evening. As I am not on watch again until midnight (for the middle watch) the rest of the evening is my own. Keepers find plenty of ways to occupy themselves. Both radio and television are available (although reception can be a bit erratic at times), but some see lighthouses as good places to tackle weighty volumes like War and Peace or The Seven Pillars of Wisdom. Making models, putting ships in

A LIGHTHOUSE KEEPER'S VIEW

STORM PETREL (right) *Living almost entirely on the ocean, petrels are resilient to most weathers. But this one may have been the casualty of a collision with a cable*

GANNETS IN FLIGHT (above right) *A series of sketches to show the variations that can be seen in plumage. Birds take several years to reach the adult state, and blotchy individuals are common. The wingspan of an adult may be as much as six feet — they spend much of the year gliding over the North Atlantic, occasionally resting on the water*

bottles, playing musical instruments, painting, embroidery, beer-making and wine-making, fishing and making the fishing tackle — they all help to pass the time, while several keepers, myself among them, have found an absorbing interest in birds and natural history. No newspapers, fresh milk, shops, traffic, neighbours or family tend to change one's preoccupations and encourage a deeper interest in the natural world outside.

It is during the migration periods that lighthouses can come alive with birds, often inundated by tired warblers, fly-catchers, chats and thrushes. In spring-time each morning brings something new. A flock of willow warblers, or bold wheatears and fiery male redstarts from wintering grounds in West Africa. Perhaps endless streams of swallows, sand and house martins moving relent-lessly north. Should the weather deteriorate then the lighthouse can have a fatal attraction to small birds, as they are drawn into its powerful beams as if by some form of optical magnetism, and many crash into the glazing and die. But far more survive and dawn will find them searching avidly for food among the rocks. By mid-afternoon most have left the island, unseen, to complete the last leg of their dangerous journeys. I make drawings and sketches of those that turn up and enter the arrivals in a separate logbook. Some I manage to catch and ring, to learn more of their migration routes and stop-over points.

South Bishop attracts a number of creatures other than birds, for during summer a regular group of up to 15 grey seals haul out on the rocks. They are part of the large colony which breeds on Ramsey and most adults return home during October when the pups are born. They seem to spend a great deal of time sleeping, occasionally scratching them-selves with a flipper. Porpoises and bottle-nosed dolphins are not infrequent visitors, passing by in small groups or feeding on the shoals of mackerel, which also attract occasional blue and porbeagle sharks.

Insects too are regular visitors, blown out to the rock by offshore winds in late summer. Butterflies and moths often turn

RINGING (above) *An adult male starling that has been attracted to the light is picked up and given a ring (Number XA 84438) before being released. Ringing is invaluable for research, but needs care and the right tools. In Britain, ringing can only be done by licence after a long training course*

up, among them migratory species like the painted lady butterfly and the hummingbird hawk moth. Daddy-longlegs, wasps, ladybirds, greenfly and blackfly and even spiders arrive —

mostly to end their days as food for hungry migrant birds.

Even when there are few birds around, the constantly changing face of the sea provides an absorbing spectacle. Winter storms on South Bishop can be ferocious, with long lines of huge breakers rolling in from the Atlantic Ocean to crash on the rocks with unrelenting force. In bad gales, the breaking spray passes right over the lighthouse. After such a storm, I have even found bits of seaweed and sand in the lantern guttering, nearly 170 feet above sea level. Fog is a real problem at some times of the year, on one occasion necessitating the sounding of the fog signal for 96 hours at a stretch. Even in summer the forces of nature provide a potential threat, for electrical storms at sea are spectacular and at times a little frightening. Lighthouses are well supplied with lightning con-ductors, but even so, South Bishop was struck twice in the space of a few hours during one July thunderstorm which raged through the night, lighting up the cliffs for miles around with an unearthly blue light at each stupendous flash, and causing a frenzy of activity among the nocturnal Manx shearwaters. These birds are attracted to the light in small numbers under normal conditions, but during this storm thousands collected around the rock, flying rapidly past the lantern, ever closer, calling raucously and occasionally misjudging and crashing into the yard, where I caught them, to be released safely at dawn.

In our world of sophisticated radar and satellite navigation systems, people some-times question the importance of light-houses to the maritime community. In fact they do have an important role to play, for many fishing boats and coasters do not have the modern equipment, and the ever-growing navy of leisure sailors relies heavily on the lighthouses' visible and audible warnings of danger. Light-houses also act as the signposts of the sea, for their different patterns of flashes (all chronicled on Admiralty charts and in almanacs) enable sailors to pinpoint their position with some confidence. The current trend in the operation of light-houses is to remove the men and make them automatic, but to maintain and supervise their working by means of a computer link to a mainland light.

This means that although lighthouses will continue to be a visible feature of our coastline, in the future the way of life of the people who have manned them diligently for the past two hundred years

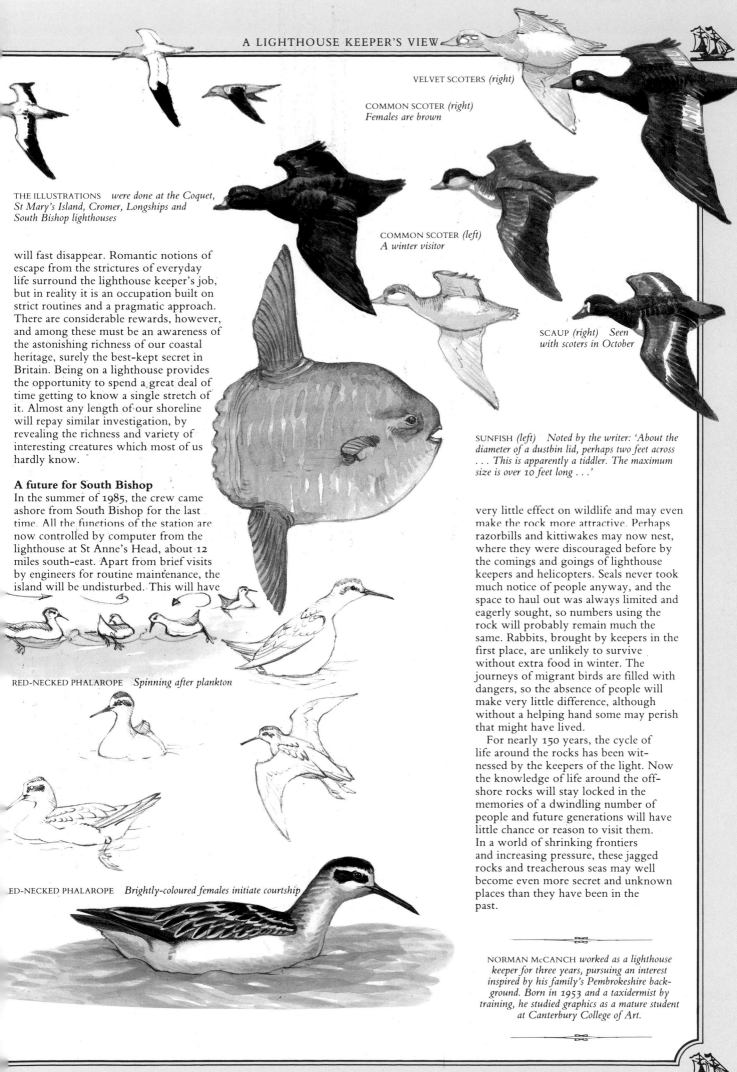

VELVET SCOTERS (right)

COMMON SCOTER (right)
Females are brown

THE ILLUSTRATIONS *were done at the Coquet, St Mary's Island, Cromer, Longships and South Bishop lighthouses*

COMMON SCOTER (left)
A winter visitor

SCAUP (right) *Seen with scoters in October*

will fast disappear. Romantic notions of escape from the strictures of everyday life surround the lighthouse keeper's job, but in reality it is an occupation built on strict routines and a pragmatic approach. There are considerable rewards, however, and among these must be an awareness of the astonishing richness of our coastal heritage, surely the best-kept secret in Britain. Being on a lighthouse provides the opportunity to spend a great deal of time getting to know a single stretch of it. Almost any length of our shoreline will repay similar investigation, by revealing the richness and variety of interesting creatures which most of us hardly know.

A future for South Bishop
In the summer of 1985, the crew came ashore from South Bishop for the last time. All the functions of the station are now controlled by computer from the lighthouse at St Anne's Head, about 12 miles south-east. Apart from brief visits by engineers for routine maintenance, the island will be undisturbed. This will have

SUNFISH (left) *Noted by the writer: 'About the diameter of a dustbin lid, perhaps two feet across . . . This is apparently a tiddler. The maximum size is over 10 feet long . . .'*

very little effect on wildlife and may even make the rock more attractive. Perhaps razorbills and kittiwakes may now nest, where they were discouraged before by the comings and goings of lighthouse keepers and helicopters. Seals never took much notice of people anyway, and the space to haul out was always limited and eagerly sought, so numbers using the rock will probably remain much the same. Rabbits, brought by keepers in the first place, are unlikely to survive without extra food in winter. The journeys of migrant birds are filled with dangers, so the absence of people will make very little difference, although without a helping hand some may perish that might have lived.

For nearly 150 years, the cycle of life around the rocks has been witnessed by the keepers of the light. Now the knowledge of life around the offshore rocks will stay locked in the memories of a dwindling number of people and future generations will have little chance or reason to visit them. In a world of shrinking frontiers and increasing pressure, these jagged rocks and treacherous seas may well become even more secret and unknown places than they have been in the past.

RED-NECKED PHALAROPE *Spinning after plankton*

RED-NECKED PHALAROPE *Brightly-coloured females initiate courtship*

NORMAN McCANCH *worked as a lighthouse keeper for three years, pursuing an interest inspired by his family's Pembrokeshire background. Born in 1953 and a taxidermist by training, he studied graphics as a mature student at Canterbury College of Art.*

NANTEOS: THE HOLY GRAIL —

The cup used by Jesus at the Last Supper — the Holy Grail — is said to have been kept at **Nanteos**.

At the Dissolution of the Monasteries, seven monks from Glastonbury fled to the Cistercian foundation of **Strata Florida Abbey**, *bringing with them an ancient bowl or cup of olive wood, much cracked and blackened. When Strata Florida too was closed, some of its monks, including those from Glastonbury, found refuge with the Powells of Nanteos. The last of the seven monks gave the cup to the head of the family, telling him that the sick could be healed by drinking from it.*

Water poured from the cup was sent to sick persons by successive heads of the family, and at some stage it began to be said that the cup was the Grail, used at the Last Supper and brought to Britain by Joseph of Arimathea.

The cup is no longer shown to visitors to Nanteos as it has gone with the last member of the family that owned the house to a new home.

NANTEOS *The handsome mansion, whose name means 'valley of the nightingale', was built for Thomas Powell, whose distinguished guests included Wagner*

Nanteos

Dyfed   SN 6178

This is a Georgian mansion with a difference. Most country houses and stately homes open to the public are more or less immaculate — but Nanteos is by no means a neat and tidy masterpiece. It is in a rather sad state of repair (though undergoing a loving restoration by its owner) and therein lies its fascination. It stands among fields and farmlands at the end of a long driveway in the green hills south-east of Aberystwyth (approach it along the B4340). Dating from 1739, it has a classically beautiful Georgian facade, and many fine interior features, their former splendour still shining through. This was the home of what was thought to be the last remnant of the Holy Grail, the cup used by Christ at the Last Supper and later entrusted to the family that owned Nanteos. In the 1950s the last member of the family took it to a new home.

Nant Gwyrtheyrn

Gwynedd   SH 3545

Myth and legend surround this shadowy spot where the steep-sided valley of Nant Gwyrtheyrn slices through the lofty headlands along the northern coast of the Lleyn Peninsula, carving one of the few breaks in the cliffs. Vortigern, the fifth-century king reputedly responsible for bringing the Saxons to Britain, paid for his mistake by dying in this gloomy hollow which has taken his name (Gwyrtheyrn in Welsh). The valley can be reached by a footpath which drops down sharply from the end of a tarmac lane, running one mile north of the village of Llithfaen.

The path eventually leads to the sea and the ghost village of Porth-y-nant, where abandoned houses rise above the shore. The position of this remote settlement is explained by the scars in the hillsides: these are the deserted quarries that once provided work for the villagers. The last inhabitants left in the 1950s. In more recent times, new lifeblood has been injected into Porth-y-nant, which is now the home of a Welsh language studies centre.

Nant-y-Moch Reservoir

Dyfed   SN 7587

High on the western flanks of the Plynlimon Mountains, a huge grey dam, stretching 172 feet across the headwaters of the River Rheidol, holds back a dramatic 7160-million-gallon lake, part of the Central Electricity Generating Board's Cwm Rheidol hydro-electric power scheme. Nant-y-Moch is accessible by car either from Ponterwyd (on the A44) or Talybont (on the A487), a giant in the heart of the remote plateaux and mist-shrouded mountains so well described in George Borrow's 19th-century classic, *Wild Wales*.

National Centre for Alternative Technology

Gwynedd   SH 7604

Less than 20 years ago, this site, hidden in thick woods north of Machynlleth, was a sad, abandoned slate quarry. Today, it is very much alive once again, thanks to a group of dedicated conservationists who work here on the development of alternative sources of heat, light and power. Windmills, water-powered generators and solar panels are among the array of 'ecologically acceptable' techniques employed in fulfilling their objectives.

Newborough

Gwynedd   SH 4265

The Isle of Anglesey's 125-mile coastline — a protected Area of Outstanding Natural Beauty — is nowhere more silent than along the sands to the south-west of Newborough, where mile after mile of sand dunes leads to a huge beach.

Next to the dunes of Newborough Warren (a nature reserve noted for its wild flowers) the regimented pines of Newborough Forest — a plantation — march right down to the beach along Llanddwyn Bay. Llanddwyn Island, at the western end, is a rocky promontory accessible on foot at low tide. A little lighthouse at the far end of this narrow neck of land keeps a watchful eye over the western entrance to the Menai Strait, the waterway that separates Anglesey from the mainland. Close to the lighthouse are the ruins of a church dedicated to St Dwynwen, an early Christian who lived there.

Parc

Gwynedd SH 8834

A hamlet in the foothills of the Arennig Mountains, Parc stands in typical hill-sheep farming country. At Cyffdy Farm, one mile away (three miles north-east of Llanuwchllyn), visitors can see this sort of farming — the backbone of Welsh agriculture for centuries — at first hand. A long-established working farm, it has a farm trail to follow, which leads through fields and paddocks stocked with cattle, pigs, poultry and, naturally, sheep, plus waterfowl and llama. Hand milking can be seen daily.

The farm is ranged around a large, stone-built, traditional farmhouse, dating from 1600. Old buildings and barns in the farmyard house exhibitions, and there are occasional displays of sheepdog handling, sheep shearing and harp playing. It is open from Easter to October.

Parys Mountain

Gwynedd SH 4490

The lunar-like, pock-marked landscape on the approach to Amlwch on the Isle of Anglesey's north coast is the remainder of the Parys Mountain, where the discovery of a rich vein of copper in the hillside had dramatic and long-lasting effects. What started as a collection of small mines in the 1760s had grown by the end of the century into the largest copper mine in Europe, employing 1500 men, women and children. Parys Mountain's pre-eminence did not last long. By 1815, the best of the ore had gone, and the mine declined and died. This scarred site, full of dangerous craters and shafts, is best viewed from the roadside.

PARYS MOUNTAIN *In the 18th century it was discovered that copper could be extracted by precipitation — hence the ponds. The windmill pumped the water*

Penarth Fawr

Gwynedd SH 4237

The farmlands north-east of Pwllheli on the Lleyn Peninsula conceal a building rare in Wales. Penarth Fawr, constructed in the early 15th century, is a stone-built hall-house, an unusual survivor from the days when most equivalent houses were in the half-timbered style rather than stone. The entire family, including servants, would have lived and slept in one large room — which makes up the interior — with servants a little apart from the rest in a gallery overlooking the main floor. Although altered over the centuries, many interesting old features survive. The house is on a minor road which joins the A497 three miles north-east of Pwllheli.

Penmachno

Gwynedd SH 7950

This small grey-stoned village, unheralded and largely unknown, sits in its secluded valley surrounded by magnificent mountain scenery. From here a minor road climbs through the trees of the Gwydyr Forest to Ty Mawr, a remote old farmhouse some two miles north-west. This humble abode, with its stone-flagged floor, rough walls and slate roof, was the birthplace in 1545 of William Morgan, later to become the illustrious Bishop Morgan, who completed the first translation of the Bible into Welsh and so gave his land 'probably the most important book in the history of language and literature in Wales'. In the care of the National Trust, the house is open daily from April to October, except Mondays and Saturdays.

Penmachno's woollen mill was a fulling mill in the mid-17th century, used by local domestic weavers to finish their cloth. Today Welsh tweed is made there. It is open daily from Easter to November.

PENMON: DOVECOTES — *The fine square dovecote at* **Penmon Priory**, *built in about 1600, is one of the best preserved in Britain.*

The building of special towers for the keeping of doves and pigeons was first introduced by the Normans, and the earliest surviving free-standing dovecote dates from 1326. Earlier dovecotes remain in the turrets of Rochester and Conisbrough (see **Sheffield***) castles.*

Only the lord of the manor might own one, and heavy penalties were meted out to any peasant who killed a pigeon. Dovecotes became popular because they ensured a supply of fresh meat in winter: most other animals had to be slaughtered in the autumn, until root crops began to be grown for winter fodder. This only began in the 17th century, and in 1659, 26,000 dovecotes were recorded in England alone.

Built by local builders from local materials, they often have character and charm. Interesting examples can be seen at **Broughton**, **Chastleton**, **Dilwyn**, *Kinwarton, Warwickshire, Willington, Bedfordshire, and Wichenford, Worcestershire. One of the biggest surviving examples is the* **Finavon Doocot**, *designed with 2000 nesting boxes.*

Penmaenpool

Gwynedd SH 6918

'Where have the trains gone?' is the question inevitably posed by visitors to this puzzling site west of Dolgellau. A signal box, signal gantry and remnants of a platform preserve the ghostly presence of a halt along an abandoned GWR railway line. When operational, this must have been one of the most scenic rail routes in Britain, for it ran along the southern shores of the lovely Mawddach Estuary. The views — and the rich bird life of the estuary — can at least still be admired from the signal box, which now serves as a Wildlife Information Centre. Walkers can also soak up scenery once enjoyed by fortunate railway passengers by following a five-mile footpath along the trackway from Penmaenpool to Morfa Mawddach, at the mouth of the estuary.

Penmon Priory

Gwynedd SH 6381

Built close to the sea, four miles north-east of Beaumaris on Anglesey, Penmon was attacked and attacked again by sea-borne plunderers during the lawless Dark Ages. The Augustinian priory founded in the sixth century was reconstructed in Norman times. Its medieval church — still in use as the parish church — forms the nucleus of a range of buildings (including a dormitory and kitchens) added in later centuries. Across the road stands an unusual-looking stone structure with a domed roof. This is Penmon's dovecote, built in about 1600, which can accommodate almost 1000 bird St Seiriol's Well, named after the sixth-century missionary associated with Penmon's earliest days, is also close by.

Plas-yn-Rhiw

Gwynedd SH 2227

Deep in a thick tangle of gardens and woodlands stands the little manor house of Plas-yn-Rhiw, a modest and charming dwelling dating from the Middle Ages, with Tudor and Georgian additions. The house is delightful — but its most memorable feature is its setting. Ornamental gardens range across the steep, sheltered hillside in Amazonian fecundity, dense clumps of rhododendron grow among the trees, and grassy paths and box hedges attempt to impose some order on profuse shrub and woodlands.

The house is near the rugged south-western tip of Lleyn Peninsula. From its hillside perch, it looks down into the stormy waters of Hell's Mouth, a four-mile-long west-facing bay with — as its name implies — a fearsome reputation as a mariners' graveyard. In the care of the National Trust, the house is open Wednesdays, Thursdays, Fridays, Sundays and Bank Holidays during the summer.

Pontcysyllte Aqueduct

Clwyd SJ 2742

When Thomas Telford came to construct the Llangollen Canal, a branch of the Shropshire Union, he was faced with the problem of spanning the vale carved east of Llangollen by the looping River Dee. His solution was a bold one. Between 1794 and 1805, he constructed Pontcysyllte Aqueduct to carry the cast-iron trough of the canal and its towpath. The result was an aqueduct 1007 feet long (the longest in Britain), 127 feet high, and with 19 sets of arches. This magnificent structure, three and a half miles east of Llangollen, is still in use, though today's traffic consists of holiday cruisers rather than commercial barges. A walk can be taken across its lofty towpath.

Ponterwyd

Dyfed SN 7481

George Borrow, who walked through Wales from north to south in the mid-19th century and wrote the travel classic *Wild Wales*, trudged across Plynlimon's desolate, boggy moorlands to reach Ponterwyd's Gogerddan Arms. The landlord used the opportunity to re-name his obscure establishment the George Borrow Hotel, in honour of its guest, soon afterwards. The little settlement is one of only a handful in the upper reaches of the Plynlimon uplands, and must have been a welcome site indeed to Borrow, despite his predilection for high, wild and remote country. The moorlands have now been partly submerged by the Nant-y-Moch reservoir.

Porth Oer

Gwynedd SH 1630

Porth Oer is one of the few places on the cliff-bound northern coast of the Lleyn Peninsula where beaches make an appearance. This isolated little crescent of sands, backed by low cliffs, is accessible by a footpath leading from a car park. It is also known by its English name of Whistling Sands, for the sand grains here are supposed to whistle — squeak is perhaps a better description — underfoot. The cove can be reached off a minor road north of Aberdaron.

Pumpsaint

Dyfed SN 6540

Traffic travelling north-westwards on the A482 towards Lampeter and the Cardigan Bay coast pass through the hamlet of Pumpsaint, unaware of its proximity to a unique site. In the hills a short distance east of the road is Dolaucothi, the only spot in Britain in which it has been definitely established that the Romans mined for gold. Although the mines were revived again in the 19th and 20th centuries (they finally closed in 1938), previous centuries of disuse have effectively disguised the Romans' efforts here. Scant evidence lies hidden in the wooded hillsides and surrounding fields. Gaping holes in the slopes reveal the entrances to 'adits' (shafts dug horizontally into the hill) and traces of a sophisticated aqueduct system can be discerned among the grass and bushes. A waymarked path leads visitors around the National Trust site. The adits should not be explored, except on the guided tours available at Dolaucothi during the summer.

Pumpsaint ('Five Saints', Pump meaning five) is named after a tale that is tall even by Welsh standards. All is revealed at the entrance to the mines where a rough old stone stands all alone on a grassy slope. The five indentations in its surface are said to correspond to the heads of a quintet of saints — Gwyn, Gwynno, Gwynnoro, Celynin and Ceitho — who used the stone as a communal pillow during a storm so terrible that their impressions were left in the surface.

Rheidol Falls

Dyfed SN 7179

For over 10 miles east of Aberystwyth, the River Rheidol carves for itself a lovely, steep-sided valley, nowhere lovelier than in the Cwm Rheidol reach, around Rheidol Falls. Here can be seen a modern building, the Cwm Rheidol Power Station. Guided tours of the station from Easter to October show that power generation is not the only concern. Brown and rainbow trout are reared at Cwm Rheidol's specially constructed fish farm; opposite the station a nature trail goes around the small reservoir (which controls the Rheidol's flow) and over the Rheidol Falls and the weir — a spectacular sight indeed when floodlit on summer nights. In the station itself, items (including the pulpit) from the drowned chapel at Nant-y-Moch are on display.

Rogerstone

Gwent ST 2688

Almost cut off by houses and the M4 motorway, Newport's northern suburb of Rogerstone has a remarkable monument to the spirit of the Industrial Revolution. In the 1790s, the builders of the Monmouthshire Canal cut a flight of no less than 14 locks within half a mile, to take barges 168 feet up and down the hill that stood in their way. This giant-sized staircase of deep locks no longer carries boats — the canal closed in the 1930s — but it has been rescued from dereliction. From the 14 Locks Centre (with information and exhibitions) at the summit, a towpath walk follows the line of the locks as they take their huge strides down the hillside, the lock chambers becoming progressively more overgrown the further they descend. The path is open at all times; the centre is open in summer, but not on Tuesdays or Wednesdays.

PUMPSAINT: A ROMAN GOLD MINE

— Dolaucothi, near **Pumpsaint**, is the site of the only known Roman gold mine in Britain.

The Romans' mining operations here have been traced by excavation. Gold near the surface was exploited by open-cast working. Deeper ore was reached by galleries underground, drained by a timber water-wheel, a fragment of which can still be seen in the National Museum, Cardiff.

Water to break down the beds of gold-bearing 'pyrites', and to wash the ore after crushing, was carried to the site by three aqueducts — one of them seven miles long — in the form of channels cut ingeniously into the hillsides.

What has been taken for a pit-head bath-house — testimony to good working conditions — probably belonged to a fort now under Pumpsaint village. Most mines were administered by an Imperial procurator with the help of the army. The miners themselves may well have been slaves or criminals, quartered underground or in caves, as at Llanymynech, Shropshire.

DOLAUCOTHI *Thousands of slaves mined gold here from about AD75, guarded by a Roman camp (now under the Dolaucothi Arms)*

ST DAVID'S PENINSULA: KING ARTHUR AND THE BOAR TWRCH TRWYTH — *Porth Clais*, **St David's Peninsula**, *is reputedly the landing-place of the legendary boar Twrch Trwyth. The story of how the boar was hunted was told in the story of 'Culhwch and Olwen' in about 1100.*

In order to win Olwen, Culhwch had to get the comb and shears which were kept between the ears of the supernatural boar, Twrch Trwyth. With Arthur helping, the great boar-hunt began in Ireland, crossed to Wales at Porth Clais, then swept across country by Prescelly Top, over the Tywi and through the valleys of Loughor and Amman, to below Pontardawe. The prizes of the chase were finally won in a battle at the mouth of the Severn, and Twrch Trwyth was driven into the sea in Cornwall.

King Arthur's dog, Cabal, came on the hunt. In about the year 800, the 'historian' Nennius mentioned Carn Cabal, a cairn whose top stone bore Cabal's footprint. If removed from the cairn, it would always return of its own accord. Carn Cabal is traditionally identified as Corngafallt, in Powys, although the route of the hunt as described in 'Culhwch and Olwen' goes nowhere near this spot. Another monument to the hunt, the Ty-newydd Standing Stones, Mynachlog-Ddu, are said to commemorate Arthur's sons, killed in the chase.

St David's Peninsula

Dyfed   SM 7227

North-west Pembrokeshire ends at a rocky, gale-tossed peninsula rich in early Christian heritage. Its name reflects its religious significance as the home of the tiny cathedral city built on the site of the monastery founded by St David — Dewi Sant in Welsh — in the sixth century. Nothing remains of the old monastery buildings. They may well have been destroyed by the Vikings, who regularly plundered and raided this coast. Yet the saint himself has exerted a powerful fascination on the Welsh mind. He is said to have died on 1 March 589, and the day has been celebrated in Wales since at least the Middle Ages. He may have founded other monasteries, but he is most closely linked with this peninsula. St David's, or Dewisland, has been a place of pilgrimage for well over 1000 years. In the days before reliable roads, pilgrims came by sea — and gave thanks for a safe passage at shrines and chapels dotted along this stormy coast.

St Non's Bay, half a mile south of the cathedral, was one of the landing points. A small white statue of Non, mother of St David, stands on a grassy headland above the cliffs. Nearby are the scant ruins of St Non's Chapel and a little holy well in which the waters still flow.

The peninsula's tough, igneous underlying rock has given it a severe, indented coastline. Sea-resistant cliffs and promontories are only occasionally worn away into bays. *Caerfai* and *Caerbwdi*, east of St Non's, are two examples. Here, the erosive hand of man is also in evidence, for stone was hewn from the cliffs to build the cathedral at St David's.

Dewisland's famous purple-stoned *cathedral* needs no introduction: some say it is best seen in the rain, which brings out and enhances the richness of colour in the stone, others maintain that dusk is the best time to visit, when it becomes a massive and powerful presence, rising from the shadows. The present Cathedral dates from the 12th century, but a container made of wood and metal, kept behind the High Altar, is believed to hold the bones of St David and St Justinian, his colleague and confessor. The fame of the cathedral is not shared by its next-door neighbour, the *Bishop's Palace*, which rarely attracts the attention it deserves. The great palace shell, roofless and ruinous in its dingle below the houses, stands as a reminder that the medieval church was no stranger to wealth, status and comfortable living. Dating from the 14th century but derelict since the 18th, this splendid medieval ruin — as impressive as any of the castles of Wales —

ST DAVID'S PENINSULA   *(main picture) Looking across Whitesands Bay to St David's Head. A monastery with a strict regime was established here by the saint: the monks lived an austere life, devoted to prayer, farming and learning, and may have been teetotallers. Over 50 'St David' placenames and dedications of ancient origin have been found in South Wales, and dedications also exist in Devon, Cornwall and Brittany.*

ST NON'S SHRINE   *(below) stands near the chapel said to mark where St Non, or Nonita, gave birth to St David. By tradition, his father was Sant, a Cardiganshire chief, and the medieval writer Rhygyfarch tells that an angel prophesied the birth to St Patrick*

ST NON'S WELL   *(below left) is a spring, rising about 40 yards north-east of the ruined chapel*

ranges itself around a large courtyard. Its arcaded parapet walls are an outstanding feature.

St David was reputedly baptised at *Porth Clais*, a narrow inlet west of St Non's Bay. This lovely little creek, its placid waters well protected from the open seas, is the safest anchorage on the peninsula. Lime kilns along the neat-and-tidy quayside (the harbour is still used by local boat-men) are a leftover from seafaring times when Porth Clais was the port for St David's.

St Justinian's, further around the peninsula, is not as accommodating. A lifeboat station, perched on tall supports, just about fits itself in amongst the cliffs. On the headland above stand the ruins of St Justinian's Chapel, dedicated to St David's confessor, who was reputedly martyred on *Ramsey Island*. The lifeboat ramp plunges straight into the waters of *Ramsey Sound*. Tides roar through this perilous stretch of water, which separates Ramsey Island from the mainland.

Ramsey, its Norse name credited to the plun-dering Vikings during the Dark Ages, is a two-mile-long island which appears to be inhabited mainly by rabbits (far too many for the likes of the enterprising couple who own it). A sanctuary for a wide variety of wildlife, the island — accessible to the public via summer boat trips — is especially noted for its colonies of guillemots, kittiwakes and razorbills, and the grey seals that bask on its rocks. *Grassholm Island*, 12 miles out to sea, is truly remote. This seemingly inhospitable rock is home to more than 20,000 pairs of gannets, one of the largest colonies in the world.

St David's Head overlooks *Whitesands Bay*, the only beach of note along this rock-bound peninsula. The headland, a promontory rising to 595 feet high at the northern end of the sands, is a repository of prehistoric remains. Long before the 'Age of Saints', Neolithic man had settled on its rugged slopes and buried his dead here, and in the Iron Age, a fort was built on the headland.

Although not strictly on the St David's Peninsula, two nearby coastal sites — no more than a few miles to the north-east — should not be overlooked. *Abereiddi's* strange, black-sand bay is a product of the dark, slatey cliffs. Ruined cottages and a flooded quarry — a deep and spooky 'blue lagoon' — are left from the times when Abereiddi had its own slate industry.

Stranger still is *Porthgain*, a mile further east. If it were not for its abandoned brickworks and quayside ruins, Porthgain would qualify as an archetypal secret cove, the kind frequented by fishermen and smugglers. Evidence of any form of industrial development in the north of Pembrokeshire is rare indeed, giving Porthgain an oddity value which eclipses the basic ugliness and intrusion of 19th-century slate and granite quarries. It was linked with Abereiddi by a rail-way. Six specially commissioned 350-ton steamers were built in the early 1900s to serve the slate quarries, but they had become redundant by the 1930s, when shipments of slate ceased to be made from here. From Porthgain's tiny harbour-side, there are magnificent coastal walks across some of Pembrokeshire's most peaceful cliffs.

ST DAVID'S PENINSULA: TWO SAINTS — *It is said that St Patrick sailed from* **St David's Peninsula** *when he went to convert Ireland to Christianity. He had been en-slaved there and escaped, but a dream commanded him to go back. Some say that a vision of Ireland came to him at the foot of Carn Llidi: it is one of the few rocky heights in this area, and from its summit (595 feet) Ireland's Wicklow Mountains can be seen on a clear day. Several chapels in Pembrokeshire are dedicated in St Patrick's name, and at Porth Mawr, a plaque near the beach marks the site of one of them.*

St David, who is said to have been born near St Non's Well on St David's Head, certainly estab-lished his most important monastery here. He was called the Waterman, possibly because he and his monks abstained from alcohol. A number of Irish saints are said to have been taught by him, so he may have been influential in the spread of Christianity in Ireland. His sign was a dove, but the traditional connection between St David's Day and leeks has existed for centuries.

MAEN MADOC *Nine feet high, this standing stone on Sarn Helen bears an inscription in Latin: '. . . of Dervacus, son of Justus. He lies here'. This dates from the fourth century, but the stone itself may be much older*

SARN HELEN: HELEN'S CAUSEWAY

*— When the Romans conquered Wales in AD74, they pinned the country down with a system of fortresses and roads. One of these roads was **Sarn Helen**, which linked South Wales with the coast road running from Chester to Segontium (see **Caernarfon**).*

The name means Helen's Causeway and has given rise to a number of explanatory stories. Helen is St Helena, celebrated as the finder of the True Cross and mother of the Emperor Constantine — who was first declared emperor by the army in Britain, hence perhaps Helen's connection with Britain. It was also long (and probably inaccurately) believed that Helen herself was British-born.

*A 14th-century Welsh story in the 'Mabinogion' (see page 139) tells how Macsen Wledig — the Roman usurper Magnus Maximus — dreamt of a girl whom he later discovered in Arfon, and married. As a wedding gift she asked for three strongholds to be built at Caernarfon, Caerleon and **Carmarthen**, to be joined by roads thereafter known as the roads of 'Elen of the Hosts'.*

*A 12th-century tradition, however, makes Helena the daughter of the founder of **Colchester** — perhaps the original Old King Cole (but see also **Colnbrook** for another contender).*

Sarn Helen

Powys   SN 8711

In certain wild and lonely corners of Wales, sections of ancient highways remain unused and forgotten — often the work of the Romans, who arrived in strength in AD74 and stayed for over 300 years. One such stretch forges a direct, single-minded path across moor and mountainside north of Glyn Neath. A minor road leading eastwards from the village of Coelbren deteriorates into a rough track at the entrance to the Coed-y-Rhaiadr Forest. From here, the Roman road of Sarn Helen, untouched and unimproved over the centuries, strikes out northeastwards beside the forest, into an uninhabited pocket of the Brecon Beacons National Park. Within just over three miles, a stone standing cross, Maen Madoc, comes into view, all alone on an exposed windy crest. After another three-quarters of a mile, Sarn Helen descends to join the surfaced country road two miles north of the hamlet of Ystradfellte.

Scwd-yr-Eira

Mid Glamorgan   SN 9310

A footpath runs behind the cascade of Scwd-yr-Eira, 'the spout of snow', one of the many falls in Ystradfellte's 'waterfall country'. Outcropping limestone rock south of this hamlet has created a distinctive part of the Brecon Beacons National Park, where rivers tumble down waterfalls in steep, wooded ravines, or disappear completely into caves and potholes. Scwd-yr-Eira, on the River Hepste, is one of the falls; a series of riverside and clifftop paths links the Hepste with another river, the Mellte, and yet more waterfalls.

Skokholm Island

Dyfed   SM 7209

Pembrokeshire's teeming birdlife is nowhere more abundant than on this mile-long island, Britain's first officially designated bird reserve. Shearwaters and storm petrels are just two of the many species of seabird that live on the island, which is not normally accessible to day visitors, although weekly stays for small groups can be arranged. Skomer, its larger neighbour, is easier to get to. This island, also a nature reserve, with one of north-west Europe's finest seabird colonies, can be visited by boat (there are daily trips in summer) from Martin's Haven.

South Stack Lighthouse

Gwynedd   SH 2082

The port of Holyhead stands on an island off an island. Holyhead Island, linked to the Isle of Anglesey by a number of bridges, is the home of a busy terminus for the Irish ferry. Ships are warned off the rocky, cliff-backed shore on the western approach to the port by the South Stack Lighthouse, built in 1808.

Here Holyhead Mountain meets the sea in no uncertain fashion — the land drops away to the surf below, the only exception being a small, rugged promontory that serves as the sturdy foundation for the lighthouse. Energetic visitors can walk the 400-odd steps cut into the cliff-face for a close-up view of the sea, lighthouse and magnificent coastal scenery. These cliffs are also renowned for their colonies of seabirds, and include an RSPB reserve which is an important breeding ground for guillemots and puffins.

Staylittle

Powys   SN 8892

One source tells us that Staylittle is so called because local blacksmiths could shoe horses so fast that impatient travellers need only 'stay a little'. Another version is that the inhospitable attitude was responsible for making visitors move through fast.

Just over a mile north, a minor road turns west off the B4518 to where the River Twymyn plunges down Ffrwyd Fawr, one of the highest waterfalls in Wales, and one of the least accessible — visitors have to take a short but strenuous walk to see the falls, and the beautiful valley into which they cascade, at their best. At Dylife, further along the minor road, a strange, scarred, grey moonscape fills the mountainside, a savage leftover of a large lead mine abandoned at the end of the 19th century.

Strata Florida Abbey

Dyfed   SN 7465

This ruined religious site was once regarded as the 'Westminster Abbey of Wales'. Strata Florida was founded in the early 13th century as a home for the Cistercians, enterprising monks, in sympathy with the traditions and culture of Wales, who saw to it that Strata Florida became much more than an introverted monastery. In medieval times, their abbey was also an influential political and educational centre.

Today, only faint traces of the abbey's former splendour survive. A miraculously well-preserved archway, decorated with bands of carved stone, is its greatest glory. Mosaic tiled floors also remain quite intact among ruins which, despite their tumbledown and fragmentary nature, still evoke a spirit of tranquillity. Its name, a Latinised version of Ystrad Fflur (The Vale of the Flowers), reflects the natural beauty of its location. A gnarled old yew tree, in the churchyard beside the abbey, is said to mark the resting place of Dafydd ap Gwilym, the celebrated medieval poet. A modest headstone near records that: 'The left leg and part of the thigh of Henry Hughes, Cooper, was cut off and interred here June 18th 1756'.

The youthful River Teifi flows beside Strata Florida. Its source lies a few miles to the north-east in the Teifi Pools, lovely lakes enclosed among silent hillsides populated only by sheep

Swansea

West Glamorgan   SS 6593

Dylan Marlais Thomas (1914-53), the great Welsh poet, spent his formative years in a quiet residential district of Swansea. The home of his childhood and youth, Cwmdonkin Drive has not changed much over the years.

The beautifully kept Cwmdonkin Park, Dylan's 'eternal park', a magic place with 'the fountain basin where I sailed my ship' is still there, complete with the cast-iron drinking fountain. And his home, from which he surveyed 'the bent and Devon-facing shore' of Swansea Bay, survives as an unusual shrine to the poet. Five Cwmdonkin Drive is not a museum, nor is it open to casual visitors — but it can be rented for a few days or a week, with breakfast and dinner provided by the housekeeper. This is strictly a treat for enthusiasts: the furniture and decor have been returned as far as possible to the way they were in the poet's pre-war childhood days. Contact the owner, Frank James, at Coynant Farm, Felindre, Swansea, for all the details.

Swiss Valley

Dyfed   SN 5103

'Swiss Valley' is the local name for the area centred around the Lliedi reservoirs. Although knocking on the northern door to the old tinplate town of Llanelli, this valley is quite untouched by any industrial or urban development. The lower reservoir, Cwm Lliedi, is accessible by a two-mile-long footpath around the lakeside. Start from the top end of the reservoir.

Talgarth

Powys   SO 1534

Parts of Talgarth are just about coming to terms with the 20th century. This quirky little village, between the Brecon Beacons and Black Mountains, is a maze of narrow streets, ancient buildings and old-fashioned shop fronts. Most ancient of all is a tumbledown medieval tower, right in the middle of the village, which looks about to fall over. Its base is taken up by a local emporium — the kind of shop that used to flourish before the days of the supermarket — which sells everything from foodstuffs to frying pans. St Gwendoline's Church stands on a rise above the village. Near the altar, a massive black slab is a memorial to Howel Harris, the fascinating 18th-century religious figure, who is buried here (see Trefeca). It was in this church on Palm Sunday, 1735, that Harris 'felt suddenly my heart melting within me like wax before a fire, with love to God my Saviour . . .' This religious experience is said to have inspired his leadership of the great Methodist Revival in Wales.

Many paths venture into the bare Black Mountains, none more directly than the Grwyne Fawr trackway. It can be joined from the minor road that runs through Rhos-fach, two miles east of the village, and climbs a sharp escarpment into the tussocky upper reaches of the mountains. Surrounded by this empty upland expanse, the path becomes little more than an indistinct sheep-walk before descending past an isolated reservoir into the conifer-clad Grwyne Fawr valley, northeast of Abergavenny. Study the map before tackling this route and go properly equipped for rough conditions.

SKOKHOLM ISLAND: THE PUBLIC LIFE OF THE RABBIT —

Among the works of R. M. Lockley (who farmed, founded Britain's first bird observatory, and wrote, on **Skokholm Island***) was 'The Private Life of the Rabbit'. Revealing the intricacies of rabbits' behaviour patterns, it later inspired Richard Adams to write his story 'Watership Down'.*

Adams' best-selling novel, which some regard as a modern classic, began with stories he told to his children during long car journeys to **Stratford-upon-Avon***. It is set near* **Newbury***, on the downs on which Adams loved to walk.*

His rabbits are as much human as animal in their epic quest for freedom, but their rabbit characteristics are soundly based on Lockley's 'Private Life', to which Adams recommends the reader for such subjects as the migration of yearlings, the effects of overcrowding in warrens and the ability of buck rabbits to fight off stoats.

◆———————◆

SWANSEA   *Frank Brangwyn's murals, depicting the people, animals and flowers of the British Empire, were commissioned by the House of Lords, but then rejected. All 16 of them can be seen in the town's Guildhall*

TINKINSWOOD: AN ANCIENT GRAVE — *Tradition says that to sleep at* **Tinkinswood** *on the night before May Day, St John's Day or Midwinter Day would cause madness, death, or the onset of the gift of poetry.*

At least 50 people were buried here in Neolithic times. Human bones, cattle bones, flints and pottery fragments have all been found on the site.

There now remain four large slabs roofed by an immense capstone, 24 feet long, 10 feet wide and 2 feet 6 inches thick. It weighs about 40 tons. In the mound itself, behind the capstone, is a stone-lined pit; corpses may have been left exposed here before the skeletons were finally interred in the burial chamber itself.

Similar to its neighbour Tinkinswood and Parc le Breos (on the **Gower Peninsula**) *is St Lythan's Cromlech. It is wedge-shaped, and consists of three massive upright stones and a capstone, which is said to spin round three times each Midsummer's Eve. The cairn stands in an 'accursed field', reputedly barren; but wishes made here on Hallowe'en are guaranteed to come true . . .*

ABOVE *A Neolithic funeral as it might have been — a reconstruction, based on available evidence, by Alan Sorrell*

Talley Abbey

Dyfed   SN 6332

A few archways and lines of ruined masonry are all that remain of Talley Abbey, founded by Premonstratensian monks in the 12th century. The ruins lie in a shallow bowl of land beside the twin lakes of Talley.

Close by is the 18th-century Church of St Michael which, from the outside, looks more or less like the usual Anglican place of worship. Twin entry doors provide the only external evidence of an unconventional interior. Instead of the usual central aisle, the main body of St Michael's is divided up by two side aisles, with pews — a layout far more characteristic of the typical Welsh chapel.

Tinkinswood Burial Chamber

South Glamorgan   ST 0973

An enormous 40-ton capstone, 24 feet long, squats protectively over a burial chamber which revealed the bones of at least 50 bodies, together with items of pottery, when excavated in 1914.

The tomb, built around 2500BC, dates from the Neolithic period. An important, well-preserved monument, it has benefited from careful restoration. All that is missing is the earthen mound which would originally have covered its stone framework and central chamber.

The exposed stonework of a second, smaller tomb known as St Lythan's (of the same period) can be seen nearby. Both prehistoric sites are in farmlands (with public access by footpath) about one mile south of St Nicholas, a village on the A48 west of Cardiff.

Trefeca

Powys   SO 1431

The only buildings of note in tiny Trefeca, one mile south-west of Talgarth, form the Presbyterian College. This was once the home of Howel Harris (1714–73), a dynamic, multi-talented character largely responsible for starting the Methodist Revival in Wales.

Harris would plant his mobile pulpit wherever and whenever an instant congregation could be gathered, but he was more than an influential evangelical preacher. He also put his religious beliefs into practice at Trefeca, where he founded a commune-like 'family' or 'Connexion', the members of which pooled their resources to farm together. Harris was a successful, innovative agriculturalist (he is credited with introducing the turnip into Wales). He is also remembered as a pioneering printer, his Trefeca Press producing many religious tracts.

Harris's 18th-century home forms the nucleus of today's college. An adjacent chapel contains a most interesting museum dedicated to this determined man and his long list of achievements.

Tregaron

Dyfed   SN 6759

Traditional, Welsh-speaking Tregaron was the last outpost of civilisation in Wales for the 19th-century drovers on their way eastwards to the livestock markets of the English Midlands. They would congregate outside the Talbot Hotel in Tregaron's large town square before driving their cattle and sheep across the wild and empty 'roof

TREGONING HILL   *The outline of Llanstephan Castle, which rises above the battlemented tower of the parish church, high above the Tywi estuary. Now just a shell, it has been a distinctive landmark since the late 13th century*

of Wales', following a rough track known as the Abergwesyn Pass.

A 20th-century road surface has in no way diluted the daunting character of this pass. It is one of Britain's most enthralling motoring experiences. The road — very narrow and steep in places — winds its way for 14 arm-bending miles from Tregaron to the hamlet of Abergwesyn, five miles north of Llanwrtyd Wells. (A recently laid link road, about half-way along the pass, also connects it to Llyn Brianne.)

North of the town is the great Tregaron Bog, no ordinary wetland but a huge, reedy expanse, and the largest bog in Wales. Ecologically, this former lake is important as an excellent example of raised peat bog. It is also an important National Nature Reserve, the bird life of which can be observed from a nature trail running along a section of abandoned railway line on the eastern edge of the bog. Curlews and sedge warblers — even the occasional rare red kite — may be seen, as well as numerous acid-loving plants. Nature Conservancy Council permits (free) are needed to explore, not least because parts of the bog are dangerous and the permits show where to walk. Contact The Warden, Minawel, Ffar Rhos, Ystrad Meurig.

Tregoning Hill

Dyfed SN 3608

A National Trust property just south of
Ferryside, Tregoning Hill stands directly above
the mouths and meeting places of three rivers —
the Tywi, Taf and Gwendraeth. Green, peaceful
farmlands sweep down to the sea as the rivers
flow into the open waters of Carmarthen Bay.

Dylan Thomas captured the haunting beauty of
this area: Tregoning Hill looks out across the
silvery waters to Llanstephan, guarded by its hilltop castle, and the sands of his beloved, sleepy
Laugharne. On a clear day, the view extends all
the way along the bay to distant Tenby. Directly
below the hill, on the rocky foreshore, is the site
of the lost village of Hawton, destroyed in a
terrible storm around 300 years ago.

Tremadog

Gwynedd SH 5640

T. E. Lawrence, better known as Lawrence of
Arabia, was born here in 1888. A plaque above
the bay window of a house on the southern
approach to the town identifies the birthplace of
this enigmatic adventurer. Although it preserves
its original façade, the house has been much
extended. It now serves as a Christian Mountain
Centre, which welcomes groups of all per-
suasions to participate in its mountaineering,
environmental and adventure courses. Would-be
rock climbers do not have to travel far to develop
their skills — the cliffs above Tremadog's roof-
tops are some of the most challenging in North
Wales.

Tremadog itself is an interesting, unusual
town. Well-proportioned, harmonious buildings
line the spacious streets, betraying its origins as a
'model town', purpose-built between 1805 and
1812. It was designed as a coaching town by local
entrepreneur William Madocks (hence Tremadog,
'tre' meaning 'town of'), to serve an intended
London to Dublin (via Lleyn) coaching and
shipping route that never materialised.

Tre'r Ceiri

Gwynedd SH 3744

The name of this Iron Age settlement means
'the town of the giants', and the inhabitants
must have been robust and hardy indeed to live
here, 1500 feet up on the rocky south-western
summit of the Yr Eifl mountains on the Lleyn
Peninsula. This native settlement, which
remained in use during the Roman occupation of
Wales, served as more than a fort. Walls — still
up to 13 feet high in places — enclosed a village
community of around 150 huts. Unlike other
ancient sites, Tre'r Ceiri has worn rather well —
probably because of its remote, undisturbed
setting, reached by a stiff climb from the B4417
south-west of Llanaelhaearn. It is a good place
for cuckoos.

— *Inscribed stones such as St Cadfan's Stone,* **Tywyn,** *often provide illuminating sidelights on history — none more so than the early memorial stones reflecting the mixed heritage of Romanised Britons in the centuries following the Romans' departure. This is the so-called Age of Arthur, since the legend of Arthur himself is believed to have grown up around a Romanised British chieftain.*

In a remote spot beside **Sarn Helen,** *the stone called Maen Madoc is dedicated in Latin to Dervacus, son of Justus, and continues the Roman practice of burying the dead along highways.*

Eliseg's Pillar *is the remainder of a stone cross (see* **Llantwit Major***) that gave its name to Valle Crucis Abbey. Its inscription (now illegible) recorded the descent of Cyngen, king of Powys, on the one side from Vortigern, the British tyrant whom tradition blames for inviting the Saxons to Britain, and on the other from the Roman usurper Magnus Maximus.*

In Cornwall, the Drustan Stone, beside the A3082 into Fowey, tells us that here lies Drustanus, son of Cunomorus. Cunomorus is probably Cynfawr, sixth-century king of Dumnonia, but his son Drustan bears a Pictish royal name. Can this be, as his ancient connection with nearby Castle Dore suggests, the grave of the Arthurian hero Tristan?

ELISEG'S PILLAR *A skull was found beneath the stone, whose message, now illegible, was noted down 300 years ago*

Tywyn

Gwynedd   SH 5800

A small seaside resort that has seen busier days, Tywyn is the unlikely home of a highly significant historical monument. Little fuss is made of the fact that St Cadfan's Church, near the town centre, contains a tall, narrow pillar of stone inscribed with what is thought to be the earliest written Welsh, if genuine.

The inscription, possibly dating from the seventh century, reads: 'The body of Cingen lies beneath'. Now safe and secure within its church, the high stone once suffered the indignity of being used as a gatepost in a farmer's field.

Vale of Ewyas

Gwent   SO 2630

The most direct, though not necessarily the quickest, route between Hay-on-Wye and Abergavenny is across the Gospel Pass and through the Vale of Ewyas. This narrow road, running through the eastern flanks of the borderland Black Mountains, just keeps itself within

Wales: in the hills above, the Offa's Dyke footpath marks the border with England.

South of Hay, the road climbs sharply on to the rounded shoulders of Hay Bluff (2200 feet) — a haunt of hang-gliders — on the way to its own summit (1778 feet) at the top of the pass. The secluded Vale of Ewyas, further south, is shut off from the outside world by the mountains. In medieval times, the Norman nobleman William de Lacy stumbled across this lonely spot and was immediately captivated.

At Llanthony, on the site of an ancient chapel dedicated to St David, he turned his back on the world and established a hermitage. This eventually developed into Llanthony Priory, the ruins of which still stand today. Much is left of this 800-year-old religious site — its well-preserved and well-proportioned row of pointed archways is particularly delightful. A small hotel-cum-inn has been built into the ruins, and is noted for its real ale.

A little further north, at Capel-y-ffin, Father Ignatius — a fascinating, self-appointed 19th-century man of religion — founded a monastery confusingly known as Llanthony Abbey. Remains of a partly finished church, which

Father Ignatius planned as a 'facsimile of old Llanthony', can be visited on the hillside next to his erstwhile, short-lived monastery (now in private ownership).

Vaynor

Mid Glamorgan   SO 0410

A reminder of the 19th-century boom years when Merthyr Tydfil was the iron- and steel-producing capital of the world can be seen in Vaynor's peaceful churchyard. Vaynor, a scattered hamlet, stands in pretty farming country a few miles north of Merthyr. Its church, in a grassy hollow, is the resting place of Robert Thompson Crawshay, who died in 1879.

He was one of the all-powerful Crawshay family, the stern ironmasters responsible for the building, in 1824-25, of Merthyr's Cyfarthfa Castle, a testament to their immense wealth and power.

Robert Thompson Crawshay's grave provides a different kind of testament to his life and times: it is marked by a massive slab of rock into which is set, in iron letters, the plea 'God Forgive Me'.

Wrexham

Clwyd   SJ 3350

Elihu Yale (1648-1721) is a far more familiar name across the Atlantic than in Britain — it lives on in the great university to which he was a generous benefactor. Yale is buried in Wrexham's Church of St Giles. His tomb is marked by a long epitaph, with the lines:

'Born in America, in Europe bred,
In Africa travell'd, and in Asia wed,
Where long he liv'd, and thriv'd; at London dead.
Much good, some ill, he did; so hope all's even,
And that his soul, through mercy's gone to heaven.'

Y Gaer

Powys   SO 0029

The name means 'The Fort' in English: it was one of the strongholds of the Romans. Originally built of earth and timber in about AD80, and then rebuilt in stone about 60 years later, it housed a garrison of 500 men.

First impressions suggest that farmlands have all but obscured the site, but closer inspection reveals a different picture. Y Gaer's plan can be clearly traced, thanks to well-preserved stretches of wall defences, complete in some cases with original gateways. It stands above the meeting of the Usk and Yscir rivers, approximately two miles west of Brecon.

Ynys Lochtyn

Dyfed   SN 3155

Running north into the water of Cardigan Bay, Ynys Lochtyn juts out from a remote stretch of cliff-backed coast, accessible by footpath from Llangrannog. The path skirts the headlands beneath the Iron Age fort of Pendinaslochdyn before descending on to the main arm of the promontory, a grassy finger of land exposed to the full force of westerly gales. Owned by the National Trust, it makes a magnificent, albeit windy, viewpoint. Be careful not to venture too far along — the rocky northern tip is often cut off by the sea.

Ystradfellte

Powys   SN 9313

Waterfalls (see Scwd-yr-Eira) and disappearing rivers distinguish the limestone area of the Brecon Beacons known as Ystradfellte. Nowhere is the scenery more dramatic than half a mile south of Ystradfellte hamlet. Here, the River Mellte flows into the gloomy, gargantuan cave called Porth-yr-ogof, reappearing from its underground course a quarter of a mile downstream in a deep, dangerous pool.

Parties of well-equipped potholers disappear into Porth-yr-ogof along with the river to explore the maze of chambers and passageways that worm their way through the limestone rock. Others must be content with following the short, steep path that drops down into a narrow gorge and the entrance of the cave.

YSTRADFELLTE   *Porth-yr-ogof, the Gateway of the Cave, leads into the great limestone cavern, 1400 feet long, which swallows up the River Mellte. Only expert potholers can venture further than the mouth of the cave, but a footpath below goes to the three lovely Clyn-gwyn waterfalls*

ERIC GILL *in 1940, and his signature, carved on a memorial in Canterbury Cathedral, 1908*

VALE OF EWYAS: ERIC GILL — *Sculptor, engraver and typographer Eric Gill came to Capel-y-ffin, in the* **Vale of Ewyas**, *in 1924. He lived with his wife in a former monastery belonging to the Benedictine abbey on Caldey Island.*

Here Gill was asked to design lettering for the Monotype Corporation, resulting in the creation of the Perpetua and the Gill Sans-serif printing types, which were developed for use all over the world.

Gill was born at **Brighton** *in 1882. Between 1900 and 1903, when articled to a London architect, he became interested in lettering, which he studied at the Central School of Arts and Crafts. From 1903, he was able to earn his living as a letter-cutter, working on inscriptions, tombstones and plaques.*

Converted to Roman Catholicism in 1913, he was next year commissioned to carve the Stations of the Cross — completed in 1918 — for Westminster Cathedral, **London**. *In 1907 he had settled with his wife at Ditchling, Sussex, and they returned there to help found the Guild of St Joseph and St Dominic, a semi-religious community of craftsmen.*

Capel-y-ffin was the Gills' next home, after which came Speen, near High Wycombe, where Gill engraved the elegant designs for 'The Canterbury Tales' and 'The Four Gospels', for Robert Gibbings' Golden Cockerel Press.

He died in 1940 and is buried in the churchyard at Speen.

NORFOLK 1935.
Watching the sea go by – occupation of fishermen since time immemorial. These are probably crab fishermen; their smocks were sometimes known as 'slops'

CENTRAL & EASTERN ENGLAND

The Devil has travelled widely through Central England. He has a chair on the Stiperstones, and is said to use it still on foggy nights; he created Meon Hill, above Upper Quinton, and a number of ghostly minions still hang around it; and he left his hoofprints on a stone at Winceby. Those not wishing to become closely acquainted with Old Nick might prefer to sample the more homely delights of the World Conker Championship at Ashton, or perhaps the notion of the Tree Dressing ceremony at Aston on Clun appeals? Some might think there is devilment to be heard at Napton on the Hill, where there is a museum of juke boxes and other mechanised music makers. They say he has the best tunes, after all.

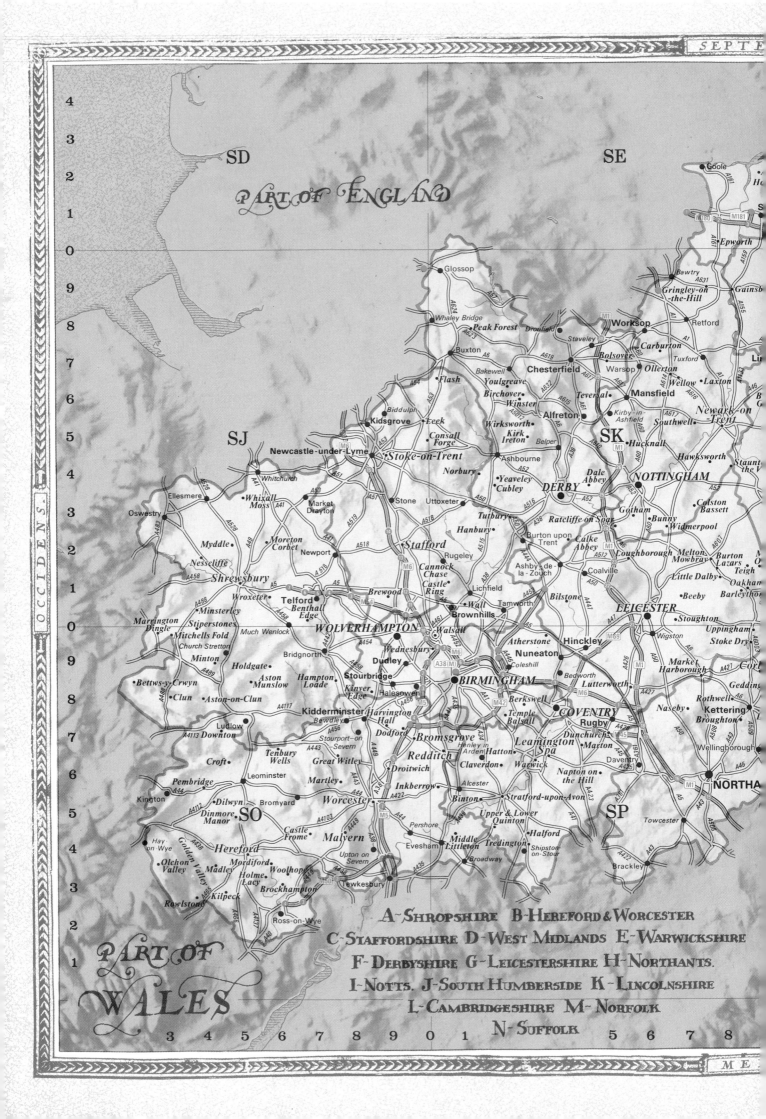

PART OF ENGLAND

SD
SE

SJ
SK

SO
SP

PART OF
WALES

A - SHROPSHIRE B - HEREFORD & WORCESTER
C - STAFFORDSHIRE D - WEST MIDLANDS E - WARWICKSHIRE
F - DERBYSHIRE G - LEICESTERSHIRE H - NORTHANTS.
I - NOTTS. J - SOUTH HUMBERSIDE K - LINCOLNSHIRE
L - CAMBRIDGESHIRE M - NORFOLK
N - SUFFOLK

OCCIDENS.

Goole
Epworth
Bawtry
Gringley-on-the-Hill
Gainsb
Worksop
Retford
Glossop
Whaley Bridge
Peak Forest
Dronfield
Staveley
Carburton
Tuxford
Li
Buxton
A6
Bakewell
Chesterfield
Warsop
Ollerton
Wellow
Laxton
Flash
Youlgreave
Bolsover
Birchover
Winster
Teversal
Mansfield
Newark-on-Trent
Biddulph
Kidsgrove
Eeek
Wirksworth
Alfreton
Kirby-in-Ashfield
Southwell
Consall Forge
Kirk Ireton
Belper
Hucknall
Hawksworth
Newcastle-under-Lyme
Stoke-on-Trent
Ashbourne
Dale Abbey
NOTTINGHAM
Whitchurch
Norbury
Yeaveley
Cubley
DERBY
Staunt the V
Ellesmere
Whixall Moss
Market Drayton
Stone
Uttoxeter
Tutbury
Ratcliffe on Soar
Gotham
Colston Bassett
Oswestry
Myddle
Moreton Corbet
Newport
Hanbury
Burton upon Trent
Calke Abbey
Bunny
Widmerpool
Nesscliffe
Shrewsbury
Stafford
Rugeley
Ashby-de-la-Zouch
Loughborough
Melton Mowbray
Burton Lazars
Teigh
Wroxeter
Telford
Benthall Edge
Brewood
Cannock Chase
Castle Ring
Lichfield
Coalville
Little Dalby
Oakham
Barleythor
Minsterley
Wall
Tamworth
Bilstone
Beeby
Marrington Dingle
Stiperstones
Much Wenlock
WOLVERHAMPTON
Walsall
BROWNHILLS
LEICESTER
Mitchells Fold
Church Stretton
Bridgnorth
Wednesbury
Atherstone
Hinckley
Stoughton
Minton
Dudley
Nuneaton
Wigston
Uppingham
Stoke Dry
Holdgate
Coleshill
Bettws-y-Crwyn
Aston Munslow
Hampton Loade
Stourbridge
Berkswell
Bedworth
Market Harborough
Col
Clun
Aston-on-Clun
Kinver Edge
Halesowen
BIRMINGHAM
Lutterworth
Rothwell
Geddin
Kidderminster
Harvington Hall
Temple Balsall
COVENTRY
Naseby
Kettering
Broughton
Ludlow
Bewdley
Dodford
Rugby
Dunchurch
Downton
Stourport-on-Severn
Bromsgrove
Henley in Arden
Hatton
Leamington Spa
Marton
Daventry
Wellingborough
Croft
Tenbury Wells
Great Witley
Redditch
Claverdon
Warwick
Napton on the Hill
Pembridge
Leominster
Martley
Droitwich
Inkberrow
Alcester
Stratford-upon-Avon
NORTHA
Kington
Dilwyn
Bromyard
Worcester
Binton
Upper & Lower Quinton
Towcester
Dinmore Manor
Castle Frome
Pershore
Halford
Hay on Wye
Malvern
Evesham
Middle Littleton
Tredington
Shipston-on-Stour
Brackley
Olchon Valley
Golden Valley
Hereford
Mordiford
Woolhope
Upton on Severn
Broadway
Madley
Holme Lacy
Brockhampton
Tewkesbury
Rowlstone
Kilpeck
Ross-on-Wye

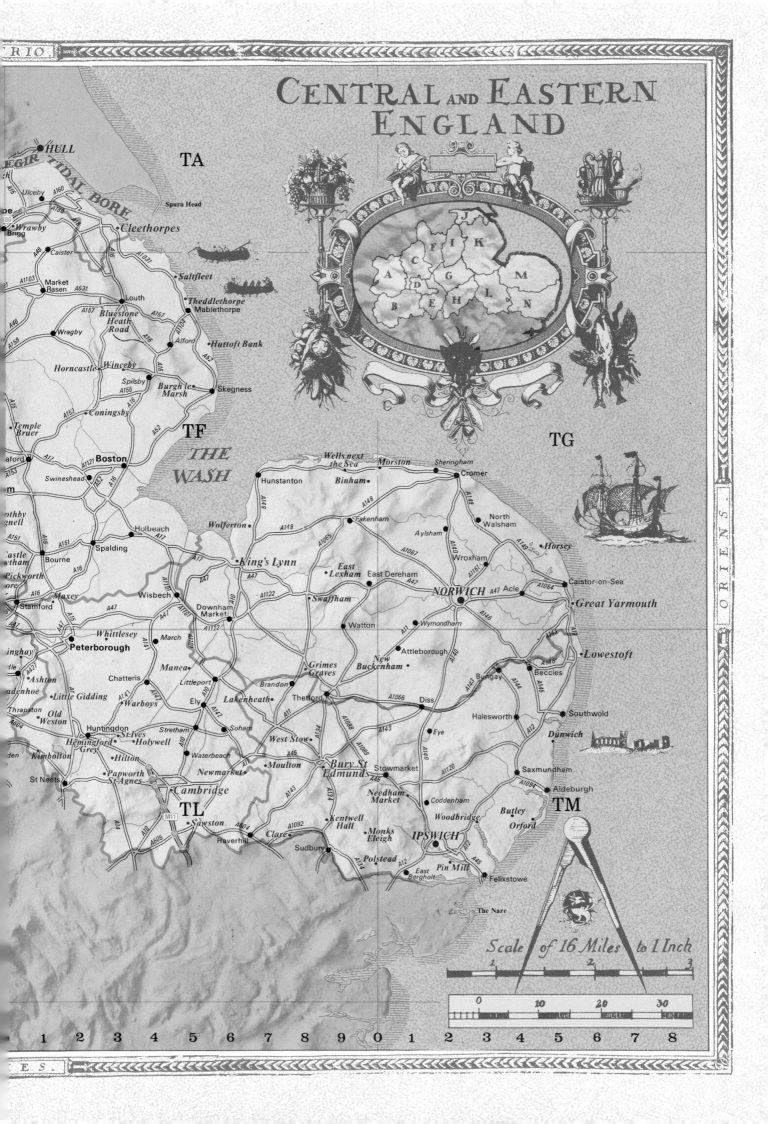

ASTON ON CLUN: ARBOR TREE — *A unique custom maintained at **Aston on Clun** is the Arbor Tree ceremony. On or around 29 May, a large black poplar tree in the village centre is decked with flags on long poles, which are left in position until next Arbor Tree Day. Local tradition has it that the custom began with the wedding of the lord of the manor in 1786. The tree was decorated for the occasion, a sight which so pleased the bride that she paid for it to be repeated every anniversary. It is very unlikely that the custom began in the 18th century, but the bride might have provided funds to help pay for an old ceremony and keep it going.*

Another tradition reported about the decorating of the tree was that it was to keep witches away. This idea may be related to the 'maypoles' of Herefordshire, which were birch trees put up outside stables and decorated with streamers on May Day, then left standing all year to ward off bad luck and stop witches riding the horses at night.

*But 29 May was also Oak Apple Day (see **Tilford**), celebrating the Restoration, but probably a revival of old customs to do with the 'guardian trees' of early settlements. A similar survival of the tree cult, which has given Britain so many of its most picturesque customs and traditions, is the intermittently performed ceremony of Bawming the Thorn, at Appleton Thorn, Cheshire. 'Bawming' is a dialect word meaning 'adorning', and on or near 5 July (Old Midsummer Day) the hawthorn at the centre of Appleton Thorn (renewed in 1967) is decked with garlands of flowers, red ribbons and flags, and danced round. Motifs which seem to originate from the tree cult can also be seen in churches — see **Coventry**.*

ALKBOROUGH *Monks probably cut the turf maze — 44 feet in diameter — and may have walked it with a pebble in their sandals as a form of penance*

Alkborough

Humberside SE 8821

The ancient turf maze of Julian's Bower at Alkborough stands on a 150-foot escarpment, overlooking the meeting of the Trent and the Humber. The traditional name of Julian's Bower is from Julius, son of Aeneas, who is said to have brought maze games to Italy from Troy (hence the alternative name, Walls of Troy). But it is more likely the work of monks from Spalding, who had a grange or cell in Alkborough, closed in the 13th century. The maze would have been regarded as a symbol of the path to salvation.

There is a replica of the maze cut into the stone floor of the entrance porch of St John the Baptist's Church nearby.

Ashton

Northamptonshire TL 0588

The World Conker Championship is held annually in front of Ashton's Chequered Skipper pub (named after a butterfly), on the second Sunday in October. No pickled or baked conkers are allowed, and each contestant takes three swipes at a time at the opponent's conker, up to a total of 12 swipes.

With its stone-built, thatched cottages huddled round a large green, Ashton looks as though it

has been here for centuries, but it was in fact rebuilt as recently as 1900, as an estate village. It was the scene of a murder mystery in 1953, when a couple who lived in the lodge cottage were killed by an intruder.

Ashton Mill, on the River Nene, is open at summer weekends and has a fish museum.

Aston Munslow

Shropshire SO 5186

Hidden up a no-through-lane north-west of the village is the White House, described as a museum but really more of an architectural time-capsule.

The homestead itself is older than any part of the building except the stone dovecote. It remained in the same family, the Stedmans of bell-ringing fame, from the 13th century until 1946. One of the family, Fabian Stedman, might be considered the father of modern changeringing: he originated many of the changes that are rung today. The present owner has researched the building and prepared the interior for display to visitors. Outside is a collection of old farming implements and household bygones.

Aston on Clun

Shropshire SO 3981

In this small village up the quiet Clun valley, three miles west of Craven Arms, there survives what is possibly the last 'Arbor Tree' in England. This is the huge black poplar in the village centre,

160

which is kept decorated with flags.

Tree-dressing takes place on or near 29 May, said to have been inspired by a local bride or by Charles II, to celebrate his restoration and remember his escape by hiding in another Shropshire tree, the Boscobel Oak.

Atherstone

Warwickshire SP 3097

Exactly 100 miles from London, Atherstone had special significance when stage-coaches plied the London to Holyhead route. But today its main street, Long Street, is more notable for a bizarre annual custom, which takes place each Shrove Tuesday. The Atherstone Ball Game is said to date back to the 13th century, and seemingly involves the entire population — men, women and children — who spend much of the afternoon endeavouring to 'smuggle' away a giant-sized football, thrown from the Three Tuns Inn, in a boisterous free-for-all game.

Also to be found in this traditional hat-making town are several hostelries surviving from coaching days.

Barleythorpe

Leicestershire SK 8409

This was the home of Lord Lonsdale, known as the Yellow Earl because nearly everything he owned was coloured in golden hues, from cars and carriages to wheelbarrows and his grooms' cardigans. Some say, wrongly, that he influenced the official colour of the Automobile Association (yellow was chosen by the Automobile Association, for signs and other purposes, because it is easily seen).

Lordy, as he liked to be known, was a great sportsman. He supported boxing and hunting, owning over 100 hunters, and Barleythorpe Stud is now renowned for its thoroughbred stock. He also had his own gasworks in Manor Lane and an inn, the Horse and Groom, now 31 Main Street, which he closed, it is said, because his staff spent too much time there.

For a period during World War II, his home, the Hall, was used by the Airborne Forces prior to the Arnhem operations, during which time Lordy lived at Catmose Cottage, next to the County Museum, which was then another of his stables. The Hall today serves as an old people's home owned by the County Council, but many elders of the village and those in nearby Langham can tell tales of Lordy's daring exploits. He died during 1944.

Beeby

Leicestershire SK 6608

The 13th-century church has an unfinished spire known as Beeby's Tub. One story goes that two brothers building the spire argued, one pushing the other off the tower to his death. In grief, the first brother then jumped from the same spot himself, eventually dying from injuries he received. Other explanations have been given.

Nearby an ancient well has a verse inscribed on it, proclaiming the many virtues of the water.

Beeby is also noted as the birthplace of Lord Chief Justice Robert Catlin, who refused to change court procedures to suit Queen Elizabeth when her favourite, Robert Dudley, Earl of Leicester, was in court in 1571.

Benthall Edge

Shropshire SJ 6602

This is the forgotten side of the Ironbridge Gorge. Many of the raw materials that made this area 'the cradle of the Industrial Revolution' were won from here, and concealed beneath today's woodland canopy are the 'adits' (horizontal entrances) of old clay mines that served brick and tile works, and limestone quarries that provided flux for the furnaces.

The geological diversity which gave this mineral wealth has also resulted in a splendid variety of plant life, explained by a nature trail.

Above Benthall Edge, at the end of a lane (or reached by the paths through the woods), lies Benthall Hall, a charming 16th-century stone house, owned by the National Trust. Alongside is the 17th-century church.

Berkswell

West Midlands SP 2479

An intriguing puzzle in this unspoilt village is why the old stocks on the green have five leg-holes. Tradition has it that they originally had four, but that a fifth was added when a local wrongdoer turned out to be a man with only one leg.

The Norman Church of St John should be visited for its mice: these can be discovered on numerous pieces of woodwork, including the oak font, and are the work of the wood-carver Robert Thompson, who used a mouse as his trademark. The church also has an unusual half-timbered porch.

Outside the 16th-century Bear Inn is another curiosity, a cannon, captured from the Russians in the Crimean War and allegedly fired only once since then — on 4 January 1859, as a spectacular prelude to a dinner for the local gentry.

A small country cottage houses an interesting museum of local life (open on summer weekends). The village lies a few miles to the west of Coventry.

ATHERSTONE: SHROVETIDE GAMES — Shrovetide, the days once known as Egg Saturday, Quinquagesima Sunday, Collop Monday and Shrove Tuesday, has always been a time of revelry and the Ball Game at **Atherstone** is a survivor of the boisterous games traditionally played to let off steam before the austerity of Lent. This wild, unruly form of football — also still played at Sedgefield, Co Durham, **Alnwick**, and

Ashbourne, Derbyshire — used to be played at other holiday times too. In pre-Christian days the 'ball' may have been the head of an animal slaughtered for sacrifice.

The Cornish people have their own ancient game called hurling which survives in **St Ives**, **St Columb Major** and **Minor**. A wooden ball, covered with silver, is tossed and carried but never kicked.

The using up of food played a large part in Shrovetide jollities — recalled in the Pancake Race at **Olney**, dating from 1445. Women wearing headscarves and aprons run from the village square to the church tossing a pancake three times on the way.

In **Scarborough**, celebrations consist of men, women and children trooping down to the foreshore after the pancake bell has rung and skipping until teatime.

ABOVE SHROVETIDE FOOTBALL at Ashbourne is played between goals three miles apart

BEEBY Another explanation of All Saints' unfinished spire is that the builder despaired of equalling that of Queniborough nearby, and jumped off the battlements

DEMON DRUMMER *of Tedworth*

BINHAM: HAUNTING MUSIC — *It used to be said that an underground passage led from* **Binham** *Priory to nearby Walsingham. A fiddler and his dog set out to explore it, he played a tune as he went so that those above could keep track of him. But at a place thereafter called Fiddler's Hill, the music suddenly stopped; and though in time the dog reappeared, shivering with terror, the fiddler himself was never seen again.*

Skeletons were found in the hill in 1932, but a similar story is told of a piper at Culross, Fife, and of a drummer at **Richmond** *Castle. Drummers who are themselves supernatural include those of* **Dover** *(headless),* **Harpham** *(drowned) and South Tidworth, where the Demon Drummer of Tedworth (as it was called) was transported in the 17th century for witchcraft, but could still be heard on Salisbury Plain.*

BINTON *'Here Captain Oates . . . unwilling to be a burden to his companions, leaves them and the shelter of the tent, to die.'*

Bettws-y-Crwyn

Shropshire SO 2086

In the remotest part of this extremely remote parish on the roof of the Clun Forest, west of Offa's Dyke but just on the English side of the border today, there stands an unusual memorial. The Cantlin Stone was erected to the memory of the pedlar William Cantlin, who died here in 1591. It lies on the centuries-old route of the cattle drovers, who came along the ancient Kerry Ridgeway and traditionally stopped at the Anchor Inn on the Welsh border (where the traveller still receives a warm welcome), before driving their stock up over the hill, en route to Shrewsbury or the Midlands.

Bilstone

Leicestershire SK 3606

A well-preserved gibbet post, one of the last in Britain, stands on the outskirts of the village. Gibbets were used for displaying the corpses of criminals, and the last person to hang on this one was John Massey, in March 1801. He murdered his second wife, and then attempted to kill his ten-year-old daughter, by throwing her into the Mill Dam.

Although the judge ordered his body to be sent for dissection, it remained on the post, eventually being buried between his two wives. Massey was a well-known wrestler, gaining the nickname Topsy Turvey from his trick of throwing opponents over his head.

Binham

Norfolk TF 9839

Surrounded by rolling, arable farmland, and on the edge of a thriving village, the remains of Binham's Benedictine priory come as a startling surprise. It was built of honey-coloured Barnack stone (from quarries near Stamford), which makes a perfect foil for the local flintwork. The great west front, built before 1244, is a superb example of Early English church architecture, and is now part of the Parish Church of St Mary and the Holy Cross, which occupies what was once the Norman nave.

On a side altar table is the Tobruk Cross, made from shell-cases to commemorate those who died in the North African campaign. Look in the ruins of the south transept for two uncovered sections of the original floor of glazed tiles, fired in the priory's own kilns. The ruins can be seen throughout the year in daylight hours, as can the parish church.

Binton

Warwickshire SP 1454

Just to the west of Stratford-upon-Avon, Binton's Victorian Parish Church of St Peter has the unexpected feature of a great west window illustrating and commemorating the last tragic voyage of Captain Robert Scott to the Antarctic.

Scott knew and loved Binton, and his last visit here was to bid farewell to his brother-in-law, the Reverend Lloyd Bruce, who was rector of the parish, before he and his fellow explorers lost their lives on the South Pole expedition in 1912. The window, which was designed by Kempe, shows a chronological sequence of episodes from this ill-fated expedition.

Birchover

Derbyshire SK 2462

Splendid rock scenery surrounds this small village, which was the scene of mysterious 'druidical' practices in the 18th century. Hence the name of the local pub — the Druid Inn.

There is a remote hermitage cave with carvings, and the Rowter Rocks are ideal for clambering. One eccentric parson carved seats in the rock and another decorated the little church with carvings and paintings.

Birmingham

West Midlands SP 0787

Among the less known delights of this vast urban sprawl is the canal network, more extensive than that of Venice, it is said, but largely hidden below the city's streets. The once busy waterways have been restored for leisure use, with Gas Street Basin (under Broad Street) and the colourful Cambrian Wharf providing evocative reminders of the canal system.

Birmingham also has a river, the Rea, which wends its way underground for much of its course. One of the few places where it can be seen is in Cannon Hill Park, not far from the BBC's Pebble Mill studios.

Transport curiosities include the Maglev, linking Birmingham International Airport to its nearest station with driverless vehicles running in a state of suspension above an elevated track, by means of magnetic levitation. A vehicular curiosity of another kind is the preserved 125-ton steam locomotive, City of Birmingham, which once an hour makes a journey of just a few feet, inside the Museum of Science and Industry.

More railway history lies deep below the Great Western Arcade in the city centre. This restored Victorian shopping arcade on two levels was built directly over the old GWR line from London to the city's now demolished Snow Hill Station. The course still lies hidden in its tunnel. Another memorial to the station is a plaque in Bull Street, at the entrance to the Quaker Meeting House. It bears the names of 49 Quakers whose coffins were removed for the railway.

Aston Hall, a Jacobean mansion, has one room which is definitely not open to the public: it measures just four feet by four feet and is said to house a 300-year-old ghost. It was here, according to legend, that a former owner, Sir Thomas Holte, imprisoned his daughter for not marrying the man of his choice. She eventually went mad and died, and her ghost has frequented this part of the house ever since.

Weoley Castle is a former fortified manor house, of which only a few impressive remains can now be seen. But there is a museum on the site, with relics discovered during excavations, including a 13th-century shoe, coins, medieval keys, and evidence of a 600-year-old chess game.

More easily missed is the weather vane on the Cathedral Church of St Philip — not the usual cock but a boar's head. It comes from the crest of the Gough family, who instigated George I's gift of £600 towards the building of the church.

Near Aston University is a street called A. B. Row, because it originally marked the boundary between Aston and Birmingham; on Pershore Road in the suburb of *Stirchley* is a terrace called

BIRMINGHAM *Beneath the Great Western Arcade — built by W H Ward in 1876 and recently restored — ran the city's old Great Western Railway line to London*

BIRMINGHAM: GUILT OF THE BLOODY HAND —

At Aston Hall, **Birmingham**, built 1618-35, there hangs a portrait of its first owner, Sir Thomas Holte. Before building Aston, he had lived at Duddeston Hall, where, according to tradition, he murdered his cook by running him through with a spit. When Duddeston Hall was razed in 1850, many expected to find the cook's skeleton under the cellar floor where Sir Thomas had buried him.

But the story was only rumour. In 1606 Sir Thomas took a neighbour to court for saying he had split his cook's head with a cleaver. Though Sir Thomas won his case, the rumour persisted — and by the 19th century it was said that it was for this that he was forced to wear the 'bloody hand' in his coat of arms.

The 'bloody hand' was actually the Red Hand of Ulster, the badge of baronetcy, but it has given rise to murder tales in other places, among them Wateringbury, Kent, and **Stoke d'Abernon**.

At Aston church, the hand — minus a finger — depicted in the Holte arms in one of the windows, was explained by saying that Sir Thomas's descendants were allowed to remove one finger or thumb for each generation, until the hand was gone.

THE BLOODY HAND *shown in the middle of the coat of arms was explained by a gory tale*

BIRMINGHAM: TOLKIEN

BIRMINGHAM: TOLKIEN — *Author of 'The Hobbit' and 'The Lord of the Rings', J. R. R. Tolkien was four years old when his family moved to Hall Green, in those days a quiet hamlet outside* **Birmingham**.

From 1896 to 1900, John Ronald and his small brother paid frequent visits to Sarehole Mill with its tall chimney, particularly admiring the great water-wheel: the Mill had recently acquired a steam engine to boost the flagging water-power when the river was running low.

This pleasant life was shattered when Tolkien was dispatched to boarding school at the age of eight. At the same time, his family moved away from Sarehole. But in 1933, he revisited the scene of his boyhood — and his diary expresses his horror. It had 'become a huge, tram-ridden, meaningless suburb'. He deplored the 'sea of red-brick' surrounding his family's cottage and the dangerous traffic on the once-quiet crossing, 'where the bluebell lane ran down into the mill lane'.

'The old mill still stands,' wrote Tolkien wistfully; and, even in the present day, the mill and river are clearly recognisable as the basis for the author's fictional village of Hobbiton, the comfortable home of his celebrated hobbits.

TOLKEIN'S *picture of 'wide respectable' hobbit-lands, perhaps inspired by Sarehole*

BIRMINGHAM *St Lazar's was built by Serbian craftsmen for the Serbian Orthodox Church. Its red sandstone pillars come from the same quarry as the stone for the original Lazarica, in Yugoslavia*

the ABC houses, because they all bear names in alphabetical order. The first pair of houses start with A, the second pair with B and so on.

Bournville, Birmingham's 'chocolate suburb', has two rebuilt timbered manor houses on the former village green — Selly Manor and Minworth Greaves, both open to the public. Not far away is a remarkable Serbian Orthodox church built in the 1960s in authentic Byzantine style and richly decorated, said to be the only European building of its type outside Yugoslavia.

In *Northfield*, another busy suburb, is the massive Northfield Stone, standing in an ancient cattle pound. Its origin is shrouded in mystery, but some say it is a prehistoric monument, others that it was a meteorite.

Outside the Barber Institute in *Edgbaston* is an equestrian statue of George I, bought for £500 by a Professor Thomas Bodkin from the authorities in Dublin, after a similar statue of George II, also in Dublin, had been blown up in 1937.

For lovers of J. R. R. Tolkien's books, *The Hobbit* and *Lord of the Rings*, the city's *Hall Green* district is a must. Tolkien lived here, and the perfectly preserved Sarehole Mill, which provided much of Tolkien's inspiration, with its mill pond and stream, is open to the public.

The *Royal Town of Sutton Coldfield* (its regal status was bestowed on it by Henry VIII) became a part of Birmingham under county boundary changes, but still retains its individual character. Most idiosyncratic of its attractions is a private domestic garden in Douglas Road. Here, the owner Donald Jones has created a complex model railway network of remarkable detail. Linked to it, and in a specially constructed building, is a scale model of Birmingham's New Street Station and much of the city centre. The model trains run

to authentic British Rail timetables. Donald Jones opens his Lilliputian world to the public on the first weekend in September, but special arrangements for parties can occasionally be made at other times.

Also worth seeing in Sutton Coldfield is its 2400-acre park, once a royal hunting ground, and now an unspoilt tract of heathland and woods.

Bluestone Heath Road

Lincolnshire TF 3975

A prehistoric ridgeway, the road follows the chalk crest of the southern Lincolnshire Wolds. To follow the route of centuries of travellers is a fine feeling — and it makes a scenic drive with wide views. It turns west off the A16 near Driby Top (west of Alford), and passes the deserted medieval village of Calceby, with the ruined chancel of the chalk-and-sandstone church on a hill. In sweeping curves the road rises to over 450 feet, with stretches of flower-rich roadside verges marked with NR (Nature Reserve) posts by the County Council and County Trust for Nature Conservation.

The isolated hamlets of Worlaby and Oxcombe are passed, tucked into deep valleys, and there is a lay-by and labelled viewpoint, with wide vistas of the scarp and outlying hills. North of the A153, on one of the highest parts of the Wolds, is the remaining Stenigot pylon — part of a Gee Chain aircraft navigation system, a very early form of radar, from the 1940s. Beyond the A157 and through Poke Holes is the classic deserted village site of Calcethorpe, which provides a clear view of the former streets and the positions of vanished cottages.

Bolsover

Derbyshire SK 4770

At one time Bolsover was famous for its buckles, and later it became a mining village — but inside the Castle, such industry seems very far away. This great Jacobean building was built by a member of the Cavendish family, and passed eventually to the Dukes of Portland. It stands on a spur and is a landmark for miles around. Only the so-called keep is intact, with exotic fireplaces and wall and ceiling paintings. The rest, much of which was built to accommodate King Charles I and his Queen when they visited the owner, is in ruins. To entertain the royal visitors a masque — *Love's Welcome at Bolsover* — was performed here. From the terraces, there are spectacular views.

Bolsover Church has interesting monuments to the Cavendish family, and Bess of Hardwick's Hardwick Hall is not far away.

Boothby Graffoe

Lincolnshire SK 9859

Somerton Castle in Boothby Graffoe Low Fields was a lavish place of imprisonment for King John I of France, for seven months from August 1359. He had been captured by the Black Prince at the battle of Poitiers and brought with him his son Philip and a household of 40 or more, whose needs were considerable. Twelve wagons were required for the baggage when they left.

The remnants of the castle now form part of an Elizabethan house, which is not open to the public. The double-moated, quadrangular structure, built in the 1280s of local limestone, with timber from as far afield as the Baltic, was very up-to-date for its period.

Boothby Pagnell

Lincolnshire SK 9730

In the grounds of Boothby Pagnell Hall, south-east of Grantham, is arguably the most important small Norman house in England. It is the chance survival of a chamber block, with later internal alterations and an extension, other buildings having long since disappeared. It was built around 1200, of Lincolnshire limestone in coursed rubble, with a defensive moat. The living quarters, consisting of a hall (with a fireplace), and solar or upper chamber (with no heating), over the rib-vaulted undercroft, are reached by an external staircase. The manor house stands on private property and may be visited *only* by permission in writing from the owner, Lord Netherthorpe, who lives at the Hall.

Brewood

Staffordshire SJ 8808

With its half-timbered houses, Brewood (pronounced 'Brood') is the archetypal picturesque English village. But visitors are surprisingly rare.

Of the many fine old buildings, the most spectacular is probably the 18th-century Gothic 'Speedwell Castle' in the main street. Actually a tall, double-fronted town house, it is supposed to have been built with the profit gained from a well-placed bet on a racehorse called Speedwell.

The Giffards have been the major landowners in the district since the 12th century, and 'Giffards Cross', south-west of the village, marks the spot where an animal described as a 'panther' was shot with a crossbow by Sir John Giffard in 1513. The beautiful Shropshire Union Canal is another attraction.

BOOTHBY PAGNELL *The hall of the Norman manor house, one of the very few Norman houses left of the smaller type, which would once have been lived in by gentry and knights of lesser rank*

OLD ROADS *An extract from the Gough Map of around 1360 shows the roads around London*

BLUESTONE HEATH ROAD: ANCIENT ROADS — *The oldest long-distance routes which can be identified, such as the* **Bluestone Heath Road**, *the Icknield Way and the Ridgeway, running from Norfolk to Wessex, probably date back to the New Stone Age. These early tracks evolved from the migration lines of wild animals and man's hunting trails. Gradually, as man became less nomadic and established settlements, more clearly defined routeways developed between populated areas. However, to think of these prehistoric ways as 'roads' is erroneous. They consisted more of hundreds of inter-linking tracks representing movement in the same general direction.*

When the Romans arrived they built well-engineered highways between their depots (see **Ilchester**), *to facilitate the movement of troops and supplies and wherever possible took the most direct line. Although many of these roads disappeared during the Dark Ages which followed, some survived to become part of our present road system.*

During this period and into medieval times the population, habitation and local trade increased, resulting in a maze of twisty, hollowed lanes which still characterise parts of the country.

With the advent of the wool trade came the extensive network of Drovers' Roads such as the **Hambleton Drove Road**. *Many followed tracks already centuries old but when in the mid-17th century road tolls brought about the resurfacing or re-routing of existing roads, a great number of the ancient routes were abandoned. Today they may be traced as footpaths and private roads, or through archaeological features and local names for tracks, such as the Drift,* **Pickworth**.

Brockhampton

Hereford & Worcester   SO 5932

The county has two Brockhamptons: one 'by Bromyard' and the other 'by Ross'. This is the latter, with a masterpiece of Arts and Crafts architecture: the church, designed by W. R. Lethaby and built in 1902. Almost every detail, both of construction and enrichment, shows inventive originality of design and workmanship at its best. External materials range through wood, stone and thatch, and the walls are enriched by the skilled choice of shrubs and creepers. Inside, a deceptive simplicity makes the most of every form beneath the concrete vault, and details range from carved wild flowers on the pews to Burne-Jones tapestries beside the altar, woven by Morris & Co.

A back road from here to Fownhope crosses Capler Hill, with a wooded prehistoric encampment and lofty views of the Wye.

The other Brockhampton also has riches however: a 15th-century timber-framed and moated manor and gatehouse, belonging to the National Trust and reached down a long lane, which appears to descend through both space and time.

Bromsgrove

Hereford & Worcester   SO 9570

In the churchyard of St John the Baptist is a double grave and memorial to two railwaymen, Thomas Scaife and Joseph Rutherford. They were killed when their engine, a locomotive of the Birmingham and Gloucester Railway, exploded in 1840. Each headstone has a realistic engraving of the ill-fated engine, and one has a long and tear-jerking epitaph beginning: *'My engine now is cold and still, no water does my boiler fill . . .'*

Another unique local railway feature is the Lickey Incline, which climbs one foot in every thirty-seven, the steepest main-line gradient on British Rail.

Not far away is Bromsgrove School, founded before the Reformation and still operating as a public school. Among its pupils was the poet A. E. Housman, who lived for a time in 18th-century Perry Hall, now an hotel.

Just to the south of the town stands historic Grafton Manor, complete with 15th-century chapel, which is now a restaurant.

BUNNY   *The monument of the wrestling baronet, Sir Thomas Parkyns, bears the lines:*
'That Time at length did throw him it is plain
Who lives in hopes that he should rise again'

Broughton

Northamptonshire   SP 8375

Today's village is an incongruous mix of old and new, but noteworthy as the setting for what must surely be one of the country's noisiest folk customs. It takes place on the second Sunday after St Andrew's Day, when the Broughton Tin Can Band turns out. This dates back to medieval times and consists of a group of 'players', banging tin cans and buckets for about an hour from midnight.

Bunny

Nottinghamshire   SK 5829

The main road between Loughborough and Nottingham rushes through this oddly-named village, but pause to look in the church at the memorial, designed by himself, of Sir Thomas Parkyns, the wrestling baronet (1662-1741). This unique monument shows the squire in wrestling pose and also thrown by Time. Founder of a wrestling contest at Bunny (with a laced cocked hat as prize), he was famed as a wrestler himself, and was also a classical scholar and amateur architect. Note the eccentric house he built for himself — Bunny Hall (not open to the public) — with an enormous semi-circular pediment across its width, surmounted by an equally massive castellated tower, and the old school with its Latin inscription between the ground and first floor.

RIDING THE STANG   *A way for the community to shame those of whom it disapproved*

BROUGHTON: ROUGH MUSIC — *At midnight on the second Sunday after St Andrew's Day, some 60 people march through the streets of* **Broughton***, banging on tin cans and buckets. The 'performance' lasts about an hour and the 'players' are known as the Tin Can Band, said to have been formed in the Middle Ages to drive out Gypsies.*

The Band is probably a survival of 'Rough Music' — an extremely noisy accompaniment to communal punishment for misdemeanours. Known as 'Riding the Stang' and 'Riding Skimmerton', this involved a night-time procession by men and boys, banging on kettles, pots and pans, and blowing on horns and whistles. Periodically a halt would be called for the leader to recite in rhyme the culprit's name and offences.

Rough Music was made for anything the community disapproved of: wife- or husband-beating, the remarriage of widows or widowers, dishonesty and blacklegging. Often prejudice was so great that the victim was forced to leave the district — which happened in a case as recently as the 1950s.

Burgh Le Marsh

Lincolnshire TF 5065

From the tower of the proud Perpendicular Church of St Peter and St Paul, at 8pm on every weekday, from Michaelmas to Lady Day, the Curfew Bell is rung. It is tolled long enough to recite Psalm 130, followed by the day of the month rung in tens. Below the handsome clock, on the north face of the tower, is inscribed in gilt letters *'Watch and Pray, for ye know not when the time comes.'*

In 1629, a ship called the Mary Rose was lost in a storm and was in danger of being wrecked on the nearby Lincolnshire coast. The sound of the church bell saved it. In gratitude, the ship's master, Captain Prohock, bought an acre of land in the Orby Field, called the Bell-String Acre, the rent on which was to provide a silken rope for the Curfew Bell.

Burton Latimer

Northamptonshire SP 8974

The encroaching tide of industry (Kettering lies just to the north) has left three remarkable survivors in Burton Latimer, all in stone.

The former school, now a private house, is a picturesque study in rustic architecture, incorporating a steeply pitched, thatched roof, attractive gables and Jacobean mullioned windows. The Church of St Mary the Virgin dates back to the 12th century and contains 14th-century wall paintings of the martyrdom of St Katherine, and the restored remains of paintings of the 12 patriarchs of Israel, dating from the early 17th century. Burton Latimer Hall, with its 16th-century dovecote and old fish ponds, has been the home of the Harpur family since 1760.

Burton Lazars

Leicestershire SK 7716

Look out for graves bearing the name Zborowski in the burial ground of the Norman church: one notable member of this titled family of Polish extraction was Count Louis, creator and driver of the legendary Chitty-Chitty-Bang-Bang car. He was killed while racing the monster at Monza in 1924. Keys to the church, which can be visited at any time, can be obtained from the duty warden listed on the door.

The village name comes from the St Lazarus leper hospital, founded here in 1146, mainly because of the medicinal sulphurous spring. Evidence of both can be seen near the church. As well as the Zborowski graves, it has several other fine headstones and monuments.

Bury St Edmunds

Suffolk TL 8564

At the north-west corner of the spacious square of Angel Hill is a red-brick Queen Anne house, Angel Corner, with one of the finest clock collections in the country.

The timepieces, lovingly preserved, span five centuries, and what is more, they all work. To stand in the elegant drawing room at noon is to be overcome by a myriad of chimes. On show is the long-case clock made by Charles II's clock-maker — the impecunious monarch was sometimes forced to reward his mistresses with such gifts — and interesting snippets of information to

CALKE ABBEY *A family of recluses and eccentrics occupied it for years — including one owner who excluded all motor vehicles from the estate*

be gleaned here include the fact that the pendulum was first used in 1660, and that it was an American writer of popular songs who first coined the phrase 'grandfather's clock', in 1864.

All the streets of delightful Bury St Edmunds — first called St Edmondsbury, after the last King of the East Angles, who was slain in AD869 — lead to Angel Hill. They were laid out on the present grid pattern by the Norman Abbot Baldwin, in the 11th century.

Butley

Suffolk TM 3651

Set between the great Forestry Commission estate of Rendlesham and the sea at Orford, this little village boasts a pleasant inn, the Oyster, and the gatehouse of old Butley Abbey. From the road the 14th-century flush-work heraldic design on the front of the building, now in private hands and not open, is easily discernible.

The road beyond leads past magnificent clumps of ancient beech to stands of twisted oak and holly trees. There are places for picnics, and foot-paths snake through the woods, their routes shown on maps obtainable from the Forestry Commission's office at Rendlesham.

Calke Abbey

Derbyshire SK 3722

This was one of the last great secret places of Britain — an immense house, hidden in a huge park, and occupied by a family which kept to itself, and hardly ever threw anything away. Some of the rooms have not been altered for a century, and the last squire to bring back a wife to Calke did so in 1876.

The interior of the classical house is filled with treasures and portraits of the Harpur-Crewe family, who owned it before it passed into the hands of the National Trust, for restoration and opening to the public in 1989. The parklands may sometimes be visited, and the estate church in the grounds has Harpur monuments.

CALKE ABBEY: A WORLD APART — *Built in 1703 by Sir John Harpur, on the site of a 12th-century Augustinian priory,* **Calke Abbey** *has housed a formidable gallery of eccentrics.*

The inter-related families of Harpur and Crewe lived in a style very far removed from accepted conventions. In the late 18th century, Sir Henry Harpur, known as the 'isolated baronet', set the precedent for the family's history of reclusiveness, cutting himself off from the outside world and ruining himself in the eyes of society by marrying a lady's maid. In a later generation, Sir Vauncey Harpur-Crewe had the habit of communicating with his daughters (who lived with him in the Abbey) by letter, sometimes carried on a silver salver by the footman and sometimes by post.

His successor, fiercely private, died in 1981, and the house came to the National Trust, for restoration and opening to the public in the late 1980s. Untouched for over a century, the rooms contained such objects as a four-poster bed still in its 18th-century packing case, bearing startling witness to the extraordinary time-warp in which the families lived.

ABOVE *Canopy from the bed which was found at Calke Abbey, still in its original packing case after 200 years*

CAMBRIDGE: HOBSON'S CHOICE

— On 1 January 1630, Thomas Hobson died. He was the **Cambridge** *carrier so celebrated in his day that two epitaphs were written on him by no less a poet than John Milton.*

Born in 1544, he had inherited from his father a carrier's business, which he continued with great success under licence from the University. For many years he plied once a month between Cambridge and the Bull Inn, Bishopsgate, in **London,** *chiefly conveying letters, but taking parcels and people as well.*

Hobson also hired out horses and became famous for his stout refusal to let a horse out of his stables, except in its proper turn. If customers objected, he would reply shortly 'This or none', whence arose a proverb 'Hobson's Choice — this or none' — nowadays simply 'Hobson's Choice'.

In 1630, Hobson's visits to London were suspended by the authorities because of the plague — and this, says Milton, was the death of him. For death could never have caught up with him if he could have gone on dodging it between the Bull and Cambridge.

Having grown rich and become a Cambridge benefactor, Hobson was buried in the chancel of St Bene't's Church, and today is remembered in the name of Hobson's Lane.

ABOVE *'This or none' was the choice offered by Thomas Hobson to those who wished to hire a horse from his stables*

CAMBRIDGE *The Botanic Gardens' Chronological Bed shows introduced species. The Globe Thistle came from Eastern Europe in the late 1500s*

Cambridge

Cambridgeshire TL 4658

A leading citizen of the town in the 17th century was Thomas Hobson, who kept horses for hire. When a customer came to rent one, he would tell them which horse to take, rather than letting them make the selection — hence the saying 'Hobson's choice'. Hobson's stables were at the George Inn, which stood between the Bull Inn and St Catherine's College, Trumpington Street.

Admiring the venerable buildings of the university today, it is hard to believe that many of the riverside colleges were built on the sites of warehouses and quays. But before it became predominantly a university town, Cambridge was a bustling port, with goods travelling along the navigable River Cam from the Wash, via King's Lynn. Stourbridge Fair, one of England's great medieval fairs, at which East Anglia's traders met their Midlands rivals, depended heavily on this river traffic.

Cambridge's colleges need no introduction here. But there are other corners well worth seeking out. Researchers into local customs and folklore should appreciate the Cambridge and County Folk Museum at the foot of Castle Hill, housed in a former inn, The White Horse; Kettle's Yard, off Castle Hill, is a must for art enthusiasts; and the Botanic Gardens have a fascinating Chronological Bed — showing the species which have been introduced over the centuries, and leaving one wondering what grew in Britain before. Entertainments such as morris dancing and Punch and Judy shows can be enjoyed in August in the spacious Victorian Leckhampton Gardens — not normally open to the public, but turned each summer into the venue for 'Music In The Trees'.

Cannock Chase

Staffordshire SJ 9710

Originally a giant Royal Forest, Cannock Chase was gradually reduced in size and grazed by huge flocks of sheep, until, by the beginning of this century, only a remnant of the old forest survived, at Brocton Coppice. Still largely unknown outside the area, the Chase now offers a fascinating and wildlife-rich combination of heathland and marshland, with Forestry Commission plantations and old woodland. The heathland plants include a bilberry-cowberry cross, noted by the naturalist who first found it in 1887 as a 'new British plant' (in fact Charles Darwin had already recorded it elsewhere).

Marsh orchids and sundew can be found in the valleys, and in Brocton Coppice can be seen the mixture of ancient oaks and birches that must once have characterised the whole of the Chase. The Forestry Commission planting has been thoughtfully planned, and wildlife to be seen includes fallow deer, badgers and red squirrels, as well as many woodland birds.

Much of the area is run as a country park, and there is an information centre at Milford.

Carburton

Nottinghamshire SK 6173

The great ducal estates of Welbeck and Clumber meet here, and sandwiched between them is the hamlet of Carburton, a quiet, almost forgotten place, with an odd and tiny church. One of the smallest in the country, it is of Norman origin. Two centuries ago, its south aisle was removed and the arches filled in — hence the curious sight of pillars and arches on an outside wall. Inside is a memorial window to a member of the Foljambe family. A former rector of the village was the Reverend F. Day Lewis, father of the late Cecil Day Lewis, Poet Laureate. Also here are the county's oldest parochial records.

Castle Bytham

Lincolnshire SK 9818

An attractive but little-visited stone village, Castle Bytham is presided over by the impressive earthworks of a motte-and-bailey castle. Built in the 11th century on a bend of a small tributary of the River Glen, the prominent mound has a ditch and bank, double in places, with a large bailey to the east.

The castle was demolished in 1221 by Henry III, although remains of the great walls could still be seen in the mid-16th century. Today no masonry remains above ground. The appealing village is tucked in a valley in the Kesteven Plateau nine miles south of Grantham, and is easily approached from the A1.

Castle Frome

Hereford & Worcester SO 6645

Seen from the A4103 from Worcester to Hereford, the straggling hamlet of Fromes Hill has little to distract the attention until, at its western end, the road drops into the valley of the River Frome and presents one of the most spectacular views in England. It is backed by the Black Mountains and Hay Bluff, and a clear day reveals the Welsh hills of Radnor Forest.

The foreground is of hopyards and orchards, dotted with black-and-white farms and cottages, and scant remains of the Hereford and Gloucester Canal (including a tunnel at Ashperton). At the bottom of the hill turn left on to the B4214, then left again where the road ends at a farm and modest church, inside which is one of the finest examples of Romanesque sculpture anywhere in Britain. The main feature of the massive font is the Baptism of Christ, in a pond with fish, above which the hand of God reaches down from a dove-filled sky. Beyond St John are the symbols of the four Evangelists and other details.

By way of contrast the church also houses an alabaster group of a certain Stuart family, detailed even down to the buttons and bookmarks.

Castle Ring

Staffordshire SK 0412

Castle Ring is one those places that preserves a haunting atmosphere of former times. It is best visited on a summer evening in fading light, when the ancient 'feel' can be quite uncanny.

It is an extremely impressive hill fort, extending over nine acres, the largest of the seven Iron Age hill-forts in the county and one of England's finest. It stands at the highest point of Cannock Chase, 800 feet above sea level, and is thought to have been used by local tribesmen as a last line of defence against invaders advancing up the Trent Valley.

The earthworks give fine views, especially to the north, while the multiple banks and ditches which follow the land's contours must have made it a formidable stronghold in its day.

Clare

Suffolk TL 7645

There is no better introduction to this large, prosperous village astride the B1092 than a walk to the top of the motte of the Norman castle, which was built in 1090. A country park surrounds it and the old railway station is used as an information centre. Across the River Stour and over the railway bridge is the confused jumble of

CASTLE FROME'S *Norman font is one of the latest surviving works of the Herefordshire School of carvers. The long claws of the birds and animals are details typical of their work*

stone and brick walls of the 13th-century Augustinian priory. Two buildings survive: the old infirmary and the church, which was reconsecrated in 1954. Lionel, the son of Edward III, was buried here in 1377.

From the motte the flint-built parish church with 13th-century tower dominates the centre of Clare and around it are clearly seen the old houses displaying the old East Anglian art of pargeting — the application of moulded plaster to timber frames. The Ancient House bears the date 1473 on its plaster, and the intricate, floral designs on the gable ends and walls are well worth seeing.

CLARE: PARGETING — Pargeting, or the art of raised ornamental plaster-work, can be seen on numerous Suffolk buildings, including some of the houses at **Clare**.

*This is one of the earlier examples of the technique, which was first properly developed by the Elizabethans and continued into the early 18th century, declining together with the popularity of timber-framing (see **Pembridge**).*

More commonly used in towns and larger villages than hamlets or farmhouses, good pargeting can be seen in Essex and Hertfordshire as well as Suffolk. The devices — generally in relief — were often made with a board stuck with pins forming a pattern, which was then dragged across the wet plaster.

*Later plasterers favoured geometric designs, but the Elizabethans preferred to depict animals, people and plants. The pargeting on the Ancient House in the Butter Market, Ipswich, is a particularly fine example of this style. On the Sun Inn, **Saffron Walden**, the pargeting portrays the Norfolk marshland hero Tom Hickathrift and his enemy, the Giant of the Smeeth.*

CLARE *Pargeting on the Ancient House. Close to the church, it was once the priest's house and is now a museum*

169

Claverdon

Warwickshire   SP 1964

The old half-timbered village forge, designed in the shape of a giant horse-shoe, is still in working order. Nearby Tattle Bank, the former meeting-place of two Ice Age glaciers, is a site of unique geological interest, as the boulders which were deposited here are unmatched by any other rocks in Warwickshire.

The ancient village, set on a gentle hill between Warwick and Henley-in-Arden, gives fine views over the Warwickshire countryside. It has expanded in recent years, thanks to the reprieve of its little country railway station. But much of the old centre survives around the Parish Church of St Michael, with its 15th-century tower.

CLAVERDON   *The Old Forge — still in use*

Cleethorpes

Humberside   TA 3207

This is one of the sites at which the Greenwich Meridian is marked. The line from which world longitude and time has been measured since 1884 is indicated by a stainless steel bar on the sea wall between Cleethorpes and Humberston Fitties, with a signpost — 2513 miles to the North Pole, 9875 miles to the South Pole.

The line also passes through Louth, where there are wall plaques in Eastgate and a strip in the pavement, and at Holbeach the Meridian is marked by a millstone in Wignall's Gate.

Clun

Shropshire   SO 3081

'Clunton, Clunbury, Clungunford and Clun, Are the quietest places under the sun' wrote the poet A. E. Housman; and it still seems true today.

Clun is a 'Peter Pan' town, Saxon or older in origin and little changed since medieval times. It gained a charter for a three-day fair in 1204, but unlike Ludlow, it did not grow as a result of this. Yet nor did Clun suffer the total eclipse that befell some boroughs of the Marches. Instead the miniature town survived as it was, with castle,

defensively solid church and medieval street grid. Trinity Almshouses still give shelter to 12 elderly men, as they have since 1618, but the corn mill now houses youth hostellers.

Colston Bassett

Nottinghamshire   SK 7033

An under-appreciated, quiet village, it lies in the heart of the Vale of Belvoir. On the approach from one side may be seen the wall and part of the neo-classical Hall with its huge conservatory. One façade resembles the Petit Trianon, the charming smaller palace in the grounds of Versailles. In the village stands the grand 'new' Victorian church, built by the Knowles family, former owners of the estate. It replaced an older church, the ruins of which are still a prominent feature on the outskirts.

Coningsby

Lincolnshire   TF 2258

On the east face of the handsome 15th-century tower of St Michael's Church is the largest one-handed clock in the world. The dial is 16½ feet in diameter and gaily coloured — so large that it is possible to tell the time to within five minutes. The framework for the mechanism is of oak beams, to which iron bars bearing wrought iron wheels are attached by wedges instead of screws. The pendulum, suspended from a bracket in the tower and linked to the clock by a connecting rod, is so long that it swings only once every two seconds, and the clock weights are big blocks of stone. Silent for many years, the clock was restored just after World War II.

Consall Forge

Staffordshire   SJ 9949

This is indeed a remote place, inaccessible by public road since a landslide in 1926. A few miles south of Leek, it can be reached by two public footpaths. Both are 'wellie-boot walks': one is tricky to follow, the other is very heavy going.

Consall Forge offers magnificent scenery, however, justifying the Churnet Valley's title of 'the Staffordshire Rhineland'. The river and the Caldon Canal meet here, and the Churnet Valley Steam Railway runs through the Forge in front of the Black Lion Inn.

Corby

Northamptonshire   SP 8988

The Poll, or Pole, Fair is held in Corby every 20 years — the next one being in the year 2002.

The reasons for its occasional appearance are lost in antiquity, but it is always held on Whit Monday. It is said that Elizabeth I granted a Fair Charter to the then tiny hamlet of Corby, after Corby men rescued her: she was lost in Rockingham Forest, and her horse had thrown her into a bog.

The Charter was confirmed by Charles II, and is read by the Rector of Corby and the Chairman of the Urban District Council, at the opening of the fair. Before the opening, all the roads into Corby are barred by gates. Visitors are only allowed to enter if they pay a toll of a few pence. Those who refuse are lifted in a chair and taken to the village stocks. Few refuse twice.

CLUN *Scott may have based the fortress Garde Doloureuse in 'The Betrothed' on the now gaunt castle, 'strong by nature and fortified by art'*

Cottesmore

Leicestershire SK 9013

The name is better known than the village — through the Cottesmore Hunt, whose hounds arrived here in 1740, and through RAF Cottesmore, whose airfield opened in 1934.

The chapel of St Nicholas' Church is dedicated to servicemen based here. The names of those who never returned from missions are recorded in a Book of Remembrance, a page of which is turned daily. Open days and group visits are organised at RAF Cottesmore, by appointment.

Cottesmore's history goes back much further, however: there have been many important archaeological finds in the area, including a Bronze Age hoard now in the County Museum at Oakham.

Coventry

West Midlands SP 3379

Quite unexpectedly in the heart of this great modern city, which rose phoenix-like from the ashes of destruction in World War II, there stands a thriving farm. Known as Coventry City Farm, it was created for those unable to visit the country, offering them the opportunity to see a variety of farm animals and poultry, and demonstrations of traditional rural skills, such as milking, cheese-making, spinning and weaving.

Coventry is best known for Lady Godiva, and for Sir Basil Spence's spectacular new cathedral, linked symbolically to the ruins of the old. In the suburbia between the Stoke and Wyken areas of the city, it also has a fragment of the former residence of a nobleman — Caludon Castle.

Croft

Hereford & Worcester SO 4565

The castle has been inhabited by Crofts since Domesday and now, with parts of its surrounding parklands, belongs to the National Trust. The interior displays the taste of the family over many generations and has a 'loved and lived-in' quality. From inside and all around are unspoilt views over rolling wooded country to the hills of Wales. Beside it the diminutive church houses Croft tombs and memories.

On the high northern edge of the estate the fine and often deserted hill fort of Croft Ambrey crowns Yatton Hill. Below it is the charmingly secluded village of Leinthall Earls.

Cubley

Derbyshire SK 1638

Well away from the main road from Ashbourne, quiet Cubley (sometimes known as Great Cubley) was the birthplace of the bookseller Michael Johnson, father of Samuel Johnson.

The church and large 18th-century rectory make a charming group, and the church itself has interesting stained glass and monuments. About a mile away is Bentley Hall (not open), now a farm but once a splendid 17th-century country house. This is all that remains of the lost village of Hungry Bentley, the outlines of which can be seen in neighbouring fields.

COVENTRY: LADY GODIVA — *Godgifu, or Godiva, was a powerful landowner in her own right, with estates in six Midland counties, the most important of which was* **Coventry***. She also happened to be the wife of Leofric of Mercia, one of the four earls who ruled England under Cnut.*

In the 12th century the story arose that Godiva, covered only by her long hair, rode naked through the market place before all the people, to fulfil a condition set by Leofric for freeing Coventry from a tax. In fact she herself would have controlled Coventry's taxes — if anything, she might have been trying to persuade him to remit the hated 'heregeld', collected by the earls for the support of Cnut's Danish bodyguard.

But the story belongs to a group: it is like explantions of the Tichborne Dole and the field-name 'The Crawls' of Bromfield, Shropshire, for example. In both of these, a husband imposes an ordeal on his wife which benefits the poor. Such traditions may record historical acts of penance, accompanied by almsgiving and endowments. Certainly Leofric was originally hostile to the Church and reconciled to it by Godiva. Possibly she performed a public penance on his behalf, clad in her shift, an event later 'remembered' as a naked ride.

DILWYN *The dovecote of Luntley Court. In 1659, England had at least 26,000 dovecotes — not for decoration but for fresh meat in winter*

DINMORE: ARTS AND CRAFTS — *Situated up a long lane from the Hereford to Leominster road,* **Dinmore** *Manor features in its cloister and hall a superb late example of the work of the Arts and Crafts Society. Founded in 1888 by William Morris, the Society marks the movement from the Gothic and Picturesque styles of the late 18th and early 19th centuries, to the blossoming of Art Nouveau, at the end of the 19th century.*

Rooted in the ideals of Morris and his circle (which included most of the Pre-Raphaelites, among them Rossetti and Burne-Jones), it advocated the return to the medievalism so central to Morris's work, and the idea of art 'by the people for the people'.

Morris's conception of labour as enjoyable handicraft, the basis of the Arts and Crafts Society, was idealistic, since hand-made artefacts are necessarily more expensive than mass-produced machine goods, and are therefore emphatically not 'for the people'. None the less, his influence, permeated through a whole generation of artists and architects, has been profound.

WILLIAM MORRIS *(on the right), founder of the Arts and Crafts Society, with Burne-Jones*

Dale Abbey

Derbyshire SK 4338

This is a survivor in the midst of development and industrial towns. Here will be found the largest surviving remnants of a dissolved abbey in the county; the smallest church in Derbyshire and one of the smallest in England; a windmill in working order; and a hermit's cave.

The church (which is half a house) has an interior unchanged since 1634, with its original arrangement of pulpit, altar and reading desk. There is a fragment of medieval wall painting to be seen and the whole ensemble is one of great beauty and interest.

In the hillside behind is a cave where dwelt a pious baker of the 12th century. He saw a vision of the Virgin Mary and came to live here, carving a crucifix in the stone wall.

Derby

Derbyshire SK 3435

Thirty years ago, Derby was a handsome county town with many fine buildings and streets. Today, much has changed, but something of the past still lingers, at Sadler Gate and Iron Gate, and best of all at Friar Gate — perhaps the most splendid piece of Georgian townscape in the Midlands, even though it has suffered some grievous blows.

Darley Abbey, on the northern outskirts, is by-passed by the main roads in and out of Derby, and is well worth exploring. Fragments survive of the old Abbey buildings, the most substantial of which have now been converted to a public house. The extensive park of Darley House is a fine open breathing space (the mansion itself, the home of the Evans family of bankers and local squires, was demolished in 1962). Particularly attractive are the rows of early 19th-century estate workers' houses.

Dilwyn

Hereford & Worcester SO 4154

Lying in the heart of an area of timber-framed buildings, less visited and less obviously pretty than Eardisland (its more famous neighbour), Dilwyn has more than its fair share of superbly preserved 'black-and-white' houses, around a diminutive green. The large, light Church of St Mary is full of interesting detail, including half an arch which supports the tower, and two medieval angels in glass.

The lane to Pembridge passes Luntley Court (not open), one of the finest of the timber-framed buildings, although it has been in disrepair in recent years. Opposite is its doll's-house-like dovecote, dated 1673.

Dinmore Manor

Hereford & Worcester SO 4850

Founded by the Knights of St John of Jerusalem in the 12th century, the manor (open to the public) is reached up a long, idyllic lane from the Hereford to Leominster road where it runs below Queen's Wood.

Beside the house stands the chapel, in which occasional concerts are given. But the glory of the manor is its west wing, a splendid late flowering of Arts and Crafts architecture and including a hall and cloister. The face of the present owner as a child peers down from the hall roof; other surprises include a grotto with stained glass palm trees and a hillside garden which flows into unspoilt landscape.

Dodford

Hereford & Worcester SO 9273

At the height of the Chartist Movement of the 1830s, which tried to give greater political power to the working classes, its proponents built an unusual settlement in the little village of Dodford, a couple of miles to the north-west of Bromsgrove.

Planned around the concept of basic single-storey dwellings in equal plots of land, the settlement still looks somewhat the same. Although nowadays the dwellings are privately owned, the original layout of the village has substantially survived intact.

Well worth visiting nearby is the early 20th-century Parish Church of Holy Trinity and St Mary, unique as old Worcestershire's only example of a church built in the style of the Arts and Crafts Movement. Dodford Priory, founded in about 1184 for Premonstratensian canons, has hardly survived at all, and its few remains are hidden in a later house.

Downton

Hereford & Worcester SO 4373

The village is set in the wildly romantic Teme Valley, in which the river flows through rocky, wooded gorges.

It also has the scant remains of a ruined Norman church, but its main claim to fame is Downton Castle (not open), built and largely designed by Richard Payne Knight, the 18th-century MP, writer, art historian and founder of the Picturesque Movement.

A footpath from Bringewood Forge passes below the terraced front of the Castle, over the contemporary Castle Bridge and close to the Hermit's Cell, all of which add up to as fine a 'Picturesque' experience as Payne Knight could have wished for.

Droitwich

Hereford & Worcester   SO 8962

Many of the buildings in the old main street of this modernised spa town seem to be defying gravity, with doors, windows and roof lines leaning at crazy angles. The reason is hidden deep below ground, in the form of vast deposits of salt and brine. These were being extracted as early as Roman times, and were mentioned in the Domesday Book — hence the subsidence to be seen in the town. The therapeutic brine bath, recently rebuilt, is said to be 12 times saltier than sea water, and 40 per cent denser than the water of the Dead Sea.

Just to the north of the town on the Bromsgrove road is the pleasant sight of a French château. Château Impney, a mixture of turrets, gables and decorative dormers, was built by a Parisian architect between 1869 and 1875, for John Corbett, the so-called 'salt king' industrialist of Droitwich, whose wife was French. It is now an hotel.

Dunchurch

Warwickshire   SP 4871

It was in the ancient village of Dunchurch, to the south of Rugby, that the gunpowder plotters awaited news of the exploits of Guy Fawkes in 1605. They met in the black and white Lion Inn,

now a privately-owned dwelling called Guy Fawkes House.

The road leading from the village to Coventry passes the old stocks on a green and then crosses mysterious Dunsmore Heath, once the haunt of highwaymen. Here a monstrous dun-coloured cow once roamed, killing cattle and terrorising the local people, until it was slain by the legendary Guy of Warwick. Today, the creature is recalled by the Dun Cow Hotel, a popular place in the village centre.

Dunwich Heath

Suffolk   TM 4770

Down a turning towards the sea from the Westleton to Dunwich road, the Heath is one of the few unspoilt places along this stretch of coast with unrestricted access.

Two miles north is a small village renowned for freshly caught fish, with chips — all that remains of the once-proud medieval town of Dunwich. The rest has been lost to the waves, for this coast, including the Heath's 60-foot cliffs, is subject to remorseless erosion by the sea.

During World War II, the first radar tower in the country was sited here. At the south end of the Heath, under the forbidding bulk of Sizewell nuclear power station, four observation hides overlook the adjacent Minsmere bird reserve. The Heath, a blaze of pink heather in late summer, is a National Trust property.

DROITWICH   *Victorian industrialist John Corbett commissioned Tronquois to design Château Impney in the style of Louis XIII. The fountain (detail below) is a centrepiece of the gardens*

DOWNTON: PICTURESQUE MOVEMENT —
*The Picturesque Movement is said to have been born at **Downton Castle** — a fine example of the Picturesque style, with its chasms and follies in the grounds, and its rugged, asymmetrical outline.*

A member of the Payne Knight family, who own it, first defined the term 'Picturesque' in a controversy with Uvedale Price, in the late 18th century. He said it was 'an aesthetic quality between the sublime and the beautiful'. Before this general definition, it was taken to signify a landscape or building similar to those in the pictures of Claude or Gaspar Poussin and their imitators.

*The movement was closely linked with the Gothic atmosphere which pervaded architecture and literature at this time, and which was satirised by Jane Austen in 'Northanger Abbey' and 'Sense and Sensibility'. It is also related to the 'Cottage Orné', a deliberately rustic style of building which can be seen at **Endsleigh**, and to the Italianate buildings of John Nash with their castellated shapes and variety of texture. His Blaise Hamlet in **Bristol** is related to the style.*

GOLDEN VALLEY: FRANCIS KILVERT

*— Opposite Merbach Hill and Arthur's Stone at the head of **Golden Valley** lies the lovely spot of Bredwardine. Here, next to the church, is the vicarage occupied between 1877 and 1879 by the Reverend Francis Kilvert, whose diary (1870 to 1879) edited by William Plomer and first published in the 1930s, is now established as a minor classic.*

It gives a fascinating portrayal of the daily life and interests of a devoted pastor and his various congregations: in Wiltshire, Clyro, Radnorshire, and finally here at Bredwardine. He records moments of piercing emotion — when he is struck by the beauty of a girl he sees (which happens often), or by the beauty of the landscape: writing after an evening walk, he recalls 'an intense feeling and perception of the extraordinary beauty of the place grew upon me . . .'

Conversations with parishioners and friends are recounted: an old man remembers seeing the oxen kneeling on Christmas Eve; on another occasion he is told that on old-fashioned farms 'a steen of butter and something particularly good' is always saved up for March, because March is reckoned a 'severe trying month' when people need extra support. Matter-of-fact descriptions of the homes and lives of poorer people are included alongside accounts of picnics and parties; nor does he leave out the ludicrous. 'A red cow with a foolish white face came up to the window by the desk and stared in while I was preaching.'

Kilvert loved this region embracing both banks of the Wye — 'Kilvert Country' as it has come to be known — and might have echoed the sentiments of 16th-century Rowland Vaughan, who thought Golden Valley 'the pride of all that country bordering on Wales'. Kilvert died of peritonitis the month after he was married, and is buried in Bredwardine under a white marble cross.

East Lexham

Norfolk   TF 8516

Known locally as the 'quarter to twelve road', the B1145 makes a pleasant route through the middle of Norfolk, and a by-road just west of Litcham leads to the hamlet of East Lexham.

Here, in early spring, the approach to the little church is a carpet of yellow aconites. The round flintwork tower, built in around AD900, could well be the oldest Saxon tower in the country. When the wall surrounding the churchyard was rebuilt in 1962, several skeletons were found under the old wall, including the skull of a young man who had clearly been shot through the head with a musket ball.

Just up the road is an eight-acre vineyard whose 1984 vintage won an award for excellence. The white wine can be bought from the Post Office stores in Litcham, and those wishing to be shown round the winery and vineyard can do so by appointment.

Another round tower graces the church at West Lexham, a mile away, and at Great Dunham, to the south, an entire Saxon church can be seen.

Epworth Turbary

Humberside   SE 7803

This is a relic of raised bog in the Isle of Axholme, an area once extensively dug for peat (a 'turbary' is a peat-digging place), and is now run as a nature reserve. Sphagnum bog, reed swamp and mixed fen vegetation may be seen, including the rare fen sedge, once widely used for ridge thatching.

The 80-acre site also includes a considerable area of birch woodland, part of which has been cleared to provide open heath. Breeding birds include warblers, finches and woodpeckers. Open pools have been created and there are bird-watching hides.

A 1¼-mile walk has been marked through the site, but access to the reserve is *by permit only* (obtainable from Lincolnshire and South Humberside Trust for Nature Conservation, Manor House, Alford, Lincs LN13 9DL).

Flash

Staffordshire   SK 0267

'Flash' meaning 'sham' probably derives from this tiny village, which was at one time a notorious haunt of thieves and forgers. Its position near Three Shire Head, where Staffordshire, Cheshire and Derbyshire meet, enabled its inhabitants to evade the various sheriffs by crossing the county boundaries.

At 1518 feet, Flash is the highest village in England, and to this day its desolate position gives it something of a sinister air, especially in bad weather, which is common.

Fotheringhay

Northamptonshire   TL 0593

Though the only reminder of the existence of Fotheringhay Castle is a grassy mound and references in history books, its site exerts a powerful fascination.

It was here that, on 8 February 1587, Mary Queen of Scots was beheaded. Legend has it that this was a messy affair, and that when the executioner went to lift her severed head aloft, he held up just her wig, while her head rolled off the platform. There is also a story that, 170 years ago, a labourer carting away stone from the castle site found Mary's betrothal ring. But the ring, if it exists, is certainly not on display anywhere.

After the gory memories of the castle site, the elegant 15th-century church, in an adjacent meadow overlooking the River Nene, is an attractive proposition with its graceful lantern tower and elaborate interior. The village itself also repays closer inspection.

Gainsborough

Lincolnshire   SK 8189

'Ware Aegir!' was the drawn-out, somewhat eerie warning, passed twice daily from wharf to wharf along the River Trent through Gainsborough. The cry is no longer heard, but the aegir, a once-feared tidal bore (named after the Scandinavian god of rushing water) can still be seen under the right conditions — when the freshwater flow of the river is least and the tides are large. The best time is likely to be in the autumn.

The form of the aegir is a smooth standing wave, breaking along the banks, followed by a train of steep rounded waves — the whelps — and a strong flow of water upstream for the next two hours or so to high tide. As the funnelling of the lower estuary begins to take effect, the aegir is more likely to be seen in the reaches above Owston Ferry, and may be looked for by checking tide tables and following the roads along the river banks to Gainsborough.

Geddington

Northamptonshire   SP 8983

An old village of stone, Geddington remains proudly independent above its sprawling neighbour Kettering. At its heart is preserved the best of the remaining three Eleanor Crosses in the country. It was built in 1294 by King Edward I, as a memorial to one of the resting places of the body of his beloved Queen Eleanor, on her final journey to London.

The village has other royal connections: north of the church there was a hunting lodge with stables and a place for falcons, when nearby Rockingham Forest was a monarchs' hunting ground. Richard I, King John and Edward I were among the visitors.

The 19th-century vicarage was once a private school and claims to number among its past pupils the Liberal Prime Minister, William Ewart Gladstone.

Golden Valley

Hereford & Worcester   SO 3535

The River Dore rises in the hills at the top end of the Golden Valley and runs its full length until it joins the Monnow near Pontrilas.

At the entrance to the valley, the remains of Abbey Dore, restored as the parish church in the 17th century, are a delight. So are Bacton, with its memorial to a maid of honour of Queen Elizabeth I, and St Margaret's, which contains a magnificent 13th-century rood screen. Both villages are approached along a web of lanes across the hills. Peterchurch, the next village after Turnastone, acknowledges the 20th century with its fibreglass church spire, and a window which

GOLDEN VALLEY *Snodhill Castle is one of a defensive chain running along the border with Wales, built by the Normans from the Severn to Cheshire. The keep was probably built in about 1200*

reflects the sunlight into rainbows on the stone.

Close to the Welsh border, and worth searching for, is Snodhill, a romantic and unrestored ruin of a castle in an area dotted with castle mounds. Above the village of Dorstone and suitably remote, an enormous stone slab and its supporting uprights, collectively known as Arthur's Stone, are the remains of a burial chamber, indicating several thousand years of human habitation hereabouts.

Gotham

Nottinghamshire SK 5330

Gotham's renown does not derive from the church's remarkable 13th-century broach steeple, nor from its monuments fashioned from local alabaster, nor from the pleasant old manor house. It is the 'Wise Men of Gotham' who have immortalised this Wolds village (rather encroached upon by Nottingham), after feigning stupidity in order to dissuade King John from settling there, and burdening them with expense. The Cuckoo Bush Inn recalls the story.

Great Witley

Hereford & Worcester SO 7566

Here stands one of Britain's most evocative ruins: the hollow shell of once-grand Witley Court, a mansion built in the 18th century, a scene of magnificent house parties in the 19th, and gutted by fire in the 20th.

Formerly the home of the first Lord Foley, it

was bought in 1838 by the Earl of Dudley, who transformed it into a truly palatial residence, frequented by the rich and royal. It was ravaged by fire in 1937, but even in decay Witley Court is an impressive sight. The terraces of the grounds can still be walked and some of the original statuary seen, including a fountain representing Perseus and Andromeda, said to be among the largest of its kind in Europe.

After the gaunt ruins and overgrown garden, it is startling to enter the adjoining Church of St Michael and All Angels, once the house chapel and reputed to be the finest Baroque church in England. Consecrated in 1735, it is a riot of stained glass, Rococo plasterwork, and a ceiling elaborately decorated with paintings and medallions by Antonio Bellucci.

Great Yarmouth

Norfolk TG 5207

Standing on the South Quay at No 4 is the house once owned and built by a rich merchant called Cooper. Completed in 1596 — the date is on the overmantel in the dining room — the present building presents to the busy street a late Georgian façade. But behind this, all is of the 17th century and in excellent condition. The largest room, an upstairs drawing room, is 30 feet long and panelled in oak. In 1648, the impressive, moulded ceiling looked down on a meeting of leading Parliamentarians, called to discuss the execution of Charles I. The owner was a Presbyterian and great friend of Oliver Cromwell.

The house belongs to the National Trust but is let to the County Museums Service, which has filled it with bygones and period furniture of relevance to this ancient port. Look out for the jug or 'gotch' used to refresh the bellringers at the parish church. It can hold 23½ pints.

HEMINGFORD GREY: GREEN KNOWE

HEMINGFORD GREY: GREEN KNOWE — *Shortly before World War II, L. M. Boston came to live at* **Hemingford Grey** *manor house. A Georgian mansion in the Huntingdonshire fens, it had a garden running down to the Great Ouse, in a landscape of islands separated by the river, dykes and brooks.*

After stripping away additions and extensions to the house, she found a 12th-century house of great historical interest and austere charm, and decided to create a garden to match.

House, garden and watery landscape come together in Mrs Boston's 'Green Knowe' books, classics of children's literature. Her almost mystical sense of place and the closeness of the past pervades the first, 'The Children of Green Knowe' (1954), in which the strong and ancient house, with its ancestral presences (the 'Children'), is a bulwark not only against floods (to which the river is prone), but against the less tangible terrors represented by Green Noah, a topiary figure, the evil spirit of the place.

The source of inspiration, the ancient house, is rectangular and barn-like, with a steeply pitched roof, one upper floor, and an outside staircase clinging to stone walls three feet thick. The large garden is planted with old roses. It is not open.

ABOVE *Illustration from 'The Children of Green Knowe'*

Grimes Graves

Norfolk   TL 8189

Four thousand years ago, Neolithic people mined the hard flint that they discovered, 26 feet below the ground, on the site now called Grimes Graves and marked by a 34-acre clearing in a forest. Shafts were sunk, and then low tunnels were driven out radially into the flint seams. Deer antlers and bones were used as picks.

Today there are two shafts open to the public and one can be descended — an eerie experience which should not be missed. Grimes Graves is well signposted off the road between Swaffham and Brandon.

At Brandon, the ancient skill of flint knapping has been practised for centuries. In the back yard of the Flint Knappers Arms pub, flints for muzzle-loading guns are still struck and exported to the USA, for the re-enactment of Civil War battles, and to Africa.

Gringley-on-the-Hill

Nottinghamshire   SK 7390

Prince Rupert is thought to have camped here before raising the siege of Newark. One hopes he had time to look at the view, for this is a place where the onlooker, like Housman, can see the 'coloured counties' which unfold into the distance.

The village, with its attractive houses, farms, dovecotes and barns, has an interesting church with Norman, Early English, Perpendicular, classical 17th-century and well-matched 20th-century features.

On nearby Beacon Hill are the remains of a prehistoric hill fort, also commanding extensive views, on a site of evident strategic value.

Halford

Warwickshire   SP 2545

By the side of the lane to the neighbouring village of Idlicote, there stands a strange house, the shape of a double octagon, said to resemble an upright knife-box of the 18th century. Called The Folly, it was built by Thomas Webb, an eccentric land surveyor, who was employed on the local field enclosures in the 1770s. He earned a substantial sum through his work in Halford, and showed his gratitude to the village by building this strange home for himself.

Also to be found in this pretty stone village by the Fosse Way are a working smithy and a medieval packhorse bridge. The latter, now dwarfed by a modern replacement, bears the scars it received during a bitter Civil War skirmish.

Hampton Loade

Shropshire   SO 7486

The last surviving ferry in Shropshire links the two small clusters of houses which lie, each one a dead-end, on opposite banks of the River Severn. The ferry, an ancient piece of ingeniously simple technology, relies solely on the energy of the stream. A ferryman or (more often) woman directs the large rudder at an angle to the current, and the box-like vessel glides across the river, restrained by a rope and pulley suspended from a cable. Today's passengers are fishermen, holiday-makers or travellers on the preserved steam line of the Severn Valley Railway. In the past they

included workers at an iron forge sited at the south end of the cottages on the east bank. The ferry is south of Bridgnorth.

Hanbury

Staffordshire   SK 1727

The small village of Hanbury lies near Tutbury, just east of the Needwood Forest. It has an interesting little 13th-century church and tombs, and has been the site of a medieval miracle and a spectacular modern disaster.

The miracle concerned the remains of St Werburgh, daughter of Wulfhere, the first Christian king of Mercia, who was buried at the nunnery here in about AD700. Her body allegedly remained uncorrupted for 200 years, after which time it crumbled into dust, to avoid, it was said, falling into the hands of pagan Danish invaders. The nuns took the additional precaution of conveying what was left of her to Chester for reinterment.

A thousand years later, in 1944, Hanbury was the scene of the worst ever munitions disaster in Britain, when 4000 tons of explosive at a nearby weapons dump blew up with the loss of over 70 lives. The resulting hole in the ground may well be one of the largest man-made craters remaining in the world, being a thousand yards across. Until recently it was possible to walk over it, but in the mid-1980s it was decided to fence it off for reasons of safety. It can be seen from the road to Tutbury.

Harvington Hall

Hereford & Worcester   SO 8774

An extraordinary complex of hiding places — not perhaps all known about — distinguishes this moated manor house. Probably built by the master of secret chamber designers, Nicholas Owen, they would have been intended especially for Jesuit priests, coming to England in the reign of Elizabeth I. In later years, the Franciscan St John Wall hid here. In 1679 he became the last Roman Catholic to die for his faith in England. Always an important centre of Roman Catholicism, the house is now owned by the Roman Catholic Archdiocese of Birmingham.

False chimneys, a false step in a staircase, a lavatory shaft and a chimney are among the devices used for hiding places. Elizabethan murals have also been found here, hidden under layers of paint. One of the wall decorations has been carried out in drops of blood — said to represent the death of Christ, or perhaps the fate of a recusant priest. The house is open to the public.

Hatton

Warwickshire   SP 2367

At George's Farm, in this village a couple of miles west of Warwick, a group of obsolete 19th-century buildings — cattle pens, hay stores, stables, tack-rooms — have been imaginatively converted into the flourishing Hatton Craft Centre. Here a diverse group of professional craftworkers perform their traditional skills, and the public are welcome to watch and to buy.

Not far away, the Grand Union Canal ascends the Hatton Flight, a series of 16 locks in the space of a few hundred yards. The towpath alongside this eye-catching memorial to the ingenuity of the early canal builders is ideal for walkers.

HAMPTON LOADE *The pulley
for the ferry, which still takes
those on foot across the Severn*

H EREFORD: NELL
GWYNNE — *A
plaque marks Nell
Gwynne's (1650-87) birthplace in*
Hereford, *but such was her
appeal during and after her lifetime that there is competition for
the same honour. Drury Lane,
which also claims the distinction,
was certainly where she worked
for many years, first as an orange-
seller, then as a comedienne at
the theatre.*

*It was during her acting career
that she became mistress to
Charles II, and increasingly
endeared herself to the public by
her high spirits, generosity and
indiscretions. The fact that she
was a Protestant also told in her
favour, especially in contrast with
her rival, the Catholic Duchess of
Portsmouth. On one occasion, a
crowd surrounded her carriage,
believing it to belong to the unpopular Duchess. Nell, with her
famous good-humoured wit, leant
out to call, 'No, my friends, this is
the Protestant whore!'*

*She bore Charles at least one
child. The King's deathbed
request, 'Let not poor Nelly
starve,' was honoured by his
brother, James II, and she became
a rich woman. But she remained
true to her lover's memory, and did
not long survive him.*

ABOVE *Nell Gwynne in the
embrace of the King's Arms at
Ockley, Surrey — the comedienne
is still a popular figure*

Hawksworth

Nottinghamshire SK 7543

Most of the church was rebuilt in the mid-19th
century, but it has an 18th-century brick tower,
and one remarkable relic, a survivor from the old
church, incorporated in the newer brickwork.
This is the Norman tympanum, set off-centre
above a small window, with a crude inscription
telling of the founders of the church, Gauterus
and his wife Cecilina. The principal feature is a
cross with splayed shafts beneath which are two
small figures, doubtless the pious couple.

Hemingford Grey

Cambridgeshire TL 2870

At the heart of this picturesque village on the
banks of the River Great Ouse, stands the Church
of St James with its curiously truncated tower,
topped by eight stone balls. This is the result of
an incident in 1741, when the former spire was
struck by a hurricane. Its masonry now lies in the
river bed and the spire was never rebuilt.

The manor house, believed to be the oldest
inhabited house in the country, dates back to the
12th century, with 16th- and 18th-century
rebuilding. Strictly private and not open to the
public, it has been fictionalised as 'Green Knowe'
in the classic children's books by L. M. Boston.

The riverside path leads to Hemingford Abbots.
The best time to visit is the last weekend in June
when the flower festival is held.

Hereford

Hereford & Worcester SO 5040

Hidden behind the many 19th-century shopfronts
are numerous much older timber-framed
buildings. Black's the clothiers in Widemarsh
Street, for example, was once the Mansion
House. In pedestrianised Church Street, with its
book, map, crafts and similar shops (do not miss
Capuchin Yard), the Old Mayor's Parlour
Gallery has a pargeted ceiling.

The Cathedral has a chained library, a world
map from 1290 when it was believed to be flat;
and a tapestry designed by John Piper and woven
in Africa. A pile of stones with fine Norman
carvings in the inner cloister is worth inspection.

Of Hereford's museums, the Bulmer Railway
Centre houses the locomotive King George V
and often has steam open days. The Cider
Museum, with its own still, is unique in Britain,
as is the Waterworks Museum. Churchill
Gardens have a fine costume collection.

THE WORDMASTER *At 20, George Borrow knew some Irish, French, German, Danish, Welsh, Latin and Greek as well as Romany*

HORNCASTLE: GEORGE BORROW
— A Hungarian jockey who threw a bottle through a window of the George Hotel in **Horncastle** *was one of the colourful types to be unknowingly immortalised by George Borrow, in his best known book 'The Romany Rye'.*

Borrow wrote about Gypsy life. Some of his accounts are supposedly fictional, but all contain large amounts of autobiographical material, gleaned from his life on the open roads.

Born in 1803 at East Dereham in Norfolk, and articled to a solicitor as a young man, he soon turned to travel, becoming almost an adopted member of the Romany race, among whom he was known as Lavengro, or 'wordmaster'. This name, earned by his extraordinary aptitude for languages, was used as the title of one of his books.

After many adventures in the company of the Gypsies — including a fight with the 'Flaming Tinman' and a narrow escape from poisoning by an old Romany woman — he became an agent for the Bible Society, travelling widely in Europe. Not until 1840, when he married a rich widow, did he begin to write up his varied experiences.

HOLDGATE *Zig-zag and scallop carvings adorn the south door of Holy Trinity. The font and a misericord have dragons*

Hilton

Cambridgeshire TL 2866

The turf maze at Hilton, just south of St Ives, is sunk below the level of the common by some inches, but cannot be missed due to the stone obelisk, with a ball, at its centre. The legend *'Sic transit gloria Mundi. Gulielmus Sparrow, Gen. natus anno. 1641'* appears on one side of the obelisk, and another side records the death of William Sparrow in 1729.

Turf mazes like this are oddly atmospheric, and some are thought to be of ancient origin, symbolising the spirit's journey and other themes. But the Hilton maze has been dated to 1660, and is perhaps an example of a less symbolic period piece, linked to a rustic game rather than to mystical symbolism.

Holdgate

Shropshire SO 5689

Amidst the network of narrow lanes east of the diminutive River Corve is a settlement which had its political heyday in the Middle Ages, but has now almost vanished. Holdgate's Norman motte formed the mound between the church and the farm. More curious is the round tower of the 13th-century sandstone castle incorporated into the rear of the farmhouse (as seen from the footpath south-west of the church). On the south wall of the church a 'sheela-na-gig' (possibly an early fertility symbol) survives, while box pews are retained within.

To conjure up the congregation that once supported this church, look over the wall across the road. The humps in the field are the house platforms of the medieval village of Holdgate.

Holme Lacy

Hereford & Worcester SO 5535

A timber-yard crane in the village is a landmark for miles around. Holme Lacy House, once the splendid home of the Scudamores, stands empty and forlorn, viewable from footpaths across its park, which once contained such wonders as a yew avenue cut to form a procession of elephants: the avenue remains but the elephants have almost departed.

A mile and a half from the village, in a bend on the Wye, the church contains fine Scudamore monuments. A 20th-century bronze knight stands with his dog in the churchyard, gazing towards the river through the old House gate.

Holywell

Cambridgeshire TL 3370

Ye Olde Ferryboat Inn is a claimant to the title of the oldest pub in England: it is also licensed to serve spirits — for on 17 March each year the pub ghost is said to walk. There are not many pubs in the area that do not claim at least one resident poltergeist, but the Ferryboat can claim more authenticity than most. Close to one of the bars is a sombre tombstone. This is the grave of one Juliet Tewsley, who, according to tradition, committed suicide more than 900 years ago by hanging herself from a riverside tree, after woodcutter Tom Zoul ignored her affections for him. As she had taken her own life, she could not be buried in consecrated ground, but was interred beneath a grey stone near the river, which became incorporated into the pub. On the anniversary of her death, her ghost rises from beneath the slab and floats down the river.

Horkstow

Humberside   SE 9818

Horkstow suspension bridge, over the New River Ancholme, is a rare gem of engineering. The archway towers are in rusticated Yorkshire stone, and suspension of the 232-foot arched wooden decking is by twin iron chains. It was designed by the great engineer, Sir John Rennie, in 1834, and built the following year by the Commissioners of the River Ancholme Drainage and Navigation, with ironwork by John and Edward Walker of the Gospel Oak Ironworks near Birmingham.

The bridge is approached by an unmetalled road from the B1204 at Horkstow. On the other side of the river are the remains of brick kilns used to burn clay from the straightening and deepening of the river. The bridge is now used only for farm traffic.

Horncastle

Lincolnshire   TF 2669

In its 19th-century heyday, Horncastle was thronged every August for the greatest horse fair in the world. Horses of all qualities were exhibited daily in the streets and in the numerous inn yards, with buyers from as far afield as Russia, Australia and America. George Borrow, author of *Romany Rye*, stayed at the George (now shops), in the Market Place, and recorded the colourful scene.

William Marwood, England's last public hangman, lived in Horncastle, and exhibited his ropes in his cobbler's shop.

This is a classic brick market-town, built in and around a Roman fort between the rivers Bain and Waring. Sections of the sandstone fort walls survive, including the north-east bastion. The canal brought prosperity, and the railway, 50 years later, began to drain it away. The nine-bayed building with the clock, in the High Street, was the town house of Sir Joseph Banks, President of the Royal Society and called 'the Father of Australia' in this area of numerous Australian connections.

Horsey

Norfolk   TG 4523

Up on the exposed coast, the B1159 follows the great sea wall of shingle thrown up after the terrible 1953 floods. Behind it shelters reed-fringed Horsey Mere, accessible by boat from the main Broads system of waterways.

At the end of a narrow arm of the mere is the mill, a drainage windpump that, until 1943, pumped water from the dykes into the mere. Lightning struck the sails and it was not until 1957 that they were restored. It is open daily in summer, under National Trust care, and, from June to September, visitors can climb up through the old machinery to the outside gallery.

Hucknall

Nottinghamshire   SK 5349

There seems to be little of subtlety, mystery or charm about Hucknall Torkard — usually known as plain Hucknall. It is a busy, bustling, industrial place, complete with a Co-op. But the Co-op is unusual in that it has a statue of Lord Byron on it, and therein lies a clue to Hucknall's other face.

The place to go to is the church. Although not the same as it was in 1824, when Lord Byron, the squire of Newstead, was brought to rest with his ancestors, St Mary Magdalen is nevertheless a quiet, dimly lit place.

Much of the atmosphere is due to the excellent late Victorian stained glass by Kempe — among the best examples of his work. A monument to the second Lord Byron, a firm royalist, may be seen, as well as the memorial slab and the marble relief bust of Byron the poet.

Huttoft Bank

Lincolnshire   TF 5477

About 10,000 years ago, eastern Lincolnshire and what is now part of the North Sea were covered with high forest. On hummocky boulder clay soils grew oak and elm, with some lime, beech and hazel, while on sandy soils pine and birch were more common.

With the inexorable post-Ice-Age rise of the sea level, the forest became waterlogged, and peat was formed. As the peat increased its stranglehold, so the forest died, fell and was entombed.

That was about 6000 years ago. Later the forest was buried by clays — but erosion in the last few hundred years has exposed the outcrop of clays and peat, together with the stumps and trunks of fallen trees. This strange remnant of a lost landscape is now submerged on every tide, and is best seen at low spring tides.

Inkberrow

Hereford & Worcester   SP 0157

Shaded by a spreading chestnut tree, by the side of a small green, is the picture-book Old Bull, a black-and-white timbered inn, the original on which the Bull was based in the BBC's 'everyday story of country folk', The Archers.

The vicarage, near the restored 15th-century Church of St Peter, provided a resting-place for Charles I when he was on his way to fight at the Battle of Naseby. In fact, he left his book of maps here and they have only recently been removed to the County Record Office in Worcester, where they are available for public inspection.

HUTTOFT BANK: DROWNED LANDS
— *The exposure at very low tide of the fossilised forest at* **Huttoft Bank** *has resulted from changes of sea level — a source of haunting legends of lost lands.*

Not far from Long Sutton, Lincolnshire, on a site near the South Holland Sluice, there was supposed to be a town called Dalproon which, according to tradition, was washed away in the Great Flood of 1236. There is no real evidence to substantiate this. But Dunwich (see **Dunwich Heath***) is known to have succumbed to 'surges of the sea' since Domesday. The sound of church bells ringing under the water can still be heard here, it is said. The church of medieval* **Walton on the Naze** *is another to have been lost under the waves.*

Traditions of a drowned forest in the bay below St Michael's Mount fuelled the legend of a lost kingdom between Land's End and the Scilly Isles, which from the 16th century was identified with King Arthur's Lyonesse. Under Cardigan Bay is the 'Bottom Cantred', with its 16 cities drowned for their sins. This widespread legend may have arisen here because of a submerged forest which is sometimes revealed between Borth and Ynyslas, and because of three 'sarnau', or causeways, running out into the bay. In the 16th century, they were believed to be stone dykes.

DROWNED CHURCH   *One of several in Dunwich, drawn in 1850 but now gone. People say the bells are heard beneath the sea*

LAKENHEATH: ANGEL ROOFS — *The Church of St Mary, Lakenheath, has some exceptional carving on the nave benches and the pulpit, but perhaps most magnificent of all is the wooden roof above the chancel arch, with its masterly carvings of angels.*

Soaring 'angel roofs' are a speciality of East Anglia, where carvers seem to have relished the opportunities provided by new types of roof design. The 'hammerbeam' roof in particular gave a feeling of space and ample surfaces for ornamentation.

At **Swaffham's** *church of Saints Peter and Paul, a chorus of 88 chestnut wood, open-winged angels grace the double hammerbeams and kingposts of the roof, while another 104 appear on the wall-plates. March in Cambridgeshire has a wonderful, fluttering array of angels watching over the congregation and at* **Furneaux Pelham** *angels seem to hold up the nave roof.* **Needham Market** *has an angel roof, and so has Blythburgh, also in Suffolk. It was damaged in 1577 by a dramatic storm (accompanied by a visitation of the Black Dog — see* **Isle of Man**) *— but has been restored this century, bringing back the full splendour of the vast roof with its angels and flowers.*

Ipswich

Suffolk TM 1744

Christchurch Mansion is an under-appreciated treasure of the town. Built of red brick in 1548, on the site of an Augustinian priory and altered substantially since, it has rooms full of riches, early English oak furniture, treen ware and fine panelling. The Wolsey art gallery attached to it has paintings by Suffolk artists — Constable, Munnings, Gainsborough and John Moore. Elizabeth I certainly twice visited the Mansion which may have belonged to her favourite, Robert Devereux, the second Earl of Essex and High Steward of Ipswich.

Only a short walk from the town's centre (where the newly restored Ancient House is a must), the Mansion is open throughout the year — a veritable free passport to Suffolk's history. It stands at the south end of Christchurch Park, with its acres of rolling green grass, ponds full of colourful waterfowl and a magnificent array of flower beds and shrubs — surely one of the finest parks of any provincial town.

Kentwell Hall

Suffolk TL 8647

A long walk up the main street of Long Melford, (where the church, more glass than mellow stone, is arguably the finest in Suffolk), brings the visitor to an entrance in an avenue of ancient limes, over 300 years old. A red–brick Tudor mansion stands at the end of it, surrounded by a moat complete with graceful black swans.

Recreations of domestic life in past centuries are undertaken here each summer, and in 1985 the front courtyard was turned into a Tudor Rose maze made out of coloured bricks set in a beguiling and symbolic mosaic. The walled gardens, themselves moated, invite quiet strolls. Rare breeds of sheep graze in the paddock. All this is the work of the young couple who acquired the house in 1971, and laboured hard to save it and open it for the public to enjoy: built in 1563, it had had a disastrous fire in the 1820s and had become derelict once more after restoration by Thomas Hopper. It is open on summer afternoons, Wednesdays to Sundays.

Kilpeck

Hereford & Worcester SO 4430

The church is modest, but with some very immodest Norman carving, from the stoup which consists of hands clasped around a pot-belly to fertility symbols among the incredible external corbels. It is, in fact, one of the most amazing collections of Romanesque sculpture to be found in Britain.

Behind the darkly overshadowed churchyard the mounds and scant masonry of the castle are almost unnoticed. In passing, look at the fine Herefordian tombstones.

KENTWELL HALL *The newly-built Tudor rose maze in the courtyard pays appropriate homage to the Tudor connections of the red-brick house: recorded as recently built in 1563, it may date from the reign of Henry VIII, and Elizabeth I stayed here on one of her tours of the kingdom*

Kimbolton

Cambridgeshire   TL 0967

The feature which makes it different from its neighbours has also given Kimbolton its biggest problem.

Access to either end of the High Street is by twin bends, which have been a feature of the scene since a market was established in 1200. The bends were put in so that all traffic had to pass through the market and pay tolls on market days (the road had formerly run straight through the village), but have been something of a hazard in the 20th century.

This is a charming community with fine period properties facing each other across the broad High Street. Alas, there is no longer a market and the Butchers Row market hall was demolished in 1873, but an annual fair brings character — and more road chaos — to the street.

St Andrew's Church boasts an unusual, modern memorial, a chapel dedicated to the American airmen who made Kimbolton their home during World War II. A book full of mementoes is kept in a glass case for inspection, and the site of the former air base can be discovered along the Stow Longa road. The church, and Sir John Vanbrugh's castle, now a school, acted as landmarks to the Flying Fortress pilots as they got near to their home base. More recently, Kimbolton School has been the centre of operations for the Reverend Ronald Lancaster, teacher, pyrotechnician and designer of firework displays on a grand scale for major celebrations.

King's Lynn

Norfolk   TF 6119

Stand in the huge Tuesday market to get first-hand experience of the importance of Lynn (as the locals call it) as a great centre for west Norfolk. Then follow King Street — once called Stockfishrow — and pass first the Guildhall of St George, where Shakespeare's touring company once performed, and then the elegant Customs House built in 1683. Lynn owes its very existence to the sea and the waterways of the Fens behind it, and the historic buildings all have strong connections with fishing and with trade, particularly with the Baltic countries.

The old warehouses stretch down at right angles to the sea: each once had its own quay or 'staithe'. Tunnels run beneath them (one under the Guildhall houses a coffee shop).

Kinver Edge

Staffordshire   SO 8383

People lived in the cave dwellings of Holy Austin's Rock on Kinver Edge until the 1950s, and in the last century some of these homes had realistic house fronts. The remains of an Iron Age fort testify to man's long occupancy of the area.

The Edge is the last remnant of Kinver Forest, one of the four ancient forests of Staffordshire — the others were Lyme, Needwood and Cannock. It is still predominantly hardwood, with oak and birch the commonest trees. Lizards can be seen on the heathland, and so can sunbathing adders.

From the Vista Seat and other vantage points, there are fine views of several counties. This is also one end of the Staffordshire Way, the 90-mile footpath through some of the loveliest parts of the county, with its other end on the Cheshire border at Mow Cop.

Kirk Ireton

Derbyshire   SK 2650

Set in a small, out-of-the-way village of attractive houses and a fine church, the gabled, 17th-century Barley Mow Inn is a genuinely traditional, old English pub, serving real ale from the wood, with a stone floor and basic furniture and a roaring fire in winter. A recent landlady refused to acknowledge decimal money and talked only in shillings and pence.

Lakenheath

Suffolk   TL 7182

During the Peasants' Revolt of 1381, three officials were killed near here and their heads stuck on the ramparts of Bury St Edmunds. In recent years, Lakenheath has come to mean an airbase. It is hard to imagine that 400 years ago the village was surrounded by 6500 acres of undrained fenland, or that from 1665 (when the fen was drained) there was flax grown, and sheep which made farmers rich. Now four squadrons of USAF fighter bombers occupy the vast airfield carved out of Lord Iveagh's estate in 1940.

There is another side to Lakenheath, however. A relic of the vanished fen remains in the interesting church, where a trimmed block of matted reed shows why the word 'hassock' means both kneeling cushion and tuft of greenery. The pew ends are amusingly carved into the weird shapes of mythical animals: look especially for the contortionist and the tiger playing with a warming pan. And look up into the lovely wooden roof, where 60 carved angels have been gazing serenely down on the worshippers for 400 years.

Laxton

Nottinghamshire   SK 7266

Laxton is renowned as the place where the medieval strip system of farming is still carried out much as it was in the Middle Ages. The method of farming can instantly be recognised by the landscape, replaced elsewhere by a (usually prettier) 'enclosed' scenery of hedges. A Court still meets once a year to determine any disputes and to make sure that all is going as it should.

The church is full of interest, not least for its series of monuments to the de Everingham family of the 13th and 14th centuries, including the county's only wooden medieval effigy. There are some fine houses, an inn — the Dovecote, where the Court holds its meetings — and a well-preserved earthwork of a motte-and-bailey castle.

Leamington Spa

Warwickshire   SP 3166

The only therapeutic natural spa facilities in Britain to be recognised by the National Health Service can be enjoyed at Leamington Spa.

It is properly known as Royal Leamington Spa, a status conferred by Queen Victoria, whose massive statue is a local oddity. It has moved one inch from its original position, owing to the explosion of a World War II bomb nearby.

In 1872 the first lawn tennis club in the world, forerunner of Wimbledon, played in the garden of the town's Manor House Hotel. Another hotel, the Regent, is reputed to have been the largest in the world when it was built in 1819.

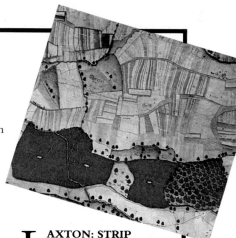

LAXTON: STRIP FARMING — The village of **Laxton** preserves some of the last remnants of an archaic way of agriculture — strip or open-field farming. It is not known where the method came from, although it is sometimes said to have been introduced by Anglo-Saxon settlers.

However it originated, in the Middle Ages each village aimed to cultivate up to three very large fields divided into several hundred strips, traditionally 200 yards long — a 'furrow-long', or furlong. These were shared out among the villagers, each receiving some good land and some bad. Tools were also shared, and common land was set aside for grazing.

Open-field agriculture was not profitable, relying as it did on community effort and producing only what was needed for subsistence. It was gradually replaced by enclosure, but in the Midlands it continued into the 17th and 18th centuries.

The Great Field at **Braunton** is one of the last surviving open fields; others exist on the Isle of **Portland**, and in Cambridgeshire at Soham. At Laxton itself, West Field, Mill Field and South Field are still farmed by a kind of open-field system, one lying fallow while the others are cultivated in strips.

ABOVE   Detail of a map of Laxton, 1635, by Mark Pierce. Today 483 acres are farmed in three fields of 165 strips

SIX GARDENS

Dr Stefan Buczacki, one of the team on Radio 4's *Gardeners' Question Time*
since 1982, unearths the secrets of six favourite gardens, from an
English vegetable patch to a tropical
Arcadia in Scotland

WE HAVE been called a nation of many different things, but whoever first decided that 'nation of gardeners' was the right name at least had the statistics to prove it. At the last estimate, the British Isles had around 18 million gardens, and, presumably, at least 18 million gardeners. For those lucky enough to have ventured through as many garden gates as I have, the wealth and quality of those gardens is plain to see; and yet so many of them must remain, understandably and rightly, unknown — except to their owners, for whom they may be sanctuary, refuge, escape, or recreation. I shall not disturb their peace.

There are also, however, the gardens that are secret like the secret garden of *Alice*. They may be small, large, familiar or obscure, but each one holds some hidden quality, a quality that sets it apart. From the 18 million gardens, therefore, I have chosen just six. All are very different, all are open at least occasionally to the public, and all have an individual secret to reveal.

Burford House

The presence of river and stream close by Burford House has enabled its owner to create fine and rich water gardens, for his streamsides positively brim with astilbes, bamboos, primulas, irises and rheums. Yet, curiously, it is more the feel of water than its actual presence that provided my first and abiding impression. Its proximity provides a soothing, almost musical accompaniment to gardening activity, and it is one of those gardens that always feels lush and moist, even at the height of summer.

Burford House lies comfortably on the banks of the River Teme at Tenbury Wells in Worcestershire, about ten miles downstream from Ludlow. When he bought the house slightly over thirty years ago, John Treasure acquired just four acres of extensive lawn, a few specimen trees, an apple orchard and meadow land. The secret of Burford House Gardens today is their uncanny deceptiveness. So many gardeners and garden designers strive to create the illusion of more space than is actually present; very few achieve it in the way that John Treasure has.

First, the formal lawns, terrace, enclosed patio and pool of the south and west fronts blend with complete harmony into the surrounding informality. Perhaps the most obvious and certainly the simplest way to create

BELOW   *Burford House, where John Treasure has created a lush green garden of 'uncanny deceptiveness'; and the Knot Garden at Barnsley House, with green box and golden variegated box interwoven around Phillyria, on a bed of coloured gravels*

the impression of space, would have been to maintain a very open centre and use some judiciously chosen plants to obscure the margins. John Treasure has, by and large, opted for the more difficult alternative of using that most misunderstood device, the island bed.

The island beds at Burford House are curved, with projections and bays. They interlock and interweave visually to create, as in almost no other garden I know, a feeling of depth, an impression of many corners, around all of which must reside something worth seeing. The garden urges you to go on and on, without ever letting you know whether you are actually walking in straight lines or circles; and often fooling you into not knowing quite where all that water is. It is a very, very clever garden; and it has some splendid plants too.

Barnsley House

There is more than one Barnsley in Britain; but thank goodness for this one. It is a Cotswold village of character, lying astride the A433 a few miles north-west of Cirencester in Gloucestershire. Here nestles Barnsley House, around which is draped one of the friendliest small gardens in the country. It is the home of one of England's best loved plantswomen, Rosemary Verey, who has created a garden that is a compelling blend of the formal and the informal, the rare and the familiar.

So much is good, so very good, at Barnsley House, that it is with some reluctance that I must take you by the hand, through a small back gate and across a lane to show you its really secret ingredient. For Rosemary Verey has the only vegetable garden that I would go many miles out of my way to see.

We British have an ambivalent attitude to our vegetables; we grow them in our gardens in greater profusion than any other nation, yet we haven't a clue how to cook them and we plant them out of sight of decent company. Rosemary Verey has brought vegetable gardening into the open and created something that is a delight to behold. She has had to plant a French *potager orné* to do it: the Barnsley vegetable garden is a chequerboard of small beds divided by narrow brick or stone paths. Here convention has been thrown out with the potato peelings. Rosemary Verey has not adhered rigidly to a vegetable garden of vegetables alone — she has

stretched her definition. Herbs such as lavender and southernwood border the paths, while strawberries grow around the feet of apple trees — for she has not restricted vertical interest to runner beans. Among the taller delights of this English version of Villandry (in the Loire Valley) are those glorious horticultural indulgences so beloved of Villandry's creator, M Lorette: fruit trees formed as winged pyramids. And there is no better test of anyone's horticultural dexterity and patience than the training of these.

To add to the visual delight, the plants are arranged in ingeniously contrasting groups, and for anyone accustomed to seeing their carrots, onions and leeks in single rows across an allotment, this is, in itself, a revelation. As a final flourish to ice the gardening cake, there are also varieties of commonplace vegetables chosen specifically for their visual appeal. Almost anyone can take at least a cabbage leaf out of Rosemary Verey's planting book and grow ornamental brassicas as she does.

FOGGY BOTTOM *A name for a Shakespearian comedy but a garden for all seasons. Contrasting with the vibrant hues of heathers are different types of Picea (blue spruce — foreground and centre back), cedar (right) and Leyland Cypress (right back — this fine species came from a chance cross in 1888). Inset picture: Picea pungens prostrata and the heather Erica cinerea Rock Pool. Foggy Bottom is open just once a year: 'the weekend is the only time I manage to garden,' says Adrian Bloom*

Foggy Bottom

'Foggy Bottom is no name for a garden' was a friend's first comment, and I agree that it could have stepped straight from a Shakespearean comedy. Yet there is nothing comic about Adrian Bloom's unique creation near Diss in Norfolk, close to the family nursery that has made the name of Bloom familiar to gardeners far and wide. For much of the appeal of Foggy Bottom belies its creator's name: it is as much a garden of leaves as of

flowers; and therein lies its very special charm.

Foggy Bottom takes its name from its low lying position by the River Waveney, and was but a meadow when Adrian Bloom began to shape and plant it in 1967. It now extends to five acres, formed mostly of the island beds so much associated with the Bloom name, in a sea of lawn. But island beds in a sea of lawn can be host to almost any plant you care to name; many gardeners have used them, some have been successful, but few have planted them as Foggy Bottom is planted.

The overall intention was to create a garden for all seasons and it almost succeeds in being more attractive in winter than in summer, largely through the contribution of winter flowering and brightly foliaged heathers. Set against these are the conifers, tall, short and dwarf, narrowly columnar, pyramidal, spherical and most forms in between; perhaps a thousand or more varieties, in a British collection without equal. There are other fine plants in abundance too,

SIX GARDENS

but the garden's magnetism, though real enough, remains elusive, and the overriding impression remains one of heathers and conifers and all the colours of the rainbow. It is also a garden of quite remarkable harmony. Just why a red heather does not clash with a golden juniper I do not know, but it is part of Foggy Bottom's and Adrian Bloom's own secret.

White Barn House

Six miles along the A133 from Colchester lies the village of Elmstead Market. Here, around their home at White Barn House, Mrs Beth Chatto and her husband have spent 26 years and inestimable labour, converting four acres of wasteland into a gardening *menage à trois*: three aspects, three soils, and now, three gardens.

From a shallow valley, containing a miserable and overgrown ditch, Beth Chatto created first, on the south-west facing slope, a hot, dry garden, a garden of the Mediterranean where assertive and pillowy euphorbias jostle with yucca spikes and where the sweet heavy aroma of pineapple broom hangs over the early summer beds. Facing it, a stand of old Essex oaks gives shelter to a deep, humus-rich loam that supports the woodland garden of erythroniums and primulas, of hellebores in bewildering variety, of Vinca, Hosta, Trillium and much, much more. Between, that trickling ditch, cleared, dammed and planted with near-incredible foresight, has become, at Beth Chatto's hands, a water garden, a horticultural wetland that, for its size, has, in the artistry of its arrangement and its abiding fascination, no peer in these islands. Many gardens have their gunneras and lysichitums, irises, astilbes, candelabra primulas and Hemerocallis. Rather fewer have cotton grasses, variegated phormiums and Miscanthus twelve feet tall. None has them as Beth Chatto has them, used like paints upon a wide wet paper that changes with the seasons and the angle of the sun to create, in a literal sense, a pattern of English water-colours.

Betwixt and between the main areas are paths, walks, beds and borders, sunken, raised or flat; and everywhere, plants of choice. White Barn House does, indeed, support a plantswoman's garden, but this is no sterile botanical collection, or showpiece of some so-called school of gardening. White Barn House is a garden that happened as its owner learned her craft, and the skills that enabled her eyes to paint a picture where others saw a wasteland have now translated that vision into something tangible, enduring, ever changing and immensely precious. The secret of White Barn House is the secret of those skills.

WHITE BARN HOUSE *(top)* *Once there was a wasteland, now Caltha polypetalia spreads by the water's edge in one of Beth Chatto's three gardens within a garden. The opposite bank is fringed by Ranunculus lingua and Pontederia cordata, with the broad hand-like leaves of Gunnera manicata behind*

STOURHEAD *(above)* *Visited by thousands every year, but with intimate vignettes of gardening glory which are often unappreciated*

Stourhead

Some will wonder by what conceivable token one of the greatest of our national landscaped gardens, extending to two and a half thousand acres, in the care of the National Trust and host to thousands of visitors each year, can possibly be deemed in any way secret. At one time, I would have wondered this too, but over the years, I have come to appreciate Stourhead in a way that I prefer to see certain other great gardens: as vast enveloping blankets of mass and obvious appeal wrapped around intimate vignettes of gardening glory, be they unexpected and surprising vistas, morsels of garden history or (my present concern), individual, choice, but often unappreciated plants.

Thus, Stourhead, Wiltshire, site of the ancient family seat of the Stourtons, but built and shaped in its present form during the 18th century, largely under the direction of one of the greatest amateur gardeners of all time, Henry Hoare II. Few of Hoare's original trees survive, but among the others, planted at various times since, there are some gems. Circumnavigate the lakes and you will see that the estate is rich in some of the finest tulip trees (Liriodendron tulipifera) in England, dating from the end of the 18th century, and which you may conveniently compare with your specimens of the variegated form, aureomarginatum, surely one of the most undervalued of all ornamental trees. Then pause and, on the wind, you catch an elusive scent: bananas? Bananas indeed, for this is the perfume of Magnolia tripetala, one of the finest magnolias, seen in inexplicably few gardens, but safely harboured here.

Conifers are a closed book to many, dismissed either as dull, which, as individuals, only a minority are, or too confusing to identify, which is partly true. Nonetheless, few will pass by a long needled conifer of any sort without remark, and fewer still will not comment with admiration upon Picea smithiana, the Morinda spruce, which at Stourhead displays its shape to perfection. But stray further from the waterside, climb the slopes and walk slowly through the woodland plantings. Pause frequently and the pathsides will reveal their hidden charms too: there, for instance, among the hollies and the oaks, are the dark red lanterns of Crinodendron, flourishing in the shelter that recreates its South American forest home. Stourhead is a landscape, true enough, but part its curtains, peer beyond the picture frame, and gardening secrets to treasure will be found.

Logan

Botanic gardens evolved from medieval gardens, for the growing of healing and culinary herbs. Most British universities have one of sorts, and there are the great national collections at Kew and Edinburgh. But a botanic garden can, despite its origins be a sadly sterile place, a living herbarium. Not so this one. Originally a country house garden, Logan has been developed over the past 20 years as an annexe to the Royal Botanic Garden, Edinburgh because, and herein lies its secret, the climate is one of the most perfect in the realm for the cultivation of plants.

Thirty five acres of the Mull of Galloway with sea on three sides, hardly any frost, hardly any snow, a slightly acid loam and 40 inches of rain would be

most gardeners' definition of Arcadia. The Arcadia is Logan. In practice, no garden is without its problems and winter gales would take a high toll in the absence of the shelter belts of protecting trees. But it is the ability of Logan to support some of the botanical gems of the Antipodes, like cordylines and tree ferns, that underline its appeal. Contrasts with Tresco are inevitable, but whilst Tresco, to me, is always a seaside garden, Logan, curiously, never seems so, and the avenue of palms by the water gives a feeling unequalled in any other British garden. To stand, in early September, among a blue sea of gently stirring Agapanthus flowers is to conjure up Africa and that other Cape, thousands of miles away.

LOGAN   *Two brothers, the last of the McDouall family which had lived here since the 12th century, collected plants from as far afield as China and Tibet for their Galloway garden*

Thus, my six gardens, an infinitesimally small fraction of an immensely rich national treasure, but six with secrets that, from time to time, are shared with a public willing and caring enough to seek them out.

DR STEFAN BUCZACKI   *A broadcaster and writer with a passion for 'science for non-scientists', he was born in Derbyshire in 1945. He lives in Stratford-upon-Avon with his family — and a large garden*

White Barn House:
Open daily, except Sundays and Bank Holidays.
Burford House:
Open daily, from March to October.
Foggy Bottom:
Open the first weekend of September each year.
Barnsley House:
Open on weekdays throughout the year, on Sunday afternoons from May to July, or by appointment.
Stourhead:
Open daily all year.
Logan:
Open daily, April to September.

L OUGHBOROUGH:
BELL LEGENDS —
Bells, the pride of
Loughborough, *traditionally
rang to accompany life and death.
They also attracted legends.*

*Inscriptions on bells at
Guilsborough, Northamptonshire,
record that their ringing warded
off plague, and at Weedon Lois, in
the same county, that the bells
averted thunder. St Aldhelm, who
came to acquire the reputation of a
magician, was said to have given*
Malmesbury *Abbey a bell that
could stop both thunder and
lightning.*

*The custom of the Passing Bell
grew out of a belief that bells drove
away demons. In England, to
protect a departing soul, nine
'tellers' are tolled for a man, six
for a woman, followed by one
stroke for each year of life. At
Ayot St Peter's, Hertfordshire, the
'Nine Tailors' and 33 strokes are
tolled for Our Lord every
Good Friday.*

The curfew bell of **Burgh-Le-
Marsh** *is remembered for saving a
ship lost at sea. At* **Newark-on-
Trent**, *'Ringing for Gofer' on six
October and November nights was
said to commemorate a merchant,
lost in Sherwood Forest and guided
home by Newark's bells. In
gratitude he left a bequest to
provide for their ringing on dark
winter nights. Curfews and special
bells were similarly explained at
Curdworth, Warwickshire,
Barton-upon-Humber and
Stamford Bridge, Humberside.*

ABOVE *The bell found in a pond
in Marden, Herefordshire, in
1848 — perhaps the one said to
have fallen into the hands of a
mermaid in earlier times. The bell
had to be drawn up in silence, by
white heifers wearing yokes of yew
and mountain ash, but an excited
driver made a noise and the
mermaid snatched it back.
Thereafter it was heard ringing in
the water*

Leek

Staffordshire SJ 9856

Thanks to its elevated position, Leek has been
known to experience a curious 'double sunset'
effect in midsummer. Called the 'Queen of the
Moorlands', it has some interesting old buildings,
notably the 13th-century parish church, St
Edward's; and the Brindley Mill, an 18th-century
working water mill with a museum on James
Brindley, the canal engineer, who spent much of
his early life in the town.

A couple of miles north-west is Lake Rudyard,
said to be where Kipling's parents first met. Not
far off, either, is the source of the Trent, on
Biddulph Moor.

Leicester

Leicestershire SK 5904

In the last century, Leicester was the home of
Joseph Merrick, the Elephant Man. He was
shown as a freak at various theatres, including
one on the corner of Wharf Street, which is now
a shop but still has remains of a stage. He also
worked at 6 Churchgate, for his uncle, but
frightened people away with his deformities.

The city sits right in the centre of one of the
smallest and least visited counties. Grand
Victorian buildings mingle with glass and
concrete tower blocks, interspersed with multi-
storey car parks. Conservation areas, parks and
museums preserve the past, and like most cities,
Leicester is best explored on foot: a Guided
Walks scheme is offered by the Information
Office in Bishop Street.

Of unusual interest is the lead casting practised
by Norman and Underwood Ltd of Freeschool
Lane. The company was established 160 years
ago. Lead is cast here just as it was in Roman
times, and the end product is used on buildings
throughout the world, including Buckingham
Palace. Viewing is by appointment.

The Lifting Bridge on Soar Lane was built by
Stephenson to take his railway across the river;
opposite it today is a similar bridge built in 1897.
Leicester also has the only gas museum in the
country — the East Midland Gas Museum at
Aylkestone Road.

An arboretum on Shady Lane has 500 species
set in 54 acres, and the University of Leicester
Botanical Gardens have 16 acres of rare plants,
many of importance to drought areas.

The Black Swan is an old, daunting building
surrounded by ultra-new offices yet steeped in
history. It now has a complete Paris street scene
in the bar, and is used by actors appearing at the
nearby theatre.

Little Dalby

Leicestershire SK 7714

This picturesque hamlet consists of a hilltop
church with spire, a large farm and Little Dalby
Hall, a fine Elizabethan building. In 1730, it was
the home of Mrs Orton, credited as one of the
first makers of Stilton cheese.

The Hall is a private home and not open to the
public, but the stable block is occupied by
furniture craftsmen who can be seen using
traditional methods and tools to make and repair
fine pieces. Visitors are welcome, but should
make an appointment with the director first.

Little Gidding

Cambridgeshire TL 1382

It certainly lives up to its name today, with earthworks indicating just the site of a deserted
village. It was here, in the 17th century, that
Nicholas Ferrar, the son of a merchant banker,
set up a small religious community of around 35
members. They took no vows, but were otherwise a strict order, attending three services daily.
Ferrar's biblical writings were influential, and
three visits to the community were made by King
Charles I.

After Ferrar's death, and as a result of the
Puritan backlash of the 1640s, the community
could not survive, though there has been a recent
revival of interest in his work. The elaborate
interior of the small church and its college seating
act as a fitting memorial.

It lies off the road from Sawtry to Hamerton: a
signpost indicates 'The Giddings' (Steeple
Gidding, Little Gidding and Great Gidding).

Loughborough

Leicestershire SK 5319

Loughborough is best known for its bells (cast at
Taylor's Foundry and used in churches and
cathedrals the world over); for the Carillon
Tower, with its 47-bell peal; for the Central
Station, where steam and old diesel engines are
run to places of interest; and for its colleges.

For a different angle on this busy market town,
try the Local Studies Photographic Collection.
Here, the changes of the last hundred years can
be studied through over 3000 prints, dating from
1870 onwards. The collection is at
Loughborough Library, Granby Street, and an
appointment should be made.

LEICESTER *The Jewry Wall was part of a Roman basilica.
Archaeologists digging when a swimming pool was proposed
found that it may have led into a public bath-house*

MALVERN: SPA WATER — *Water from the* **Malvern** *Hills has been celebrated for centuries for its health-giving properties. Doctor Wall's analysis in 1757 was summed up in the following rhyme:*
'Malvern water, says Doctor John Wall,
Is famed for containing just nothing at all.'
— not an insult, but a tribute to its remarkable purity.
Taken on tour by the Royal Family, it is widely sold today along with other waters such as Ashbourne and Cwm Dale. The latter is thought by some to be the best tasting — it rises from the foot of the Long Mynd in Shropshire, having percolated through ancient rocks from the plateau above and collected such minerals as calcium, magnesium, potassium and fluorides.
Real or supposed health-giving properties have made 'taking the waters' popular for centuries. The Romans developed curative springs, most notably at **Bath** *and* **Buxton**; *and the National Health Service has approved of the springs at* **Leamington Spa**. **Llanwrtyd Wells** *offers strong-smelling water from a sulphur well; but one spa town owes its mineral-rich water to St Dunstan. He seized the Devil by the nose with a pair of red-hot pincers, causing the fiend to flee shrieking to Tunbridge Wells, where he cooled his nose in the water — hence its reddish tinge.*

MALVERN   *Three rats hang a cat on one of the Priory misericords — perhaps the carver was making a satirical joke, whose meaning has been lost*

ST DUNSTAN   *scorched the Devil's nose with pincers and gave Tunbridge spa water*

Lowestoft

Suffolk   TM 5593

North of the swing bridge is the real town, built on a hill with the narrow alleys or 'scores' leading steeply down to the Denes. Trawlers are continually on the move in the harbours; there is a pervading smell of fish, and at the fish market can be bought big packs of some of the cheapest — and freshest — fish in the country. But the kippers are all from Scotland.

A testimony to seafaring interests is the elegant row of painted shields belonging to the honorary vice-consuls of the Low Countries, displayed outside one of the many shipping agents' offices.

Lowestoft Ness, the most easterly point in Britain, is surmounted by the old Martello lighthouse, which is now closed to the public. Down the adjacent Cart Score and through pleasant gardens is the Maritime Museum, open in summer and a must for anyone wanting to appreciate how Lowestoft remains a lively fishing port.

Madley Tracking Station

Hereford & Worcester   SO 4138

Five giant dish aerials rise like insects from a strange planet, out of the flat farmlands between the B4352 and the B4348, and the villages of Kingston and Madley. Built in this 'electrically quiet' and pleasant place, its largest disc (105 feet in diameter) tracks a communications satellite in stationary orbit over the Indian Ocean, from which it feeds the telecommunications network.

Although the station is not open to the public, the aerials can be seen for miles, and are particularly spectacular at night when they are floodlit. A good vantage point is the B4348 where it rises to cross into the Golden Valley.

Madley church has an annual music festival.

Lutterworth

Leicestershire   SP 5484

John Wycliffe, translator of the Bible into English, was rector here. His outspoken criticism of Rome gained Wycliffe many enemies, to such an extent that 43 years after he died, his remains were dug up, burnt and thrown into the River Swift. The church has many items believed to have belonged to Wycliffe and several monuments and carvings recall times in his hectic life.

On the outskirts of town is Bitteswell Aerodrome, still operational, where Sir Frank Whittle tried his jet engine prototype.

Malvern

Hereford & Worcester   SO 7845

High up on the wind-blown ancient hills that Elgar walked above the town are the remains of a hill-fort of the second century BC, known as British Camp. Much of the detail of its former layout can be discerned.

In the ancient Priory, seek out the misericords (hinged choir-stall seats). They are carved with representations of day-to-day life in medieval times, and one depicts the only known example of early urinoscopy — the testing of a urine specimen by a physician.

KNILLIAN *The bequest of John Knill provided for music and dancing at his mausoleum*

MARKET HARBOROUGH: BEQUESTS

— In 1786, William Hubbard bequeathed a guinea a year forever to the choir of St Mary's in Arden, Market Harborough, to pay for the singing of the Easter Hymn over his grave, every Easter Eve. The conditions are still fulfilled, though the church is derelict.

John Knill's bequest required children of St Ives in Cornwall to dance at his mausoleum; at Leighton Buzzard a will requires a choirboy to stand on his head, and at St Ives in Cambridgeshire children play dice for a bequest of bibles.

More dicing takes place in Guildford, for a bequest to two deserving women. The bequest has so developed that today the loser wins the most money.

A bequest to a bell is found at Burgh Le Marsh, where the rent on a piece of land went to pay for a new bell rope. At Old Bolingbroke in Lincolnshire, a piece of land was left to be bought at intervals by 'candle auction' — bids could be made until the candle had burnt a certain length — the price paid going towards a dole. Siamese twins founded the dole at Biddenden, Kent, and moving stories are attached to the doles at Tichborne, Hampshire and else-where (see Coventry).

At the Theatre Royal, Drury Lane, London, the Baddeley Cake is still eaten on each Twelfth Night, in fulfilment of a will of 1794 (for ceremonies at London churches see page 88).

The hoods for which teams compete in the annual Hood Game at Haxey, Humberside, are said to have been paid for origi-nally by a bequest of Lady de Mowbray, whose hood was retrieved by Haxey men — but this may be a later explanation of the custom.

Manea

Cambridgeshire TL 4889

So isolated was this fen island village, that the compilers of the Domesday Book failed to find it.

Charles II knew of its whereabouts, and planned a town called Charlemonte here, though it never got further than the planning stage.

In the 19th century the Manea Colony proved slightly more successful than the king's dream. It was founded in 1838 by William Hodson, and based on the principles of the Co-operative movement. With a motto *'Each for All'* and clad in green uniform tunics, the colonists set up their humble dwellings and started working the land. They were paid in vouchers for the colony store. Hodson was unable to secure an outside market, and within a decade the colony was abandoned.

Market Harborough

Leicestershire SP 7387

The world's largest industrial battery maker, Tungstone, was founded here in 1898. The first car battery, tested on a vehicle through the town, ran for under a mile and stopped outside the cemetery. The company has a colourful history: it was run by a trickster at one stage, and a director was murdered. Tours can be arranged.

Gartree, the top-security prison is passed on the road to Foxton locks — worth seeing for fine canal engineering. Boat-building also flourishes at the Basin.

Market Overton

Leicestershire SK 8816

A superstition holds that the last person to be buried has to watch over the churchyard until the next arrival. This is said to have given rise to the occasional scramble for funerals.

Sir Isaac Newton regularly visited his grand-mother here, and donated the sundial now on the west wall of the church. A Roman kiln and a Saxon cemetery can be seen on the outskirts, while the centre of the village has a restored Manor House, thatched cottages, stocks and whipping post.

MARKET HARBOROUGH *The little 17th-century grammar school was built on stilts to give space and shade to market stalls. Close by, the church is reckoned to have one of the finest spires in England*

Marrington Dingle

Shropshire SO 2797

The Dingle was gouged out by the rushing waters of an overflowing glacial lake which stood south-east of Churchstoke during the last Ice Age. Today the steep-sided, flat-floored gorge is hung with woodland. A footpath follows close to the River Camlad (the only river to rise in England and flow into Wales), providing a walk which is splendidly rich in birds and plants. Dippers bob in the rushing waters, kingfishers whizz from perch to perch, pheasants strut beneath the trees, and the keen botanist should keep an eye open for some rarities that survive in this isolated haven of wildlife.

Martley

Hereford & Worcester SO 7559

When the red sandstone parish church of St Peter was being restored, earlier this century, the builders uncovered impressive wall decorations, with heraldic designs and other paintings. Two of the most striking depict the Adoration of the Magi and the story of St Martin and the beggar. Although they have been described as some of the best wall paintings in Britain, they have been seen by relatively few, as Martley, a few miles north-west of Worcester, is not on a major tourist route.

The early 14th-century rectory nearby was once the home of Sir Charles Hastings, founder of the British Medical Association.

Marton

Warwickshire SP 4069

One of the views across the fields towards Marton includes an old barn, in front of which, summer and winter alike, a farmer guides an early plough, pulled by two sturdy farm horses.

Farmer, horses and plough are an illusion — an appealing example of *trompe l'oeil*, painted on the barn's massive wall and merging perfectly into the surrounding landscape. The picture's purpose is to give a flavour of what is inside the barn: the Marton Museum of Country Bygones, re-capturing traditional ways of life. It is open during the summer.

Maxey

Cambridgeshire TF 1208

Maxey Mill is a rare example in this area of a working water mill. The mill, the third one on the site, dates from 1779, and has a 15-foot diameter wheel, two feet wide, driving two pairs of stones. About a ton of corn is milled there daily. In 1984 the mill won a Civic Trust award for conservation. While not generally open to the public, it can be viewed by appointment with the owners (a donation to charity is requested).

The Church of St Peter stands almost a mile from the present village, but was undoubtedly closer to the original settlement. Square-towered, it is mainly of the 12th century, though its low mound site is possibly an ancient burial ground. Maxey is a place of long occupation: gravel excavations have revealed that the area has been populated since Neolithic times. A field pattern of Iron Age and Roman times has been discovered near the church.

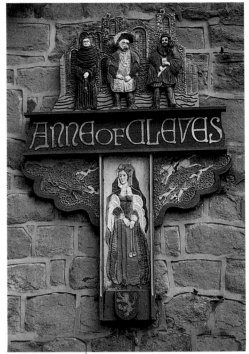

MELTON MOWBRAY *The sign of Anne of Cleves House — dating from before her time, it was given to her by Henry VIII as part of the divorce settlement*

Melton Mowbray

Leicestershire SK 7518

One of the world's top Western authors, J. T. Edson, lives in the town and will meet visitors at his home, where his collection of replica guns can be seen. Appointments are essential.

The oldest and and busiest cattle market in the country is held in Melton on Tuesdays. It is controlled by a 400-year-old charity called the Town Estate, which owns and runs much of the town, including parks, sports fields and street markets.

Classics of English food — the renowned pork pies, Hunt Cake, Stilton cheese and crumbly Red Leicester can be seen being made locally. Within the town, Burton Street offers most of interest. The Bedehouses are well preserved and Anne of Cleves House, now a restaurant, dates from 1378. During alterations, two corpses were found.

Further along is the beautifully maintained Harboro Hotel and a small inn, the Boat. It was the haunt of boatmen who stopped at the Basin, part of the now defunct Oakham Canal.

Also in Melton, the Production Engineering Research Association — PERA — has special facilities for visitors interested in seeing the latest technology at work, including computers and robots. Arrangements must be made through the Visits Liaison Officer.

Middle Littleton

Hereford & Worcester SP 0747

A tithe barn of enormous proportions, said to be one of the largest and best preserved in Britain, can be admired here. It was built for the Abbot of Evesham in the 14th century, and a loaded hay-cart hauled by four horses could enter through the giant doors and turn round inside.

The barn, now owned by the National Trust, is open daily, and shares its delightful setting with the village's 17th-century Manor House and the ancient Parish Church of St Nicholas.

MELTON MOWBRAY: HUNTING —

According to foxhunting enthusiasts, the best sport is found in the Shires, *which makes* **Melton Mowbray**, *meeting place of three of the largest hunts (the Quorn, the Cottesmore and the Belvoir), perhaps the 'foxhunting capital' of the world.*

Hunting foxes — increasingly a matter of controversy — has only comparatively recently been seen as a 'sport' worthy of the aristocracy. (Where it is still felt to be chiefly a necessity, the style of hunting is very different — see **Parc**.) *William Twici, chief huntsman to Edward II and author of 'Le Art de venerie', mentions foxes only as inferior sport, and it was not until the mid-18th century that hounds were bred solely for foxhunting. The fact that this form of the sport is now the best known may be partly because other game has been made scarce by centuries of ruthless pursuit by hunters.*

Like falconry (still to be seen at **Weyhill**), *other kinds of hunting used to be subject to strict class controls. The 'higher chase' (of deer and other superior animals) was reserved for the upper classes, from Anglo-Saxon times.*

From the Norman Conquest onwards, illicit hunting brought severe penalties, by means of harsh forest laws. William the Conqueror, who 'loved the tall deer as if he were their father', and outlawed bows and arrows in the New Forest, introduced such punishments as the loss of both eyes for unauthorised slaughter.

CLUMBER SPANIEL

FOXHOUND

HUNTING DOGS *The Clumber Spaniel (top), bred at Clumber Park and noted for silence, and the Foxhound*

MINSTERLEY: MAIDENS' GARLANDS — *At Minsterley and Ashford in the Water, Derbyshire, some pieces of maidens' garlands have survived. Probably because it was considered unlucky to dispose of them, they were left in their places and any bits that dropped off were buried in the churchyard.*

The garlands were originally wreaths of flowers, carried as a symbol of virginity before the coffin of an unmarried girl. They are referred to as 'crants' (German kranz) in Shakespeare's 'Hamlet': 'She should in ground unsanctified been lodg'd . . . yet here she is allow'd her virgin crants'.

Later, the flower wreath came to be replaced by something less perishable — commonly a crown-shaped wooden frame covered with linen or paper and decorated with artificial flowers. Sometimes it had streamers hanging down and might include a kerchief or single white glove, symbolic of 'clean hands'.

After the funeral, the maiden's garland would be hung in the church. If the girl's right to be thus honoured remained un-challenged, the garland would be found a permanent place.

Widespread in Elizabethan England, the practice was still current in some parts in the 18th century, with a few later survivals. At Abbots Ann, Hampshire, the last garland was carried at a funeral in 1953.

The garlands may have been an imitation of bridal flowers, reflecting a belief that young people who died before their time — before marriage — were under a kind of curse, which could be lifted by the pretence of a wedding ceremony, with bridal flowers put on the corpse, and bridal garlands hung in the church. In 1603 it was reported that the streets 'were strawed with flowers when maids of any sort are buried . . . and for batchelors, they wear rosemary, as if it were a marriage.'

Minsterley

Shropshire SJ 3705

Inside the 17th-century church (which attracts attention by its unusual brick construction and neo-Classical design) is a collection of seven 18th-century 'Maiden's Garlands', wooden frames supporting paper flowers, ribbons and gloves. They were carried at the funerals of girls and young women who had died before marriage. Why so many are preserved in this one church remains a mystery.

Over the west door is a frieze decorated with skull-and-cross bone carvings.

Minton

Shropshire SO 4290

Perched on the flanks of the Long Mynd, this cluster of farms and cottages around its triangular village green exudes timelessness as few other settlements do. The name is Saxon, but traces of cultivation terraces suggest Celtic origins. The mound of a Saxon motte still stands behind the manor house.

When goods travelled by packhorse, and a dry route was more important than a level one, Minton was on a major trackway across the Long Mynd to Bishops Castle and Welshpool. The rutted path still leads clearly up the hillside for today's walker to follow. As it levels off on the shoulder of the hill, the Packetstone can be seen, traditionally the point at which the drivers stopped to adjust the packhorses' loads.

Mitchell's Fold

Shropshire SO 3098

Shropshire's most conspicuous Bronze Age monument (dating from about 1500BC) is a stone circle standing in brooding isolation on the lonely southern spur of Stapeley Hill. Fifteen stones remain out of a complete circle of about twice that number, in silent testimony to our ancestors who congregated here, it is thought, for unknown religious ceremonies.

Monks Eleigh

Suffolk TL 9647

The village green is almost perfect, complete with a pump, erected in 1854, that stands forlorn in the middle. The parish church overlooks the scene.

Beyond the church on rising ground a mile away is the moated site of the medieval manor. As so often in Suffolk, many of the cottages flaunt walls of many colours. Down by the river there are old mill buildings.

Mordiford

Hereford & Worcester SO 5637

Local legend tells of the Mordiford Worm (dragon) which descended from the hills to devour local maidens, until killed by a criminal, who was pardoned but died in the fight.

Today, tranquillity prevails. Church, rectory and a house and cottages look across the water meadows where the Lugg joins the Wye through a long-decayed lock. A narrow 14th-century bridge carries the B4224 towards Hereford.

On the hillside, Sufton Court (open summer Sundays) overlooks the village and its park, designed by Humphry Repton. Behind it, the remains of Old Sufton include a barn, manor house, cider mill, timber yard, and dovecote in an overgrown garden. Paths lead off into the woods and to Blackbury Hill encampment.

Moreton Corbet

Shropshire SJ 5523

Off the main road north from Shawbury village, and disturbed more by the shriek of jet planes from the RAF base than by visitors, are the extra-ordinary red sandstone ruins of Moreton Corbet Castle. Although it is of 13th-century origin, the 16th-century walls with large windows and ornamentation are clearly the remains of an Elizabethan house rather than a defensive structure. In rebuilding their home, the Corbets extinguished the immediately surrounding village, except for the rectory and church, which has elaborate tombs and monuments.

Morston

Norfolk TG 0043

One of the many delightful coastal flint villages along the North Norfolk coast, it is the best place from which to visit Blakeney Point, a long spit of sand and shingle jutting out from the shore at Cley. To walk to the Point along four miles of pebbles is hard, but a boat can be taken from Morston Quay. Local fishermen run ferries an hour each side of high tide, and can take visitors to view the 400-odd seals that live on sand banks off the coast, or drop passengers on the Point itself, near the old Lifeboat Station.

A wooden walkway circles the dunes, leading to observation hides, on the seaward side, that overlook terneries. It is suitable for disabled people, but let the Warden know first.

A pagoda-like boatstore and information hut on Morston Quay has a viewing gallery and tide and ferry timetables.

Moulton

Suffolk TL 6964

In the early 15th century, a pack-horse bridge of brick and flint with four pointed arches was built to span the river, now reduced to a small stream. This bridge and a smaller footbridge further up-stream towards the church both remain in remarkably good condition.

The churchyard of St Peter's is entered through an elegant wrought iron 'kissing gate', helping to contain the sheep that nibble the grass around the graves. Atop the square tower is a splendid weather vane in the shape of a large pike.

Myddle

Shropshire SJ 4623

This little village off the Ellesmere to Shrewsbury road, with its red sandstone buildings and frag-mentary castle, is pleasant enough but un-exceptional — except in its chronicler. Richard Gough lived here in the 17th century, and wrote the *Antiquities and Memoires of the Parish of Myddle*.

This is a racy account of village history, life and gossip of the period. It was hard to find copies until the work was recently unearthed by Penguin. Re-published in 1981 as *Gough's History of Myddle*, it was suddenly in the best-seller lists.

MITCHELL'S FOLD: MAGIC COW — *It was said that in lean times a beautiful white cow appeared at the partly dismantled stone circle of* **Mitchell's Fold**. *No matter how many came to milk her, so long as each person filled only one pail, she never ran dry. But when an old witch named Mitchell milked her dry by milking her into a sieve, she vanished.*

The story of the magic cow is found all over the country. A tower at Doddington Park, **Audlem**, *is supposed to have one of her bones, and a church at Stanion, Northamptonshire, has another — the Dun Cow's Rib. In some versions, the White Cow of Mitchell's Fold was said to have been transformed into the rampaging Dun Cow of* **Dunchurch**, *which was killed by Guy of* **Warwick**.

The white cow is also linked with Callanish stone circle on **Lewis**. *A woman was on the point of drowning herself in the sea at a time of famine, when the cow appeared from the sea. It ordered her to take her milking pail to Callanish, where she and her neighbours were able to milk it each night. Everyone was able to fill a single pail, until a witch milked the cow into a sieve and milked it dry. The cow vanished from the island and never came back.*

The story of the witch and the cow was attached to Mitchell's Fold by the 18th century. Another story of the same date, or perhaps earlier, is that Medgel's or Medgley's Fold was where a giant (presumably Medgley) kept his cows. The name of another pre-historic enclosure — Grimspound, at Manaton, Devon — suggests that it too was thought to be the 'pound', or fold, of a giant.

MITCHELL'S FOLD   *is linked with the tale of a magic cow, and remains an enigma even for those in search of more prosaic explanations. An axe factory has been found nearby*

NEW BUCKENHAM:
THATCH — Today,
thatch on buildings is
regarded as unusually picturesque,
but until the 17th century this was
the commonest form of roofing in
Britain. Old Buckenham (see
New Buckenham) still has a
thatched church; many more
churches must once have been
roofed in this way. Large and
important buildings were also
thatched, for instance Pevensey
Castle in the 14th century, and
the word derives from the Saxon
'theac' for any roofing material.

Most thatched buildings today
are in rural areas, because of the
fire risk which caused thatch to be
banned in towns. In London, it
became compulsory by 1212 to
whitewash any thatched roof as
protection, and thereafter it was
forbidden to thatch new houses. In
later years other towns followed
this example, until only country
villages were permitted to practise
this traditional craft.

The counties which have the
most thatched buildings today are
Cornwall, Devon, Somerset and
Norfolk — where thatching is
considered to be at its best. Norfolk
reed gives the sharper outline of
thatching in the eastern counties;
the more rounded profiles of the
west come from wheatstraw.

REVIVAL THATCH   *The church
of All Saints at Little Stretton,
Shropshire, was built in 1903,
after the style of Norman Shaw*

NESSCLIFFE   *Kynaston's Cave, the hideout of Wild
Humphrey Kynaston, or 'Kynnyson'. He is said to have
robbed from the rich but enriched the poor, sold his soul to
the Devil, and shod his horse backwards, to leave a baffling
trail for his pursuers*

Napton on the Hill

Warwickshire   SP 4661

Perched on top of a conical hill, Napton is the
home of a remarkable museum — a working
collection of vintage juke-boxes, symphoniums,
musical boxes and other exotic machines,
including a restored cinema organ, complete with
hydraulic lift, from the Regal, Hammersmith. It
is installed in a replica 1930s cinema, and the
owner, Graham Whitehead, plays it during the
authentic early film shows he offers visitors. The
Napton Nickelodeon is usually open on the last
Saturday evening and the last Sunday afternoon
and evening of every month, except in July and
August, but visitors are advised to check first.

Other attractions are views of the surrounding
countryside, through which runs the picturesque
Oxford Canal. The Church of St Lawrence dates
back to Norman times, and there is a carefully
restored windmill (privately owned and not
normally open to the public).

Naseby

Northamptonshire   SP 6878

The story goes that after the state funeral of
Cromwell at Westminster Abbey in 1658, his
body was taken secretly at night to his birthplace
at Huntingdon and then on to Naseby, the site of
his great Civil War victory.

A secret grave, nine feet deep, was dug, and the
ground was carefully levelled to leave no trace of
its whereabouts. It has not been found.

Needham Market

Suffolk   TM 0855

At the bottom — the east end — of the main
street, is the Victorian railway station whose fine
buildings are now sadly neglected. A low tunnel
under the railway line gives access to a pleasant
park and lake. At the opposite end, a road sign
points to the Creetings and down to the old mill
of 1887, also derelict, on the Gipping river. A
bygones museum (open in summer) en route
contains a hotch-potch of items. Beyond the mill,
the towpath makes a very pleasant walk. The
parish church on the High Street offers a 15th-
century timber roof, and Quakers will wish to
see the Friends' Meeting House.

Nesscliffe

Shropshire SJ 3819

Shropshire's 'Robin Hood' of the 15th century was Humphrey Kynaston, the outlawed member of a prominent county family.

His headquarters is traditionally said to have been the cave cut out of the red sandstone of Nesscliffe Hill. North of the busy A5 and concealed in the woods on the steep slope is a flight of rough steps leading to the two-roomed cave. Legend says one room was the stable for his remarkable horse, on which he performed such miraculous feats as jumping the Severn at Montford Bridge to escape his pursuers.

The summit of Nesscliffe Hill is crowned with an Iron Age fort.

Newark-on-Trent

Nottinghamshire SK 7953

Close to the Great North Road, this is not a place where the average person stops. Hardly a tourist centre, it is arguably among the most attractive small towns in England.

The River Trent runs right through the town, whose heart is the wide Market Place and dignified town hall, designed by John Carr of York. All four sides of the Market Place have distinguished Georgian houses and inns, and soaring to the heavens behind is the spire of St Mary Magdalen, described as 'among the two or three dozen grandest parish churches of England'. Leading from the Market Place are numerous interesting streets and alleys.

At the edge of the town is the ruin of the huge castle, vigorously defended for the King in the Civil War, but finally captured and slighted.

New Buckenham

Norfolk TM 0890

Set in the heart of rural Norfolk, this quiet village was 'new' in the 15th century. It was laid out to a practical design around the green, in the middle of which is a Market House, complete with a whipping post. Off one corner the street leads to a 13th-century church, which positively gleams with polish and is the pride of the church councillors. The records of this parish are exceptional and amongst its possessions is a Vulgate — a translation of the Bible in fourth-century Latin — of around 1270. In the bell tower, a small window called a 'sacring squint' enabled the bell to be rung at the same moment as the Host was offered, to silence conversation.

Only a mound remains of the castle built here by d'Albini, who was reputed to be butler to William the Conqueror. Cricket lovers should visit Old Buckenham, just down the road, where the turf for the cricket pitch was brought over from Australia. The thatched church has a Norman door, stained glass by Kempe, and interesting bench-ends.

Newmarket

Suffolk TL 6463

A visit to the Horseracing Museum in the High Street is essential. Charles II helped to establish Newmarket as the headquarters of horse racing and set a precedent — later royalty owned two of the three Arab and Turkish stallions which are the ancestors in a direct male line of each of the

110,000 (approximately) thoroughbred foals born annually throughout the world.

The present museum is housed in the 'New' Subscription Rooms, built in 1844 by the Jockey Club, as a suitable place for betting debts to be settled by racing men. All the great jockeys are portrayed here in their gaudy silks, among the spread of other turf memorabilia. Also to be seen is the small pistol with which Fred Archer, the greatest of them all, shot himself. He was only 29, and the champion jockey. A video film of great races runs continually.

Norbury

Derbyshire SK 1242

The church is not large, but it has some of the finest stained glass in the country, and is filled with magnificent monuments to the Fitzherbert family who lived in the Manor House — Norbury's other outstanding building. Elizabethan, it has recently been rescued and restored by a descendant of the Fitzherberts, but is only open occasionally by appointment. Close by is the family's original 13th-century hall-house, a very rare survivor. The owner has built a gazebo in the garden.

Norwich

Norfolk TG 2308

In Georgian times, this fine city had over a thousand pubs, and it still boasts an impressive 200-plus. Twenty-eight of the most interesting form the route of one of the town trails for which guides can be bought at the Information Centre in the old Guildhall (beside the colourful open market). The Adam and Eve, down by the Cathedral, dates from 1249.

A silver trail unlocks the secrets of fabulous collections on view in the City Hall, the Cathedral and other places. There is a trail of the macabre, and one of door knockers. At Strangers Hall, a wonderfully preserved medieval mansion in St Andrews, the round knocker on the front door has been in use since 1450 and opens the way into a fascinating museum of furniture and domestic life through the ages.

There are also numerous medieval churches, from the days when Norwich was one of England's largest cities. St Julian's has the site of the cell of the 15th century anchorite and mystic, Lady Julian.

Nottingham

Nottinghamshire SK 5741

'Seek and ye shall find' is a useful motto to keep in mind when visiting Nottingham. Maid Marion Way cuts a vast swathe of road through the city centre, and is only one example of the city's development. But still lurking are some fascinating places, such as the restored 18th-century castle, and medieval pubs — the Salutation Inn, the Flying Horse and, most amazing of all, the Trip to Jerusalem. It dates from crusading times and is built into the castle rock.

High Pavement, Middle Pavement and Castlegate have fine Georgian houses, and the Lace Market is an oasis of Victoriana. The Park is a unique ducal housing development, a quiet, enclosed area, full of magnificent Victorian houses built for the Duke of Newcastle.

NORWICH: NORFOLK WHERRIES —
*During the 19th century the old Adam and Eve in Bishopgate, **Norwich**, was run by a Mrs Howes, who was also a wherry-owner. Her wherry — also called the Adam and Eve — used to fetch sand from Yarmouth for sprinkling the floors of the pubs of Norwich.*

Like others on the Norfolk waterways, the Adam and Eve became a 'wherrymen's pub' — a meeting-place for men who, like those who worked canals in narrowboats, were almost a race apart. They worked alone except for the mate (often a wife) and were always on the move.

Most of the wherries were built at small boatyards like that of William Petch, commemorated at Petch's Corner, on the riverbank opposite Norwich's medieval Cow Tower. Here were built wherries

such as the Jessie, the Hand of Providence and the Jenny Morgan — the heroine of a popular song — from whose windvane (a girl in Welsh costume) all wherry vanes of whatever design came to be known as 'Jenny Morgans'.

The last Norfolk wherry to be built was the Ella in 1912; and by 1949 not one trading wherry remained under sail. But a black-sailed wherry called the Albion is still maintained by the Norfolk Wherry Trust, and can sometimes be seen on the Broads.

ABOVE ALBION, – *last of the wherries. They carried three-ton cargoes in shallow inland waters*

PEAK FOREST: A GATE TO THE UNDERWORLD —

Peveril Castle, north of **Peak Forest** *in the heart of the Peak District, is said to stand over one of the gateways to the underworld. The gate is Peak Cavern, known by a more indelicate name in the 16th century.*

A 12th-century story tells how a swineherd, working for the lord of Peveril Castle, lost a sow about to farrow one winter's day. Frightened of what his master would say, he decided finally to investigate the cave, despite its eerie reputation. When he was some way in, he emerged into a broad plain where the harvest was being gathered, and discovered his sow safe and sound, and delivered of her piglets. He was kindly dismissed by the lord of the country, and returned with the sow and piglets through the cave, emerging into the same wintry weather that he had left behind.

Similar tales current at the same time — of the Green Children who appeared out of a pit at Woolpit, Suffolk, and Elidyr who visited the fairies in their underground kingdom in the Vale of Neath — seem to stem from the Celtic idea of the 'otherworld' as a lovely subterranean land — very different from the underworld suggested by **Binham.**

PEAK CAVERN *below Peveril Castle. Apparently at one time the great cave sheltered an 'underground' village.*

'Stacks both of hay and turf, which yields a scent Can only fume from Satan's fundament' (Charles Cotton)

Oakham

Leicestershire SK 8509

Jeffrey Hudson, the world's smallest man, was born in a thatched cottage on Melton Road (not open to the public) during 1619. When Charles I and Queen Henrietta stayed at Burley, Hudson was served up in a cold pie. So pleased was she with the dwarf that the Queen took him into her care. He led an active life: twice captured by pirates, he was sold into slavery, escaped and died at Oakham aged 63, having reached the height of three feet six inches.

Mysterious carvings enrich the capitals of the nave in All Saints Church. The subjects include angels singing, a fox running off with a goose, a monkey, a beast, Adam and Eve, and a man with a broom.

The town is a place of wide streets and fascinating passageways. The castle has a collection of horseshoes; in the Market Place are the Buttercross and stocks; and at Rutland Farm Park, a collection of rare breeds can be seen.

OAKHAM *The Great Hall, home of a horseshoe collection, is the oldest English castle hall left intact — but the rest of the castle has been lost*

Olchon Valley

Hereford & Worcester SO 2931

The Olchon rises on the hillside beneath Black Hill (scene of Bruce Chatwin's novel *On the Black Hill*). The spur known locally as the Cat's Back (with a picnic site at the lower end) joins the main ridge and the long-distance footpath on Offa's Dyke, running along the Welsh border towards Hay Bluff.

Flowing through a mesh of lanes and footpaths, the river joins the Monnow between Longtown, with its castle, and Clodock, where the river curves on a rocky bed round pub and churchyard. On the hillside above the Mountain Road, a picnic site between the outcrops of Red and Black Darren offers the prospect of steep climbs and distant views. This feels about as remote a place as one can find in England.

To the west are the Black Mountains.

Old Weston

Cambridgeshire TL 0977

On the Sunday after the feast of St Swithin (mid-July), the nave floors of St Swithin's Church are covered with hay, from a meadow bequeathed by an old lady in the 17th century. She disliked the sound of new boots on the floor.

In recent years, a different kind of peace protestor has come to nearby Molesworth.

Ollerton

Nottinghamshire SK 6567

Five main roads meet at Ollerton, in a constant swirl of traffic. But only yards away is an unspoilt village, well worth exploring.

Red brick predominates, and there are several very attractive little houses, with a splendid old coaching inn — the Hop Pole. The small church was rebuilt in 1780, or perhaps slightly later, with 18th-century Gothic plasterwork.

Orford

Suffolk TM 4250

On the wall of the tiny Captain's Room, in the waterside Jolly Sailor Inn, is a copy of the handbill offering a reward for the capture of Margaret Catchpole, whose involvement with smugglers and horse stealing led to her transportation to Australia in 1801. There are also frightening pictures of the scene in 1963, when a tornado deposited the roof of the inn in Quay Street.

Rare avocets breed on Havergate Island, next to the long shingle bank that shelters Orford from the sea but also contributed to its decline as a port. The area is a nature reserve. A climb up the steep staircases of the polygonal 12th-century castle keep provides fine views.

PICKWORTH *Losecoat Field, the only battleground in the old county of Rutland, was the scene of a massacre after an uprising in Lincolnshire*

Papworth St Agnes

Cambridgeshire TL 2862

At the end of a dead-end lane, just five miles south of Huntingdon, this lonely hamlet feels like a place caught in a time warp.

A former farming community, it was in danger of becoming one of the lost villages, with the church and manor in a state of decay and some of the cottages in need of repair. But the last few years have brought a new lease of life. The church has been restored, its stone and flint chequerwork resplendent once more under a repaired roof. The magnificent manor house, also a scene of restoration, has a moat, and behind the 17th-century brick front is a stone house dating back to the 12th century.

On the village green are a communal bake-house of the mid-19th century, built for all the villagers to use, and a Victorian letter-box.

Peak Forest

Derbyshire SK 1179

Lying in the Peak District National Park between Tideswell and Chapel-en-le-Frith, Peak Forest was the scene of many a runaway marriage, as the Vicar could grant marriage licences. The custom stopped in the early 19th century.

An old chapel dating from 1657 was erected by a fiercely Royalist Countess of Devonshire. Windows commemorate the Martyr King and Lord Frederick Cavendish, assassinated in Phoenix Park, Dublin, in 1882.

Just over a mile away is one of the Wonders of the Peak — the 'bottomless pit' of Eldon Hole.

Pembridge

Hereford & Worcester SO 3858

Once a market town which was feared for its witches, Pembridge now enjoys comparative peace, being missed by the many visitors who flock to neighbouring Eardisland. A fine, mainly medieval, assortment of black-and-white buildings, a pub and a market house make the place worth a stop, but its glory is the detached bell tower in the spacious churchyard. It is a marvel of late 14th-century timber construction, externally a pagoda-like series of roofs and stages, and inside a forest of great beams. Take a torch in to see the details.

All around are explorable lanes, crossing and re-crossing the River Arrow towards Wales.

Pickworth

Leicestershire SK 9913

The poet John Clare, who worked as a lime burner here in 1812, wrote '. . . and the place where we dug the kiln was full of foundations and human bones'. They were the remnants of a thriving village, reduced to a hamlet by 1490.

A 14th-century arch from the medieval church stands alone in a field. Nearby is the Drift, an old drovers' road, favoured today for walks.

Follow the Empingham road south-west to its junction with the A1 for Losecoat Field. In 1470, rebels were cornered here by the forces of Edward IV. The site is said to owe its name to the discarding of their distinctive jackets by the desperate rebels, who hoped to be mistaken for locals. Bloody Oaks Wood, on the other side of the A1, is where the King executed the ringleaders, including Lord Welles and Sir John Hussey. Tales abound of screams in the woods. Visits may be made at any time, but do not tread on the field if it is sown.

PEMBRIDGE: TIMBER-FRAMING — The timber-framing to be seen at **Pembridge** is an outstanding feature of northern and western England. The most elaborate example is probably Little Moreton Hall in Cheshire, and the same county also has medieval timber-framed churches, at **Marton** and **Lower Peover**. Outside stone areas, dovecotes (as at **Dilwyn**), barns and even palaces (like Henry VIII's now-vanished Nonesuch) were timber-framed, as well as houses, until brick began to become widely available in the 18th century.

The cruck frame — an inverted 'V' made by putting two curved timbers together — can be found all over England, except in the south-east and East Anglia, where box-frames are typical. It might be covered with plaster and decorative pargeting (see **Clare**).

The timber used was unseasoned hardwood: it was cut down, sawn up and assembled into flat frames on the ground. The carpenter drilled holes for the joints, making marks (still to be seen) where the frames should be fitted together. Large buildings were also pre-fabricated — notches in the timber of barns may show where one side was propped up while the others were fitted on to it.

Wattle and daub — woven shoots of hazel, coated with clay — filled in the spaces. As the unseasoned wood dried out, it shrank and pulled the structure together, making the building

crooked perhaps, but stronger.

Traditions have arisen around the frames: the cruck is said to have been a gift from a manorial lord, and hence a status symbol — surviving today in the V-shaped chevron as a badge of rank.

ABOVE *Timber-frames with windows added later, at Lavenham, Suffolk, incomparably rich in medieval timber-framing*

POLSTEAD: MARIA
MARTEN — *The
murder of Maria Marten at*
Polstead *became the subject of
one of the best known of all
melodramas.*

*The crime was committed by
her lover, William Corder, in
1827. In the play, Corder first
seduces Maria and then shoots her
to avoid a scandal. The plot's truth
is not fully established.*

*'Maria Marten', versions of
which have appeared on the
English stage since 1840, particularly appealed to the Victorians,
for whom 'melodrama' had ceased
to mean 'drama with music' and
simply signified especially sensa-
tional theatre. Irving, who had a
great success with 'The Bells', did
much to establish the genre's
artistic credibility, but even he
could not prevent the terms
'melodrama' and 'melodramatic'
from becoming derogatory.*

*Meantime Maria Marten's sad
story remained so popular that her
gravestone at Polstead was stolen
piecemeal by souvenir hunters.
Now that the Red Barn has been
demolished, the only memorial of
the tragedy is a book bound in
Corder's skin in Moyses Hall
Museum, Bury St Edmunds.*

ABOVE *Lover turned murderer.
The insignificant appearance of
William Corder belies the evil that
drove him to seduce, then kill,
Maria Marten — supposedly*

PIN MILL *'We Didn't Mean To
Go To Sea' — Arthur Ransome's
sailing adventure — starts here.
The Ransomes had a house near
the Orwell, and sailed to Holland
in the 'Nancy Blackett' to get
authentic material*

Pin Mill

Suffolk TM 2037

Follow the B1456 away from the southern edge
of Ipswich, and at Chelmondiston turn left,
down to the shore of the River Orwell (from
which the writer Eric Blair took his pen-name).
A steep, mixed woodland backs the muddy foreshore, where a strange variety of barges and
hulks forms a colony of houseboats. Even the
sleek hull of a six-metre yacht has been transformed into a snug berth here.

A circular footpath runs from Pin Mill car
park, through the wood, over the adjoining
fields, and back, conveniently, to the Butt and
Oyster, arguably one of the finest East Anglian
pubs. Old Thames sailing barges are often
moored to the jetty, their rust-coloured sails
furled along massive spars. Over all hangs the
evocative tang of mud and salt water.

Polstead

Suffolk TL 9938

It is not the unique Norman arches of the 12th-
century church that have spread Polstead's name
to the world, but the tale of Maria Marten.
Daughter of Polstead's molecatcher, she was first
seduced and then murdered in the notorious Red
Barn that once stood near her cottage. Her
murderer was subsequently caught at Brentford
and hanged in 1828 at Bury St Edmunds, before a
crowd of 10,000.

Morbid interest satisfied, the arches of the
church should be inspected: they are fashioned
from bricks and tufa, a porous stone probably
taken from the hearths of Roman villas. Polstead

('place of pools'), straggles from a green at the
top of the hill to a large pond at the foot, where
witches were once 'swum' with their thumbs tied
up behind, and where boys now fish.

The stream flows out of the pond into the
River Box, beside which stands a very
picturesque mill, now in private hands. A footpath leads up the hill beside the road to the Cock
Inn, facing, across the green, an old smithy
complete with chestnut tree. The inn is unpre-
tentious and echoes to soft Suffolk voices.

Ratcliffe on Soar

Nottinghamshire SK 4928

Overshadowed by vast cooling towers and close
to the M1 motorway, the village church has
remarkable Sacheverell family tombs, painted by
John Piper for Sir Osbert Sitwell. These tombs
are worth a pilgrimage to see, and the village is
not bad either.

Not far away is Thrumpton Hall, which has
Byron connections and is open for parties by
appointment.

Raunds

Northamptonshire SP 9972

In March 1905, a protest march set off from
Raunds — a landmark in working-class history.

Employment in the town depended heavily on
the production of boots and shoes, which reached
a peak during the Boer War, when the demand
was high from the army. A slump followed, and
wages dropped alarmingly. When a strike failed
to restore them, an ex-soldier named James

Gribble organised the march, from Raunds to the War Office in London.

Gribble planned the march with military precision, and was known as 'General' Gribble. The campaign was successful and, for a while, trade picked up again in Raunds, still making shoes several decades later.

The mainly 13th-century church has a 15th-century, 24-hour segment clock supported by angels, and some large wall paintings.

Redditch

Hereford & Worcester SP 0468

Old Redditch has been transformed into an impressive New Town, but has retained some idiosyncratic reminders of its long history. One of these is a museum devoted to the local industry of needle-making. It is housed in the early 18th-century Forge Mill on the edge of the town, where the only water-driven needle-scouring mill in the world still operates.

Less unusual craft skills can be seen at the Wynyates Craft Centre, housed in a group of old farm buildings on the outskirts of the town.

Rothwell

Northamptonshire SP 8181

One of the largest of the traditional fairs is held at Rothwell on the week following Trinity Sunday. It starts at six on the Monday morning, when the agent of the Lord of the Manor rides on horseback from the manor house to the market house, to read out the proclamation. He is accompanied by musicians and halberdiers.

ROWLSTONE *Upside-down figures, perhaps a lapse by the carver whose masterly work is also seen in the doorway. His favourite subject seems to have been birds*

Rowlstone

Hereford & Worcester SO 3727

Orchids grow in the churchyard and Christ in Majesty sits above the entrance of the church — a gem of Norman building, in the shadow of the Black Mountains about two miles from Pontrilas. The carved chancel arch is supported on one side by a stone with a cock and two saints, the latter two inexplicably upside down. The sculpted tympanum depicts Christ in Glory; this subject, with the Tree of Life, dragons and the Harrowing of Hell were popular themes with early carvers. Overall, the church offers one of the best collections of the Herefordshire School of Norman sculptors.

Also to be seen, in the chancel, are two medieval candle brackets, each nearly five feet long, on which sit iron cocks and fleurs de lys.

St Ives

Cambridgeshire TL 3171

The two-storey stone structure on the 15th-century bridge spanning the Great Ouse is well known as a chapel. It was consecrated in 1426, and restored in the 1930s. But it has had other uses. It was an inland lighthouse when the river was navigable for sea-going barges as far as the bridge; it once had an additional brick storey and was used as a house; and for a while in the last century it served as an inn.

At the west end of town, All Saints' Church observes a Whit Sunday ceremony started by the will of one Dr Robert Wilde, who died in 1675. He left provision for the income from £50 to be spent each year on 12 Bibles, to be awarded to six boys and six girls of 'good report, under 12 years of age and able to read the Bible'. Eligible children have to roll dice to qualify.

Another benefactor, Robert Langley, bequeathed money on his death in 1656 to provide bread for the town's poor, after St Ives' church bells had helped him find his way when lost in the snow. The 'Langley Bread' is still distributed in early January, in the form of groceries, given mainly to the elderly.

At nearby Fenstanton on Plough Monday (the first Monday after 6 January), molly dancing has been revived, with dancers following a horse-drawn plough around the village.

RATCLIFFE ON SOAR: JOHN PIPER — *The Sacheverell tombs in Holy Trinity Church,* **Ratcliffe on Soar** *are the subject of a celebrated picture by the artist John Piper (born in 1903), whose work was frequently inspired by and for cathedrals and churches. Like his contemporary, Chagall, he became interested in stained glass and designed windows for Oundle,* **Plymouth, Coventry** *and* **Liverpool**.

One of the most versatile and experimental British painters of the twentieth century, in 1933 he came under the influence of Braque, one of the founders of classical Cubism, and from this abstract discipline evolved his own representational style.

Some of his most interesting work has been for the theatre — his first ballet was 'The Quest' in 1943 for Frederick Ashton. In 1948 he was a collaborator on 'Job', a re-staging at the Royal Opera House, Covent Garden, of the masque with libretto (after William Blake) by Geoffrey Keynes, choreography by Ninette de Valois, and music by Ralph Vaughan Williams.

World War II meantime had seen the production of his dramatic records of bomb damage to churches in Coventry, **Bristol** *and* **London**, *and also a series of topographical paintings including watercolours for the Queen.*

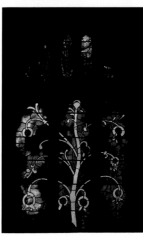

JOHN PIPER *(top) works in many media. The window in Totternhoe Church (above) typifies his style*

STAUNTON IN THE VALE: CHURCH MONUMENTS

The effigies in **Staunton's** *church are typical of the life-size memorials to notable figures which began to feature in British churches during the 13th century. The earliest carvings made no attempt at realistic portrayal and the figure, nearly always shown in death, was only identifiable by heraldry and details of costume. A knight was always represented in his armour, with his feet resting on his heraldic beast or another animal of some kind. Purbeck marble was generally used at first but alabaster, which is easier to work, became more popular. There are a few wooden effigies surviving, as at* **Danbury** *and* **Pamber**, *but these are comparatively rare. Whatever material was used the figures were always painted.*

From the 14th century the design began to vary and became progressively more informal; figures adopted different poses and individual characteristics were included. The Fettiplace family at Swinbrook in the **Windrush Valley** *for instance are shown leaning casually on their elbows. At* **Aldworth** *the effigies lie beneath vaulted stone canopies, an embellishment which became increasingly common as monuments became more elaborate and reflected the importance of the subject. The wealthier and more noble a person the nearer the effigy would be placed to the altar.*

From the late 13th to 15th centuries monumental brasses were a popular alternative to stone as they were less expensive and more durable — they are not actually made of brass, but an alloy called latten, and the craftsmen were called latteners. Because these were cheaper they represent a much wider cross-section of medieval society than stone effigies. The oldest surviving brass monument can be seen at **Stoke D'Abernon's** *church.*

SHROUDED EFFIGIES
Thomas Beresford and his wife, at Fenny Bentley, Derbyshire

Saltfleet

Lincolnshire   TF 4593

The caravan camp near the shore is part of a long resort tradition. In the 17th century, Saltfleet was 'frequented by the Gentry in the Summer season for the eating of fish' at the New Inn, built on a line of ancient dunes. A three-storey brick building, the inn became a sea bathing hotel in the 1770s for travellers from Nottingham and Leicester. The dining room could seat 100, and had bay windows offering a 'beautiful and extensive view of the German Ocean'. Access to the shore was lost in 1854 when the saltmarsh frontage was enclosed.

Opposite is Saltfleet Manor, where Lord Willoughby is said to have entertained Oliver Cromwell before the battle of Winceby (1643). On a small window pane of a sitting room on the first floor are scratched the names of Richard ffox and Jane Hardy, with a lovers' knot and the date 1673. Not open to the public, it dates from the 14th century.

The old church of Saltfleet disappeared into the sea in the 16th century.

Sawston

Cambridgeshire   TL 4849

On the death of Edward VI, his half-sister Mary Tudor fled to East Anglia, a fugitive from the Duke of Northumberland, who wanted his daughter-in-law, Lady Jane Grey, to be queen. On 7 June 1553, the princess was at Sawston Hall, a guest of John Huddleston, when Northumberland's men and a Cambridge mob attacked. Disguised as a maid, she left by a back door and reached the Gog Magog hills in safety — only to look back and see the hall in flames. 'Let it blaze,' she told her host, and promised to build him a better house when she was queen.

The result is the Sawston Hall we see today, built with stone taken from Cambridge Castle. It has now become the 'Cambridge Centre for Languages', but remained with the Huddleston family for almost 500 years, and saw little change — mainly because the family could not afford to keep up with the latest trends.

The house is said to be haunted by Mary Tudor; rather more interestingly, the hall also has a priest hole in the masonry of the tower. It was designed by Nicholas Owen, the great architect of hiding places for Catholic 'recusants' in the reign of Mary's sister, Elizabeth I.

Shrewsbury

Shropshire   SJ 4912

A renownedly lovely town, Shrewsbury nevertheless has secluded corners, thanks to a network of pedestrian alleyways, or 'shuts', running between the medieval streets.

In the heart of the town Grope Lane leads off the High Street through to Fish Street and the splendidly restored medieval hall known as Bear Steps. Rescued by the Shrewsbury Civic Society in 1972, the hall houses a changing exhibition and provides information, as well as being an appropriate base for several local conservation organisations. The 16th-century extension to the hall encloses part of St Alkmund's Square with the church of that name on the eastern side. Next door to St Alkmund's, the redundant Church of St Julian has found a new lease of life, and is a thriving craft centre.

STIPERSTONES   *The Devil is said to have flung the rocks scattered over the landscape from the 'Devil's Chair', the largest rocky outcrop*

Southwell

Nottinghamshire   SK 7053

With its bishop and its great church, called the Minster, Southwell looks perhaps as cathedral towns such as Canterbury and Winchester used to, before World War II.

One of the least known places of its kind, it has several beautiful Queen Anne and 18th-century houses in close proximity to the Minster. Nearby are the ruins of the old palace of the Archbishops of York. The fine Saracen's Head Inn has been visited by several monarchs, including Charles I, and Burgage Manor (not open) was once lived in by Byron and his mother.

But the glory of the place is Southwell Minster, with its great Norman nave and its chapter house, filled with glorious medieval stone carving, most notably the foliage called the 'Leaves of Southwell'.

The Bramley seedling apple is supposed to have first been grown in a garden in the town belonging to Bramley Tree Cottage.

Stafford

Staffordshire   SJ 9223

A novel by a local author suggested Stafford Castle as the site of Arthur's Camelot. The theory is dubious, but in recent years, the castle's undoubted historical interest has belatedly been recognised, and it has been intensively 'dug' by archaeologists. Amongst the finds have been a medieval village, and a medieval garden.

A trail round the castle gives details of its history and construction. The earthworks, a third of a mile in length, are excellently preserved, and give fine views of town and country. Pleasant walks can also be had in Castlefields.

Staunton-in-the-Vale

Nottinghamshire   SK 8043

There have been Stauntons at Staunton Hall since 1041. The last of the male line died in 1807, but the estate has been passed down in the female line, and the name perpetuated.

Monuments to the family can be seen in the north aisle of the 14th-century church, including a chain-mailed knight of about 1300 and a monument to the last of the male line, by Westmacott.

Three counties meet near here and views can be had from Folly Hill of the Vale of Belvoir.

Stiperstones

Shropshire   SO 3699

A jagged ridge of stark white quartzite tors, the Stiperstones are steeped in myth and legend. When the summit is shrouded in mist, it is said that the Devil occupies his craggy Chair.

The dramatic quality of the landscape was brought to a wide audience in Mary Webb's novel, *The Golden Arrow*. Trackways past ruined cottages once echoed to the steps of miners, who worked the lead on the western flank of the ridge. Today the scientific interest of the summit moorland is recognised in its designation as a National Nature Reserve. It is a prime example of the very restricted range of plants characteristic of extremely exposed and acid conditions. At the northern end of the ridge is 'the Hollies', an area of immensely old pollarded holly trees.

Stoke Dry

Leicestershire   SP 8597

The RAF's Dambusters used Eyebrook Reservoir (overlooked by Stoke Dry) for practice prior to their raids on the Ruhr dams in 1943. Today it offers trout fishing.

A notice in St Andrews Church asks the visitor not to believe the tale that a previous vicar sealed a witch in the little room above the porch, and starved her to death. Another tradition, better founded, is that the Gunpowder Plot was hatched in the room: one of the plotters was Sir Everard Digby, of the Digby family whose monuments ornament the church.

Stoke-on-Trent

Staffordshire   SJ 8745

Stoke-on-Trent is the centre of the Potteries today — but its oldest industry is coalmining, which dates back at least 600 years. The Chatterley Whitfield Colliery, near Tunstall, is now a mining museum, providing unusual insights into this unexpected facet of Stoke: visitors are provided with their own helmet and cap lamp, and taken 700 feet below ground, to view the Holly Lane coal seam. It has been worked in North Staffordshire since the 14th century. On the surface, exhibits include the Hesketh Steam Winding Engine, used at the pit from 1915 until coal production ceased here, in 1976.

Those who believe that no visit to Stoke is complete without pottery should try the Gladstone Pottery Museum in Longton, a Victorian pottery with demonstrations of traditional skills.

STOKE DRY   *Eyebrook Reservoir, where the Dambusters practised their bombing of the Mohne and Eder dams, an exploit celebrated in the squadron badge*

STOKE DRY: DAMBUSTERS — *In World War II, the 617 Squadron of the RAF, better known as the Dambusters, gathered at Eyebrook Reservoir, **Stoke Dry**, to rehearse the skills which were to make them legendary. Having practised to perfection, on the night of 16 May 1943, they executed their precision raid on the Mohne and Eder dams, vital sources of electric power and water for the Ruhr industries.*

The scientist Barnes Wallis had designed a new form of circular bomb which bounced along the water, arriving in the correct spot to explode the dam walls. Wing-Commander Guy Gibson personally started the attack, diving his plane down past the high mountains which hemmed in the dams and levelling it out at 60 feet above the water. He then dropped the single heavy bomb. The operation was repeated again and again, although the turbulent water had to be allowed to settle before each new attack, and pilots had to gauge their exact height above the water in the dark.

The operation was undoubtedly ingenious — but its strategic value has come to be questioned.

SWAFFHAM: THE PEDLAR

SWAFFHAM: THE PEDLAR — *On the south clergy stall in* **Swaffham** *parish church, a pedlar with his pack is represented. Once part of the family pews of John Chapman, a 15th-century benefactor of the church, the carving is a pun on his name, which means 'merchant'. 'Rebys' puns on names were popular in the Middle Ages.*

Attached to it is an old story, also told at Dundonald Castle, Strathclyde, and Upsall Castle, North Yorkshire, but best-known from at least the 17th century as 'The Pedlar of Swaffham'.

He is said to have dreamt that if he stood on London Bridge, he would hear 'something to his advantage'. Once he was there, however, nothing happened, until a shopkeeper seeing him asked what he wanted. The pedlar related his dream, at which the shopkeeper replied that he himself had dreamt that if he dug under a certain tree in a certain pedlar's orchard at Swaffham, he would find a treasure — but he wasn't fool enough to try.

The pedlar hurried home, dug beneath the tree and found a pot of treasure. Some time later, a passer-by read the pot's Latin inscription:
'Under me doth lie
Another much richer than I.'
Thus made even richer than before, the pedlar repaired Swaffham church, where his effigy stands today as a memorial.

THE PEDLAR *who 'by a dream found a great treasure'. Carved on a bench-end in Swaffham's parish church, he can also be seen on the colourful town sign*

Stoughton

Leicestershire SK 6402

In 1919, Bella Wright, aged 21, was found dead near her bicycle on Gartree Road, Stoughton — she had been shot.

A man was tried but found not guilty in what became known as the Green Bicycle Mystery. Bella was buried in Stoughton churchyard, since when sightings have been reported of a young woman riding an 'old-fashioned bike' along the road. The Information Office in Bishop Street, Leicester, has issued a booklet about this unsolved crime.

STRATFORD-UPON-AVON *Rolls-Royce 1926 Phantom I, specially commissioned from Barkers for His Excellency Nawab Wali-ud Dowla Bahadur, Prime Minister of Hyderabad — one of the exhibits at the Motor Museum, displayed alongside other vintage cars, sports cars and motorcycles, in a period setting*

Stratford-upon-Avon

Warwickshire SP 2055

With the Royal Shakespeare Theatre, Shakespeare's birthplace and Shakespeariana at every turn, Stratford-upon-Avon is one of the world's great places of pilgrimage. There is something appealing about seeing items like the desk in King Edward VI Grammar School on which Shakespeare's name is written — but at times, even the most devoted visitor needs a change from the playwright.

Then is the time to turn to Stratford's less familiar delights. A realistic replica of a 1920s garage, and some exotic Rolls-Royces and other cars once owned by Indian Maharajahs, are among the attractions in a motor museum housed in a former chapel. An early 19th-century railway wagon near the river recalls a lost horse-drawn railway: this ran to Moreton-in-Marsh, and its former track, including a narrow brick bridge over the Avon, is now a picturesque route for walkers. The restored Stratford Canal, a sequestered waterway with a towpath for walkers, and characteristic canalside architecture, like 'guillotine' bridges and barrel-roof cottages, meanders through unspoilt countryside to join the Avon here.

Swaffham

Norfolk   TF 8109

The big country market held every Saturday is one of the diminishing number of open markets remaining in Britain where *caveat emptor* — 'buyer beware' — is the watchword for all who buy from the varied stalls. That said, there can be few better places for such articles as cheap second-hand bicycles.

The refurbished circular Market Cross majestically overlooks the great open triangle of the 'square' and in 1783 cost £400 to build.

In recent years, Fakenham Road has been renowned for octogenarian Oliver Meek, deftly weaving baskets from withies and osiers while discussing the weather, sitting next to an ever-burning coke stove, on a wooden platform in a little room at the back of the shop.

The large church, of beautiful proportions, is exceptionally rewarding.

Teigh

Leicestershire   SK 8616

Holy Trinity is by far the most unusual church in the region. The 1782 interior has pews in tiers, facing inwards, enabling the congregation to turn their eyes to either end of the church easily. The carved pulpit is some 13 feet up on the west end, and is flanked by two prayer desks, all overlooked by a painted landscape and window. Anthony Jenkinson, the first Englishman to penetrate Central Asia, is buried in the graveyard; exactly where is not known. The church keys are available from Sycamore Cottage.

Temple Balsall

West Midlands   SP 2076

The medieval Knights Templar — a curious mixture of soldier and monk, whose duties included guarding the old pilgrim routes to Jerusalem — had a preceptory (or estate) with farm buildings, a granary and a church here.

Parts of the early buildings survive, including a 13th-century hall with roof supports made from tree trunks. The beautifully restored church of St Mary also remains, and so do several later buildings like the 'hospital', or almshouses, set in a delightful courtyard and still in use. Since World War II, the residents have not had to wear

the regulation bonnets and shawls of their predecessors, although examples of these uniforms have been preserved.

The Master of the Hospital is also the vicar of Temple Balsall, and can take visitors round by prior arrangement.

Temple Bruer

Lincolnshire   TF 0053

As the name suggests, this, like Temple Balsall, was the site of a preceptory of the Knights Templar. It was founded on Lincoln Heath, six miles north-west of Sleaford, in the mid-12th century, to farm the former wilderness ('Bruer' comes from the Norman French word for heath). In its heyday, the centrepiece was a great round church, surrounded by other buildings and defended by a wall and gatehouse, with a village outside. It was dissolved in 1541, and all that remains of the church is the three-storey southeast tower with spiral staircase, built of the local oolitic limestone. Restored in 1961, it is open at all reasonable times, and is reached through a farmyard.

Tenbury Wells

Hereford & Worcester   SO 5968

Queen Victoria called Tenbury Wells 'my lovely town in the orchard'. Standing by the sylvan River Teme, it still deserves the description, and it also possesses an extraordinary building, resembling a bizarre, metal-clad Chinese pagoda. This landmark was built in 1862 to house the water-cure facilities, when Tenbury Wells was aspiring to become a leading spa town. But its therapeutic days were short-lived, and the building had a variety of uses before being abandoned. It is in a dilapidated state, although officially listed as being of architectural and historic interest. The local district council has acquired it for preservation.

Teversal

Nottinghamshire   SK 4861

Surrounded by collieries and housing estates, Teversal's riches are well worth seeking out.

The church has a squire's pew, hatchments and memorials to the Molyneux family who were baronets. Near the church is a very fine Rectory, and the Hall of 1767 was made to look Jacobean in the last century.

Theddlethorpe

Lincolnshire   TF 4788

From the door of Curlew Cottage, a single-storey brick dwelling in the dunes, the smuggler had a clear view to the sea and over the Marsh, where a 'Preventive Officer' could easily be seen. Horses and carts would meet shallow draught Dutch galliots carrying contraband on the edge of the wide sandy beach, and 'caves' in the dunes were used to hide the goods.

Curlew Cottage has a framework of ships' timbers and was later the lifeboatman's cottage. It is private property and not open to the public, but there is access to the dunes and shore in the adjoining National Nature Reserve, to the north at Rimac. In late May to early June, it gives one of England's great displays of marsh orchids.

KNIGHTS TEMPLAR   *The tower is all that survives of their church at Temple Bruer. It was round, like the Templar churches which still stand in Cambridge and the Temple, London*

TEMPLE BALSALL: KNIGHTS TEMPLAR — *When, as in* **Temple Balsall** *and* **Temple Bruer***, Temple appears in the name of a village, it is often an indication that land and property in the area belonged to the Knights Templar. This religious military order was founded early in the 12th century to guard the shrines and pilgrim routes in the Holy Land. Although one of their official seals depicted two knights on one horse — implying brotherhood and poverty — they rapidly acquired massive wealth and subsequently great power and influence throughout Europe.*

In England, the Grand Master, who resided at the Temple, **London***, regularly attended the king's Parliament and was regarded as head of all religious Orders.*

Another Order of the time was the Knights of St John, originally the Knights Hospitaller, but their regime was less military and was founded on the care and welfare of pilgrims. Nevertheless, by the end of the 12th century the two were equals (and rivals) in wealth and power, and in many ways similar. The Templars wore white garments with a red cross and the Knights of St John white crosses on a red background.

Charges of heresy, homosexuality and blasphemy were levelled at the Templars, and myths, legends and an aura of mystery and supernatural power evolved and survived for centuries. When the Latin Kingdom of the East was lost, they lost their 'raison d'etre' and were suppressed, finally disappearing (or so it was believed) in the early 13th century. Much of their property passed to the St John Knights, whose fortunes can be traced in a museum at Clerkenwell, London.

UPPER AND LOWER QUINTON: WITCHCRAFT —

The villages of **Upper and Lower Quinton**, *within a short distance of Long Compton and the ancient* **Rollright Stones**, *have a lugubrious modern, as well as an ancient, tradition of witchcraft.*

In 1945, on St Valentine's Day (the date when the Druids sacrificed to ensure a rich harvest), Charles Walton, an elderly labourer, was found murdered beneath a willow tree, a pitchfork hammered through his throat and into the soil. His body had been viciously slashed with the sign of the cross (witches were traditionally 'bled' thus to immobilise their powers).

Fabian of the Yard, arriving as chief murder investigator, found the local residents uneasy and unwilling to offer clues as to Walton's enemies. It emerged that he had been a solitary person, credited with second sight. Allegedly, he bred large toads and let them loose in the countryside, harnessed to miniature ploughs. This, said superstition, blighted crops, and the local harvest had indeed been poor in 1944.

A black dog was also found, hanged, quite near Walton's corpse — it was probably believed to be his 'familiar'. This notorious 'witchcraft murder' remains unsolved to this day.

FABIAN OF THE YARD
(on the right) was baffled by the mystery of Meon Hill

Tredington

Warwickshire SP 2543

The ancient Parish Church of St Gregory, with its slender 15th-century spire, has the remains of doorways and archways, high up on the inside walls. They date from before the Norman Conquest, when villagers had to enter the church by ladder and pull it up behind them, to escape marauding Danes. Also in the church are the old village stocks, and in the main door are marks of bullets fired in the Civil War.

Tutbury

Staffordshire SK 2129

It is small but rich in interest. The castle is one of many where Mary Queen of Scots spent part of her long imprisonment; and there are beautiful views, a museum and a nature trail. The Priory Church has a superb 12th-century west front, and several other outstanding features, including rare 16th-century leaded lights.

Other places worth a visit include the glass-works and the Chapman Sheepskin Shop, situated in a Georgian cornmill together with a traditional tannery.

Upper and Lower Quinton

Warwickshire SP 1746

Looming above the Quinton villages, to the south of Stratford-upon-Avon, Meon Hill is crowned by ancient earthworks. It is said to have been created by the Devil, who saw Evesham Abbey being built from nearby Ilmington Hill, and was so infuriated by the sight that he kicked a mighty mass of earth at it, with the intention of demolishing it. But the timely prayers of the monks caused it to fall short near the Quintons, and it became Meon Hill. Phantom hounds, a ghostly cow, and a black dog which is alleged to portend local disaster are among the apparitions reported here.

Another mystery dates only from 1945, when the body of a local farmworker was discovered on the hill, impaled by his own hay-fork. Even Fabian of Scotland Yard could not solve the mystery and to this day the killing is attributed to ritual witchcraft and the sinister influence of Meon Hill.

Uppingham

Leicestershire SP 8699

Past the town boundary on Stockerston Road, the large wood was once part of a Royal Forest, and is now in the shape of England, as can be seen from the other side of the valley.

Uppingham is full of pleasant buildings from all periods, and has a 13th-century market place and many fine hostelries with interesting signs. A 'town trail' starts at the library.

Wadenhoe

Northamptonshire TL 0083

The King's Head is the sort of country pub one dreams of, but rarely finds. Its cosy bar has a Northamptonshire skittles table, and the large gardens meander down to the river bank.

In other ways too, this is an idyllic village with a picturesque mill (now a private dwelling), a multi-sided toll house, old cottages and barns, an ancient dovecote, and a Norman-towered church, standing aloof on a hillside.

Inside the church is a sad memorial: '*Sacred to the memory of Thomas Welch Hunt, late proprietor of the estate and manor of Wadenhoe, and of Caroline his wife, eldest daughter of the Rev Charles Eusbey Isham, Rector of Polebrook in this county, who were both cruelly shot by banditti near Paestrum in Italy on Friday the third of December 1824. He died on the evening of the same day having nearly completed his twenty-eighth year. She died on the morning of the following Sunday in the twenty-third year of her age after a union of scarcely ten months. Affording an impressive and mournful instance of the instability of human happiness.*'

Wall

Staffordshire SK 0906

Wall (Roman Letocetum) lies on the Roman road of Watling Street, near the more frequented tourist attraction of Lichfield. The small Roman settlement here was a posting station on the road from London to Wroxeter and Chester. There are remains of the hostel and bath-house, and a small museum housing objects discovered at the site.

Today a little church stands at the top of the hill with a cornfield alongside.

Walsall

West Midlands SP 0198

Tunnelling under the east end of St Matthew's Church is an odd archway, which local tradition says once spanned the main road to Birmingham, although early maps disagree. A more likely explanation is that when the church was extended to the limit of the churchyard, the archway was built to provide an uninterrupted processional route round the outside of the church.

Inside the building, whose medieval walls are hidden beneath later stone cladding and plaster, slender cast iron pillars support the nave roof and galleries. Like the window tracery, they were made from the local iron of the Black Country, newly discovered when they were added in the early 19th century. Look under the hinged seats of the choir stalls for the misericords, including a pelican pecking her own breast (a symbol of Christ), a hart, and a miller with a sack.

The town also has an arboretum.

Warboys

Cambridgeshire TL 3080

This sprawling Fen-edge community was rocked in 1593 by the episode of the 'Witches of Warboys', when John Samuel, his wife Alice and his daughter Ann were tried for sorcery.

The children of Squire Throgmorton had accused Alice Samuel of being a witch and causing them to have fits. Lucy Cromwell, wife of Sir Henry Cromwell, took a lock of Alice's hair to counteract the spells. Afterwards she suffered nightmares and fits, and died within two years. After questioning — more likely torture — Alice confessed and was hanged with her husband and daughter on 4 April 1593. Sir Henry Cromwell provided for a sermon on sorcery each Lady Day, which continued until 1814.

The manor house is striking, with huge Dutch gables, and the village also has a slightly eccentric clock tower.

Warwick

Warwickshire SP 2865

There is more to Warwick than one of the finest castles in Britain. Deep below an iron ventilation grille at the Shire Hall, an ancient dungeon survives complete with foot-shackles around a central cess-pit. It can be inspected by arrangement. Nearby in Barrack Street is the original sturdy door of the town's lock-up, giving a glimpse of the forbidding interior through the cracks caused by the ravages of weather and time.

In the Saltisford area of the town, the building with two diagonal towers has recently been restored for offices, but the towers originally held early 19th-century gasholders.

Hidden between the lofty walls of the castle and the River Avon is the Mill Garden, nestling by the remains of an old mill and creeper-clad stones. Its opening times, in season, are on a notice at the entrance to Mill Street.

Victorian pillar-boxes are still to be seen in use in the town.

WARWICK: SIR GUY THE MONSTER-SLAYER — The town's lofty castle has long been associated with the great hero of medieval romance, Sir Guy of **Warwick**. Originating in France around 1200, his story was well known to Chaucer, but the first printed version in English appeared in the reign of Elizabeth I, by which time the legendary Guy had been confused with the historical Guy Beauchamp, Earl of Warwick.

Sir Guy was said to have lived in Saxon times and been, like Dick Whittington of **Pauntley**, a poor boy who made good, eventually winning the hand of the Earl of Warwick's daughter, Felice. Among his many adventures, the most celebrated was his slaying of the terrible Dun Cow of **Dunchurch**, perhaps the fairy cow which appeared at **Mitchell's Fold**, and was turned into a raging monster by having been milked dry. In the 16th century, relics of the Dun Cow were shown at Warwick and **Coventry**, and at Guy's Cliffe Chapel, Warwickshire, where her gigantic 'rib' was found.

Both 'Guy of Warwick' and the 'Dun Cow' became popular inn signs up and down the country — at Dunchurch itself there has been a Dun Cow Inn since at least 1665. Relics of Guy also abounded. In the 17th century, at Warwick Castle, his sword and cooking pot were discovered. Both can still be seen there.

WARWICK   The old castle mill and the elegantly disguised gasholders (below) — England's oldest surviving gasholders

WELLOW: MAY-POLES — Dancing round the maypole on May Day has been revived at **Wellow** and Kingsteignton, Devon. Elsewhere the custom is usually seen in a prettified form — with children plaiting ribbons round a short, continental-style pole, which seems to have been introduced in 1888 by Ruskin.

English poles, often permanent and annually refurbished, were immensely tall — St Andrew Undershaft in Leadenhall Street, **London**, was so named because the pole outside its south door was higher than the church. The periodically renewed poles at Welford-on-Avon, Warwickshire, and Barwick-in-Elmet, West Yorkshire, are respectively 70 feet and nearly 90 feet tall. Possibly connected with the ancient tree-cult (see also **Coventry** and **Tilford**), the poles may have symbolised the 'World Tree'. The Saxons had just such a symbol, called Irminsul — it was a wooden post, which Charlemagne cut down.

The Puritans likewise gave short shrift to 'this stinking idol', as Philip Stubbes called the maypole in 1583, because licentious customs attended it; the worst being the practice of staying out all night to 'bring in the May'. Of the maidens who went to the woods to cut hawthorn for decking the houses and maypoles, says Stubbes, scarce a third returned in the same condition. Cromwell banned maypole dancing altogether.

DANCING ROUND THE MAYPOLE
An illustration from the 17th century, for a ballad

Wednesbury

West Midlands   SP 0095

This is the home of the largest collection of model buses in the world, amassed in a modern suburban house in Comberford Drive, Tiffany Green. Here the Prices have more than 2600 buses from Britain and over 30 other countries around the world on display: viewing is by telephone appointment only.

From the medieval Parish Church of St Bartholomew, which shares its hilltop site with the Roman Catholic Church of St Mary, there is an unsurpassed Black Country panorama.

Weldon

Northamptonshire   SP 9289

An inland village seems a strange place to find a lighthouse — but Weldon was once surrounded by a sea of trees, the formerly extensive Rockingham Forest.

The story goes that a traveller was hopelessly lost in the forest, when he spotted the church tower at Weldon in the Woods, as it was then known. In gratitude, he paid for a lantern to be placed at the top of the tower to help fellow travellers, and it is still there.

A Roman villa with mosaic pavements was discovered close to the A42 at Chapel Field. One of the pavements is now a wall decoration at the British Steel Corporation offices at Corby.

Wellow

Nottinghamshire   SK 6666

Round a corner from Ollerton Colliery, the unexpectedly peaceful village of Wellow has a very wide green with a very tall, colourful maypole. Dancing takes place once a year, usually around Whit Monday.

The village lies on the edge of Rufford Country Park, formerly a seat of the Savile family and now open to visitors. Rufford Abbey, the house, is partly in ruins.

Wells-next-the-Sea

Norfolk   TF 9143

Despite a short strip of Blackpool-style entertainments along the quay, this delightful town remains a working port with a strong local identity. Coasters — over 200 came in 1985 — load grain from silos in the old warehouses, and unload fertilisers and timber, while clinker-built open fishing boats venture far into the North Sea for whelks which are boiled up in huge coppers in sheds by the quay.

Two miles west, there is access to miles of sand and pine-clad dunes. On a warm day, a delicious scent comes from these trees, planted by the Earl of Leicester in the last century.

West Stow

Suffolk   TL 8170

Only a few miles east of the congested A11, down the B1101 and across the ancient Icknield Way, is a quiet land of forest and heath, administered by the Forestry Commission and with several access points. A 23-mile long-distance walk through Breckland begins at the Kings Forest picnic area (there is an information office

in season) — and the less energetic can saunter over 2¼ miles of waymarked paths. Nearby is the West Stow Country Park, covering both a site of settlements since 2000BC, and a man-made hill built above a reclaimed rubbish tip. Timber and thatch dwellings have been built in the style of AD750. This Anglo-Saxon hamlet is open in summer, and crops of the Roman period are grown in sandy plots.

Whittlesey

Cambridgeshire   TL 2797

A bemused crowd gathered on Saturday, 12 January 1980, as a man dressed from head to toe in straw took to the streets of Whittlesey with morris dancers, to raise money for the local conservation society and charities.

The Straw Bear is a variation on Plough Monday celebrations. It had been suppressed at the end of the first decade of this century, after police found the antics of the bear and his supporters too boisterous.

Whixall Moss

Shropshire   SJ 4935

Hidden away astride Shropshire's northern boundary with Clwyd, the four square miles of Whixall Moss (or Fenns Moss as the Welsh side is called) form the largest survivor of the peat bogs (known locally as mosses) left after the retreat of the glaciers in the last Ice Age. Most of them are now drained off for agriculture or forestry, but Whixall Moss is cut commercially only on a small scale. It is a wilderness that the casual visitor should treat with the utmost caution. The insectivorous sundew and cranberries that creep over its spongy surface are separated from the few safe trackways by deep and often concealed ditches.

Widmerpool

Nottinghamshire   SK 6327

Be prepared for a shock on visiting the church. Visitors suddenly encounter Mrs Robertson, a frighteningly lifelike recumbent lady with pillows, made of marble. She lies in the gloom of this lovely Victorian edifice, built by her husband's family.

The Robertsons also built the eccentric-looking Hall, with its tower and 'Elizabethan' gables. Note particularly the little *cottage orné*.

Winceby

Lincolnshire   TF 3268

On the road verge alongside the A1115 three miles east of Horncastle is a large sandstone block known as the Druid Stone. It once stood in the field, and the legend was that treasure lay beneath: the Devil's hoofprints on the stone were the result of trying to move it.

Where the road dips through a hollow it is known as Slash Lane. One thousand Royalists were slaughtered here in the rout following the battle of Winceby on 11 October 1643. The Parliamentary cavalry commanded by Sir Thomas Fairfax and Colonel Oliver Cromwell had chosen the battleground well — a restricted plateau by the ravine of Snipe Dales (now a nature reserve).

WING *A burial mound lies near the maze, which may point to prehistoric origins, but why or when it was made is unknown*

Wing

Leicestershire SK 8903

Cut into the turf at the east end of the village (close to Rutland Water) is a maze, 40 feet across, the same in design as the mazes found in French cathedrals such as Chartres. Some say it was used as a punishment for wrongdoers — they would be put in the maze to find their own way out; others suggest that it was originally used for rustic games.

The village church has stout Norman pillars, with zig-zag decoration.

Winster

Derbyshire SK 2460

Years ago Arthur Mee said that Winster 'hides itself from the world'. It still does, but there are many fine houses which tell of its former prosperity as a lead-mining centre. The best, externally, is the Hall: this is now a public house and its interior has been virtually destroyed. Also of special interest is the Market House, a prominent feature of the village and a property of the National Trust.

Winster is a good centre for lonely walks on the surrounding moors. On Winster Moor is an Anglo-Saxon barrow, and there are fine views.

Wirksworth

Derbyshire SK 2854

Wirksworth, a lead centre since Roman times, went to sleep in the 1840s. The Great Barmoot Court still meets in the Moot Hall to settle disputes, and the town abounds in quaint corners, alleyways and fine old buildings. There is now a Heritage Centre, housed in the old silk mill, and a flourishing Civic Society.

The church, founded in AD653, is one of the finest in the county and filled with interest. It contains monuments to the Gell family, who claim a Roman descent, and interesting modern stained glass. The great treasure is the Wirksworth Stone — a carved Anglo-Saxon coffin lid, which may have come from the sarcophagus of a contemporary saint.

WHITTLESEY: RITUAL ANIMAL DISGUISE — *The Straw Bear, an example of ritual animal disguise ceremonies, has recently been revived in* **Whittlesey** *and other Fenland villages. The Bear celebrates Plough Monday, the first Monday after 6 January, when work on the farm was traditionally resumed and a decorated plough was dragged through the streets by young men fancifully attired.*

The coming of May is celebrated with the Hobby Horse which appears in Padstow and Minehead. 'Old Oss', covered with a hoop-shaped frame draped with black tarpaulins, wears a fearsome mask crowned with a tall, conical cap. Various attendants follow him as he prances lewdly through the streets, chasing young girls. An 'Oss' known as the Hob-Nob sometimes appears at **Salisbury** *as well, and the equivalent in South Wales seems to be the winter 'Mari Lwyd' (perhaps meaning the 'grey mare') — a horse's skull decorated with ribbons, carried on a pole by a man draped in a sheet.*

The Ram or Tup disguise which flourished in Derbyshire, Nottinghamshire and South Yorkshire during winter months, varies considerably according to ingenuity and availability of materials. A brief performance entailed an Old Man, his wife and a butcher, whose task was to catch and slaughter it

Folklorists have linked animal disguises with fertility rites and with the winter solstice — some think that the Cornwall celebrations have strayed from their original place. Collecting money always seems to have been an important part of the rituals, so perhaps the entertainment value of the disguises should not be underestimated in the search for explanations.

ROSA MUNDI *Rose of the world, said to be named after Henry II's mistress Fair Rosamund*

WOODBRIDGE: ROSES — Two poets are remembered by Omar Khayyam, a damask rose propagated from a plant growing on the grave at Boulge, near **Woodbridge**, of Edward FitzGerald (1809-83). Planted there in 1893, it was grown from seed gathered at the tomb, at Nishapur, of the 11th-century Persian astronomer and poet, Omar Khayyam.

One of the earliest and still most evocative of all old roses is the pink-and-white striped Rosa Mundi ('R gallica versicolor') said to commemorate Fair Rosamund, of **Frampton-on-Severn**, mistress of Henry II, kept hidden in a maze at Woodstock.

Gardens in and around Kelso, Borders, may still preserve descendants of 'Prince Charlie's White Rose' — possibly 'R alba maxima', the Great Double White or Jacobite Rose — traditionally planted by him in his host's garden on his road south in 1745.

Later came the 'poet's' roses, first the Old Blush or Monthly Rose, a pale pink China, introduced in about 1790, smelling of sweet peas and sometimes still flowering at Christmas — the 'Last Rose of Summer' of the Irish poet Thomas Moore (1779-1852). Elegiac, too, is Nuits de Young, a dark maroony-purple moss rose from 1851 believed to recall the 'Night Thoughts' of widowered Edward Young (1683-1765), rector of Welwyn.

WOLFERTON *A superior urinal — formerly used by kings and princes at the royal station now preserved as a museum, on the Sandringham estate*

Wolferton

Norfolk TF 6528

Through the dense woodland and thickets of rhododendron of the royal Sandringham estate, a maze of roads leads to the village of Wolferton, on the edge of the Wash. An elaborate village sign shows Fenrir, the great wolf of Viking mythology, whose howls, the locals claim, can be heard above the wind in the pine forests.

When the Prince of Wales (later Edward VII) bought the Sandringham estate in 1862, this halt on the branch railway line from King's Lynn to Hunstanton became a royal station, and through its substantial buildings came kings, queens and heads of state. Today the 'Down Side Royal Rooms' and the signal box are lovingly preserved by an enthusiast, who has a fascinating display of royal memorabilia, from train tickets to letters and from furniture to children's toys. This unusual museum (which is also the owner's home) is open from April to September, every day except Saturdays. The owner offers an entertaining running commentary to parties who make a polite request.

Wolverhampton

West Midlands SO 9198

In busy Queen Street, there survives the shop of a Victorian tea merchant which has not changed for over 150 years. This is the business of W. T. M. Snape, a Dickensian world of gas lamps, brass scales, dark mahogany counters, wrought iron fittings, and tea dust.

Tettenhall Towers, in the town's Tettenhall district, is another notable Victorian survivor. Now occupied by Tettenhall College, it was once the home of the eccentric Thomas Thorneycroft, better known as Colonel Tom. His exploits included the invention of 'flying wings', which he persuaded his butler to test by jumping off the roof; a hair-raising trip by balloon which ended at nearby Smethwick; the design of a folding carriage, a patent shower-bath and a glass umbrella; and a scheme for making warships impervious to cannon balls. He also constructed, as part of his home, a theatre in which a built-in waterfall and a fireplace capable of producing flames ten feet high provided the special effects.

Woodbridge

Suffolk TM 2749

With its new weatherboarding, the rare, working, tide-operated mill ranks high among the town's fine buildings — many built by Elizabethan merchant Thomas Seckford. Amusing masks and figures gaze down from houses built some 300 years later; and New Street has a wagon-weighing machine dating from the 1740s when an Act of Parliament levied extra tolls on wagons loaded over a certain limit.

A few miles north-west is Boulge, where Edward Fitzgerald, who translated the work of the Persian poet Omar Khayyam, lies buried.

Woolhope

Hereford & Worcester SO 6135

The village is at the heart of the Woolhope Dome, a humpy volcanic region loved by geologists. On Marcle Hill a 16th-century landslip is still called 'The Wonder'.

To the south, Chapel Farm, Yatton, has a Norman church reached by a footpath — it is administered by the Redundant Churches Fund, and is open to the public. To the east, just outside Much Marcle, Weston's Cider Mill can be visited.

Worcester

Hereford & Worcester SO 8555

The escape route of Charles II after the Battle of Worcester (1651) can still be traced through the town, and the buildings associated with it are well worth visiting. Charles's lodgings were at Rowland Berkeley's house (now a restaurant) at the corner of the Cornmarket and New Street. It was from here, as Cromwell's troops were entering through the front door, that Charles fled through the back, before escaping from the city through St Martin's Gate, then on to Boscobel. The 15th-century Commandery, headquarters of the Duke of Hamilton (in which he was killed), has been restored and now contains historical displays, including one on the battle.

Wrawby

Humberside TA 0108

The post mill at Wrawby, near Brigg, is the last remaining example in Lincolnshire, where once there were nearly 800 windmills of all types. Built in the late 18th century, it worked first with cloth sails and later, until 1940, with heavier spring shutter sails. On the verge of collapse by 1960, it was restored by vigorous local effort. The mill stands on a commanding, breezy hillside on a slight mound to enable the miller to push the tail pole when turning the 30-ton mill into the wind. Two pairs of millstones are on the top floor. The mill is open and working on certain advertised weekends in summer.

Wroxeter

Shropshire SJ 5608

The visible section of entrance wall to the bath house has always indicated the presence of a sizeable Roman town at Wroxeter, known to have become the regional capital of the Cornovii tribe Excavations show that it was a fortress, around which grew a city, Uriconium, the fourth largest

— *It seems quite right that today not only are wells dressed, but also pumps and more up-to-date sources of water. In* **Youlgreave**, *the five public taps are dressed on the Saturday nearest 24 June. At* **Wirksworth** *even the taps have disappeared, but the well-dressings are put up at Whitsuntide, in the traditional positions.*

Springs and wells have been venerated in Britain from ancient times. Although when Christianity came, the worship of well spirits was forbidden, most of the holy wells were 'Christianised' — they were rededicated to the Virgin Mary or one of the saints. The wells continued to be decked with garlands and honoured with processions at festivals.

Well-dressing in Derbyshire continues the ancient (though not unbroken) tradition. Tissington claims to have the longest record, going back to 1350, with a revival in 1615. At Buxton, well-dressing is said to have begun only in 1840, although St Anne's Well, a healing spring in the Middle Ages, has Roman origins.

Since about 1818, well-dressing garlands have been replaced by elaborate pictures made of flower petals and similar plant materials, pressed into damp clay on wooden boards.

WELL-DRESSING *at Tissington in about 1900, showing pictures of Bible scenes*

WOLVERHAMPTON *Time has stood still in the charming old shop of W. T. M. Snape, where tea leaves are displayed in small wooden chests and countless varieties of tea are blended and sold — even by the ounce if required. The fragrance is wonderful*

in Roman Britain. The forum, public baths and market hall have been excavated.

Most Roman towns have been built over by later generations, but Uriconium (like Silchester) was deserted, except for the small Saxon settlement of Wroxeter (whose church and other buildings incorporate fragments of Roman masonry). Much of the city has yet to be excavated, but the area is preserved by the National Trust and English Heritage and there is an Information Centre on the site. Finds are displayed at the site museum and at Rowley's House Museum in Shrewsbury.

Yeaveley

Derbyshire SK 1840

Outside the village and down a muddy track is what Henry Thorold has described as a 'remote and altogether mysterious place'. Stydd Hall, a Gothic building (not open to the public) is now a farmhouse, but has in the garden the remains of a chapel, which served a community of Knights Hospitallers of St John of Jerusalem.

The village is said to be the birthplace of Henry Yevele, the architect of Canterbury Cathedral and Westminster Abbey.

Youlgreave

Derbyshire SK 2164

About a mile out of the village is Derbyshire's version of the mysteries of Stonehenge and Avebury. The henge monument of Arbor Low is a fine Bronze Age ritual ring of 46 stones — not upright, but almost certainly meant to be — in a circumference of 812 feet. Other earthworks and barrows are to be found in the surrounding countryside, perhaps because of the sanctity of the ring, and there are good views.

The village, which has well-dressings, is quiet and charming. The large church contains a small effigy of Thomas Cockayne (was he a midget?) and there are stained-glass windows by Burne-Jones and Kempe. An aisle is dedicated to King Charles the Martyr; and in the churchyard is the grave of Captain H. S. Wheatley-Crowe, the eccentric Royalist who dedicated his life to the memory of 'my Royal Master' — King Charles I.

LIVERPOOL *circa* 1870.
Lime Street Railway Station. The station's cast iron roof is still there. As for the locomotives, their like can now only be seen in museums and on preserved railways. Early locos did not have cabs, since it was believed that protection from the weather would make the crews lose concentration – a notion which the crews themselves accepted for a long time

NORTHERN ENGLAND

*T*he North . . . where sheep may safely graze, even on factory roofs (or at least they did). That was at the Marshall Mill in Leeds. Where a notable local landmark is actually a huge sewage lift. That is at Christleton. Where England's last professional court jester, who went by the name of Maggoty Johnson, is buried. That's at Gawsworth. Where Wigan Pier is now a tourist attraction. Where a stone 'saddle' can be seen that was once used by fairies to ride the vicar's horse (or so the story goes). That's at Douglas, on the Isle of Man. And best of all, perhaps, where if you go to Scarborough on Shrove Tuesday you can skip along the sands with the locals.

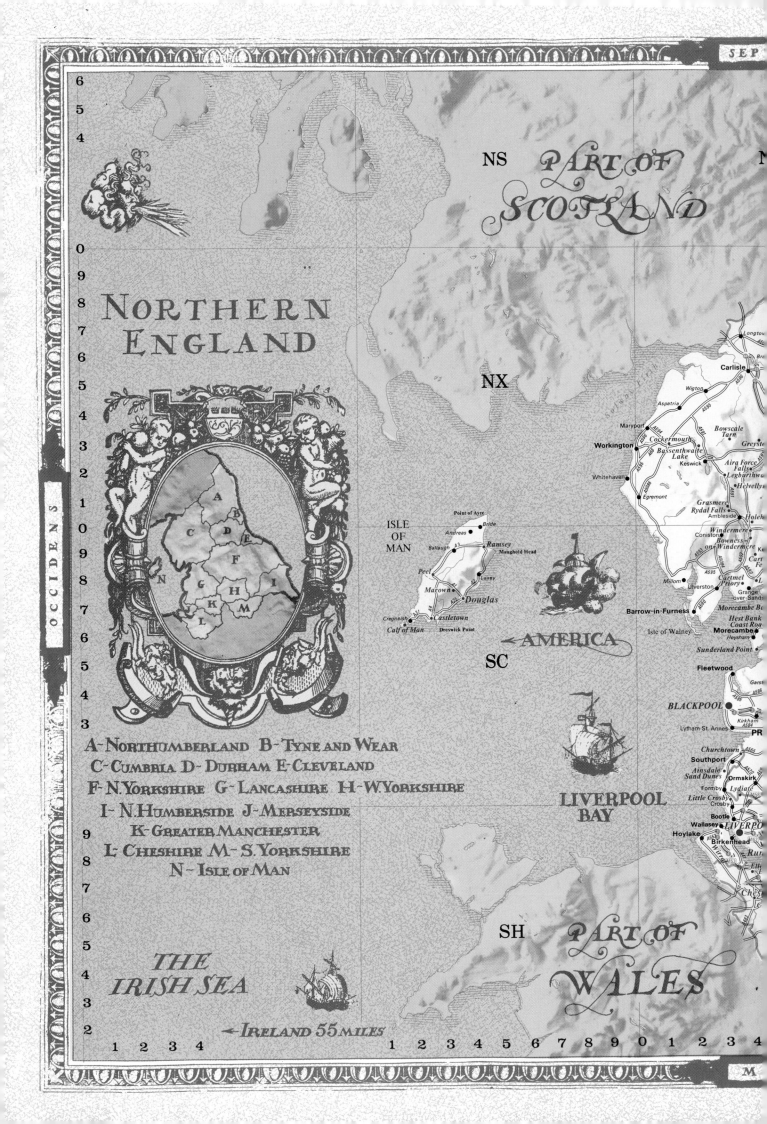

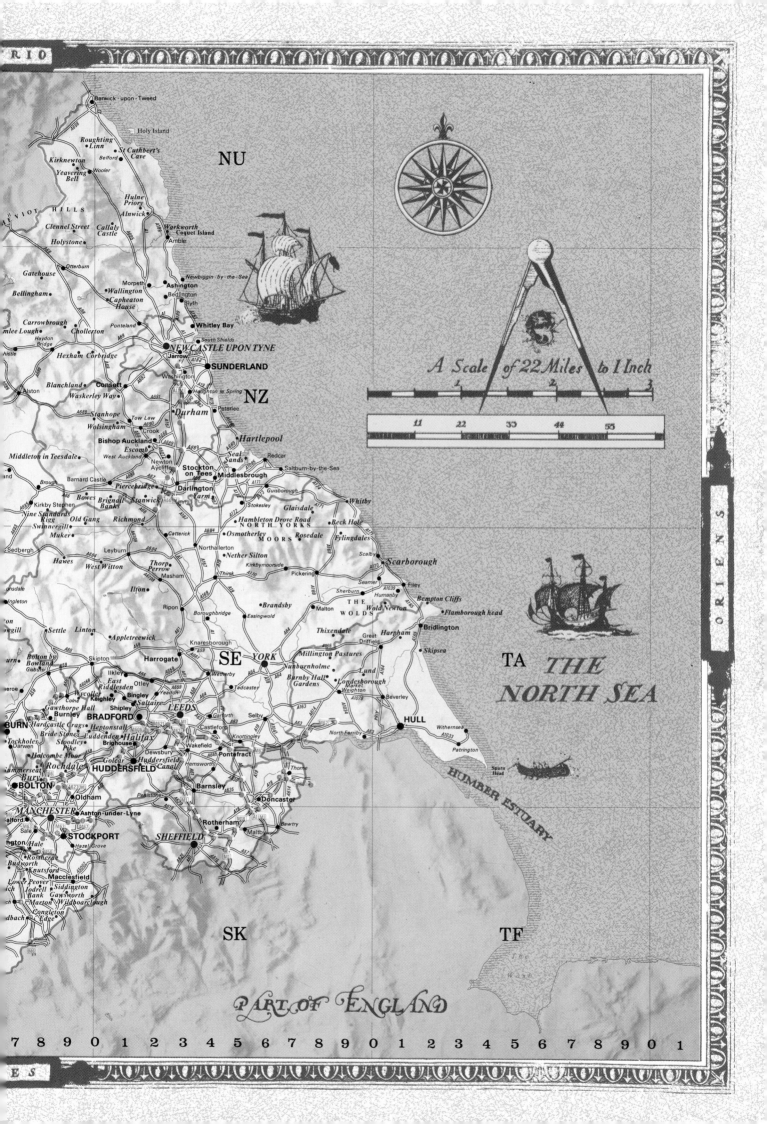

BASSENTHWAITE: A NON-EXISTENT SAINT

BASSENTHWAITE: A NON-EXISTENT SAINT — *The church at* **Bassenthwaite** *is dedicated to St Bega, whom tradition claims was an Irish princess shipwrecked off Cumbria with her nuns. When the Lord of Egremont Castle was asked by his wife to help them, he mockingly promised them as much land as snow fell on next morning. Next day, to his surprise — for it was midsummer — the ground was white with snow from Egremont to the sea. He duly built St Bees (Bega's) Priory, endowing it with land, including the site of Whitehaven.*

Suspiciously, St Bega's 'bracelet' was kept in St Bees Priory church in medieval times, and oaths were sworn on it — just as they were on arm-rings in pagan Scandinavian temples. Norsemen may have brought the custom with them when they settled in Cumbria, and 'Bega' may have been no more than a venerated arm-ring (Old English 'beag' means a ring).

If so, she is not the only non-existent saint. Two Yorkshire churches, Giggleswick and Middleham, are dedicated to St Alkelda, reputedly strangled by the Danes. Some authorities claim, however, that her name is a corruption of 'Halig Keld', for in each of these places is a holy well or 'keld'.

St Kilda is another British saint who began life as an error. Originally called Hirta, the island was later known by the Norse name of Skildir, 'shields', which by the 16th century had been corrupted to St Kilda.

Oddest of all was Wilgefortis, who owed her name and legend to a crucifix at Lucca which showed Christ in long robes with a beard. The story got about that this was really a princess crucified by her father after miraculously growing a beard to avoid being married. Because she liberated people from care, she was also called Liberada, in English 'Uncumber'. Her cult centre at Chew Stoke, Somerset, was chiefly visited by women who wanted to be 'uncumbered' of their husbands.

Ainsdale Sand Dunes

Merseyside SD 2912

Between Formby and Southport lies one of the largest areas of unspoiled duneland left in Britain. Some 1200 acres of beach, dunes and woodlands have been designated Ainsdale Sand Dunes National Nature Reserve, under the control of the Nature Conservancy Council; another 500 acres is a Local Nature Reserve controlled by the local authority. Though access is restricted in parts to specified paths, it is possible to see red squirrels, rare plants and insects and, particularly, the rare natterjack toad and sand lizard.

Aira Force

Cumbria NY 4020

The tumbling waterfalls at Aira Force close to Ullswater rarely disappoint, plunging down into a frothing pool. De Quincey relates the mysterious adventure of one Miss Smith who, on a solitary scramble, found herself 'cragfast' on a precipitous ledge. Neither retreat nor advance seemed possible; she was surrounded by perpendicular rocks 'all glazed with trickling water or smooth as porphyrie'. On the verge of despair, she saw a woman appear, dressed in white muslin, who calmly and confidently led her to safety. Although Miss Smith's white-robed saviour kept her distance, she was close enough for Miss Smith to recognise her as her own sister. Back safely on the path and pausing for breath,

AUDLEM *Medieval St James's Church, built in the Perpendicular style, and the Shambles — the former market place — at the heart of the village where the Mayor used to be chosen for drunkenness*

she looked up to thank her; but neither sister nor anyone else was to be seen. On returning home Miss Smith received strong assurances that the whole family had never stirred out that day.

Alnwick

Northumberland NU 1912

The vast castle of the Dukes of Northumberland is still a family home, a paternalistic presence. A massive town gate survives, cobblestones border the main street, and an 18th-century town hall, arcaded below on one side like a cloister, with small shops, overlooks the market place. Elegant streets, good shops, the brooding splendour of the castle and its wooded parklands combine to make Alnwick one of the most satisfying of small northern towns.

Anderton

Cheshire SJ 6475

The River Weaver and the Trent and Mersey Canal almost come together at this point — except that the canal is just over 50 feet above the river. In the early days salt, the principal product of the area, was transferred from canal barge to

river boat by a simple chute, but in 1875 the boat lift was built. The first major boat lift in the world, it was driven hydraulically, and by using watertight 'caissons' it allowed one boat to be raised from river to canal as another was lowered from canal to river. Between 1906 and 1908 it was modernised and electrically powered.

Appletreewick

North Yorkshire   SE 0560

A legend over much of Britain and Europe concerns a spectral hound, known in the Dales as Barguest. Traditionally a huge woolly dog with large eyes, it was said to appear silently by the water in a steep-sided limestone ravine called Trollers Gill, two miles north-west of this pretty Dales hamlet which sits in the shadow of Simon's Seat (1590 feet). Barguest usually ran silently beside travellers, then vanished, but left a visible trail. A Barguest incident was believed to portend some serious trouble. The legend of the Trollers Gill Barguest has been revived recently in a dance by the local Burnsall Morris men.

Audlem

Cheshire   SJ 6543

The curfew bell and the pancake bell still toll in this ancient and very attractive village. There was a time when it had its own Mayor — an honour bestowed for the ensuing year on the first man to get drunk on Audlem Wakes Sunday.

The 14th-century, massive, red sandstone church on its prominent grassy mound dominates the village and at its gate is the Shambles, a 17th-century market hall (now a shelter with seats), its roof supported by eight Tuscan columns. The narrow streets exude an air of history, and interest is heightened by the adjoining Shropshire Union Canal (the 'Shroppie'), which rises over 90 feet in a flight of 15 locks.

Bassenthwaite Lake

Cumbria   NY 2230

Close to the east shore of Bassenthwaite Lake, on the Mirehouse Estate, is the lovely Norman church dedicated to St Bega. Why this ancient building enjoys so remote a site, with no signs of settlement nearby, is a mystery. One suggestion is that the ninth-century saint herself chose the spot, either for her home or for her burial place. Certainly there are no other dedications to St Bega in England, apart from the priory near St Bees Head (where she reputedly landed on fleeing from Ireland) and the associated chapel at Ennerdale. Little wonder that Tennyson, staying at Mirehouse, should use this atmospheric setting for the opening of *Morte d'Arthur*:

'The bold Sir Bedivere uplifted him,
Sir Bedivere the last of all his knights,
And bore him to a chapel in the fields
A broken chancel with a broken cross,
That stood on a dark strait of barren land
On one side lay the Ocean, and on one
Lay a great water, and the moon was full.'

Beck Hole

North Yorkshire   NZ 8202

Quoits is still played in this charming hamlet below the edge of the moors near Goathland. The village green, with two quoits pitches, occupies a raised position near the Birch Hall Inn, where photographs of quoits teams adorn the walls. A cottage by the green has a quoit door-knocker.

The quoits are saucer-shaped iron rings with the centre knocked out. Weighing just over five pounds, they have to be thrown to land cleanly over an iron pin, in the centre of a yard-square patch of clay about eight and a half yards away. A colourful terminology includes 'ringers', 'gaiters' and 'Frenchman', and scoring is '21 up', as in bowls.

Bellingham

Northumberland   NY 8383

Local legend has it that in 1723 a pedlar called at Lee Hall, between Bellingham and Wark, begging a night's lodging. The owner, Colonel Ridley, was away, and the maid refused the request but allowed the pedlar to leave his pack in the kitchen. After he had left she saw the pack move, called for help, and a ploughboy fired a gun at it. Blood gushed forth, and the body of a small man was found inside. Obviously a robbery had been planned. Other servants were summoned, and when the robbers came they were ambushed and defeated.

St Cuthbert's Church, long and low, mainly a 17th-century rebuilding, has a stone-ribbed roof of 22 arches. An easy walk (three miles return) from the village follows a wooded glen to the beautiful waterfall of Hareshaw Linn.

OFF THE RAIL   'King' Hudson — the overweight, little-liked railway tycoon — ridiculed by Punch in 1849

BOWES: HAND OF GLORY — *A maid sitting up one night with a lady guest at the Old Spital Inn on Stainmore, near* **Bowes,** *suddenly noticed a man's trouser leg beneath her companion's skirt.*

Suspecting foul play, the maid pretended to be asleep, whereupon she saw the man — actually a robber — take from his pocket a severed hand, fix a candle on to it and light it, saying: 'Let those who are asleep be asleep, and those who are awake be awake!' When

he moved towards the door to call his accomplices, the maid jumped up, pushed him out, and locked the door behind him. She then tried to wake the sleeping family, but without success until, remembering the burning candle, she dowsed the flames with skimmed milk. This neutralised the 'spell' so that the family woke up.

The severed hand was a 'Hand of Glory', actually used as a charm by burglars in many parts of Europe. It had to be cut from the corpse of a hanged felon as it hung on the gibbet, pickled in salts and dried until it was hard. It was then used as a holder for a candle made of, among other things, a hanged man's fat, which while it burnt would render a household unable to wake.

❖

Bempton Cliffs

Humberside TA 1974

Britain's chalklands end dramatically in 400-foot-high cliffs six miles north-west of Flamborough Head. Bempton Cliffs, part privately owned, part an RSPB Nature Reserve, form the only mainland British cliff where gannets breed, and the most southerly major seabird colony on the east coast. From specially constructed viewing areas you can watch the arrogant grace of swooping gannets, the noisy flight of herring gulls, busy guillemots and kittiwakes, and the crowds of puffins and razorbills precariously perched. The scene above the restless waves is white with stirring wings, raucous with calls and cries and the air pungent with guano.

Blackpool

Lancashire SD 3035

Blackpool gets blasé about thrills and spills, but one of its newest has rescued the town's Olympic-sized Derby Pool from closure. Splashland is an import from American leisure parks and it entails zooming down translucent, water-filled polyester tubes in a twisting, spinning, whirling 300-foot journey to the pool.

Since it opened in 1984, business at the pool has boomed. You climb 68 steps up to the top of the tubes before launching yourself down the fast and furious Black Hole or the slower, gentler Knuckleduster. Even non-swimmers are safe, however.

BOLTON-BY-BOWLAND *Figures of Sir Ralph Pudsey, his three wives and the 25 children they produced between them, carved in relief on the large grey marble slab of the family's monument, in the Church of St Peter and St Paul. The names of the children are carved above them*

Blanchland

Northumberland NY 9650

In the Derwent Valley, the squares of this austerely beautiful village occupy the site of inner and outer courts of a 12th-century monastery. In about 1750, Lord Crewe, Bishop of Durham, created a new village for leadminers on his estate, re-using the old stone for neat, two-storey houses. A former monastic gatehouse, now housing the Post Office and shop, is a splendid focus. The Lord Crewe Arms with its thick walls, huge fireplaces (one with a secret chamber) and tales of the ghostly red-robed figure of Dorothy Forster of late Stuart times, is set in the former west range of the abbey.

Bolton-By-Bowland

Lancashire SD 7849

A stroll round the village church will reveal quirky details like the 'hagioscope', or leper's squint, through which sad wretches watched gentry take communion. Marks on the doorpost show where bowmen sharpened their arrows, and there are still yews round the church supple enough, perhaps, to fashion a strong longbow — said to be how the area, Bowland, got its name.

The Pudseys were lords of the manor here and Sir Ralph Pudsey's tomb commemorates his three wives and 25 children. The stone altar dates from pagan times, and the font cover is carved by the modern craftsman, Robert Thompson of Berkswell, who 'signed' his work with a mouse carving. In the woods round this appealing village are feral sika deer which call to each other in voices someone once described as sounding like 'pencils squealing on slate'.

Bowes

Co Durham NY 9913

Surrounded by wild, desolate scenery, the village straddles the Roman road beneath the towering walls of a 12th-century keep. One of the stone houses here (now a café) was the model for Dotheboys Hall in Dickens's novel *Nicholas Nickleby*. At that time it was a school called Shaw's Academy and one of the pupils, George Taylor, inspired his character Smike. The grave of this sickly 19-year-old can be seen in the churchyard. Inside the church there is a Roman slab bearing a lengthy inscription 'in honour of Emperors and Caesar . . .' and a Roman altar — testimonies to the fact that both church and castle stand on the Roman fort of Lavatrae. A gruesome custom of using a hanged man's hand — the 'Hand of Glory' — to commit a robbery, is associated with Stainmore, to the west.

Bowness-on-Windermere

Cumbria SD 4096

The inspiration of the United States flag can be seen in the east window of St Martin's Church at Bowness. In the fifth of the seven 'lights' is a section of glass showing the heraldry of local families. The second of the seven shields shows the arms of John Washington, an early ancestor of the first president of the USA. Although not easy to discern (binoculars are recommended), they represent the two red bars and three stars of the Washingtons.

Among the other church treasures at St

BRIDESTONES *is a name often given to distinctive, weathered outcrops such as those on the moor north of Todmorden. It is thought to derive from 'brinka', a Norse word meaning edge, or hillside. But what the significance may be of the devil's head carved on the rock (right), no one knows*

Martin's is a rare copy of a bible known variously as the 'Breeches', 'Braine Pan' and 'Cratch' Bible — referring to the unorthodox renderings of certain words: 'breeches' for aprons (Genesis iii; 7); 'braine pan' for skull (Judges IV; 53); and 'cratch' for manger (Luke II; 7 & 10).

Bowscale Tarn

Cumbria   NY 3331

A walk up to this wildly beautiful mountain lake was a popular excursion for Victorian tourists. The easy path from the hamlet of Bowscale is probably an old peat track or a route to a now abandoned mineral working. Bowscale is the most northerly of Lakeland's tarns and the romantic travellers of yesteryear made the trek to its wind-ruffled surface to view the legendary home of two seemingly immortal fish, and to gaze on a mountain lake which is said to reflect the stars at noon.

Another legend tells of the beautiful Ermengarde who, prompted by the Devil, received two scales from the fish and wore them on a chain next to her heart, until the chain broke and she drowned in the River Greta.

Brandsby

North Yorkshire   SE 5872

On the grass verge of a minor road along the Howardian Hills between Easingwold and Malton is North Yorkshire's only surviving turf maze. Locally known as 'City of Troy' or 'Troy Town', its origins are unknown. Roughly circular in plan and measuring 27 feet by 24 feet, it is regularly cared for and in good condition. A traditional derivation of its name is that the walls of ancient Troy were designed so that an enemy, once inside, was trapped and could neither progress further in nor yet get out again. Although it may have had some ancient significance, during medieval times and later it seems to have been used for rustic games which probably merely consisted of contests to get to the centre first.

Bridestones

West Yorkshire   SD 9326

A spectacular gritstone outcrop on the moors above Todmorden, Bridestones is a strange, deserted spot. Odd-shaped rocks rise out of the heather: climbers can be seen practising on them, and the tiny caves and passages make this an exciting natural playground for children — or adults — who enjoy scrambling. There are also several sheltered crevices, out of the wind, for picnics, and those in search of a challenge can try and find the devil's head carved on one of the rocks. Clue: look for the 'balancing' stone. (See also Congleton Edge, page 219.)

Brignall Banks

Co Durham   NZ 0511

Sir Walter Scott, a frequent visitor to nearby Rokeby between 1809 and 1832, described the scene:

'O Brignall Banks are wild and fair,
And Greta Woods are green,
And you may gather garlands there,
Would grace a summer queen.'

There is riverside scenery here to delight in all seasons, but the Banks are especially good in summer and autumn. They can be explored on the footpaths which follow both banks of the River Greta for four miles between Greta Bridge (A66) and Rutherford Bridge to the west; tiny Brignall village is a good starting-point for Brignall Banks along the north side of the river.

BRANDSBY: TURF MAZES — *Close to Brandsby is a small turf maze known as the 'City of Troy'. It is the most northerly turf maze known in England — another on Ripon Common was ploughed out in 1827.*

This has been the fate of many turf mazes — today only eight survive, some deliberately destroyed, others lost by neglect and even by Shakespeare's time 'for lack of tread . . . indistinguishable'.

Like church mazes (see **Bristol***), turf mazes were perhaps used in the Middle Ages as a substitute for pilgrimage. But they seem ultimately to descend from a cult symbol, probably representing both the Path of the Dead to the Underworld and an actual path followed by initiates. A tradition exists of a 'Game of Troy', said to have been introduced into Italy by Aeneas, and performed at funerals.*

CITY OF TROY *The turf maze at Brandsby, and (top) a diagram of 'Julian's Bower', Alkborough*

THE DEVIL *is said to have carried off the church at Over, and dropped it when the monks of Vale Royal rang their bells*

Callaly Castle: Supernatural Sites

CALLALY CASTLE: SUPERNATURAL SITES — *In the 1890s, the remains of a medieval building were found, close to* **Callaly Castle***, on Callaly Castle Hill. It may have been the 'Castle of Old Callaly' mentioned in the 15th century.*

This could explain a folk-memory that workmen tried to build the castle on the hill, but every morning found their previous day's work destroyed. Setting watch, they heard a voice saying:

'Callaly castle stands on a height,
It's up in the day, and down at night:
Build it down on the Shepherd's Shaw,
There it will stand and never fa'.'

Tales of supernatural interference with the builders' choice of a site are most often told of churches, for example St Brannoc's Church, **Braunton***. The Devil carried off the church at Over, Cheshire, but dropped it when the monks pealed their bells. A story was attached to Barn Hall, Tolleshunt Knights, Essex in which the Devil destroyed each day's work until overcome by a knight set to watch the site with his dogs. Even in the moment of defeat, the Devil snatched a beam from the building and hurled it, crying out:*

'Whereso'er this beam shall fall,
There shall stand Barn Hall!'

—◦◦⊙◦◦—

Broomlee Lough

Northumberland NY 7969

Treasure is supposed to lie in Broomlee Lough, one of three lakes north of Hadrian's Wall near Housesteads. Follow the Wall eastwards for a mile to Sewingshields Crags with their panoramic views: a castle once stood on lower ground nearby, whose owner, needing to flee hurriedly but not wanting his heirs to have his riches, put his valuables in a box, cast a spell on it, and threw it into the water. Recovery was possible only by using twin oxen, twin horses, twin youths, and a chain forged by a seventh-generation smith. It was tried once, but the chain broke, having been wrongly made. So the box remains, lying beneath a patch of water that stays calm even when the wind ruffles the surface of the rest of the lake.

Burnby Hall

Humberside SE 8247

A wonderful scene of water-lilies greets the visitor to the Hall's gardens, on the eastern outskirts of Pocklington. These gardens were the outcome of decades of work by their creator, Major Stewart, who began in about 1904. Two acres of lakes (initially stocked with trout) were planted from 1935 onwards with the lilies, which now form one of Europe's largest collections. There are some 5000 plants, of over 50 species, flowering from late May to October, but they are at their best between mid-June and early September.

BURNBY HALL GARDENS *are famed for their water-lilies. The white flowers, once sought out by apothecaries, symbolise purity of heart*

Bury

Greater Manchester SD 8010

Bury's market is one of England's oldest — and best, say locals. Held on Wednesdays, Fridays and Saturdays, it is renowned for its cheapness and sheer variety of goods.

Bury is home of the black pudding and of Simnel cake, both of which are well represented on stalls here. Lovers of his work might like to follow the example of Walter (*Love on the Dole*) Greenwood, who used to eat black pudding with hot black peas, mustard, diced dollops of bacon fat and ice cream.

Callaly Castle

Northumberland NU 0509

This 17th-century mansion is one of the county's few great houses open to the public. Externally, it is a conundrum: it has a 14th-century pele-tower, but also represents various buildings and architects from 1675 to 1835. Internally, the showpiece is the entrance hall, redecorated with superb plasterwork by the same artists employed at Wallington in about 1750. A huge ironwork spiral staircase reaches to the roof, and one of the chimneys has a false flue which was used as a priest hole. The castle lies in the Aln valley between the A697 and the Cheviots.

Capheaton House

Northumberland NZ 0380

Just off the A696, this remarkable house was the ancestral home of the Swinburnes, and the Victorian poet, Algernon Charles Swinburne, was a frequent visitor. The Newcastle architect Robert Trollop designed the present mansion (for a £500 fee) in 1668, creating a building of great character, with exuberant Baroque detail. The south front deserves the closest appraisal — especially the carved faces of Northumbrian masons which surely show a likeness to the footballing Charltons — a very old local family. The embracing parkland was landscaped, perhaps by a former neighbour, 'Capability' Brown, in the 18th century.

Carrawbrough

Northumberland NY 8671

In a field near the 'Military' road, on the site of the Roman fort of Brocolitia, a local farmer discovered, in 1949, the foundations of a Mithraic temple. It was excavated to reveal three altars which had lain buried since the fourth century. These are now in the Museum of Antiquities at Newcastle, copies having replaced them on the original site. Nearby is Coventina's Well, opened up in 1876 to reveal 13,487 Roman coins and a variety of other objects — one of the most remarkable Roman hoards ever discovered in Britain. Many of the treasures are now displayed at the Chesters Museum, three miles away.

Cartmel Fell

Cumbria SD 4188

Elusive and lonely, the 16th-century fell-side church was built originally for the herdsmen and tenants of Cartmel Priory, a few miles south. At one time people tramped or rode here — women riding pillion behind their husbands — but today they come by minibus, to see St Anthony's beautiful east window, the three-decker pulpit and a quaint epitaph to Betty Poole. The surrounding hill country is scattered with tucked-away sheep farms and fine old houses.

Cartmel Priory

Cumbria SD 3778

The striking tower of Cartmel Priory, set diagonally on a square base, is the most memorable feature of this ancient and picturesque building. But curious observers will find the church has other claims to their attention. A

CARRAWBROUGH: SACRED WELLS — *Near* **Carrawbrough** *on Hadrian's Wall is Coventina's Well, a spring in a stone tank once covered by a temple, in which it served as a central shrine. Amongst the objects which have been found in it are a sculpted slab showing the goddess reclining on a floating leaf, and worshippers' offerings, mainly brooches, bronze coins (nearly 14,000) and pins.*

When the Romans arrived in Britain and encountered native Celtic cults, they followed their customary play-it-safe policy of propitiating the local gods.

These included the many in-dwelling spirits of the rivers and springs, often goddesses, like Verbeia of the Wharfe, whose altar, dedicated to her by Roman legionaries, can still be seen in Ilkley church, West Yorkshire. At Buxton, known in Roman times as Aquae Arnemetiae ('the Waters of Arnemetia'), the goddess's temple may have stood near the Roman bath, at what was later St Anne's Well.

The modern practice of throwing coins into a wishing well is a relic of ancient worship. The traditional offering at holy wells was often a pin, usually bent (a ritual 'killing' which rendered it harmless). A number of wells are still called Pin Well, notably Pin Well, Wooler, Northumberland.

memorial to William Myers on the north wall records that he died on *30 February 1762*. The effigy of Lord Frederick Cavendish, assassinated in Phoenix Park, Dublin, in 1882, stands in the north-west corner of the nave. A brass memorial relates that Rowland Briggs gave sufficient money to distribute bread to the parish poor every Sunday and on the shelves of the wooden 'bread cupboard', rolls and loaves are usually to be found. Among the interesting misericords is a fine carving representing Alexander's Flight, showing how Alexander the Great cunningly enlisted the help of two large birds by harnessing them to a basket which they pulled high into the air. He encouraged the birds by dangling a spear baited with meat in front of their beaks.

Chester

Cheshire SJ 4066

King Harold lived at Chester after the Battle of Hastings — or so a local tradition maintains. It is said that he settled as a recluse in the Anchorite, a small rectangular house perched on top of a sandstone outcrop. This supposed former hermit's cell can be seen down a footpath alongside the Church of St John, leading to a riverside walk which is called the Groves.

The church is half in ruins, but the rest was restored in the last century. The Norman nave with its massive columns is most impressive — of cathedral-like dimensions, this actually was the cathedral church of the Chester diocese from 1075 to 1102.

But first and foremost, Chester is a Roman centre built around the Roman fort of Deva. As well as the best-known evidence of their tenure — on view at the Grosvenor Museum, the Roman Gardens (where part of an excavated bath-house heating system and columns have been re-erected) and in a partly excavated amphitheatre opposite the Visitor Centre — there are less obvious ancient reminders, exciting to seek out. Roman parts remain of the city's encircling walls: east of the North Gate, Roman facing rises some 16 feet high, and a length of the original Roman wall can be seen in Kaleyards. The inside

CHESTER The medieval crypt of Brown's of Chester now serves a modern cup of coffee. Subtle lighting shows up the old stonework

angle turret of the south-east corner of the walls near the Newgate is also Roman and between Nun's Road and the Roodee racecourse, near the stands, are the remains of a Roman quay.

Across the medieval Old Dee Bridge at Handbridge, on the south side of the river in Edgar's Field, are the remains of a quarry dating from about AD100, when the Romans largely rebuilt their wooden fortress in stone. In a niche in the rock face is a sculpted figure, very weather-worn now but probably unique. It is thought to be a representation of the goddess Minerva, whom the quarry workers may have worshipped.

Medieval crypts from the 13th century (largely restored in Victorian times) still turn up in unlikely places: the 'Crypt' coffee bar, for instance, in Brown's of Chester, the department store in Eastgate Street, and in Bookland, the bookshop in Bridge Street. Some medieval arches form part of the first floor of the department store of Owen Owen, also in Bridge Street.

Among the unusual features of the town, look out for the sedan chair porch (with a door on each side) at Sedan House. It is one of a number of Georgian houses in Stanley Place, close to Stanley Palace in Watergate Street, which is occupied by the English Speaking Union. This is open to view and dates from 1591.

Chollerton

Northumberland NY 9372

Chesters Roman fort supplied the pillars for the unusual wooden-spired church, and the font was a Roman altar. A low building by the lych-gate was a stable for parishioners' horses, a coffin-house and later a post office. In the churchyard may be seen the headstone of John Saint, a fuller, which bears a fine representation of a fulling-mill together with tools of the fuller's trade. More of a farming community than a village, Chollerton lies north of Hexham.

CLOOTIE WELL *on Culloden Moor, where people tie a rag or 'clootie' to a nearby tree after a wish has been made. The clootie must be left to rot*

CONGLETON: WAKES WEEKS — *The annual Wakes once celebrated throughout Britain were parish festivals held on the anniversary of the church's consecration or on the feast-day of its saint.*

They were so-called because originally the parishioners 'waked' or watched in the church on the eve of the festival. At **Congleton** *in Cheshire, where this fell on Lammas Day, the feast of St Peter-ad-Vincula, the congregation was summoned at midnight by lads who ran through the streets wearing belts hung with bells, whose jangling supposedly represented the clanking of St Peter's chains.*

The most important event of the next day in most places was the Rush-bearing, which unlike the vigil managed to survive the Reformation. (The Church of St Mary Redcliffe, **Bristol***, is still strewn with rushes to receive the Lord Mayor at Whitsun.) The secular entertainments accompanying the festival also often survived — dancing, feasting, bear-baiting, races, wrestling and other sports.*

The festival became increasingly secular and possibly more rowdy. In Congleton the old bell-belts passed into the hands of a family of sweeps who would parade the streets with them at the head of a cheerful drunken procession. When the family split into rival groups disputing ownership of the belts, each Wakes Day brought its fights, until in the mid-19th century the belts were confiscated by the Corporation.

ABOVE *The bearing of rushes to church often marked the first full day of Wakes Week*

DARESBURY *A dormouse, a Mad Hatter, a March Hare and other Wonderland characters are celebrated in stained glass in the village where Lewis Carroll was born*

Christleton

Cheshire SJ 4365

On the side of the A41 Chester-Whitchurch road at Christleton, three miles east of Chester, is a structure which puzzles many passing motorists who have long looked upon it as a landmark. It resembles a conical-roofed dovecote on top of a very tall pole. This is Christleton Sewage Lift — an outsize lavatory flush, in fact. Local sewage once drained into a large underground tank and at intervals the automatic flush would force it up into the Chester city sewage system.

Churchtown

Merseyside SD 3618

An ancient village (and conservation area), Churchtown has two attractive old pubs and Meols Hall, home of Colonel Roger and Lady Fleetwood-Hesketh, Lord and Lady of the Manor. Southport's Botanic Gardens are also here, with a museum.

Claughton

Lancashire SD 5666

England's oldest working bell (1296) tolls in the little church in this village, whose name is pronounced 'Claffton'. The bell was a feature of the original Church of St Chad, built in 1100, but most of that was obliterated in the rebuilding of 1815. The chief idiosyncrasy of the village is a 17th-century mansion which was split in two — half being rebuilt on the other side of the valley, where views were considered better, and half staying where it was.

Clennel Street

Northumberland NT 9206

For centuries Upper Coquetdale was a convenient way through the Border Hills, and Clennel Street one of its best-known tracks. Developed by pioneering Cistercian monks in medieval times, it saw its busiest years during 18th-century droving days. Today it makes a splendid walk with a fine sense of following in the footsteps of past generations: follow it northwards from Alwinton to Wholehope,.

Cockermouth

Cumbria NY 1230

Birthplace of William Wordsworth, the area is less boastful of two other remarkable 'sons'. At the outlying hamlet of Eaglesfield, a carved stone plaque above the door of a cottage reads:
'John Dalton DCL LLD
The Discoverer of
The Atomic Theory
Was born here 5th September 1766
Died at Manchester 27th July 1844'
On the farmhouse of Moorland Close, another

plaque marks the birthplace of Fletcher Christian, leader of the mutiny on the Bounty.

Traditional English food and more recent culinary fashions are brought together at 7 Market Place in the town: set in the wall high above a Chinese takeaway is Cockermouth's historic 'Butter bell', which was formerly rung on Market Days.

On the car park near the information centre a memorial reads:

> 'On 17th May 1568
> There came to this house
> as a guest of Henry Fletcher Esq
> Mary Queen of Scots
> On her journey from
> Workington to Carlisle.'

Every year, during the third week in August, the Cockermouth Festival is celebrated. Concerts, exhibitions, cattle auctions and sheep fairs are held.

Congleton Edge

Cheshire   SJ 8760

Just south of Bosley Cloud looms the megalithic burial chamber known as the Bridestones, dating from about 3000BC and once covered by a cairn, said to be over 100 yards long. The portion which remains consists of a chamber, six yards long and divided into two compartments. The forecourt has been lost in the undergrowth. (Not to be confused with the Bridestones above Todmorden — see page 215.)

Corbridge

Northumberland   NY 9964

A friendly little town, given half a millenium's start over neighbouring Hexham by the Roman supply-base and fort of Corstopitum. The Romans also provided the massive squared stones for the Saxon tower of the church, and for the 13th-century Vicar's Pele in the churchyard, now housing the Tourist Information Centre.

The small, central market place has a cast-iron cross of 1814 bearing the Percy crescent. Nearby runs a pant (water-conduit), while the adjoining streets show neat 18th-century stone houses.

Daresbury

Cheshire   SJ 5782

Watch out for the White Rabbit and the Dodo, the Dormouse and the March Hare — and the Mad Hatter, the Knave and Queen of Hearts, the Mock Turtle and the Cheshire Cat. They are all here, in All Saints Church, in a stained glass memorial window to Lewis Carroll, the writer of *Alice in Wonderland*.

Charles Lutwidge Dodgson, as he was known to the everyday world, was born in Daresbury parsonage on 27 January 1832. His father was the incumbent from 1827 to 1843, so young Dodgson spent his formative years in and around this little village. The window was erected with subscriptions from all over the world to mark the centenary of his birth.

The tall tower in Keckwick, on the other side of the dual carriageway, marks the Daresbury Laboratory of the Science and Engineering Research Council.

Durham

Co Durham   NZ 2742

The Norman cathedral and castle must not be missed, dominating as they do this medieval citadel on a rocky peninsula, high above the wooded, looping Wear. But as well as these sights, seek out the field path south-west of Prebend's Bridge: it climbs a hill to Durham Observatory, with the reward of a magnificent panorama to distant majesty beyond fields and woodlands. The city's riverside paths should also be tried: they yield their own surprises, in beech green or autumn gold.

To the south of the city, among the new University buildings, is the Gulbenkian Museum of Oriental Art, a unique collection ranging from the Egypt of the Pharoahs to Japan.

East Riddlesden Hall

West Yorkshire   SE 0742

Ghostly traditions of the house tell of a Grey Lady who 'comes to people in trouble' and of the Elizabethan Rishworth cradle which is said to rock itself every New Year's Eve.

A mid-17th-century manor house on Keighley's northern edge, East Riddlesden Hall has fine panelling, plasterwork and furnishings, with two splendid examples of rose windows in the north and south porches — they were regarded in Yorkshire then almost as architectural badges of rank. Across the fishpond are two barns, the larger of around 1640–50, stone-built, with two round-arched cart entrances and a superb timber-framed interior.

DURHAM: CURIOUS TENURES — *When a Bishop of* **Durham** *first entered his diocese, it was customary for him to cross the Tees at Croft Bridge, or the ford at Neasham, where he would be met by the Lord of the Manor of Sockburn, riding a horse and carrying a falchion in his hand. He would then present this falchion — a kind of short sword — to the Bishop, and receive it back from him again as his feudal service.*

Many medieval tenures — the terms on which land was held from an overlord — were purely nominal. Manors could be held by the service of presenting a sword, as at Sockburn and Bishop Auckland or perhaps a horn as at Boarstall, Buckinghamshire, or by 'flower rents' of a garland or single flower. Such services often had legends attached to them. That of Sockburn was said to have been won by Sir John Conyers, Lord of the Manor in the 14th century, when he slew a dragon. At Bishop Auckland, a boar was killed — the Pollard Brawn — as it was at Boarstall.

The ceremony of the falchion at Sockburn is first mentioned in connection with the death of Sir John Conyers in 1396. It was performed for the last time in 1826, after which the falchion was deposited in Durham Cathedral Treasury.

ABOVE   *The falchion presented as rent to the Bishop of Durham, on display in Durham Cathedral*

ELLESMERE PORT:
ART IN WOOD — *The
unique life-style and culture
of the narrowboat people is recalled
in **Ellesmere's** Boat Museum,
including their distinctive Canal
Art — the roses and turreted
castles traditionally painted on the
boats themselves, and on utensils,
such as watercans and lamps.*

*England has a long tradition of
carving and painting wood, to
which medieval funerary effigies
(see **Danbury**) and trade signs
belong. It expressed itself too, in
the semi-protective figures made
for houses and ships. The Valhalla
Museum, Tresco, among others,
preserves many ships' figureheads,
often thought of as their 'luck'.
They ranged from classical heroes
such as Ajax to the jolly Jack Tar,
wearing the first uniform issued by
the Navy to ratings, of HMS
Cruizer (1852), and the witch
from Tam o'Shanter on the Cutty
Sark. Like figureheads, windvane
figures on Norfolk wherries often
referred to the vessel's name —
hence the 'Jenny Morgans' in
Norwich's Bridewell Museum.*

*A crowned lion symbolising
power and aggression was once
almost standard on smaller ships,
and on the Red Lion, Martlesham,
Suffolk, an early 18th-century
example has been used as a corner
bracket to support the oversailing
storey. This continues the medieval
tradition of adding carved 'grotesques' to buildings with the intention of warding off evil. Surviving
grotesques are the chained devil of
Stonegate, **York**; and in Essex
the bearded man on The Maltings
farmhouse, Terling, and the
cloven-footed 'Hag' on George
Boote's House, Felsted.*

Ellesmere Port

Cheshire   SJ 4077

In the early years of the 19th century Thomas
Telford built a dock system and warehouses here,
where the Ellesmere Canal reaches the River
Mersey. Ellesmere Canal Port was soon
shortened to Ellesmere Port, and the canal, (under
the ownership of the Shropshire Union Railways
and Canal Company) became the Shropshire
Union — or 'the Shroppie'.

Despite a disastrous fire in 1970, which
devastated Telford's spectacular arched warehouses, the top basin and other buildings have
been most imaginatively brought to life again as
the Boat Museum. It has over 50 narrow boats of
all descriptions, and the restored Island Warehouse holds a splendid exhibition depicting life
on the canals in their heyday. Special events and
exhibitions are held throughout the summer
season.

Escomb

Co Durham   NZ 1829

In unpromising surroundings two miles west of
Bishop Auckland stands one of the best-
preserved Saxon churches in England. Restored
with tactful restraint and care, its tall, narrow
nave and chancel are little changed from the
seventh-century years of Bede and Cuthbert.
Some of the masonry is older still, many large
stones having come from the Roman fort at
nearby Binchester.

Flamborough Head

Humberside   TA 2670

This most renowned east coast promontory has
two lighthouses. The older, near the 11th hole of
the golf course, is octagonal in section and was
built in 1674 as a coal-fired beacon tower. The
'new' lighthouse of 1806, built in nine months by
John Matson of Bridlington, using no scaf-
folding, still stands 214 feet above the sea, its
light visible 21 miles away.

Church Cave and Smugglers' Caves to the
north, their interiors colour-veined and cold, can
be visited on foot at low tide; to the south, Robin
Lythe's Cave has its roof almost 50 feet above the
ground. Many more caves are accessible only by
boat, ideal for the busy trade of smuggling
carried on here for centuries.

Fylingdales

North Yorkshire   SE 8898

Space-age geometry has given the North York
Moors National Park its most distinctive feature.
The 'golf balls' of the Fylingdales' Ballistic
Missile Early Warning Station have, since 1964,
been scanning for missiles as well as monitoring
the hundreds of satellites and other space debris
circling the earth. Each 'radome', weighing
around 100 tons, is 154 feet high, 140 feet across,
and made of 1646 laminated glass-fibre panels
mounted on a steel frame. Inside each is a highly
sensitive, rotating radar dish 84 feet wide with a
range of 3000 miles.

Ellerbeck Bridge on the Whitby-Pickering road
is a fine viewpoint. Nearby a moorland path leads
to Lilla Howe, a prehistoric tumulus, with the
seventh-century Lilla Cross — a reminder of
early Christianity in the 20th-century scene.

Gatehouse

Northumberland   NY 7988

Three centuries of conflict up to 1603 brought a
proliferation of defensive structures to the Border
country. At Gatehouse, a hamlet in upper
Tynedale, two rare 16th-century 'bastle-houses'
still stand on opposite sides of the road. One is
splendidly preserved: a two-storey building with
thick walls, a ground-floor entrance for livestock, and an external staircase leading to an

GRASMERE *The island where the Wordsworths baked fish and boiled a kettle on an open fire. From a rowing boat, the minute-looking lake feels vast*

upper door for humans. Bastle-houses were temporary refuges during the short but sharp Scottish raids. They must once have been desirable assets, but few have survived.

Gawsworth

Cheshire   SJ 8869

'There is nothing in Cheshire to compare with the loveliness of the church above the pool and the three great houses and one small house grouped round two further pools,' declared Sir Nikolaus Pevsner in the Cheshire volume of his *Buildings of England* series. No-one who has seen Gawsworth would argue with that. The beautiful black-and-white timbered Gawsworth Old Hall dates from the 15th century, though it has been the seat of the lords of the manor since the Norman era. Mary Fitton, of the Fitton family who lived here from 1316 to 1662, is one of those said to have been Shakespeare's mysterious 'Dark Lady of the Sonnets'. Now owned by the Richards family, the Hall is open to the public.

Across the road, the Old Rectory is also 15th-century, and the present Rectory dates from 1707 when it was built as a school. The other building, the New Hall, was begun in 1707 for Lord Mohun — but building was interrupted in 1712 when his lordship figured in a remarkable duel against the Duke of Hamilton: both adversaries were fatally wounded. It is described in Thackeray's *Esmond*.

Along a lane off the Macclesfield road lies Maggoty Johnson's Wood, with the grave of the eccentric Samuel Johnson, England's last professional court jester, who was employed at the Old Hall until his death in 1773. One tombstone bears his own epitaph, another alongside bears a later one by Lady Harrington who did not approve of Johnson's own words.

Gawthorpe Hall

Lancashire   SD 8034

Gawthorpe Hall, a stately home belonging to the National Trust, resonates with the personality of Rachel Kay-Shuttleworth, descendant of the Reverend Lawrence Shuttleworth who built the hall in 1600. Rachel, a much-loved woman, who started lecturing at the National Gallery when she was only 17, assembled here a collection of embroidery and needlework from all over the world. It is now used by scholars who come to Gawthorpe to study. Rachel Kay-Shuttleworth died in 1967.

Glaisdale

North Yorkshire   NZ 7705

A single, graceful, stone arch of Beggar's Bridge spans the River Esk in its wooded valley near Glaisdale station. A worn stone records the date, 1619, and 'TF' — for Thomas Ferries. This farmer's son fell in love with Agnes Richardson, daughter of a rich landowner who gave consent to the marriage only on condition that Thomas became wealthy. Ferries forthwith went to sea, fought against the Armada, joined Drake in piracy around the West Indies, and did become rich, only returning to England and Glaisdale in 1592 after six years away.

Golcar

West Yorkshire   SE 0915

Terraces of houses cling tenaciously to a steep hillside facing across the Colne valley, narrow streets slide between high gables of dark stone, and scores of weavers' cottages retain their large, top-floor windows which illuminated weaving-rooms. Once these would have been bedrooms, but in around 1800, the new three-storey houses had upper-floor loomshops cut off from the rest of the building, with separate entrances from outside staircases at the back. This was a noted centre of the weaver's trade, and the Colne Valley Museum recreates the domestic and working conditions of 1800 in a group of three converted weavers' cottages.

Grasmere

Cumbria   NY 3307

A row out to the island in the middle of Grasmere is a guaranteed way of finding solitude even on the busiest days of summer. Stamina, rowing boats and time are all limited, resulting in this blissfully peaceful spot lying right in the heart of Lakeland. The Wordsworths and their friends much enjoyed such excursions — often catching pike from their boat to supplement their picnic. Dorothy writes of seeing some charred stones on the island — the makeshift fire-grate of a previous visit when she had boiled a kettle there and baked fish.

Also in this most popular area is the coffin stone, a large flat-topped boulder by the road, a couple of hundred yards south of Dove Cottage, close to Grasmere. This is one of several stones on which hearses were rested, during the arduous journey through the hills to the final resting-place in the churchyard. Such journeys were often very long in areas like the Lake District, where one parish church served a large and sparsely populated area.

ESCOMB: ANGLO-SAXON CHURCHES — St John's Church at Escomb *was little-known and neglected until 1875, when the Reverend Hoopell recognised it for an Anglo-Saxon building. It is one of over 200 pre-Conquest churches that have been found in the 19th and 20th centuries, many of them concealed by later additions. St Lawrence's Church, Bradford-on-Avon, Wiltshire, for example, was part school and part cottage before being 'found' in 1858.*

England's oldest church may be St Martin's, Canterbury, *where, according to the Venerable Bede, the King of Kent's Christian wife used to pray, before St Augustine's mission to the English in AD597. Parts of it may be late Roman.*

Anglo-Saxon ground plans varied from the single cell of Jarrow (see Newcastle upon Tyne) *through the double cell with elaborate apsed buildings with lateral chambers (as at* Bradwell-on-Sea *and Escomb), and occasionally aisles, as at* Hexham *and* Wing, *Buckinghamshire.*

Wing also has one of the few surviving crypts — others are at Brixworth, Northamptonshire, and Hexham — originally used to house relics.

Towers became prevalent only during late Saxon times (from about 885 to 1066). Earl's Barton, Northamptonshire, Barton-on-Humber, Lincolnshire, and Sompting, Sussex, have exceptionally grand examples.

ST LAWRENCE *Bradford-on-Avon. The long-forgotten Saxon church was rediscovered in 1858*

HAMBLETON DROVE ROAD: DROVERS' ROADS

*— For centuries the most important long-distance travellers, the drovers, used the **Hambleton Drove Road**, driving huge herds of cattle between **Durham** and **York**. They were regarded, in the days when few people ventured far from home, with a mixture of admiration and suspicion.*

*Some drovers, such as the Highlander Rob Roy, immortalised by Sir Walter Scott, and the Welsh outlaw Twm Shon Catti of the **Doethie Valley**, attained almost legendary status as roving adventurers. Travellers of all sorts would join the procession for companionship and safety — country lads eager to see the world, and women such as Jane Evans, who went under the protection of the cattlemen to join Florence Nightingale and sail to the Crimea to be a nurse.*

The cavalcades of animals, urged on with the traditional cry 'Hoo-hoo!', were accompanied by cattle dogs, generally highly intelligent. They were often left to find their own way home from the south, when their masters stayed on for the harvest, and as late as the mid-19th century could be seen making their unaccompanied way on the long roads to the north.

SCOTTISH DROVERS *Travellers in years when few went far from home; drovers were held in awe*

Great Budworth

Cheshire SJ 6778

This is one of those villages that may seem inexplicably familiar. Film and television companies looking for ready-made 'olde worlde' sets frequently come here, as did the BBC for *Hinge and Bracket*, renaming the village 'Stacton Tressell'. It is a very picturesque place. The oldest building is the beautiful Church of St Mary, which dates from the 14th century, and there are timber-framed houses (and cottages in School Lane) which date from the 17th century.

One of the lords of the manor in the first half of the last century has left examples of his poetry above the main door of the George and Dragon, and over the village spring, where High Street meets the main Northwich road. Also to be seen are words of wisdom carved in the wooden rails round the pub — not all of them are as old as they seem.

Greystoke

Cumbria NY 4330

The 5000 acres of Greystoke Park are said to form the largest tract of countryside in England which is not crossed by public roads or paths. Encircled by walls, the park and castle are only revealed to the public on occasional charity fête days. But something of the spirit of this former home of the 11th Duke of Norfolk can be enjoyed at the nearby 'folly' farms of Bunker's Hill and Fort Putnam, picturesque testimonies to his eccentric temperament. As a Whig aristocrat he named them after events in the American War of Independence, to inflame his Tory landowning neighbour, Lord Lonsdale of Lowther Castle. Similarly he dubbed one of his plantations 'Jefferson'. Another farm, Spire House, is likewise whimsically picturesque. It was built by the Duke to house a tiresome tenant, a member of an obscure religious sect, who maintained that churches were unnecessary for worship. All three follies seem to function happily today as normal farmhouses. They can be seen from the road, but are not open.

Hale

Cheshire SJ 7786

The Childe of Hale was a giant, reputed to have grown to a height of nine feet three inches. His name was John Middleton and he lived from 1578 to 1623. In 1620 he wrestled at the Court of James I and is mentioned in the diary of Samuel Pepys. The cottage where he was born still stands and his grave can be seen in the churchyard.

Interesting 17th-century thatched cottages add to the pleasures of this small village on the edge of Liverpool Airport (moved into Cheshire in 1974 as the other, much larger Hale was moved into Greater Manchester) and there is a walk to the disused lighthouse on Hale Point.

Since the 14th century, Hale has elected its own Lord Mayor from among its Freemen, an honour for a long time confined to tenant farmers but now bestowed more widely for services to Hale.

Halifax

West Yorkshire SE 0825

Britains's most ornate chimney must be Wainhouse Tower, completed as a dyeworks chimney in 1875, and overshadowing the district called Kings Cross. It has a conventional circular brick flue surrounded by a stone casing, with a 403-step spiral staircase between leading to balconies — intended as observation platforms — at the top, 250 feet above ground. Since the structure was never connected to the dyeworks and thus never used as a chimney, perhaps John Edward Wainhouse designed it as a folly.

The Piece Hall is renowned as a 315-room cloth market. Built in 1779 round an open quadrangle, it has recaptured something of its old purpose, with an open-air market on Fridays and Saturdays, and the colonnaded galleries house shops, a Textile Museum and a Modern Art Gallery.

HAWES *Nineteenth-century nodding head toys in the Upper Dales Folk Museum. Most of the exhibits were collected by Marie Hartley and Joan Ingilby during years of research into Dales life*

Hambleton Drove Road

North Yorkshire   NZ 4702

Probably part of a route used by prehistoric people, this moorland ridgeway along the crest of the Hambleton Hills saw its busiest days from the early 18th century to about 1870. Along it plodded Scottish drovers taking their cattle to the markets of York, the Midlands and London. From above Swainby to south of Sutton Bank it lies within the North York Moors National Park, and part of this 15-mile stretch is still unmetalled — a broad, green track inviting walkers to experience its well trodden, windy heights, with wide, sweeping views to the west.

Hardcastle Crags

West Yorkshire   SD 9730

The 'Crags' are actually rather insignificant out-crops on the northern side of the Hebden Water a few miles from Hebden Bridge, but the area is full of interest. Miles of footpaths thread the woodlands here, including the Slurring Rocks Nature Trail. Natural history, wildlife, and industrial archaeology are nicely balanced; oak and ash woodland includes stands of beech and pine, and in late spring a bluebell carpet contrasts with the previous autumn's tawny-tinted bracken.

In the 19th century, dams and weirs on the Hebden Water controlled the water supply to mills like three-storey Gibson Mill of 1800, still to be seen with its cottages. Originally water-driven, it was converted to steam in about 1860, but closed down at the end of the century.

Much of the valley is owned and managed by the National Trust, with car parking at Midgehole in the valley-bottom and at High Greenwood beyond Heptonstall.

Harpham

Humberside   TA 0961

Six miles south-west of Bridlington, the village has two notable wells. The sound of drumming from the 'drumming well' was said to foretell deaths in the St Quintin family, the lords of the manor (their monuments are in the church). A drummer boy was drowned in the well by a St Quintin, whereupon his mother said he would drum the family to their deaths. Also here is a healing well, dedicated to St John of Beverley, who by tradition was born in Harpham. Some say its waters calm wild animals.

Hartlepool

Cleveland   NZ 5032

The town represents a 1967 marriage between 'old' Hartlepool, and its mid-Victorian neighbour, West Hartlepool, which by 1900 was Britain's fifth-largest shipping port. 'Old' Hartlepool is a quirky mixture of old and new. Its greatest glory is the early 13th-century St Hilda's Church, close to the site of a seventh-century monastery where a Northumbrian princess, Hilda, presided over a community of monks and nuns. A good length of medieval town wall of 1322 now fronts the harbour; near the breakwater early 19th-century houses recall past prosperity. A plaque near the lighthouse commemorates 16 December 1914, when three German warships bombarded Hartlepool, killing over 100 and injuring over 200 civilians.

HELVELLYN   *Red Tarn, the lake embraced by Striding Edge and Swirral Edge on the eastern flank of the mountain — once thought to be England's highest*

Hawes

North Yorkshire   SD 8789

With a splendid situation and a busy livestock and open street market every Tuesday, Hawes is a classic market town. Near the National Park Information Centre in the old station yard is the Upper Dales Folk Museum, with displays on cheese-making and other skills, and the Rope-works where visitors can see ropes being made. A sense of challenge and purpose emanates from the Pennine Way, passing through the town: here, northbound walkers are not yet half-way along their punishing trail.

Helvellyn

Cumbria   NY 3415

Dramatic, glaciated scenery abounds on Helvellyn, a mountain which artists and photo-graphers have been attracted to since the earliest days of tourism.

In April 1805 Charles Gough, a young gentleman artist, fell to his death from the dangerous cliffs above the mountain lake of Red Tarn. His body was not discovered until a full three months later, guarded by his loyal pet terrier. That same year the eminent physicist, Humphry Davy, accompanied Walter Scott and William Wordsworth on an ascent of Helvellyn. They were all much moved by the tragedy, and Scott and Wordsworth (unknown to each other) both composed poems on the incident. Wordsworth particularly admired Scott's poignant lines describing the dog's dashed hopes on these forlorn and windswept slopes:

'How long didst thou think that his silence was
     slumber?
When the wind waved his garments, how oft didst
     though start?'

HELVELLYN: FAITHFUL DOGS — *A remarkable instance of canine fidelity occurred in 1805 at Helvellyn, when a man named Gough died while crossing the mountains. The body, discovered after three months, was still being guarded by his emaciated dog.*

More widely remembered is the poignant tale of Greyfriars Bobby, a Skye terrier who returned to his master's grave every night for 14 years, and has been immortalised in book and film, as well as by a statue in Edinburgh.

Dogs have also taken a more active part both in avenging their owners' death and in protecting their lives. In 1361 a duel took place in Paris between a dog and his master's murderer. The dog won. Three centuries later, a Royalist, Henry Bishop, hiding from the Roundheads during the Civil War, took refuge with his dog in a priest's hole in Parham House, Pulborough. A single bark would have betrayed them, but despite the long confinement, the dog stayed silent.

ABOVE   *So devoted was Prince Rupert's dog, Boy, that enemies claimed sorcery was involved*

HEXHAM:
SANCTUARY — *The
ancient abbey of
Hexham was founded by Wilfrid
of Ripon in AD674. One of the
few surviving features of the
original church is the bishop's
throne, known as St Wilfrid's
Chair, or the Frith (Saxon for
'peace') Stool. It was an important
refuge: all churches held limited
rights of sanctuary, but at
Hexham they were particularly
strongly enforced. Anyone who
harmed someone sitting in the
Frith Stool faced the death
penalty, and canons regularly
watched from the choristers' robing
room at the top of the Night Stair
in order to open the church door to
fugitives.*

*A so-called Sanctuary Stone in
Liverpool can be seen in the
road outside the National
Westminster Bank, which has a
plaque on its wall explaining the
stone. Ely Place, London, was a
sanctuary: not even in the Old
Mitre pub, in the alleyway of Ely
Court, could anyone be arrested.
Adel (see Leeds) has a sanctuary
handle on the door.*

*Another London church, St
Mary's in Eversholt Street, was
recently the scene of a claim for
sanctuary, when a Greek Cypriot
couple spent several months there
in 1985, in an attempt —
ultimately unsuccessful — to
avoid deportation.*

⊷◦⊷◦❈◦⊷◦⊶

ABOVE *A fugitive at the Frith
Stool, Hexham, where sanctuary
rights were strongly enforced*

Heptonstall

West Yorkshire SD 9827

This austerely handsome hill-top village of dark
stone houses is full of architectural delights and
surprise views across steep, wooded valleys to
patterned hillsides beyond. The buildings of a
domestic weaving community of the 18th and
19th centuries have survived almost intact; there
are rows of weavers' houses, a 16th-century
former Cloth Hall, a 17th-century Grammar
School, now a museum, an octagonal Methodist
Chapel in continuous use since 1764, and a full
churchyard, shared by the ruined 15th-century
church and its proud, mid-Victorian successor.

Hest Bank coast road

Lancashire SD 4766

'The world stretcht out' was an old way of
describing the wondrous views along this bit of
Lancashire's coast north of Morecambe and up to
Silverdale. From Hest Bank the seven-mile span
of sand over the bay to Kents Bank looks eerie
and near. This is where a guide takes organised
groups of ramblers over the quicksands when
tides are right. (See Morecambe Bay, page 243).

The road slides below Warton Crag, a great
limestone face where caves inhabited by Bronze
Age settlers have been discovered. The crag itself
was an Armada beacon and hilltop fort, and has a
'bride's chair' (a limestone ledge) where newlyweds raced to sit down first. It was supposed to
decide who would be boss.

Hexham

Northumberland NY 9364

An abbey town turned lively market town, it
grew up round St Wilfrid's great seventh-century
church, whose crypt has masonry from Roman
Corstopitum. In the present building (mainly
Early English) the unique Night Stair was used
by medieval monks for very early services.
Violent days of Border strife are recalled in the
formidable 14th-century Moot Hall, and the
Manor Office, later a prison. The town spread
round the Market Place to meet the needs of local
trade and farming, and an 18th-century covered
Shambles and some good Georgian and Victorian
shop-fronts contribute to its charm.

Holcombe Moor

Lancashire SD 7618

Ellen Strange's cairn, just off the Rossendale
Way, marks where she was murdered by her
lover, Billy. Spotted with Billy while calling at
the Whitehorse Hotel in Helmshore for a pint on
the way home from Haslingden Fair, Ellen was
never seen alive again. Billy the Pedlar confessed
his guilt at his trial in Lancaster, where he was
later executed. His body was hung on a gibbet at
Bull Hill, half a mile from the murder scene, and
the cairn was raised from stones brought by
people visiting the spot.

Nearby Stake Lane was named after the gruesome practice of tethering bulls to stakes while
terrier dogs attacked them. It was said to
tenderise the meat. Also here is Robin Hood's
Well — a peculiar structure no-one seems able to
explain. A Robin Hood festival was celebrated
annually in Bury, until 1810 another of several
North Country reminders of the hero.

Holehird Gardens

Cumbria NY 4000

Visit soon after breakfast or in the early evening
to rediscover the atmosphere of the gardens as a
secret, half-forgotten place. (At other times, the
official gardens of the Lake District Horticultural
Society become rather thronged, being deservedly popular.) These are good times of the day
to admire the pocket handkerchief tree — *Davidia
involucrata*, and in the twilight, especially, this fine
specimen deserves its other name — the ghost
tree. During the summer, the five-inch-long
bracts are very conspicuous.

Originating in China, the first tree was
brought to England in 1897. Holehird's tree must
have been planted about this time, and is one of
the largest in the country.

A guidebook available here shows the vista
from the fountain, with some of Lakeland's most
evocatively-named peaks indicated on the
viewfinder: Crinkle Crags, Pike O' Stickle,
Pavey Ark.

Holystone

Northumberland NT 9502

In Coquetdale above Rothbury, tall beeches and
rhododendrons shelter a quiet, clear pool,
rimmed by 18th-century masonry. Lady Well,
source of Holystone's water supply, is reputed to
have been the site of early seventh-century
baptisms, when Northumbria was the cradle of
northern Christianity. A nunnery was founded
nearby five centuries later. Beyond the village the
Forestry Commission's car park is a good base
from which to enjoy short waymarked walks in
plantations and deciduous woodlands. ·

Huddersfield Narrow Canal

West Yorkshire SE 1416

A three-and-a-half-mile walk along the towpath
of the Saddleworth section of this canal — now a
recreational waterway — reveals an interesting
succession of buildings and scenes illustrating the
industrial archaeology of the upper Tame valley,
particularly from 1790 to about 1850. Bridges,
wharfs, locks, a viaduct, cottages, mills, and the
entrances to the Standedge tunnels can be seen. A
Local Interest Trail leaflet, obtainable from the
Saddleworth Museum, details the route.

Hull

Humberside TA 0929

Since May 1983, masts and sails have restored the
city's skyline to something of its glory 170 years
ago, when Hull merchants and the Corporation
completed their ambitious dock projects. Until
recently, the old docks and their Victorian warehouses were redundant, but in the past few years
a continuous conservation and redevelopment
programme has been restoring the core of the
'Old Town'.

Most of this Conservation Area lies south and
east of Queen's Gardens, itself created from the
18th-century Queen's Dock. A walk through the
streets around Holy Trinity Church gives
glimpses of Hull's seafaring importance and
prosperity — Trinity House, the Humber Pilot's
Office, fine Georgian houses in the High Street
including Wilberforce House, Maisters House
and Cowle House. Off Alfred Gelder Street is

the Land of Green Ginger, a street name redolent of Eastern trade, while north of Queen's Gardens the Charterhouse, and Albion Street/Jarratt Street/Kingston Street conservation scheme continue the revitalisation.

A fine warehouse of 1745 at High Street's northern end (converted with great restraint into apartments) is another sight to stir the imagination — as perhaps the commercial buildings dominating the city's centre will do in years to come.

Hulne Priory

Northumberland   NU 1615

Ruins of a rare, 13th-century Carmelite friary lie by the river, hidden in the walled parklands of Alnwick Castle. No vehicles are allowed in the Duke of Northumberland's estate, but a free permit from the estate office allows you to walk through. The walk to the ruins, and their glorious situation, are ample reward for the effort involved. Unusually, the friars never migrated to a town, and the site's isolation probably saved it from plunder at the Dissolution.

Ilton Temple

North Yorkshire   SE 1878

This Stonehenge is not scheduled as an ancient monument. In a woodland glade four miles west of Masham, Squire William Danby of Swinton Hall made this folly of standing stones, loosely grouped around the entrance to a little hillside cavern. A curved monolith on a raised central platform is too symmetrical to be convincing, but the whole concept is delightfully whimsical, in the best folly traditions. It looks very ancient, but dates from about 1820.

Ings

Cumbria   SD 4498

The fast modern highway which now by-passes the church at Ings has in recent years cut it off from the itinerary of present-day travellers. Not so in the 18th century, when the inlaid Italian marbles of the altar floor brought admirers from far and near. Entering the church, one is immediately struck by the similarity of the interior to the far better known City of London churches.

A brass plaque on the wall by the pulpit tells in verse the 'Dick Whittington' story of the local boy made good: Robert Bateman left the tiny hamlet of Ings to become a successful merchant (according to Wordsworth he 'grew wondrous rich'), but paid homage to his humble origins by financing the building of this splendid church in 1745. The marble paving was imported from Leghorn, which was where Bateman lived.

An old painting hanging by the entrance confirms the church's former position on the main coach road, now just a byway. If the church is locked, a key may be obtained from the nearby cottages.

ILTON TEMPLE   *Trilithons encircle a monolith and mark the entrance to a cave — looking like a charming miniature Stonehenge, the 'Temple' was built only in the early 19th century*

HEXHAM: A DAY IN THE LIFE OF A MONK — *In Dark Ages monasteries throughout Europe, the monks lived spartan and orderly lives centred round a daily sequence of prayer.*

In summertime at Anglo-Saxon **Hexham***, a monk would rise at about 1.30 am for the night office, 'Nocturns' (modern Matins) at 2am, followed at daybreak by the first of the day offices, Matins (modern Lauds).*

He might thereafter have a chance to rest or meditate, then at 6am came Prime, at 8am Tierce, followed by the daily Chapter meeting, and at 11.30, Sext.

The first meal of the day was at noon, after which he might again get some rest or the opportunity for private prayer before None at 2.30. But somewhere in between Tierce and Sext, None and Vespers in the evening, he had also to fit in five hours of intellectual or manual labour.

The second meal of the day came at 5.30, then the last day offices, Vespers, at about 6pm and Compline, at 8pm. The monk would go to bed in the common dormitory at about 8.15pm.

There were many additional daily services, among them High Mass and the Offices for the Dead, and feast days and holy days brought special services and ceremonies.

The Isle of Man

The independent Isle of Man — it has its own parliament and laws — is, like all Celtic countries, a magical hunting-ground for seekers of the legendary and bizarre. Few natural features in this beautiful island with its windswept hills and thickly-wooded glens are without a story. The native population are a quiet but proud race who have managed to hold on to many of the twists of imagination and delightful turns of phrase inherited from their ancestors.

The Calf of Man

SC 1565

Now a wildlife sanctuary belonging to the National Trust, this stormy but very beautiful islet has one modern lighthouse and two old ones, one of them built by the father of Robert Louis Stevenson. On the island was found the Calf Crucifixion, one of the finest pieces of early Christian Manx art, and a relic known as 'St Patrick's footprint' is preserved there. An odd structure, a long narrow trench with two transepts, is attributed to Thomas Bushell, a scholar of Balliol College, Oxford, and follower of Francis Bacon, who voluntarily exiled himself for three years to the Calf in 1621. He was a man of some scientific ingenuity and it has been suggested that he intended setting up a telescope on the island.

Castletown

SC 2667

Castle Rushen, dating from the 12th century, is the second of the island's great castles: there is a legend of a monster-haunted tunnel linking it with the Cistercian monastery of Rushen Abbey at Ballasalla, two miles away. In the square outside its walls the last Manx witch, with her young son, was burned alive in 1617. A house on the opposite side of the square was the home of Captain Quilliam, who steered the *Victory* for Nelson at the Battle of Trafalgar.

Bridge House, the tall, brooding building (now owned by an insurance company) next to the footbridge across the harbour, was the home of the Quayle family, leading citizens involved during the 18th century in both banking and smuggling. A concealed stairway and passage lead to a strongroom that was used in the former activity, and there is a secret cellar, below high water mark under the front lawn, used in the latter. An armed yacht, the *Peggy*, was also found some years ago: it had been walled up in the boathouse.

An odd grave in Malew churchyard, about a mile from the town, has a heavy cat's-cradle of chains hanging above it. There is no well authenticated explanation, but they were probably either to deter body-snatchers or to prevent the occupant getting out — hence the popular local name of the 'Vampire's Grave'.

Douglas

SC 3876

A curious edifice on a tiny island in the middle of Douglas Bay (rowing boats may be hired for a trip there in the summer) is the Tower of Refuge built by Sir William Hillary, founder of the RNLI, for the use of sailors wrecked on the treacherous St Mary's Rocks.

Harold Tower, one of the castellated private houses on Douglas Head, was said until recent years to be haunted by the ghost of a young

servant girl. She was seen by occupants on stormy winter nights, gazing from the window of a first-floor bedroom: she would then turn, run 'through' a wall and be heard to rush down a staircase no longer in existence, to fall with a terrible crash to the floor below.

The Nunnery Mansion House (strictly private) a mile from the town on the Old Castletown Road, is built near the site of a nunnery founded by St Bridget. Her well is still in the grounds, with a portion of the ancient chapel walls.

Another mansion, Kirby Park, a mile inland on the Saddle Road, Braddan, was the home of Colonel Mark Wilks, Governor of St Helena at the time of Napoleon's imprisonment. Flowers are still placed regularly on the grave of a black slave of his, Samuel Ally, buried in the nearby Braddan graveyard. Old Kirk Braddan is an extraordinarily picturesque church.

Protruding from the wall, also in Saddle Road, is the large and curiously shaped stone which gives the road its name. Legend has it that it was the saddle which was used by a fairy to ride the Vicar of Braddan's horses during the night, and which turned to stone at daybreak.

North of Douglas is the village of Onchan, where Captain Bligh (of *Bounty* fame) was married in 1781.

PEEL *St Patrick's Isle, reached by a causeway, where stand the ancient ruins of Peel Castle and the Cathedral of St German, said to have been appointed by St Patrick*

DOUGLAS *The fairy saddle of Braddan, used for nocturnal gallops by the Little People — the same ones perhaps as the dancing, fungus-hued creatures reported by a Manxman in 1932*

MAROWN *Romantically overgrown and not well known even to local people, Eyreton Castle was the work of an eccentric Methodist preacher, and saw service as a boys' school. It is now in ruins*

DOUGLAS *Groudle Glen (to the north) was 'the' place to visit for the Victorians. A waterwheel and narrow gauge railway can still be enjoyed*

valley the figure of a man is crudely picked out in white quartz — his horse is similarly depicted nearby. Nobody seems to know how long the figure has been there, but it is known as the 'Deemster in the Wall' and is said to have been built to commemorate a Deemster (Manx judge) who perished in a snowstorm as he was riding to court over the mountains.

Peel

SC 2484

Across a causeway from the town of Peel lies St Patrick's Isle, colonised more than a thousand years ago and today one of the most fascinating archaeological sites in Europe, with layer after layer of pagan and Christian buildings and burials in and around the ruined castle and cathedral. A mysterious handprint can be seen below St German's Cathedral, in the crypt, a noisome place used as a prison for centuries. The castle was supposed to have been haunted by the Moddey Dhoo, a gigantic black dog.

On the headland above is a windswept tower known as 'Corrin's Folly', built as a mausoleum for a Freechurchman who objected to being buried in bishop-consecrated ground. His friends were forbidden to bury him here: there are differing stories as to whether they did or not.

At Lag-ny-Keilley, the remains of an early Christian chapel on spectacular cliffs to the south of Peel were said to be haunted by the ghost of an illegitimate child born to a local heiress. It died soon after birth and she buried it, un-baptised, in the ruined chapel. A tiny ghost carrying a lighted taper haunted the coastline until enterprising fishermen, spotting it from the sea, called out a blessing and a choice of baptismal names. It disappeared gratefully, never to be seen again.

The area of Dalby became briefly famous in the 1930s when a local farmhouse, Doarlish Cashen below Dalby Mountain, was said to be haunted by one Gef, a talking mongoose. It attracted the attention of the psychic investigator Harry Price, amongst others, and he wrote a book about it, *The Haunting of Cashen's Gap*.

Marown

SC 3278

Eyreton Castle, Crosby, is an extraordinary crenellated ruin in a grove of trees — although what was to have been its imposing entrance lodge is clearly visible on the main Douglas-Peel road. It was built in the 1830s by an eccentric Methodist evangelist, the Reverend Robert Aitken, who had heard the voice of God from a nearby mountain top. He operated the Castle briefly as a boys' school according to his own precepts, but then left the island to become a renowned saver of souls in the West Country.

St Trinian's Church is a picturesque, roofless ruin a little further towards Peel down the same main road. The story is that it has never been covered, the roof being repeatedly thrown off by a buggane, a species of Manx monster who disapproved of Christianity.

Slieu Whallian, the steep wooded hill above St John's, provides a magnificent view of the Tynwald Hill, on which the annual Tynwald Day ceremony is held; it was also traditionally a place of punishment down which witches were rolled in spiked barrels.

In a drystone wall high above the East Baldwin

Ramsey

SC 4694

The handsome stone tower on the hilltop above the town (worth a climb for the view towards Scotland on a clear day) is the Albert Tower, erected to mark the spot to which Prince Albert climbed in 1847 while Queen Victoria stayed resolutely on board the Royal Yacht.

The family homes of two notable sons of Man were not far from Ramsey. Fletcher Christian, the second main protagonist in the *Bounty* saga, was descended from the Christian family of Milntown (not open to the public) at the foot of Glen Auldyn; and Myles Standish, Pilgrim Father of the *Mayflower* and military leader in New England, was born in a house on or near the site of the present Ellenbane, on the Road of the Ayres in Lezayre. Above Milntown looms Sky Hill, scene of the great Viking defeat of the Manx in 1079.

Cashtal yn Ard, above the Cornaa valley south of Ramsey, is a spectacular megalithic gallery grave, one of the largest in Britain. Pottery and stone fragments were found in early excavations, as well as pieces of bone, including part of the skull of a young woman.

ISLE OF MAN: MODDEY DHOO — *Because Sir Walter Scott used the story in 'Peveril of the Peak',* **Peel** *Castle's Moddey Dhoo is the most famous phantom Black Dog in Britain.*

The Moddey Dhoo was a big black curly spaniel that, in the mid-17th century, visited the guardroom so regularly at night to sit by the fire that the soldiers grew used to him. However, they would never risk meeting him alone, and after dark always went in pairs along the passage near his lair. A soldier who defied this precaution in his cups, returned after a commotion had been heard, and died three days later without speaking. The passage was blocked up and the Moddey Dhoo was never seen in the castle again.

Peel Castle is the only place apart from Blickling Hall, Norfolk, where the Black Dog has habitually appeared indoors — though in 1577 he did blast through the Suffolk churches of Bungay and Blythburgh, leaving burn-marks (still visible) from his talons on Blythburgh's north door.

Known in East Anglia as Shuck, perhaps an old word for 'demon', he normally haunts lonely roads, bridges and cross-roads, and is thought in origin to be the guide of the dead on their journey to the Underworld. Hence in most places he is feared: it is an ill omen to see him, certainly fatal to speak.

⚬⚬❀⚬⚬

ISLE OF MAN: THE BUGGANE — *The roofless grey stone church of St Trinian's,* **Marown,** *used to be called Keeill Brisht, 'the Broken Church', because, so it was said, it was never finished.*

Every time anyone attempted to roof it, a buggane (a Manx bogey), with coarse black hair and eyes like torches, rose up out of the ground and demolished it.

Finally, a tailor called Timothy sat in the church all night (with his sewing) to confront the buggane — tailors were traditionally good at dealing with fairies. The buggane duly heaved itself out of the floor bit by bit in order to frighten him, but Timothy just sewed on. This put the buggane in a rage and when Timothy finally leapt out through a window — just before the roof came crashing down — it chased him to Marown churchyard. Unable to enter sacred ground, it tore off its head and threw it at him over the wall.

The head burst into flames, the buggane disappeared and has not been seen since. Still, no one likes to risk putting a roof on St Trinian's, and unbelievers are shown Timothy's thimble and scissors in a pub on the Peel to Douglas road.

KNUTSFORD: SAND IN MAY — *In Knutsford, the pretty custom of decorating the pavements with patterns of coloured sand — flowers, love-knots, and so forth — was practised in the 19th century to celebrate a wedding.*

The story explaining the custom, and also the name of the town, is that King Cnut once forded the river (hence 'Knutsford') and, getting sand in his shoes, stopped to shake it out. Just then a wedding-party went by, and he wished the couple as many descendants as there were grains of sand in his shoe.

Although primarily a wedding-custom, sanding was also employed on special occasions, and is now practised only on Royal May Day, which, despite its name, may be any convenient date in May or early June. Patterns of the traditional brown and white sand are made on the pavements outside St John's Church, in front of the Sessions House, and outside the May Queen's house and some of the shops.

The practice of sanding is an ancient one, connected with the belief that complicated patterns ward off evil spirits. In Shropshire, to the end of the 19th century, doorsteps and hearthstones were decorated with designs made with the dye from elder leaves, to bring good luck and keep the Devil away.

LANCASTER *Atkinson's tea and coffee importers in China Street — one of the many places specialising in good traditional fare, in a city better known for its castle and Georgian houses*

Jodrell Bank

Cheshire SJ 7971

Difficult to miss, this giant radio telescope is 250 feet in diameter. It is one of the world's largest steerable instruments and its purpose is to detect radio waves from the depths of space. Those intrigued by this bizarre feature of the landscape can go inside: there is a Visitor Centre with an exhibition of astronomy, optics and space, including weather maps from Meteostat and a demonstration of satellite television. There is also a planetarium, gardens set aside for picnics and the 30-acre Granada Arboretum, containing thousands of trees and shrubs.

Kirknewton

Northumberland NT 9130

Below the Cheviots' northern slopes a few miles west of Wooler, Kirknewton Church has an un-usual tunnel-vaulted chancel, with side walls only three feet high, while those of the south transept rise directly to a pointed vault. One of two rare carved reliefs depicts the Adoration of the Magi in which the Wise Men seem to be clad in kilts. The churchyard has graves of British and Commonwealth airmen from the nearby airfield at Milfield, killed in action, and of German air-men killed when their bomber crashed in the Cheviots in 1943.

Knutsford

Cheshire SJ 7578

This ancient town is known as Mrs Gaskell's *Cranford*. She lived in a house called 'Heathwaite' on what is now Gaskell Avenue, and her grave can be seen in the graveyard of the quaint 17th-century Unitarian Chapel, which has two outside staircases leading to the balcony.

Less familiar is the work of Richard Harding Watt, an eccentric Manchester glove manufac-turer, who was wealthy enough to employ four architects to execute his whimsical ideas for buildings and houses which have echoes of archi-tectural styles seen on his travels in Spain, Southern Italy and the Near East. In King Street

are his Gaskell Memorial Tower and the fanciful Ruskin Rooms, while in Legh Road Watt built a number of houses, including one for himself called 'The Old Croft', which Sir Nikolaus Pevsner described as 'the maddest sequence of villas in all England,' in the *Cheshire* volume of his *Buildings of England* series.

The town's Royal May Day Festival is one of the oldest of its type in the country. No mechanical vehicle is allowed to take part in the procession and the ancient custom of patterning the pavements of certain streets in brown and white sand still prevails. Characters include 'Highwayman Higgins' and 'Jack-in-the-Green', and the May Queen is crowned on the heath.

Lancaster

Lancashire SD 4761

Scores of writers and artists have documented Lancaster's history and architecture. But few have mentioned its food, which is a pity — because Lancaster specialises in excellent examples of the county's traditional fare. In its lively market can be found delicious Lancashire cheese in four strengths: mild, medium, tasty and tasty tasty. Also here are Morecambe Bay shrimps, while down Penny Street is Kinloch's, the traditional pork butchers. People come from miles around for home-made pies, sausages, hams, bacon and black pudding. For Lune smoked salmon, visit St George's Quay where they smoke it traditionally, and for a time-stood-still-at-1900 experience, try Atkinson's tea and coffee importers in China Street. Blends are concocted to order, and if unsatisfactory can be taken back. The shop is also worth visiting for the sight of the old tea bins and roasters.

Back at the market, Grandad Daly's fish shop is locally famous for 'fish from the Bay', and specialises in local salmon, shrimps, plaice and whitebait. The grandson, Douglas, still wears clogs and a striped apron. 'Not for any trendy reason,' he says, 'they're just the most suitable.'

Leeds and around

West Yorkshire SE 3033

In the city a mill masquerades as an Egyptian temple, in the country the real Robin Hood might have lived, and in between an ancient church has a sanctuary handle nearly a thousand years old

An attractive feature of the city is its arcades, two of which, Thornton's Arcade and the Grand Arcade, contain magnificent mechanical clocks made by the city firm of William Potts and Sons. Busy strangers shopping in Thornton's Arcade may fail to notice, high above them, the 'Robin Hood' clock installed in 1878. Here a gallery of figures from Sir Walter Scott's novel *Ivanhoe* strike the hours and the quarters.

Even more impressive is the clock installed in the Grand Arcade in 1898. Two armoured knights emerge to strike the quarters with battle-axes. But the main attraction comes when the hours sound and a door opens to admit a pageant of figures that pass before the onlooker then vanish through another aperture. A guardsman appears and salutes, a Scotsman in tartan bows, as does an Irishman complete with shillelagh. Then comes a Canadian and finally a turbanned Indian. An inscription beneath the clock reminds spectators that 'Time and tide wait for no man'.

Other interesting marks of the city's Victorian past are the key stones on some of its older buildings. As new buildings replace the old, these ornaments become fewer, but Burley Road still bears a fine crop of carved heads on a terrace of 13 houses.

Sheep used to graze, though not always safely,

it seems, on the roof of the Marshall Mill, *Holbeck* — an amazing construction on the lines of an Egyptian temple. It was built around 1840 by Ignatius Bonomi, who had spent eight years in Egypt studying the temples of Karnak, Edfu and Philae. The extraordinary choice of design is explained by the vogue enjoyed at the time by all things Egyptian, due to Napoleon's campaigns in Egypt. Even the chimney was designed to resemble Cleopatra's Needle. But the Marshall Mill was not just a curiosity. A great, single-storey building adorned with magnificent pillars, it had a flat roof equipped with 66 glass windows to provide lighting and ventilation for the whole building. The roof was covered with earth and grass (kept neatly trimmed by the sheep) to help warm the workroom below. All went well until — so the story goes — one of the sheep fell from the roof into the machinery. The Marshall Mill is still in commercial use.

On Cardigan Road in *Headingley*, once a village but now a suburb of north-west Leeds, is a quaint-looking structure consisting of two small, battlemented towers with narrow apertures like arrow slits, and, between them, a wall with an arched entrance in the centre flanked by what appear to be two low, square doors. These are the 'Bear Pits', the only relic of the old Leeds Zoological and Botanical Gardens, which, in early Victorian days, was one of the places to

BEARS *Victorian Bear Pits and 17th-century bear baiting*

LEEDS: BEAR BRUTALITY — A souvenir of the national fascination with bears can be seen in **Leeds**, where the old Bear Pits are still intact. Sole survivors of the once-famous Leeds Zoological and Botanical Gardens, they still have the two towers from which the bears could be viewed in safety.

The Pits had no provision whatsoever for the animals' comfort, but even these were an improvement on earlier 'entertainments', when bears, sometimes blinded, would be set on by bulldogs and men with whips. Occasionally a bear would escape, causing havoc among the crowd, but such accidents were speedily terminated with the death of the creature.

Bear-baiting was a popular English sport from Norman times onwards, and carvings depicting it are to be found in churches.

It was banned by Parliament in 1835, but continued secretly for some time, discreetly ignored by the law. Even when it finally died out, there were still the dancing bears, whose performances continued into the 20th century.

LEEDS *Sheep grazed here, on the roof of the Marshall Mill, and there used to be a roof garden*

LEEDS: ROBIN HOOD — *South-west of* **Leeds**, *a stone in the park of Kirklees Hall is said, since at least the 16th century, to have marked the grave of Robin Hood, the most renowned of the medieval outlaw heroes (see* **Doethie Valley** *and* **Nesscliffe**). *He is also remembered by Robin Hood's Well, so-called by 1622, on the A1 south of Barnsdale Bar (north-east of Barnsley), and at Hathersage is Little John's Grave.*

Despite the strong tradition of Nottinghamshire, West Yorkshire seems to have been the likeliest home of the outlaw. The earliest ballads refer to 'Robin of Barnsdale', and go back well before any Sherwood Forest traditions. But **Nottingham** *had a 'Robynnode Close' by 1485 and a Robin Hood's Well by 1500. Sherwood Forest has acquired a Larder, two Caves, a Grave, a Well and a Stable, none of them traceable before 1700.*

Other reminders of the outlaw abound all over England. Robin Hood's Stride, between two stone pinnacles south of **Birchover**, *testifies to his giant-like prowess. Burial mounds were called his Butts (for archery practice) at Otterford in Somerset, Bromfield in Shropshire, and numerous others. His cave is at Creswell Crags, Derbyshire, and there is the Bay named after him near* **Whitby**. *The earliest known relic of Robin, the 'Stone of Robert Hode', mentioned in a deed of 1422, stood in the fields of Sleep Hill between Skelbrooke and Wrangbrook — but has now vanished.*

ABOVE *Yorkshire's Robin Hood tradition seems stronger than that of Sherwood Forest*

ADEL *'And behold a door opened in heaven . . .' The church porch illustrates St John's vision in the Book of Revelations*

visit during the hard-won leisure time of citizens of Leeds. When the construction of Cardigan Road was being planned it was clear that the end was in sight for the zoo, which closed in 1858. But the path of the road was not impeded by the Bear Pits and so they remain, a pit in which 'wild beasts' were viewed by onlookers safe in the tops of the towers. Leeds University students, a great many of whom live in Headingley, felt a certain affection for the Bear Pits and undertook their restoration.

A collection which may be unique is housed at the Abbey House Museum at *Kirkstall*, north-west of Leeds. Its theme is the era of the 'chimney boys' who used to be sent up chimneys to dislodge the accumulated soot. This collection of over 4000 models, prints, books and pamphlets is the work of Dr S. A. Henry, and is called the Henry Collection. Dr Henry amassed it while he was engaged in research into the causes of industrial cancer. Some exhibits show that far from being horrified by the sufferings of the 'climbing boys', the Victorian saw them as picturesque, sometimes cherubic figures suitable as decorations for tiles, egg-timers and ornaments. The collection is often on tour but may be viewed on application.

In the churchyard of *Otley* (ten miles north-west of the city centre), is the large, elaborately carved memorial to the victims of a disaster which cost the lives of several navvies working on the construction of the Bramhope Tunnel of the Leeds and Thirsk Railway from 1845 to 1849. The memorial, which perfectly represents the entrance of the tunnel, with its mock castle design, complete with battlements, was erected 'at the expense of . . . the director . . . agents, sub-contractors and workmen', some of whom may have felt a sense of guilt, since the disaster is said to have happened on Good Friday. It was seen locally as divine retribution on the men for working on such a holy day.

The ancient days of sanctuary are recalled by the great bronze ring on the door of St John the Baptist Church at the village of *Adel*, on the northern outskirts of Leeds. One of the most perfect Norman churches in Yorkshire, it is renowned for the south doorway, fantastically carved with zigzag or chevron markings, beaked heads and the figure of Christ in majesty flanked by four beasts. The bronze sanctuary handle on the door is made up of a circular plaque on which the head of a beast is seen devouring a human head. Through the mouth is set a movable ring.

LINTON *A clapper bridge and a packhorse bridge cross the stream running through the green, overlooked by the almshouse of the Fountaine Hospital*

Legburthwaite

Cumbria   NY 3219

At the entrance to the lovely Vale of St John, where the B5322 branches off from the main A591 near Legburthwaite, stands Castle Rock, steeped in legend and folklore. Walter Scott made the magical place famous in his *Bridal of Triermain* but long before that this noticeable outcrop had mysterious associations. An 18th-century history book asserts that local residents believed the rock was a 'fairy fortress' where King Arthur was beguiled into wasting his time under the spell of the resident witch. Engravings of the rock from the 19th century actually depict a great chateau-like castle perched on its summit, with knights in shining armour on horseback and sporting pennants.

To appreciate its mystery to the full it is recommended that the crags are viewed 'in morning or evening maze' (in the full brightness of a summer's day the imagined parapet and portcullis dissolve away). Today adventurous rock climbers are the main visitors, no doubt scorning the old belief that certain genii of the place perform 'supernatural acts and necromancy' on the Rock.

Lindale

Cumbria   SD 4180

Neglected for years, damaged by lightning and abandoned in a shrubbery, the remarkable obelisk of John ('Iron Mad') Wilkinson has recently been restored and given pride of place in Lindale.

One of the great ironmasters of the Industrial Revolution, Wilkinson (1728–1808) was iron-mad indeed: he expressed a wish (eventually fulfilled) to be buried in an iron coffin, and carried out experiments, despite derision, to float an iron ship. Again he succeeded, on the nearby River Winster.

The obelisk itself is an early example of box casting. Newly painted and with an inscription picked out in gold, it states that 'his different works in various parts of the United Kingdom are lasting testimonies of his unceasing labours'.

Linton

North Yorkshire   SD 9962

Scenically and architecturally one of the finest villages of the Yorkshire Dales, it has a layout which probably dates from Anglo-Saxon times. Houses are informally grouped round a green with Linton Beck chuckling by. It is crossed by stepping stones, a clapper bridge, a packhorse bridge and a modern road bridge.

Dominating Linton is the Fountaine Hospital of 1721, one of the first examples of classical architecture built in the Dales. At the other end of the green, Old Hall shows how the new ideas and proportions were grafted on to a 17th-century house.

Half a mile away, Linton's 13th-century church continues to serve four townships in the surrounding district: Linton, Grassington, Threshfield and Hebden.

Little Crosby

Merseyside   SD 3101

One and a half miles north of Great Crosby, this estate village has hardly changed over the past 200 years. It has been the seat of the Blundell family of Crosby Hall, lords of the manor of both Great and Little Crosby, since 1362. The church and most of the residents are Roman Catholic because, it is said, the Reformation never got this far.

Nearby are Ince Blundell and Ince Blundell Hall, until the 1960s the seat of the Weld-Blundell family, who were also Roman Catholic. The hall is now a nursing home. The Round House on the main A565 was formerly the Priest's House. All its rooms are circular.

Little Leigh

Cheshire   SJ 6175

Two hundred years ago it was not uncommon for farmers in Cheshire to brew and sell beer as a sideline, and there were quite a number of farmhouse inns. Now the only one left is the Holly Bush, at Little Leigh, off the A49 near Northwich. The listed, thatched-building is thought to be some 500 years old and in traditional style has no bar, just a tiny tap-room measuring ten feet by three feet.

LEGBURTHWAITE: CASTLE ROCK — *From 1805 onwards, the poet and novelist Sir Walter Scott was a regular visitor to the Lake District. At* **Legburthwaite***, he found inspiration for his narrative poem 'The Bridal of Triermain'. The fairy castle seen by King Arthur in the poem was based on a snippet of local superstition, attached to a rock once called Green Crag, in the middle of the Vale of St John, near a rock formation known as Watson's Dodd.*

Green Crag, says the Cumberland historian Hutchinson (1794), looked like a castle, with towers and ruined battlements. It was a place best not approached too closely, since it was supposed to be protected by 'genii', who would transform it by magic into the semblance of a rock.

Out of this Scott created the fairy castle visited by King Arthur, since when — though no castle, fairy or otherwise, ever existed on this natural outcrop — Green Crag has been known as the Castle Rock of Triermain.

CASTLE ROCK   *An engraving that suggests a castle where no castle was ever built*

THE GYPSIES

They came to Britain 300 years ago, and said they were descended from the Pharaohs of Ancient Egypt. Their language and way of life are still mysterious to housedwellers. Who are the Gypsies? Denis Harvey unravels some of the enigma

Looking at a scattered mess of discarded scrap by the roadside it is easy to be cynical about any romantic concept of the roving life and to disbelieve in the old-fashioned Gypsy in much the same way as one doesn't believe in fairies. But I stumbled on the Gypsy scene when I was 17, back in the days the Travellers now call 'Wagon-time', when the cavalcades of Gypsy vans still rolled along the roads, and at night the smoke from their fires would rise and hang in the air in the lanes, up against the woods or on the open common. One morning in late summer I picked damsons with a gang of Gypsy youngsters and went back with them to the wagons to eat my sandwiches . . .

Who, and what, are the Gypsies? Since well before they entered this country in the 16th century, claiming to be descendants of the Pharaohs of Ancient Egypt, it has been part of their way of life and livelihood to surround themselves with an aura of mystery, fostering a mystique that even today can play a part in their relations with the *gauji*, the non-Gypsy house-dwellers.

But cynicism notwithstanding, after a while one discovers that there really *is* some mystery. Their old speech, a derivation of Sanskrit, suggests they originally came from India. In Britain today the Romani language — *Romanes* old Gypsies call it — survives at best in a debased form; nevertheless a remarkable number of Sanskrit words have remained almost unchanged, over perhaps more than a thousand years of wandering, handed on orally down the generations, without the aid of a written language.

The ability to communicate in a secret language has been an important aid to survival and the Gypsies remain even today a somewhat secret people. In some ways this has militated against them. The cultural differences in their way of life give rise to misunderstanding and inappropriate legislation followed by increasing problems.

In Britain there is still much confusion regarding who are the 'true Gypsies'. Broadly speaking the travelling population of Britain can be divided into three groups of roughly equal proportion: Anglo-Saxon/Celtic (the indigenous nomad population); the people with some Romani blood — descendants of the 'Egyptians' who began to arrive in the 16th century; and the Irish Travellers, who have been entering the country sporadically for over a century and in increasing numbers since World War II. The first two groups, now mainly of mixed blood through intermarriage, for the most part share the same customs, traditions, manner of speech and domestic taste. The third group, the Irish, are separate and different, and in general are viewed with a certain amount of resentment by the others.

Shiftless and dirty rate-evaders' is the opinion held of travelling people by some

THE THREE BASIC TYPES   *of Traveller in Britain today. Above, from left to right: Romani, Anglo-Saxon-Celtic, Irish*

LIVING WAGON *(below)   A typical example of those built in around 1915 by Dunton of Reading for well-to-do Gypsies*

house-dwellers — but it might surprise those accusers to know that most Gypsies consider housedwellers themselves to be 'dirty people', and they generally disapprove of *gaujo* concepts of cleanliness. They have a word *mockadi* in their vocabulary, which sounds like slang ('muckety') but the word is Romanes and has its root in Sanskrit. It is used in the sense of 'unclean' rather than merely dirty. It is *mockadi* to wash vegetables and food utensils in a bowl or sink that has ever been used for washing yourself or your clothes. Each operation must have a separate bowl assigned to it. Cats and dogs are *mockadi* and any utensil that has been licked by one is destroyed forthwith, as also is any china that becomes cracked or chipped. Horses are not *mockadi*. Whether this is because the horse has long been at the centre of Traveller culture, or simply because a horse cannot lick its own backside, is open to specu-

lation. I believe these customs and attitudes are occupational rather than racial in origin, the instinctive response to a way of life. As one Gypsy woman put it to me: 'Livin' like we does you got to keep clean.'

Gaujos are often shocked by the untidiness outside some Gypsy trailers and do not see further — that the trailer itself, both inside and out, is kept spotlessly clean. For the Traveller, always self-employed, the ground outside the trailer is considered a work area and is casually treated as such, although the work itself is all-important.

Up until the twilight of Wagon-time, craft manufacture of clothes-pegs, baskets and artificial flowers provided a steady supplementary income. Dealing in horses, vehicles and almost any other commodity and (for the women) selling lace and small domestic articles and materials from door-to-door, with fortune-telling on the side, made and still can make a fair living. Today handcrafted items have had to give place to cheap mass-production, but scrap-dealing, tarmac-ing, tree-surgery, logging and contract gardening, with door-to-door sales and collection of cast-offs ('rags and woollens') by the women, all contribute to an adequate family income. Little national provision is made for recycling scrap-metals, and many Travellers have developed an expert knowledge of metallurgy, playing an important part in the economy by their recycling. They also form a mobile labour force, male and female, old and young alike, still much in demand in some areas of agriculture from June through to October.

Fortune-telling ('dukkerin') is as popular as ever and the skill of the Gypsy woman at reading character, at discerning the kind of person you are, and consequently the kind of experiences you have had and are likely to have in the future, sometimes borders on the uncanny. Certainly intuition plays a part in dukkering, and there have been instances of what looks like genuine clairvoyance. Though such cases are rare, the customer usually gets good value for money.

At the age of 21 I had a personal, if somewhat doubtful, experience of magic at the hands of a Gypsy witch. I had offered to carry her two heavy four-gallon water-jacks back across the Common to the vans. ''Old up, love!' she commanded before I set off, and ran her hands lightly over my shoulders and down my arms. 'There now!' she said, 'I seed it won't pain yer. Let 'em 'ang, my love . . . just 'ook yer fingers.' She walked beside me over the half-mile of rough heathland to the camp and I never felt a trace of tiredness. Supernature? Or just mechanical know-how? A bit of both perhaps.

The 'Carmen' syndrome — the operatic or musical-comedy concept of the Gypsy girl — has nourished the romantic imaginations of housedwellers for at least 150 years. I find the truth more beguiling. In Britain girls of Traveller stock still tend to be by temperament fastidious and restrained. It is this and other conservative social attitudes, as well as domestic style and taste, that has earned the Gypsy people the title 'the last Victorians'. In the late 1970s, a young family of horsedrawn Travellers in the south-west, when passing along the road below where the Cerne Abbas Giant is cut into the chalk hillside, would discreetly shepherd their children into the barrel-top and close the door, shielding young eyes from this unseemly pre-historic display of nudity.

The most colourful and glamorous element of Gypsy life — and the one that distinguishes the English Gypsies from even their most flamboyant counterparts on the Continent — is the carved and painted wagon. (Gypsies do not use the word 'caravan' except when talking to the *gauji*.) The so-called Gypsy caravan with its tall wheels, elaborate chamfering, carving and paint-decoration is peculiar to Britain; wagons in Europe are of far less elegant and specialised design. But the Gypsies did not take to the living-wagon until late in the last century. Until then they had travelled with tents, carts and pack-animals. 'Bender-tents' were made from fresh-cut hazel pushed into the ground and bent over, forming a resilient frame to be covered by blankets or water-proof sheets. They probably

pre-date recorded history and are far from obsolete even today. Gypsies actually adopted the one-horse, one-roomed living-wagon from the travelling showmen of the late 19th century, and they used and developed it long after the showmen had graduated to the heavy two- and three-roomed wagons pulled by a traction engine, or, later, by Foden and Scammell lorries.

The 'Gypsy caravan' engendered a considerable amount of mystique, not without help from the Gypsies them-selves. If *gaujos* were reckless enough to ask an innocent question, they were told exactly the kind of thing they wished to hear, such as that most wagons are over a hundred years old and painted with the colours and secret symbols of the tribe they belong to, or that they are con-structed of 365 boards (one for each day

---

A HORSE-DEALING FAMILY *(right)* which has given up motors and gone back to horse-drawn wagons. Their taste in clothes reflects a thousand-year-old connection with the Orient

A FAMILY REUNION *(below)* Epsom Downs in Derby Week, 1948. The girls are making daisy chains

---

of the year). A magazine article in the sixties contained the startling information that 'the true Gypsies' proof their bow-top caravans with varnished otter-skins.

In fact most proprietary-built Gypsy wagons were as practical as sea-going craft, and had a structural elegance that is the by-product of sound functional design. But nearly all aspired to a degree of decoration, and some which were built to order for well-to-do Gypsies were ela-borately carved and painted, and often embellished with gold-leaf. The interior of one of these could be like a Renais-sance palace in miniature, with gilded carving, french-polished mahogany, cut-glass mirrors and ornamental brasswork.

After World War II, when the old

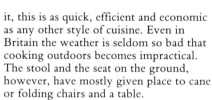

OLD AND NEW STYLES *(above)*   *The father (seen here) is a horse-dealer and breeder, the son-in-law, whose truck is in the background, is a scrap metal merchant*

VICKERS LUXI-TRAILER *(above right)*   *One of several makes of 'Travellers' Special' designed to cater for Gypsy needs and often extravagant tastes*

wagons were falling apart and most of the old builders were 'finished and gone away', some Travellers developed the necessary skills and took to building a somewhat modified wagon to their own design, the 'open-lot'. Constructed on an existing dray (the four-wheeled trades-man's cart), the design developed until today some of them rival the best products of the past. And so, though only a few families are horsedrawn now (chiefly in the Midlands and North), the traditional Gypsy van is neither extinct nor obsolete. Some families, anxious to avoid the rising costs of petrol, tax and insurance, have sold their trailers and returned to the life with horses and wagons. A horse fills its own tank over-night, and overheads can be kept to a minimum by those with generations of horse-experience. Horse-drawn Travellers carry out their own shoeing, harness repairs and veterinary treatment. Such families also find that today the decorated Gypsy vans and carts, with horses quietly grazing, are more readily tolerated on the roadside than the lorry and trailer with a pile of scrap-metal. But horsedrawn Travellers are as hard to locate as the wild otter, mostly hidden away in the hinterlands along narrow, twisting lanes in the very heart of the country.

Most Gypsies changed from horse-drawn vans to lorries and trailers (again the word 'caravan' is not used) when petrol came off the ration in the early fifties, and it was not long before firms started manufacturing motor caravans specifically to meet their requirements — quite different from those of the holiday caravanner. Few Travellers would tolerate a loo inside their trailer, let alone one close to where food is prepared, but they do require a solid-fuel stove for heating in winter. A sink is not an essential feature and though there usually is one, Travellers often place a board over it to accommodate stainless steel bowls for the separate washing operations. During the seventies these trailers, 'Travellers' Specials', reached a peak of baroque splendour and opulence, with luxury interiors and every available space of the outside panelled and embossed in stain-less steel, coloured plastic, chrome and glitter. Both inside and out, they were the equivalent of the style of Wagon-time, translated into the materials and techniques of the motor-age. Today the trend is towards more sleek, sophisticated lines and trailers are often imported from Germany.

Although most trailers are fitted with calor gas for cooking and lighting, cooking is still sometimes carried out on a stick-fire outside, with large oval 'boilers', iron kettles and bucket-handled frying pans suspended from a kettle-prop. For those who are accustomed to it, this is as quick, efficient and economic as any other style of cuisine. Even in Britain the weather is seldom so bad that cooking outdoors becomes impractical. The stool and the seat on the ground, however, have mostly given place to cane or folding chairs and a table.

Horses are still the favourite emblem of Traveller culture, and horses are present in effigy inside most trailers, sharing the shelves with Crown Derby china, Chelsea, Staffordshire and Capo-di-Monte figures. The family motor itself, nick-named the 'Soster Grye' (Iron Horse), sometimes still has horses' heads painted or in transfer on the cab doors.

There is space only to make mention in passing of some things powerfully redolent of the Travellers' life in this country — of trotting races on summer evenings (or at dawn on dual-carriageways before the traffic starts); of nightly hedgehog hunts; of the soft-eyed lurcher dogs so friendly and reliable in the family, but guarding the wagons and trailers with the ferocity of a tigress defending her young (they can be taught to catch or retrieve game, carry it straight to the wagons and lay it down by the fire); of a thousand ways and attitudes strange to housedwellers but an integral and valuable part of a rich culture that Gypsies still hold fast to against all the odds.

Stuart Mann wrote in *Encyclopaedia Britannica*: 'Society has always found the Romanies an ethnic puzzle and has tried ceaselessly to fit them, by force or fraud, piety or policy, coaxing or cruelty, into some framework of its own conception, but so far without success.' Though he was writing over fifty years ago, his words are as true today.

DENIS HARVEY   *Sculptor, writer, lecturer, photo-grapher and illustrator, his books include 'The Gypsies; Wagon-time and After' and 'The English Gypsy Caravan', a standard work.*

Liverpool and the Wirral

Merseyside and Cheshire SJ 3591

King Midas pours out gold where tons of gold were hidden, secret gardens lie close to a floating road, and over the Mersey, the factories hide model villages and ancient village greens

MERSEYSIDE'S OWN ENTERTAINMENTS PAPER
MERSEY BEAT
Vol. 1 No. 13   JANUARY 4–18, 1962   Price THREEPENCE
Beatles Top Poll!
FULL RESULTS INSIDE

LIVERPOOL: MERSEY SOUNDS — *Between 1962 and 1970, four young Liverpudlians — Paul McCartney, John Lennon, George Harrison and Ringo Starr — took the world of pop music by storm.*

In early days they performed at **Liverpool's** *Cavern Club, just a dank cellar, which had become the musical centre of the area. A 14-year-old fan of those days later opened the Cavern Mecca in the same street, incorporating a reconstruction, complete with arches, of their old the venue.*

Today the Beatles and their history are a leading tourist attraction of Liverpool, with Beatle City the world's first permanent Beatles exhibition. Not the least visited is the controversial statue of the 'Fab Four'.

But the city at the time of the Beatles' rise to fame was swarming with other pop groups. With bands abounding, such as the Searchers, the Hurricanes and Gerry and the Pacemakers (with whom the early Beatles had a lively but friendly rivalry), it is easy to see why Liverpool has been regarded ever since as one of the most fertile areas for pop music. As a friend of Lennon's said, 'Look at anybody who's made it, and if they came from Liverpool, it's partly **because** *they came from Liverpool.'*

ABOVE *Beatles, 1962. They began as just one of many new bands at a fertile time and place for music*

Liverpool may have lost its eminence as a world seaport: modern handling methods mean that ships arrive, are unloaded, reloaded and depart within a few hours rather than days so that the River Mersey no longer provides a spectacle of ships waiting at anchor for berths. But it is still a city of riches to discover, with some splendid Victorian buildings, odd corners to explore, and a unique atmosphere, made all the more poignant in these days of change.

Those ferries across the Mersey still ply between Liverpool and Birkenhead and Wallasey, and in the summer months, when the tide allows, there is a service up-river to Otterspool and the Festival Gardens which were born out of Britain's first International Garden Festival in 1984.

Canning Dock and part of the vast Albert Dock Warehouses (Britain's largest group of Grade I listed buildings) houses the Merseyside Maritime Museum. The rest, now called Albert Dock Village, has become the scene of an exciting restoration, with a wide variety of shops, places to eat and drink, exhibitions and entertainments, including Tate in the North — the northern arm of London's Tate Gallery — planned for the late 1980s.

On the Pier Head the oldest of the trinity of well-known buildings is that of the domed Port of Liverpool Building, headquarters of the Mersey Docks and Harbour Company, with an interior every bit as impressive as its exterior. The second to be built was the Royal Liver Building, topped by the Liver Birds. It was the world's first multi-storey building in reinforced concrete (but granite-faced) and its clock is Britain's largest.

Near the Floating Roadway (which gives vehicles access to the Landing Stage and rises and falls with the tide), are two 'secret' gardens. One of them has a sculpture called 'The Seven Seas', symbolising Liverpool's trading links with the world. A plaque in the wall above the roadway commemorates the use of the Port of Liverpool by American Forces during the last war. Above the roadway on the opposite side, in St Nicholas Place, is the Engineers' Memorial, designed by Sir William Goscombe John RA, and originally intended to commemorate the engineers and firemen (mainly from Liverpool) lost in the sinking of the *Titanic*. Eventually it was dedicated to 'all heroes of the engineroom who were lost at sea'.

On the far side of the dual-carriageway dock road in Brunswick Street, behind Wilberforce House, is the Piazza Waterfall, a unique and ingenious cascading water contrivance known to Liverpudlians as 'the bucket fountain'. India Buildings has an arcade running through the ground floor, with a beautiful barrel-vaulted ceiling and small shops. On the other side of Water Street is Oriel Chambers, highly regarded by present-day architects for its unusual oriel windows. Also here is Barclays Bank — originally the head office of Martins Bank and full of surprises, both outside and in. Note the sculptural detail — especially King Midas pouring coins from a cornucopia — and the splendid bronze doors. Inside, the banking hall, with much marble and gilded scrollwork, is magnificent. At knee-level on the Town Hall side of the building is a plaque above a vault door recording that Britain's gold reserve (280 tons of it) was secretly lodged in the vaults prior to shipment to Canada for safety during World War II.

In Castle Street, in the roadway near the National Westminster Bank, is the Sanctuary Stone, encircled in yellow. This marked the limit of Liverpool's ancient Martinmas fair. The Co-operative Bank at the junction with Brunswick Street has a distinctive onion-shaped dome and unusual bronze doors, sculpted by Stirling Lee, depicting sets of famous historical twins (Romulus and Remus, for example).

At the junction of Lime Street and William Brown Street, the Wellington Monument is said to have been cast from guns captured at the Battle of Waterloo. In one corner of the base, low down, are the Standard Imperial Measurements — lest we forget, perhaps, as the country goes steadily metric.

Southwards of the city centre stands the Ancient Chapel of Toxteth, built in 1619. There are some fine woodcarvings inside, and a memorial to Jeremiah Horrox (1618–41), said by some to be Britain's finest astronomer, who at the age of 23, two years before his untimely death, discovered the Transit of Venus. The first minister of this church was Richard Mather, a prominent Pilgrim Father on the *Mayflower*.

In Sefton Park, outside the Palm House, is a large statue of Christopher Columbus, inscribed *'The Discoverer of America was the Maker of Liverpool'*. The park also has replicas of

CENOTAPH *'To the men of Liverpool who fell in the Great War'.*

ALBERT DOCK VILLAGE   *Restaurants, shops and entertainments have brought new life to the massive Dock buildings, once described as architecture of 'rough cyclopean masses'*

Piccadilly's *Eros* and Kensington Gardens' *Peter Pan*. Still going south through an almost continuous green belt of public parks, Calderstones Park has the Allerton Oak, reputed to be more than 1000 years old.

Five miles from Liverpool city centre in *West Derby* is Croxteth Hall and its 530-acre estate. The seat of the Molyneux family, Earls of Sefton, for nearly four centuries until the death of the last earl in 1972, it is now in the possession of the local authority. The hall, the gardens and parklands (especially recommended at rhododendron time), a walled garden and a Victorian-style working farm are all open to the public. Special events and exhibitions are also held at various times.

In *St Helens*, long famed as a glassmaking town, the main manufacturer, Pilkington Brothers, has established the Pilkington Glass Museum (a striking building mostly made of glass) at their head office in Prescot Road. Just south is *Prescot*, where a museum devoted to the former clock- and watchmaking industry was opened in 1982. At neighbouring *Rainhill*, a plaque on the station platform recalls the locomotive trials which were held in 1829, to determine which locomotive should be used for the world's first regular passenger railway service between Liverpool and Manchester. George Stephenson's *Rocket* was the winner, but it ran down William Huskisson, Liverpool's Member of

Parliament and the world's first railway accident victim. A memorial marks the spot where the accident happened, 250 yards along the track from the station. The road across the railway line by the station runs obliquely over the world's first ever skew bridge, a considerable engineering feat at the time since all the stones had to be cut 'on the skew' to fit.

Wirral

Merseyside and Cheshire   SJ 3591

In the 12th century, Benedictine monks built *Birkenhead Priory* on leafy Birchen Head which jutted out into the Mersey. Only one wall and the steeple of the church now remain but services are still held in the Chapter House, Merseyside's oldest place of worship, every Sunday morning. Hidden away among industrial buildings, the Priory can be reached through the Priory Industrial Estate in Chester Street.

Birkenhead Park (1847) was Britain's first municipal park (and the inspiration for New York's Central Park), and in the 1860s the town had Europe's first street railway (with horse trams). Hamilton Square with its stone-built terraces is very fine.

Bidston Hill's restored windmill is the last of many on the same site and went on grinding corn until 1975. A lighthouse was erected on the hill in 1771, and before that it was the site of a semaphore signal station. On the lower slope are Bidston Hall, built by the fourth Earl of Derby in about 1580 (rescued from near-dereliction) and Tam O'Shanter's Cottage, a squatter's cottage from about 1670, now a Field Study Centre.

In *Bidston Village*, Church Farm has 13 windows all at different levels, and Stone Farm, opposite, was once the Ring O'Bells pub.

At *New Brighton*, the massive red sandstone Fort Perch Rock was built in 1826 to guard the mouth of the River Mersey. Now privately owned but open to the public, it has a restaurant and a museum of wartime aircraft salvaged by the Aircraft Recovery Group. Perch Rock Lighthouse is in the same ownership, and has accommodation for an unusual get-away-from-it-all holiday. Access to both is affected by the tides.

Hillbark, *Frankby*, is a beautiful pseudo-Elizabethan, black-and-white timbered house, first built in Birkenhead in 1891 for Robert

LIVERPOOL: GREAT SHIPS — *The huge emigration to America in the 19th century was handled in England chiefly by* **Liverpool**, *and helped to make it one of the world's most eminent seaports. Vast steamships like those built by Isambard Kingdom Brunel carried great numbers of Irish people to Boston and New York, and many of the great liner companies based themselves in the city, including Inman and Cunard. The latter, founded by Samuel Cunard in 1840, helped to revolutionise the shipping industry, with steam ships such as the Britannia. Made in Glasgow, she was the first ship to sail to an exact timetable, between Liverpool and Boston.*

A less fortunate Cunard ship was the Lusitania, a liner sailing between Liverpool and New York, and sunk by German torpedoes during World War I, killing 1198 civilians.

White Star, another Liverpool-based company, owned the Titanic, victim of the greatest tragedy in shipping annals. Outstanding in size, power and luxury, and reputedly unsinkable, she sailed in 1912 from **Southampton** *on her maiden voyage to New York, and five days later ran into huge icebergs. The liner sank, drowning 1503 passengers. All might have been saved by a ship which was just ten miles away, but the wireless operator was asleep and failed to hear the SOS.*

UNTO·ALL·THE·PEOPLE

LIVERPOOL: SIR GAWAIN AND THE GREEN KNIGHT —

The 14th-century author of 'Sir Gawain and the Green Knight', a tale of King Arthur's court, tells how Sir Gawain, going in search of the mysterious Green Chapel, embarks on a perilous winter journey through the 'wyldrenesse of Wyrale' — or **Wirral** *(starts page 237).*

Gawain sets out from Camelot in the south and rides through North Wales, keeping Anglesey on his left. He crosses the mouths of Conwy and Clwyd by fords, and via 'Holy Head', somewhere on the Dee, enters the Wirral.

The Wirral was truly a 'wyldrenesse'. Made into a forest

by Randle Meschines, third earl of **Chester***, it remained wild to the 16th century. To Gawain it offers many dangers: dragons, bears and boars, wolves and wildmen, and fell-haunting trolls.*

But at last he enters Cumbria, sleeping in his irons among the bare rocks, frozen burns hanging overhead in 'hard iisse-ikkles'. There he comes to a hoary oak-wood hung with ragged moss (possibly Inglewood Forest), and ultimately to the Green Chapel, perhaps the Chapel of the Grene, marked on old maps on the coast not far from Skinburness. Nearby was Volsty Castle, where the magical books of Michael Scot (see **Melrose***) were kept — an appropriate region for Gawain's encounter with the supernatural Green Knight.*

ABOVE *Sir Gawain 'rides . . . into a deep forest, which was wondrous wild'*

BIDSTON VILLAGE
Church Farm, with its irregular windows, is one of several 17th-century buildings in this rural corner close to central Birkenhead

Hudson, the soap manufacturer, and later bought by Sir Ernest Royden, a shipowner, who had it dismantled, moved and re-erected on its present site in 1929–31. A good view of it can be had from Royden Park.

A mile out in the estuary of the River Dee lie *Hilbre Island, Middle Hilbre* and *Eye*, all famed as bird-watching centres. During the winter months some 100,000 wading birds make their home on the salt marshes of the estuary. Now owned by Wirral Metropolitan Borough Council, Hilbre Island has a resident warden. It is accessible at low tide with permits obtainable from the Visitor Centre, Wirral Country Park, Thurstaston.

The old village of *Burton* consists of a single street with a variety of ancient cottages, several of them thatched and half-timbered, and Burton Manor, now a college of adult education. The Church of St Nicholas (1721) has a one-handed clock and an 18th-century sundial in the graveyard. Beside a footpath immediately behind the church are the Quaker Graves, dating from the time when Quakers were not allowed to be buried in consecrated ground.

The first Thursday in June every year in *Neston* sees Ladies' Walking Day, the annual procession through the town to the parish church, of the unique Neston Female Friendly Society (1717), all simply dressed in white and carrying white garlands. Rules decree that the Treasurer must always be a man. The register in the Parish Church of St Mary and St Helen records the birth on 26 April 1765 of Emy Lyon, daughter of the blacksmith at neighbouring Ness, who grew up to become Lady Emma Hamilton.

The little isolated hamlet of *Shotwick*, with a population of less than three dozen, has remained virtually unchanged for the past 200 years. It has no shop, no Post Office, no school, no pub and no bus service, but once it had a castle and in the Middle Ages it was the port for Ireland and the gateway to Wales. Henry II and Edward I passed through the Norman porch of St Michael's, although the tower is 16th-century and the nave was restored in 1871. There are score-marks in the sandstone, made, it is said, by archers sharpening their arrows. At the end of the only other lane is Shotwick Hall, built of brick in the shape of the letter 'E' during 1662; it was later used as a farmhouse.

It is thought that an Anglo-Saxon chief named Wiglaf settled in *Willaston* in the seventh century and that the place derives its name from 'Wiglaf's Tun'. Another theory is that it comes from 'Wirhael Stone' — 'Wirhael' being the ancient name for Wirral. The so-called Wirral Stone can be found on the grass verge in Hadlow Road where it meets the Chester High Road (A540). It looks like — and many say it doubtless is — an old mounting block, but others maintain it marks the meeting place of the Wirral Hundred. An Elizabethan hall can be seen in Hadlow Road, and Willaston Mill (now a residence) was the Wirral's tallest mill.

Wirral Country Park (based on an abandoned railway line and the country's first linear park) passes along the edge of the village. Hadlow Road Station has been restored to look just as it did on the day it closed in the 1950s.

Eastham is one of Wirral's oldest villages. In the churchyard, a yew bears a plaque recording a visit made in 1898 by the Royal Archaeological Society, and their opinion that it was at least 1000 years old.

Wirral has three outstanding purpose-built workers' villages. *Price's Village* was built between 1853 and 1901 for the employees of Price's Patent Candle Company. Totally hemmed in by industry, it offers a delightful prospect of neat, orderly streets and a village school, church and village hall facing a spacious green. Access (signposted) is via Pool Lane off the A41 New Chester Road near *Port Sunlight* — a beautiful garden village built by William Lever, the first Viscount Leverhulme, for his soap works employees, and named after one of their best-known products. The architects included Lutyens. *Thornton Hough* is the handiwork of two men: Joseph Hirst, a retired Yorkshire woollen manufacturer, and William Lever. Hirst built Thornton House (for himself), the parish church (which has a clock with a fifth face because Hirst could not see any of the first four from his window), a school, a terrace of houses and a village store. Lever built the rest, including the beautiful Norman-style Congregational (now United Reformed) Church, cottages in the Port Sunlight style, another shop and a village club. He also provided a large village green and a smithy complete with a spreading chestnut tree.

Londesborough

Humberside SE 8645

The Wolds Way, a long distance footpath, goes through parkland created by the third Earl of Burlington in the early 18th century. Sample it by walking from the park gates in Londesborough village southwards for a mile, east by field paths to pick up the drive from Towthorpe Corner, and back through the park. Burlington's house was demolished in 1819, but rebuilt — with his private station at Shiptonthorpe — in 1845 by George Hudson, the 'railway king', whose empire collapsed four years later. The estate is now in private hands.

Lower Peover

Cheshire SJ 7474

Pronounced Lower Peever, this tiny hamlet tucked away off the B5081 has had a chapel since at least 1269. The very attractive black-and-white St Oswald's Church probably dates from a century later, with the tower dating from 1582. With St James' and St Paul's at Marton, it can claim to be amongst the three oldest timber-framed churches in Europe. The Bells of Peover Inn was once renowned for its own ale.

Lowgill

Lancashire SD 6564

Reputedly the quietest village in Lancashire, Lowgill does not even have a pub now. Once the old Roman road from Ribchester to Carlisle ran right through it, and Lowgill would have shuddered with the tramp of legionaries.

The village, with 60 listed buildings in the parish and notable vernacular architecture, is at the end of a superb, wild road slicing right through the fells of central Lancashire. This is sheep country, with very little sign of civilisation, and rights of way are hard to follow without a detailed map. An alternative is to try schemes like the 'Bowland Treks' started here by Sue and Dick Frost, who 'sherpa' small groups of walkers through the surrounding fells.

LOWER PEOVER St Oswald's Church was built in the 14th century or perhaps earlier — a chapel referred to in 1269 may have been this building

Luddenden

West Yorkshire SE 0425

This is a charming village of narrow streets, steep hills, weavers' houses of dark stone and hillside farms, in a landscape of contrasting colour and moods. The Lord Nelson Inn dates from 1754 and was a favourite haunt of Branwell Brontë when he worked as booking clerk at the station in Luddenden Foot. The village school has a double lock-up beneath it — not for pupils, but for wrongdoers in the adjacent townships of Midgeley and Warley.

Lund

Humberside SE 9648

A few miles north of Beverley, this well-kept village is centred on a small, triangular green with a market cross and sycamores known as the 'Cockpit Trees', marking the site of a former village feature. The old smithy has been sympathetically converted into a bus-shelter, and nearby the Wellington Inn has two signs, the hanging one showing a much younger duke than its fellow on the wall.

Lydiate

Merseyside SD 3604

Built in 1320 round a massive tree which still supports part of the thatched roof, the Scotch Piper Inn is the oldest pub in old Lancashire. Originally the Royal Oak, its name changed, it is said, when one of Bonnie Prince Charlie's wounded men took refuge here and was nursed back to health. One family — the Moorcrofts — held its licence for 500 years, until in 1945 an only surviving daughter sold it to a brewery and married a local farmer. Fire destroyed part of it recently, but it is a listed building and has been immaculately restored.

LIVERPOOL: WIRRAL COUNTRY PARK — *Above the Dee estuary, Cheshire County Council have established the* **Wirral Country Park**, *England's first linear park.*
It follows 12 miles of disused railway line from Kirkby to Hooton, and Hadlow Road Station, situated in the park, has been preserved exactly as it looked in the 1950s, with authentic time-tables, tickets and furnishings including milk churns and wooden trolleys.

The trains themselves no longer run, partly on account of the wild-life which inhabits the area in rich variety. There are badger setts, fox earths and frog ponds in the grounds, while the views over the Dee mudflats provide excellent birdwatching. Waders and wild-fowl of many kinds frequent the marshes, including wigeons, knots, dunlins, curlews, godwits and such rarities as the day-flying short-eared owl and the hen harrier.

Since the success of the Wirral Country Park, another linear park, the **Middlewood Way**, *has been developed along the same principles, following the old rail-way track from Marple to Macclesfield.* **London** *also has a railway path, from Crouch End to Highgate. The technique may be repeated elsewhere in the future — since the 1960s, 2300 miles of track have been taken out of service, and now form a wildlife-rich network of green walkways, as yet unprotected, through Britain.*

ABOVE Hadlow Road Station — still as it was in the 1950s. The railway line now forms part of the Wirral Country Park

Manchester and around

From a Gothic fantasy to rustic Daisy Nook, by way of brass bands, curry restaurants and a duchess's pince-nez, with country walks to take where trains once ran

MANCHESTER: PHANTOM FOOT-PRINTS — *In the reign of Queen Mary, the Protestant martyr George Marsh was brought for interrogation to Smithill's Hall, Bolton, Greater* **Manchester**. *Before being taken to the stake, he stamped on the stone-flagged floor, praying for a proof of his enemies' injustice. His footprint was miraculously left there (it can still be seen) and according to Nathaniel Hawthorne, it becomes 'wet with fresh blood' once a year.*

Brindle church has a footprint stamped on the wall, which some say was made by the Devil. Two bare spots on the ground by Cerne Mill Stream, Cerne Abbas, Dorset are said to be the last footprints of a man who drowned himself there. The grass would not grow, either, in the footprints left by Black Vaughan (Herefordshire's most notorious ghost) under an oak near Hergest Court. But probably the most celebrated footprints burnt into grass are the Brothers' Steps left in the reign of Charles II in Southampton Fields, **London**, *by two brothers duelling over a woman. These are said to survive in the south-west corner of Tavistock Square, Bloomsbury.*

ST COLUMBA'S FOOTPRINTS
Two right feet near Keil are said to mark where the saint landed on Kintyre, but may have been where pagan chiefs took their vows

Many visitors to Manchester ignore the Town Hall and thus miss one of the city's treats. Variously described as a 'civic Gormenghast', 'a set from The Slipper and the Rose', and 'detestably lovable', Waterhouse's Town Hall is a cadenza of ornament, leaded glass, spires, towers, turrets, staircases and pre-Raphaelite murals. The great hall is used for concerts and recitals and there are guided tours of the building twice daily at 10am and 2.30pm on weekdays. A recent addition to this Victorian Gothic fantasy is the Sir John Barbirolli triptych, which represents the work of the man who conducted the Halle Orchestra for over 25 years.

There are two theories about why the delightful Catholic Church of St Mary is known as 'the hidden gem'. One is because it was so tucked away down Mulberry Street and overshadowed by larger buildings on either side. The other is that a bishop once said: 'No matter what side of

THE HIDDEN GEM *is the name affectionately given today to St Mary's Church, perhaps because of its rich decoration — although Pugin for one disliked its 'strange styles'*

MANCHESTER: BOGGART'S FLIT — *On the outskirts of* **Manchester** *is Boggart Hole Clough, once the haunt of a malicious boggart, and now part of one of the city's parks.*

The story is that he made such trouble in a farmhouse that once stood in the valley, that the farmer and his family decided to move. They had packed their belongings on to a cart, but just as they were setting off, a neighbour asked what they were doing. The farmer explained that they were 'flitting' or moving, at which a sepulchral voice was heard from the cart saying 'Aye, neighbour, we're flitting!' Seeing it was useless to try and leave the boggart behind, they decided to stay where they were.

The clough certainly had its boggart — a kind of domestic bogey, much like a poltergeist — but this particular tale may be an import from Yorkshire. It was also well known in Lincolnshire, where it was heard by Lord Tennyson and retold in 'Walking to the Mail' (1842).

The same tale is attached to a bogle called Jesse at West Lands Farm, near **Hexham**, *Northumberland and to the Hobthrush of Obtrusch Tumulus, Farndale West, North Yorkshire.*

BARTON ARCADE *(above)   Resplendent with Victorian wrought iron and glass, topped by a glass roof and two domes, the arcade (built in 1871) has been restored to its former glory following a recent renovation, and is lined with luxury shops*

ST JOHN STREET *(right)   Georgian terraces enrich the 'Harley Street of Manchester', where Charlotte Brontë's father came for treatment and she began to write 'Jane Eyre' while waiting for him*

the church you look, you behold a hidden gem'. Kindly developers have now given the little church polite breathing space. The elaborate altar, ornate doorway, hundreds of candles and statues make it worth visiting. It was built in 1794 and rebuilt in 1844.

'Manchester's Harley Street' — as St John Street is known — is one of ten conservation areas in the city. With help from the National Trust, this beautiful street of Georgian houses has been restored complete with brass plates and elegant front doors. There is a braille library at one end and Charlotte Brontë wrote the first lines of *Jane Eyre* here while waiting for her father to come out of his operation for cataracts.

John Rylands Library is a magical, marbled, funereal place, full of amazing things like papyrus scripts, books written on rice paper, stone, bamboo and silk. It has Bibles by the thousand and vaults of pre-1501 manuscripts, as well as jewelled bindings and priceless records.

Several television, book and film researchers come to the Platt Hall Gallery of English Costume for all their facts and ideas on period clothes. Of its kind, the museum is certainly one of the finest in the country and you can see examples of anything from a maid's knickers to a duchess's pince-nez. Apart from permanent exhibitions, they have temporary shows. The museum is in a Georgian house with a Shakespearian garden in front of it, which is always tranquil and full of roses in summer.

Newly restored, glassy Barton Arcade is an excellent example of how exuberant Victorian architecture often was: there is hardly a straight line in it and it gives some idea of how soothing buildings based on concepts other than the right angle can be. The arcade is full of classy shops and businesses.

Manchester Jewish Museum, in Cheetham Hill Road, tells how Jewish people settled in Manchester and gradually integrated into the community without losing their own identity. The museum is housed in a 19th-century Spanish/Portugese synagogue and it is England's only Jewish museum outside London.

At *Droylsden*, Fairfield's Moravian Settlement is worth visiting. Founded in 1785 — the oldest in England — it is an 18th-century oasis of gentleness and calm where the sedate Christian community even buried men and women separately.

A mile or so out of the city centre are *Rusholme's* many curry restaurants where you can get a superb meal at a very reasonable price. In this Manchester suburb every other shop seems to be an Indian restaurant and the atmosphere is usually fun because the restaurants are full of the people who actually live in the bustling community.

MANCHESTER: REFORMERS AND REVOLUTION-

ARIES *In 1793, publicans in* **Manchester** *banned 'any clubs or societies that have a tendency to put in force the DESTRUCTION of the country.' The cause? Fear of the unrest fuelled by the French Revolution. Artisans and tradesmen formed clubs to talk about Tom Paine's book 'The Rights of Man' (which criticised the power of the rich and was read by thousands), evading the law against national groups by 'corresponding' with fellow clubs in* **London**, **Sheffield**, *Manchester,* **Norwich** *and elsewhere. Tom Paine was outlawed in 1793 — but his book was still read in secret trade union meetings, themselves illegal under the Combination Acts of 1799 and 1800. The long-standing mutual help societies of artisans like the weavers, with their traditions of solemn oath-taking and strict ritual, became a disguise for secret committees to discuss reform and plan campaigns for a minimum wage. Although many might still be harmless benefit clubs, artisans' societies were regarded with suspicion and were subject to infiltration by government spies. Some have said that it was spies and 'agents provocateurs' who turned the reform movement into a near-revolution during the Luddite disturbances of 1812, but workers' committees may have been involved. The disturbances took the form of machine-breaking around* **Nottingham***; in Yorkshire and Lancashire 12,000 troops were called in to keep order, and informers reported nocturnal arms collections in Lancashire and arms manufacture in Sheffield. Whole districts on the Yorkshire-Lancashire border, says E. P. Thomson in his 'The Making of the English Working Class', were under martial law.*

ABOVE   *At the height of the riots Luddite men dressed as women, calling themselves 'General Ludd's wives'*

DAISY NOOK *(right)   was a name invented by dialect-writer Ben Brierley for this stretch of the Medlock Valley. Teas are served in his old home, Hen Cote Cottage*

Queen magazine once called Lowry 'the sanctifier of Mancunian depression' and you can see if you agree with this view by going to *Salford* Art Gallery, to see the largest collection of Lowry paintings in the world. Inspired by the distinctiveness of the north's industrial civilisation, Lowry grumbled that 'today everything's light industry'. Also at the Salford Gallery is Lark Hill, a Victorian street of shops using all the original materials, costumes, cobbles and appropriate produce of the day.

Cotton mills are what one might expect of Lancashire, but visitors may be unprepared for the scale and classical formality of these temples to commerce. Elk Mill at *Royston* was the last mule spinning mill ever built (in 1926) and with it ended an era which had, quite literally, changed the world. The mill is not open, but its proportions convey something of the cotton industry's rule and dominance during the 19th century. Nearby is Tandle Hill Country Park and from the top of Tandle Hill you can see a panorama of all the mills in this area. Two of them — Manor and Kent, built in 1906 and 1908 — at Victoria Street, *Chadderton* — are now owned by Courtaulds. Architecturally, they are probably the best examples of cotton mills in the whole of Lancashire. Terraced houses opposite complete the picture of life as Lowry might have painted it.

Dobcross is one of a group of villages in the area called Saddleworth, a compelling example of a complete and totally unspoiled Pennine settlement from the 18th and 19th centuries. Built randomly on the hillside at the junction of two packhorse routes, Dobcross has weavers'

cottages, clothiers' and merchants' houses, and the former headquarters of Saddleworth Bank — forerunner of the National Westminster. All the surrounding area is rich in a mixture of industrial archaeology and countryside. Radio and television playwright Henry Livings lives here, and brass bands are a way of life.

When industry exploded in Oldham and Ashton-under-Lyne, land was gobbled up for mills, houses and canals. But a few acres, known as *Daisy Nook*, along the Medlock Valley between Oldham and Tameside, miraculously survived. Millworkers called it the 'weavers' seaside' because they spent Sundays here among the woods and streams away from the clatter and pandemonium of machinery. The area is now owned by the National Trust and it has locks, hides for wildlife watching, a dramatic aqueduct, a garden centre and lots of walks. A book was written about the area and called *Daisy Nook*; the name stuck and pubs and streets were called after characters in it. It lies on Newmarket Road, two miles off the A627 between Oldham and Ashton.

You might think that ghostly trains would shudder through you as you wander along Middlewood Way, the one-time railway track from Marple to Macclesfield, but the atmosphere is quiet and mellow. The trains stopped running in 1970 and the line fell into dereliction — until two local councils decided to convert the area into an amenity. Over three years the whole 11 miles of the line was transformed into a sort of linear park for cyclists, riders and walkers. You can stick to the Way itself, or explore the network of alternative paths.

Marton

Cheshire   SJ 8568

Along with St Oswald's Church at Lower Peover, the beautiful Church of St James and St Paul, mainly 14th-century, shares the distinction of being one of the oldest timber-framed churches in Europe. This superb example of a wood and plaster building is typical of Cheshire's black-and-white architecture.

Middleton in Teesdale

Co Durham   NY 9425

This small town of dour, yet attractive rows of cottages and houses developed early last century with the expansion of lead mining, mainly under the paternalistic Quaker London Lead Company. Company offices, workers' housing, non-conformist chapels, a Mechanics' Institute, at least a score of structures with arches (miners were very skilled in building these), and an ornate, cast-iron memorial fountain, are all to be seen.

Millington Pastures

Humberside   SE 8454

Until the early 1960s, a 400-acre field of rich, close-cropped grass sloping down to the dry valley of Millington Dale was used as common pasture by farmers in the district — a rare survival of open-pasture sheep-farming on the Wolds. Later it was enclosed, but public rights of way can still be followed through Wold country filled with lark song.

Morecambe Bay

Cumbria/Lancashire   SD 3975

From Kents Bank to Hest Bank, across the treacherous sands of Morecambe Bay, must be one of the most exciting of Britain's 'forgotten' routes. Official guides were once appointed by the Duchy of Lancaster; they had detailed knowledge of the tides and quicksands and moving river channels, but parish records and Cartmel

MUKER   *Traditional hay meadows near the village are at their flower-filled best in late June or early July. They are easily seen from the footpath that leads to the river*

tombstones record tragic drownings, and local newspapers of the period relate tales of near escapes for travellers and horses. A painting by Turner shows a motley crew of men, women and children — some walking, others in coaches or with horse and cart, and dogs barking at seagulls. The present guide takes occasional summer crossings: details from Guides Farm, Cart Lane, Cart-in-Cartmel.

Muker

North Yorkshire   SD 9198

Cottages of grey-brown stone, a popular pub, a church of Elizabethan times, a chapel and an Institute added during the lead mining boom last century make a memorable group in their setting by Muker Beck, against a backcloth of Swaledale hills. The district inspired the Kearton brothers, Richard (1862–1928) and Cherry (1871–1940), who went to the village school and became great naturalists and pioneers of wildlife photography.

Nether Silton

North Yorkshire   SE 4592

In a field behind the church is Yorkshire's mystery stone, bearing the enigmatic inscription:

H T G O M H S
T B B W O T G W W G
T W O T E W A H H
A T C L A B W H E Y
A D 1765
A W P S A Y A A

Not a code nor yet a series of anagrams, the letters are thought to be the initials of words, carved on Squire Hickes's orders in the 18th century:

'Here the grand old manor house stood,
The black beams were oak, the great walls were good;
The walls of the east wing are hidden here.
A thatched cottage like a barn was here erected year
   AD1765
A wide porch spans a yard and alcove.'

MIDDLETON IN TEESDALE: CHEESE — *The area around* **Middleton in Teesdale** *is known for its production of Cotherstone cheese. The name was first used in this century, but the recipe is older, going back to days when a black snail might be used in emergencies instead of rennet — a discontinued practice, though the cheese is otherwise the same. Cheese-making seems to have been going on in Wensleydale for the best part of 2000 years, to judge from a curd-strainer found in the Roman fort at Bainbridge. Swaledale farmers still make a cheese softer than the well-known Wensleydale, but other traditional Dales cheeses, such as Craven, Dentdale, Garsdale and Niddersdale, may now be extinct. Cleveland cheese, from the North York Moors, is still to be found in Thirsk, while Danbydale appears regularly at Guisborough market.*

Traditional farmhouse cheeses can still be bought in Neal's Yard Dairy, Covent Garden, **London** *and at Wells Stores,* **Streatley**, *but many are extinct or vanishing. Green Fade, a variant of Blue Cheshire described as 'a cheese fit only for heroes' and first appreciated by Yorkshire miners, was rare even in 1922, while real Dorset Blue Vinney, supplied for years in Colston Basset, is now made privately on only one farm. Some rarities, however, have been*

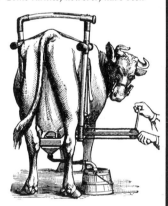

revived, like the Scottish Crowdie and Caboc (see **Tain***).*

Better-known products include Stilton, Britain's most renowned cheese. Records of its making around **Melton Mowbray** *date back to 1720. Enormous care was taken in its production: as an Edwardian cheesemaker told Rider Haggard, 'Stiltons, with the exception they make no noise, are more trouble than babies.'*

MILKING MACHINE   *A late 19th-century model from Denmark — designed to speed up milking but found to be no quicker than by hand*

Newcastle upon Tyne and around

Tyne and Wear NZ 2464

Victorian splendour and quayside bustle give way to golden sands and commonland where 'Hoppings' take place annually, with an Athenian temple and the Venerable Bede's Chair — centuries old — on the way

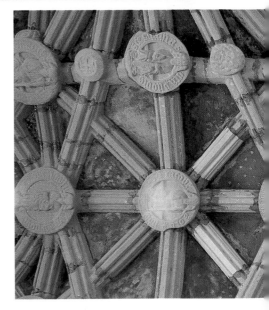

NEWCASTLE UPON TYNE: VENERABLE BEDE

— *The Venerable Bede (about AD672–735), born near Jarrow, now on the edge of* **Newcastle upon Tyne**, *was sent at the age of seven to the new monastery of Wearmouth. When he was about ten, he seems to have been moved to its sister house of Jarrow. Here he remained as a monk for the rest of his life, probably venturing no further south than* **York**, *no further north than Lindisfarne.*

But it was also here, with only the libraries of Wearmouth and Jarrow at his disposal, that he made himself perhaps the most learned man in Western Europe.

His greatest work was his 'History of the English Church and People', without which England's early past would be a matter largely of bare dates and archaeology.

GIBSIDE CHAPEL *(above)   at Rowlands Gill, in the Gateshead District, was built in the Palladian style by Paine*

JESMOND DENE *(above right)   With its mill, stream and wooded banks, it lies between Heaton and Jesmond — a village until the 19th century*

Regional capital and working-class town, Newcastle evokes intense local pride. It has a vitality, warmth and friendliness which can be seen and felt in pubs and shops, at the Sunday-morning Quayside market and the June 'Hoppings' on Town Moor; and nowhere is there so much lilt of music in voices.

The river gives Tynesiders their sense of place and Newcastle a reason for being. To understand the town (it achieved city status in 1882) and its history, start on the Quayside beneath the coat-hanger girders of Newcastle's most familiar bridge — easternmost of six spanning the river within a mile. This was the hub, near the Roman crossing and the medieval ford where the Swing Bridge stands idle now.

Nearby, in Close and Sandhill, 17th-century half-timbered houses and the Guildhall recall merchants' prosperity. A warren of 'chares' and steps climb, canyon-like, between cliffs of warehouse and office walls, towards the darkly massive Norman castle keep and the lantern-tower of St Nicholas' Cathedral beyond. In Broad Chare is the cobbled and flagged courtyard of Trinity House, with scrolls, inscriptions and an 18th-century chapel. 'Dog Leap Stairs' leads to All Saints' Church, whose tall steeple of 1786 dominates the skyline.

But all around change and development have continued ever since 1849, when Robert Stephenson threw his High Level bridge across the river, reversing 15 centuries of history to bring road and rail high above the water and shifting Newcastle's heart away from the Tyne.

Grey's Monument is the focal point for the neo-classical, early Victorian city, all elegance and stone dignity in Grey Street, and Grainger Street and the Grainger Market (1830–40). Nearby Eldon Square is the largest enclosed shopping and recreational complex in Europe, and five minutes walk away are the medieval Town Walls and Dominican Blackfriars friary, restored to sensible modern use.

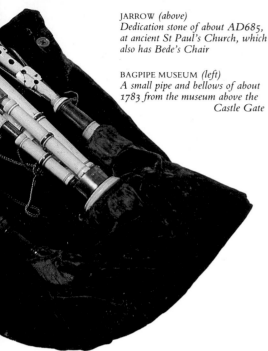

JARROW (above)
Dedication stone of about AD685, at ancient St Paul's Church, which also has Bede's Chair

BAGPIPE MUSEUM (left)
A small pipe and bellows of about 1783 from the museum above the Castle Gate

TYNEMOUTH PRIORY (below) *The intricately vaulted roof of the Percy Chantry is studded with carved roof bosses around a central figure of Christ*

The floodlights of St James' Park Football Ground are a guide to one of Newcastle's best streets — Leazes Terrace, a huge, inside-out, Regency rectangle. Beyond is the wonderful urban commonland, Town Moor. Newcastle University campus above Barras Bridge forms part of the town, while the new Civic Centre nearby has a carillon which plays traditional Tyneside tunes. 'Blaydon Races' was first heard in Balmbra's Music Hall in 1862 — the place was rebuilt in Clothmarket 40 years later and has now become a restaurant.

An Athenian temple of soot-blackened stone crowns *Penshaw Hill*, south-west of Newcastle. The 1844 monument commemorates the first Earl of Durham, a great Liberal parliamentary reformer, and is now owned by the National Trust. Local legend associates the river with the monstrous Lambton Worm which 'wrapped its tail ten times round Penshaw Hill', although another version reduces this to 'three times round Lambton Hill'. A young Lord Lambton, returning from a Crusade, is credited with slaying the worm.

Jarrow, in South Tyneside, celebrates its connections with both ancient and very 20th-century writers. Catherine Cookson, one of the best-selling writers ever, comes from the area. She left it when she was 22, returned almost 50 years later, and intends to remain here. All her 64 books are set locally and recently a 'Catherine Cookson Trail' has been established, based on places associated with her life and writings. Signs, information panels and plaques identify these, many being in and around Jarrow.

Near the southern approach to the Tyne Tunnel is St Paul's Church, one of Christendom's great sites, where Benedict Biscop founded a monastery in 681. The Venerable Bede spent most of his life there, and for 200 years Jarrow, with St Peter's, Monkwearmouth, and Lindisfarne, formed a centre of European culture and learning. Near the church 18th-century Jarrow Hall has been restored to house the Bede Monastery Museum, with various visitor facilities and an Information Centre.

Alongside the Tyne Tunnel itself is the Pedestrian Tunnel, with the longest pedestrian escalator in the world.

Newcastle's Victorian middle-class families took to the water at *Tynemouth*, east of the city where the river meets the sea. Golden sands beneath the headland give a resort flavour, while within the town dignified 19th-century terraces reflect its popularity. Tynemouth was once important for its clifftop monastery-fortress, an influence which went at the Dissolution, but the abbey ruins within the later curtain walls, on the sunny side of the estuary, are an ideal spot for watching the spectacle of Tyne shipping going about its business.

Three miles south of Sunderland is the *Ryhope Engines Museum*. Scheduled as a historic monument, this triple-gabled brick extravaganza, with adjoining tall chimney, houses two 1868 double-acting beam-engines which formerly pumped Sunderland's water supplies. Cared for by a devoted local trust, and occasionally steamed, the engines can be seen most weekends.

At Springwell, just north of Washington, the *Bowes Railway* can be visited, one of the many colliery railways developed to carry coal from local mines to the Tyne or Wear for shipment. Part of the line was designed by George Stephenson in 1826 and, subsequently extended, the railway continued working until 1968. Engine houses, lineside cabins and 40 wagons can be seen, on one-and-a-quarter miles of track, together with various buildings and equipment, including one diesel and two steam locos.

The display is open daily. Various Sundays and Bank Holidays from April to October are 'operational days', guided tours are available, and short train trips allow visitors to see the Rope Haulage Engine at Blackman's Hill — the only preserved standard-gauge rope-hauled railway working as it was in the coal-producing days. To get there, leave the A1(M) at Washington, take the B1288 Birtley road, and turn north to Springwell.

NEWCASTLE UPON TYNE: THE LAMBTON WORM
— Penshaw Hill, south of central **Newcastle upon Tyne**, *was once known as 'Worm Hill', recalling the legend of the Lambton Worm. This tells how the heir of Lambton caught a strange fish, which he threw into a well, where it turned into a dragon (worm, in early English). The monster chose to live in the River Wear and every now and again would emerge and wrap itself about Worm Hill, just like the dragon of* **Linton**.

When young Lambton returned from the Crusades to find the neighbouring countryside laid waste by this monster, he took a wise woman's advice and studded his armour with blades. He then stood in the river, whereupon the Worm, coiling about him, cut itself to shreds. Unfortunately, Lambton had promised the wise woman that he would kill the first creature he saw after his victory, but broke his vow when this proved to be his father. As a result, the family was cursed for nine generations, during which time no Lord of Lambton died naturally in his bed.

The Lambton Worm was just one of many dragons terrorising the north-east, according to old local tales. They lurked at Bamburgh Castle, Northumberland; Sockburn, County Durham; Slingsby, Kellington and Nunnington, North Yorkshire; Wharncliffe Side, South Yorkshire; and Handale, Cleveland.

ABOVE *The worm '. . . grew and grew, An' got to an awful size. He'd great big teeth, a great big mouth, And great big goggle eyes,' says the Northumbrian song 'The Lambton Worm'*

NINE STANDARDS:
MAGIC NINE —
*North Yorkshire. The
group of nine stone cairns known
as the* **Nine Standards** *is one of
several such 'Nines' in Britain.
The actual number sometimes
varies, and some say 'nine' is a
corruption of 'noon'.*

*This is suggested by the tradi-
tion that groups of standing stones
were women petrified for dancing
on the Sabbath, and more particularly by the Nine Maidens of* **St
Columb Major***, said still to
dance at midday. The Nine Stones
of Harthill Moor, Derbyshire, also
known as the Grey Ladies, dance
at midnight.*

*But 'nines' include other sorts of
antiquities. There really are Nine
Barrows at* **Priddy***, but the Nine
Barrows of Corfe Castle, number
eighteen. Superstitions surround
other numbers, but three, seven
and nine most of all.*

NINE STANDARDS *A line of
unexplained stone cairns*

Nine Standards Rigg

Cumbria   NY 8206

Over 2000 feet up, almost on the North
Yorkshire-Cumbria boundary, the Nine
Standards still pose a mystery. Various theories
exist about the origin of this line of nine stone
cairns on the hill called Nine Standards Rigg.
Shown on 18th-century maps, they give their
name to this lonely hill overlooking the Vale of
Eden. Most likely they were built as boundary-
markers or beacons, for the old boundary passed
through them. Now they mark the watershed of
the increasingly popular 'Coast to Coast' Walk
from St Bees' Head to Ravenscar. The easiest
approach is from Hartley, near Kirkby Stephen.

Northwich

Cheshire   SJ 6573

The imaginative Salt Museum in London Road
vividly tells the story of Cheshire's salt trade and
contains a life-size reconstruction of part of a salt
mine. Two miles away at Marton the privately-
owned Lion Salt Works were the only producers
of block salt in the United Kingdom still using
the age-old natural brine pumping method, until
closure in 1986.

Nunburnholme

Humberside   SE 8548

Small, attractive cottages are strung out along the
road which borders a clear chalk-stream in a
sheltered valley. Named after a former convent
for Benedictine nuns, the village was home for
Victorian ornithologist, the Reverend F. O.
Morris, rector from 1854 to 1893. In the house by
the church he wrote his six-volume *History of
British Birds*.

The church, whose Norman nave is only 15
feet wide, possesses a fine Anglo-Saxon cross
which has worn carving showing a Madonna and
Child and several animals including small
monsters. The cross dates from about the year
AD1000, and is a good example of its kind.

Old Gang

North Yorkshire   NY 9501

In a remote valley between Swaledale and
Arkengarthdale (reached from a minor road
between Low Row and Langthwaite) are the
ruins of the Old Gang complex of lead-smelting
mills and lead-mines.

The main period of local lead-mining was in
the 18th and 19th centuries, peaking between

1790 and 1860. The buildings at Old Gang are probably of early 19th-century date and include the remains of furnaces, chimneys, flues, workshops, smithy and stables. Beyond, on the hillside, are the stone piers of the old peat-store which originally had a timber-framed roof of ling thatch, 340 feet long (peat was used to fuel the furnaces). Adits and levels run into the hillsides along the former veins from which lead-ore was mined.

Osmotherley

North Yorkshire SE 4597

Gloriously situated on a shelf below the western edge of the Hambleton Hills, Osmotherley is as warm and inviting as its name. Three streets of stone houses of dark yellow sandstone meet at the market cross, while cobbled pavements and tree-lined verges vary the visual appeal. Behind and to the south are the moors; northwards is the start of the Cleveland Way, and nearby a delightful walk leads to a charming, early 16th-century Lady Chapel, which became a place of pilgrimage after the Reformation. It may have been built by a prior of Mount Grace Priory, to the north-west, a 'charterhouse' for Carthusian monks, who took vows of silence and lived in seclusion.

Piercebridge

Co Durham NZ 2115

A triple-arched bridge carries the road from Scotch Corner across the River Tees from North Yorkshire into Durham. The elegant George Hotel and a row of colourful cottages are in Yorkshire, but most of the village is in Durham, with neat, whitewashed cottages facing one another across a rectangular green on the site of an important third-century Roman station. The rounded north-eastern corner walls of the fort can be seen in a field north of the church. An earlier fort guarded the river-crossing to the east, where recent excavation has revealed a paved ford and the south abutment of the timber bridge carrying Dere Street.

Plemstall

Cheshire SJ 4570

The Church of St Peter is noteworthy for the work of the Reverend J. H. Toogood, rector from 1907 to 1944. It is not so much his spiritual work as his handiwork for which he is remembered, for during his long incumbency he made most of the furnishings — all the box pews, the choir stalls, the rood, the altar, the reredos, the war memorial and much else. The church lies at the end of a lane off the B5132 outside Chester.

Richmond

North Yorkshire NZ 1701

On Low Moor, a mile north-west of the town centre, is Richmond's former racecourse, established there in 1765 to 1776 after two centuries on High Moor. When Whitcliffe Pasture was enclosed in the early 19th century, the 82-acre racecourse and 44 acres of training gallops were secured, not only for horse racing but also for common grazing. Their fine turf and hillside situation are still an attraction today, and the remains of the 18th-century grandstand, and of the almost complete Judges' Box of 1814, evoke the atmosphere and excitement of racing in late Georgian times.

Richmond has another impressive survivor from the 18th century in its Georgian playhouse, built in 1788 by Butler — and the castle is one of the oldest stone forts in the country. There is a story of an underground passage, leading to Easley Abbey, along which ghostly drumming can be heard.

Rochdale

Greater Manchester SD 8913

After a bitter and humiliating strike, local flannel-weavers in Rochdale each subscribed a sovereign and opened the first Co-op in Toad Lane in 1844. It is called Toad Lane after Rochdale's way of pronouncing 'the old lane' or 't'owd lane'. Inspired by Chartist principles, customers shared all profits — and so one of the world's big businesses was born. There is even a Château Rochdale wine sold in Normandy by the French Co-op. The Rochdale shop shows documents, mementoes and pictures of the pioneers.

Also in Rochdale, the magnificent and grandiose town hall, reckoned to be one of the best in the country, is worth walking across town for. It is a soaring, Victorian Gothic fairy-tale building with a clocktower 191 feet high.

RICHMOND: SLEEPING KING — *The story goes that one Potter Thompson met a stranger at* **Richmond** *Castle, who let him into a vault below the walls. There he saw many people, seemingly asleep. Potter was given a horn and a sword, but as soon as he began to draw it, the sleepers stirred and so terrified him that he jammed it back into its sheath. A mysterious voice then reproached him for neither blowing the horn nor drawing the sword, either of which would have released the sleepers. They were King Arthur and his Knights, and a long time must elapse before the spell could again be challenged.*

All over northern England and into southern Scotland there are 'sleep sites' where traditionally King Arthur and his Knights lie, not dead but sleeping: Sewingshields Castle, Brinkburn Priory and Dunstanburgh Castle, Northumberland; Freebrough Hill, North Yorkshire; the Sneep, County Durham; Threlkeld Fell, near Keswick, Cumbria; and the Eildon Hills, Borders.

The prevalence of 'sleep sites' in the north lends strength to the suggestion that Arthur fought his last battle, Camlann, here, at Roman Camboglanna (Birdoswald). The same legend is, however, found elsewhere, notably at Cadbury Castle, South Cadbury, Somerset, and in Wales at Craig-y-Ddinas, Mid Glamorgan, Caerleon, Gwent, and on Lliwedd in Snowdonia.

ABOVE *Deep in the Eildon Hills there is a cave where Arthur himself is alleged to sleep*

ST CUTHBERT'S CAVE: CAVE GHOSTS AND TRADITIONS —

On the side of Cockenheugh near Hazelrigg is **St Cuthbert's Cave**, said to be haunted by the ghost of reiver — a Borders cattle rustler (see also **Woodcock Air**). He mislaid a great treasure hereabouts, and thereafter roamed the neighbourhood lamenting, sometimes as a dun-coloured horse, the bogey known as the Hazelrigg Dunny.

Others who 'haunted' caves were outlaws such as Twm Shon Catti of **Doethie Valley** and 'Wild Humphrey Kynaston', said to have frequented Kynaston's Cave, **Nesscliffe**.

In Runswick Bay, Yorkshire, there is a natural cavern called Hob Hole, haunted by a 'hob', here a beneficent kind of spirit, but often associated with mischief-making. The Hob of Hob Hole was believed to cure whooping cough and well into the 19 century, mothers would take their children into the cave, and exclaim in a loud voice

'Hob Hole Hob!
My bairn's gotten't kink-cough,
Tak't off, tak't off!'

Caves all over Britain have their legends. In some King Arthur sleeps (see **Richmond**), in others Merlin — as at **Carmarthen**. Perhaps the most notorious has disappeared under the suburbs of **Leicester**. Black Annis's Bower, in the Danes Hills, was the lair of an ogress who caught little children in her claws, sucked their blood and hung up their skins to dry.

Welsh folk lore in particular abounds with tales concerning treasure hidden in caves and other subterranean regions. One, the Cavern of Ravens in Glamorgan, is said to be guarded by two ravens who can summon the elements to defend their prize. A drover once ventured into the cave; immediately terrific thunder and lightning rent the air and the hapless man — scared out of his wits — rushed out gibbering.

ST CUTHBERT'S CAVE
The ghost of a cattle rustler is said to frequent the cave where St Cuthbert's body rested

Rosedale

North Yorkshire   SE 7296

This serenely lovely valley of the little River Seven, flowing southwards from the North York Moors, is appropriately named. But from 1856 until 1926 it was a Klondyke of ironstone mining, with millions of tons of ore sent by rail to Durham's blast-furnaces. Hundreds of miners worked in hillside tunnels, and plundered the ruins of Rosedale Abbey for building stone for their houses. Hillside scars are healed, but ruined kilns at Rosedale West and Rosedale East are stirring reminders of the busy past. Pony tracks and the route of the Rosedale railway are invitations to explore the lonely upper valley.

Rostherne

Cheshire   SJ 7483

Rostherne Mere, the largest and deepest of Cheshire's meres, is a National Nature Reserve: access is *by permit only* (details are given on notice boards). But a splendid elevated view of the mere can be had by going through the churchyard to the rear of St Mary's Church.

Rostherne Post Office and village store is the only shop in the village, but it compensates by specialising in the sale of English wines, of which it boasts one of the largest selections in the land — together with home-made cakes, jams, chutneys, relishes and the like, made to old English recipes.

Roughting Linn

Northumberland NT 9737

On sandstone ridges and outcrops of rock in northern Northumberland, strange carvings can be found, probably of early Bronze Age date. In a wooded grove near Ford the surface of a huge rock is covered with a variety of shapes — grooves, ridges, flowers and concentric circles known as 'cup-and-ring' marks. Their significance is not known, but may be religious. Experience the enigma at dusk in autumn; it is quiet, mysterious, even 'fey'.

Runcorn

Cheshire SJ 5182

Eleven years work on the site of Norton Priory has resulted in a museum which houses the most comprehensive exhibition of medieval monastic life anywhere in Britain. Visitors can see the excavated remains of the cloister, church, chapter house, kitchen and the undercroft, and in a purpose-built building there is a model of the priory as it was before the Dissolution, plus other exhibitions. Seven acres of woodland lead down to the historic Bridgewater Canal.

Rydal Falls

Cumbria NY 3606

When the Dowager Queen Adelaide visited Rydal in 1840, the first place she was taken to was the lower waterfall, so important an attraction had it become. Today the Rydal Falls are scarcely visited. Even guidebooks specifically devoted to listing and describing Lakeland's best waterfalls usually omit them. But during the heyday of landscape painting they were among the most painted subjects in the area — so popular that a summer-house was built to enable artists to carry on working even in the rain. The study by Wright of Derby is perhaps the finest.

Strictly speaking there are two falls — the Upper and Lower. For many years the Lower Falls have been inaccessible to the general public, but the grounds of Rydal Hall have recently been reopened to visitors on two days each week. The Upper Falls are part of an access area and are open at all times.

St Cuthbert's Cave

Northumberland NU 0635

Good navigation and a pleasant mile-long walk on the Kyloe Hills lead to this remote spot with its saintly and brigand-ish associations. The large, natural cave in 13 acres of open woodland is said to have been one of the resting-places of the body of St Cuthbert, on its journey from Lindisfarne to Durham but is also said to be haunted by an outlaw. Park the car at Holburn Grange Cottages, four miles north of the B6349.

Saltaire

West Yorkshire SE 1338

Sir Titus Salt's ideal of an industrial community far from Bradford's smoke consisted of mills like Renaissance palaces, good-quality housing, opportunities for education and advancement, and care for the sick and old. The huge mill was opened in 1853, and in the next 20 years 792 houses were built, together with almshouses, a school, a hospital, churches and chapels, public baths, Turkish baths, a steam laundry and a 14-acre park (with essential bandstand), all in a rural setting by the River Aire. Strangely, the visionary's statue shows him looking away from the town he created.

Sandbach

Cheshire SJ 7560

In the attractive cobbled square in the centre of Sandbach stand two sandstone pillars known as the Sandbach Crosses. Dating from about the ninth century, they are of uncertain origin, and though they are akin to others elsewhere none is so elaborately decorated as these. In the late 16th and early 17th centuries they were vandalised by religious extremists, but the scattered fragments were rescued and the pillars were rebuilt on their original site in 1816.

Around and just off the square itself are half-a-dozen old and picturesque pubs (with the Lower Chequer inn dating from 1570) and several cobbled streets with timber-framed houses.

Scarborough

North Yorkshire TA 0388

At the foot of the cliffs below the castle, in the old part of the town, Quay Street is tucked behind the brash façades and glitter of noisy Sandside. The timber-framed, plaster-fronted Three Mariners, now a numbered feature on Scarborough's History Trail, was a famous pub, with secret passages and probably large cellars, and a reputation for being a smugglers' haunt from the 14th century until 1910.

On Shrove Tuesday, Scarborough people may be seen skipping with long ropes beside the sea — an old Shrovetide custom.

Seal Sands

Cleveland NZ 5225

Teeside claims the doubtful privilege of possessing Europe's largest petro-chemical complex, yet on the north bank of the estuary, six miles south of Hartlepool, 1000 acres of mudflats and marshes at Seal Sands form an important bird sanctuary between the Farne Islands and the Humber. As a pausing point for migrants, from autumn onwards waders crowd the shoreline and gulls find little loneliness among the giant gantries. All seem unconcerned at the movement either of tankers in the river, or of watchers by the shore.

Settle

North Yorkshire SD 8263

This small market town of grey stone buildings stands on the edge of the largest area of limestone landscape in Britain — a southern gateway to the Yorkshire Dales National Park. It is also on the busy A65 Leeds-Kendal road, yet it has retained a friendly, family atmosphere. Small, compact and faithful to its past, its life and buildings are centred on the market place whose focus is the unusual, two-storey, arched Shambles, overlooked by the limestone crag called Castlebergh. Reached by steep paths, the summit rewards the energetic with panoramic views.

SIR TITUS SALT *thought comforts for workers would benefit industry — a new idea*

Sheffield and around

South Yorkshire SK 3587

A hotel bar adorned with 'wanted' posters of an arch-criminal and Mary Queen of Scots' lodgings can be seen in the steel city, while round about, Little John's grave, England's oldest circular keep and four strange monuments are to be found

SHEFFIELD: GABRIEL HOUNDS — *When a child was burnt to death in* **Sheffield**, *in the 19th century, neighbours remembered that the 'Gabriel Hounds' had passed over the house not long before.*

The Gabriel Hounds are packs of spectral dogs, also known in Cornwall as Dandy Dogs, and in Devon as Yeth or Wisht Hounds. The Wisht Hounds of Wistmans Wood on Dartmoor were the inspiration for Sir Arthur Conan Doyle's 'Hound of the Baskervilles'.

'Gabble' and 'Gabriel' are thought to come from an old word for 'corpse'. In the neighbourhood of **Leeds** *they were said to be the souls of unbaptised babies, doomed to flit forever round their homes.*

A more prosaic explanation is that the name imitates the gobbling sound they made as they passed overhead and that the 'hounds' were in fact flocks of wild geese. Also known as the Sky Yelpers, they may be the same as the mysterious Seven Whistlers, of whom only six were ever heard at one time. When all seven whistle together, the world will come to an end.

Sometimes the hounds were black with staring eyes, like the lone Moddey Dhoo of the **Isle of Man**, *and Black Shuck of East Anglia. They too were a portent of disaster.*

Twentieth-century Sheffield boasts of its remarkably clean air ('as clear as many a seaside resort'), its museums and galleries, its Crucible Theatre, its parks (there are 52 of them) and its fine modern civic architecture. Its tradition of steel and cutlery-making was celebrated by the placing of the blacksmith god Vulcan on the 192-foot tower of the Town Hall, and until the 1970s the express train to London was called the *Master Cutler*.

But reminders of a murkier side to Sheffield's past survives.

Charles Peace, (1832–79) arch-criminal and master of disguise (despite a grotesque appearance), became enamoured of Mrs Catherine Dyson at Banner Cross, Sheffield, and when her husband, Arthur, tried to chase him off, shot him in the head. Peace escaped, was re-arrested under a false name, and had his cover blown when his mistress wrote to the authorities identifying him and claiming £100 reward.

The smoke room at the Banner Cross Hotel, Ecclesham Road, Sheffield, near the spot where Peace shot Arthur Dyson, is now decorated in memory of Charlie Peace. The exhibits include 'wanted' posters (one of which gives 'Paganini' as one of Peace's aliases), and an enlargement of the official police photograph of Charlie, who indeed appears as 'monkey-faced', as contemporary observers said he was.

Mary Queen of Scots was 14 years in the area of the steel city when in the custody of the sixth Earl of Shrewsbury. Much of her captivity was spent at Sheffield Castle (now destroyed). She relieved the tedium of her imprisonment with lengthy visits to Sheffield Lodge, beside which still stands the Turret House, believed to have been built specially for the royal prisoner.

Sheffield's attractive south-western suburb of *Dore* appears a peaceful enough place, but it was the setting for a great battle to decide who should be the first man to wear the crown of all England. The conflict is commemorated by a stone inscribed: 'King Ecgbert of Wessex led his army to Dore in the year AD829 against King Eanred of Northumbria by whose submission King Ecgbert became first overlord of all England.' (In those days Northumbria meant the whole of England north of the River Humber.)

To the west the city abuts the moors which stretch down from the High Peak. Just into Derbyshire is *Hathersage*, where a grave, 14 feet long, near St Michael's Church porch, is reputed to be Little John's. A human thigh bone 30 inches long was found inside it. It is said that he was born in Hathersage and died here, broken hearted after the death of Robin Hood at Kirklees, near Leeds.

At the peaceful little village of *Bradfield*, further north, the gateway to the churchyard of St Nicholas is a sturdy, fortress-like building with windows overlooking the churchyard. It was once a watch-house, built to foil the 'resurrectionists' — or body-snatchers.

A few miles east of Sheffield, *Babworth* was the home of two of the Pilgrim Fathers: William Brewster, of Scrooby Manor, and William Bradford sailed in the *Mayflower* after their friend and parson, Richard Clyfton, had been deprived of his living for his beliefs. Manor Farm at *Scrooby* bears a plaque to say it was Brewster's home, and 'Brewster's Pew' can still be seen in the church at Scrooby, north of Babworth.

The first circular castle keep built in England is reputed to be at *Conisbrough*, between Doncaster and Rotherham. It appears as the home of Athelstane in Sir Walter Scott's novel *Ivanhoe*. The keep has six buttresses to support the walls (15 feet thick), in one of which is set the oratory Scott described in his novel. The castle was built by Hamelin Plantagenet in the 12th century. In 1321 a 'small feast' was held here by a later owner, Earl Thomas of Lancaster. For a total cost of £12.10½d, the feasters consumed four gallons of wine, twenty-eight gallons of ale, two geese, eight fowls, bread, eggs and meat. And that figure also took into account candles, provender for the horses and a tip for the woman who fetched the ale.

In the park of *Wentworth Woodhouse*, a great house near Rotherham, are four strange monuments. The Needle's Eye is said to have been built so that a gambler could drive a coach and horses through its arch, and was once used in local exercises of the Royal Horse Artillery. Hoober Stand, a three-sided construction, was built in 1748, in honour of George II and to commemorate Culloden. Cigar-shaped Keppel's Column was erected by the first Marquis of Rockingham to demonstrate his belief that a friend, Admiral Keppel, had been unjustly court-martialled; and the Mausoleum (in private woodland) is a tribute of 1788, by 'the first of the Fitzwilliams' (Earl Fitzwilliam) to his forebear, 'the last of the Rockinghams'.

CONISBROUGH CASTLE
A conical roof once topped the 90-foot keep. Walls 15 feet thick, massive buttresses and the round shape gave it strength

SHEFFIELD: BODY-SNATCHERS — *So concerned were they about the prevalence of body-snatching that the people of Bradfield, near* **Sheffield**, *built a watch-house in the churchyard.*

Body-snatchers, also known with black humour as 'resurrection men', used to dig up corpses in secret from graveyards, and sell them for medical research. Before the Anatomy Act was passed in 1832, anyone in Britain could open an anatomical school, without training or licence, and there was no formal provision of corpses for dissection.

Body-snatching was illegal and those who embarked on it risked fines and prison sentences. Most

notorious were Burke and Hare, who began by selling the dead body of their aged lodger, but soon proceeded to murdering healthy strangers.

Relatives of the deceased, perturbed at the activities of resurrectionists, would take the precaution of burying their loved ones in iron coffins or with the kind of protection still to be seen at Bradfield, and in Greyfriars churchyard, **Edinburgh** *(where Burke was hanged in 1829) which has a framework of iron bars, or 'mortsafe', enclosing the grave.*

ABOVE *Mr and Mrs Hare. Hare (who died a beggar) and Burke (who was hanged) provided fresh bodies for the anatomist Dr Robert Knox*

WENTWORTH WOODHOUSE *The Needle's Eye, built for a gambler who had rashly claimed that he could drive his coach through a needle's eye — or so the tale goes. The folly may well have pre-dated the story*

SLAIDBURN: SALT —
The salt roads around
Slaidburn *recall that salt
has always been a staple of human
existence. For a long time it was
the only means of preserving meat,
a necessity in the days when cattle
had to be slaughtered every
autumn because they could not be
fed during the winter.*

*Domesday Book informs us of
many salt-pans or 'salterns' in
Sussex and along the east coast,
and in Cheshire and north
Lancashire. At the salt-pans, fires
would be burned to evaporate seawater which had been channelled
into shallow enclosures ('pans').
The salt was then transported by
pack ponies along tracks known as
salterns roads or salt-ways.*

*One of the most important salt-
ways in the North was that from*
Manchester *to Salthill,
Clitheroe. One branch ran over
Waddington Fells to Newton and
Slaidburn, thence to Croasdale
and down the Roeburn from Salter
Fell, through High Salter and
Salter to Salterwath.*

Northwell, Cheshire and
Droitwich *were the major
inland salt-producing centres in
Anglo-Saxon times: at least six
salt-ways radiate from Droitwich,
one of them the present A38
between Worcester and
Birmingham.*

Siddington

Cheshire   SJ 8470

One of Cheshire's strikingly beautiful black-and-
white churches, All Saints is not quite what it
seems. The original 14th- or 15th-century
timber-framing was enveloped in a brick
cladding in 1815 when it was discovered that the
heavy flag-stone roof was causing the nave to
bulge dangerously. The traditional black-and-
white herringbone pattern was then painted on
the brickwork both inside and out. The chancel
and the south porch are in their original state,
however.

Adjoining the churchyard is a small farm, the
owner of which is known in Cheshire as a corn-
dolly maker, and invites inspection of his garden
and corn-dolly studio.

Skipsea Castle

Humberside   TA 1655

Soon after the Norman Conquest, William
granted the lordship of Holderness to Drogo de
Brevere, a Flemish adventurer who built a motte-
and-bailey castle at Skipsea Brough. Its enormous
earthworks remain, their outer ramparts, a
300-yard crescent, linked to the motte (36 feet
high) by a grassy, raised causeway. Elder and
hawthorn grow on the motte's steep sides, and
from its plateau top, 100 feet across, evening
sunlight picks out the distant lighthouse at
Flamborough.

One medieval historian claims that de Brevere
killed his wife.

SLAIDBURN   *The old salt road on Croasdale Fell, where
packhorses took vital salt to outlying farms*

SIDDINGTON   *Timber-framed churches are one of the
glories of Cheshire — but this one owes its black-and-
white appearance to painted brick*

Slaidburn

Lancashire   SD 7152

The Hark to Bounty inn is named from the story
of a local squire who recognised the voice of his
favourite hound, barking from afar, above the
rest of the pack. Two whips used by the official
parish dog-whipper, whose job was to separate
fighting dogs, are on display.

Coiling up over the fells around Slaidburn are
wild and deserted salt tracks which can be identi-

north and across Stainmore from Roman attack. Over 850 acres are enclosed by six miles of ditches and ramparts, some rising to over 20 feet in height. Excavation has revealed rock-cut ditches and some masonry walling.

Stoodley Pike

West Yorkshire   SD 9724

Dominating the southern skyline above the Calder Valley between Hebden Bridge and Todmorden, this 120ft-high monument was built in 1814 to commemorate the surrender of Paris in the Napoleonic Wars. It collapsed in 1854, and had to be rebuilt. Today it is conveniently reached from Lumbutts or Mankinholes, as well as being on the Pennine Way, and makes a superb viewpoint.

Summerseat

Greater Manchester   SD 7914

Bottoms Mill, one of five in this once-typical Lancashire textile village, closed in 1969 and hundreds of people lost their jobs. For years no-one knew what to do with such an enormous white elephant of a building, but now it has been converted into 55 flats. The frontage has been preserved and it is a fascinating example of turning old into new for people to use and enjoy. Part of the mill houses Bottoms Restaurant — once the old weaving shed — which offers meals every day of the week, and a real Lancashire cabaret on Saturdays.

Sunderland Point

Lancashire   SD 4255

High tides can whoosh over the road to Sunderland Point, so visits have to be timed carefully. This was once Lancaster's seaport, and ships unloaded here rather than negotiate the shallow River Lune up to the city itself. Cottages, 17th-century warehouses and a bath-house (now a garage) where slaves and sailors were de-loused still survive. Most poignant attractions, though, are a 50-foot high cotton tree which must have germinated from an imported bale of cotton, and Sambo's grave. Sambo arrived from the West Indies and willed himself to die shortly afterwards when his master left him to go away on business. He was buried in a lonely grave because Christians objected to a heathen lying in their consecrated ground.

Nearby at Middleton is the Old Roof Tree Inn — built in the first place by monks, it was reconstructed in 1440, and converted into an inn in 1953. A massive tree supports the cruck roof.

Swinnergill

North Yorkshire   NY 9000

Two miles east of Keld in upper Swaledale, reached by a footpath passing behind the ruins of Crackpot Hall, the wild ravine of Swinnergill cuts deep into a hillside. At the head of this secret valley is Swinnergill Kirk, a widening of the gorge below a waterfall hiding a cave entrance. It was a secret meeting-place for zealous nonconformists in the 17th century, when they were fined for holding services. A look-out warned of anyone approaching.

fied by their names: Salter Fell, Higher Salter Close, High Salter. The latter leads on to Hornby Castle, over the River Lune, to Gressingham. Pack ponies would follow these recognised salt-ways from Cheshire, south Lancashire, or the coastal salt-pans; salt was the only way of preserving meat during the winter and each farm needed plenty of it.

Stanhope

Co Durham   NY 9939

Steep roads climb to wild moorlands, but woodlands soften the hills enfolding Stanhope, whose broad main street leads to a small square near the parish church. Here the stump of a fossil tree guards the graves.

In the last century lead mining, ironstone working and quarrying brought prosperity and Methodism to this Pennine Dale, formerly used as hunting forest by successive Prince Bishops of Durham. Stanhope Castle (1798) is now a reform school; Stanhope Hall to the west is an unusual mixture of dates and styles; early 17th-century Stone House, north of the church, was once the old Rectory.

Stanwick

North Yorkshire   NZ 1811

Six miles north of Richmond is an impressive site of the Brigantes tribe constructed in about AD69–72 by Venutius as a tribal rallying point, and to protect the important trade routes to the

SUNDERLAND POINT: SLAVE TRADE — *The first British shipload of black West African slaves arrived in the colony of Virginia in 1619, and 17th-century buildings for de-lousing slaves can still be seen at* **Sunderland Point**.

During the 17th century, slavers of the specially formed Royal Africa Company would sail from **London, Bristol** *and* **Liverpool** *loaded with rum, guns, cloth and beads, to land on the Gold Coast or the estuary of the Calabar and Niger rivers.*

There they exchanged their cargo for natives captured in the hinterland by African slave-traders, and loaded up again for the 'Middle Passage', to the Americas.

Between 200 and 500 slaves would be manacled together between decks, each in a space about five feet long and eighteen inches wide. With neither ventilation nor sanitation, up to 40 per cent might die if the voyage were slow.

The survivors who reached the West Indies were kept in stockades or auctioned off at once, to work on the sugar plantations. Slaves were also used on the tobacco and cotton plantations of Maryland and Virginia, and the Southern States.

The slavers themselves returned to their home ports on the third leg of the notorious 'Atlantic Triangle' laden with tobacco and molasses. They were never empty and the profits were enormous: one reason why the Slave Trade was not abolished until 1807.

ABOVE *'Here lies Poor Sambo . . .' a slave who died at Sunderland Point and acquired this stone 'Full sixty Years' later, in 1796*

WEST WITTON: BURNING OF BARTLE — *One story connects the Burning of Bartle at* **West Witton** *with a giant, another with a local robber, Old Bartle, who used to steal the village pigs. One day as he was being pursued down the hillside, he fell and broke his neck, and was burnt at the stake at Grassgill End.*

An effigy of Old Bartle is still made in secrecy every year and carried through the village after dark. The procession stops outside any open door to show him to those within, while someone recites a verse recounting the chase. When it reaches Grassgill End, Bartle is thrown onto a large bonfire where he burns amid the explosions of hidden fireworks.

The ceremony bears an obvious resemblance to the burning of Guy Fawkes, and to 'Burning Judas' on Good Friday in **Liverpool's** *South End. Both are ritual punishments, but behind the 'punishing' of Bartle may be something else.*

'Bartle' is evidently St Bartholomew, patron saint of the parish church, whose day once ushered in a week's festival. Possibly his festival replaced that of a local harvest god, and the burning may stem from rites to this deity.

Burning forms part of another festival, the Burning of the Clavie, held at **Burghead** *in January. In this the aim is to drive out evil spirits lingering from the year before. The Clavie — a fire lit in half a barrel — is carried through the town by different people and if the bearer stumbles or falls bad luck will follow.*

Thixendale

North Yorkshire   SE 8461

This single-street village, nestling in a chalk-stream valley at the heart of the Wolds, has sixteen small dry valleys and six minor roads converging on it. The nearest town, Malton, is ten miles away. A timeless tranquillity pervades the characteristic grouping of church, lych-gate, vicarage and school, all designed by G. E. Street for Sir Tatton Sykes in about 1870.

Thorp Perrow

North Yorkshire   SE 2686

Approached by a long drive through well-wooded, sheep-grazed parkland, one of the finest arboreta in northern England numbers over 2000 trees in its 70 acres. Avenues and glades of different species lead from the main drives, their setting enhanced by an ornamental lake in front of the house. Beeches, silver birches and maples reveal special glories in autumn, while clouds of pink and white blossom adorn the cherry walk in spring.

Tockholes

Lancashire   SD 6622

Hidden in Tockholes woods are the ruins of Hollinshead Hall. Nearby a stream comes tumbling out of a lion's mouth at the restored Well House. The whole site is one of ancient habitation, and even when winds are howling off the moors people say it always feels quiet and peaceful here.

There are nature trails and breezy walks round Roddlesworth reservoirs nearby.

Wallington

Northumberland   NZ 0384

This large, square house of cool grey stone, built in 1688 by Sir William Blackett, was extensively remodelled in the 1740s. In 1855, on Ruskin's advice, it had its courtyard roofed and was given Italian arcades and an arched gallery. Contemporary decor by William Bell Scott illustrates scenes from Northumbrian history, and the pre-Raphaelite flavour of the Central Hall comple-

WARKWORTH   *A castle with some comfort inside its bold angles — it was built at a time when strength did not have to be the only consideration*

ments the 18th-century plasterwork, paintings, procelain and furniture of the main rooms. The walled garden has a conservatory with fine fuchsias, stone heads of the famous Wallington beasts glare at passing motorists from the gardens, and the extensive woodlands opposite are always open.

Warkworth

Northumberland   NU 2406

The great castle above the Coquet was a favourite home of the Percy family in the 14th century. Late in the century the second earl built the sophisticated keep where needs of comfort displaced those of defence. Narrow passages and secret stairs in the thick walls linking the various floors add lively interest, and upper windows afford lordly views of village, valley and coast. Up river, accessible only by boat from below the castle, is a 14th-century hermitage with relatively comfortable rooms hollowed out of a low, sandstone cliff.

Waskerley Way

Co Durham   NZ 0847

High on the windy Pennines of West Durham, the Waskerley Way is a footpath, bridleway and cycle track along the former Stanhope and Tyne railroad. The railroad was built in 1834 to carry lime from the Stanhope limekilns to the Tyne near South Shields. Much of it was worked by inclined planes, self-acting or using stationary engines, or, on some stretches, horse-power. The summit was at 1445 feet; Waskerley Station at 1150 feet brought into being a small village to house workers employed on the railway and in the engine sheds, which operated from 1846 to 1940.

Waskerley and Rowley Station, near Castleside, are access points for the Way. A station house at Waskerley bears the plaque K9, probably of about 1860, when the Stockton and Darlington Railway took control of the line.

West Witton

North Yorkshire   SE 0688

An annual three-day feast took place in this Wensleydale village in Victorian times. Now reduced to the Saturday in late August nearest to St Bartholomew's Day, the feast is a one-day sports event, ending late in the evening with the 'Burning of Bartle'. This ceremony involves an effigy, carried down the village street with pauses at many points (usually the pubs) before being burnt on a bonfire. A rhyme which is recited during the procession probably refers to a chase, traditionally involving the Giant of nearby Penhill, his wolfhound, a shepherdess called Gunda, the wise man of Carperby, and the local villagers, who were tenants of the Giant.

Whitby

North Yorkshire   NY 8911

At 9am on the eve of Ascension Day the custom of planting the Penny Hedge, or Horngarth, takes place. Three gumbooted countrymen, one holding a horn, the others carrying hazel stakes and branches cut from a wood at Eskadaleside near Sleights, tramp into the mud of the upper

harbour of the old town. The horn is blown by the Manor Baliff who then cries 'Out upon ye!' twice, the stakes and branches thrust into the mud to make a primitive fence — and so the traditional Horngarth is planted.

Legend takes the custom back to 1159, but it is more likely that it marks a practical tradition whereby tenants of land belonging to Whitby Abbey were reminded of the duty to keep their garths well maintained by the blowing of a horn, and possibly by the staking of the Abbot's land to low-water mark. It is thought that the knife for stake-cutting cost a penny, and that the hedge had to withstand three tides.

Perhaps the most curious of the town's pleasant buildings was demolished some fifty years ago — it was supported on the massive jawbones of whales.

Wigan

Greater Manchester   SD 5805

Wigan Pier has long been a joke. When George Formby senior strode the boards in Wigan, audiences roared with delight at every mention of it. The idea of a town 20 miles inland having a pier — with all the glamour that implied — tickled men and women who lived and worked in the industrial north.

Wigan Pier was actually a large, wooden coal

WIGAN   *Trencherfield Mill, where one of the world's largest engines is the pride of Wigan Pier — once a gantry, now the name of the refurbished canal-side, a far cry from George Formby senior's jokes and George Orwell's study of poverty*

gantry over the canal and railway. Not only were gantries often called piers in those days, but a barge picked up passengers from this one and took them to Liverpool. So it was, at least a little bit, like a seaside pier.

Today, the name Wigan Pier embraces the surrounding part of town. The council has transformed the derelict and dangerous canalside into a historical and recreational complex housing exhibitions, a heritage centre, a pub, a restaurant, a study centre, and Trencherfield Mill.

One of the mill's major assets is its superb engine — among the largest in the world. Volunteers from the Northern Mill Engine Society cleaned 80 years of grease off it, and the council spent £65,000 rescuing it from rusty redundancy, with the result that it can be seen in steam every weekend. 'Invigorating', 'symphonic', and 'majestic' are amongst the adjectives used to describe the sight.

Wigan Council have also pioneered land reclamation and nature conservation in areas most blighted by toxic waste and tipping, and barges from the pier carry people to 'the Flashes', now rich in wildlife and flora.

WHITBY: WHALES' BONES — 'Great ghastly whale-jaws', *Mrs Gaskell said of the numerous whalebone arches erected since 1750.* **Whitby** *possessed an edifice (demolished in 1930) whose principal supports were seven pairs of jawbones — doubtless taken from one of nearly 3000 whales landed here.*

Penton, Cheshire, had a bridge made from the jawbones of a whale, and arches still survive at **Cellardyke**, *in* **Edinburgh**, *in* **Hull** *and the public park at* **Cleethorpes**. *Most spectacularly sited are the jaws on top of North Berwick Law, Lothian.*

Jaws were the bones whalers brought back most frequently as they had the highest content of oil, which could be drained out on deck during the homeward voyage. St Mary Redcliffe, **Bristol**, *had a rib, and the Dun Cow's Rib in Stanion, Northamptonshire is probably a whale's bone, though said to belong to the fairy cow of* **Dunchurch** *and* **Mitchell's Fold**.

WOLD NEWTON: METEORITES — The meteorite which fell on 13 December 1795, at **Wold Newton**, is kept at the Natural History Museum, **London**. It is the earliest meteorite in the collection.

Other places in Britain hit by meteorites include **Perth** and **Middlesbrough**, where the stone fell on a railway line a mere 40 yards from some workers. The Wold Newton meteorite missed a labourer by no more than ten yards, while a man in India was actually killed by one in 1827.

Not unnaturally, these 'bolts from the blue' have in the past often acquired a mystical significance. For generations a meteorite which fell in Phrygia was worshipped as Cybele, the Great Mother. One of the holiest Muslim relics, built into a corner of the Kaaba at Mecca, is also thought to be a meteorite. Beliefs in the holiness of meteorites may be echoed in a tradition attached to the Rudston Monolith, Humberside, the tallest standing stone in Britain at 25 feet 9 inches high (it was probably once higher). One explanation said that the stone had fallen from the clouds and buried some people desecrating the churchyard — quite possibly an embroidered memory of the Wold Newton meteorite.

DIGGING FOR METEORITES, seen as celestial cannonballs, at Hatford, near Oxford, in an illustration of 1628

WYCOLLER The ancient clapper bridge — uncrossed for years when the village was abandoned by its people

Wildboarclough

Cheshire SJ 9868

This little village, lying in a secluded fold of the hills of the Peak District, has been described as 'the most beautifully placed of all Cheshire villages'. The post office occupies a part of a three-storey former mill. The legend that the village was the scene of the last boar hunt in England has now been largely discounted.

Windermere

Cumbria SD 3994

Four admirals are honoured by the Temple of Heroes, an octagonal stone building lapped by the waters of England's longest lake, off the shore of Storrs Hall Hotel, on Windermere.

Linked to the hotel grounds by a substantial stone jetty, the open, unglazed windows frame unrivalled views to the north, south and west. At the side of each window are the names of the admirals who secured celebrated victories during the Napoleonic Wars: Nelson, Howe, Duncan and Vincent.

The hotel itself was built in 1790, and visited by some of the country's most important statesmen in the early years of the 19th century. Among them was William Huskisson, President of the Board of Trade, and the first person to be killed in a railway accident, when he attended the opening ceremony of the Liverpool to Manchester Railway.

Wold Newton

Humberside TA 0473

At 3pm on 13 December 1795, a meteorite landed with a loud explosion and made a hole 19 inches long and 28 inches wide in a field, three-quarters of a mile south-east of this Wolds village. It was analysed and sent to the Natural History Museum in London, and the spot where it landed is marked by an obelisk.

Wolsingham

Co Durham NZ 0737

Together with four other markets granted by the Bishop of Durham, Wolsingham had its goods subjected to an early form of consumer protection. The Marshall of the Markets controlled standards, awarding goods a seal of approval.

Among good houses in Front Street, Whitfield House and Old Bank House date from the late 17th century, contemporary with the finely carved headstones in the churchyard. A 19th-century cast-iron milestone in the main road is a reminder of Weardale's iron industry, which developed during Victorian times.

Wycoller

Lancashire SD 9339

Writers have always been drawn to Wycoller — probably because of its eerie past. During the Industrial Revolution the people of Wycoller, who were handloom weavers, abandoned it and moved to nearby towns to work on the power looms of textile-booming Lancashire. They never returned, and the village fell derelict. Goldsmith is said to have based his poem *The Deserted Village* on it. For years no-one crossed the three bridges here: the Iron Age clam bridge (just a single slab of gritstone across the back), the 'weavers' bridge, and the packhorse bridge. Wycoller Hall crumbled — watched only by the Brontës who walked round here on hikes from Haworth. Caught by the stories of a mad woman who set the hall on fire, and a dispossessed heir called Thomas Eyre, Charlotte Brontë wrote *Jane Eyre* and made Wycoller Hall the Ferndean Manor of her novel.

Today, volunteers have restored much of the village and many of the cottages are now inhabited again. The 16th-century hall has a superb fireplace, window and cockfighting pit. Once a year a ghost horseman gallops through to atone for the murder of his wife. He found her embracing a long-lost brother, and mistook him for a lover.

On the moorland around can be seen 'vaccaries' — vertical stone slabs used as cattle enclosures in the 13th century.

Yarm

Cleveland NZ 4111

To drive along the busy High Street takes a minute; to saunter and savour may occupy a pleasant hour. Three-storey buildings reflect the prosperity of Georgian merchants; coaching-inns retain arched entrances to courtyards and stables. In Chapel Wynd is the octagonal Methodist Chapel of 1763; St Mary Magdalene's Church, a simple Georgian building of 1730, overlooks the river. A huge viaduct dominates the town, where, in the George and Dragon, the Stockton and Darlington Railway was first promoted in 1820.

Yeavering Bell

Northumberland NT 9229

A few miles west of Wooler, this northern outpost of the Cheviot Hills, accessible from the road and relatively easy to climb, has thoroughly rewarding wide views northwards across the Tweed basin. In pre-Roman times Northumbrian Celts liked its defensive qualities; and their rampart walls, visible among the heather and bilberry, enclosed 17 acres around the summit, with 130 timber huts housing a large community.

York

North Yorkshire SE 6052

More than most historic cities, York has a profusion of secretive paths and alleys for which Mark Jones has coined the evocative word 'snickelways'. Almost all evolved as the paths that people took, to church, to market and to work. Following them is fun, giving a glimpse of hidden intimacies behind and between the shopfronts and busy streets. Over 50 short 'Snickelways' lie within quarter of a mile of York's most famous street, the Shambles; almost every one is a tiny oasis of quiet, more often in shadow than in sun. Footsteps echo on the flags of Lund's Court, Pope's Head Lane, Coffee Yard and Straker's Passage, doubtless as they did centuries ago. Here, perhaps, are the real ghosts of York.

After exploring the city at ground level, take to the walls for the longest snickelway of all, a three-mile circuit above the noise and bustle of city streets.

YEAVERING BELL: ANGLO-SAXON PALACES — One of the most exciting archaeological finds ever made in England was the discovery at **Yeavering Bell** of what the Venerable Bede (see **Newcastle-upon-Tyne**) called 'villa regalis ad Gefrin', the royal house of the Northumbrian kings.

Excavations from 1953 to 1957 produced the plan of a complex series of buildings. Outside a large timber fort of the late sixth century stood a long, rectangular wooden hall (rebuilt six times) and a wooden structure thought to have been a grandstand.

Another building was probably a temple, turned into a Christian chapel after the court had been converted by Paulinus in AD627. The grandstand may be where he preached.

The scale of the Yeavering complex — abandoned in about 685, after perhaps three generations — reflects the early political supremacy of the Northumbrian kings.

A Mercian palace has been traced at Hatton Rock, near **Stratford-upon-Avon**, and the kings of Wessex and England — perhaps even Alfred himself — lived at Cheddar.

Here the site was dominated until about AD930 by a long timber hall, which may have been two-storeyed and as much as 78 feet long — 'towering high and horn gabled', perhaps, like the royal hall described in the Anglo-Saxon epic 'Beowulf'.

GLASGOW *circa* 1880.
The Broomielaw – the steamers in the foreground are
'going doon the watter'; beyond are boats for Ireland.
One paddle steamer – the Waverley – sails the Clyde today,
and its mooring is not far from the Broomielaw. It is the
only sea-going paddle steamer in the world

SOUTHERN
SCOTLAND

*T*he Lowlands, where local imagination runs riot:
*Maggie the Witch annoyed the Devil so was turned to stone and
stands on the Lomond Hills; Linton church sits on a hill
squeezed out of the ground by a dragon's tail, and is Alva Glen
still full of fairies? Less fanciful but no less fascinating is the cave
at Pittenweem where St Fillan lived and services are still
occasionally held; the mysterious brochs scattered about —
built by Iron Age tribes, or not? A land too, of surprises.
Sculptures by Epstein, Moore and Rodin on the hills at
Glenkiln, a Tibetan Centre at Eskdalemuir and Britain's
shortest street at Falkirk.*

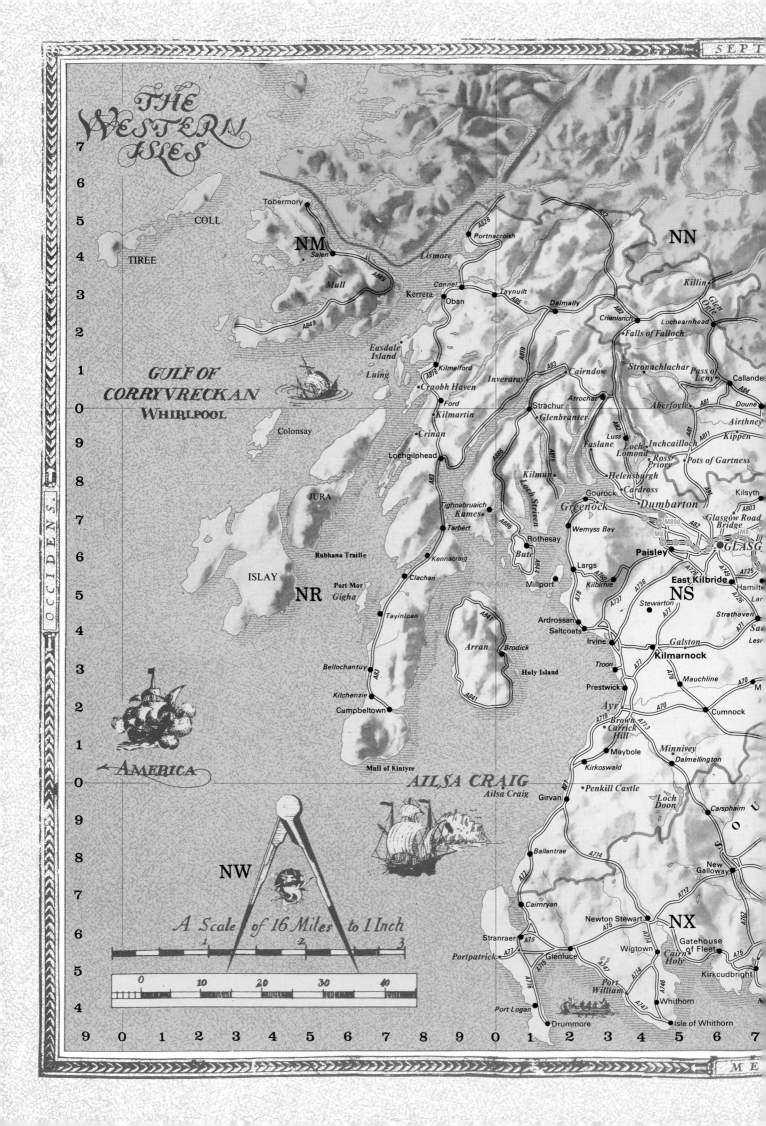

THE WESTERN ISLES

COLL

TIREE

Tobermory

NM

Salen

Mull

Kerrera

A849

A849

GULF OF
CORRYVRECKAN
WHIRLPOOL

Colonsay

JURA

ISLAY

NR

Port Mor
Gigha

Rubha na Traille

Easdale
Island

Luing

Kilmelford

A816

Craobh Haven

Ford

Kilmartin

Crinan

Lochgilphead

A83

Tighnabruaich
Kames

Tarbert

Kennacraig

Clachan

Tayinloan

A83

Bellochantuy

Kilchenzie

Campbeltown

Mull of Kintyre

Portnacroish

A828

Lismore

Connel

Oban

A85

Taynuilt

Dalmally

A85

A819

Inveraray

A83

Strachur

A886

A83

A815

Cairndow

Atrochar

Glenbranter

Luss

Faslane

Loch
Lomond

Kilmun

Loch Striven

A886

Rothesay

Bute

A844

Sound of Bute

Millport

Arran

A841

Brodick

Holy Island

A841

Crianlarich

A82

Falls of Falloch

Stronachlachar

Ross
Priory

Helensburgh

Cardross

Greenock

Gourock

Wemyss Bay

Largs

Kilbirnie

Ardrossan

Saltcoats

A78

Irvine

A737

Troon

Prestwick

Ayr

A719

Brown
Carrick
Hill

Maybole

Kirkoswald

AILSA CRAIG

Ailsa Craig

Girvan

A77

Penkill Castle

Ballantrae

A714

A77

Cairnryan

A77

Stranraer

A75

Portpatrick

A77

Glenluce

A716

A715

Port
William

Port Logan

Drummore

A742

Killin

NN

Glen Orle

Lochearnhead

A82

Pass of
Leny

Callande

A84

Aberfoyle

A81

Doune

Airthrey

A811

Kippen

Inchcailloch

Pots of Gartness

A81

Kilsyth

A803

Dumbarton

Glasgow Road
Bridge

M898

M8

M8

Paisley

GLASG

East Kilbride

A726

A736

A760

A77

Stewarton

A78

Galston

Kilmarnock

A76

Mauchline

A70

Cumnock

A70

A713

A719

Minnivey

Dalmellington

Loch
Doon

Carsphairn

A712

New
Galloway

A712

Newton Stewart

A75

NX

Gatehouse
of Fleet

A75

Wigtown

A714

A746

Cairn
Holy

Kirkcudbright

Whithorn

A747

Isle of Whithorn

Hamilte

Lar

Strathaven

A71

Sa

Lesr

NS

A728

A726

Kilsyth

AMERICA

NW

A Scale of 16 Miles to 1 Inch

1   2   3

0   10   20   30   40

OCCIDENS

9 0 1 2 3 4 5 6 7 8 9 0 1 2 3 4 5 6 7

SOUTHERN SCOTLAND

NO

A·Central B·Fife
C·Strathclyde D·Lothian
E·Borders
F·Dumfries and
Galloway

MICAT INTER OMNES IVLIVM SIDVS

ORIENS

Newport-on-Tay

Newburgh
Moonzie
Auchtermuchty
Kembäck
Scotstarvit
Ladybank
Bannet Stane
St Andrews
Fife Ness
Crail
Cellardyke
Glenrothes
Buckhaven
Pittenweem
Elie
Isle of May
Cowdenbeath
Wemyss Caves
Kirkcaldy

FIRTH OF FORTH

Glen Dollar
Menstrie
Dunfermline
Bo'ness
South Queensferry
Inverkeithing
Kinghorn
Falkirk
Linlithgow
Cairnpapple
EDINBURGH
Ratho
Almondell
Shotts
Carluke
West Linton
Corra Linn
Broughton
Kirkton Manor
Lamington
Abington
Peebles
Innerleithen
Galashiels
Melrose
Mertoun
Selkirk
Harestanes
St Mary's of the Lowes
Jedburgh
Hawick

Cockenzie and Port Seton
Garleton Hills
Pencaitland
Dalkeith
Musselburgh
Haddington
Pencraig
Abbey St Bathans
LAMMERMUIR HILLS
Manderston
Polwarth
Lauder
Greenlaw
Coldstream
Kelso
Roxburgh
Linton

Luffness
North Berwick
Athelstaneford
Dunbar
Barns Ness
Cove Harbour
Fast Castle
Eyemouth
Foulden

CHEVIOT HILLS

Durisdeer
Moffat
Eskdalemuir
Thornhill
St Ann's
Bentpath
Keir Mill
Craigcleuch
Langholm
Lochmaben
Lockerbie
Hightae
Canonbie
Dumfries
Woodcock Air
New Abbey
Annan
Gretna

NY

PART OF ENGLAND

Solway Firth

9 0 1 2 3 4 5 6 7 8 9 0 1 2 3 4 5 6 7

ABBEY ST BATHANS: BROCHS

*— Edin's Hall Broch, near **Abbey St Bathans**, is one of a series of fortresses built in a style unique to Scotland.*

The mysterious brochs were erected by Iron Age tribes. They were essentially tall, circular, dry-stone towers with a thick ring-base enclosing a courtyard. Here a central hearth was surrounded by wooden buildings, clinging to the inner face of the wall.

The ring-base was divided above first-floor level into an outer and inner wall, the hollow between being occupied by galleries with flagstone floors, through which a staircase wound clockwise to the walltop. The Clickhimin Broch, Shetland, housed perhaps 30 to 50 people.

There are something like 500 brochs in Scotland, all similar in design. It has been suggested that professionals built them, or that they are evidence of the rise of a new ruling class, imposing its ideas on disparate local populations. The origin of brochs was hotly debated, until the excavation of Clickhimin from 1953 to 1957 showed that this broch had developed from an earlier type of fort, seeming to confirm the view that brochs were military in origin, not defended farmsteads.

Until the 19th century nothing was known of them. They were popularly judged to be 'Picts' castles' or 'Picts' hooses'. In the Hebrides they were associated with the fairies. Edin's Hall, a rare Borders broch, has some claim to be the lair of an ogre, the Red Ettin of an old fairy tale told in the nursery of the infant James V.

◆ ⸻ ◆

ABOVE *Mousa broch, Shetland: 40 feet high, with stairs winding inside the walls to the top*

◆ ⸻ ◆

AIRTHREY HERMITAGE
Looking towards the Wallace Monument, 362 feet high, built in 1869 at a cost of £1600

Abbey St Bathans

Borders   NT 7562

Toot Corner is not something from A.A. Milne, but a sharp bend near this attractive village in the winding valley of the Whiteadder Water. An early road sign was erected here, with the cut-out word 'TOOT', giving the same cost-effective message in both directions.

Around the village, copper beeches contrast with the fine natural oakwoods. An estate information centre and trout farm are open to visitors. The coast-to-coast Southern Upland Way passes through; less ambitious walks include a hillside stroll from Toot Corner to the remains of Edin's Hall Broch, an Iron Age tower standing high over the valley.

Aberfoyle

Central   NN 5200

Up above the tourist village of Aberfoyle there are waymarked trails running through the conifer plantations of Achray Forest, reached by the pass constructed by the Duke of Montrose and known as the Duke's Road. It climbs, at first, through a beautiful birchwood fringe; near the summit of the pass, trees screen the massive spoil heaps of the series of quarries which produced up to a million and a half roofing slates a year, until they closed in 1958.

In these lonely and slightly eerie surroundings stand the remains of the abandoned village called Slate Quarries, which in its heyday in the 1920s had a bigger population than Aberfoyle itself.

Ailsa Craig

Strathclyde   NX 0299

Gannets nest by the thousand on the great southern and western sea-cliffs of Ailsa Craig. Until well into the 19th century, the tenant of the great rock raised the rent due to the Marquis of Ailsa by gathering and selling their feathers.

Known to passengers on the old Glasgow-Belfast steamers as Paddy's Milestone, this towering granite outcrop in the Firth of Clyde is reached by a ten-mile boat trip from Girvan. Visitors land near the Victorian lighthouse, which has an array of fearsomely loud modern foghorns. Since quarrying for curling stones finished, the lighthouse-keepers are the only regular inhabitants.

An exposed footpath climbs past a ruined castle and an unexpected high-level lochan, to the magnificent viewpoint summit, at 1110 feet.

Airthrey Hermitage

Central   NS 8196

Below the rock-face of the Witches Craig, the monuments of the Grahams of Airthrey make an aisle in the old churchyard of Logie. Nearby, a lane follows the wall of the family's one-time estate, and footpaths climb a steeply wooded hill to the stone hermitage built by a Graham laird, who then advertised for a hermit to occupy it.

With its three, arched, window openings, the hermitage provides a splendid viewpoint over the estate to the outstanding Wallace Monument, silhouetted on a neighbouring hill. The estate, surrounding a sailing loch, was taken over in the 1960s as the campus of Stirling University.

Allan Water

Central   NS 7896–NS 8909

The most beautiful stretch of the river can be seen from the wooded and wildflower-rich Darn Road, actually a footpath, which follows the east bank towards Dunblane. A riverside cave here was a favourite boyhood haunt of Robert Louis Stevenson, whose family brought him to 'take the waters' at the Bridge of Allan spa.

Bridge of Allan itself, on the banks of Allan Water, grew up around a well-house — it was built in 1820 at the spring of mineral-rich water, which, like Airthrey Hermitage, was one of the features of the Airthrey estate. The water flowed from an abandoned copper mine.

Almondell

Lothian   NT 0868

Within a mile of the wilderness of red spoil-heaps around the old Pumpherston shale-oil works, Almondell is a 90-acre country park where beautiful, wooded ridges of pine and larch, elm, chestnut, oak and lime look down on meadows beside the winding River Almond. There are woodland and riverside walks, interesting bridges and abundant wildlife.

Outside the visitor centre in the restored Stables Cottage stands the Kirkhill Astronomical Pillar, erected in 1777 by the Earl of Buchan. His remarkably accurate calculations about planetary movements can still be seen carved in the stonework today.

Alva Glen

Central   NS 8897

Most spectacular of the southern glens in the Ochil Hills, this sheer-sided ravine is reached by an easy high-level footpath from a public park around the lowest waterfalls of the Alva Burn. Mosses and ferns flourish in the chasm which nevertheless has a long history of service to industry. A pipeline, on which the early part of the footpath is built, used to direct water to Alva's textile mills. Above the top reservoir is the grassy upper glen, where a side-path plunges downhill again towards another waterfall crashing into an inaccessible rocky chamber.

Arran

Strathclyde   NR 93

Around 2000 red deer roam the northern glens and golden eagles soar overhead, while offshore there are regular sightings of porpoises, whales and plankton-eating basking sharks, 30 feet long.

Arran is one of Scotland's grandest islands, with a remarkable variety of landscapes, from the jagged skyline of the northern granite mountains to the moorlands and forest plantations of the south. Prehistoric man settled early here, and impressive Bronze Age stone circles on Machrie Moor. A modern sculptor has used a similar design at the Thomson Memorial Seat by the roadside south of Brodick. For industrial archaeologists there is the abandoned barytes mine, last worked in 1939 and overlooked by the rugged mountains of Glen Sannox. In North Glen Sannox are the remains of what was once the biggest village on the island: all 500 residents were evicted in 1832. They settled, successfully, in Canada.

Natural formations include the Fallen Rocks, a massive sea-cliff landslip reached by a forest walk north of Sannox, and a fine waterfall in Glenashdale near Whiting Bay. Other excursions include visits to the National Trust for Scotland's splendid Brodick Castle and its colourful woodland gardens; a stiff walk to the summit of Goat Fell (2866 feet) which rises above them; a tour of the Arran Heritage Centre at Rosaburn and a sail from Lamlash to Holy Island, which rises to 1030 feet.

ALVA GLEN: A PLACE OF FAIRIES — Long known as a beauty spot, **Alva Glen** lies in a part of the Ochil Hills which was once remarkable for its fairies.

A few miles west of Alva, and still marked on the map on the northern edge of Bridge of Allan, is Fairy Knowe, an artificial mound in which (as elsewhere in Britain) fairies were believed to live.

It was in Menstrie Glen, between Bridge of Allan and Alva, that the Black Laird of Dunblane, returning late one night from Alloa, fell in with the fairies and flew with them to Cruinan, mounted on a plough-beam.

But the most celebrated fairy tale connected with the district is that of 'The Miller of Menstrie', which tells how the miller's pretty wife was abducted by the fairies. Every morning, though he could not see her, he could hear her chanting over his head:

'O! Alva woods are bonnie,
Tillicoultry Hills are fair
But when I think on the braes
   o' Menstrie,
It makes my heart ay sair.'

One day as he was standing at his mill door sifting chaff, the miller happened to stand on one foot — whereupon she appeared beside him, for his action had broken the spell.

FAIRY GLENS   *Illusion, enchantment and a wicked sense of fun — the stock-in-trade of fairies*

ATHELSTANEFORD: MIRACULOUS FLAGS

ATHELSTANEFORD: MIRACULOUS FLAGS — *A flag seen in the sky at* **Athelstaneford** *gave new heart to the Scots who were fighting King Athelstan in the ninth century — a story which echoes the legend of 'Constantine's Cross', according to which Constantine, on his march to Rome, saw a cross in the sky with the motto 'In hoc vinces' — 'By this conquer'. On the night before the battle of Saxa Rubra (AD312) he was told in a vision to inscribe the cross and motto on his soldiers' shields, which he did — and won.*

A similar account is given of the Dannebrog or 'Strength of Denmark'. King Waldemar II, leading his troops into battle against the Estonians in 1219, saw a fiery cross in the sky which he took as assurance of victory. The sign was adopted as the Danish flag — legend aside, the flag has been in use since the 13th century, and is therefore the oldest in existence.

Pagans also had their holy flags, notably the Vikings, who often fought under a raven — the sign of Odin. A banner called 'Raven', said to have been woven by the daughters of the semi-legendary hero Ragnar Lothbrok, which fluttered for victory but drooped for defeat, was captured in Devon by Anglo-Saxon forces in AD878.

Another magical raven banner, 'Landwaster', belonged to the Danish Earl Siward ('Old Siward' of 'Macbeth'), who ruled Northumbria in the decades before the Norman Conquest. A giant of a man, he was alleged to be the grandson of a great white bear, and his father was said to have had bears' ears hidden under his helmet.

A rather less warlike but no less miraculous banner was the fairy flag of Dunvegan Castle (see **Skye***). As well as bringing victory, it was locally believed to be a fertility talisman. Once asked by his peasantry to wave it at the time of a potato famine, the Macleod of the day refused. But perhaps because of his association with the banner, the Macleod himself was thought of as a fertility bringer: his return to Dunvegan after a long absence was in the 18th century believed to be always followed by an exceptionally good herring catch.*

—∘:∘✕∘:∘—

Athelstaneford

Lothian   NT 5377

The name comes from the loser in a battle fought around the year AD815. The Saxon king Athelstan was defeated by an army of Scots, who are said to have been heartened by the appearance of an omen in the sky — a formation of white clouds arranged in a cross against the blue background. This was the cross of St Andrew which, ever since, has been the national flag of Scotland. One flies, day and night, over a memorial in the parish churchyard.

A sensitively restored estate village of the 18th century, Athelstaneford still has its lines of single-storey cottages with mellow, red-pantiled roofs.

Ayr

Strathclyde   NS 3322

Dodgem cars, a helter-skelter and a merry-go-round can be seen in Ayr Cemetery in Holmston Road: all are carved on the gravestones of carnival folk buried here. Also immortalised on a headstone are a horse and jockey, a reminder that Ayr is the main centre of horse-racing in Scotland. Early-risers can see stable-lads exercising their charges in the morning on the resort's two-mile sands.

The character that dominates Ayr is Robert Burns: he is featured all over this old-established county town, having been born in what is now the suburb of Alloway. But other Scots have also made an impression locally. William Wallace, for instance, wiped out an English garrison here during the independence battles of the late 13th century; an incident recalled by the striking Victorian baronial monument to him on the lonely viewpoint hilltop at Barnweill, six miles north-east. Keys for it are available from the information centre in Miller Road, Ayr.

BALCARY HEUGHS   *Once a vantage point for smugglers. Offshore lies Hestan Island; further round the coast are Rough Island bird sanctuary and Mote of Mark, a vitrified fort (both National Trust for Scotland)*

Balcary Heughs

Dumfries and Galloway   NX 8249

Balcary Bay, a beautiful inlet of the Solway Firth, was a hot-bed of smuggling until stern measures finally extinguished the contraband trade in the 1820s. An invigorating right-of-way leads over fields and through woodlands on to the hills called Balcary Heughs.

The footpath rises above seabird cliffs to a headland. A concealed watcher used to signal with a lantern from the rock formation called Adam's Chair, to let smuggling boats approaching from the Isle of Man know if the coast was (literally) clear, for the landing of illicit cargoes of wines, brandy, lace or tobacco.

Bannet Stane

Fife   NO 1807

Easiest to reach of the weird rock formations on the Lomond Hills is the Bannet Stane or Bonnet Stone, a massive 'table' of sandstone poised on top of a slim supporting pillar.

On the west side of the hills is Carlin Maggie — Maggie the Witch — who so annoyed the Devil that he hurled a bolt of lightning to turn her into stone for all eternity. She still stands there, a 40-foot column of shattered basalt, with boulders balanced on top.

Barns Ness

Lothian   NT 7277

Although in sight of the huge cement works at Oxwellmains and the nuclear power station at Torness, the coastal reserve at Barns Ness takes visitors back to an earlier industrial environment. Its eight different bands of limestone led to the setting up of the Catcraig Limekilns, which remained in operation until 1921. One of the kilns has been restored as part of a fascinating geology trail. A wildlife reserve links it to a grassy parking area leading to Barns Ness lighthouse, established in 1901 as the second light along the dangerous North Sea coast.

BANNET STANE *The curious bonnet shape — whence its name — was caused by the erosion of a layer of softer stone lying beneath the sandstone*

Beeswing

Dumfries and Galloway   NX 8969

A 19th-century butler who gambled regularly on the same chestnut mare was eventually able to retire on his winnings — she had won 51 out of her 64 races, including the Ascot Gold Cup and a succession of events at Doncaster. He used his money to buy an inn here, on the main Dumfries-Dalbeattie road, and in gratitude, called it Beeswing — after the horse. Later the village grew up along the roadside, hence its name.

Bentpath

Dumfries and Galloway   NY 3190

Thomas Telford carved one of the headstones in the churchyard of this little village, which stands beside a bridge over the Esk. He did it for his father's grave, in his early days as a stonemason.

Telford was born in 1757 at Glendinning on the Meggat Water, reached by the road from Bentpath bridge. He went on to build roads, docks and canals all over Britain, was the first president of the Institution of Civil Engineers, and is buried in Westminster Abbey — but he always regarded this little Dumfries-shire valley as his home, and there is a substantial memorial to him beside the Eskdalemuir road.

Blairlogie

Central   NS 8296

Visitors used to come for healthy draughts of the beverage which gave it the nickname Goat's Milk Spa. On very rare occasions, a dozen gardens are open to view as part of Scotland's Garden Scheme. There are rock, heather and water gardens, orchards, espaliered pear trees, herbaceous borders and, beside a house which started life in 1543 as a castle, camellias and magnolias on a terrace overlooking the whole village. This is an attractive, old-fashioned place, with a few narrow lanes, sheltered from the north winds by the steep, craggy slopes of the Ochil Hills.

Bo'ness

Central   NS 9981

Borrowstounness flourished for many years as a port with industries as varied as ironfounding, coal-mining, salt-making and pottery, recalled in a fine museum in the restored stable block of Kinneil estate. It is now a public park above the town, with lawns and woodland walks and extensive views to the hills of Fife. An excavated Roman fort on the Antonine Wall can be seen in the park. Much later, James Watt worked at Kinneil on some of his early steam engine experiments. Appropriately, the Bo'ness and Kinneil Railway, run by volunteers, operates steam-hauled services on summer weekends along its rebuilt line by the shore.

BARNS NESS: JAMES HUTTON — *Siccar Point, on the coast south-east of* **Barns Ness***, is the site where James Hutton (1726–97) developed the theory of 'unconformity' — for which he is known as the founder of modern geology. The site shows Old Red Sandstone resting on the upturned edges of the Silurian, from which Hutton deduced a picture of erosion, sedimentation and folding of rocks over the ages — in contrast to the 'Catastrophist' theory, which explained geological structures by reference to the single event of the Biblical Flood.*

It was by a roundabout route that Hutton became interested in rocks. Apprenticed to an **Edinburgh** *lawyer, on his employer's advice he sought a more congenial profession and chose medicine as being closest to his greatest interest, which was chemistry. After attending the universities of Edinburgh, Paris and Leyden, he qualified as a doctor in 1749, but seeing few openings decided instead to take up agriculture.*

He went to Norfolk to learn practical farming, and travelled in the Low Countries and France before settling in 1754 on his own farm in Berwickshire, where he remained for the next 14 years. It was while he was learning to be a farmer that he became interested in soil and rock formation. In 1768 he gave up farming and returned to Edinburgh to pursue his scientific interests.

First delivered in two papers in 1785, and published three years later as the 'Theory of the Earth', his ideas were not at first wholly grasped because he expressed himself obscurely. Fortunately, his friend John Playfair prepared a clearer and more concise version of the theory, published in 1802 as 'Illustrations of the Huttonian Theory of the Earth.'

ABOVE *James Hutton suggested rock formations were due to causes still seen at work*

CARDROSS: BIRD MEN — *Percy Pilcher's pioneer hang-gliding flights at* **Cardross** *were preceded in Scotland when King James IV (1473–1513) witnessed an unsuccessful demonstration of flight from the top of Stirling Castle, by John Damien, Abbot of* **Tongland**.

The Greek myth of Daedalus who constructed wings for himself and Icarus, shows an early conviction that people might be able to fly. In Britain the idea was accepted, with magicians such as Michael Scot (see **Melrose***) being credited with the power of flight. Practical experiments, however, legendary or otherwise, met with varying degrees of failure. King Bladud of* **Bath***, the first recorded 'tower jumper', is supposed to have leapt to his death, inadequately supported by feathered wings, from the Temple of Apollo in Trinovantum (***London***) in the ninth century BC. In around AD1020 Oliver, 'the Flying Monk', broke his legs trying to fly from* **Malmesbury** *Abbey.*

It was Sir George Cayley of Brompton Hall near **Scarborough** *who constructed the first man-carrying glider, in 1849. The 'man' was actually a boy, but in 1853 Cayley sent aloft his coachman, who on landing promptly gave notice, declaring he was hired to drive, not fly.*

Broughton

Borders   NT 1136

Better known for the John Buchan Centre which recalls the life and work of the novelist who spent part of his boyhood here, this attractively placed village, overlooked by rolling hills, owes a great deal to the architect and antiquarian James Grieve. Between the wars he was involved in many restoration projects, and he rebuilt the arch-roofed cell beside the old parish church as it might have been in the days of its founder, the seventh-century missionary-bishop St Llolan. Painstakingly researched biographical details of the saint are on display; the key to St Llolan's Cell is kept in the village shop.

Brown Carrick Hill

Strathclyde   NS 2916

For the length of a mile on the southern side of the hill, the present public road is the same one as was given the world's first experimental 'macadam' surface, the predecessor of tarmac. The historic stretch is where the sharp cornered minor road, which has scrambled up from south-west of Ayr, passes the driveway to Sauchrie House — the home of the road-maker John Loudon Mcadam.

On the flanks of Brown Carrick Hill there are picnic places with magnificent views over Ayr Bay, the Firth of Clyde and the peaks of Arran.

Bute

Strathclyde   NS 06

Prince Charles is the present-day Duke of Rothesay — the resort of the island, built around a 13th-century castle used by Stuart kings. Among the town's Victorian buildings there are intriguing architectural fancies, like the birds' nests in stone which decorate a house at Bourtree Place; and one of the oddest streets in Scotland is Serpentine Road, virtually a hairpinned staircase by which cars reach the open spaces of Canada Hill. A viewpoint on the golf course here — where people used to gather for a last sight of the emigrant ships heading for the Atlantic — offers a splendid panoramic outlook over the Cumbraes and the mountains of Arran.

Bute is the largest island in the Firth of Clyde, after Arran and has a far gentler landscape. There are walks and nature trails beside the attractive lochs and reservoirs at the centre. On the west side of Loch Fad is Woodend House, built in the 1820s by the actor Edmund Kean as a refuge from creditors and heckling mainland audiences. At Ascog on the east coast of the island, an actor who gave up the stage because it seemed a sinful occupation lies in lonely state: Montague Stanley, who died in 1844, is the only occupant of the churchyard. South of Ascog is the English-style model estate village of Kerrycroy, at the entrance to the wooded grounds of the Marquess of Bute's mansion-house of Mount Stuart. His family have owned most of the island since the 12th century.

Prehistoric sites include the vitrified fort on a hilltop at Dunagoil on the south-western tip of the island. Half a mile inland is the atmospheric ruin, complete with Norman archway, of St Blane's Chapel. It is an easy walk along a field-edge from the road end, and a visit to it before dusk means that the return downhill stroll may be made in full view of a glorious sunset over the jagged peaks of Arran.

Cairndow

Strathclyde   NN 1810

Although open hillsides look down on this pleasantly placed village near the head of Loch Fyne, the great attraction is the woodland garden at Strone, laid out beside the Kinglas Water as it curves round to meet the loch. It was established more than 100 years ago, and a Grand Fir here, at over 200 feet, is reckoned to be the tallest tree in Britain. There is a fine pinetum, the displays of azaleas, camellias and magnolias add brilliant colour, the riverside footpaths lead past a salmon leap, and the picnic area is carpeted with bluebells in spring.

Nearby on a tributary of the River Fyne is Eagle's Fall (1278 feet) and, one mile south-west, Ardkingles House, a fine modern mansion built by Sir Robert Lorimer, the Scottish architect who designed the famous war memorial crowning Castle Rock at Edinburgh.

Cairn Holy

Dumfries and Galloway   NX 5154

Off the main Solway Firth coast road between Creetown and Gatehouse — which Thomas Carlyle confusingly claimed to Queen Victoria was, in both directions, the two most beautiful roads he'd ever travelled on — a side-turning leads up a narrow, wooded glen, where deer sometimes dart across to reach the Kirkdale Burn, trickling far below. Up above, high over the woods, is one of Galloway's finest ancient monuments — the Cairn Holy group of chambered tombs. Marked by upright stones, they were used for burials for more than a millenium, from about 3000 to 1800BC.

Cairnpapple

Lothian NS 9871

Sharing the ground with an incongruous transmission mast on this rounded summit of the Bathgate Hills is one of the most important prehistoric sites in Scotland. An entrance in a modern protective dome leads to a sanctuary and burial place, used for around 3000 years from the Late Neolithic Age to the first century BC.

The significance of Cairnpapple to early man may be explained by its height: on a clear day, the view extends all the way across Scotland, from the Isle of May in the Firth of Forth to Goat Fell on Arran.

Cardross

Strathclyde NS 3477

This dormitory village was where Percy Pilcher made several pioneer hang-gliding flights in the 1890s. But the really historic place here is the little whitewashed chapel of St Mahew which stands on a site first used for worship in the sixth century. The derelict 15th-century building was completely restored in 1955, but its interior has retained an authentic, late medieval look.

Cellardyke

Fife NO 5703

Many visitors to the old Fife coastal town of Anstruther concentrate on the Scottish Fisheries Museum by the harbour. Fewer explore its eastern 'suburb' of Cellardyke, once a separate burgh, where narrow streets lead to a sturdy, if smaller-scale, harbour, where, on gala day, the

CELLARDYKE *One of the royal burghs — close-knit communities of merchants who shared the town's responsibilities in exchange for special privileges*

Sea Queen is brought by fishing boat to her coronation on the quayside.

Cellardyke produced some famous whaling and tea-clipper captains, and one house has an archway formed from the jawbone of a record-size Arctic whale. Along the coast to the north-east at Caiplie are sandstone caves still showing crosses carved by the monks who lived there.

CAIRNPAPPLE: BEAKER FOLK —

Towards the end of the third millennium BC, great folk movements took place throughout much of Europe. The most widespread and easily recognised of the migrants were the Beaker Folk, so-called by archaeologists because of their distinctive pots.

One of their burials was found on **Cairnpapple** Hill, a ritual site used for over three thousand years. Within a henge (see **Woodhenge**) built around 2500 to 2000BC, a large grave was discovered, bounded by stone kerbs and a tall, upright footstone. Here a body had been buried with the burnt oak remains of what may have been a funeral mask over its face, and a club beside it.

Wherever the Beaker Folk went, they buried their dead individually under round cairns, sometimes re-using, but never themselves building the megalithic communal tombs of their predecessors. The Cairnpapple grave was probably covered with a small cairn, later incorporated entire into a larger cairn of the Bronze Age. This has been reconstructed and the Beaker grave with its stones can be seen inside it.

Originating, some say, in Iberia, others in central Europe, the Beaker Folk imposed themselves as a military aristocracy on native communities, and did much to introduce copper and bronze working into northern and western Europe.

Indeed they ushered in the Bronze Age, bringing with them not only flint daggers and barbed arrowheads, but daggers of copper and bronze.

Great areas of forest were cleared by them and became grassy — it was perhaps then that Salisbury Plain as we see it today came into existence.

And here is one of their grandest memorials. It seems to have been the Beaker Folk, coming perhaps direct from the mouth of the Rhine, where there are many timber circles of this period, who adapted the techniques of shaping wood to dressing stone, inaugurating an era of great stone engineering. It was certainly they who soon after 2000BC undertook the extraordinary feat of transporting to Stonehenge from the Prescelly Mountains in South Wales the celebrated bluestones.

CAIRNPAPPLE *Cremated bodies were interred inside the chamber. Flint arrowheads, a cup-and-ring marked stone and Beaker Folk pottery have helped to date it*

CRAOBH HAVEN:
WHIRLPOOLS — *The
roar of the whirlpool of
Corryvreckan can sometimes be
heard for miles along the coast by*
Craobh Haven. *'Brechan's
Cauldron' (as Corryvreckan
means) is said to have swallowed a
fleet of Viking ships.*

*Whirlpools have long been the
stuff of 'wonder' tales. No doubt a
sailor's yarn lies behind the
monstrous Charybdis of classical
legend, who sucked the seawater in
and belched it out, swallowing any
ships which happened to be
passing, three times a day. It is
thought that Charybdis was
Garafalo, off northern Sicily, in
which case she was not a true
whirlpool, as she forms no vortex.*

*The same is true of that arche-
typal 'whirlpool', the Maelstrom,
off Norway. It appears on
Mercator's map of 1595, and was
said by the 17th-century mystic
Athanasius Kircher to be the
entrance to a subterranean world,
its water resurfacing in the Gulf of
Bothnia.*

*In fact the Maelstrom
('Moskenesstraumen' in modern
Norwegian) is a strong tidal
current which rips past
Moskenesay in the Lofotens. Most
dangerous between high and low
tide, when the wind blows against
it, Moskenesstraumen can sink
large ships. But its power has been
greatly magnified by writers,
notably Edgar Allan Poe, whose
'Descent into the Maelstrom'
popularised the image of the whirlpool as a 'terrific funnel', capable
of devouring entire fleets.*

Cockenzie and Port Seton

Lothian   NT 4075

Since 1880, the fishing fleet of these two villages
has been based at Port Seton. The fishermen
financed their own harbour here, after the owner
of Cockenzie caused consternation by starting to
charge harbour dues. Port Seton's original
harbour has the terminus for Scotland's first
railway, laid in 1722. Also of interest is the
Chalmers' Memorial Church: opened in 1905, its
ceiling resembles an up-turned fishing boat.

Outside the villages, the Seton Collegiate
Church was built — but not completed — in the
14th century. It has some fine Renaissance tombs
of the Setons, who were major landowners here
until the 12th Lord Seton's estates were forfeited
because of his support for the 1715 Jacobite
Rising.

CORA LINN   *In 1708 a 'hall of mirrors' was built on the
eastern bank of the falls, to give visitors the illusion of being
totally surrounded by water. Minks, otters and kingfishers
live in the gorge*

Corra Linn

Strathclyde   NS 8841

The splendidly restored cotton-milling village of
New Lanark, below the falls of Clyde, is the
access point to a spectacular Scottish Wildlife
Trust reserve, and has footpaths on both wooded
banks of the precipitous rock-walled gorge. First
of the falls up-river is Corra Linn, overlooked
from the western cliffs by a ruined 15th-century
castle. In 1708 a 'hall of mirrors' was built where
visitors would seem to be entirely surrounded by
water. Although it is usually diverted to a power

station, on four days every year the full force of the River Clyde is released into its natural channel and the gorge resounds to the crashing roar of water, a spectacle which delighted Landseer and Turner, Wordsworth, Coleridge and Scott.

Cove Harbour

Borders   NT 7871

The very idea of a harbour seems absurd: the old fishing village and coastguard station at Cove stand on top of cliffs, which plunge down to an often wave-lashed shore.

But there is in fact a winding road (no visitors' cars allowed), which dips out of sight towards the sea. Some way down it, a masonry arch set in a grassy headland leads into a 60-yard tunnel (open), which comes out quite unexpectedly through a delicately-shaded pink sandstone cliff above Cove Harbour. After two previous break-waters were pounded to debris by northerly gales, the present harbour, now used by lobster fishermen, was opened in 1831. The access road and a footpath above the cliffs (filled with seabirds) lie on the route of the Southern Upland Way.

Craigcleuch

Dumfries and Galloway   NY 3486

This Scottish Baronial mansion house is a museum of souvenirs, no ordinary souvenirs, but the intriguing objects brought back by explorers, from Africa, America and Asia. The Craigcleuch Collection — open daily from May to September — includes intricately-fashioned wooden figurines from Zaire and the Ivory Coast, ceremonial masks and staffs, wall-hangings, weapons, antelope horns, ivories and a cabinet of oriental jade. One major exhibit features ornamental pipes gathered from North American Indian tribes; another, a series of dragon figures from Sri Lanka.

Craobh Haven

Strathclyde   NM 7907

Craobh (pronounced Croove) Haven is a new arrival. This holiday and watersports village is built on ancient MacDougall lands, with colour-washed houses and shops in an old vernacular style, based on a sheltered marina. It was created by the imaginative linking of a string of little islands, by causeways, to the mainland.

On the approach road there is a fine viewpoint looking over to the Gulf of Corryvreckan where, between the islands of Jura and Scarba, Scotland's most infamous whirlpool spins ominously in the tide-race.

Crinan

Strathclyde   NR 7894

One of the grandest sights in Scottish sailing occurs early on the morning of Glasgow Fair Monday in July, when the second leg of the Tobermory Race starts from Crinan. On the turn of the tide, the whole fleet of around 200 yachts races for the channel which marks the beginning of their course, threading through the maze of islands, towards the Sound of Mull.

The village itself is tiny, but beautifully situated in woodland around the locks and basin at the western end of the Crinan Canal.

Dalserf

Strathclyde   NS 7950

At the start of the road past the fruit farms and market gardens in the Clyde Valley, a lane turns off through a fringe of conifers to the parish church of Dalserf, a scattered hamlet where fields run down to the riverside. The whitewashed church was built in 1655, then remodelled and extended in the 19th century. It has no fewer than four outside staircases, and an elegant and whimsical little belfry.

Dumbarton

Strathclyde   NS 3975

High-level attractions include the climb to the viewpoint of Dumbarton Rock overlooking the mouth of the River Leven, where the fortress-capital of the Kingdom of Strathclyde was established about 1500 years ago and a much later castle is maintained as an ancient monument; and the wooded riverside trails in the glen at Overtoun House. In the heart of the town itself there is a fascinating industrial museum: the Denny Experiment Tank. This is where Dennys of Dumbarton, who were also pioneers in heli-copter, hydrofoil and hovercraft design, used to test scale models of their latest ships, in a 330-foot channel simulating stormy seas.

An ancient arch known as College Bow was originally in St Mary's collegiate church, but has been re-erected in Church Street.

Durisdeer

Dumfries and Galloway   NS 8903

The Ordnance Survey's 39-year re-mapping of Britain was ceremonially completed on 25 May 1982, in Durisdeer's tiny village square. It was once on the line of a Roman road, a pilgrims' way to Whithorn and an 18th-century coaching road. Through-traffic now goes elsewhere, but Durisdeer still has its fine parish church of 1699, and a famous extravagant black-and-white marble monument to the second Duke and Duchess of Queensberry. The village stands at the foot of a glen, on the south side of the rounded Lowther Hills.

Easdale Island

Strathclyde   NM 7317

Reached by a five-minute passenger ferry crossing from Ellanbeich on the island of Seil, Easdale, just 650 yards by 500, once supported a population of more than 450 people who were employed by a flourishing slate industry. At its peak in the 18th and 19th centuries, Easdale slate was shipped to Canada, the United States, Australia and the Caribbean. The quarries were sunk to a depth of 180ft below sea level; but during a ferocious storm in November 1881 these quarry pits were completely flooded and the industry petered out. The quarries had closed down by 1911.

Easdale still has a small, resident population, and there is an excellent folk museum devoted to the domestic and industrial life of the villagers during the heyday of the slate industry.

CRINAN: THOMAS TELFORD — *The village of* **Crinan** *marks the north-west end of the Crinan Canal, begun in 1793 and completed by the engineer Thomas Telford (1757–1834).*

A shepherd's son born near **Bentpath**, *Telford was apprenticed to a stonemason at 15, and educated himself, not only in engineering but also in languages and literature. His verse was published several times, and one of his poems, addressed to Burns, was included in James Currie's 'Life' of the poet.*

A versatile and dynamic personality, Telford was involved in many aspects of building, not least the construction of Somerset House. However, it is as an engineer that he is best remembered, for his canals — among them the Caledonian (which took 44 years to build and has 29 locks, all still in working order), and the Ellesmere, or Shropshire Union, which first established his reputation (see **Ellesmere Port** *and the* **Pontcysyllte Aqueduct**). *Along with McAdam, he is also remembered as one of the foremost British roadbuilders (see* **Kames**).

Telford was consulted by the King of Sweden on the Gota Canal and received a Swedish knighthood for his services. But in spite of his renown and his many honours, he remained a lonely man, never marrying and living alone for 21 years at the Salopian Coffee House, Charing Cross, **London**.

Edinburgh

Lothian   NT 2573
Within the elegant city are nature trails and a railway line to walk. An Edinburgh professor was the original Sherlock Holmes, an Edinburgh saint gave away her eyes, and nearby a Stuart king played skittles

SAINT LUCY *holding eyes — detail of painting by Francesco del Ferrarese (c1435–1477)*

EDINBURGH: EYE WELLS — *Most holy wells in Britain were also healing wells, the greatest number of them being sought for eye troubles.*

One of the Scottish eye wells (now dry) was St Triduana's Well, Restalrig, **Edinburgh***, in a chapel adjoining the parish church.*

St Triduana was invoked for curing diseases of the eye because of the tale that when a local prince became enamoured of her beautiful eyes, she had them cut out and given to him — she is probably a Scottish version of St Lucy. According to one version of her legend, St Triduana came to Scotland in the fourth century with St Rule. Her relics at Restalrig were sought by pilgrims (see **Hailes Abbey***) up to the Reformation.*

Whether it was simply the bathing of the eyes in cold water that was efficacious, or whether it was a matter of faith, eye wells were visited up and down the country. The Eye Well at **Llandrindod Wells***, reputedly in use since Roman times; St Gudula's Well, Ashburton, Devon; St Edith's Well, Kemsing, Kent; St Mary the Virgin's Well,* **Dunsfold***; St Anthony's Well, Forest of Dean; Ffynnon Cybi (St Cybi's Well),* **Llangybi***, are just a few of them.*

The *High Kirk of St Giles* in Scotland's capital city is probably the only Presbyterian church to give space to a Chinese dragon. Knights of the Thistle, in effect the Scottish equivalent of the Garter, have their crests on display in its Thistle Chapel, and Lord MacLehose — a former Governor of Hong Kong — selected the dragon emblem as the most appropriate for himself.

Edinburgh has innumerable literary associations. Scott and Stevenson were both born here, and so was Sir Arthur Conan Doyle, who based Sherlock Holmes's remarkable powers of observation and deduction on those of an Edinburgh professor of forensic medicine.

Open spaces within the city include pleasant walks on *Corstorphine Hill*, nature trails in the wooded glen at the *Hermitage of Braid*, and, most spectacular of all, grassy paths in *Holyrood Park*, which rise by the exposed rock-faces of an old volcano to the summit of Arthur's Seat.

In 1778, mutineers from the Seaforth Highlanders encamped on the hill until they were assured that the rumour that they were going to be shipped to slave plantations was false.

Below the basalt columns of Samson's Ribs, part of the track-bed of Edinburgh's first railway, from an unsuspected tunnel under the southern perimeter road, has been turned into a footpath. Opened in 1831 as the Edinburgh and Dalkeith line, the *Innocent Railway* carried a quarter of a million passengers every year in its busiest times, and gained its name because the trains were horse-drawn and accident-free.

Outer Edinburgh is really a collection of villages. At *Cramond*, Scotland's shortest ferry-trip takes less than a minute as the ferryman, using a single oar, rows across to the jetty on the far bank of the Almond, where footpaths extend into the beautiful Dalmeny estate.

At *Duddingston*, skittles are played in the Sheep Heid Inn, where at least one of Scotland's Stuart kings came to relax at the skittle alley after a hard day spent going over state papers at Holyrood Palace. This is the oldest pub site in Scotland, dating back 600 years.

A walkway follows the Water of Leith, past the

DEATH of RIZZIO.

CRAIGENTINNY *(top)* *Miller's marble-decorated mausoleum overlooking the bowling green was designed, it seems, to foil body-snatchers*

CRAMOND *(above and right)* *The Romans used the village as a supply base for the Antonine Wall; today a one-minute ferry ride crosses the Almond*

THE INNOCENT RAILWAY *(left)* *at the heart of the city in Holyrood Park. It earned its name because horses pulled the carriages and few accidents occurred. The old track is now a footpath*

old paper, meal and snuff mills in the south-western fringe villages of *Currie* and *Colinton* and *Juniper Green*, and the delicious half-hidden *Dean Village* in the heart of the city itself, in former times the preserve of Edinburgh's 'baxters', or bakers.

The 13½-acre, *Dean Gardens*, which are privately owned, are open to the public twice a year on a Sunday.

Not all Edinburgh's spectacular memorials are in the city centre. A remarkable 19th-century mausoleum, whose marble panels are carved with Biblical scenes, stands beside a bowling green in *Craigentinny*. It was built for a wealthy land-owner, William Miller. Perhaps because of his fear of the body-snatchers who were none too fussy about where they acquired their supplies for Edinburgh's anatomy classes, he lies 40 feet down in a solid, stone-built chamber.

Another village now gathered within the city

boundaries is *Granton* on the shores of the Forth. Here, the United Wire Group's headquarters (not open) are based on the 1898 Madelvic motor works, almost certainly Britain's first purpose-built car factory. William Peck constructed curious electrically-powered carriages here; he was also the city astronomer and — until he resigned hurriedly after some embarrassing newspaper publicity — the highly-regarded astrologer of an occult society, which was called the Hermetic Order of the Golden Dawn.

Further out, within a stone's throw of one of the busiest roundabouts in Scotland, where the M8 and the M9 motorways meet, directly under the flight path to nearby Edinburgh Airport, *Huly Hill* is passed daily by thousands of travellers who have never actually visited it. When the roundabout was built, the planners were careful to avoid this Bronze Age monument (it is reached via the little village of Newbridge, on the A89), where a 100-foot grassy cairn, circular pathways and three ancient standing stones have an atmosphere remarkably apart from the buzz of road and air traffic which surrounds them.

E DINBURGH: INDELIBLE BLOOD-STAINS — *Provoked to levity by the 'Gothick' school of novel, Sir Walter Scott has a Cockney salesman of patent cleaners tackling the celebrated bloodstain of Holyrood House,* **Edinburgh**, *in his 'Chronicles of the Canongate'(1827–28).*

This, the most famous of all 'indelible bloodstains' — tradition-ally impossible to remove — was said from at least 1722 to mark the spot where fell David Rizzio, the murdered Italian secretary of Mary Queen of Scots. Indelible or not, the stain has now been removed and its place taken by a brass tablet.

At one time scarcely a great house was without its bloodstain. The gore of Lord Knyvett, stabbed by his son in the reign of Henry VIII, marked the boards of Condover Hall, Shropshire, while in a room at Calverley Hall, West Yorkshire, a bloodstain was witness to 'The Yorkshire Tragedy'.

According to this melodramatic tale, adapted by Harrison Ainsworth in 'Rookwood', Walter Calverley had a fit of madness, and stabbed his wife and children. As he galloped off to find and kill the remaining child, his horse stumbled and threw him, allowing him to be caught by pursuing villagers and pressed to death at **York** *Castle.*

ABOVE *Death of Rizzio — hacked to pieces by over 50 dagger strokes at Darnley's behest*

Eskdalemuir

Dumfries and Galloway   NY 2597

In 1967 two Buddhist abbots from Tibet founded Europe's first Tibetan Centre at Eskdalemuir. Kagyu Samyé-Ling now offers resident courses in Buddhist teachings and meditation, and a fine new Tibetan-style temple should be completed by the end of the 1980s. Books, woodcarvings, paintings and pottery are all produced here to authentic Tibetan designs.

Sheep farms on the moorlands around this scattered village take second place to thousands of acres of forestry plantations. Eskdalemuir Observatory (not open) is Britain's main seismological station. Its duties include tracing other countries' underground nuclear explosions.

Eyemouth

Borders   NT 9464

This prosperous fishing port on the rocky North Sea coast has its own fish market, ice-factory and ships' chandlers right in the heart of the town. When the Burgh Chambers were built in 1880, a stone carving of the *Supreme*, the town's most successful fishing boat, was placed above the entrance. But a year later, 129 Eyemouth men were drowned when the fishing fleet was caught in a violent storm, a disaster recalled in detail in the local museum.

Gunsgreen House, a Georgian mansion above the lifeboat quay, was heavily involved in the 18th-century smuggling trade. Across the bay, the site of a 16th-century fort occupies a flat-topped grassy headland where two cannons still point defensively out to sea.

EYEMOUTH   *seemed made for smuggling. It became a free port in 1597, and its alleys and twisting streets provided good cover when Customs men were alerted*

Falkirk

Central   NS 8879

A wooded ridge running alongside Tamfourhill Road in Falkirk — the B816 to High Bonnybridge — is worth exploring. Footpaths signposted Watling Lodge reveal it to be a substantial section of the Antonine Wall, the northern boundary of the Roman Empire.

Nearby, Lock 16 on the Forth and Clyde Canal is the site of several canal-boating events. The Union Inn here looks over a landscaped grassy area which used to be Port Downie, the former basin where a string of locks (also disappeared) took boats uphill to join the Union Canal.

In the centre of the town itself, Tolbooth Street manages to accommodate a tearoom, a pub and a shoe shop while being, at around 20 paces end-

GARLETON HILLS   *above the pastures of East Lothian*

to-end, the shortest street in Britain. The parish church, spanning eight centuries, has some interesting carved stones and a pair of crude effigies of unknown origin.

Callendar House, to the south-east, has five trees in the grounds planted by Mary Stuart and her four attendants — all called Mary.

Falls of Falloch

Central   NN 3320

A picnic site marks the start of a short footpath to the hidden but impressive falls where the River Falloch, striking off angled ledges, plunges into a dark and shadowy rock pool. Originally a cattle-drovers' route, the Glen Falloch road was improved in the 1750s as part of the pacification of the Highlands after the final Jacobite Rising. There was a battle of sorts here as late as 1845 when supporters of one proposed railway line set upon surveyors working for a rival company. Eventually, the West Highland line, above the road, was opened in 1894.

Faslane

Strathclyde   NS 2489

Beside the Clyde Submarine Base on the Gareloch, wooded Faslane cemetery has a memorial to a chilling event — the sinking, during its acceptance trials in 1917, of the unluckily numbered K13. Air-inlets were accidentally left open before a dive, the boiler-room filled with water, and the submarine plummeted to the bed of the loch. Trapped behind watertight doors, 32 of the 80 men on board were drowned within the first few minutes; but after 55 hours almost all the others were rescued. The memorial and the surrounding headstones form the outline of a submarine, complete with conning tower.

Fast Castle

Borders NT 8670

It was built, probably, in the 14th century in its dramatic position on a dizzy and steep-sided rock, flanked by reefs, scree-runs and precipitous seabird cliffs.

Logan of Fast Castle was one of the personalities involved in the bewildering Gowrie conspiracy of 1600, which was either a plot to kidnap James VI or a plot by the king himself to 'frame' some of his courtiers. According to the first version, Fast Castle was where the conspirators planned to imprison the king. An exhilarating headland walk leads from a parking place near Dowlaw, dipping steeply to the castle itself, now just a few fangs of ominous masonry balanced high above the sea.

Foulden

Borders NT 9255

The parish church of this village overlooking the low-lying Merse of Berwickshire stands on the site of an earlier church where, in 1587, commissioners from Elizabeth I came on a delicate, diplomatic errand. They had to explain to representatives of James VI why the English queen had ordered the execution of the long-since abdicated and exiled Mary Queen of Scots, who was James VI's mother.

Nearby is an architectural survival very rare in Scotland, a well-preserved, two-storey, crow-stepped tithe barn from medieval times.

Galston

Strathclyde NS 5036

In this Irvine valley town, Barr Castle is a restored sandstone tower, 80 feet high and now serving as a masonic temple, where John Knox and George Wishart preached to enthusiastic out-door crowds before the Reformation. Close to it, St Sophia's Roman Catholic Church is in unexpected Byzantine style. It was built in 1886 in memory of Sophia, third Marchioness of Bute, and is modelled on the church of the same name in Istanbul.

More prosaically, a Victorian parish minister of Galston invented the external-combustion Stirling engine, now being redeveloped because of its quiet and pollution-free running.

Garleton Hills

Lothian NT 5076

These neatly-proportioned hills rise abruptly from the rich East Lothian farmlands. At the west end, a footpath climbs through oak and ash, elm, larch and beech to the 560-feet-high viewpoint at the summit of Byres Hill, crowned by a soaring memorial tower. It was set up in 1824 to the fourth Earl of Hopetoun.

The walled gardens of West Garleton House are usually open to the public one weekend in June.

Gigha

Strathclyde NR 6449

Gigha is noted for its ancient standing stones — one notched example being, according to tradition, the 'hanging stone' where executions used to be carried out — and for fine Celtic carvings, springy shell-sand turf and peaceful northern beaches. Views extend from the mountain peaks of Jura to the hills of the Irish coast, faint on the south-west horizon. But best of all on this island, reached by car and passenger ferry from Tayinloan in Kintyre, is the beautiful woodland garden at Achamore House, where the collection of rhododendrons, azaleas and other exotic flowering shrubs, is in the hands of the National Trust for Scotland.

Glasgow

Strathclyde   NS 5865

Where Tobacco Lords once swaggered in scarlet, where a spotted ladybird — the gift of a torpedo boat crew — still perches in the ancient cathedral, while nearby weavers made a speciality of growing pinks.

GLASGOW: JAMES NEILSON — *Born at Shettleston, near* **Glasgow***, in 1792, James Neilson was one of the pioneers of the Industrial Revolution.*

The son of a millwright, with only an elementary education, he nevertheless managed to attend Glasgow's Andersonian University and become foreman and then manager (1817–47) of Glasgow gasworks.

He became interested in solving the great problem of iron smelting in his day — its huge consumption of coal. By experiment he discovered that if, instead of pumping cold moist air into the furnace to help combustion, as was the practice, the air was made hot and dry, and temperatures within the furnace maintained at a maximum, the iron was smelted more efficiently.

He was eventually allowed to test his theory at the Clyde ironworks and so successful were the results that several businessmen helped him patent his invention in 1828.

After improvement, the Hot Blast was found to reduce coal consumption to a quarter of its previous level. So dramatic was this reduction and the accompanying increase in production, that by 1835 the Hot Blast was used in all but one Scottish furnace.

ABOVE   *Nineteenth-century blast furnaces at the Summerlea Ironworks, Glasgow*

BOTANIC GARDENS   *A rare collection of tree ferns and other plants from temperate climates thrive in the Kibble Palace glasshouses, built in 1873, where bananas and orchids have also been grown*

One of the surprising statistics about Glasgow is that it has more than 70 public parks, from *Whiteinch* with its multi-million-year-old Fossil Grove to the *Botanic Gardens* with their exuberant series of domed Victorian glasshouses, called the Kibble Palace. These were originally installed on a private estate on Loch Longside and sailed by barge, in carefully numbered pieces, to the city.

The 361-acre *Pollok Country Park*, site of the Burrell Collection (Scotland's most popular tourist attraction), is also the home of the city's pedigree herd of shaggy Highland cattle which, with Gaelic names like Angus Og of Glenogle, are regular prize-winners at agricultural shows all over the country.

Oldest of the city's public open spaces is *Glasgow Green*, established in 1662 on a site bounded by the River Clyde. Here, the *People's Palace* is a museum concentrating on Glasgow's own history.

While many people think the city's fortunes were based on engineering and ship-building, displays in the People's Palace show that the first great money-spinner was tobacco. Glasgow's 18th-century 'Tobacco Lords' were mercantile grandees who controlled half of all the tobacco trade between the American colonies and Europe.

They were men of immense influence in the city, and even regarded one specially paved area

of the *Trongate*, known as the Plainstanes, as their exclusive preserve. Tobacco Lords in scarlet cloaks would promenade along it, taking a swipe with their elegant canes at any of the hoi polloi who tried to follow suit.

Stirling's Library, a building with an intricately decorated ceiling, is based on the mansion of one of these Tobacco Lords, William Cunningham. He made his biggest killing in the nervous times after the American War of Independence, when the Glasgow merchants' plantations had been confiscated. His colleagues were delighted when he offered them twice the slumped rate for the tobacco they held in store, but he sold it again later — at a 700 per cent profit. Glasgow's *Mitchell Library* — the biggest public reference library in Europe — was endowed in 1874 by another tobacco baron.

Other notable buildings which can be visited in the city centre (details of guided tours from the information centre in St Vincent Place) include the *Merchants' House*, home of the oldest Chamber of Commerce in Britain or America; the Robert Adam *Trades House*, where the 14 Incorporated Trades of Glasgow — now largely charitable

The handloom weavers of Paisley, to the south-west of **Glasgow***, are remembered for the distinctive shawls they wove to a colourful basic design brought back from Kashmir by the East India Company. The shawls were internationally popular in the 19th century, and a collection of over 700 can be seen in the local museum.*

In their own time, however, the weavers were also highly skilled as 'florists' — flower-growers who aimed at producing blooms of perfect shape and size. The skill of growing 'florist's' flowers had come to Britain in the 17th century with French and Flemish refugees, and in the 18th century, floristry clubs, with attendant flower shows, sprang up in many parts of the country. By the end

of the 18th century, there were eight official florist's flowers, including pinks. Because they fell short of the ideal — a perfect circle — earlier fringed pinks were despised, but by the middle of the century, a pink of solid outline, with a band of darker colour at its eye and near the petal-margin, had been developed. The cultivating of this, the laced pink, became the special art of the Paisley handloom weavers around the turn of the 18th and 19th centuries.

Florists' societies flourished particularly around the manufacturing towns, because for weavers and other cottage workers, growing flowers for show proved an ideal recreation. The florist's art required little space but intense cultivation, the weaver was on hand all day to give the plants attention, 'and this', said William Hanbury in 1770, was 'an ease and a pleasure to him' in his repetitive work.

ABOVE   *Paisley weavers found 'ease and pleasure' in the growing and perfecting of flowers*

---

organisations — carry on their business; the extravagant Venetian Gothic *Stock Exchange*, with its completely modernised interior; the sumptuously furnished *City Chambers*, whose marble and alabaster main staircase shows no sign of the plasterwork repairs made to it after a wartime air-raid; and the *School of Art*, which was Charles Rennie Mackintosh's greatest contribution to the skyline of his native city.

His Edwardian *Willow Tearoom* in Sauchiehall Street has been restored to its original use, and the interior of his own house has been brilliantly reconstructed inside the tower of Glasgow University's *Hunterian Art Gallery*.

Oldest of all the city's buildings is *Glasgow Cathedral*, on the site of the original chapel founded in the sixth century by St Mungo, Glasgow's patron saint. The present building dates largely from the 15th century. In amongst all the grand historic monuments there are numerous interesting little details. During World War II, for instance, a motor torpedo boat crew found a 'lucky' ladybird on board. It turned out to be lucky indeed, because when their MTB was attacked and sunk, every single member of the crew survived.

In gratitude, they presented a canopied chair to the cathedral; and there, resting permanently on the underside of the canopy, is a full-colour ladybird delicately carved in the wood.

CITY CHAMBERS   *Opened by Queen Victoria in 1888, they are so grand it has been said that officials prefer to enter by the less formidable side door*

GLASGOW CATHEDRAL   *A ladybird carved in wood remembers the lucky insect, found on board, that brought good fortune to a torpedo boat crew when hit*

Glasgow Road Bridge

Strathclyde NS 6373

Half a mile on the Glasgow side of Kirkintilloch, a sturdy two-storey Georgian building stands at a bridge over the Forth and Clyde Canal. Now a bar and restaurant, it was originally a stable-block for the horses which hauled the early passenger barges.

Glasgow Road Bridge is the base of two converted Glasgow river ferries: the *Ferry Queen* runs weekend cruises, and the *Caledonian* is a cruising restaurant. There is also a pleasant walk along the towpath, which becomes a winding woodland stroll on the way to the village of Cadder, one and a half miles to the south-west.

Glenbranter

Strathclyde NS 1197

In the heart of the mountains of Cowal, Glenbranter forestry village stands on the site of Glenbranter House, the home for several years of Sir Harry Lauder, the world's highest-paid music-hall star. The Lauder Monument, on a little viewpoint hilltop above the main road south of the village, was set up in memory of his only son, an officer in the Argyll and Sutherland Highlanders who was killed during World War I.

Glenkiln

Dumfries and Galloway NX 8477

Carefully placed on hillside sites north-west of the village of Shawhead, are sculptures by Epstein, Henry Moore and Rodin. They stand in the Glenkiln estate, and were bought in the 1950s by the laird, Sir William Keswick. One of the most striking, easily seen from the public road across the estate, is Epstein's 'King and Queen'. The pair gaze out over the extensive valley and moorland view near the Glenkiln Reservoir.

Glen Ogle

Central NN 5725

On the main road out of Lochearnhead, this is a wild-looking glen whose heathery hillsides are broken by lines of rocky cliffs. A five-and-a-half-mile waymarked trail, starting just outside Lochearnhead, follows riverside and woodland footpaths, and an 18th-century military road, on the east side of the Ogle Burn, comes back along the birch-fringed track of the old Callander and Oban Railway, through the spectacular rock-fall which closed the line in the 1960s.

Grangemouth

Central NS 9281

The world petroleum industry began in Scotland, with Young's Paraffin Light and Mineral Oil Company, established in 1851 by Dr James ('Paraffin') Young (he was also the anonymous financier of David Livingstone's African explorations). Today, the Paraffin Young Heritage Trail starts at Grangemouth and goes the rounds of sites connected with that old shale-oil-based industry. At its peak, the shale-oil business employed 40,000 at 120 different works. It dried up in the face of competition from foreign oil-wells whose oil simply gushed out of the ground, instead of having to be refined from shale, and

GLASGOW ROAD BRIDGE *The Forth and Clyde Canal was built to cut through Scotland from the Clyde shipyards. It closed in 1962, but is being restored*

the last shale-mine closed in 1962 — but Young's Paraffin Light and Mineral Oil company is still going, as part of the BP group.

Now the site of a massive oil-refinery and chemical works, Grangemouth has a BP information centre, with displays on the Scottish shale-oil companies.

Greenlaw

Borders NT 7146

For a small town with no official status, Greenlaw has some mystifyingly ambitious Georgian buildings, like the domed town hall and the Castle Hotel facing it. The parish church behind the village green has a curious tower, which has nothing to do with the church itself, but was built as a jail. The reason for all this is that, late in the 15th century, Berwick-upon-Tweed — originally the county town of Berwickshire — was transferred to England, and there were arguments for hundreds of years between Greenlaw and Duns about which of them should take its place. Greenlaw held the position for many years, but in 1903 the decision went finally in favour of Duns.

Harestanes

Borders   NT 6424

The Woodland Centre at Harestanes features displays on timber-growing, woodworking and wildlife on the extensive Monteviot estate, as well as on plant explorers and natural history needlework. It is open on Sunday to Friday afternoons in July and August, otherwise on Sundays, Wednesdays and holiday Mondays between Easter and October. Waymarked walks lead to a Pinetum, the Roman road called Dere Street, an old dovecote on the banks of the Teviot and, most spectacularly, to the summit of Peniel Heugh.

This hilltop, still ringed by the crumbled walls of an ancient fort, is a conspicuous sight for miles around because of the 150-foot Waterloo Monument, built of locally quarried whinstone and dedicated to 'the Duke of Wellington and the British Army'. Peniel Heugh is a magnificent viewpoint over the Border hills, valleys, farms and wooded estates.

Helensburgh

Strathclyde   NS 2982

The outstanding architectural treat is Hill House, designed by Charles Rennie Mackintosh, and open to the public. But there are minor curiosities too, like the red-painted devils on the roof of a house in William Street, arranged so that they grimace at the church across the road.

Television pioneer John Logie Baird was born in this residential town on the Firth of Clyde, and one of his 'televisors' is displayed in the Templeton Library. Henry Bell, designer of the world's first sea-going steamship, the *Comet*, also lived here; his monument stands on the esplanade, and the *Comet's* flywheel is preserved in Hermitage Park.

Hightae

Dumfries and Galloway   NY 0978

Both the inn and the public hall in this pleasant village of trimly-painted cottages bear the name Royal Four Towns. This is no delusion of grandeur, because the tenants of Hightae — like those of the now much smaller Greenhill, Smallholm and Heck — were given special privileges by King Robert the Bruce in the 14th century. As recently as 1965, an Act of Parliament confirmed that local residents are still, after six and a half centuries, allowed free fishing on the Royal Four Towns stretch of the River Annan.

Greenock

Strathclyde   NS 2776

On Lyle Hill above this industrial town on the Firth of Clyde, where the World War II convoys used to assemble, there stands a handsome Cross of Lorraine. Sailors from the Free French naval base at Greenock raised it in memory of comrades who died in the Battle of the Atlantic.

View indicators on Lyle Hill point out not only mountains, forests and sea lochs, but also the sites and statistics of four nuclear bases across the water. Inverclyde District has declared itself a nuclear-free zone.

Haddington

Lothian   NT 5173

This elegant county town is a treasury of restored Georgian architecture, and its history is explained in an exhibition in a dovecote beside the Nungate bridge over the River Tyne.

Haddington House has gardens laid out in 17th-century style. In St Mary's Church, the Lauderdale Aisle — a chapel for all members of the Maitland family — has wood carvings by craftsmen from Oberammergau, and is the destination, on a Saturday in May, of the 11-mile ecumenical pilgrimage walk from the parish church of Whitekirk.

HELENSBURGH: CHARLES RENNIE MACKINTOSH —
In the late 19th century, new artistic movements began to spring up all over Europe, from the German Bauhaus school of design to the English Arts and Crafts movement. A prime mover in this artistic revolution was the Scottish architect Charles Rennie Mackintosh (1868–1928), designer of Hill House, **Helensburgh**.

After winning a competition in 1896 to design the **Glasgow** *School of Art (now his most famous work), Mackintosh and his associate McNair, with the Macdonald sisters who later became their wives, contributed hugely to the development of contemporary architecture.*

Influenced by Voysey and by the current English 'Wrenaissance', Mackintosh combined the languid curves of Art Nouveau with the crisply rectangular practicality of traditional Scottish building.

Hill House, commissioned in 1902 by the publisher Walter Blackie, gave Mackintosh the chance to integrate exterior and interior design according to his own ideas. However, it is a rare monument to his style, since he was a difficult and erratic man to work with, and after 1913, when he left the firm Honeyman and Kepple in which he had been a partner since 1904, he never recovered his architectural practice.

ABOVE   *Charles Rennie Mackintosh, more admired abroad than in his native Glasgow*

HELENSBURGH   *A devout Roman Catholic is thought to have placed the devils on his house in William Street to taunt the rector (with whom he fell out) of the Episcopal church opposite*

KAMES: ROAD-
BUILDERS — *An old
tar works near* **Kames***,
once owned by John McAdam, is a
reminder of one of the three men
who revolutionised road-making by
their methods and force of
character.*

*McAdam (1756–1836) is
probably the best remembered of
the three, commemorated as he is
by the name of the process he per-
fected — 'macadamizing', which
laid emphasis on the strength of
the surface rather than the
foundation.*

*His contemporary, Thomas
Telford (1757–1834) (see*
Crinan*), by contrast, relied on a
strong base. More expensive than
McAdam's, his work has been
more popular with motorists, who
used to claim that you could tell if
you were on a Telford or
McAdam road by the number of
times you had to change gear.*

*The orthodox system followed
by Telford was also used by his
predecessor, John Metcalf
(1717–1810). 'Blind Jack of
Knaresborough' was an extraordinary personality, whose blind-
ness never seemed to hamper him
in a career which included fighting
for George II at the Battle of
Falkirk, and eloping with a pub-
lican's daughter on her wedding
eve. Celebrated as the builder of
over 180 miles of road, he once
claimed that his road over
Crossland Moor needed no repairs
for 12 years.*

ABOVE *John Loudon McAdam,
portrayed by the English engraver,
Charles Turner*

INVERARAY *In 1773
Dr Johnson was entertained at the
castle as a guest of the Duke of
Argyll*

Inchcailloch

Central   NS 4190

Fallow deer have been established here since the
14th century; and an ancient burial ground
surrounds a ruined church, which was the centre
of a mainly landward parish until 1621.

Reached by boat from Balmaha, Inchcailloch is
one of a string of islands in the Loch Lomond
National Nature Reserve which mark the line of
the Highland Boundary Fault, dividing Highland
and Lowland Scotland. A two-and-a-half mile
nature trail explores its oakwoods, once
harvested commercially, and there are splendid
views of the loch, the other islands and the
mainland hills from the viewpoint at the 250-foot
summit.

Inveraray

Strathclyde   NN 0908

Visitors to Inveraray usually admire its lochside
situation, the Georgian elegance of this former
royal burgh's buildings, and the many public
rooms of the Duke of Argyll's Inveraray Castle.
Also much admired is the Combined Operations
Museum, which recalls the town's World War II
role as a training centre for assault landings in
Norway, Italy, North Africa and France.

But starting at the castle, a different view can
be had of the town, from the vantage point of
three excellent waymarked walks. A fine selection of trees, wild flowers and bird habitats are
noted; and the longest walk climbs to the summit
of Dun na Cuaiche, where an 18th-century skyline folly is a magnificent viewpoint over the
town, the castle and the hillsides around Loch
Fyne.

Isle of May

Fife   NT 6599

Weather permitting, boatmen from Anstruther
take visitors to this National Nature Reserve
island owned by the Northern Lighthouse Board,
where Scotland's first-ever coal-fired warning
beacon is preserved as an ancient monument.

The Isle of May is noted as a nesting ground
for all kinds of seabirds. Place-names like
Pilgrim's Haven, Kirk Haven, Angel Stack and

Holyman's Road recall its long religious history,
but the caves on its cliff-bound coast have also at
various times been the resort of wreckers,
smugglers and honest fishermen evading the
press gangs.

During World War II, the waters around the
island provided a practice range for torpedo-
bomber crews. In the mainland churchyard at
Crail, there are 21 gravestones of aircrew who
died when their planes crashed into the sea
during these dangerous training runs.

Jedburgh

Borders   NT 6520

A major Border burgh, renowned for the ruins of
its 12th-century abbey, Jedburgh has an oddity in
Jedburgh Castle — despite appearances, it was
built in 1823 as a model prison, and is now a
museum.

South of the town, Ferniehirst Castle is a
splendidly situated 16th-century fortress,
standing in woods above the Jed Water. Owned
by the Marquess of Lothian, head of the Kerr
family, it is open to visitors on Sunday afternoons in summer. Like Queen Mary's House
(Jedburgh's museum devoted to Mary Queen of
Scots), the castle has 'wrong way round' spiral
staircases — said to be in order to suit left-
handed swordsmen defending it. Hereabouts,
Kerr is pronounced Karr, to match an old word
for left-handed.

Kames

Strathclyde   NS 6926

Although the industries which sustained this
village from the 18th century onwards have been
abandoned, the strikingly designed red-sandstone
Ironworks Cottages and Institute have survived.
Most of the original village area is now covered
by a small motor-racing circuit.

Beyond Kames, a minor road peters out into
bleak moorland, where a tar-works was once
owned by John Loudon McAdam. Strangely, he
never struck on the idea of using tar to bind his
gravel 'macadam' road-surfaces. A McAdam
memorial cairn was erected here in 1931 from a
few remaining stones of his old tar-kilns.

Keir Mill

Dumfries and Galloway   NX 8593

A handsome church, with battlemented tower
and pencil steeple, stands in this village where the
Keir Hills begin to rise from the valley of the
Scaur Water. But head for the older churchyard,
down a leafy footpath towards the river. The
long inscription on one family gravestone ends,
almost casually, with 'Kirkpatrick Macmillan,
inventor of the bicycle' — at least, of the modern
pedal-powered cycle. Macmillan, the local
blacksmith, built his first bicycle in 1839, and
three years later pedalled all the way to Glasgow,
where he caused so much disturbance in the
streets that he was fined for dangerous behaviour.
Amazingly enough, he made no attempt to patent
or exploit his invention, but continued happily
enough as the village blacksmith. Other people
copied his idea, and it was only after his death in
1878 that Macmillan was acknowledged as the
true pioneer. Wall plaques mark his old smithy
(now a private house) at Courthill, on the north
side of the village.

KEIR MILL:
BICYCLES — *The first
mechanical bicycle,
operated by pedals which turned
the rear wheel via rods and cranks,
was the invention of the Scottish
blacksmith, Kirkpatrick
Macmillan of* **Keir,** *in 1839.*

*It was preceded by the
'draisienne', exhibited at Paris in
1818 by Baron Karl de Drais.
This was an improvement on the
earlier 'vélocifère', a two-wheeled
machine, with saddle and hand-
bars, pushed along with the feet.
In Britain, where it enjoyed a
vogue in the 1820s as the 'hobby-
horse', it was ridden by the Prince
Regent.*

*It was not until the 1860s,
when the cranks and pedals were
connected to the front wheel, that
the bicycle really became popular.
The pioneer in this field was
Ernest Michaux, who opened a
factory in France for producing the
'vélocipede', on which the front
wheel was slightly larger than the
rear. An exaggeration of this
feature resulted in the penny-
farthing of the 1870s.*

*This had to be mounted with
such care that it gave way in 1874
to Lawson's safety cycle, with
cranks and pedals between the
wheels, and the chain connected to
the rear axle. Comfort finally
came in 1885 with John Dunlop's
patented pneumatic tyre.*

KILMARTIN *Carved medieval stones in the churchyard
commemorate Malcolm of Poltalloch. To this day there is
a member of the family with the same name*

THE DANDY HORSE, *the first
rear-driven bicycle, invented by the
blacksmith Macmillan in 1839*

Kemback

Fife   NO 4115

From the enclosed and winding valley of Dura
Den, with its relics of a 19th-century yarn-
spinning industry, a minor road slants up a
wooded bank to the attractive and tucked-away
village of Kemback.

Unobtrusive footpaths pass the old churchyard, backed by yew trees, and the present
church of 1814, to which the original bell-tower
was transferred. Behind the church, a flight of
steps leads to the higher settlement of
Blebocraigs, across a ridge where roe deer
browse among the woods.

Killin

Central   NN 5732

Overlooked by the peaks of the Tarmachan
range, the burial ground of the chiefs of Clan
MacNab is on Inch Buie, a wooded island below
the spectacular Falls of Falloch. The present
MacNab chief lives nearby; but of the
400,000-acre estate of the Campbell Earls and
Marquesses of Breadalbane, nothing remains in
that family's hands.

Finlarig Castle, a shattered ruin across the
River Lochay, was where the Earls exercised the
power of 'pit and gallows', and their beheading
pit can still be seen.

Killin also has a strong connection with the
missionary St Fillan. His 'healing stones' are kept
in the village, as they have been for the last 1300
years. It is said that the various stones have
similar shapes to the different parts of the body
they heal.

Kilmartin

Strathclyde   NR 8398

In the valley, fanning out towards the sea at Loch
Crinan, can be seen the most concentrated site of
prehistoric memorials in Scotland. Bronze Age
burial cairns and standing stones are reached by
country roads around the Poltalloch estate.
Further south, a footpath goes up to the outstanding rock of Dunadd, where an Iron Age fort
became the capital of the sixth-century kingdom
of Dalriada. The path leads to the hilltop where
the earliest kings of Scotland were crowned.
Kilmartin is also noted for its church and churchyard, with their fine recumbent gravestones and
fragments of crosses.

LAMINGTON: ROBERT BURNS —

*Few places in Scotland are without some reminder of the country's national poet, Robert Burns (1759–96). The church at **Lamington** is mentioned in a poem written after he attended a service there, while Ayrshire is crowded with the subjects of his verse, among them Poosie Nansie's Inn at Mauchline and Soutar Johnie's cottage, Kirkoswald.*

*Burns is more than a poet: he is an institution, his birthday commemorated every 25 January with haggis and whisky (see **Arbroath** and **Auchroisk** for traditional food and drink) and at least one of his poems is known around the world — 'Auld lang syne'.*

*Some common references to his work may not even be recognized as such. The grave of 'Tam o' Shanter', the hero of his most successful long poem, can still be seen at Kirkoswald, but an episode from the poem is also preserved in the name and figurehead of the Cutty Sark, in dry dock in Greenwich, **London**.*

Burns travelled all over Scotland collecting old verses and melodies to work into his songs, and in the last years of his life, when disapproval of his radical views had left him in a state of debt and depression, he produced some of his best-known work, including 'My love is like a red, red rose'.

ABOVE *'Ae spring brought off her master hale, But left behind her ain grey tail' — from 'Tam o' Shanter'*

Kilmun

Strathclyde NS 1781

Facing the submarine base in the Holy Loch, this strung-out village is backed by the Forestry Commission's Kilmun Arboretum, where hillside paths reaching almost 1000 feet above the loch go through specimen plots of European, North and South American, Asiatic and Australasian trees, from Alaskan mountain hemlock to Antarctic beech — which is actually a native of Tierra del Fuego. The Arboretum is part of the Argyll Forest Park, covering about 100 square miles of mountain, forest and coast on the Cowal Peninsula.

Kilmun churchyard is the burial place of several Dukes of Argyll, and of Dr Elizabeth Blackwell, who overcame fierce prejudice to become the first woman graduate of medicine in 19th-century Britain.

In the 1820s, the first steam-powered omnibus in Scotland was based in Kilmun, taking passengers to inland Lock Eck, where the attraction was a cruise on the *Aglaia*, the world's first iron-built passenger steamboat.

Kinghorn

Fife NT 2687

A family holiday resort, with sandy beaches and shoreline walks, it merges with the village of Pettycur, which plays a mysteriously prominent part on the old milestones retained in many parts of Fife. The explanation is that Pettycur was at the northern end of a long-gone ferry route across the Firth of Forth to Leith.

West of Kinghorn, road and railway run below towering cliffs. A memorial marks where Alexander III, the last of Scotland's Celtic kings, fell to his death from the clifftop when his horse stumbled on a night of furious winds, in the spring of 1286.

Kippen

Central NS 6594

Kippen is an old-fashioned crossroads village, with a lively annual street fair. Its parish church is one of the most meticulously restored in Scotland. A renovation, completed in 1926, was inspired by the artist Sir Donald Cameron, who lived in the village for almost 50 years. Wood and stone carvings, ironwork, stained glass, vases and needlework in profusion have been given to the church by individual parishioners in a tradition which continues to the present day. There is a grave in the churchyard which belongs to Jean Key, the woman abducted by Rob Roy's youngest son — Robin Oig.

Kirkton Manor

Borders NT 2237

South-west of Peebles, the quiet farming valley of the Manor Water shows traces of many hill forts and ancient settlements.

Kirkton Manor churchyard has two literary connections. The burial aisle of the old lairds of Barns behind the parish church is a reminder of *John Burnet of Barns*, one of John Buchan's first novels. Beside the church is the grave of David Ritchie, on whom Sir Walter Scott based his novel *The Black Dwarf*, after an eerie meeting with him in his cottage at Woodhouse, farther up the Manor Valley, in 1797.

Lamington

Strathclyde NS 9731

A model estate village, with a burn running through to join the Clyde, hardly seems the place to catch an echo of Benjamin Disraeli; but the landowner who built it a century and a half ago — Alexander Baillie Cochrane, later Lord Lamington — was a political disciple of Disraeli's who figured as Buckhurst in Disraeli's novel *Coningsby*. Lamington church has a Norman doorway transferred from an earlier building and a bell inscribed with the date 1647. Robert Burns attended a service here and wrote a grumpy verse about the chill of the morning, the minister, the building and the congregation alike.

Leadhills

Strathclyde NS 8815

This is an 18th-century lead-miners' village high in the Lowther Hills with the gravestone of John Taylor, who died at the ripe old age of 137; the monument to William Symington, who designed the world's first steam-boat engine; and an irreplaceable collection of lead-mining records in the library. But gold was the first great local attraction, as early as Roman times. James V's second wife Mary of Guise helped to swell the royal treasury by importing miners from her native Lorraine. James VI and I tried and failed to attract extra finance by creating a new order of chivalry called the Knights of the Golden Mines. And there was a faint recollection of those great days when, in 1956, the present Queen was presented with a brooch made of gold laboriously panned from one of the Lowther burns.

LOCH DOON *Some five miles long and half a mile wide, it was enlarged to form a reservoir for the Galloway Hydro-Electric Scheme which includes six other reservoirs and five power stations*

Linton

Borders NT 7726

In the foothills of the Cheviots, Linton Kirk figures in a hazy tale about how a 12th-century Somerville laird killed a fearsome dragon which, in its death-throes, squeezed its massive tail around a rise of ground — one explanation of how the church happens to stand on a curious sandy hillock. A weathered stone carving above the door is said to illustrate this, but sterner authorities dismiss the story as something to explain the carving, rather than the other way round. And yet . . . a reference to the incident does seem to have been carried down through the centuries on the Somerville coat of arms.

Thomas Elliot, buried in a lonely corner of the churchyard, was a later landowner who, in 1895, bought a Panhard-Levassor car from France and became Scotland's first private motorist.

Lismore

Strathclyde NM 8441

The long, narrow and often cliff-edged island, with rocky satellites offshore, is reached by a Monday to Saturday car ferry (booking advisable) from Oban to Achnacroish on its eastern coast, and by a ten-minute passenger ferry from Port Appin to a jetty at the north end.

An Iron Age broch stands at Tirefour and the 13th-century ruin of Castle Coeffin is perched on a headland facing the mainland hills of Kingairloch. The Pictish St Moluag brought Christianity to Lismore in the sixth century, and the parish church, on the site of the 13th-century cathedral of the diocese of Argyll, retains his name. So does the nearby hollowed boulder known for hundreds of years as St Moluag's Chair. North of the restored cottages of Port Ramsay, a long-redundant lime-kiln recalls once-lucrative trading days.

Loch Doon

Strathclyde NX 4998

Reached by an attractive hummocky glen, and surrounded by forested hills, Loch Doon played a major part in a military planning disaster during World War I. It was selected as the site for a very ambitious aerial gunnery school. Thousands of men — civilian labourers, members of the Royal Flying Corps and German prisoners — worked through 1917 on an airfield, target areas, service railways, hangars, a seaplane shed, a hospital, officers' and other ranks' quarters and even a cinema, before the whole project was unceremoniously scrapped as a massive waste of public money. Almost nothing remains, apart from some concrete foundations.

In the 1930s, however, contractors were back at Loch Doon, raising its level to make it a reservoir for the Galloway Hydro-Electric Scheme. This would have inundated the 14th-century Loch Doon Castle, which originally stood on an island, so the castle ruins, with their curious design of 11 irregular-length walls, were carefully dismantled and re-erected by the roadside above the western shore.

Loch Lomond

Strathclyde NS 4190

As well as afternoon cruises and the ferry to Inchcailloch (see page 278), MacFarlane's boat-yard at Balmaha on the east side of Loch Lomond is the base of the mailboat which sets off at 10.50 every Monday, Thursday and Saturday morning, going round the inhabited islands in the beautiful southern part of the loch. A few passengers can be carried. Only a handful of people live on the islands, most of which are splendidly and heavily wooded; but there are farms on some of them too, and the mailboat provides an essential year-round link.

LINTON: THE LINTON WORM — *A tympanum over the south door of* **Linton's** *old parish church, incorporated into the later church on the same site, represents a knight carrying a falcon and encountering two monsters. The sculptor perhaps intended it to show St Michael overcoming the Devil — often shown as a dragon in Christian symbolism. But the parishioners interpreted it otherwise and, as with the tympanum of St George and the Dragon at Brinsop Church, Herefordshire, made it the subject of the tale of a local hero.*

A mile south-east of Linton church was the lair of a dragon or 'worm', which one John Somerville undertook to destroy. Armed with a lance tipped with a wheel, to which were affixed burning peats, he encountered it on a green hillock and thrust the peats down its throat. For dispatching the monster he was knighted by King William the Lion, and thereafter the Somerville crest bore a wheel with a dragon on it.

An effigy of the dragon-slayer — known as the Somerville Stone — was placed on Linton church, and the green hillock was long remembered as 'Wormiston'. To this day, like Mote Hill at Dalry, Dumfries & Galloway, Linton Hill bears the marks left on it by the dragon's coils.

ABOVE SERPENTS *on a 16th-century map, perhaps to mark a hill with a dragon legend*

REINETTE PIPPIN.

ONE difference of opinion exists, amongst pomologists, respecting the progressive natural decay of Apple-trees, in proportion to the time that has passed since their origin, individually, from seed. The Ribstone Pippin is generally considered to be approaching a state of decrepitude. It must not be forgotten, as we have previously explained, that a tree propagated from a graft, is still a part of the original tree, and inherits much of its infirmities, whether from age or otherwise; and certain it is, that trees of this variety, now propagated from grafts will not continue in healthy growth a third of the number of years that usually belong to a seedling tree. A renovation, for a few years, is obtained by grafting it on a fresh stock, or even by re-grafting the same stock with the same

MELROSE: TRADITIONAL APPLES —

*Cowsnout, Catshead and Foxwhelp, Old Wife and Apple John — such were the names bestowed on the 500 or more varieties of apples once grown in Britain. Rarely seen in shops, traditional and regional types like these are still grown at Priorwood Garden, **Melrose**, maintained by the National Trust for Scotland.*

The cultivated apple probably arrived with the Romans, who knew how to bud and graft and are unlikely to have settled for the native crab and wild apples. Their introductions are said to include 'Court Pendu Plat', and 'Pomme d'Api', brought to Rome from the Peloponnese by Appius Claudius.

Such apples were kept in cultivation by the monks, who also experimented with new varieties. The first named English apple was the Pearmain (about AD1200), followed by the Costard (1292), whence came the word 'costardmonger', and then 'costermonger', for fruitseller.

*Interest in apples, whether for eating or cider (see **Tedburn St Mary**), was at its height between the 16th and 18th centuries. A romantic survival from this period is the Wyken Pippin (1700), reputedly grown from the pip of an apple eaten by Lord Craven, builder of **Ashdown House**, on one of his Holland journeys.*

Amongst old local apples that still exist are Yorkshire's 'Improved Cockpit', the Sussex 'Forge Apple', the Essex 'D'Arcy Spice', the East Anglian 'Dr Harvey', and the 'Flower of Kent' — the one that fell on Sir Isaac Newton.

Loch Striven

Strathclyde   NS 0871–NS 0583

Three roads follow the shoreline of this sea loch in the hills of Cowal, but none of them links up with the others.

In the early years of this century, Scottish car manufacturers liked to publicise successful ascents of the road that makes a steep climb at Loch Strivenhead. The road up the eastern shore passes the old parish church of Inverchaolain, where generations of Lamonts are buried — this was the heart of their clan territory — and finishes beside an unexpected deep-water anchorage, reserved for laid-up merchant ships far from the busy sea-lanes.

Luffness

Lothian   NT 4780

This miniature district surrounds the estuary of the Peffer Burn, which flows into the nature reserve of Aberlady Bay. A footbridge crosses the mouth of the Peffer, where a box labelled 'left wings only, please' shows that there is controlled wildfowling here, and leads on to the gentle slopes of Gala Law.

The wooded grounds of 16th-century Luffness House, including a fruit garden built by French prisoners during the Napoleonic Wars, are occasionally open to visitors. Luffness Links, once a rabbit warren, were turned into a fine golf course in Victorian times.

Luing

Strathclyde   NM 7410

Reached by car-ferry across the white-capped tide-race of Cuan Sound, the north end of 'Ling' looks wild and inhospitable, but its well-kept southern farmlands are the home of the hardy and individually registered Luing breed of pedigree cattle.

North of the main village of Cullipool, massive canyons have been excavated from the now-abandoned cliffs of slate. Cullipool looks out over a magnificent island view: to the roofless houses of Belnahua, evacuated early this century just before the sea inundated its slate quarries; Ru'a Fiola with its adventure centre; and, along the horizon, the Isles of the Sea rising sheer from the open waters of the Firth of Lorn. Highest island nearby is Scarba, soaring to nearly 1400 feet above sea level. The most impressive view of it is from the harbour at Black Mill Bay.

Manderston

Borders   NT 8154

John Kinross was told money was no object when he remodelled Manderston into the most sumptuous Edwardian country house in Britain. The mansion and its 56 acres of gardens are open to visitors on Thursdays and Sundays from May to September, and are a perfect illustration of *Upstairs, Downstairs* Edwardian life. In the basement, for instance, there are 56 bells to summon servants to different rooms, each bell with its own distinctive tone. A magnificent marble dairy and the world's most lavishly constructed stables stand in the grounds. On a more homely scale, a small museum of Huntley and Palmer biscuit tins recalls that Manderston passed by marriage to the Palmer family.

Maxwelton House

Dumfries and Galloway   NX 8289

The heroine of the world-famous love song *Annie Laurie* was born in this Cairn Valley mansion-house in 1682; but she and the suitor who wrote the original poem both happily married other people. The song itself was not written until the 1830s. When the gardens of Maxwelton are open to the public, on one Sunday in April and another in August, the little room called Annie Laurie's Boudoir can be visited. So can a little courtyard museum of early household, dairy and farming implements. Maxwelton chapel, built in 1868 and recently restored, is open most of the year.

Melrose

Borders   NT 5434

Centrepiece of this mellow Border town, where the grassy banks of the Tweed are overlooked by the soaring Eildon Hills, is ruined Melrose Abbey where a wizard and the heart of Bruce are said to be buried. After lying abandoned for several centuries the ruins were repaired in 1822 under the supervision of Sir Walter Scott, and the Duke of Buccleuch subsequently donated the abbey to the nation. Beside it, an ornamental wall with wrought-ironwork designed by Sir Edwin Lutyens encloses the National Trust for Scotland's Priorwood Garden. Priorwood specialises in growing flowers for drying. But the monks' orchard has also been re-established, with a display of apples including ancient strains like Pomme d'Api and Court Pendu Plat, perhaps brought to Britain by the Romans, whose palates rebelled at the sour-tasting fruit they encountered here.

MELROSE: THE WIZARD MICHAEL SCOT —

In the South Transept chapel nearest the Presbytery in **Melrose** *Abbey is the traditional grave of the wizard Michael Scot.*

He was a leading European scholar of the 13th century, and his reputation as a wizard, like those of learned men before and after him, including Vergil and Roger Bacon, was built on his known interest in astrology and science. Later folklore named his

birthplace as Balwearie Castle, Fife, and his home as Oakwood Tower, on Ettrick Water. It was said that aided by his imps, Prim, Prig and Pricker, he cleft the Eildon Hills into three and 'bridled the Tweed' with a barrier (near Maxton). The Devil himself helped him build Hadrian's Wall and Watling Street, once known as 'Mitchell Scott's Causeway'.

According to one tradition, Scot in old age retired to Holm Cultram Abbey, Cumbria, and his 'secret works' were reputedly stored by the abbots at Wolsty Castle. In the 17th century one of 'Sir Michael's' works could be seen 'hanging on an iron pin', in the castle of Burgh-under-Bowness. No one had dared to read it.

Like St Aldhelm of **Malmesbury**, *he was reputed to have the art of flight. When he flew to Rome, the Pope was amazed to see the snow still on his bonnet.*

Menstrie

Central NS 8496

Early in the 17th century, James VI and I created Scotland's first baronetcies — of Nova Scotia. Money raised by selling the titles was to finance the development of this 'New Scotland' in Canada. Although the scheme failed, the baronetcies were confirmed. The idea had been Sir William Alexander's, and his Menstrie Castle — converted into flats and a library — contains a Nova Scotia Room, open to visitors on Wednesday, Saturday and Sunday afternoons from May to September. More than 100 baronets' shields are on display.

Mertoun

Borders NT 6131

Mertoun House (not open) is a very fine Georgian mansion, completed in 1705 for the Scotts of Harden from whom Sir Walter Scott was descended. Its gardens, open at weekends and on holiday Mondays, include an arboretum, woods and parkland, herbaceous borders and shrub roses, footpaths with views to the Tweed, and a well-preserved circular dovecote of 1567.

The 17th-century Mertoun parish church is half-hidden in the estate woodlands, far from any of the villages.

Minnivey

Strathclyde NS 4707

The coal and ironstone mining which once sustained the town of Dalmellington have come to an end; but at Minnivey, the Ayrshire Railway Preservation Group has a collection of industrial

MINNIVEY *The industrial 0-4-0 locomotive at the old colliery is hard to identify without its nameplate or number, but it would have been used to transport coal and iron ore to and fro*

locomotives which on open days are 'in steam' on a surviving stretch of line.

Beyond Minnivey, a remarkable hill road climbs towards the sites of two lonely villages built in the mid-19th century by the Dalmellington Iron Company. Corbie Craigs, which originally housed the men who worked a mineral tramway, is now a line of ruined cottages on a grassy headland overlooking Dunaskin Glen. Higher still, at 1100 feet above sea level, Benwhat — even after World War II — had 130 houses, a Post Office and shop, an 80-pupil school, two libraries and a men-only beer and whisky store. This lively if remote settlement with its own championship-winning silver band, football and athletics teams, survived under National Coal Board Ownership until 1951. All that remains are lines of grass-covered foundations on a breezy moorland, with splendid views to the hills around Loch Doon.

Moonzie

Fife NO 3417

The Old Kirk of Moonzie, standing on a viewpoint hilltop, used to be known as the 'Visible Kirk', because sailors often caught sight of it on the skyline. Ruined Lordscairnie Castle was the stronghold of a 15th-century Earl of Crawford, a fearsomely whiskered character known — behind his back — as Earl Beardie. After joining an ill-fated plot to overthrow James II, Crawford was forced to dress in beggar's rags and grovel for forgiveness in front of the Court.

PEEBLES: EXPLORERS OF THE DARK CONTINENT

Some of the most notable explorers were Scottish, including Mungo Park and James Young from **Peebles**. *The Dark Continent was Africa, whose great rivers — the Niger, the Congo and the Nile — had a powerful fascination for explorers in the late 18th and 19th centuries. Mungo Park (1771–1806) began his exploration of the Niger in 1796, having been captured by and escaped from a chief, and after a year and a half away was helped back by a slave trader, having falling ill. He described his experiences in his 'Travels in the Interior of Africa' in 1799, and became a doctor in Peebles, where his Arabic teacher alarmed the locals; but becoming restless once more, he set off again in 1805. By November of that year, his band of 45 companions had been reduced to four, and he drowned in the river in 1806.*

James Young served with the Nile expedition which brought back the Rosetta Stone, but the most renowned explorer of the Nile was Dr David Livingstone (1813–73). Born in Blantyre, Strathclyde, he worked in a cotton factory to subsidise his education at **Glasgow** *University, and in 1840 he was sent to Africa by the London Missionary Society. (His travels were also financed anonymously by Dr James 'Paraffin' Young of* **Grangemouth**.*) Livingstone was driven on throughout his travels by his Christian fervour, and although he failed and died in the attempt to find the river's source, he inspired both explorers and missionaries, and was influential in stopping the slave-trade.*

James Bruce, who found the source of the Blue Nile, though not of the river's main stream, was born in Kinnaird in 1730, and was known as 'the Abyssinian' from his travels. So curious were the descriptions of the Abyssinians in his 'Travels to Discover the Source of the Nile' that they were disbelieved by Dr Johnson among others, but have since been proved true.

A collection of items brought back by explorers of Africa, America and Asia can be seen at **Craigcleuch**.

Mull

Strathclyde NM 53

Many parts of the coast — like the highly unstable cliffs at Gribun, where the ruins of an 18th-century cottage still lie crushed under a boulder which killed a young couple on their wedding night — are easily seen from the main roads. But more adventurous expeditions can be made to MacKinnon's Cave on the roadless shoreline south of Gribun; to McCulloch's Tree, a fossil imprint 40 feet high and something like 50 million years old, on the coast of the massive headland called The Burg; and to the rock arches of the towering cliffs near Carsaig.

There are also the attractions of Mull's mountains, and many lower-level places to see — Duart and Torosay Castles, Tobermory with its colour-washed houses facing the bay, where the Tobermory yacht race finishes, Mull Little Theatre, and the Byre Heritage Centre. Most visitors arrive on the car-ferries from Oban and Lochaline; but in summer, smaller passenger ferries also run from Oban to Duart, Torosay and Grass Point. Cruises continue the process westward, to Fingal's Cave on Staffa, and the seal and seabird colonies on the Treshnish Isles.

Scotland's only island railway has started to run summer services on its narrow-gauge line between Craignure and Torosay Castle. But as darkness falls, the lonely roads of Mull can take the imagination back to a far different world; like the road through frowning Glen More, traditionally haunted by a decapitated horseman.

New Abbey

Dumfries and Galloway NX 9666

Prayers for its founders John and Devorgilla Balliol are regularly offered in the chapel of Balliol College, Oxford. In Scotland, the most notable building connected with this fabulously wealthy 13th-century couple is Sweetheart Abbey — the first use of the word 'sweetheart' in the English language. In the Abbot's Tower (not open) across the river behind Sweetheart, the last of its abbots plotted to have the Spanish Armada make a subsidiary landing in Galloway. New Abbey also has a recently restored 18th-century corn mill and an impressive Museum of Costume.

Newburgh

Fife NO 2318

The ruin of 12th-century Lindores Abbey stands untended on the edge of the village, on the south side of the Tay. Newburgh has many fine architectural details, like the marriage lintel at 60 High Street, where the names of the newlyweds of 1758 have a carved sailing-ship alongside, to show that the husband was a master mariner. Newburgh harbour looks across to the extensive reed-beds on the north shore, harvested every winter for roofing thatch.

Pass of Leny

Central NN 5809

There are several waymarked walks in the forested hills above the north bank of the River Leny. Less well known is the woodland footpath from the signposted Ben Ledi car park, which follows the other side of the brawling river to an abandoned 18th-century settlement called Coire a'Chrombie — the Bent Birch Corrie — whose cattle-raising tenants were evicted in one of the early clearances to make way for sheep.

Peebles

Borders NT 2540

Like any long-established county town — its oldest building is the quietly-located ruin, set among pine trees, of the 13th-century Cross Kirk — Peebles has many intriguing corners. Mungo Park, explorer of the River Niger, was a doctor here; his surgery in the High Street and house in Northgate are marked by wall plaques. Thomas Young, a military surgeon, served with the expedition in the Nile Delta which brought back the Rosetta Stone, whose parallel Greek and Egyptian texts eventually solved the problem of deciphering ancient Egyptian hieroglyphics. In 1807 he built the neat Georgian mansion called Rosetta on the north side of the town. Although the estate is now a caravan and camping site, visitors are welcome to see the plaster-cast of the Rosetta Stone (the original is in the British Museum) which he installed in the house.

Pencaitland

Lothian NT 4468

Both Easter and Wester Pencaitland have well-planned, mostly 17th-century domestic buildings. In the earlier churchyard, east of the River Tyne bridge, little outhouses with red-pantiled roofs were built as a guard against 19th-century body-snatchers. The old schoolhouse opposite the market cross in Wester Pencaitland has the statue of an industrious schoolboy over a porch — the gift of a grateful former pupil. Pencaitland Railway Walk follows the track-bed of the Gifford and Garvald Light Railway.

Pencraig

Lothian NT 5776

Beside the A1, this is a layby with its own woodland walk and viewpoints. Northwards, there is a fine view towards the Firth of Forth. To the south, the land dips steeply into the Tyne Valley, with the beautifully situated ruin of Hailes Castle beside the river, then rises sharply again to Traprain Law, whose heavily-defended hilltop town — was the capital of the people the Romans called the Votadini.

Penkill Castle

Strathclyde NX 2398

The Order of the Owl is a newsletter devoted to Pre-Raphaelite art, and the Penkill Foundation which publishes it is centred on this astonishing castle above the Girvan Valley. In Victorian times, Penkill was remodelled and decorated by Pre-Raphaelite artists like Holman Hunt, William Morris, Edward Burne-Jones and William Bell Scott, all close friends of Spencer and Alice Boyd, whose family were lairds of Penkill for more than 550 years. The castle is open for pre-booked guided tours which show off, among other art treasures, the Boyds' portrait, protected — effectively — by the Curse of Penkill. A carved owl, one of the Pre-Raphaelites' symbols, perches on a roof overlooking the castle lawn.

PITTENWEEM   *The gate to St Fillan's Cave, with its altar and well. A light is said to have shone from his arm when he was writing in dim light one day*

Pittenweem

Fife   NO 5402

In this attractive fishing port, several narrow wynds, or lanes, descend from the High Street to the harbour. In Cove Wynd there is a gate set in rock (key from the Gingerbread Horse craft and coffee shop in the High Street). It opens into a series of caverns, traditionally the cell of the seventh-century St Fillan, and maintained until the Reformation by Augustinian monks as a shrine in his honour. After years of ill-use, the caves were cleared and re-dedicated in 1935. Still used for occasional underground religious services, St Fillan's Cave gave the town its name: Pittenweem is Pictish for Place of the Cave.

Polwarth Kirk

Borders   NT 7450

Although this has been the site of a church since the year 900, its most significant historic connection is with Sir Patrick Hume, the noted Covenanter.

For several weeks in 1684, Hume hid in his family's burial vault while troops searched the countryside for him. His daughter Grizel supplied him secretly with food. Restored to favour when William III, previously Prince of Orange, came to the throne, Sir Patrick was created first Earl of Marchmont, and gratefully included a heraldic pun in the shape of a crowned orange in the Marchmont coat of arms. A stone carving of that curious device tops the east gable of the church, which he extended and rebuilt.

The church is in the grounds of Marchmount House, which was built by William Adam, father of the more famous Robert Adam.

PITTENWEEM: PICTS — Those mysterious people the Picts, who gave **Pittenweem** its name, have left traces both real and imagined of their activities in Scotland.

Most dramatic are the sculptured stones with scenes of horsemen and animals, and symbols of unknown meaning — double discs, crescents, Z-rods, mirrors and combs.

Many stones remain in their original position, as at Aberlemno kirkyard, Tayside; others have been gathered into collections, as at St Vigeans and Meigle, Tayside. Their heyday was probably in the seventh century AD. Whether the stones are upright slabs or unshaped boulders, their purpose is uncertain: they are as enigmatic as the Picts themselves. But where archaeology has no answers, folklore supplies them. Martin's Stone, Tealing, Tayside, carved with fantastic beasts, was said to mark the spot where, after a chase covering half the neighbourhood, one Martin killed a dragon:
'I was tempted at Pittempton, Draiglit (wetted) at Baldragon, Stricken at Strike-Martin (Strathmartine), And killed at Martin's Stone.'
An Earth House at Tealing also recalls the Picts, popularly identified in Scotland with the fairies. Throughout Britain, the fairies were believed to live underground, and underground chambers such as the souterrains of Tealing and Culsh, Grampian, were known as 'Pecht's', or Pict's, houses.

PICTISH SYMBOLS   *on a stone by the road at Aberlemno, showing a mirror, a serpent and discs*

IMAGINARY BRITAIN

The landscapes that lie behind the pages . . . Barbara Littlewood looks at the lives of favourite fiction writers and the scenes from which they drew the inspiration for their work

JANE AUSTEN

One of the most 'private' novelists who ever lived, Jane Austen made no parade of her writing. Her books were not published under her own name, but only described as being 'By A Lady' on their title pages. In due course the secret leaked out, but very few of the people who called at the modest family home in the little village of Chawton in Hampshire knew what it was that she was writing at the small round table which stood in a corner of the living room. The table is still there, and the door into the sitting room still creaks, as it did in her day, to give her warning, it is said, of any intrusive visitors.

By the time the family came to live at Chawton in 1809, Jane was in her 30s, and in the estimation of the day, approaching middle age. Her distant relative and fellow-writer Mary Russell Mitford has left this description of her as '. . . no more regarded in society than a poker or a fire screen or any other thin, upright piece of wood or iron that fills the corner in peace and quietness.'

Yet by this time Jane Austen had written the first drafts of three of her novels, commenting acutely on the society of her day, *Sense and Sensibility*, *Pride and Prejudice* and *Northanger Abbey*. She had written them at Steventon, a village even tinier and more secluded than Chawton, where her father was rector and where she had spent the first 25 years of her life. Nothing in her correspondence helps to identify any of the characters and events in the novels with people or experiences in her own life, although, like Anne Elliot in *Persuasion*, she had had an intense and unhappy love affair. In Jane Austen's case there was no happy ending: the young man died before he had 'spoken'. Her novels are mostly set in places that she knew well: Bath in *Northanger Abbey* and *Persuasion*; Devon, which she knew from visits to Dawlish and Sidmouth, in *Sense and Sensibility*; Surrey and Kent in *Emma* and *Pride and Prejudice*. Jane Austen knew Kent very well, since she often stayed with her brother Edward Austen Knight at Godmersham Park, said by some to be Rosings Park in *Pride and Prejudice*. Others claim Chevening for the model. Jane Austen knew this house too, since at the time it belonged to a second cousin of the family.

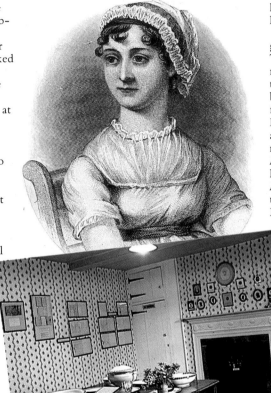

JANE AUSTEN *(top)* and her house at Chawton *(above)*, now a Jane Austen Museum

ABBOTSFORD *(below)* A farmhouse transformed into a Scottish baronial fantasy. Building expenses were one reason for Scott's prolific output

SIR WALTER SCOTT

Although a sociable man, he loved to keep the often conflicting strands of his life separate and had a love of mystery.

He spent most of his childhood at his grandfather's farm near Kelso in the Tweed Valley, feeding his imagination on romantic Border ballads and memories of the Jacobite Rebellions. He dreamed of becoming a soldier, but lameness and family pressure obliged him to study law. His love of ballads persisted, however, and in 1805 he published his first great narrative poem, *The Lay of the Last Minstrel*, becoming almost overnight a literary celebrity. After he had written *Marmion* and *The Lady of the Lake*, which told the story of Ellen, the Lady of Loch Katrine, Scott became Britain's best-selling poet.

He later reproached himself that his verse brought hordes of tourists to the hitherto almost unknown scenery of the Trossach hills and their hidden lochs. It was said that a large hotel was built at Callander solely to cater for them.

His children grew up almost in ignorance of his literary activities. When he turned his talents to the novel, his love of secrecy made him publish the first of a long line of immensely popular historical novels, *Waverley*, anonymously in 1814, only acknowledging his authorship publicly in 1827 when faced with financial ruin. By this time he had written more than 20 novels, among them *Guy Mannering*, *Rob Roy*, *The Antiquary* and *Ivanhoe*, driven partly by his ever-increasing need for money to finance the grandiose building of Abbotsford, his private 'folly'. He had bought the property, a modest farmhouse called Clarty Hole, in 1811, and transformed it into the vast Scottish-baronial-style turreted mansion that is his monument. With this and unfortunate investments, in 1826 Scott found himself ruined. Although he struggled to repay debts of over £116,000, his health broke down and he died at Abbotsford in 1832.

He created the character of Dandie Dinmont, thought to be Jemmie Davidson of Hindlee, who kept a breed of terriers, all called Old, Young or Little Mustard or Pepper. The name Dandie Dinmont is now given to all Border terriers of this breed.

CHARLES DICKENS *(left)* 'No words can express the secret agony,' he wrote, recalling the childhood experiences which influenced his work

THOMAS HARDY *(below)* mocked literary pilgrims

CHARLES DICKENS

Buried many feet deep under what is now the site of Charing Cross Station on the south side of the Strand are the remains of Warren's Blacking Factory. Here, as a child in the 1820s, Charles Dickens spent four desperately unhappy months after his father was imprisoned for debt, washing bottles and sticking on labels with a set of companions who were to reappear in 1837 in exaggerated form, as Fagin's band of child pick-pockets in *Oliver Twist*. This period of his life was so painful to Dickens that for the rest of his years he could never hear or see the name of Warren's without a feeling of despair, and he kept it a secret from everyone but his closest friend, John Forster.

He was able to use the experience in *David Copperfield*, where Warren's appears, thinly disguised as Murdstone & Grinby's Warehouse: the young David Copperfield is sent to work here in a similar menial capacity after his mother's death.

'Its decaying floors . . . the dirt and rottenness of the place; are things, not of many years ago, in my mind, but of the present instant.'

From his experiences in Gray's Inn and as a reporter, Dickens knew London well, and many of the locations of his novels can still be traced: the Inns of Court in *Bleak House*; Camden Town in *Dombey & Son*; Clerkenwell in *Little Dorrit*; Limehouse, lair of the ferocious dwarf, Quilp, in *The Old Curiosity Shop*. What is said to be the original of the Old Curiosity Shop, where Little Nell and her grandfather lived, still stands in Portsmouth Street, south of Lincoln's Inn Fields, and Dickens' own home in Doughty Street is now a Dickens Museum.

The place that he most loved, however, was his childhood home in Chatham, and the towns and countryside around it. Eventually he was able to buy a house he had often admired near Chatham, Gad's Hill Place. The description of the dreadful prison hulks in *Great Expectations* owes something to memories of similar ships in Chatham Docks, and Dickens' last, unfinished novel, *Edwin Drood*, is set in nearby Rochester.

THOMAS HARDY

Born at Higher Bockhampton near Dorchester, Hardy spent almost all his life, apart from brief periods in London, in his native Dorset. Before he turned novelist, however, he trained as an architect, and his first literary recognition came with an award for an essay *On the Application of Coloured Bricks and Terracotta to Modern Architecture*.

Having tried and failed to win fame as a poet, Hardy turned to the novel. Following an idea of the Dorset poet William Barnes, Hardy first referred to 'Wessex' in *Far from the Madding Crowd*, published in 1874. Three years later, the terrain was firmly enough established in his mind for him to draw the first map of Wessex for *Return of the Native*. Eventually Hardy's Wessex covered about two-thirds of southern England, although in the early days it was confined to the Dorset and Wiltshire area. The 'Hardy' trails of today are not new: even in his own day, Hardy was besieged by literary pilgrims seeking out the locations of the novels. Egdon Heath of *Return of the Native* was equated with Puddletown Heath; Casterbridge in *The Mayor of Casterbridge*, with Dorchester; Weatherbury in *Far from the Madding Crowd* with Puddletown; Stourcastle of *Tess of the D'Urbervilles* with Sturminster Newton; and the Isle of Slingers in *The Well Beloved* with the Isle of Portland.

Hardy took all this with a pinch of salt and once said that, to satisfy questions as to where exactly was the original of Little Hintock in *The Woodlanders* he 'once spent several hours on a bicycle with a friend in a serious attempt to discover the real spot, but the search ended in failure.'

RUDYARD KIPLING

Born in 1865, Rudyard Kipling was named Rudyard after the Staffordshire lake where his parents had fallen in love. His schooldays were not particularly happy, but he did remember with some affection his time at the United Services College at Westward Ho! near Bideford in Devon. Here he made a lasting friendship with two boys who were later to become distinguished men: G. Beresford and Major General Dunsterville. In his novel *Stalky & Co*, published in 1899 and describing the enclosed and secretive world of the Victorian public school, Kipling immortalised not only the school, but also his friends, as M'Turk (G. Beresford) and Stalky (Dunsterville); he himself was the bespectacled Beetle.

After his years in India, Kipling came in 1902 to live at Batemans, near Burwash in the Sussex Weald. A 17th-century ironmaster's house, it is rooted firmly in the history of the region, a history he brings vividly to life in *Puck of Pook's Hill* and *Rewards and Fairies*. The 'bare, fern-covered slope of Pook's Hill that runs up from the far side of the mill-stream to a dark wood' can be seen from

Batemans, and Puck, 'the oldest Old Thing in England' is an earth spirit belonging to an ancient legendary tradition. Puck takes the children into the distant past, showing them the

hidden events that have shaped the history of Sussex. With him they meet figures from Norse mythology, a Romano-British soldier, a Norman knight, and even the last of the ancient fairy folk who fled from Britain across the Romney Marshes, taking ship for France at Dymchurch.

BEATRIX POTTER

Children visiting Beatrix Potter at Hill Top Farm after she had become famous were always amazed to find themselves walking up Tom Kitten's garden path, through his front door and into his house. Beatrix Potter portrayed her house and garden, the village of Sawrey and the surrounding fells of the Lake District in all but a few of her many children's stories. In books such as *Mrs Tiggy-Winkle* and *Pigling Bland*, the Cumbrian hills form a marvellously detailed background, and Pigwig, the Black Berkshire pig of *Pigling Bland*, lived on Hill Top Farm. In *Jemima Puddleduck* we see the farm again, and the village inn; in *Ginger and Pickles*, the village shop appears. In *Squirrel Nutkin*, Owl Island is taken from Derwentwater; the squirrels had been observed while Beatrix Potter was staying at Melford Hall in Suffolk.

A stay at Harescombe Grange near Stroud provided the inspiration for *The Tailor of Gloucester*. and the shop, now a Beatrix Potter bookshop, can be seen in an alley off the Cathedral close. Curiously enough, the story that earned her the money to buy Hill Top Farm, *Peter Rabbit*, published in 1902, was originally written not in the Lake District but at Dunkeld in Scotland and later revised at her brother's farm in Roxburghshire.

RUDYARD KIPLING *(left)   After the years in India that inspired such works as 'The Jungle Book', he found a fertile source of inspiration in rural Sussex*

DERWENTWATER *(above)   Squirrel Nutkin and friends paddled across it to Owl Island, using their large tails as sails*

E. NESBIT *(above right)   cut her hair short, rolled her own cigarettes and was a life-long Socialist*

E. NESBIT

No-one looking at the London district of Kennington now would imagine that, little more than 100 years ago, when Edith Nesbit lived here as a child, there were fields and farms all around. The family travelled round quite a lot after leaving Kennington, but in 1871 they settled at Halstead in Kent for several happy years. Edith loved this house, and many years later she wrote:

'My book of memory lies open always at the page where are pictures of Kentish cherry orchards, field and farm and gold dim woodlands.'

Exploits with her brothers furnished episodes for *The Wouldbegoods*, the sequel, set in Kent, to the Bastable family's adventures, first described in *The Story of the Treasure Seekers* in 1899: E. Nesbit also had a secret rooftop hideyhole and adventures with home-made rafts. Memories of playing around the railway line at Knockholt, near Halstead, probably gave her the idea for *The Railway Children* — ups and downs of fortune were not unknown in the Nesbit family, although nothing so dramatic as her father being imprisoned.

By the time *The Wouldbegoods* was published in 1901, she and Hubert Bland were living at Well Hall, in what is now the south-east London suburb of Eltham, and the old moat here, part of a house which had once belonged to Thomas More's daughter, Margaret Roper, gave her the name for the Bastable's house in

The Wouldbegoods and served as a model for the Red House in the story of that name. Well Hall has long since been demolished, but the site of the house is now a public garden, named Well Hall Pleasaunce.

J. M. BARRIE

'Oh for an hour of Herod,' the novelist Anthony Hope is reported to have said, on leaving the theatre after *Peter Pan*, first produced in 1904. The idea of the 'boy who never grew up' had been in J. M. Barrie's mind since 1897, when he first made friends with George, Jack and Peter Llewelyn Davies. With their mother, Sylvia, Barrie had a relationship so intense (though platonic) as to exclude her husband.

For the three boys, Barrie created a world of fantasy in the prosaic surroundings of Kensington Gardens. There was an island in the lake called Birds' Island where, he pretended, all the birds that were born waited to be transformed into human babies. At about this time, the name Peter Pan began to slip into the stories, although the character was not yet fully formed. As his friendship with the family prospered, Barrie eventually invited them to stay with him at his country cottage on Tilford Road, near Farnham in Surrey. The games of pirates and redskins they played in the woods also furnished material for the later version of *Peter Pan*, which began as *The Boy Castaways of Black Lake Island*, a sort of scrapbook with photographs taken during the holiday.

His Newfoundland dog Luath was the model for the nursemaid-dog, Nana, in *Peter Pan*. The costume-makers used Luath as their model, and the actor who played Nana came to see her and conscientiously studied her movements.

A. A. MILNE

Where was The House at Pooh Corner? The Milne family lived at Cotchford Farm in Ashdown Forest, Kent, between East Grinstead and Tunbridge Wells, and the Christopher Robin of the poems and

stories was A. A. Milne's own son. The real Christopher Robin was to be deeply embarrassed throughout his schooldays, especially by the notorious *Vespers* which contained the lines most often quoted:

'Hush! Hush! Whisper who dares!
Christopher Robin is saying his prayers.'

In *The Enchanted Places*, C. R. Milne's own account of his childhood, he identifies some of the fictional places where his and Pooh's adventures took place:

'I could see Gill's Lap from my nursery window . . . a clump of pines on the top of a hill. And of course you can see it as Shepard drew it in *The House at Pooh Corner*.'

In the book, its name is thinly disguised as Galleon's Lap. Christopher Robin and Edward Bear, or Winnie the Pooh, as he soon became universally known, first appeared in Punch from 1924 onwards, in a series of humorous verses, later collected as *When We Were Very Young* and *Now We Are Six*. The two story books, *Winnie the Pooh* and *The House at Pooh Corner* were woven around Christopher Robin's toys.

Chiefly a writer for adults, A. A. Milne was surprised by the popularity of his books with children. He was not naturally at ease even with his own son, and C. R. Milne describes him as often, at home, being banished 'Eeyore-like' to 'gloomy places'.

AGATHA CHRISTIE

Heralded for 50 years as the Queen of Crime, Agatha Christie was, in real life, the heroine of a mystery as strange as any that she ever wrote, and to which no adequate solution has ever been found. In 1926, at the beginning of her fame (she had just written *The Murder of Roger Ackroyd*) she and her husband were living in Sunningdale, Berkshire, at 'Styles', named after her first crime novel, *The Mysterious Affair at Styles*. Their 12-year-old marriage was breaking up. On 3 December Colonel Christie left to spend the weekend with Nancy Neele, with whom he was having an affair, and

LAKE WINDERMERE *'No matter where I was, wandering about the world, I used at night to look for the North Star and, in my mind's eye, could see the beloved skyline of great hills beneath it . . .' wrote Arthur Ransome. From memories of the Lakes, 'Swallows and Amazons almost wrote itself'*

Agatha drove off in her car and vanished.

The next day her abandoned car, with her suitcase in it, was found at a local beauty spot called the Silent Pool. A massive search by the police of four counties, and by 15,000 volunteers who combed the Downs in groups of 30, failed to find any clues. Then rumour leaked out that she had been seen in Harrogate, and a 20-year-old Daily News reporter, Ritchie Calder, identified her as a guest staying at the Hydropathic Hotel, where she had registered as . . . Mrs Neele.

Most of her 85 crime novels and collections of short stories are set in the southern counties, in a now-vanished England of large country houses, inhabited by people of independent means and a sprinkling of doctors, solicitors and eccentric vicars and their wives. This was the world into which she was born in 1890 at Ashfield, a rambling, detached house in the Tor Mohun district of Torquay — the 'St Loo' of *Peril at End House*. At the beginning of World War I there was a large colony of Belgian refugees living in Torquay, and this was one reason for her detective Hercule Poirot's nationality.

ARTHUR RANSOME

The Lake District that Arthur Ransome wrote about in the 1930s, when he began his *Swallows and Amazons* stories, is the secret country he knew as a child at the turn of the century, a place only beginning to be known by tourists; where farming on the fells was still carried out by traditional methods; where

charcoal-burners still practised their craft deep in the woods around Nibthwaite and old miners could talk of the copper mines on Coniston Old Man.

He was born in Leeds in 1884 and had spent his childhood holidays on the Swainson's farm on Lake Coniston. Every time he arrived there, he had, as he later wrote in his autobiography, 'a private rite to perform. I had to dip my hand in the water, as a greeting to the beloved lake or as a proof to myself that I had indeed come home.'

In fact, Arthur Ransome did not 'come home' until he was 41 and married, with a distinguished career as a journalist and war correspondent — he was in Russia for many years — behind him. In 1925 he bought his first Lake District home, a cottage near Lake Windermere, and in 1931, wrote *Swallows and Amazons*. Lake Windermere, not Coniston, is the lake of the five Lake District stories. However, he borrowed Peel Island from Coniston and set it down as Wild Cat Island, the secret camp of the Amazon pirates, Nancy and Peggy. He borrowed the charcoal burners for an episode in *Swallowdale*, and an old miner, Slater Bob, for *Pigeon Post*. He also took the farming families of his own childhood holidays and made them into the Dixons and the Jacksons with whom the Callum and Walker children stayed. Perhaps he also included himself as Uncle Jim, the traveller and would-be writer whom the children involve in their exploits.

Some of his stories are set in East Anglia, where the Ransomes lived for several years from 1935, and the River Orwell, near one of their homes, is the setting for *We Didn't Mean to Go to Sea* in which the Walker children are carried out to sea.

BARBARA LITTLEWOOD *has worked in publishing since 1964, except for three years as a press officer with a Norfolk construction company. She worked with Methuen and with Weidenfeld and Nicolson after leaving Oxford University.*

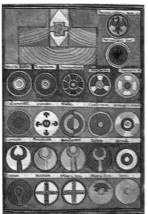

ROUGH CASTLE: ANTONINE WALL — *Less than ten years after the completion of Hadrian's Wall in the second century AD, the Emperor Antoninus Pius reversed an earlier decision to abandon Scotland to its barbarians and ordered the building of a new wall.*

The result had over 16 forts (among them **Rough Castle**), *together with fortlets and beacon platforms. Stretching from Bo'ness on the Forth to Old Kilpatrick on the Clyde, the new Antonine Wall was half the length of Hadrian's and was built wholly of turf. It was manned in the main by auxiliaries, but constructed by more heavily armed legionaries, from the three legions stationed in Britain: II Augusta from Caerleon, VI Victrix from* **York** *and XX Valeria Victrix from* **Chester***. Each squad commemorated the completion of its length by erecting inscriptions. Eighteen of these 'distance slabs' are preserved in* **Glasgow** *University's Hunterian Museum.*

While the legions were originally recruited from Italy, and auxiliary units from frontier tribes, in the second century most recruiting was local. One of the Second Cohort of Thracians stationed at Mumrills was actually a Brigantian from northern England, and most of the troops patrolling the Wall were pobably British.

ABOVE *unit shields — emblems of an administrator of Britain under the Romans*

PORTPATRICK *So short is the crossing from here to Ireland that Thomas Blower swam it in 16 hours in 1947. Irish couples, taking advantage of the proximity, used to elope across*

Portpatrick

Dumfries and Galloway   NX 0054

Until the 1860s, this beautifully placed harbour on a cliff-bound coast was the Scottish port on the short sea crossing to Donaghadee in Ireland. Runaway Irish couples often married here, as English ones did at Gretna Green.

Although the old connection has gone, the lights of Donaghadee can be seen reflected on the underside of clouds 21 miles across the water. Steps up Portpatrick's North Cliff are the start of a very long walk — all 212 miles of the Southern Upland Way. But the first few miles make a pleasant stroll past the clifftop radio station, alongside the breezy golf course and down to a series of rocky bays. At Laird's Bay, a remote-seeming cottage was built to house equipment for the submarine cable to Ireland.

Port William

Dumfries and Galloway   NX 3343

Sir William Maxwell of Monreith built this harbour village, named after himself, in the 1770s. Many of his tenants hereabouts — as he knew perfectly well — were engaged in the smuggling trade. Once, as an election candidate, Sir William paraded through the streets of Whithorn with his smuggling tenants at his heels. This so annoyed his opponent that he convinced the government to build a barracks at Fort William, with troops to come down hard on the smugglers; and that building survives as part of the Monreith Arms Hotel.

Pots of Gartness

Central   NS 5086

These rocky falls on the River Endrick are renowned as a 'leap' during the autumn run of salmon. Downstream, only the site remains of Gartness Castle, where the great mathematician John Napier often worked. He is usually credited with having invented both logarithms and the word itself; but his log tables were intended for working out navigational calculations at sea. Modern logarithms are based on a system first published by Henry Briggs, after Napier's death in 1617.

Ratho

Lothian   NT 1370

The Bridge Inn at Ratho stands beside the Union Canal, which opened in 1822 as a link between the Forth and Clyde Canal at Falkirk and the heart of Edinburgh. A restaurant barge, the *Pride of the Union*, cruises slowly westwards, overtaken by pedestrians on the towpath, to the elegant Almond Aqueduct from which there are fine high-level views over a wooded river valley. Ratho is also the base of two barges operated for disabled visitors by the Seagull Trust. East of Ratho, the canal is used by the punts of the Honourable Society of Edinburgh Boaters.

In either direction, towpath walking could hardly be easier — the Union was built as a 31-mile 'contour' canal, with no locks except at each end, and maintains a constant height along its length of 242 feet above sea level.

RATHO   *The Almond Aqueduct, one of three carrying the Union Canal, stretches 800 feet across the River Avon over 12 arches 86 feet high*

Ross Priory

Strathclyde   NS 4187

This Loch Lomondside mansion dates originally from the late 17th century, but was given its present appearance in 1812. At that time, it was owned by Hector Buchanan, a colleague of Sir Walter Scott's at the Court of Session in Edinburgh. Scott came here several times, while working on *The Lady of the Lake* and *Rob Roy*.

Ross Priory is now owned by the University of Strathclyde, and its very fine sheltered gardens, with lawns, flowering shrubs, glasshouses and alpine beds, are open to visitors one Sunday in May. There are excellent views from here of the mountains flanking the upper reaches of the loch.

Rough Castle

Central   NS 8479

Approached from the west by a minor road from Bonnybridge, Rough Castle is surrounded by railways, power lines and industrial spoil heaps. But it is a significant and carefully protected site — the earthworks of a full-scale Roman fort on the Antonine Wall. No trace of the stone and timber buildings survives, but grass-covered mounds and terraces mark the site of the high-set barracks and headquarters block, granary and bath-house. Running through the centre is the clearly defined military road which linked all the forts, placed at two-mile intervals along the wall. Excavations have revealed the identity of only one Roman unit definitely stationed here, the Sixth Cohort of the Nervians.

Roxburgh

Borders   NT 7133

Between the Tweed and the Teviot opposite Kelso stood long-lost Roxburgh. No trace remains, although it was important enough in the 12th century to be the home of the royal mint.

On the wooded ridge which guards the narrow isthmus, reached by a riverside footpath from near the Teviot bridge, only isolated archways and fragments of once-mighty walls show where Roxburgh Castle used to stand. It changed hands many times between the Scots and the English. For four long years starting in 1306, Robert the Bruce's sister was imprisoned — by direct order of the English king — in a cage slung over its outer wall. In 1460, while bombarding the castle from what are now the grounds of Floors Castle across the Tweed, James II took too close an interest in his ordnance, and was killed when one of the cannons blew apart.

St Andrews

Fife   NO 5016

Three different factors combine to give St Andrews its interest, variety and historic buildings — Scotland's oldest university, founded in 1411; the ruined cathedral; and its undisputed status as the home of golf. The older colleges are right in the heart of the town, where their grassy quadrangles lie behind anonymous walls. Red-robed students follow the centuries-old tradition of walking out along the stone piers at the harbour, as they did when prominent visitors used to come and go by sea. As well as its escape-proof bottle-shaped dungeon, St Andrews Castle has a mine hacked into the rock underneath it by medieval besiegers, and the counter-mine dug outwards by the defenders to cut it off.

There are five golf courses on the links turf behind the two-mile stretch of the West Sands. Visitors are often astonished to find that they are owned by a public trust. An old-established right of way — Granny Clark's Wynd — runs across the revered first and eighteenth fairways of the Old Course. Legally, it may be used at any time — even in the middle of a major tournament, but no St Andrews resident would be so insensitive as to disrupt play.

St Ann's

Dumfries and Galloway   NY 0793

This is an estate village in a parish which has been called Johnstone — after the principal land-owners — as far back as records go. In 1985 the Hope Johnstones of Raehills, a splendid mansion (not open) across the Kinnel Water, had the Earldom of Annandale revived in their favour.

Previous generations of the family enjoyed building ornamental footbridges. The most notable is reached by a path from St Ann's. Three walkways arranged like the spokes of a wheel meet at a rustic rest-house in the centre.

St Mary's of the Lowes

Borders   NT 2320

Reached by a signposted footpath, this ruined churchyard stands on a breezy hillside over-looking the curve of St Mary's Loch. It was the parish church of Yarrow from the 12th century until the present church, in a much more convenient situation down the valley, was built in 1640. But the old church is not forgotten. Every year on the fourth Sunday in July an open-air service is held here — a 'blanket preaching' which recalls the 17th-century Covenanters. As was their custom, the minister is still sheltered from the weather by a blanket draped over a wooden framework.

MARY QUEEN OF SCOTS *plays golf at St Andrew's in 1563 (picture after Dornestier)*

WOODCOCK AIR: BORDER WARFARE

WOODCOCK AIR: BORDER WAR-FARE — *The architecture of the Border country reflects a prevailing concern for security, from the grim 14th-century fortress of Hermitage Castle in Liddesdale to* **Woodcock Air's** *Repentance Tower, built in 1560 as a fire-beacon.*

From the 12th century onwards, the Borders have been a battle-ground for the rival English and Scots. Although the almost per-manent state of warfare often amounted merely to the skirmishes of cattle-rustling Border 'reivers', there was also conflict on a larger scale. In 1388 for instance, the Scottish Earls of Moray and Douglas launched a raid through Northumberland to Durham, burning and pillaging as they went. Met by the northern English forces at Otterburn, they fought the battle commemorated in the most celebrated of the old Border Ballads, 'Chevy Chase'.

Even the comparatively small dwellings of farmers and modest lairds were defensive in nature. In the 16th century, the bastle-house, a fortified farmhouse, appeared on the English side of the border, while on the Scottish side the pele or tower-house was characteristic. Greenknowe Tower, Berwickshire, is a fine example. Even the Church was not immune, and fortified 'vicars' peles' (from the Latin 'pilum', for palisade) were built for the clergy. One still stands at **Corbridge,** *Northumberland.*

HOLLOWS TOWER *The home of Johnny Armstrong, a Border reiver, it has walls six feet thick. It stands near Canonbie*

Sandford

Strathclyde   NS 7143

From this village on the Kype Water, a road open to walkers follows the north bank to the rocky 50-foot falls called Spectacle E'e, or Spectacle Eye.

In the 18th century, the flow of water worked a corn mill. A young Sandford man, rebuffed as a suitor for the miller's daughter, secretly fixed a pair of spectacles to its thatched roof. The sun shining through the lenses — or 'eyes' — set fire to the roof and gutted the mill; hence the name.

Scotstarvit Tower

Fife   NO 3711

South of Cupar, the National Trust for Scotland owns the estate called Hill of Tarvit, where an Edwardian mansion is surrounded by fine gardens and high-level viewpoints. The house and its contents epitomise the taste of the period and serve as an almost perfect record of Edwardian life.

At Hill of Tarvit, the key is available for the older Scotstarvit Tower, about three-quarters of a mile away. This much sterner building was the home of Sir John Scot, the 17th-century author of a book of political memoirs, *Scot of Scotstarvit's Staggering State of Scots Statesmen*, which was so libellous that publication was delayed until decades after he and all the people referred to in it were safely dead.

Stronachlachar

Central   NN 4010

With a half-timbered 'big house' and cottages in sheltered woodland around it, Stronachlachar was built in the 1850s as the headquarters of the Loch Katrine water scheme. In summer, the lovely turn-of-the-century steamer *Sir Walter Scott* — which was brought overland to Stronachlachar as a kit of parts and reassembled here — calls on its regular excursion runs.

Beyond the village, the road (open to walkers and cyclists) follows the lochside past Glengyle, the house at the foot of the northern mountains which was the birthplace of Rob Roy MacGregor.

Just off Stronachlachar pier, the tiny Factor's Island is where he once held the Duke of Montrose's factor to ransom. A masonry wall protects the island whenever the water level rises.

Tongland

Dumfries and Galloway   NX 6953

John Damien, Abbot of Tongland in the reign of James IV, once made himself wings of birds' feathers and, flapping his arms energetically, stepped off the battlements of Stirling Castle to show the king that here was a way for man to fly. Dusting himself down after the inevitable impact, he pinpointed the basic flaw in his design: he had used chicken feathers, when eagle feathers would have performed much better.

Approached from Kirkcudbright by Telford's fine bridge over the Dee, Tongland power station offers summer-time guided tours which show off many engineering and wildlife aspects of the Galloway Hydro-Electric scheme, like the 29 pools of the salmon ladder at Tongland dam.

TYNRON   *William Smith's grave in the village church-yard. A rough slab on Racemuir, Moniaive, records that he was shot in 1685*

Tynron

Dumfries and Galloway   NX 8092

The churchyard in this tiny, secluded village has an 'Old Mortality' (the name of the carver and renewer of numerous martyrs' memorials) stone to the young Covenanter William Smith, who in 1685 refused to talk under questioning, was shot in dubious circumstances, and then buried 'under the doorstep of Hill'. Only after the Revolution was he given a proper grave. Tynronkirk was also the name of a whisky, first marketed in the 1850s. The explorer Joseph Thomson, who came from nearby Penpont, reported finding an empty bottle near Lake Chad, in the heart of Africa.

Wanlockhead

Dumfries and Galloway NS 8712

With some of its houses at 1400 feet above sea level, Wanlockhead is the highest village in Scotland, as well as the home of the Museum of Scottish Lead Mining. From the museum, a silver- and lead-mining trail follows the valley of the Wanlock Burn, visiting the walk-in Loch Nell Mine, the site of the Bay Mine where an early steam engine once pumped water from galleries 600 feet deep, and Straitsteps Mine, where the 19th-century beam engine has been restored. The museum's address is Goldscaur Row, a reminder that gold was panned from the Wanlock Burn.

East of Wanlockhead, the grassy slopes rise to 2378 feet at Lowther Hill and 2404 feet at Green Lowther. In winter, the telecommunications station on Green Lowther — the highest in Britain — can be reached only by snow-tracked vehicles. British Telecom engineers feelingly call it Ice Station Zebra.

Wemyss Caves

Fife NT 3496

Like Pittenweem, farther along the Fife coast, the parish of 'Weems' takes its name from the old word for its sea-cliff caves. Their story is told in the Environmental Education Centre at East Wemyss, where Open Sundays — usually one per month in summer — include walks and displays on history, wildlife and industry.

The ruins of Macduff's Castle stand on the site of an earlier fortress, probably occupied by the historical original of the Thane of Fife in Shakespeare's *Macbeth*.

East Wemyss was on the line of the intriguing town-and-country Wemyss and District Tramway, whose yellow 'mustard box' trams ran from 1906 till 1932. Parts of the old route can still be discerned.

Woodcock Air

Dumfries and Galloway NY 1672

At the Hoddom and Kinmount estates visitor centre beside the River Annan, maps indicate the network of footpaths on this wooded hill to the south-east. Plantations of oak and beech, larch, pine and spruce attract a varied birdlife, including the woodcock from which the hill possibly takes its name, although it may have come from a family called Wodecoc, mentioned in 13th-century records.

One walk through the Hoddom estate climbs to the hilltop viewpoint of Repentance Tower. Whatever the reason for its much-discussed name, this was built in the 1560s as a fire-beacon tower from which a watch was kept on any English incursions over the border. It still has a superb outlook over the upper Solway, the coast of Cumbria, the Lake District hills and even — in really clear weather — to the faraway Isle of Man.

WEMYSS CAVES *'They were built by the Pechs — short wee men wi . . . feet sae broad that when it rained they served as umbrellas,' says an old legend*

Sir WILLIAM WALLACE, GENERAL and GOVERNOR of SCOTLAND 354

WILLIAM WALLACE — *The Border warfare recalled by Repentance Tower,* **Woodcock Air***, owed much to Scotland's fight for independence, whose greatest champion was Sir William Wallace 1274–1305. He spent his early manhood in* **Ayr** *and was brought up in* **Dundee***. According to Blind Harry, his 15th-century chronicler, Wallace's love of independence was fostered by his uncle and fanned into flame by his outlawry following the slaughter of an Englishman who insulted him.*

In exile, he gathered a band of patriots who joined him in the burning of the 'Barns of Ayr', the first incident in the Scottish War of Independence.

In 1297 he avenged his wife's death by killing the English sheriff Hazelrig and went on to a great victory over Edward I at the Battle of Stirling Bridge. Afterwards, he had the hated English chief justice, Sir Hugh de Cressingham, flayed and a sword-belt made of his skin — a rare historical example of the practice of flaying (see **Hadstock***).*

The English were thereafter expelled from Scotland, and Wallace was elected governor. However, in 1298 he was defeated by Edward at the Battle of Falkirk and, though he escaped, he was taken in 1305 and executed in Smithfield, **London***, where a plaque commemorates the event. In Scotland, memorials in* **Edinburgh***, Barnweill and Stirling are reminders of his heroism.*

WESTERN ISLES (date unknown).
A group known locally as the 'village parliament'. The picture was taken on St Kilda, now deserted. The last islanders had become unable to make a living by 1930, and were evacuated to the mainland

NORTHERN SCOTLAND

*A*re there really monsters lurking in the icy depths of the
Highlands' lochs? A man who thought so tried to drain Loch na
Beiste to find one. Travellers through these often lonely, but
hauntingly beautiful parts will see turreted, fairy tale castles –
at Dunvegan there is a rare treasure, the fairy flag –
and wild seascapes where the cry of seabirds never fades. On the
way there'll be stone circles, a monument to a cow at
Lendrum, the Earthquake House at Comrie, and the chance to
pan for gold in the Strath of Kildonan . . .

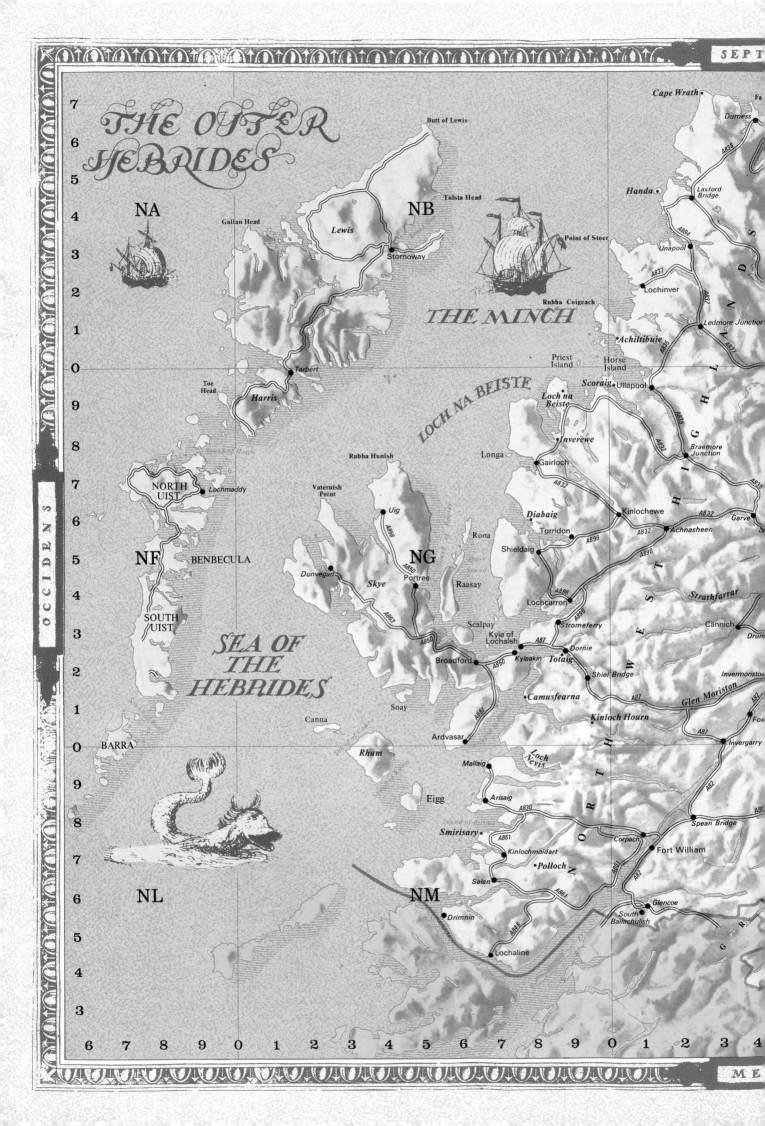

THE OUTER HEBRIDES

Cape Wrath
Fa
Durness
A838
Handa
Laxford Bridge
A894
Butt of Lewis
Tolsta Head
NB
NA
Gallan Head
Lewis
Point of Stoer
A837
Unapool
Lochinver
A837
Rubha Coigeach
Stornoway
THE MINCH
Ledmore Junction
A835
Priest Island
Horse Island
Achiltibuie
Tarbert
Toe Head
Harris
Loch na Beiste
Scoraig
Ullapool
A835
A832
Braemore Junction
Sound of Harris
Inverewe
Longa
Gairloch
A832
NORTH UIST
Lochmaddy
Rubha Hunish
Diabaig
Kinlochewe
A832
Garve
Vaternish Point
Uig
A866
Torridon
A896
A832
Achnasheen
A890
NF
BENBECULA
Rona
Shieldaig
Strathfarrar
NG
Portree
Raasay
A896
Dunvegan
Skye
A850
Lochcarron
A890
SOUTH UIST
Scalpay
Stromeferry
Cannich
Drum
A863
Kyle of Lochalsh
SEA OF THE HEBRIDES
A850
Broadford
Kyleakin
A850
Dornie
Totaig
A87
Invermoriston
Soay
Camusfearna
Shiel Bridge
Glen Moriston
A82
Canna
A851
Kinloch Hourn
A87
Fo
BARRA
Loch Nevis
Invergarry
Rhum
Mallaig
A82
Eigg
Arisaig
A830
Spean Bridge
A82
Smirisary
A861
Corpach
Fort William
Polloch
Kinlochmoidart
A861
A82
NL
Salen
NM
A861
Glencoe
Drimnin
South Ballachulish
A884
Lochaline
G

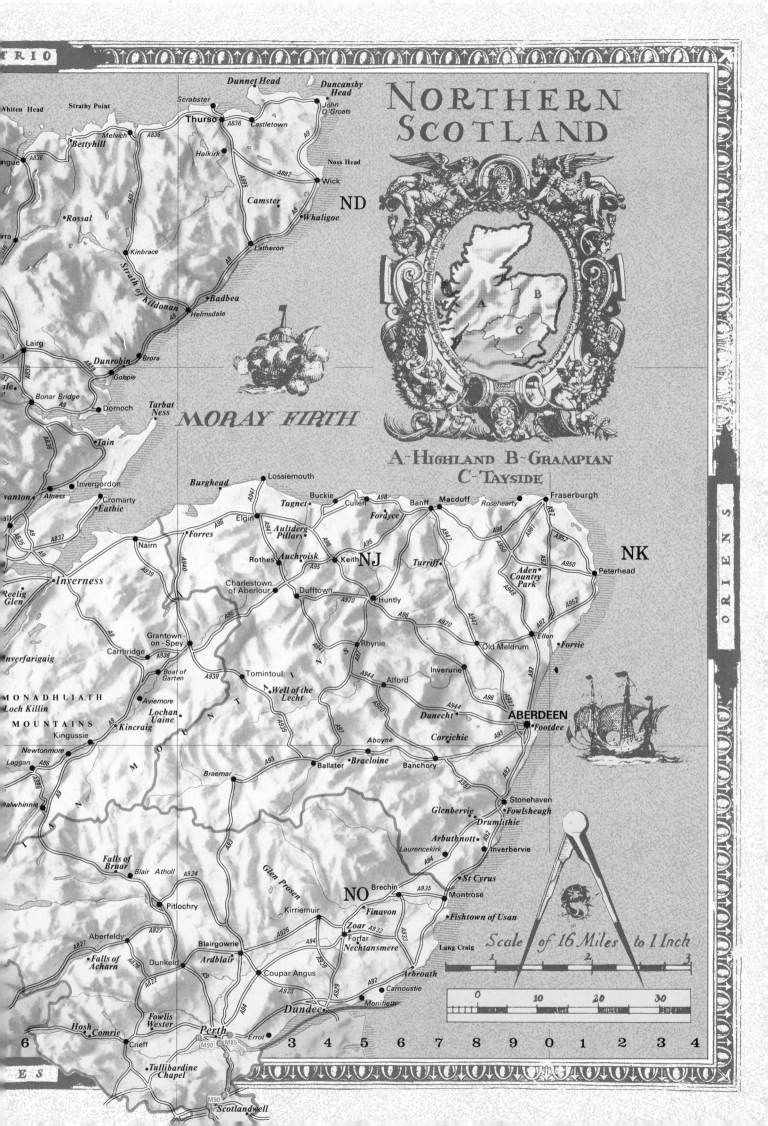

NORTHERN SCOTLAND

A·HIGHLAND B·GRAMPIAN
C·TAYSIDE

MORAY FIRTH

ND

NJ

NK

NO

Scale of 16 Miles to 1 Inch

Whiten Head · Strathy Point · Dunnet Head · Duncansby Head · Scrabster · John O'Groats · Thurso · Castletown · Melvich · Halkirk · Bettyhill · Noss Head · Wick · Rossal · Camster · Whaligoe · Kinbrace · Latheron · Badbea · Helmsdale · Lairg · Dunrobin · Brora · Golspie · Bonar Bridge · Dornoch · Tarbat Ness · Tain · Invergordon · Cromarty · Eathie · Alness · Burghead · Lossiemouth · Buckie · Cullen · Banff · Macduff · Rosehearty · Fraserburgh · Tugnet · Fordyce · Elgin · Forres · Aultderg Pillars · Rothes · Auchroisk · Keith · Turriff · Peterhead · Nairn · Aden Country Park · Inverness · Charlestown of Aberlour · Dufftown · Huntly · Reelig Glen · Grantown-on-Spey · Rhynie · Old Meldrum · Ellon · Forvie · Carrbridge · Inverfarigaig · Boat of Garten · Tomintoul · Alford · Inverurie · MONADHLIATH · Aviemore · Well of the Lecht · Dunecht · ABERDEEN · Loch Killin · Lochan Uaine · Corrichie · Footdee · MOUNTAINS · Kincraig · Kingussie · Aboyne · Newtonmore · Braeloine · Laggan · Braemar · Ballater · Banchory · Dalwhinnie · Stonehaven · Glenbervie · Fowlsheugh · Drumlithie · Falls of Bruar · Arbuthnott · Blair Atholl · Inverbervie · Laurencekirk · Pitlochry · Kirriemuir · Brechin · St Cyrus · Montrose · Aberfeldy · Finavon · Fishtown of Usan · Blairgowrie · Zoar · Forfar · Nechtansmere · Arbroath · Lang Craig · Falls of Acharn · Dunkeld · Ardblair · Coupar Angus · Carnoustie · Hosh · Comrie · Fowlis Wester · Dundee · Monifieth · Perth · Errol · Crieff · Tullibardine Chapel · Scotlandwell

6 3 4 5 6 7 8 9 0 1 2 3 4

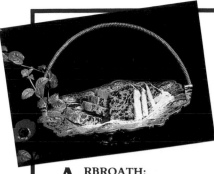

ARBROATH:
SCOTTISH FOOD —
*Some of the world's finest
saltwater fish is landed at Scottish
ports, whence regional specialities
such as 'Finnan haddie' (haddock)
and Loch Fyne kippers, and the
haddock smoked over a beechwood
fire peculiar to* **Arbroath**, *and so
known as 'Arbroath smokies'.*

*From the butcher's come black
puddings and 'mealies', made of
oatmeal and fat (also served dished
up in batter at the chippy), and
that most 'Scottish' of foods apart
from porridge — haggis. This
mixture of oatmeal and chopped
meat in a sheep's stomach-lining
— nowadays normally plastic —
is traditionally served on Burns
Night, accompanied by 'bashed
neeps' (mashed swede), and
'tatties'.*

*From the bakers come mutton
pies, 'bridies' (pasties with suet
and onions) and 'Lothian slice' (a
sandwich of minced meat in
pastry).*

*But the glory of Scotland is its
sweet baking — not for nothing is
it called the 'Land o' Cakes'.
High tea brings everything from
oatcakes (flat oatmeal biscuits)
served with a traditional cheese
(see* **Tain**), *to potato pancakes,
scones and Selkirk Bannock. A
sweeter version of this is the
peculiarly Scottish Black Bun,
made of pastry wrapped round
currants, chopped apples, nuts,
candied peel and spices.*

ABOVE *Black bun, one of the
rich, spiced specialities served up
for the Scottish high tea*

Achiltibuie

Highland NC 0208
During the mackerel and herring seasons, fishing boats from the Minch are constantly passing by, taking their catches to the massive East European factory ships anchored in the loch. Not their entire catches though: Achiltibuie has a reputation for gourmet food, and in summer, visitors are shown round the Smokehouse, where fish, meat and game are cured. And the Summer Isles Hotel has gardens where vegetables are grown without soil. Guided tours demonstrate the processes used in the imposingly named Achiltibuie Hydroponicum.

Aden Country Park

Grampian NJ 9848
Something like 220 acres of an estate which used to cover 10,000 acres in the heart of Buchan have been turned into this very attractive country park.

Footpaths explore broadleaved and conifer woodland, pass a wildfowl lake which used to provide a head of water for a mill, and cross footbridges over the winding South Ugie Water.

The mixture of habitats attracts many kinds of birds, from goldcrests and tree creepers to dippers, moorhens and sparrowhawks. Visitors to the park early or late in the day can sometimes catch sight of roe deer feeding on the open ground.

Aden's beautifully restored semi-circular range of farm buildings houses a series of displays illustrating the lives of estate workers.

Arbroath

Tayside NO 6440
The ruined 12th-century abbey is well known, as are Arbroath smokies — haddock deliciously cured over a beechwood fire. But there are many additional attractions. Kerr's Miniature Railway operates steam and diesel-hauled trains on a 10¼-inch line at the West Links Park. Nearby, the Regency-style Signal Tower (now a museum) was the original communications link with the Bell Rock lighthouse 11 miles offshore. For expectant fathers on the faraway rock, special signals used to be hoisted on the flagstaff — a pair of trousers to show the safe arrival of a son, a petticoat for a daughter.

The Stone of Scone, sensationally stolen in 1950, came briefly to Arbroath in 1951.

Arbuthnott

Grampian NO 7975
The upland farms of Arbuthnott parish were the setting for Lewis Grassic Gibbon's novel *Sunset Song*. It was written while he was in exile in Welwyn Garden City, was published in 1932 and was followed at yearly intervals by *Cloud Howe* and *Grey Granite*. Gathered into a trilogy called *A Scots Quair*, these books have been reprinted several times, and Gibbon's work gained a wider audience through adaptations serialised on television during the 1970s.

Arbuthnott church, attractively situated above the Bervie Water, played the part of 'Kinraddie kirk' on television, and the author's ashes are interred under a memorial giving his real name of Leslie Mitchell, in this churchyard he knew so

AULTDEARG PILLARS *Natural sculpture on the Spey*

well as a boy. The handsomely-restored building is one of the few pre-Reformation parish churches still in use in Scotland.

Ardblair

Tayside NO 1644
No house is more steeped in Jacobite memories than this 16th-century castle, home of the Blair Oliphant family. Laurence Oliphant was aide-de-camp to Prince Charles Edward Stuart, and Ardblair contains many personal mementoes of the prince. In a later generation, Carolina Oliphant, Lady Nairne, wrote the words for many Jacobite songs like *Charlie Is My Darling*, *The Hundred Pipers* and that most famous of all Scottish farewells, *Will Ye No' Come Back Again*. Many of her possessions, including the piano at which she worked, are still at Ardblair. During her lifetime, the authorship of these best-selling songs was a complete mystery. Even her publisher knew her only by the pen-name of 'Mrs Bogan, of Bogan'.

Ardblair is open to visitors on Thursday afternoons from Easter to October, but guided tours are arranged only through the Tourist Information Centre in Blairgowrie.

A UCHROISK: WHISKY — *Fifteen million gallons of whisky can be stored in the distillery at* **Auchroisk** — *a relative new-comer in a land where the art of distilling alcohol from barley has been known for over a thousand years.*

By 1700 the production of whisky as we know it was well established, but it was not taxed until the Union of Parliaments in 1707. Taxes were regarded as an 'English' imposition: the Malt Tax of 1725 caused serious rioting and the Scots began to make whisky in secret. In the 18th century, customs officers estimated there were more than 200 illicit stills, hidden away in remote glens in the Highlands. The barley was soaked in a mountain stream for a couple of days, then the grain would be spread out to germinate in a cave or other safe place. After ten days it was dried at a peat fire and this 'malted' grain was put in a barrel with boiling water. Yeast was added to the resulting liquid, which was then distilled a few times to produce raw whisky.

Among the legal distillers were the Haigs of Leith, who made whisky from oats, potatoes and turnips to avoid the taxes on malt.

DISTILLING *in the Highlands, 1883 — an illicit still is captured, then seized and destroyed*

Auchroisk

Grampian   NJ 3351

Set among farm and forest land, Auchroisk malt whisky distillery above the Burn of Mulben is not open to visitors, but the white-walled complex of buildings is well worth admiring from the roadside.

Auchroisk went into production in 1974, and has won architectural awards for its modern expression of traditional Victorian distillery design. Slated roofs slope at attractively varied angles, and the conical yeast-house tower provides a contrasting centre piece.

Aultdearg Pillars

Grampian   NJ 3356

From a forest car park south of Fochabers, a footpath leads through pinewood, birch and rowan to a viewpoint over the lower Spey. It is also a good vantage point for the curious Aultdearg Pillars: columns of sandstone, clay and gravel, protected by capping stones, which have stayed in place while the surrounding material has been eroded away by rain over thousands of years.

Further south, the narrow public road winds in steep, hairpin bends down to the foot of an unsuspected gorge.

Badbea

Highland   ND 0819

A sturdy memorial on the sloping moorland recalls the lost settlement of Badbea — built by people who had been moved out of their homes in sheltered inland glens, to make way for flocks of Cheviot sheep. It was a harsh, high and wind-swept spot: dangerous sea-cliffs meant that children had to be tethered for their own safety, and farming was always difficult. The settlers came here towards the end of the 18th century; later generations gave up the struggle, although the last inhabitant did not leave until early in this century.

Bettyhill

Highland   NC 7061

The Betty who gave her name to this village was Elizabeth, Countess of Sutherland, during the implacable Sutherland Clearances of 1806-20.

Strathnaver Museum at Bettyhill is open from July to September and has displays on the clearances, as well as on the district's wildlife and prehistory. Invernaver Nature Reserve, crossed by a footpath, was created to protect the rare wild flowers, but is also a fine place for bird-watchers and has the remains of an Iron Age broch.

CAMSTER: CAIRNS

Like earthen long barrows, cairns were family or community graves for multiple burial. But while a long barrow would be used once, the chambered cairn, with its stone-built chamber and entrance from outside, could receive successive generations of the dead.

*At **Camster**, a long cairn and a round cairn, both Neolithic, can be compared. Inside the round cairn, a low narrow passage, crept down on hands and knees, leads into a tall, circular burial chamber. The long cairn, approached by steps, contains two burial chambers, which seem originally to have been encased by separate round cairns, later combined into one.*

Long and round chambered cairns can also be seen at South Yarrows and Corrimony, Highland. In England and Wales, the chambered long cairn is virtually the rule.

The Grey Cairns of Camster (as they are called) have been restored and present an unusually complete appearance. Very often most of the stone has been robbed, leaving only the slab-built burial chamber as a 'cromlech' or 'dolmen'.

ABOVE *Inside one of the cairns. Ashes, bones, pots and skeletons were found in excavations of 1865*

COMRIE *Earthquake House — built in 1869 to house equipment used to record the earth tremors which shook this area over a period of nearly a hundred years*

Braeloine

Central   NO 4896

Glen Tanar estate's visitor centre at Braeloine, open from April to September, preserves the name of a disappeared village by the Water of Tanar. The stone bridge beside it was on the old Firmounth road, one of the great rights-of-way across the Grampians. The people of Braeloine were not only farmers; they also had a mill and an inn, a provision store and shoemakers' shops, to supply travellers on the road. In the late 18th century, traffic began to move to newer roads elsewhere, and the need for Braeloine's services gradually faded away. Around 1870 the by-then derelict village was dismantled, but some of the stones went into the building of St Lesmo's Chapel, which is occasionally open to visitors.

Burghead

Grampian   NJ 1168

At the north-west end of King Street, an anonymous door (key available at a nearby house) leads into one of the most baffling ancient monuments in Scotland. Stone steps descend a grassy hillside to the Burghead Well — a rock-hewn and spring-fed pool surrounded by a massive stone-built chamber, erected after the well was rediscovered in 1809.

The Burning of the Clavie ceremony on 5 November is a highlight of the village calendar.

Camster

Highland   ND 2644

Standing by the roadside on a bleak Caithness moorland are the Grey Cairns of Camster — Neolithic monuments, dated to the third millennium BC. One of them survives only as a partly rebuilt wall, but the other two have not only been re-roofed in modern materials but also have skylights, so that visitors, crawling in by the original entrance tunnels, can stand upright and look around in the central chambers. The round cairn is regarded as the finest chambered tomb in mainland Britain.

Camusfearna

Highland   NG 7714

This is a name which appears on no maps. It was invented by Gavin Maxwell to preserve the anonymity of Sandaig, where he wrote *Ring of Bright Water* and other best-selling books about his otters. But some readers worked out from geographical references where Camusfearna had to be, and Maxwell once accidentally allowed the name Sandaig to appear in print. His house burned down one winter's night when the nearest fire engine was almost 40 miles away over the mountains. A memorial marks the site, and readers still make nostalgic pilgrimages to Camusfearna, the last mile or so on a walk down a winding forest road.

Cape Wrath

Highland   NC 2574

From May to September, a minibus operates from the ferry slip on the west side of the Kyle of Durness along one of the loneliest roads in Europe — the 11-mile stretch to this north-western tip of the British mainland. Much of the wild moorland country is used at times as a Ministry of Defence firing range.

Cape Wrath lighthouse was built in 1827 of locally quarried granite. Standing on a clifftop almost 400 feet above the sea, it has a spectacular outlook from Orkney to the Western Isles. Along the north coast, back towards Durness, the great seabird cliffs of Clo Mor are the highest in mainland Britain. Guillemots, razorbills, kittiwakes, fulmars and puffins share the 900-foot sandstone walls.

Carbisdale Castle

Highland   NH 5795

Carbisdale's dominant position was carefully chosen by the former Duchess of Sutherland, who had it built before World War I. She had fallen out with the rest of the family and wanted her new castle to be as close as possible to the edge of their estates. When they travelled, by road or rail, to or from their own castle near Golspie, Carbisdale was annoyingly within sight.

Now serving as the grandest-looking youth

hostel in Scotland, it stands on a wooded hill above the beautiful Kyle of Sutherland. Although the castle is not normally open to visitors, a forest walk starting north of Culrain station passes nearby.

Comrie

Tayside   NN 7722

Situated at the foot of Glen Lednock, exactly on the Highland Boundary Fault, Comrie was the first place in Britain where earthquakes were systematically studied. Records kept here from 1789 showed an increasing number of tremors caused by movements on the geological fault line. Dishes rattled in cupboards and houses shook. After the worst disturbances, in 1839, the Comrie postmaster invented the world's first seismo-meter. As the shocks continued, it was decided in 1869 that a special building should be set up to house more advanced recording equipment. Almost as soon as that was done, the earthquakes began to peter out. But tremors are still felt from time to time, and the Earthquake House has been retained, with documents, reports and old illustrations on display.

Corrichie

Grampian   NJ 7301

At a clearing in the roadside spruce forest, a massive granite pillar commemorates the Battle of Corrichie, 1562, when Mary Queen of Scots' army, commanded by her half-brother, heavily defeated the forces of the Earl of Huntly. Huntly, chief of the Gordons, was advancing on Aberdeen, where the Queen was in residence, to avenge an insult to himself in a redistribution of territory. He died on the field of battle, although his corpse, meanly dressed, is said to have been dragged into court to have the charge of treason read over it.

Later, Mary visited Corrichie, and maps still show a Queen's Chair, from which, so the story goes, she surveyed the scene.

Diabaig

Highland   NG 7960

Down a remarkably steep hill to the sea, this village with the Viking name is scattered round a spectacular rocky amphitheatre. A shortage of cattle grazing meant that goats were often kept here for milking. Their descendants have gone half-wild, roaming the lonely country to the north-west, where a rough footpath leads past the isolated youth hostel at Craig.

Drumlithie

Grampian   NO 7880

In his novel *Sunset Song*, the author Lewis Grassic Gibbon (see also Arbuthnott) jokes that the people of this Mearns village were so proud of their steeple that whenever the rain started, they ran out and took it inside. Drumlithie is a pleasant place of haphazardly angled streets and lanes, and many of its modernised cottages were the homes and workshops of handloom weavers. It was for them, and not for the church, that the elegant little pencil steeple was built in 1777. The bell tolled to let the weavers count the passing hours of the working day.

C ORRICHIE: MARY QUEEN OF SCOTS — *A pillar in the forest at* Corrichie *marks the scene of a major triumph for Mary Queen of Scots, when her army defeated the Earl of Huntly in 1562.*

One of the most romantic figures of her day, Mary seemed at this point to have the world at her feet. Renowned for her beauty, the Queen of France and Scotland was seen by many as rightful heir to the throne of England.

But her wheel of fortune was to turn. She never forgave her second husband Lord Darnley for the murder of David Rizzio, her secretary and confidant (whose bloodstains at Edinburgh *were thought indelible), and only three months after Darnley died in 1567, she married his suspected murderer, the Earl of Bothwell.*

Such a marriage set the country against her. Defeated at Carberry Hill, she was forced to abdicate and was imprisoned at Lochleven Castle. She escaped and stayed for one night at Dundrennan Abbey, then fled in a tiny fishing boat across the Solway Firth to seek protection from her cousin Elizabeth I.

After eighteen years' imprisonment (much of it spent in Sheffield*), she was finally convicted of conspiracy through letters found hidden in ale casks, and went bravely to her execution at* Fotheringhay *Castle in 1587.*

ABOVE   *Mary with Darnley, who held her while her favourite, Rizzio, was murdered, and died himself in suspicious circumstances in 1567*

DUNDEE: COMICS

D UNDEE: COMICS — Desperate Dan was born in **Dundee** on 4 December 1937 when the publishing house of D. C. Thomson launched 'The Dandy' comic.

The firm already had a reputation in the juvenile publishing market through their range of boys' papers — 'Rover', 'Skipper', 'Adventure', 'Wizard' and 'Hotspur' — and 'The Dandy' was produced for younger readers. Such was its success that it was soon followed by the 'The Beano'. During the war, which brought a drastic cut in paper supplies, 'The Dandy' and 'The Beano' appeared on alternate weeks. In 1940, a survey of children's reading habits, published by A. T. Jenkinson, showed how widely read the Dundee publications were, and 'The Beano' and 'The Dandy' are still the most popular comics in Britain today.

Forerunners of modern comics were publications like the 'Boys Own Magazine', launched in 1855, which had stories and competitions for prizes such as pencil cases. In 1879 came the 'Boys' Own Paper', soon followed by the 'Girls' Own Paper', with 'Marvel' in 1893 and 'Magnet' in 1908. Contributors to children's periodicals included Sir Arthur Conan Doyle, Jules Verne and R. M. Ballantyne, and in the words of one writer, their message was that 'the strong fellows must look after the weak'. Alongside these magazines was a vigorous tradition of colourful weeklies filled with astonishing tales — the so-called 'penny dreadfuls' — whose roots may lie in the tales of folk heroes sold by pedlars from the 16th century onwards.

© D. C. THOMSON & CO. LTD., 1986

Duncansby Head

Highland   ND 4073

This is the extreme north-eastern tip of mainland Britain, far more memorable than nearby John o'Groats. The high-set lighthouse gives magnificent views, north towards Orkney and south to where the red-sandstone sea-cliffs are matched by the superb offshore Stacks of Duncansby. These jagged pillars with pointed summits rise as much as 300 feet out of the sea. A walk from the lighthouse gives closer views of the Stacks, which, like the mainland cliffs and sheer-sided inlets, are crowded with seabirds. At migration time, more pass by on their long flights to and from the Arctic. Sightseeing boats come here from the harbour at John o'Groats.

Dundee

Tayside   NO 4030

It is famous for 'jute, jam and journalists' (although it is also where marmalade was invented when an 18th-century grocer, John Keiller, bought a cargo of bitter Spanish oranges and gave them to his wife, to boil in the same way that she prepared jam) and for the characters who have appeared in its long-established comics like *The Beano* and *The Dandy*. Scotland's best-known Sunday newspaper strips — *Oor Wullie* and *The Broons* — used to be drawn by the illustrator Dudley D. Watkins at his home in the suburb of Broughty Ferry.

Dundee built most of the whaling ships which operated from British ports, and sent many crews to the Arctic and Antarctic whaling grounds. The museum at Broughty Castle, near the harbour where the Firth of Tay cruises begin, recalls that long-gone industry.

In 1986, after years on the Thames, the Polar expedition ship *Discovery* returned to Dundee's Victoria Dock, where she was built. Nearby, the frigate *Unicorn*, launched in 1824 and the oldest British warship afloat, is a fascinating museum of Royal Navy shipboard life.

Among Dundee sea-dogs was Admiral Duncan, who defeated the Dutch fleet at the Battle of Camperdown in 1797. In the extensive Camperdown Park, an adventure playground has the battle as its theme. In the city, a recent programme of wall decorations has put coloured mosaics on the wall of an indoor bowling centre, and vintage bus scenes on painted tiles at a modern transport depot. An older plaque marks the house where a girl called Mary Wollstonecraft once lived. In later life, she married the poet Shelley; and during a pleasant Continental holiday she wrote *Frankenstein*.

Dunecht

Grampian   NJ 7509

This Victorian estate village has neat granite cottages, large gardens and — on its principal building — heraldic carvings. It was built by an Aberdeen paper magnate who made newspaper headlines for a different kind of landowning in Wester Ross: in 1879 he repossessed from the crofters of Leckmelm all the land they had worked for generations. This late 'clearance' led indirectly to the government legislation which gave crofting tenants firm security of tenure.

South of the village, the gardens of Dunecht House, set among woods and parkland, are open to visitors some Sundays in June and August.

Dunnet Head

Highland   ND 2076

Caithnessians claim that this most northerly point on the British mainland was the first place in Scotland mentioned in writing: the author was a Roman geographer reporting to Julius Caesar in 53BC. The headland is ringed by seabird cliffs, with more than a dozen freshwater lochs on its grassy top, and a lighthouse with superb views over the Pentland Firth to Orkney. Before the days of radio, ships passing by used to make flag signals to watchers on Dunnet Head, who would relay the messages by telegraph to their home ports. On the south side, the recently rebuilt Dwarwick pier looks across the breakers beating on the two-mile surfing beach at the head of Dunnet Bay.

Dunrobin

Highland   NC 8500

Perhaps the most exclusive railway halt in Scotland: attractively rustic Dunrobin Castle station was built as a private halt for Dunrobin's main attraction: the palatial Victorian castle — but is worth seeking out in its own right. Last used regularly in the 1960s, it does not appear on timetables or maps; but British Rail arranges summer excursion trains from Inverness, which stop here.

The Franco-Scottish style castle, created in the 19th century for the second Duke of Sutherland, is open to visitors in summer.

DUNCANSBY HEAD *The astonishing sandstone stacks are perpetually gnawed away by the sea*

Eathie

Highland   NH 7763

Discoveries in the fossil beds of Eathie made Hugh Miller of Cromarty world-famous among 19th-century geologists. His birthplace there is now a National Trust for Scotland museum, and the site of his early fieldwork is still accessible. South of Eathie Mains, where parking is available on request, a field-edge track leads to a splendid clifftop viewpoint, hairpins dizzily down to the shore, then turns north-east past a salmon-fishing station to the opening of the Eathie gorge. Fossil fish and plants can still be uncovered, but the overgrown gorge should not be tackled.

Evanton

Highland   NH 6066

Above the Novar estate plantations on the summit of Fyrish Hill (north of Evanton) stands a replica of the arched gateway of the Indian city of Negapatam. It was built in 1782 by General Sir Hector Munro of Novar, who had commanded the siege of the original. West of the village, the spectacular Black Rock Gorge is a two-mile ravine, 200 feet deep in places and occasionally only 12 feet wide. Evanton airfield, to the east, was used briefly in the 1960s as the most northerly motor-racing circuit in Britain.

Falls of Acharn

Tayside   NN 7543

A half-mile walk up from the old mill village of Acharn on Lochtayside leads to an artificially constructed cave.

In the heyday of the Breadalbane estates, guides used to pause at a junction halfway through, and usher unsuspecting visitors along the alleyway to the right. They came out on a belvedere with a fine view through the woodlands to the waterfalls of the Acharn Burn; the guide, having followed the other branch of the cave to a secret exit, would suddenly leap over the wall at them, simulating a heart-stopping attack by wild clansmen.

Falls of Bruar

Tayside   NN 8266

When Robert Burns came this way, he admired the waterfalls but saw that something was missing. His *Humble Petition of the Bruar Water* asked the Duke of Atholl, a great arboriculturalist, to clothe its banks in trees. The Duke obliged, and now the falls cascade through pinewoods, with footpaths and bridges. There are three sets of falls in the group; the upper one is the most impressive, with a combined drop of 200ft.

By the main road, the Clan Donnachaidh Museum (open April to October) illustrates the history of the Robertsons and allied families who make up the clan, and of the Jacobite Risings in which they played a prominent part.

DUNDEE: FRANKENSTEIN — *Born in London in 1797 and brought up in* **Dundee***, Mary Wollstonecraft Shelley created Frankenstein's monster in a competition between friends.*

The fashion for heavily romanticised fiction, typified by novels such as Horace Walpole's 'The Castle of Otranto' (1746) and Mrs Radclyffe's 'The Mysteries of Udolpho' (1794), paralleled the Picturesque Movement in architecture (see **Downton***). Both were born of a pervading taste for the 'Gothick' in the late 18th and early 19th centuries.*

It was in spirited response to this, while they were in Switzerland, that Mary, her husband the poet Shelley and Byron competed together to write a supernatural tale. Shelley seems to have produced nothing, Byron never finished his vampire tale, and Mary won by default. Her story was 'Frankenstein, or The Modern Prometheus' (1818), one of the most celebrated horror stories ever written.

The fame of 'Frankenstein' has fuelled the 'horror' fiction of the 20th century — and several generations of horror films, from James Whale's 'Frankenstein' with Boris Karloff in 1931, to the Hammer Horror films of the 1950s. The claim of 'Frankenstein' to be the father of 'horror' is rivalled only by Bram Stoker's 'Dracula' (1897).

ABOVE *'His eyes, if eyes they may be called, were fixed on me . . .' Illustration from the original 'Frankenstein'*

FINAVON: VITRIFIED FORTS

*The vitrified fort at **Finavon** is one of several in eastern Scotland. A source of speculation for two centuries, they are stone forts, which have clearly been burnt at a great heat, so that the stone has become fused into a solid mass. But whether the fires which caused the heat were accidental or deliberate remains a mystery.*

The stone seems to have become vitrified because in Scotland in particular the dry-stone walls of Iron Age forts were often strengthened with internal timbers. There is evidence to suggest that lean-to wooden houses were built against the inner faces of the walls, and when these caught alight the flames spread to the wall-beams. Because of the lack of oxygen in the wall cavity, the internal timbers burnt at a tremendous heat, melting any meltable stones around them and fusing them.

It is not known whether the fires were the result of enemy attack or started by the fort-builders themselves to make strong defences.

*Folk traditions seem to have favoured the theory of enemy action. It was said of the vitrified fort at Knockfarrel, Highland, that giants once lived there. On a day when they were hunting in **Skye**, they spied flames and hurried home just in time to save their wives from burning to death in a hut fired by their enemies.*

ABOVE *Knockfarrel vitrified fort, said to be the home of giants, burnt by enemies*

Finavon

Tayside NO 4957

The scattered hamlet has two features of a kind prominent in Angus. A side-road to the south-east starts deceptively straight and level, but then hairpins steeply up the Hill of Finavon. On the summit, the grass-grown site of a vitrified fort of the eighth century BC gives a glorious view north over the wooded farmlands of Strathmore.

Looking over the main road is the largest dovecote in Scotland. It houses an exhibition, open in summer, of 'The Doocots of Angus'. Details from the Doocot Shop, on the other side of the main road.

Fishtown of Usan

Tayside NO 7254

Today most of the houses are roofless ruins, like the original coastguard watch-tower, having been abandoned in the 1930s. The name of Ulysseshaven — as this fishing village was once known — was lost long before.

Usan was confusing to outsiders because almost all the families in it shared the surname Paton. In the 18th century, tens of thousands of lobsters were sent to London, and there was a fair amount of smuggling too. The narrow creek which formed Usan's natural harbour is still used, though on a smaller scale. To the south,

near a bay where semi-precious stones are often found, the Elephant Rock really does deserve its name. Where the 'elephant' has backed into the grassy clifftop, the breezy, ruined churchyard of St Skeoch can be seen.

Footdee

Grampian NJ 9505

Protected by the sea-wall at the south end of Aberdeen esplanade, and bounded on the other side by the bustling quays of Aberdeen harbour, 'Fittie' is a peninsula village quite separate in atmosphere from the rest of the city. Its sturdy stone cottages ranged round squares were built early in the 19th century for fishermen and harbour pilots, and the pilotage authority is still based at the Round House. Pocra Quay is a land-ward supply base for North Sea oil platforms, and the shipyard nearby launched many of the phenomenally quick Aberdeen tea-clippers, whose times were virtually unrivalled in the races to bring back the first crop of the season from China in Victorian times.

FINAVON *Seen by thousands from the main Perth-Aberdeen road but seldom identified, the Doocot — or dovecote — is the largest in Scotland with 2000 nesting boxes still in place. It was probably built in the 17th century, and now houses an exhibition on similar buildings in Angus*

Fordyce

Grampian   NJ 5563

Country roads with banks of yellow-flowered gorse lead to this quiet and unspoiled village which featured in the European Architectural Year of 1975. Fordyce Castle (now a private house) dates from 1592 and is — unusually — right in the middle of the village. Near it is the restored ruin of a church dedicated to Talarican or Tarquin, a sixth-century Pictish saint. One of the burial aisles has a very fine effigy of a knight in armour. An outside stairway on the belfry tower leads to a first-floor room, used from 1682 as a jail.

Forres

Grampian   NJ 0358

Sueno's Stone at Forres is one of the most magnificent early monuments in Scotland, more than 20 feet high and carved around 1000 years ago with intricate scenes of hunting and battle.

A later monument is the Nelson Tower, an imposing octagonal viewpoint on one of the summits of the thickly wooded Cluny Hills, which rise, ringed by footpaths, a few hundred yards to the south. It commemorates, with slightly dog-Latin inscriptions, Nelson's death at Trafalgar. The view here over the great sweep of Findhorn Bay and the coastal Culbin Forest which borders it to the west is the only high-level views in the district over the Bay.

Forvie

Grampian   NK 0226

In the heart of the Sands of Forvie nature reserve, 2500 acres of dunes and tussocky grassland on the east side of the Ythan estuary, the partially re-built walls of its old parish church are all that remains of the vanished village of Forvie. Relentlessly advancing dunes forced out the last inhabitants in 1416. But there were earlier settlements too: Iron Age hut sites and burial places have also been discovered under the sands.

Near the ruined church, the remote salmon-netting station at Rockend has been worked for more than 200 years. It looks out towards the first of the North Sea oil platforms. As the wild geese fly low over the reserve, they sometimes seem to be outnumbered by the helicopters servicing the production platforms and exploration rigs beyond the horizon.

Fowlis Wester

Tayside   NN 9224

'Fowls Wester' used to be a handloom-weavers' village supporting around 400 people. Much reduced in size, it retains a neat, old-fashioned appearance. The restored pre-Reformation church has a 'leper squint', a window through which lepers forbidden entry to the church itself could still see and hear the services. In the centre of the village, a very fine Pictish cross has weathered carvings of horsemen and animals, as well as characteristic (and unexplained) symbols. Uniquely, this stone is actually in the shape of a cross; other so-called Pictish crosses simply have the cross carved on them. Inside the church is another Pictish cross; this one is much better preserved, having been discovered embedded in the church well in 1931.

Fowlsheugh

Grampian   NO 8879

At the all but abandoned fishing village of Crawton, a footpath leads down over a burn, then along the grass-topped cliffs of the RSPB's Fowlsheugh reserve. For a mile and a half, the red-sandstone cliffs, rising in places to over 200ft, form a striking series of sheer faces, overhangs and old sea caverns of which the roofs have long since collapsed.

In early summer, Fowlsheugh is a nesting site for thousands of guillemots, razorbills, kittiwakes and other seabirds. A total of something like 10,000 pairs of birds nest here, making it one of the biggest seabird colonies in Britain. Care is needed on the clifftops, but the full length of the nesting colonies can also be seen from boats hired at Stonehaven harbour.

Glenbervie

Grampian   NO 7680

In 1420, John Melville, laird of Glenbervie, so exasperated James I that the king commented he would not be too much bothered if Melville were boiled up for soup; and the story goes that five neighbouring landowners did exactly that.

But in the beautiful old Glenbervie churchyard, it is the graves of generations of Robert Burns's relatives which take the attention. His cousins worked the hill farm of Brawliemuir, in the north of the parish, until the early years of the 19th century.

Although there is a modern food-processing factory here, Glenbervie remains a quiet village. It is approached by beech-lined roads above the Bervie Water.

The gardens of Glenbervie House, an extended 15th-century castle, are open to visitors on one Sunday in May and one in July.

Glen Moriston

Highland   NH 2210

A memorial cairn near the head of this rugged and forested glen stands opposite the riverside grave of Roderick Mackenzie. He told the soldiers who killed him here in 1746 that he was Bonnie Prince Charlie, a ruse which made them call off their pursuit of the real prince.

Further down the glen, a little gate in the deer-fence bordering a birchwood leads to the place where a travelling preacher, challenged on some point during an outdoor service in 1827, insisted that the ground itself would bear him out. Behind another cairn, his footsteps remain clearly marked in the grass.

Glen Prosen

Tayside   NO 2967

Dominating the entrance to this narrow Angus glen, the Airlie Monument tower commemorates the eleventh Earl of Airlie, who was killed while leading a cavalry charge during the Boer War. It is built to resemble the Earls' residence, Cortachy Castle, whose beautiful gardens and riverside walks are usually open to visitors on one Sunday early in the summer.

A smaller roadside memorial recalls that Captain Scott and Dr Wilson conferred in Glen Prosen while planning the ill-fated South Pole expedition.

FORDYCE: SCOTTISH CASTLES — The 16th-century castle at Fordyce, noted for its fine corbelling, is one of a great variety of castellated structures to be found in Scotland, from the simple Border pele (see **Woodcock Air**) to castle-mansions such as Thirlestane, Borders, elaborate complexes of wings and keep such as Cawdor, Highland, and the massive, battlemented and forbidding Black Douglas fortress of Hermitage in the Borders.

Rugged walled enclosures like the one at Mingary, Highland, derived from the Norman motte-and-bailey. They were followed, mainly in the 14th century, by the independent keep without significant outer defences. Taller, more tower-like keeps followed in the 15th century — plain towers built between about 1370 and 1450 include Drum, Grampian, Craigmillar, Lothian, and most notably Threave in Stewartry, built by Archibald the Grim, Lord of Galloway. Between 1550 and

1650 came the most characteristic Scottish style — the elaborate tower-house, with wings and turrets projecting from the main block, stepped gables and corbelled stonework, square caphouses and conical roofs. These are Scotland's fairy tale castles: Claypotts, Tayside, once the home of 'Bonnie Dundee', John Graham of Claverhouse; Crathes, Grampian, built by the Burnetts of Leys; and, perhaps the most beautiful of Scottish castles, soaring Craigievar, also in Grampian.

ABOVE   Craigievar — a fairy tale-like castle of the 17th century. 'Do not vaiken sleeping dogs' is inscribed inside

HARRIS: WEAVING
— *The hand-made
tweeds of* **Harris** *and its
neighbouring islands have been
manufactured for centuries, and
sold in London since the 1830s.
Weaving has been the main
industry of the islands since World
War I, and reached the height of
its success in the 1960s, when over
five million metres were produced
each year. The Harris Tweed
Association was formed in 1909 to
discourage imitators, but it was not
until 1964 that the Court of
Session passed judgement that the
'orb' trademark of Harris tweed
could only be used if the cloth was
'made from pure virgin wool,
produced in Scotland, spun, dyed,
finished and handwoven by the
islanders at their own homes in the
. . . Outer Hebrides.'
Vegetable dyeing was still
common in the 1930s, and
although modern colouring
methods are now in general use,
the rest of the manufacture is
traditional. Proposals made in
1975 for modernising production
with power-driven looms were
emphatically rejected by the
weavers.
Though demand for the cloth is
currently in decline, it is to be
hoped there will always be a
market for traditional handwoven
tweed.*

ABOVE *New Harris Tweed
awaits collection outside the home
of the weaver who made it*

Handa

Highland NC 1348

As late as the first half of the 19th century, the 12
families living on this island accepted as their
leader the eldest widow, who was referred to as
the Queen of Handa. Birds used to be the
islanders' main crop, providing meat and eggs,
and feathers which were bartered for wool; now
uninhabited, Handa is an RSPB reserve which
can be reached from April to August, except on
Sundays, by boat from the village of Tarbet. Seabirds crowd its 300-foot northern and western
coasts; the gentler bays on the south and east are
favoured by divers, waders and eider ducks.

The spectacular Great Stack is an isolated
wave-dashed pillar in a U-shaped inlet on the
north coast. Its flat, grassy top was first visited
by 19th-century bird-catchers, who reached it by
a hair-raising hand-over-hand crossing on a fixed
rope — 300 feet above the sea.

Harris

Western Isles NB 10

Harris has its crofters, still weaving Harris
Tweed, and it has a wonderfully varied landscape, of magnificent Atlantic beaches to the west
and rocky fishing villages to the east, with a
wildernesss of peat lochans in between.

It also has some splendid, unfrequented hill
walks, like the one from Hushinish above the
narrow Sound of Scarp. In 1934, when the island
of Scarp was still inhabited, a German inventor
pioneered a rocket mail service for it, which
ended in a shower of charred paper when the
rocket exploded.

A tougher walk along a four-mile track over a
pass leads to remote Rhenigidale.

From the island of Scalpay in East Loch
Tarbert, reached by a Monday-Saturday car
ferry, a boat can be hired to reach Rhenigidale the
easy way, and also for cruises to the Shiant
Islands. Here are weird silhouette of steep hills,
cliff faces and a single house on a natural causeway just above the sea, where Sir Compton
Mackenzie, who owned the islands, occasionally
retired to write.

Hosh

Tayside NN 8523

Just as the hydropathic hotel at Crieff was built
to take advantage of the pure waters of the
Turret Burn, so the malt whisky distillery in the
nearby hamlet called The Hosh needed the same
high-quality water supply. The whisky came first
— Glenturret distillery started in 1775 and is the
oldest in Scotland.

Inverewe

Highland NG 8681

The National Trust for Scotland's splendid
woodland gardens beside Loch Ewe are world-
famous, but they do not occupy anything like the
full extent of the Trust's Inverewe estate. In
summer, guided walks are occasionally arranged
around the hill lochs to the east, and a footpath
inland runs above the shore of Loch Kernsary.

A quite different view of the area is given by
the little cruise boat which operates in summer
from Aultbea, around the wartime anchorage
where Atlantic convoys gathered in Loch Ewe.

HARRIS *Made up of some of the oldest rocks in the world,
Harris was later scoured by glaciers, leaving a landscape of
mountain, rock and water. In fine weather it has an austere
beauty, but lowering clouds make it forbidding indeed*

Inverfarigaig

Highland NH 5223

This forestry village is perched on a promontory
above Loch Ness, at the foot of the precipitous
gorge of the River Farigaig. Fine viewpoints over
the loch and the gorge can be reached by waymarked footpaths from the forest exhibition
centre in the deep-cut Pass of Inverfarigaig.
North of the Farigaig bridge, a remarkable road
hairpins sharply up a hillside of birches, bare rock
and heather. Near a grassy car park above the last
hairpin there are excellent views down to Loch
Ness and, across the wooded gorge, to the
striking cliffs where the Picts built their stronghold of Dun Dearduil almost 3000 years ago.

Inverness

Highland NH 6645

One of the football teams, Inverness
Clachnacuddin, takes its name from Clach-na-
Cuddain — the stone of tubs — where women
used to rest their tubs of washing while having a

KINCRAIG: SWAN CHILDREN OF LIR

— One of the most haunting of Ireland's Celtic legends is the tale of the Swan Children of Lir, who are said to have come to Loch Insh, where the River Spey widens at **Kincraig**.

King Lir (pronounced the same as Lear, and perhaps the same person) was one of the ancient kings of legend. He married a witch, who put a curse on his children (her stepchildren), transforming them into swans for 300 years. The enchantment took place on Lough Derravarragh, in County Westmeath, but the Swan Children lived on the Waters of Moyle, in the sea below Fair

Head. From here, the coast of Scotland can be seen — one reason, perhaps, for the link with Loch Insh.

The story is similar to Hans Christian Andersen's fairytale, 'The Wild Swans', in which a malicious queen casts a spell to turn her 11 stepsons into swans. But the story of Lir's children would originally have been told not to the young, but to the kings and nobles of the ancient Celts, who regarded storytelling as a noble art.

In some other countries, early Christian missionaries were hostile to the old Celtic tales. They survived in Ireland because the early monks retold them, in beautifully illuminated manuscripts. St Patrick is said to have encouraged them to listen to old men's stories and set them down before they were forgotten.

gossip on the way back from the River Ness. The stone is preserved outside the Town House.

The buzz of traffic around the streets of the Highland capital tends to divert attention from its many other interesting features, like the Town House itself in ornamented Victorian Gothic where Lloyd George called the first cabinet meeting ever held outside London, and the flood-lit Bank of Scotland opposite, with its Corinthian columns and statuary. Inverness Castle stands on the same hilltop as the long-since disappeared fortress where Macbeth murdered Duncan in the play. After the Reformation, Cromwell's citadel in the lower part of the town was enthusiastically demolished. Only the clock-tower, now restored, was allowed to remain.

Footbridges link up the wooded Ness Islands, a quiet and old-established public park, which makes a fine place to watch anglers casting for salmon in the fast-flowing water. Another beautiful place is more unexpected: a local boast is that Inverness has the best-placed burial ground in the world. Tomnahurich cemetery occupies a wooded hill above the Caledonian Canal, and a favourite walk is to the viewpoint at its summit.

An exhibition in Falcon Square 'correlates the fossil evidence of the Plesiosauridae with advanced studies of the morphology of the biomass' — in other words, illustrates research into the Loch Ness Monster.

Kincraig

Highland   NH 8305

Kincraig is a village set among pine and birch-wood on a slope down towards Loch Insh. The church, which stands on a little hill on the far side of the loch, retains a 1000-year-old Celtic handbell. Loch Insh features in an ancient Irish story about the Swan Children of Lir, and swans still arrive every November, flying from Iceland. The loch itself is really a widening of the River Spey, and a footpath down-river from Kincraig offers splendid views to the Cairngorms.

Kinloch Hourn

Highland   NG 9506

This tiny settlement is at the end of one of the loneliest roads in Scotland, which passes no other houses in its last 12 miles from Glen Garry, becoming steeper and twistier as it makes the final descent to the head of Loch Hourn. This is classic fjord country, where rugged hillsides rise directly from the shores of the sea loch. Thomas Telford himself surveyed the line of the road in 1803; the idea was to provide a route for cattle-drovers and for the produce of the rich herring-fisheries near the mouth of the loch. There is very little regular traffic here now, apart from the Land Rover post-bus, three days a week.

LOCH NA BEISTE: WATER MONSTERS

— Water-dwelling monsters are an ancient tradition in Britain. **Loch na Beiste** *is one of several Scottish lochs with occupants, while 'Nessie', looking like the sea-serpents of early maps with its humps, has been known about since at least the sixth century, when it met St Columba. It now has its own research displays at* **Inverness** *and* **Drumnadrochit.**

The monster most feared by Shetland fishermen was the **'brigdi'**, *a huge flat sea creature with fins, which reduced the boat of a Fetlar crew to splinters in 1840.*

Then there was Nuckelavee, who would come ashore in lonely places. He had a huge lolling head and lower quarters like a misshapen horse with flippers. He was skinless and his black blood visibly pulsed through his veins. Memories of him remained in Hoy and Sanday up to this century. In England, the Knucker of Knucker

Hole, **Lyminster**, *was a species of dragon, and seems to reflect beliefs held by the Anglo-Saxons before the eighth century. The connection of dragons with wells (see* **Newcastle upon Tyne**) *may have been handed down to us by our Indo-European ancestors.*

Welsh lakes were sometimes haunted by the 'afanc' — whose nature is unclear, though he may have been humanoid.

ABOVE *The orchum (left) was a sea monster that preyed on whales, especially females, illustrated in 1491 with a nymph*

Lewis

Western Isles   NB 33

Most of the crofting and fishing villages in Lewis are round the coast, while the interior has a number of well-guarded sporting estates where the river and loch systems provide some of Europe's best and most expensive salmon fishing.

Lewis also has many museums and ancient monuments, notably the well-preserved broch at Carloway and the mysterious, atmospheric stone circle at Callanish.

On the Atlantic coast, Uig Sands stretch for a mile and a half; this is where a set of Viking chessmen were discovered in 1831 — modern copies of these are made in local craft workshops. The sands at Traigh na Berie are overlooked by a burn where the remains of a Viking meal-mill can still be seen. And one of the finest outlooks in the Hebrides is from the beach at Bosta on the island of Great Bernera, linked to the rest of Lewis by a bridge.

Stornoway is the only town in the Western Isles, and has the only substantial area of woodland, planted in Victorian times. Two waymarked nature trails in the 600-acre grounds of Lews Castle, mostly a public park, show off tree species and birds seen nowhere else in the islands.

Lochan Uaine

Highland   NJ 0010

The waters of this 'little green loch' are a greeny-blue, and the story is that this is where the fairies wash their clothes. Rougher stories are told of the days when it was on the Thieves' Road, along which raiders from Lochaber hurried the cattle they had stolen from the rich lands of Moray.

Lochan Uaine lies in a narrow defile called the Pass of Ryvoan, with a steep, forested hill on one side and equally steep scree-runs on the other. It is an easy two-mile walk from the information centre at the heart of the Glenmore Forest Park.

Loch Killin

Highland   NH 5210

In the hill country east of Loch Ness, this smaller loch is reached by a dead-end road where lines of fencing fend off the wind-blown winter snows. At Garragie Lodge it begins to follow the eastern shore; opposite, there are deeply-eroded gullies, scree runs and rock ledges with scattered birch trees. Until the early 19th century, people from Loch Ness-side took their cattle to high summer pastures beyond Loch Killin. In Gaelic, they called one side of the loch Rocky and the other Necessity.

Loch na Beiste

Highland   NG 8894

Its name means the Loch of the Beast, which, indeed, it seems to be. In the 1840s a story arose that there was a monster in its depths. The landlord spent two years trying to drain the loch. Once that had proved to be an impossible task, he had barrel upon barrel of lime emptied into it. Greatly annoyed by an article in *Punch*, which ridiculed his efforts, he increased his tenants' rents so that, having (as he was convinced) made a fool of him, they would meet at least some of the cost.

Loch Nevis

Highland   NM 79–NM 89

No road approaches this west coast sea loch; but on three days a week, a mailboat from Mallaig takes passengers to Inverie, the Knoydart estate village on the north shore. On certain days it continues — passing the adventure centre run by Atlantic rower and temporary resident of Rockall, Tom McClean — to the tiny settlement of Tarbet, on the south shore; and it sometimes makes afternoon runs in summer to the very head of the loch. The mountain scenery there is superb, with the shapely peak of Sgurr na Ciche, 3410 feet high, dominating the upper reaches.

Nechtansmere

Tayside   NO 5048

In front of the church at Dunnichen, a substantial monument was erected in 1985, on the 1300th anniversary of the Pictish victory at the Battle of Nechtansmere, fought on what is now arable land stretching to the north-east. Northumbrian forces invading Pictland were probably lured into an ambush below the unsuspected fort on Dunnichen Hill. Their king and most of his army were killed, and the Northumbrians never again ventured beyond the Firth of Forth — their boundary for more than three centuries, until the border between Scotland and England was pushed south to the Tweed.

LEWIS *Legend explains Callanish stone circle as giants who were turned to stone when they refused to be baptised by St Kieran. It is also linked with a tale of a fairy cow, but most mysterious of all is the legend of a 'Shining One', who walked along the avenue at sunrise on midsummer morning, heralded by a cuckoo*

THE FAIR MAID   *'listening in . . .
devout attention to the instructions
of a Carthusian'*

Perth

Tayside   NO 1123

One of the most intriguing buildings in this town full of interest happens to be the tourist information centre. It occupies the Round House, a classical rotunda which was built in the 1830s as an indoor waterworks. The tall pillar beside it, with a Grecian urn on top, was the chimney for the steam engine which worked the pumps, and the scheme operated until 1862.

The water was pumped from filter beds on Moncreiffe Island in the Tay — another curious place, because the James VI golf course which occupies most of it can only be reached along a walkway running along on the Perth-Dundee railway bridge.

Elsewhere is an abundance of parks, gardens, sports grounds, museums, historic buildings and churches, stretching along both banks of the Tay. The summit of Kinnoull Hill is laid out with woodland walks and nature trails. At one beautiful viewpoint, the 'ruined' Kinnoull Tower can be seen. It was built in this condition simply as a picturesque addition to the view.

Polloch

Highland   NM 7968

Motorists arriving at this remote village built by the Forestry Commission might be impressed to learn that the timber houses here were brought in, ready-made, by lorry, over the same narrow, steep and twisting hill-road from Strontian. On the way to Polloch, the road climbs past the excavations of abandoned hillside lead-mines. Across the summit, a forest viewpoint opens up a magnificent outlook over conifer plantations, valleys and faraway peaks.

A walk can be taken along a forest road to give a closer view of the mountain-crowded shores of Loch Shiel.

Reelig Glen

Highland   NH 5543

The only winery in the Highlands operates at Moniack Castle; from Mondays to Fridays visitors can see how it produces elderflower, silver birch and meadowsweet wines, and liqueurs distilled from honey and sloes.

An unusually interesting forest walk goes through the Glen: the Frasers of Reelig, who owned the estate till 1949, planted ornamental trees, built an Italian-style footbridge over the gorge of the Moniack Burn, and employed landless Highland crofters to construct stone summer houses along the footpaths.

ROSSAL: HIGHLAND CLEARANCES —

After the failure of the 1745 Rebellion, brought to an ignominious end on 16 April 1746 at Culloden, the Scottish clans were disarmed and the hereditary powers of their chiefs removed. At the same time, increased demand for food brought Lowland farming methods into the Highlands. Instead of turning the stony soil for crops, cattle were to be grazed on it, and if not cattle, sheep. For this purpose, small units were combined into large ones, casting many off their land. Changes like these altered Scottish farming out of all recognition, and with them came a policy of deliberate depopulation — the Highland Clearances.

*Around **Rossal** alone more than 2000 people were evicted to make way for eleven, as more land and fewer hands were needed for the keeping of sheep.*

This was not exclusively the work of the English, but also of the Highland chiefs, no longer content to live as their forefathers, as they looked towards the more civilised life of Edinburgh. By the end of the 18th century, three-quarters of Hebridean landlords were absentee.

The land was farmed by tenants known as 'tackmen', and under them by sub-tenants. As the chiefs made heavier and heavier demands to support their new life-style, so began what Samuel Johnson called the 'fever of emigration'. Hard-pressed tacksmen often left, taking with them sub-tenants and landless cottars too, to become future tenants in the New World. One such was John MacDonald of Glenalladale, who, bitterly resenting the land-grabbing of the Clanranald family, bought land on the Island of St John in the Gulf of St Laurence, and in 1772 led there an expedition of tacksmen and sub-tenants from South Uist, Moidart and Arisaig. 'Emigrations are likely to demolish the Highland Lairds,' he wrote, 'and very deservedly.'

Others were less fortunate. In the Isles in 1739, Macdonald of Sleat and Macleod of Dunvegan sold some of their people as indentured servants for the Carolinas. The bookseller John Knox spoke to families he had seen in the 1780s, travelling to the ports, and was told they had been driven from their lands by their chiefs, their cattle seized and their furniture taken in lieu of rent. 'Our fathers were called out to fight our masters' battles, and this is our reward!'

*Clearances were connected especially with the Sutherland estates (see also **Bettyhill**) and consequently were also known as the 'Sutherland evictions'.*

Rhum

Highland NM 39

Entirely owned by the Nature Conservancy Council, this spectacular island is a red-deer research centre and the place where sea-eagles have recently been re-introduced to Scotland. Boats arrive at Kinloch Bay from Mallaig and Arisaig.

Work parties are organised for various island projects: information on these and on all matters of access and accommodation is available from the Nature Conservancy warden at Kinloch Castle — an almost unbelievably lavish building, created for the millionaire Bullough family, who used to own Rhum and used it as a holiday and deer-stalking preserve.

Nature trails go north through woodland and south up a hairpinned track, towards the Norse-named peaks like Hallival and Askival, which make up the 'Cuillin of Rhum'. An old estate road crosses to Harris, where, at a bay which breaks the cliff-bound west coast, the family built a grand, pillared mausoleum.

Rossal

Highland NC 6841

In the heart of the modern Naver Forest, an interpretation trail explores the site of the lost village of Rossal. It was one of nearly 50 separate settlements in the valley of Strathnaver, where something like 2000 people grazed cattle and raised crops, before they were turned out and replaced by just 11 Border shepherds. This was one of the valleys most severely affected by the Sutherland Clearances; and Patrick Sellar, the Sutherland estate factor who cleared Strathnaver, became a wealthy sheep-farmer by renting the very lands from which he had evicted the entire native population.

St Cyrus

Grampian NO 7464

A car park by the bypassed mouth of the River North Esk is the best access point to the St Cyrus nature reserve, where a long sandy beach with stake-nets set for salmon is backed by rugged cliffs full of seabirds. An old churchyard at the foot of the cliffs has the grave of George Beattie, a poet, lawyer and star-crossed lover, who shot himself in 1823, but left the diary of his un-availing courtship of a higher-born lady to be published posthumously, delighting gossips for miles around.

Scoraig

Highland NH 0096

The original residents abandoned the place in the 1950s; but incomers arrived with ideas of self-sufficient living.

There is crofting, some holiday accommodation, a meditation centre, boat-building and a maker of electricity-generating windmills. But no road — the people of Scoraig firmly turned down an offer by the local authority to have one built. Traffic comes and goes by boat, and a mailboat crosses from Badluarach three days per week.

Another way to approach it is to take an exhilarating walk by a footpath which runs high above Little Loch Broom from Badrallach.

Scotlandwell

Tayside NO 1801

Near the airfield at Portmoak, where gliders take advantage of the air currents sweeping up the edge of the Lomond Hills, this pleasant village has a spring of clear water the Romans knew. The well is still in fine condition, protected by a 19th-century rustic-style canopy.

Every year in July, the parish church has a memorial service for Michael Bruce, the 18th-century poet and author who wrote two fine Scottish hymns: *O God of Bethel* and *Behold! The Mountain of the Lord*.

Bruce actually lived in the next village at Kinnesswood, also the birthplace of the Victorian meteorologist Alexander Buchan. People all over Scotland still swear by Buchan's 'cold spells' of February 7-10, April 11-14, June 29-July 4, August 6-11 and November 6-12, and the 'warm spells' of July 12-15, August 12-15 and December 3-9, which he publicised after years of observation.

Skye

Highland NG

On Skye, stunning mountain and sea-loch views are almost taken for granted. MacLeods come from all over the world to Dunvegan Castle, MacDonalds to the Clan Donald Centre at Armadale; and this is the island of Bonnie Prince Charlie and Flora MacDonald.

But Skye also played a part in the grimmer story of Lady Grange. In 1730, having overheard her husband discussing secret plans with his Jacobite friends, she was kidnapped from her home in Edinburgh and imprisoned, first of all, on a series of utterly remote Hebridean islands, and eventually on Skye. She died out of her mind in 1745 and was secretly buried in the faraway churchyard at Trumpan.

Beside the hydro-electric power station at the Storr Lochs, more than 650 steps lead down to a beach; at Loch Cuithir there are the intriguing remains of the three unprofitable attempts in the last hundred years to work the diatomite deposits which form the bed of the loch. Over on the lovely island of Raasay, reached by car-ferry from Sconser, an ironstone mine was in operation from 1913 to 1919. Afterwards, nobody took responsibility for removing the buildings and other industrial fabrications; but Raasay has more than enough forest and hill walks, waterfalls and historic ruins for the dereliction to be absorbed.

Boat trips from Elgol, towards the jagged sky-line of the Cuillin peaks, make for a landing place near the towering inland cliffs around Loch Coruisk. There is a footpath too, passing the bay at Camasunary where, in misty weather, it is comforting to remember that the ritualistic mountainside throat-cuttings in Mary Stewart's book *Wildfire at Midnight* were entirely imaginary.

Smirisary

Highland NM 6477

In the days when this tiny settlement on the exposed Moidart coast was cultivated by crofting families, the only approaches were by a rough pony-track over a little pass, or by boat to an even rougher, harbourless shore. The last permanent residents left a generation ago, but the pony track still opens up magnificent views. In the 1940s, Wendy Wood wrote *Mac's Croft* in a

SKYE: THE FAIRY FLAG OF DUNVEGAN

— *The Fairy Flag of Dunvegan, preserved at Dunvegan Castle,* **Skye***, ancestral home of the Macleods since the 13th century, is Britain's most interesting fairy relic.*

The usual tale is that the silken banner (now a mere fragment) was given to Iain, the fourth chief, by his fairy wife on parting. An earlier tradition said that the 'Benshi', identified as the Queen of the Fairies, had bestowed it on the family to bring them success on three occasions. The third time it was waved, both the banner and its bearer would mysteriously vanish.

It is said to have been produced at the Battle of Glendale in 1490 and at Trumpan, 1580. Like the magical flag of **Athelstaneford***, it brought victory both times. Photographs of the flag were carried during World War II by Macleods on active service with the RAF.*

The story that the flag came from a fairy wife may stem from the Highland tradition of banshees as guardian spirits attached to families. From a banshee, it is an easy step to a fairy. The Saxon hero Edric Wilde (see **Doethie Valley***) likewise had a fairy wife, and the Physicians of Myddvai (see* **Llyn-y-fan Fach***) a fairy mother.*

Many great men of the Middle Ages — among them Henry II — traced their descent from a fairy. Henry counted Melusine, the fairy of Lusignan Castle, ancestress of the Counts of Poitou, among his forebears.

ABOVE *The flag which was given to the Macleods by a fairy and is still kept at Dunvegan*

---

cottage near the start of the track, and Margaret Leigh, crofting at Smirisay itself, wrote the classic *Spade among the Rushes*.

Strathfarrar

Highland NH 2238

Since 1962, the River Farrar which flows through this majestic glen has been tapped for a hydro-electric power scheme. By agreement with the landowners, the 14-mile private road to the Loch Monar dam is open to visitors' cars from Easter to October, except on Sundays and Tuesdays:

RHUM *The Bullough family mausoleum*

passes can be purchased but there is a limit of 25 cars a day. A 5500-acre National Nature Reserve protects a substantial area of Caledonian pine forest. This is red deer country, and the hills are out of bounds to walkers during the stalking season. Access to this area requires a permit from the Nature Conservancy Council in Inverness. However, advance bookings can be made for guided tours of the deer-farm belonging to the Culligran Estate and holiday cottage accommodation is available. Contact F. Spencer Nairn, Culligran, Struy, nr Beauly.

TAIN: CLANS — The Ross clan has its centre at **Tain**; MacLeods converge from all over the world on Dunvegan Castle, and Macdonalds flock to Armadale (both on **Skye**). All take pride in the tradition of the Scottish clan, whose name comes from the Gaelic for 'family', and which was the basis of Highland society from the sixth century to the eighteenth.

By this time 'clan' had come to mean the followers of a particular chief, and its members were not necessarily related — not all the Donald clan were called Macdonald, and clansmen named Gordon were not always kin.

This allegiance to a chief, which customarily entailed fighting for him in return for one's land, led the Government to suppress the clans following the Battle of Culloden. The Disarming Act of 1746 prohibited the bearing of arms, in 1747 the hereditary powers of clan chiefs were removed and tenure of land by military service was abolished. Another Act forebade the kilt and clan tartan.

Though the Highland Clearances (see **Rossal**) meant the departure of many Highlanders, a nostalgic cult began around Highland costume and customs. Today's kilt is a simplified version of wearing a plaid — a matter of pleating 16 yards of tartan on the ground, lying on it and then fastening it round the body.

The extent to which tartans were individual to clans is doubtful, but today all principal clans have official tartans, with subdivisions for smaller 'septs', or parts of clans.

GATHERING OF CLAN MACLEAN 1912 *The MacLeans land at Duart Point, on the way to Duart Castle*

Strath of Kildonan

Highland NC 8726

Place-names like Baile an Or — the Village of Gold — recall an unexpected turn in the fortunes of this narrow valley of the River Helmsdale. Years after the brutal Sutherland clearances (see Bettyhill), gold was found in the gravel beds of several tributary burns. In 1869, prospectors rushed to take out monthly licences, gold in some quantity was produced, and Baile an Or and other hut and tent settlements made the Strath look like a miniature Klondyke.

Sheep-farming and sporting interests soon gained the upper hand: on the first day of 1870 the issue of licences stopped, and the prospectors dispersed. But modern prospectors can now take out free licences at Kildonan Farm to pan along the Kildonan Burn.

Strathpeffer

Highland NH 4858

As Britain's most northerly spa, in a beautiful situation, Strathpeffer in its Victorian and Edwardian heyday attracted fashionable visitors from all over the country. Elegant hotels, boarding houses and villas were built, but it has no street names.

Visitors, whether or not they were here for the baths and the sulphur and chalybeate water cures, were expected to keep to a strict timetable. A march by the official piper began the day. Golf, walking and angling were encouraged, and still are, in the present-day resort. A small pump room and the pavilion remain.

Tain

Highland NH 7882

In 1966 the people of Tain chose a colourful way to mark the town's 900th anniversary as a royal burgh, by creating the 900 Roses Garden. The small but well-stocked local museum, open in summer, is also a historical centre for Clan Ross. Incidents recalled include the Earl of Ross's shameful handing over, in 1306, of Robert the Bruce's womenfolk to the anything but tender mercies of Edward I of England. They had taken refuge in what should have been a sanctuary, the chapel of Tain-born St Duthus, which survives as a ruin.

The small Highland Fine Cheeses factory at Tain works to traditional recipes for its Crowdie, Galic, Hramsa and the oatmeal-rolled Caboc which was first made for the family of the Lords of the Isles. The factory does not advertise its products, relying solely on word-of-mouth recommendations. Visits and free tasting sessions can be booked.

Tarbat Ness

Highland NH 9487

The peninsula between the Dornoch and Moray Firths is a fine place for bird-watching: in the migration seasons, rare species can be seen pausing at this convenient resting place. Almost at the tip, the tall white and red lighthouse tower, approached by stone-walled roads and then a walk between gorse thickets, is a splendid view-point. The alignment of Tarbat Ness provides unusual views west to the mountains of Sutherland. At the last left turn before the car

park, an unsignposted road ahead drops down immediately to the tiny fishing station at Wilkhaven, where the low sea-cliffs briefly recede.

Totaig

Highland NG 8725

At the end of the beautiful but finally very narrow road along the south-west shore of Loch Duich, Totaig is simply an old ferry-house and jetty. Until World War I, Glasgow steamers used to anchor offshore, unloading passengers and freight into a rowing-boat. The small ferry across the mouth of Loch Duich to Dornie — which on occasion transported precariously balanced cars — survived for some years longer. A forest track leads uphill to the remains of a dry-stone broch, from which there is an unfamiliar, high-level view of Eilean Donan Castle across the loch. Also in view is the little Eilean Tioram, where gravel and shingle used to be dug for ballast which was used to weight sailing ships.

Tugnet

Grampian NJ 3465

Walking into the Ice House at Tugnet makes it instantly clear how both the place and the building came by their names. The Ice House, with its thick walls and vaulted, turf-topped roof, was built in 1830 as an early refrigerator to store salmon netted at the mouth of the Spey, and continued in use till 1968. Now, linked exhibition rooms illustrate the history and techniques of salmon-netting.

The gravel beds at the shifting mouth of the Spey and the long shingle beach to the east are ideal habitats for shelduck, oystercatchers and curlews. Tugnet is also the starting point of the Speyside Way long-distance footpath.

Tullibardine Chapel

Tayside NN 9013

Close to the international hotel and golf courses at Gleneagles, this restored but unfurnished ancient monument is an unusual survival for Scotland. It was founded in the 1440s by Sir David Murray of Tullibardine. He intended it as a collegiate church whose college of priests would have the duty of saying regular masses for his soul. The church never actually achieved that status, but it was never a parish church either. It remained the private chapel and often the burial place of the Murrays and their descendants, who became Marquesses of Tullibardine, Dukes of Atholl, Viscounts of Strathallan and Earls of Perth.

Turriff

Grampian NJ 7249

This is the red-sandstone market town for West Buchan, with a major two-day agricultural show every August; so it is appropriate that the hero and heroine of a favourite local story are a farmer and a white cow. In 1913 Robert Paterson of Lendrum, about four miles south-east of Turriff, refused point-blank to pay for his farm-workers' newly-introduced health insurance stamps. One of his cows was impounded and offered for sale in Turriff. The local farmers declined to bid. The

WHALIGOE *A sharp-bend in the staircase up the cliff can be seen on the left. Women climbed it with baskets of herring for market*

authorities then put it up for auction elsewhere; unexpectedly, Turriff farmers turned up and this time they did buy the cow, returning it to Robert Paterson. Undisturbed thereafter, the 'Turra Coo' lived out her life at Lendrum, and has her own memorial there.

Well of the Lecht

Grampian NJ 2315

In 1754 the soldiers who built the high-level Lecht Road carved a stone in curious shorthand to mark the occasion. It still stands at a well across the main road from a picnic area beside the Conglass Water.

A half-mile footpath up the heathery glen leads to the well-restored crushing mill of a remote manganese mine operated in the 1840s. Westwards, the main road passes a ruined cottage which was briefly, in 1920, the hiding-place of Percy Toplis, who had fled north after being suspected of a murder in Hampshire. He shot two men who came to question him, and escaped — by bicycle.

Whaligoe

Highland ND 3240

In the middle of the 19th century, more than 150 fishermen lived in this high-set village, but landed their catches at the foot of the cliffs, down a hairpinned flight of more than 300 stone steps. Women carried herring-baskets up the whole weary staircase before trudging another six miles to the fish-market in Wick. Later, the Wick and Lybster Light Railway made part of the journey easier.

Whaligoe harbour has been abandoned, but the steps have been repaired and the cliffs around it echo to the screaming cries of nesting seabirds.

Zoar

Tayside NO 4551

Local enthusiasm for Old Testament references gave what is now a northern suburb of the town of Forfar the only village name in Scotland to begin with the letter Z. It is evident in the names of a filling station and an inn, and in at least one street name-plate. Biblical Zoar was the City of the Plain to which Lot escaped just before burning sulphur rained down on Sodom and Gomorrah.

TAIN: SCOTTISH CHEESES — *The traditional Scottish cheeses to be found at* **Tain** *remain little known, despite the fact that the Scots have been making cheese since at least the 13th century. At one time, cheese could even be used to pay university fees.*

The oldest is probably the skimmed-milk Crowdie (porridge) cheese, but the oldest record of a still-existing cheese is a recipe for the oatmeal-coated Caboc, or 'Chieftain's Cheese', made in the 15th century by Mariota, daughter of a Macdonald of the Isles. The recipe was passed down to Mariota's descendant Susannah Stone, who began making it again in the 1960s, on the farm of Blarliath, on Dornoch Firth, near Tain. The Stones went on to mix Crowdie (a sort of cottage cheese) with chopped wild garlic and cream to produce Hramsa — so-called from the Gaelic name of the herb.

The first full-cream hard cheese came from the parish of Dunlop, in Ayrshire. It is said to have been made by Barbara Gilmour, who learned cheesemaking in Ireland and settled in Dunlop with her husband in 1688. The spread of Ayrshire cattle led to cheese 'after the Dunlop manner' being made on almost all the farms of south and south-west Scotland, including that of Robert Burns (see **Lamington***). But today genuine Dunlop is hard to find — it is only the name that survives on the little plastic-wrapped creamery-made cheeses from Arran and Orkney. Until recently, true Dunlop was virtually made only for shows, but Scottish Milk Marketing Boards show signs of attempting a revival.*

The only Scottish cheese widely known before Dunlop was Orkney, a hard, flat, round cheese much sought after for funeral feasts. In the Grampians, a few small farms still make 'cabics' (six-to seven-pound cheeses) according to traditional methods. Hard wholemilk cheese (formerly they would have been made of skimmed milk), they are sold as Aberdeenshire or Banffshire Farmhouse, for example in Mossat.

LONDON STREET INDEX

*Index to Central London Map on page 86. Names in **bold** are mentioned in the text and shown on the map in red.*

A
Abbey Street K3
Abercorn Place A7
Abingdon Street F3
Acton Street F7
Adam's Row C5-D5
Albany Street D7
Albemarle Street D5-D4
Albert Bridge B1
Albert Embankment F2
Albion Street B5
Alderney Street D2-E2
Aldersgate Street H6
Aldford Street C4
Aldgate High Street K5
Aldwych F5-G5
Alie Street K5
Allsop Place C6
Appold Street J6-J7
Argyll Street D5
Argyll Street F7
Artillery Row E3
Ashmill Street B6
Astell Street B2
Atterbury Street F2
Ave Maria Lane H5
Aylesford Street E1-E2

B
Baker Street C6-C5
Balcombe Street B6-C6
Baldwin's Gardens G6
Bankside H5
Banner Street H7-J7
Basil Street C3
Basinghall Street J6
Bath Street H7-J7
Bath Terrace H3
Baylis Road G3-G4
Bayswater Road A4-A5-B5-C5
Beak Street E5
Bear Lane H4
Beauchamp Place B3-C3
Beaufort Street A1-B1
Bedford Avenue E6
Bedford Place F6
Bedford Square E6
Bedford Way E7
Beech Street H6
Belgrave Place C3-D3
Belgrave Road D2-E2
Belgrave Square C3-D3
Bell Lane K6
Bell Street B6
Bell Yard G5-G6
Belvedere Street F4-G4
Berkeley Square D5-D4
Berkeley Street D5-D4
Bermondsey Street J4-K4-J3-K3
Berners Street E6
Berwick Street E5
Bethnal Green K7
Birdcage Walk E3
Bishop's Bridge Road A5-A6
Bishopsgate J6-K6
Black Prince Road F2-G2
Blackfriars Bridge H5
Blackfriars Road H2-H4
Blandford Street C6
Blomfield Road A6
Bloomsbury Street E6-F6
Bloomsbury Way F6
Bolsover Street D6-D7
Bolton Crescent G1
Bolton Street D4
Boltons, The A1-A2
Bond Way F1
Borough High Street H3-H4-J4
Borough Road H3
Boswell Street F6
Bourdan Street D5
Bourne Street C2
Bouverie Street G5
Bow Street F5
Bowling Green Lane G7
Bray Place C2
Bressenden Place D3
Brewer Street E5
Brick Lane K6-K7
Brick Street D4
Bridge Street F3
Britten Street B2
Brixton Road G1
Broadley Street B6
Broadwick Street E5
Brompton Road B2-B3-C3
Brook Drive G3-H3
Brook Street D5
Brown Street B5-B6
Brunswick Square F7
Brushfield Street K6
Bruton Place D5
Bruton Street D5
Bryanston Square C5-C6
Buckingham Gate D3-E3
Buckingham Palace Road D2-D3
Buckingham Street F4
Bunhill Row J7
Byward Street J5-K5

C
Cadogan Gardens C2
Cadogan Lane C2-C3
Cadogan Place C2-C3
Cadogan Square C2-C3
Cadogan Street C2
Cale Street B2
Calthorpe Street F7-G7
Calvert Avenue K7
Camberwell New Road G1-H1
Cambridge Street D2-E2
Cannon Street H5-J5
Carburton Street D6
Cardigan Street G2
Cardington Street D7-E7
Carey Street G5-G6
Carlisle Lane G3
Carlisle Place D3-E3-E2
Carlton House Terrace E4
Carlyle Square B1
Carnaby Street D5-E5
Carroun Road G1
Carter Lane H5
Cartwright Street J5
Castle Lane E3
Cathcart Road A1
Cavendish Square D5-D6
Caxton Street E3
Central Street H7
Chamber Street J5
Chancery Lane G5-G6
Chandos Place F5
Chandos Street D6
Chapel Street B6
Chapel Street C3-D3
Charing Cross Road E6-E5-F5
Charles II Street E4
Charles Street D4-D5
Charlotte Street D6-E6
Charlwood Street E2
Chart Street J7
Charterhouse Square H6
Charterhouse Street G6-H6
Cheapside H5
Chelsea Bridge D1
Chelsea Bridge Road C2-C1-D1
Chelsea Embankment B1-C1-D1
Chelsea Manor Street B1
Chelsea Square B1-B2
Chesham Place C3
Chester Road C7-D7
Chester Row C2
Chester Square D2-D3
Chester Street D3
Cheyne Row B1
Cheyne Walk B1
Chilworth Street A5
Chiswell Street H6-J6
Christchurch Street C1
Church Street B6
Churchill Gardens Road D1-E1
Circus Road A7
City Road H7-J7
Clabon Mews C2-C3
Clapham Road G1
Clarendon Street D2
Clarges Street D4
Claverton Street E1-E2
Claylands Road G1
Clayton Street G1
Clerkenwell Close G7
Clerkenwell Green G7
Clerkenwell Road G6-G7-H7
Cleveland Square A5
Cleveland Street D7-D6-E6
Cleveland Terrace A5
Clifford Street D5
Clifton Gardens A6-A7
Clifton Street J6-J7
Clink Street H4-J4
Clipstone Street D6
Club Row K7
Cobourg Street E7
Cock Lane H6
Coin Street G4
Cole Street J3
Coleman Street J6
Columbia Road K7
Commercial Street K6-K7
Compton Street H7
Conduit Street D5
Connaught Street B5
Constitution Hill D4
Conway Street D6
Copperfield Street H4
Cork Street D5
Cornhill J5
Cornwall Gardens A3
Cornwall Road G4
Cosser Street G3
Courtenay Street G2
Courtfield Road A2
Covent Garden F5
Coventry Street E5
Cowcross Street G6-H6
Cranley Gardens A1-A2
Craven Hill A5
Craven Road A5
Craven Terrace A5
Crawford Street B6-C6
Cresswell Place A1-A2
Cringle Street E1
Cromer Street F7
Cromwell Road A2-B2
Cross Road F7-G7
Cubitt Street F7-G7
Culross Street C4
Cumberland Street D2-D1
Curtain Road J7-K7
Curzon Street D4
Cut, The G4-H4

D
Davies Street D5
De Laune Street G1-G2-H2
De Vere Gardens A3
Dean Street E5
Decima Street J3
Denbigh Street E2
Deverell Street J3
Devonshire Street C6-D6
Dingley Road H7
Dolben Street H4
Dorset Road F1
Dorset Street C6
Doughty Street F7
Douglas Street E2
Dovehouse Street B1-B2
Dover Street D4-D5
Downing Street F4
Draycott Avenue B2-C2
Draycott Place C2
Drayton Gardens A1-A2
Druid Street K3-K4
Drummond Street D7-E7
Drury Lane F5-F6
Dufferin Street H7-J7
Duke Street C5-D5
Duke's Place K5-K6
Durham Street F1-G1

E
East Smithfield K5
Eastbourne Terrace A5
Eastcastle Street D6-E6
Eastcheap J5
Eaton Place C2-C3-D3
Eaton Square C2-C3-D3
Eaton Terrace C2-D2
Ebury Bridge Road D1-D2
Ebury Street C2-D2-D3
Eccleston Place D2-D3
Eccleston Square D2
Eccleston Street D3-D2
Edgeware Road A6-B6-B5-C5
Edith Grove A1
Egerton Terrace B3
Elder Street K6-K7
Eldon Road A3
Eldon Street J6
Elizabeth Street C2-D2
Elm Park Gardens A1-B1
Elm Park Road A1-B1
Elm Tree Road A7
Elvaston Place A3
Ely Court G6
Ely Place G6
Elystan Place B2-C2
Elystan Street B2
Emerson Street H4-H5
Endell Street F5-F6
Enid Street K3
Ennismore Gardens B3
Epworth Street J7
Erasmus Street E2-F2
Euston Road D7-E7-F7
Evelyn Gardens A1
Eversholt Street E7
Ewer Street H4
Exhibition Road B2-B3
Exmouth Market G7

F
Falmouth Road H3-H4
Fann Street H6-H7
Farm Street D4-D5
Farringdon Lane G7
Farringdon Road G7-G6
Farringdon Street G6-H6-H5
Fashion Street K6
Fawcett Street A1
Fenchurch Street J5-K5
Fentiman Road F1-G1
Fernshaw Road A1
Finborough Road A1
Finsbury Circus J6
Finsbury Square J6
First Street B2
Fisherton Street A6-A7-B7-B6
Fitzalan Street G2-G3
Fitzroy Street D7-D6
Fleet Street G5
Flood Street B1-C1
Floral Street F5
Foley Street D6
Folgate Street K6
Fore Street H6-J6
Foulis Terrace B2
Fournier Street K6
Frampton Street A6-B6-B7
Francis Street E2-E3
Frazier Street G3
Frederick Street F7
Frith Street E5
Fulham Road A1-B1-A2-B2

G
Gainsford Street K4
Garrett Street H7
Gee Street H7
George Street B5-C5-C6
Gerrard Street E5
Gertrude Street A1
Gilbert Road G2
Gilbert Street D5
Gillingham Street D2
Gilstan Road A1
Giltspur Street H6
Glasshouse Walk F2
Glebe Place B1
Gloucester Place B7-C7-C6-C5
Gloucester Road A2-A3
Gloucester Square B5
Gloucester Street D2-E2
Gloucester Terrace A5
Golden Lane H6-H7
Goodge Street E6
Gordon Square E7
Gordon Street E7
Gosfield Street D6
Gossett Street K7
Goswell Road H6-H7
Gough Street G7
Goulston Street K6
Gower Street E6-E7
Gracechurch Street J5
Grafton Way D7-E7
Grange Road J3-K3
Grange Walk K3
Grays Inn Road F7-G7-G6
Great Castle Street D5-D6
Great Cumberland Place C5
Great Dover Street J3-J4
Great Eastern Street J7-K7
Great George Street E3-F3
Great Guildford Street H4
Great Marlborough Street D5-E5
Great Ormond Street F6-F7
Great Peter Street E3-F3
Great Portland Street D7-D6-D5
Great Queen Street F5-F6
Great Russell Street E6-F6
Great Smith Street E3
Great Suffolk Street H4
Great Titchfield Street D6
Great Tower Street J5-K5
Greek Street E5
Green Street C5
Greencoat Place E2-E3
Grenville Place A2-A3
Gresham Street H6-J6
Greville Street G6
Grey Eagle Street K6-K7
Greycoat Street E3
Grosvenor Gardens D3
Grosvenor Place D3
Grosvenor Road D1-E1-E2
Grosvenor Square C5-D5
Grosvenor Street D5
Grove End Road A7
Guilford Street F7
Gunter Grove A1
Guy Street J4

H
Halkin Street C3-D3
Hall Place A6
Hall Road A7
Hallam Street D6
Halsey Street C2
Hamilton Place D4
Hamilton Terrace A7
Hampstead Road D7
Hanover Square D5
Hans Crescent C3
Hans Place C3
Hans Road B3-C3
Harcourt Terrace A1
Harewood Avenue B6
Harley Street D6
Harleyford Road F1-G1
Harleyford Street G1
Harper Road H3-J3
Harriet Walk C3
Harrington Gardens A2
Hart Street K5
Hasker Street B2
Hastings Street E7-F7
Hatfields G4
Hatton Garden G6
Hay's Mews D4
Haymarket E4-E5
Henrietta Place D5
Hercules Road G3
Hertford Street D4
High Holborn F6-G6
Hill Road A7
Hill Street D4-D5
Holbein Place C2
Holborn G6
Holborn Circus G6
Holborn Viaduct G6-H6
Holland Street H4-H5
Hollywood Road A1
Hopton Street H4-H5
Horse Guards Avenue F4
Horse Guards Road E3-E4
Horseferry Road E3-F3
Houndsditch K5-K6
Howick Place E3
Howland Street D6-E6
Hoxton Square J7
Hugh Street D2
Huntley Street E6-E7
Hyde Park Crescent B5
Hyde Park Gate A3
Hyde Park Square B5
Hyde Park Street B5

I
Inner Circle C7
Ivor Place B6-B7-C7
Ixfield Road A1
Ixworth Place B2

J
James Street C5-D5-E5
Jermyn Street D4-E4-E5
Jockey's Fields G6
John Adam Street F5
John Islip Street E2-F2
John Street E5
Jonathan Street F2-G2
Jubilee Place B2
Judd Street F7

K
Kempsford Road G2
Kennington Lane F1-G1-G2-H2
Kennington Oval G1
Kennington Park Place G1-H1
Kennington Park Road G1-G2-H2
Kennington Road G1-G2-G3
Kensington Road A3-B3
King Charles Street F4
King James Street H3
King Street E4
King William Street J5
King's Road A1-B1-B2-C2-C3-D3
Kingly Street D5-E5
Kingsway F5-F6
Kipling Street J4
Knightsbridge B3-B4-B5

L
Lambeth Bridge F3
Lambeth High Street F2-F3
Lambeth Palace Road F3-G3
Lambeth Road F3-G3-H3
Lambeth Walk G2-G3
Lambs Conduit Street F7-F6
Lamont Road A1
Lanark Road A7
Lancaster Gate A5
Langford Street D7
Langham Place D6
Langley Lane F1
Langton Street A1
Lant Street H4
Launceston Place A3
Lavington Street H4
Law Street J3
Lawn Lane F1
Lawrence Street B1
Leadenhall Street J5-K5
Leather Lane G6-G7
Leather Market Street J4
Leicester Square E5
Leigh Street E7-F7
Leinster Gardens A5
Leman Street K5
Lennox Gardens C3-C2
Leonard Street J7
Lever Street H7
Limerston Street A1
Lincoln's Inn Fields F6-G6
Lisle Street E5
Lisson Grove A7-B7-B6
Little Boltons, The A1-A2
Liverpool Street J6
Lloyd Baker Street G7
Lodge Road B7
Lollard Street G2-G3
Lombard Street J5
London Bridge J4-J5
London Road H3
London Wall H6-J6
Long Acre F5
Long Lane H6
Long Lane J3-J4
Lovat Lane J5
Lower Belgrave Street D3
Lower Marsh G3-G4
Lower Sloane Street C2
Lower Thames Street J5-K5
Lowndes Square C3
Lowndes Street C3
Ludgate Hill G5-H5
Luke Street J7
Lupus Street D1-E1-E2
Lyall Street C3

M
Maddox Street D5
Maida Avenue A6
Maida Vale A7
Maiden Lane F5
Malet Street E6-E7
Mall, The E4-F4
Maltby Street K3-K4
Manciple Street J3
Manette Street E5
Manresa Road B1
Mansell Street K5
Marchmont Street F7
Margaret Street D6-E6
Margery Street G7
Mark Lane K5
Markham Street B2
Marshall Street E5
Marshalsea Street H4
Marsham Street E3-F3-F2
Martin Lane J5
Marylebone High Street C6
Marylebone Lane C6-C5-D5
Marylebone Road B6-C6-D6-D7
Meadow Road F1-G1
Mecklenburgh Square F7
Medway Street E3
Melton Street E7
Methley Street G2
Middlesex Street K6
Miles Street F1
Milk Street H5-H6
Millbank F2-F3
Millman Street F7
Milmans Street A1-B1
Minories K5
Mint Street H4
Monck Street E3
Monmouth Street F5-F6
Montague Place E6
Montague Square C5-C6
Montague Street F6
Montford Place G1-G2
Montpelier Street B3
Moore Street C2
Moorfields J6
Moorgate J6
Moreton Place E2
Morley Street G3
Morpeth Terrace E2-E3
Mortimer Street D6-E6
Motcamb Street C3
Mount Row D5
Mount Street C5-D5
Museum Street F6
Myddelton Street G7

N
Neal Street F5
New Bond Street D5
New Bridge Street G5-H5
New Cavendish Street C6-D6
New Change H5
New Compton Street E5-F5
New North Street F6
New Oxford Street E6-F6
Newburn Street G2
Newcomen Street J4
Newgate Street H6
Newington Causeway H3
Newman Street E6
Newton Street F6
Nine Elms Lane E1-F1
Norfolk Crescent B5
Norfolk Square A5-B5
North Carriage Drive B5-C5
North Gower Street D7-E7
North Row C5
Northington Street F6-F7-G7
Northumberland Avenue F4

O
Oakley Street B1
Old Bailey H5-H6
Old Bond Street D4-D5
Old Broad Street J6
Old Brompton Road A2-B2
Old Church Street B1
Old Compton Street E5
Old Marylebone Road B6
Old Park Lane D4
Old Pye Street E3
Old Street H7-J7-K7
Onslow Gardens A2
Onslow Square B2
Ontario Street H3
Orchard Street C5
Orchardson Street A6-B6-B7
Outer Circle B7-C7-C6-C7-D7
Oval Way G1
Oxford Street C5-D5-E5-E6

P
Paddington Street C6
Page Street E2-F2
Palace Gate A3
Palace Street D3-E3
Pall Mall E4
Parade, The C1-D1
Pardoner Street J3
Paris Garden G4
Park Crescent D6-D7
Park Lane C5-C4-D4
Park Road B7-C7
Park Street C5-C4
Park Street H4
Park Walk A1
Parker Street F5-F6
Parry Street F1
Pascal Street F1
Paul Street J7
Pavillion Road C2-C3
Pavillion Street C2-C3
Pearman Street G3
Pelham Crescent B2
Pelham Street B2
Penfold Street B6
Pepys Street K5
Percival Street H7
Petty France E3
Piccadilly D4-E4-E5
Pilgrimage Street J3-J4
Pimlico Road C2-D2
Pitfield Street J7
Pocock Street H4
Poland Street E5
Pond Place B2
Ponsonby Place E2-F2
Pont Street C3
Ponton Road E1
Porchester Terrace A5
Portland Place D6
Portman Square C5
Portman Street C5
Portugal Street F5-G5-G6
Poultry J5
Praed Street A5-B5-B6
Princelet Street K6
Princes Gardens B3

Q
Quaker Street K6-K7
Queen Elizabeth Street K4
Queen Street H5-J5
Queen Victoria Street H5-J5
Queens Gardens A5
Queens Gate A2-A3
Queens Gate Gardens A2-A3
Queens Gate Terrace A3
Queens Square F6-F7
Queensborough Terrace A5-A4
Queenstown Road D1

R
Radnor Street H7-J7
Radnor Walk B1-C1
Randolph Avenue A6-A7
Rathbone Place E6
Rawlings Street B2-C2
Red Lion Square F6
Red Lion Street F6
Redburn Street B1-C1
Redchurch Street K7
Redcliffe Gardens A1
Redcross Way H4-J4
Reeves Mews C5
Regency Street E2-E3
Regent Street D6-D5-E5-E4
Renfrew Road G2-H2
Riding House Street D6-E6
Riley Road K3
Riley Street A1-B1
Rivington Street J7-K7
Robert Street D7
Rochester Row E2-E3
Rockingham Street H3
Roland Gardens A2
Romilly Street E5
Roseberry Avenue G6-G7
Rossmore Road B6-B7
Rothsay Street J3
Rotten Row B4-C4
Rouel Road K3
Roupell Street G4-H4
Royal Avenue C2
Royal Hospital Road C1-C2
Royal Mint Street K5
Royal Street G3
Rupert Street E5
Russell Square E7-F7-E6-F6
Rutland Gate B3

S
Saffron Hill G6-G7
St Andrews Hill H5
St George Street D5
St George's Circus G3-H3
St George's Drive D2-E2
St George's Road G3-H3
St George's Square E1-E2
St Giles High Street E6-F6
St James's Square E4
St James's Street D4-E4
St John Street H6-H7-G7
St Johns Lane H6-H7
St Johns Wood Road A7-B7
St Leonards Terrace C2
St Martin's Lane F4-F5
St Mary Axe J5-J6-K6
St Michaels Street B5-B6
St Thomas Street J4
Salisbury Street B6
Sancroft Street G2
Savile Row D5
Savoy Place F5
Scala Street E6
Scalter Street K7
Scrutton Street J7-K7
Sekforde Street G7
Seymour Place B6-B5-C5
Seymour Street B5-C5
Seymour Walk A1
Shad Thames K4
Shaftesbury Avenue E5-F5
Shelton Street F5
Shepherd Market D4
Shepherd Street D4
Shoe Lane G5-G6
Shoreditch High Street K7
Sidmouth Street F7
Sidney Street B1-B2
Silk Street H6-J6
Skinner Street G7
Sloane Avenue B2-C2
Sloane Gardens C2
Smith Square F3
Smith Street C1-C2
Snows Fields J4
Soho Square E5-E6
South Audley Street C5-C4-D4
South Carriage Drive B3-C3-C4
South Eaton Place C2-D2
South Lambeth Road F1
South Parade B2
South Street C4-D4
South Terrace B2
Southampton Row F6
Southwark Bridge H5
Southwark Bridge Road H3-H4
Southwark Street H4
Spa Road K3
Spencer Street G7-H7
Spital Square K6
Stag Place D3-E3
Stagnes G1-H1
Stamford Street G4-H4
Stanhope Gardens A2
Stanhope Street D7
Stanhope Terrace B5
Stannary Street G1-G2
Star Street B5-B6
Store Street E6
Strand F4-F5-G5
Strand Lane G5
Stratton Street D4
Sumner Place B2
Sumner Street H4
Sun Street J6
Sussex Gardens A5-B5-B6
Sussex Place B5
Sussex Street D2
Sutherland Street D2-D1
Swanfield Street K7

T
Tabard Street J3
Tabernacle Street J7
Tachbrook Street E2
Tanner Street K4-K3
Tavistock Place E7-F7
Tavistock Square E7
Tavistock Street F5
Tedworth Square C1
Temple Avenue G5
Theed Street G4
Theobald's Road F6-G6
Threadneedle Street J5-J6
Throgmorton Street J6
Thurloe Place B2-C2
Thurloe Square B2
Tite Street C1
Tooley Street J4-K4
Torrington Place E6-E7
Tottenham Court Road E7-E6
Tower Bridge K4
Tower Bridge Road J3-K3-K4
Tower Hill K5
Trafalgar Square E4-E5-F4-F5
Tregunter Road A1
Trevor Place B3
Trigon Road G1
Trinity Square K5
Trinity Street H3-J3
Tudor Street G5-H5
Tufton Street F3
Turk's Row C2
Turnmill Street G6-G7
Tyers Street F2-G2

U
Ufford Street G4
Union Street H4-J4
Upper Berkeley Street C5
Upper Brook Street C5
Upper Grosvenor Street C5
Upper Ground G4-G5
Upper Thames Street H5-J5
Upper Woburn Place E7

V
Vale, The B1
Vauxhall Bridge F1-F2
Vauxhall Bridge Rd D3-D2-E2
Vauxhall Street G1-G2
Vauxhall Walk F2
Vere Street D5
Victoria Embankment F4-F5-G5
Victoria Road A3
Victoria Street D3-E3-F3
Vincent Square E2-E3
Vincent Street E2-F2
Vine Lane K4
Virginia Road K7

W
Walnut Tree Walk G2-G3
Walton Street B2-B3-C3
Wandsworth Road F1
Wardour Street E5
Warren Street D7-E7
Warrington Crescent A6-A7
Warwick Avenue A6
Warwick Square D2-E2
Warwick Street E5
Warwick Way D2-E2
Waterloo Bridge F5-G5-G4
Waterloo Road G3-G4
Watling Street H5-J5
Webber Street G4-H4
Welbeck Street C6-D6-D5
Wellington Road B7
Wells Street D6-E6
Wentworth Street K6
West Carriage Drive B4-B5
West Square G3-H3
West Way A6-B6
Westbourne Terrace A5-A6
Westminster Bridge F3
Westminster Bridge Road G3
Westmoreland Terrace D1-D2
Weston Street J3-J4
Wetherby Gardens A2
Weymouth Street C6-D6
Wharton Street G7
Whitcomb Street E4-E5
Whitechapel Road K6
Whitecross Street H6-H7
Whitefriars Street G5
Whitehall F4
Whitehall Place F4
Whitehead's Grove B2-B3
Whitfield Street D7-E7-E6
Wigmore Street C5-D5
Wild Street F5
Willow Place E2-E3
Wilson Street J6-J7
Wilton Crescent C3
Wilton Place C3
Wilton Road D3-D2-E2
Wilton Row C3
Wimpole Street C6-D6-D5
Winchester Street D2-E2
Wincott Street G2
Woburn Place E7-F7
Wood Street H6
Worship Street J7-K7

Y
Yeoman's Row B3
York Gate C6-C7
York Road G4
York Street B6-C6
York Terrace C6-C7-D7

PLACE INDEX

Page numbers in roman *type show main headings. Page numbers in italics refer to place names within the text. A Subject Index starts on page 317*

A

Abbey Cwmhir 126
Abbey Dore *174*
Abbey St Bathans 262
Aberdulais Falls 126
Aberfoyle 262
Abergorlech 126
Aberystwyth 126
Achiltibuie 298
Adel *230*
Aden Country Park 298
Adlestrop *12*
Ailsa Craig 262
Ainsdale Sand Dunes 212
Aira Force *212*
Airthrey Hermitage 263
Aldworth 56
Alfold *56*
Alkborough *160*
Allan Water 263
Alloway *264*
Almondell 263
Almondsbury *12*
Alnwick *212*
Althorne *56*
Alton Barnes *12*
Alva Glen 263
Amersham *56*
Anderton *212*
Anstey *56*
Appletreewick 213
Arbroath 298
Arbuthnott 298
Ardblair 298
Arran 263
Artists' Valley 127
Ascog 266
Ashdown House *56, 57*
Ashmore *12*
Ashton *160*
Asthall *120*
Aston on Clun *160*
Aston Munslow *160*
Athelney *13*
Athelstaneford 264
Atherstone *161*
Auchroisk 299
Audlem 213
Aultdearg Pillars 299
Avington *56*
Aylesbury *57*
Ayr 264

B

Babworth *250*
Bacton *174*
Badbea 299
Balcary Heughs 264
Bannet Stane 264
Banstead *58*
Barkway *58*
Barleythorpe *161*
Barmouth 127
Barns Ness 264
Barnweill *264*
Barwick Park *13*
Basildon *58*
Basingstoke Canal *58*
Bassenthwaite Lake 213
Bath *13*
Beaconsfield *59*
Beauchamp Roding *59*
Beaupre Castle 127
Beck Hole 213
Beckley *59*
Beeby *161*
Beer *14*
Beeswing 265
Bellingham 213
Bempton Cliffs 214
Benington *59*
Benthall Edge *161*
Bentpath 265
Benwhat *283*
Berkeley *14*

Berkswell *161*
Bersham *127*
Berwick, East Sussex *60*
Berwick St John *14*
Bettws-y-Crwyn *162*
Bettyhill 299
Bidston Hill 237
Bidston Village 237
Biggleswade *60*
Billericay *60*
Bilstone *162*
Binham *162*
Binton *162*
Birchover *162*
Bird Rock 127
Birkenhead 237
Birmingham *162-4*
Bisham *60*
Bishop's Waltham *60*
Bisley *14*
Blackpool 214
Blairlogie 265
Blanchland 214
Blockley *15*
Bluestone Heath Road *164*
Bocking *61*
Bodmin *15*
Bolnhurst *60*
Bolsover *165*
Bolton-By-Bowland 214
Bo'ness 265
Boothby Graffoe *165*
Boothby Pagnell *165*
Botallack *15*
Boughton Malherbe *60*
Bourne Valley *60*
Bowes 214
Bowness-on-
  Windermere *214*
Bowscale Tarn 215
Bradfield *250*
Bradwell-on-Sea *61*
Braeloine 300
Braintree *61*
Bramber *62*
Brandsby 215
Braunton *15*
Bray *62*
Breamore *62*
Brecon 128
Bremhill *15*
Brentford *100*
Brewood *165*
Bridestones 215
Bridge of Allan 263
Brightling *62*
Brighton *63*
Brignall Banks 215
Bristol *16*
Britford *16*
Broadhembury *16*
Brockham *63*
Brockhampton *166*
Bromsgrove *166*
Brookland *63*
Brooklands *64*
Broomlee Lough 216
Broughton, Hampshire *63*
Broughton,
  Northamptonshire *166*
Broughton, Tweedale 266
Brown Carrick Hill 266
Brownsea Island *17*
Brympton d'Evercy *17*
Bryn Tail Lead
  Mine *128*
Buckfastleigh *17*
Buckingham *64*
Bunny *166*
Burford *120*
Burgh Le Marsh 167
Burghclere *64*
Burghead 300
Burnby Hall 216
Burpham *64*
Burton *238*
Burton Bradstock *18*
Burton Latimer 167
Burton Lazars *167*
Bury 216
Bury St Edmunds 167
Bute 266

Bute Town *128*
Butley 167

C

Cadder *276*
Caeo *128*
Caernarfon 128
Cairn Holy 266
Cairndow 266
Cairnpapple 267
Calceby *164*
Calf of Man, The 226
Calke Abbey *167*
Callaly Castle 216
Cam Long Down *18*
Cambridge 168
Cameley *18*
Camerton *18*
Camster Cairns 300
Camusfearna 300
Candleston Castle *129*
Candovers, The *64*
Cannock Chase 168
Canterbury *64*
Cape Wrath 301
Capheaton House 216
Carbisdale Castle 301
Carburton 168
Cardross 267
Carmarthen 129
Carn Euny *19*
Carrawbrough 216
Carreg Cennen Castle *129*
Carreg Wastad Point *129*
Cartmel Fell 216
Cartmel Priory 216
Castell Coch *130*
Castell-y-Bere *130*
Castle Bytham *168*
Castle Cary *19*
Castle Frome *168*
Castle Ring *169*
Castleton 226
Cellardyke 267
Chadderton *242*
Chaldon *65*
Chalford *19*
Chalgrave *65*
Charfield *19*
Charlbury *65*
Chastleton House *66*
Cheesewring, The *28*
Cheriton *132*
Chertsey *66*
Chester 217
Chichester *66*
Chicksands Priory *66*
Chilworth *66*
Chipping Campden *20*
Chittlehampton *20*
Chollerton 217
Christleton 218
Church Norton *67*
Churchtown 218
Cilycwm *130*
Cirencester *20*
Clare 169
Claughton 218
Claverdon 170
Claydons, The *67*
Clayton *67*
Cleethorpes 170
Clennel Street 218
Cliffe *78*
Clun *69*
Cockayne Hatley *67*
Cockenzie 268
Cockermouth 218
Codford St Peter *20*
Coire a'Chrombie *284*
Colchester *68*
Colinton 271
Colnbrook *69*
Colston Bassett 170
Come-to-Good *21*
Comrie 301
Congleton Edge 219
Congresbury *21*

Coningsby 170
Conisbrough *250*
Consall Forge 170
Cookham *69*
Cooling *78*
Corbie Craigs *283*
Corbridge 219
Corby 170
Corhampton *106*
Cornwell *69*
Corra Linn *268*
Corrichie 301
Corscombe *21*
Corton Denham *21*
Cottered *69*
Cottesmore 171
Cove Harbour 269
Coventry 171
Craig-yr Aderyn 127
Craigcleuch 269
Craigentinny *271*
Cramond *270*
Cranleigh *69*
Craobh Haven 269
Cregennen Lakes *130*
Crinan 269
Croft 171
Crofton *23*
Crowcombe *23*
Crowlink *69*
Cubley 171
Cullipool *282*
Currie *271*
Cwm Bychan *130*
Cwm Einion 127
Cwm Tudu *130*
Cwmystwyth *131*
Cynghordy Viaduct *131*

D

Daisy Nook *242*
Dale Abbey *172*
Dalserf 269
Danbury *70*
Daresbury 219
Dean Village *271*
Derby 172
Diabaig 301
Dilwyn *172*
Dinmore Manor 172
Dinton *70*
Dobcross *242*
Dodford 172
Doethie Valley *131*
Dolaucothi *147*
Dolton *23*
Dorstone *175*
Douglas 226
Dove *250*
Dover *70*
Dowland *23*
Downton *172*
Dozmary Pool *23*
Drewsteignton *23*
Droitwich *173*
Droxford *106*
Droylsden *241*
Drumlithie 301
Dumbarton 269
Duncansby Head *302*
Dunchideock *23*
Dunchurch *173*
Dundee 302
Dunecht *302*
Dunnet Head *302*
Dunrobin 302
Dunsfold *70*
Dunstable *70*
Dunwich Heath *173*
Durham 219
Durisdeer 269

E

Easdale Island 269

East Ilsley *71*
East Lexham *174*
East Riddlesden Hall 219
Eastham *238*
Eathie *303*
Edinburgh *270-1*
Eggesford *23*
Eilseg's Pillard *132*
Ellesmere Port 220
Elsfield *71*
Elstow *71*
Emmetts Garden *72*
Endsleigh House *23*
Epworth Turbary *174*
Escomb *23*
Eskdalemuir *272*
Evanton *303*
Exeter *24*
Exton *106*
Eye *238*
Eyemouth *272*

F

Falkirk *272*
Falls of Acharn *303*
Falls of Bruar *303*
Falls of Falloch *272*
Falmouth *24*
Faringdon *72*
Farleigh Hungerford *25*
Farley Mount Country
  Park *72*
Faslane *272*
Fast Castle *273*
Felin Geri Flour Mill *132*
Finavon *304*
Fingest *72*
Finkley Down Farm *72*
Fishtown of Usan *304*
Flamborough Head 220
Flash *174*
Fleet Pond *73*
Footdee *304*
Fordwich *73*
Fordyce *305*
Forres *305*
Forvie *305*
Fotheringhay *174*
Foulden *273*
Fowlis Wester *305*
Fowlsheugh *305*
Frampton-on-Severn *25*
Frensham *73*
Fulking *73*
Furneaux Pelham *74*
Fylingdales 220

G

Gainsborough *174*
Galston *273*
Ganllwyd *132*
Garleton Hills *273*
Garsington *74*
Gateholm Island *132*
Gatehouse 220
Gawsworth 221
Gawthorpe Hall 221
Geddington *174*
Gigha *273*
Glaisdale 221
Glasgow *274-5*
Glasgow Road Bridge *276*
Glen Moriston *305*
Glen Ogle *276*
Glen Prosen *305*
Glenbervie *305*
Glenbranter *276*
Glenkiln *276*
Gloucester *25*
Glyme river *74*
Glympton *74*
Godshill *79*
Golcar 221

Golden Valley *174*
Golitha Falls *25*
Goonhilly Downs *26*
Gotham 175
Gower Peninsula *132*
Grangemouth *276*
Granton *271*
Grasmere 221
Grays Thurrock *75*
Great Amwell *75*
Great Barford *75*
Great Bedwyn *26*
Great Budworth 222
Great Durnford *51*
Great Munden *75*
Great Witley 175
Great Yarmouth 175
Greenlaw *276*
Greenock *277*
Greystoke 222
Greywell *59*
Grimes Graves 176
Gringley-on-the-Hill *176*
Gwaun Valley *134*
Gwynfynydd Gold Mine *134*

H

Haddington *277*
Hadleigh *75*
Hadstock *76*
Hafren Forest *135*
Hailes Abbey *26*
Hale 222
Halford *176*
Halifax 222
Hallsands *26*
Halstead *76*
Hambleton Drove Road *223*
Hamdon Hill *26*
Hampton Loade *176*
Hanbury *176*
Handa *306*
Harbledown *65*
Hardcastle Crags *223*
Harestanes *277*
Harpham *223*
Harrietsham *76*
Harris *306*
Hartlepool *223*
Hartlip *76*
Harvington Hall *176*
Harwell *76*
Hascombe *76*
Hastings *76*
Hathersage *250*
Hatton *176*
Hawes *223*
Hawkesbury *27*
Hawksworth *177*
Headingley *229*
Hebden Bridge *223*
Helensburgh *277*
Helford River *27*
Helvellyn *223*
Hemingford Grey *177*
Hempstead *77*
Henley on Thames *78*
Heptonstall *224*
Hereford *177*
Hest Bank Coast Road *224*
Hexham *224*
Higham *78*
Hightae *277*
Hilbre Island *238*
Hilton *178*
Hinton St George *27*
Holcombe Moor *224*
Holdgate *178*
Holehird Gardens *224*
Holme Lacy *178*
Holsworthy *27*
Holystone *224*
Holywell,
  Cambridgeshire *178*
Holywell, Clwyd *135*
Hook Norton *78*

315

T

Taddiport 48
Tain 312
Talgarth 151
Talley Abbey 152
Tarbart Ness 213
Tedbury St Mary 49
Teigh 201
Telscombe 116
Temple Balsall 201
Temple Bruer 201
Tenbury Wells 201
Tendring Hundred 116
Tennyson Trail 80
Tenterden 117
Teversal 201
Tewin 117
Thameshead 49
Thaxted 117
Theddlethorpe 201
Therfield 117
Thixendale 254
Thornton Hough 238
Thorp Perrow 254
Tilford 117
Tinkinswood Burial
    Chamber 152
Tisbury 49

Tobermory 284
Tockholes 254
Toddington 117
Tongland 292
Tortworth Chestnut 49
Totaig 312
Totternhoe 117
Tredington 202
Trefeca 152
Tregaron 152
Tregoning Hill 153
Tremadog 153
Tre'r Ceiri 153
Trotton 118
Tugnet 312
Tullibardine Chapel
    312
Turriff 312
Turville 118
Tutbury 202
Tyneham 49
Tynemouth 245
Tynron 292
Tywyn 154

U

Upper Quinton 202

Uppingham 202
Upton Country Park 49
Upwey 49
Usan 304

V

Vale of Ewyas 154
Valency Valley 49
Vaynor 155
Veryan 49

W

Wadenhoe 202
Wall 202
Wallington 254
Wallops, The 63
Walsall 202
Walton on the Naze 118
Wanborough 118
Wanlockhead 293
Wansdyke 49
Wantage 120

Warboys 202
Wardour 50
Ware 118
Warkworth 254
Warleggan 50
Warnford 106
Warnham 119
Warwick 203
Waskerley Way 254
Weare Giffard 50
Wedmore 50
Wednesbury 204
Weldon 204
Well of the Lecht 313
Wellow 204
Wells-next-the-Sea 204
Wemyss Caves 293
Wentworth Woodhouse
    250
Weobley Castle 132
West Challow 120
West Clandon 119
West Dean 50
West Stow 204
West Witton 254
West Wycombe 119
Wey and Arun Junction
    Canal 119
Weyhill 119
Whaligoe 313
Whitby 254
Whiteley Village 120

Whiteway 50
Whittlesey 204
Whixall Moss 204
Wickham 120
Widmerpool 204
Wigan 255
Wildboarclough 257
Willaston 238
Wilsford 51
Wilts and Berks Canal
    120
Winceby 204
Winchcombe 51
Windermere 257
Windrush Valley 120
Wing, Bucks. 120
Wing, Leics. 205
Winslow 120
Winster 205
Wirksworth 205
Wirral 237
Witham 120
Witley Court 175
Wold Newton 257
Wolferton 206
Wolsingham 257
Wolverhampton 206
Woodbridge 206
Woodcock Air 293
Woodford Valley 51
Woodhenge 51
Woolhope 206

Wotton Rivers 51
Worcester 206
Worth 121
Wrawby 206
Wrexham 155
Writtle 121
Wroxeter 206
Wycoller 257

Y

Y Gaer 155
Yarm 257
Yarmouth 80
Yeaveley 207
Yeavering Bell 257
Ynys Lochtyn 155
York 257
Youlgreave 207
Ystradfellte 155

Z

Zoar 313

SUBJECT INDEX

*Page numbers in **bold** show where subjects are given extended coverage in a side panel or four-page feature*

Animals
Arran 263
bats **58**, 59
bear-baiting **229**
Beware Chalk Pit 72
Brownsea Island 17
Cannock Chase 168
Child-Beale Trust 58
coypus 121
deer **121**, 312
faithful dogs **223**
Greyfriars Bobby **223**
introduced from overseas **121**
Jumbo the elephant **68**
lighthouse keeper's view **140-3**
Marrington Dingle 189
mink 17
pigs 25
rabbits **151**
rare breeds **25**
Rhum 310
salmon ladder 292
scorpions 121
seals 190
sheep on rooftop, Leeds 229
Timothy Tortoise 110
whales' bones **225**, 267
Wirral Country Park **239**

Archaeology
ancient memorial stones 154
ancient routes **165, 222**
Anglo-Saxon palaces 257
Antonine Wall **290**
Beaker Folk **267**
Belle Tout 69
Bridestones 219
brochs **262**
Burghead well 300
burial cairns **133**
Cairn Holy 266
Cairnpapple **267**
cairns **300**
Castle Ring 169
Cathole Cave 132
deneholes **74**
Dolaucothi **147**
fogous **19**
Grimes Graves 176
Hembury Fort 16
henges **51**
Huly Hill 271
Hurlers, The 28
Kestor 29

Kilmartin 279
Lanyon Quoit 34
Men-an-Tol 34
'missing link' hoax 12
Mitchell's Fold 190
moats **116**
Offa's Dyke **134**
Parc Le Breos 133
pecht houses 19
Pictish stones **285**
Red Lady of Paviland 132
Rollright Stones 110-11
Roman roads **28**
Rosetta Stone 284
St Patrick's Isle 227
Stanton Drew 47
Tinkinswood **152**
Tre'r Ceiri 153
vitrified forts **304**
Wansdyke 49
Woodhenge 51
Yeavering Bell 257

Architects
Burges, William **130**
Cubitt, Thomas 92
Deacon, George 60
Grieve, James 266
Lethaby, W.R. 166
Lutyens, Sir Edwin 23, 76, 238, 282
Mackintosh, C. R. 275, **277**
Nash, John 16, 101
Owen, Nicholas 198
Picturesque movement **173**
Soane, Sir John 100
Spence, Sir Basil 171
Stirling, James 109
Street, G.E. 254
Trollop, Robert 216
Vanbrugh, John 57, 98, 181
Waterhouse, Alfred 240
Williams Ellis, Clough 69
Wren, Sir Christopher 90, 120

Artists
Arts and Crafts Society **172**
Bell, Vanessa 60
Bellucci, Antonio 175
Burne-Jones, Edward 166, 284
Constable, John 75
Epstein, Sir Jacob 276
Forbes, Stanhope 34
Gill, Eric **155**

Grant, Duncan 12, 60
hoaxes 12
Hogarth, William 100
Hunt, Holman 284
John, Sir William 236
Lee, Stirling 236
Lowry, L.S. 242
Morris, William 100, 101, **172**, 284
Newlyn School **34**
Penkill Foundation 284
Piper, John 177, **197**
Reynolds, Sir Joshua 108
Ruskin, John 109
Scott, William Bell 284
Skeaping, John 12
Spencer, Stanley **64**
Van Dyck, Sir Anthony 120
Watkins, Dudley D. 302
Whistler, Lawrence 23
wood, art in **220**

Birds
Aden Country Park 298
avocets 194
Bempton Cliffs 214
Bird Rock, Gwynedd 127
doves, Faringdon 72
Epworth Turbary 174
falconry **119**
Fleet Pond 73
Fowlsheugh 305
gannets 214, 262
Handa 306
hawk conservancy 119
herons 17, 78, 119
Hothfield 78
Isle of Grain 78
lighthouse keeper's view **140-3**
Marrington Dingle 189
peacocks 17
Savernake Forest 46
Seal Sands 249
Skokholm Island 150
Tarbat Ness 312
terns 190
Wirral 238, 239

Buildings
bastle houses 220
fortified, Border counties **292**
materials 18

pargeting **169**
Scottish castles **305**
thatch **192**, 284
timber-framing **195**
tithe barns **49**, 189
see also **Churches**

Canals & Rivers
aegir, River Trent 174
Basingstoke Canal 58
Birmingham 162
boat lift 213
Boat Museum 220
Bridgewater Canal 249
canal art 220
Crinan Canal 269
Ellesmere Canal 220
Forth and Clyde Canal 272, 276, 290
Foxton locks 188
Grand Union Canal 176
Hampton Loade ferry 176
Hatton Flight 176
Horsey Mere 179
Huddersfield Narrow Canal 224
James Brindley museum 186
London **101, 102-3**
Monmouthshire Canal 147
Oxford 109
Pontcysyllte Aqueduct 147
Sapperton Tunnel 46
Shropshire Union 213, 220
Stratford Canal 201
Telford, Thomas **269**
Thames barges **98**, 196
Trent and Mersey Canal 212
Union Canal 290
Wey and Arun Junction Canal 119
wherries **193**
Wigan Pier 225
Wilts and Berks Canal 120

Churches
angel roofs **180**
Anglo-Saxon **221**
brasses 115, 118, 120, **198**
curious tenures **219**
customs
    Aylesbury 57
    bequests and **188**
    Boy Bishop **45**
    City of London **88**

Clipping the Church **38**, 114
dole 76, 188
rush-bearing **218**
wakes **218**
yew trees 118
detached belfry 63, 195
effigies **56, 70, 198**
graffiti **81**
Herefordshire school of craftsmen **43**, 169, 197
holy wells 212, 223, **270**
human skin on doors 76
items stored in **73**
lych gates 82
mazes 17, 160, 205
memorials to foreigners **95**
misericords **24**
mythical beasts **37**
sanctuary **224**, 230
Sandham Memorial Chapel 64
sites, supernaturally chosen **15, 39, 79, 216**
stone crosses **137**
timepieces **120**
tombstone inscriptions **16**
unfinished spire, Beeby 161
wall paintings 18, 60, 63, 64, 65, 67, 76, 79, 115, 118, 120, 130, 172, 189

Crime
body snatchers **251**
Border reivers **248**
murder
    Charles Peace 250
    of Ellen Strange 224
    Green Bicycle Mystery 200
    Jack the Ripper 89
    John Massey 162
    Judge John Johnes 128
    of Maria Marten **196**
    Percy Toplis 313
outlaws **131**
    Dick Turpin 77
    Lady Katherine Ferrers **83**
    Humphrey Kynaston 193
    Owain Llawgoch 131
    Robin Hood **230**
    Twm Shon Catti 131
pirates, women as 115
smuggling 110
    Balcary Heughs 264
    'Battle of Brookland' 63
    Carter gang 43

ACKNOWLEDGEMENTS

The Automobile Association also wishes to thank the following photographers, organisations, museums and libraries for the use of their material

Aberdeen University Library 258/9 *Glasgow*. **Aerofilms** 116 *Little Moreton Hall*, 134 *Offa's Dyke*. **Bass Worthington** 175 *The Cuckoo Bush*. **Vic Bates** 226 *Peel, Groudle Glen*. **BBC Hulton** 23 *Death of Arthur*, 41 *Admiralty*, 50 *West Wycombe*, 60 *Bisham Abbey*, 63 *Pavilion*, 91 *Russell*, 92 *Dan Lemo*, 108 *Windmills*, 120 *Hampton in Arden*, 128 *Arthur*, 153 *Lawrence of Arabia*, 155 *Eric Gill*, 172 *Burne-Jones & William Morris*, 197 *John Piper*, 202 *Fabian*, 224 *Hexham Frith Stool*, 308 *Monster*, 312 *MacLeods*, 263 *Fairy Glen*. **Birmingham Museum** 163 *Holte Coat of Arms*. **Janet & Colin Bord** 15 *Braunton church*, 17 *Church porch*, 19 *Culsh*, 28 *Roman Road*, 44 *St Germoe's Chair*, 46 *Stone circle*, 75 *Monolith*, 82 *Bench ends*, 147 *Pumpsaint*, 154 *Eliseg's pillar*, 155 *Gill's signature*, 170 *Bench end*, 192 *Little Stretton*, 216 *Over church*, 247 *Eildon Hills*, 262 *Mousa Broch*, 304 *Vitrified fort*, 276 *Witch*, 285 *Pictish symbols*. **Bodleian Library** 165 *Gough Map*, 181 *Strip Farming*, 238 *Sir Gawain*, 290 *Roman insignia*. **Bridgeman Art Library** 104/5 *Metropolitan railway*. **Brighton Pavilion** 63 *Menu*. **Burford House** 182. **Buxton Museum** 194 *Peak Cavern*. **Canterbury Heritage Museum** 65 *Pilgrim badge*. **Valerie Cottle** 226 *Fairy Saddle*, 227 *Eyreton Castle*. **Dunvegan Castle** 311 *Fairy Flag*. **Dunwich Museum** 179 *Drowned church*. **Durham Dean & Chapter Library** 219 *Falchion*. **Eastern Daily Press** 193 *The Albion*. **Ellesmere Port Boat Museum** 220 *Canal Art*. **Keith Ellis** 135 *Bible*. **Robert Estall** 217 *Well*. **E T Archive** 95 *Pocohontas*. **Faber & Faber** 176 *Green Knowe*. **Gloucester County Museum** 25 *Pig*. **George Allen & Unwin** 164 *The Mill*. **Denis Harvey** 232, 233, 234, 235. **Herefordshire Museum** 186 *Bell*. **I L N Library** 26 *Grand Master*, 68 *Jumbo*. **Liverpool Maritime Museum** 237 *White Star Line*. **London Transport** 101, 105. **Norman McCanch** 140/3 *illustrations*. **The Mansell Collection** 13 *Alfred*, 39 *Sir Richard Whittington*, 42 *Jack*, 47 *Robinson Crusoe*, 51 *Stonehenge*, 57 *Elizabeth*, 61 *Weaving room*, 71 *Bunyan's dream*, 77 *Dick Turpin*, 102 *Despatch tube*, 102/3 *railway*, 115 *Emily Faithfull*, 117 *Boscobel Oak*, 138 *Herb*, 162 *Demon Drummer*, 166 *Rough Music*, 215 *Maze*, 223 *Dog's elegy*, 231 *Castle Rock*, 249 *Sir Titus Salt*, 251 *William Hare*, 299 *Whisky still*, 301 *Mary, Queen of Scots*, 303 *Frankenstein*, 309 *Fair Maid*, 265 *James Hutton*, 269 *Thomas Telford*, 271 *Rizzio*, 278 *J Macadam*, 281 *Linton Worm*, 288 *Kipling*, 289 *Edith Nesbit*, 286 *Jane Austen*, 287 *Dickens*, 287 *Hardy*, 291 *Golf*, 293 *Wallace*. **Mary Evans Picture Library** 12 *Diplomat*, 29 *Dinosaurs*, 36 *Sing a song*, 37 *Mantichora*, 38 *Painswick*, 59 *Sherlock Holmes*, 67 *Fairies*, 72 *Stool*, 80 *Tennyson*, 103 *Tunnel*, 109 *Wind in the Willows*, 111 *Rollrights*, 114 *Shire Moot*, 119 *Falconry*, 127 *Mermaid*, 157 *Fisherwomen*, 168 *Tobias Hobson*, 178 *George Borrow*, 189 *Foxhound, Spaniel*, 196 *William Corder*, 204 *Maypole*, 207 *Well Dressing*, 213 *George Hudson*, 214 *Hand of Glory*, 222 *Drovers*, 244 *Venerable Bede*, 256 *Meteorite*, 307 *Swans*, 266 *Birdman*, 274 *Furnace*, 279 *Bike*, 280 *Tam O'Shanter*, 282 *Pippin*. **Museum of Antiquities Newcastle** 126 *Head*. **Museum of Cider** 48 *Cider making*. **Museum of London** 89 *Carved stone*, 97 *Poster*, 102 *Rat catchers*, 104 *Tickets*. **Museum of Wales** 152 *Tinkinswood*. **National Gallery of Art Washington** 270 *St Lucy*. **National Museum of Labour History** 242 *Luddite*. **National Trust** 167 *Calke Abbey bed, N.T.S.* 277 *Charles Rennie Mackintosh*, NT W.R. 184 *Stourhead Gardens*. **Nature Photographers** 58 *Natterer's Bat*, 107 *Yellow Flag*. **Paisley Museum** 275 *Weavers*. **Pembrokeshire Museum** 129 *Carreg Wastad* **Penzance Town Council** 34 *School Is Out*. **Principal and Fellows of Jesus College, Oxford** 39 *Red Book of Hergest*. **RAF Museum** 199 *617 Squadron*. **Doc Rowe** 161 *Games*, 188 *John Knill*, 218 *Rush cart*. **Royal Commission on Historical Monuments of England** 30/1 *Fosse Way*, 76 *Church door*, 83 *Markyate*. **Rural Life Museum Reading** 243 *Milking Machine*. **Saffron Walden Museum** 112 *Cockatrice*. **Scottish Tourist Board** 298 *Black Bun*, 273 *Eyemouth, Garleton*. **Scunthorpe Museum** 20 *Haxey Hood Game*. **Brian Shuel** 88 *John Stow*. **Sunderland Museum** 245 *Lambton Worm*. **D C Thompson & Co** 302 *Desperate Dan*. **Topham Picture Library** 8/9 *Cavedwellers*, 52/3 *Hop pickers*, 84/5 *Milkbar*, 122/3 *Fisherwomen*, 236 *Beatles 1962*, 294/5 *St Kilda*. **University of London** 187 *St Dunstan*. **Universal Pictorial Press** 30 *Tom Vernon*. **V & A Museum** 206 *Rosa Mundi*. **Warwick Castle** 203 *Sir Guy*. **West Country Tourist Board** 14/15 *Botallack*. **W. Wilson** 239 *Willaston Station*. **Mrs E Wood** 98/99 *Thames barge*.

The photographs listed below were commissioned by and are copyright of the Automobile Association Picture Library

Martyn Adelman 56 *Aldworth*, 57 *Aylesbury*, 64 *Frescoes*, 73 *Wayland's Smithy*, 74 *Church roof*, 99 *Little St Pauls*, 114 *Moot Hall*, 160 *Alkborough*, 197 *Tottenhoe*, 198 *Fenny Bentley*, 286 *Chawton*, 302 *Duncansby Stacks* 308/9 *Standing stones*, 311 *Rhum*, 306 *Harris Tweed*. **Stephen Beer** 236/7 *Cenotaph*, 237 *Albert Dock village*, 238 *Farm*, 240 *St Marys Church, Barton Arcade*, 241 *St John's St*, 242 *Daisy Nook*. **P & G Bowater** 271 *Kilmartin*. **E A Bowness** 220/1 *Grasmere Island*, 223 *Red Tarn*, 246/7 *Nine Standards*, 264 *Balcary Heughs*, 282/3 *Minnivey engine*, 292 *Covenanters Memorial*. **R Czeja** 18 *Cottages*, 27 *Horton Tower folly*, 39 *Okeford Fitzpaine*, 41 *Plush*, 43 *Rampisham*, 48 *Tyneham*. **Robert Eames** 127 *Bird Rock*, 136 *Tomb*, 139 *Bardsey Island*, 145 *Parys Mountain*, 217 *Crypt*, 218, 219 *Tea party*, 239 *Church*, 252 *Church*. **Robin Fletcher** 113 *Town Hall*. **Alan Greerley** 35 *Lydney Park*. **Dennis Hardley** 185 *Port Logan*, 277 *Helensburgh*, 278 *Inverary Castle*. **Bob Johnson** 40 *Penzance*. **Sarah King** 289 *Windermere*. **A. Lawson** 12/13 *Burrowbridge Mump*, 13 *Barwick Park follies*, 16 *Henbury grave, Goldney Grotto*, 16/17 *Blaise Hamlet*, 17 *St Mary Redcliffe*, 19 *Carn Euny fogou*, 22 *Dozmary Pool*, 24 *The Cygnet*, 25 *Frampton-on-Severn*, 26/7 *Helford River*, 28/9 *The Cheesewring*, 37 *Morwenstow*, 38/9 *Oldbury-on-Severn*, 42 *Portreath*, 43 *Puxton Church*, 45 *St Nectan's Glen*, 46 *Sapperton Tunnel*, 46/7 *Stanton Drew*, 47 *Stanway House*, 50/1 *Warleggan Church*, 79 *Mump*, 120 *Clock*. **S Lund** 20 *Chipping Campden*. **S & O Mathews** 4/5 *Hay Meadow*, 18 *Round House*, 21 *Cirencester Park*, 21 *Potter's Museum*, 32/3 *Fosse Way*, 33 *Jupiter column, Dolphin mosaic*, 49 *Tithe Barn*, 58 *Milestone*, 58/9 *Benington Lordship*, 61 *St Peter's Chapel*, 62 *Brightling church*, 63 *Dovecote*, 64/4 *Wall painting*, 66 *Claydon House*, 70 *Crusader*, 70/1 *Dunsfold church*, 71 *Saddlery*, 72/3 *Farringdon House*, 73 *Devil's Dyke*, 74/5 *Manor garden*, 76 *Silk mill*, 77 *Fishermen's huts*, 68 *Timperleys*, 69 *Ostrich Inn, Cat's Head*, 78 *Bass Brewery, Isle of Grain*, 79 *Needles*, 80/1 *Lewes Castle*, 82 *Lead Font*, 90 *Fat boy*, 96 *Thomas More*, 99 *View from Bankside*, 100 *Dinosaurs, Wimbledon Mill*, 101 *Holland Park, Widow's Son, Admiral's House*, 108 *Windmill*, 109 *Botanic Gardens*, 110 *Church*, 111 *Cave carving*, 113 *Shalford Mill*, 114/5 *Stadhampton*, 118 *Grotto*, 118/9 *Wey & Arun Junction Canal*, 121 *Worth church*, 146 *Willington dovecote*, 182 *Knot garden*, 184 *Beth Chatto's garden*, 212/3 *Buttercross*, 222 *Hawes Museum*, 243 *Muker*, 280/1 *Loch Doon*, 286 *Abbotsford*, 287 *Old Curiosity shop, Batemans*, 290 *Portpatrick*, 306 *North Harris*. **Colin Molyneaux** 146 *Dovecote*. **Rich Newton** 134 *Offa's Dyke*, 162 *Scott window*, 163 *Birmingham*, 164 *Orthodox church*, 170 *Claverdon Forge*, 171 *Castle*, 177 *Foot ferry*, 178 *Coverdale church*, 179 *The Old Bull*, 173 *Droitwich*, 186 *Jewry Wall*, 191 *Mitchell's Fold*, 192 *Cave*, 200 *Motor Museum*, 203 *Gasworks, Castle Mill*, 205 *Turf maze*, 207 *Tea shop*, 194 *Oakham Castle*, 274 *Gardens*, 275 *City Chambers, Ladybird chair*, 276/7 *Clyde canal*, 268 *Cora Linn*. **Franki Raffles** 266/7 *Cairnpapple*, 270 *Innocent Railway*, 270/1 *Cramond Ferry*, 271 *Craigentinny Marbles, Cramond river*, 291 *Union Canal*. **Rod Richard** 300 *Camster Cairns*, 313 *Whaligoe*. **Peter Russell** 130 *Moorish room*. **Richard Surman**, *Friars Crag*, 187 *Misericord*. **Martin Trelawny** *Cover Adel church door*, 61 *Fournier Street*, 88 *Spitalfields, Sweetings*, 89 *St Olave's, St Katherine Cree window*, 90 *Twinings, St Paul's*, 91 *Society of Apothecaries*, 90/1 *Wig & Pen*, 91 *Fox & Anchor, Well of Clerkenwell*, 92 *Temple lamplighter*, 93 *Watch House, Wellcome Institute, Middle Temple Lane, Toy Museum*, 94 *War room, The Mall, Tradescant Museum*, 95 *Lock's, Lobb's*, 94/5 *Sotheby's, House of St Barnabas*, 96 *Albert Bridge*, 97 *Rotten Row*, 97 *Physic Gardens, Albert Memorial, Pagoda, Royal Hospital*, 99 *Operating Theatre*, 214 *Tomb*, 215 *Bridestones*, 225 *Ilton Temple*, 228 *Atkinsons shop*, 229 *Leeds, Bear pits*, 230 *Adel Church*, 231 *Linton*, 255 *Wigan Pier*, 256 *Bridge*, 252/3 *Slaidburn*, 253 *Sunderland Point*. **Wyn Voysey** 107 *Basing House seige*. **R W Weir** 262/3 *Airthrey Hermitage*, 265 *Bannet Stane*, 267 *Cellardyke*, 285 *Pittenweem*, 292/3 *Wemyss Cave*, 298/9 *Aultdearg Pillars*, 300/1 *Earthquake House*, 304 *Dovecote*, 305 *Castle*. **Harry Williams** 1 *Llanstephan*, 2/3 *Cwm Bychan*, 36 *Lynmouth*, 43 *Kilpeck church*, 67 *Windmills*, 126 *Camera Obscura*, 128/9 *Candleston castle*, 130/1 *Roman steps*, 133 *Parc le Breos*, 133 *Culver Hole*, 136/7 *Nash Point*, 137 *Crosses*, 138/9 *The Rivals*, 140 *Nash Point*, 144 *Nanteos Mansion*, 148/9 *St David's Head*, 148 *St Non's Well, & Shrine*, 150 *Meon Madoc*, 151 *Murals*, 152/3 *Castle*, 154/5 *Cave*, 169 *Font*, 175 *Snodhill Castle*, 172 *Dovecote*, 197 *Carving*, 198 *Stiperstones*. **Trevor Wood** 66 *Topiary*, 74 *Grimes Graves*, 200 *Pedlar*, 195 *Lavenham church*. **Tim Woodcock** 26 *Mason's Marks*, 161 *All Saints*, 166 *Father Time*, 167 *Calke Abbey*, 165 *Manor House*, 168 *Botanic Gardens*, 169 *Pargeting*, 180 *Kentwell*, 183 *Adrian Bloom's garden*, 188 *Market Harborough*, 189 *Anne of Cleves House*, 196 *Pin Mill*, 199 *Eyebrook Reservoir*, 201 *Temple Bruer*, 206 *Wolferton Station*, 194/5 *Pickworth*, 215 *Turf Maze*, 216 *Burnby Hall*, 248 *Cave*, 244 *Chapel, Old Mill, Priory*, 245 *Dedication stone*, 250 *Castle*, 251 *Folly*, 254 *Castle*. **Jon Wyand** 40 *Bread Stones*, 116 *Streatley*.